THE GERMAN PEOPLE

THE TRANSLATION OF *THE GERMAN PEOPLE* FROM THE ORIGINAL GERMAN WAS MADE BY OLGA MARX. THE ENGLISH TEXT HAS BEEN EDITED BY DOROTHY TEALL IN CONSULTATION WITH THE AUTHOR AND WITH HIS ASSISTANCE UPON MANY GENERAL PROBLEMS AND SPECIFIC DETAILS.

VEIT VALENTIN

The German People

THEIR HISTORY AND CIVILIZATION FROM THE
HOLY ROMAN EMPIRE TO THE THIRD REICH

ALFRED A. KNOPF NEW YORK

1952

Manufactured in the United States of America

Published in Canada by McCLELLAND & STEWART LIMITED

PUBLISHED JULY 11, 1946
SECOND PRINTING, APRIL 1949
THIRD PRINTING, MAY 1951
FOURTH PRINTING, MAY 1952

THIS IS A BORZOI BOOK,
PUBLISHED BY ALFRED A. KNOPF, INC.

To

J. K. de R.

PREFATORY ACKNOWLEDGEMENT

THE FRIENDS, professional and personal, whose aid I have had in the years of writing this book are legion. The first draft, based on courses given at the University of London, 1933–9, was completely recast with the very stimulating advice of Dr. Minna Falk, Professor of History at New York University. George Shuster, President of Hunter College, and Sidney B. Fay, Professor of History at Harvard University, read and criticized the manuscript. I have good reason also to be grateful to Charles and Mary Beard.

To these and many others, my warmest thanks.

VEIT VALENTIN

APRIL 1946   LIBRARY OF CONGRESS, WASHINGTON, D. C.

CONTENTS

IX THE GERMAN REFORMATION

X THE COUNTER-REFORMATION
AND THE THIRTY YEARS' WAR

CONTENTS

XIII   GERMANY AND THE FRENCH REVOLUTION

XIV   THE WAR OF LIBERATION AGAINST NAPOLEON

XV THE GERMAN RESTORATION

XVI THE FIRST TWO GERMAN REVOLUTIONS

CONTENTS

THE GERMAN PEOPLE

Chapter 1

BASIC PROBLEMS OF GERMAN HISTORY

GERMAN HISTORY is hard to understand and therefore hard to write. Why? Somewhere in central Europe lies Germany. Any more exact specification is likelier to confuse than to clarify. Germany's boundaries are ambiguous and transient to a degree that has not been experienced by any other country. The Britons are identified with their great island; the geopolitical unification of the British Isles marked the beginning of almost absolute definiteness and security for the boundaries of Great Britain, and with that her historical greatness dawned. The Italians became a nation in filling up their peninsula and making it politically effective; no one with a shred of sense will ever want to dismember this land again. France possesses clear, sharp boundaries on at least three sides; they had to be made secure politically, but the result was so definitive that it was possible for the term "natural boundaries" to arise in France. There are, in truth, no absolute boundaries but seacoasts. Neither rivers nor high mountains have constituted immutable boundaries through the history of the ages.

THE BOUNDARIES OF GERMANY

As the heartland of central Europe, Germany has more boundaries than any other comparable large country. She has more neighbours. Her boundaries are formed by seacoasts to only a very minor extent. The Baltic is a small inland sea whose coasts increase rather than decrease the number of neighbours. The German stretch of North Sea coast is broken by many island groups. Germany was at a disadvantage here in comparison with England, Holland, and Denmark. Whenever she sought to improve her unfavourable situation she immediately encountered lively resistance from these neighbours. The North Sea coast was thus more a handicap than a safeguard.

In the course of centuries all the German land boundaries have shifted this way and that. They were defined by mere accidents of history, and never for more than a short period. Conquest, colonization, inheritance, division, purchase, and exchange served to set them for longer or shorter periods. Often the boundaries contradicted geographical facts and economic interests, and military and dynastic considerations further confused the situation.

The lack of homogeneity and of definiteness in the geopolitical structure of Germany had its counterpart in topography. The stretches along the Rhine and the Main are among the most beautiful and fertile in Europe or indeed the whole world. From time immemorial Germany has been a land of forests; the famous forest wealth of her secondary mountain ranges has been preserved to this day. But these very forests hindered efficient development of the land. First-class agricultural soil existed, indeed, in only a few regions of the west and the northwest. The east and the northeast were handicapped by light sandy soils, a condition that carried significant economic, political, and sociological consequences. The Rhine, the Weser, and their tributaries direct the interest of the country toward the west and the northwest. This core of Europe lay within the cultural sphere of western Roman civilization; here the after-effects of the imperial and humanitarian temper were clearly traceable. The Danube with its tributaries connected southern Germany with the Alpine region and the Balkans; this part of Germany also looked instinctively toward the Mediterranean. The Elbe, for its part, both united and separated the northwest, cultivated from of old, and the newly colonized northeast. Finally the Oder and the Vistula, which both have their sources in Slavic countries, gave the northeast and the east their special character, even from a geopolitical point of view — their emotional tone and their fields of action, which contrasted with those of the west and entered into competition with the Danubian lands with so much the greater energy. Only a strong political will could hold the divergent parts of central Europe together.

Napoleon once said that geography is destiny. The dictum seems to have been misapprehended and misapplied by a certain modern school of thought. Geopoliticians tend to explain historical and political problems on the basis of geographical conditions with a kind of scientific determinism. Actually, however, history is not a simple fulfilment of an inevitable destiny, but a struggle against the definable or indefinable elements that constitute the brute impersonality of the environment. The issue of the conflict between differing possibilities is then an adaptation, an intelligent adjustment, a harmony. The bitterest reproach that is likely to be made against National Socialism in Germany is that it has made false historical deductions from German geography. What are the basic realities?

The arbitrary course of the great German rivers clove the country apart instead of binding it together, and the forests of the numerous mountain ranges fostered distinctive peculiarities in the tribes and districts. Valleys and plateaus, river mouths, glens and basins, all created local centres — governments, markets — that lived unto themselves and persisted for centuries without any larger patriotic connections. Thuringia and Württemberg are the best instances of such enduring peculiarities, which, however, had some practical point and were therefore able to hang on tenaciously. Even here in the tiniest territorial units there were boundary disputes. Count quarrelled with bishop, abbot with free city; each had his claims, and disputatiousness ate up all other passions.

In these conditions lies the probable cause of one of the most curious phenomena of German history. The German has been distinguished by his very deep love of his native spot. The city with its fountains and inns, the cheery streets crowded with workers and tradesmen, the jokes and gibes uttered in fresh, lively dialect, all went straight to the typical German's heart. It was part of himself, astir with memories of his old home, of zestful youth, of care, striving, and aspiration. If it were a German who hailed from the vineyard country along the banks of the Moselle, from the slopes of the Black Forest, from a heath village of Lower Saxony, or from a lake in Bavaria or in the Mark of Brandenburg, his life was saturated with the freshness of the true German landscape. It would be difficult to say what all these landscapes have in common; the outward look of things has very little indeed to do with it. The great point was the feeling of rootedness, of connection. The German soul clung to the maternal warmth of just this bit of earth, and its yearning was allayed by the simplicity, the homely and enduring reality, of the native soil.

A feeling so vivid, given form and enhanced as it was by the poets

3

and musicians, could be carried over to the dominant local forces even in a political sense. But it broke down before just that form of state that destiny appointed for Germany—to wit, territorial dominion. A few examples will show what is meant. The people along the Lower Rhine, in Cleve and in the County Mark, or those of East Friesland felt a decided attachment for the hereditary princely houses that belonged to the land as it were by the course of nature, but they were wholly indifferent to the Hohenzollerns, who, suddenly coming forward as heirs, were regarded with the suspicion and hatred that were the due of foreigners. The citizens of Nürnberg loved their venerable city in spite of many reactionary abuses of an ancient regime; but the kings of Bavaria, when on one ground or another they tried to take it over, were looked on as intruders. Perhaps the German's love for his native spot remained so strong just because for a long time there was no collective German political form around which a feeling of nationality might have crystallized. The Prussians demanded a monarchical Prussian brand of patriotism, the Hessians a grand-ducal Hessian variety. No wonder that sentiment set against such artificialities. Something broader and loftier was needed. And so, to balance the strong love of home, the German developed his yearning for the emperorship as something all-embracing. Only a very few knew what emperorship actually had and had not been in olden times. The fragmentation went deep, and because of it the ultimate fulfilment was bound to be overwhelming.

ETHNICAL COMPONENTS OF THE GERMAN PEOPLE

It took a long time for German land to become German and nothing else. Germans needed a long while for their evolution into the German people. German history does not begin with the Cimbri and the Teutons or even with Hermann the Cheruscan. At that time there were Germani, Celts, and Romans, but no Germans as we use the word today. The Germani of the Latin historians were not Germans, and the Germans are not Germani. Only a small part of the Germans are of predominantly Germanic descent.

The most various components fused in the full light of history to form the German people. The four most important are the residue of the pre-Indo-European population, the Celts, the Germani, and the Slavs. There were also some subsidiary elements: a variety of strains lumped together as Romans, as well as Scandinavians, Lithu-anians, and, from the middle of the eighteenth century, Jews, who had been almost completely segregated till then. The Huguenots who immigrated from France were themselves either Celtic and Germanic or Celtic and Roman blends, and thus they constituted a new factor only from a cultural point of view. Among the principal elements of the German people the remnant of the pre-Indo-Euro-pean population must not be underestimated.

The great migrations were actually conquests that ended with the destruction of the upper class who had ruled up till then and with the enslavement of the lower class, along with the wives and children of the upper layer. Killing was usually confined to the extermination or sacrificial murder of dangerous characters. These facts must also be kept in mind with regard to the colonization of the Slavic east. It was to the advantage of the new ruling class to conserve as much manpower as possible. To define the part played by the Romans in Germany it would be necessary to deal separately with case after case. During the Roman period Syrians and Spaniards, Africans and Illyrians, and of course Italians settled in western and southern Ger-many. Such were the original components of the urban population of Germany. What was left of the pre-Indo-European inhabitants survived, by contrast, in the mountains as a rule, while Slavic ele-ments predominated in the open country. All this may have been a partial cause of the sharp contrasts between city and countryside, be-tween east and west.

In general it may be said that the west and southwest of Germany are Celtic and Roman in character; the northwest, Germanic; central and southern Germany, Celtic and Germanic; the southeast, Celtic and Slavic; and the east, Germanic and Slavic. The pre-Indo-Euro-pean strain made itself felt especially in the Alpine regions and in the secondary mountain ranges, the Scandinavian in Schleswig and Pom-erania, and the Lithuanian in East Prussia. No other great European people is woven of so many different strands as the Germans.

Here, indeed, lies the psychological reason why the idea of race has commanded so great a following in Germany of late. In a his-torical work that seeks to be at all scholarly, discussions of race are best avoided. The enumeration of races and the description of racial characteristics can be properly handled only by competent specialists in the natural sciences. For present purposes it is enough to state that beyond all doubt a comparatively small pre-Indo-European factor combined with a very large number of various Indo-European factors. The mixture was more diverse than anywhere else, and this fact had two important consequences.

Germany has more boundaries and therefore a larger borderland population than any other European country. The borderland inhabitants, repeatedly swayed this way and that, are strikingly like their neighbours on the other side of the line—often more like them than like the other Germans who are nearest to them. The Celtic-Roman inhabitants of the Rhineland are first cousins to the Celtic-Roman elements in Lorraine, Burgundy, and other parts of eastern France, but they are foreigners to the Westphalians and the Hessians. The East Frisians and the Franconians on the Lower Rhine resemble the Dutch; the Alemanni of the Breisgau resemble the Swiss and the Alsatians. The German Bohemians and the Czechs are blood relatives, and so are the eastern Germans and the western Poles; the members of these groups accordingly know each other well and feel no mutual fondness. In the old days many of the regions mentioned belonged to some neighbouring state on the other side of the national border, and the close similarity of the inhabitants, based on a like ethnical character, led to much political friction. The effect was emphatically centrifugal.

The second consequence of the pronounced ethnical diversity of the Germans raises one of the most significant problems in German history. German stocks are more foreign to one another than is the case elsewhere. Peculiarities have been developed further, and tension between stocks was sharpened by the deep sentiment for home. As a result civil wars were frequent and long-drawn-out. It is true that individual groupings changed within themselves, but nevertheless they were reluctant to adapt themselves to others. This factor of intrinsic physical and psychic discord caused the bitterest hatred between religions, professions, parties, and classes, a phenomenon characteristic of the destiny of the Germans to this very day. It appeared that the Germans could be forced into some sort of unity only in combat with an inner or an outer foe. Expeditions of the emperors to Rome united the vassals in one great object; crusades blotted out feuds between neighbours; Reformation and Counter-Reformation

6

split Germany into two camps instead of twenty; the War of Liberation against Napoleon welded Germany together as it had not been unified for a very long while.

The ethnical diversity of the Germans is the cause of their best qualities and of their most fatal. No other European people embraced the universalism of late antiquity so intimately, and it became for Germany a natural impulse of feeling and action. The ideas of emperorship, of Rome, of world dominion — yes, even the claim to world redemption — belong to German history. Again and again such ideas were invoked to lay the spectres of predestined discord. The particularism of the stocks, dynasties, and cities, the dualisms of west and east, of Protestants and Catholics, of Lutherans and Reformed, of Prussia and Austria, of imperial patriotism and colonial expansion eastward, of mysticism and scholasticism, of rationalism and faith, of nobility and bourgeoisie, of civilian and military, of bureaucracy and public opinion, of capitalism and labour—all these tensions in German history needed to be resolved. The attempt would be made at first in a provisional way by a claim to supremacy put forward as a missionary concept; only after such an effort failed would compromise be tried.

Physically there is no such thing as a German type. There is, however, a German facial expression, a German spiritual attitude, a German destiny. The German people is torn with inner conflict and is at once happy and unhappy. It has produced more profound music and creative thought than any other great people. Its soldiers and bureaucrats have been distinguished. Many of its businessmen and scholars deserved and won the highest respect. Its rulers, however, were often weaklings and all too often tyrants. Its unquestionable political gifts were squandered on organization and seldom achieved a confident freedom. The Germans were readily intoxicated with success and boldly ventured the impossible. But they steeped themselves in self-torment at every misfortune, and brave though they were in battle, they took refuge in that spiritual world that was always so close to them, the secret realm of creative and visionary excitement. The Germans were never placid or pleasant neighbours. They did not want to be liked and, by and large, lacked the gift of arousing such feelings; they enjoyed being right about things, and they could not resist the pedantic urge to instruct others in the con-

7

duct of life. Individuals were indeed accorded the recognition and even the admiration of the entire civilized world. But precisely their stalwart individualism made the Germans politically quarrelsome and obstinate. In the course of recent developments the nation as a whole has become more and more controversial. Today it is the focus of world interest as the begetter of a world-wide movement that has had incalculable effects. The world has one more reason to ponder this people: it is the problem people of our epoch.

Chapter 2

THE ORIGIN OF GERMAN NATIONALITY

THE GERMANS are not Aryans. In the scientific sense of the word only the Persians and the people of India can be called Aryans. Nor are the Germans Indo-Germanic. The term "Indo-Germanic" is misleading and is therefore no longer used by scholars. The Germans belong to the Indo-European family of peoples, though the pre-Indo-European element is probably stronger among the Germans than farther west in Europe. The Germans are not Germani, though the nationality contains a strong Germanic element. To venture an estimate, probably a bare thirty per cent of the German people of today can be set down as predominantly Germanic. The next strongest component is the Celtic; then comes the Slavic. The growth of the German nation was slow; the beginnings go back to the time of Charles the Great (742–814). It was not until 1300 that the German people emerged historically, and its ethnical structure certainly underwent great changes even after that time. The origin of a German language and the origin of German royal rule together mark the beginning of German history.

THE HERITAGE OF THE KINGDOM OF THE FRANKS

German history is rooted in that of the Kingdom of the Franks. Here was a heritage, a claim, but also a cleavage. What did it signify? Among all the kingdoms founded by the Germani and the tribes who accompanied them on their migrations, the Kingdom of the Franks was the only one that endured. Its longevity was due to favourable geographical and ethnical conditions, but above all to alliance with the orthodox Athanasian form of Christianity, which maintained the divinity of Christ. The Roman concept of empire and of civilization persisted here; the fusion of old and new in a fresh and vigorous form of existence could come to pass. Arian Christianity,

9

with its heretical questioning of the absolute divinity of Christ, was overborne by the orthodox hierarchy of the bishops rather than by sheer doctrinal theology. The Catholic or universal Roman and orthodox spirit of the Frankish Kingdom made it possible for its kings to extend their dominion triumphantly and to found the new Carolingian Empire.

Charles the Great was neither German nor French, because at that time there were no Germans and no French. But he is the father of German, of French, and also of Italian history. Posterity saw in him the incarnation of imperial majesty: his mighty head, rendered even more venerable by his long, flowing beard, bore the holy crown of the eternal and universal Roman Empire. The actual appearance of this robust, domineering prince of the Franks was quite different. The famous equestrian statue in the Cluny Museum shows the real man as moustached and thick-necked, sturdy and vigorous, a man of the moment, an executive type. "This king of the Franks mounted the steed of the Roman emperors," but he remained always wholly himself. He was not a saint until the romantic admiration of the Hohenstaufen period made him one. The Carolingian period was great because temporal and spiritual interests coincided in it. This harmony dominated the West up to Martin Luther's time. Even though conversion to Christianity was often very superficial and a wild pagan spirit persisted for a long while, yet up to the triumph of the Cluniac Reform in the eleventh century politics rested on the co-operation of the temporal ruler with the clergy. Small wonder that the self-conceit of the clergy, as vessels of the concept of imperial unity, became acute enough to annoy many dukes and tribes. The cultural significance of the so-called Carolingian renaissance did not at all correspond to this political pattern. The longed-for reconciliation of the Christian, Roman, and Germanic ideologies and the release that would have come with the attainment of such unity has always remained visionary.

Those regions east of the Rhine that were to become the stage of German history were drawn into the Kingdom of the Franks. The Bavarians, the Alemanni, the Thuringians, and finally the Saxons were all seized by this growing kingdom; they were converted, subjugated, and as far as possible won over. Among all the Germani the Franks proved the cleverest colonizers. Their rough social dealings acquired, from contact with the Romans in Gaul, a form of organization that was imperious, yet considerate. Anyone who was ready to conduct himself honourably toward the Frankish powers could keep his personal liberty and his land. The Roman cities in the Rhineland were allowed to continue as well as those in Gaul; there was no real break in civilization. The Celtic substratum in the Rhineland and in the Roman-settled part of southern Germany made it possible for the old ruling class to be at peace with the Frankish kings. The bishops and the Frankish officials took what they regarded as a suitable share of land and then let the Germani and the Celts live as they would.

The Franks had difficulty in establishing their supremacy only in regions where there were neither Roman cities nor a Celtic substratum — in Saxony and in the land of the Chatti. For several reasons the arduous and bloody Saxon campaigns of Charles the Great (772–814) offer the most significant introduction to German history. The Saxons, a purely Germanic component of the population, were won over by the Franks to their orthodox Christianity. This was the prerequisite for the coalescence of the Saxons with other Germanic tribes. On the other hand the cruelty of this conquest and conversion were never forgotten; it proved a strong stimulus toward particularism in the Germany of the future. A generation later the conversion of the Saxons would have assumed a milder form, like that of the Scandinavian peoples, but then the Saxons might very possibly have joined this group of peoples and remained independant of the growing German state. In that case Germany in the historical form we know, Germany in central Europe, would never have arisen, for politically it is the creation of the Saxon dukes.

THE RISE OF THE GERMAN LANGUAGE

The forced removal and resettlement undertaken as a method of taming the obstreperous Saxons marked the beginning of the fusion of the Germanic tribes and was thus another factor in the development of the German people. All these tribes spoke their own native tongues, mutations of what we call Old High German and Old Low German. For a long time the official language remained Latin. When Charles and Louis, the sons of Louis the Pious, made common cause against their elder brother Lothair, they sealed their confederacy by the Strassburg Oaths (842). Each swore his oath in the language of his partner's vassals. There was then no one popular tongue prevalent throughout the world of the Franks; there were East Frankish and West Frankish — that is, Old German and Old French. When the kings pronounced their oaths, each used an idiom that was commonly understood by the other side, though it was not so commonly spoken, let alone written. Charles the Great had shown much feeling for and understanding of the old poetic language of the people and had encouraged literary production. But Louis the Pious, in his narrow orthodoxy, permitted zealous priests to destroy these pagan treasures. The monasteries in East Francia were art schools, universities, and economic centres. West Francia had a richer intellectual life; here aristocratic laymen made themselves felt, while the cathedral and monastery schools diffused education of a high level, and Romance culture found little difficulty in carrying forward that of ancient Rome. In East Francia this was possible only to a limited degree; the Germanic and Celtic population was unresponsive, and it had to be courted.

For a long time traces of the old pagan ways persisted. Lax marriage customs, for instance, reflected the bland pre-Christian attitude toward law and society. It was not a question of immorality, but of morality of a different kind, primitive and naïve, obedient to its own norms. The work of Christianizing had been carried out chiefly by Irish monks, who were mistakenly called Scotch; the Scotch monastery in Vienna survives as a reminder of them. In reality, however, the East Franks never became Christians in a religious, spiritual sense. It was rather that their unwarped, vigorous emotions and actions appropriated Christian symbols, words, and rites as the newest and most potent magic, which had already shown itself superior to heathendom. But faith in gods and witches persisted with secret strength under all surface changes. A witch was originally a woodland spirit that was hostile to humankind. Now, under the infection of the Oriental contempt for women, something hellish and demoniacal was apprehended in the nature of the female, though such a feeling was altogether foreign to the Germanic spirit.

The word *deutsch* (*theod*) first appeared in 786 to designate the language of the people of East Francia. It was not until the middle of the twelfth century that the terms *deutsch* (*dieutsch*) and *Deutsch-*

land (*Diutskland*) were commonly applied to the people and the land of the East Frankish state. A German nation was first spoken of in the reign of Frederick Barbarossa.

Latin lyrics and epics of the early East Frankish period were written and read by the clergy and by the few laymen who had secured a scholar's education. The *Hildebrandslied* is the only surviving fragment of real Old German folk poetry. Characteristic of the German bent toward self-destruction, it tells the affecting tale of the father whose own son opposes him in mortal combat. Even more remarkable is the spiritual poetry that set out to win lay souls with the help of the people's language. The author of the *Heliand,* for example, tried to adapt Christian doctrine to the ideas of his audience and his readers. His Christ is no Jewish or Oriental ascetic who flees the world and overcomes its stresses through mental and spiritual sufferings that are a model for the ages: rather, Christ was here the people's king, receiving the oath of allegiance from a new subject through the rite of baptism—a brave warrior who sacrifices himself and so assures victory to his vassals. In the end he dies only to extend his triumphal progress to the very gates of hell.

THE RISE OF THE EAST FRANKISH KINGDOM

German history begins with the Saxon wars (772, 782, 792) and with the *Heliand,* but all this was still by way of preparation. The fact that one of the sons of Louis the Pious was called Louis the German (Germanicus, died 876) is somewhat misleading. His East Francia, the land east of the Aar and the Rhine, was a part of the Empire that had no definite form as yet, and Louis's selfish ambitions reached out beyond its borders. There was something accidental about its very nature, and its provisional existence was threatened by the King's contentious sons. Conditions were still more unsettled in West Francia, and Lothair's central part of the Empire broke up into three subdivisions: Lorraine, Burgundy, and Italy. Lorraine was gradually taken over by East Francia, which accordingly pressed deeper and deeper into the Romance language sphere. Partitionings, discord, treachery, and changes of front are typical of the end of the Carolingian period. The idea of an imperial unity, the dynastic interests of the Carolingian house, the claim of the bearers of the imperial crown to exercise supremacy, and over against this the tendency of the different tribes to flock around their local leaders for the sake of security in the midst of all the disorder—these are the main features of the time of transition. The imperial authority dwindled steadily, and not even a very efficient and honest man, such as the Emperor Arnulf of Carinthia (died 899), could succeed in building it up again. Invaders pressed in on East Francia: the Normans, the Moravians, the Hungarians. Each part of the Empire was forced to defend its own interests. And thus the concept of Carolingian sovereignty perished from within. Duke Conrad of Franconia made a last attempt to realize it (911–8). But his kingdom, which set out with the help of the episcopate to enforce centralization in spite of the tribal dukes, came to a sad end. The Frankish era was over. Either the ingrained particularism of the different tribes would carry off the victory—and there were many factors that made this probable— or a kingdom would arise of itself in the east. Such a kingdom would have to be based on the co-operation and coalescence of the tribes in a new unity. This is what came to pass, and with it the true beginning of German history.

EAST FRANKISH
KINGDOM
c. 919

Prussians

Slavic peoples

Saxony

Lorraine

Franconia

Swabia

Bavaria

Panonia

West
Frankish
Kingdom

Burgundy

Italy

Dalmatia

Chapter 3

THE SAXON RULERS

THE EMPIRE of Charles the Great did not fall apart solely because his successors were weak. This Empire was a unique creation that had been hammered together by an almost superhuman personality, who exerted a magic as of legend while yet he lived. From a practical point of view the economic conditions and communications of the Carolingian Empire were far too rudimentary for a permanent imperial regime. Any strong local authority necessarily took precedence over the distant chief who was now here, now there, and equally over his authorized representatives, who appeared and disappeared unpredictably.

The boundaries of the Empire continually called for defence. What a chance for young nobles to distinguish themselves! At these boundaries the margraves gathered armed forces and matériel of war, and this in turn was felt in the interior and increasingly challenged the central power. At this time the only important and permanent form of power was the possession of land. The officials around the king were assigned land; the counts transformed their feudal fiefs into hereditary estates. The mass of freemen mattered less and less in political life. The king whittled down his own property in order to reward devotion. Aristocratic families arose which, holding numerous offices and large possessions, became allied among themselves by marriage and thus developed territorial power. These groups pushed themselves in between the king and his officials. Such was the origin of the new tribal duchy, which was rooted in the soil, in local tradition, and in personal attainment. In a way this phenomenon revived the old Germanic provincial kingdom.

In this Germany-in-evolution there were still many free peasants. Even where large estates prevailed, there were no agricultural operations on a large scale. The land was let out to people who were required to work it. These were in part serfs and bondsmen who were inferior ethnically; or, again, free men who had lost their land; or, finally, free men who owned some land but needed more if they were to make a comfortable living, and who preferred to get it from the church, since dependency was least disagreeable in relation to that institution. Churches and monasteries encouraged the clearing of the land and the planting of orchards and especially vineyards, since wine was required for the sacrifice of the Mass. In market towns, particularly in the Rhineland, there were many independent artisans, whereas in purely agrarian regions the artisan was subject to the landed proprietor. Commerce followed the old roads in the Rhine region and across the Alps, where the Roman tradition was never entirely broken. Itinerant merchants visited the Slavic and northerly regions with increasing regularity. The Frisians excelled at maritime trade, in which they competed with the Normans and Anglo-Saxons. Along the Rhine much buying and selling was done by Jews, who had settled there from the second and third centuries. Their communities survived the storms of the great migrations and were as useful to the new lords as to the old.

At the beginning of the period of the Saxon rulers this Germany-in-evolution was a completely unhomogeneous entity in the midst of central Europe. For a while it seemed as if a kingdom would never again be set up. The tribal duchies had a very decided character of their own. They lived unto themselves as political organizations of tribal particularism. In Saxony and Bavaria the dukes appropriated almost all the royal prerogatives. In Lorraine, Swabia, and Franconia several great families struggled for power and held one another in check. The Saxon Liudolfingers were nobles of the Harz region who enjoyed the privileges of margraves and had proved their military leadership in war with the Slavs. They prevented the formation of a Thuringian duchy, annexed this land to their own, and thus made their position in northern and central Germany too powerful for the Franks to dispute.

Henry, who became the first Saxon King of Germany, held aloof from the scholastic culture of his era and was cool toward the church. His two marriages greatly increased the lands he held, till only the Frisians were still independent of the rule of the Duke in northern

Germany. The East Frankish King Conrad I had sent from his death-bed, by his own brother, Duke Eberhard of Franconia, the symbols of kingship—lance, robe, crown, and sword—to the Saxon Duke, who was his bitterest and most determined foe, and had thus singled him out as his only possible successor. Alleged descent from Charles the Great was also in the Saxon Duke's favour. The requirement of legitimacy, still most pressing, wrapped its tendrils around the necessities of politics. Now the old calamitous evil of the Saxon wars found a late atonement. Would the Saxons be able to create a true East Frankish, a German, or even a Carolingian and Roman Empire?

During his whole lifetime Henry I remained a Saxon peasant duke, sober, quiet, soldierly, calm, strong, and majestic, an enemy to all visionary undertakings. His first need was to gain recognition. Bavaria and Swabia were cool and accorded him mere feudal homage. West Francia was still under Carolingian rule. Lorraine, thanks to its geographical position, could swing like a pendulum between West and East Francia. To gain the recognition of the West Frankish Carolingians, Henry I sacrificed Lorraine at the beginning and then exploited the weakness of the West Frankish Kingdom to bring it under his sway again. The Duke of Lorraine was more fortunate in his relations with an evolving Germany than in those with a growing France; in token of his loyalty he married one of Henry's daughters. At this time the parishes of the Rhenish bishoprics became purely German from a political point of view, though still not so linguistically. No danger threatened the Saxon Kingdom from the west; it came instead from the east. Repeated invasions of savage Hungarians were a plague and a torment to East Francia. Henry had to proceed slowly. First he made a treaty with the Hungarians; it provided that for nine years Saxony and Thuringia should pay tribute, but it could not save the rest of Germany. At the end of the truce the Hungarians reappeared in northern Germany. Henry did not pay tribute again, but, armed and prepared, he struck at his dangerous adversary in two encounters, which, to be sure, gave him only a brief breathing-spell. His victories over the Slavs were more substantial. In the course of the truce the King had strengthened Saxony by establishing citadels. These were not cities, since, economically speaking, the time was not yet ripe for cities: they were only places of refuge for the country folk—large fortified structures without distinct administrative status. In many cases convenient bishoprics, monasteries, and imperial palaces were used for them. As a standing garrison for these new places Henry settled in them every ninth man among his retainers. A powerful impetus toward the creation of this new defence system was provided by the example of the Anglo-Saxon King Edward, with whom Henry was connected through the marriage of his son Otto to the Anglo-Saxon Princess Edith.

The Hungarian invasions had split into two divisions the Slavs who bordered on growing Germany, and this development decisively weakened the Slavic peoples. There was now a northerly group of Slavs, comprising Sorbs, Czechs, and Poles, and a southerly group. Henry was concerned only with the northern Slavs. He subjugated small tribes in what was later Brandenburg and founded the Mark of Meissen (Saxony). In company with the Duke of Bavaria he then attacked Bohemia, where the Přemyslids had established themselves. This Czech ducal house was forced to recognize the supremacy of the German King and to pay tribute, much to the satisfaction of the exigent Duke of Bavaria. Henry's victory over the Slavs was his most notable achievement. He led no crusade; there was too much ancient heathenism in Saxony itself. But in his fight against the Slavs he was the first to raise the local feuds of the Saxon nobility to the level of a national German enterprise. No longer were the Slavs exterminated; they kept their own princes, though they were compelled to receive German merchants, advisers, and settlers.

Henry also had a certain amount of success in his struggle against the Danes. As a result of his work his last years were peaceful; there was friendly or at least tolerable co-operation with the princes and bishops. The church respected this sober, silent man, and he smilingly accepted its support and willingly promised to put down abuses. The realm seemed to him so well stabilized that he planned an expedition to Italy. Relations between southern and southwestern Germany and Italy had always remained close—closer than between southern and northern Germany. Anyone who wanted to be German king must have his part in this circle of interests. Henry I was prepared to join in it, and not as a dreamer, but as a man of action. But his early death (936) put an end to his plans.

Except for Otto I, who died at sixty-one, none of the rulers of either the Saxon or the Salic dynasty reached the sixties. Both lines died out quickly. They produced a series of extraordinary characters who swiftly burned out; there was a sort of youthful exuberance about them. Talent, faith, task and destiny, environment and opposition — all gave them a dash of greatness, but also imposed on them the curse of wasted strength and premature exhaustion. The nature of the sources compels later commentators to say a great deal about these sovereigns themselves, for their foes and their supporters alike seem faint and blurred, while the great mass of subjects led an anonymous existence in which, at best, only typical features can be traced. What actually took place was neither quite simple nor wholly heroic. Since it is possible to know only a little, it is necessary to venture some guesses.

According to old Germanic law the king was elected. The leading families did not care for this arrangement, since they were ambitious to become dynasties. Moreover, a limitation was imposed by the king's prerogative, as he lay dying, of indicating as his successor the man whom he regarded as the aptest and the most worthy to continue his work.

OTTO THE GREAT (936–73)

King Henry had designated his oldest son by his second marriage as his successor — not his son Thankmar by his first marriage, which had been dissolved because his first wife, the Countess of Merseburg, had already been married and had then taken the veil. In his father's opinion Otto, his eldest son by his second marriage, had the best claim, although Henry, who was younger, had been actually born in the purple, after his father had become king — a substantial consideration from the mystical outlook of the period. Thus from the very outset the choice of Otto was open to question and indeed to the charge of illegality.

The election itself went off smoothly. Only the lay nobility participated, but the young King had himself crowned and anointed in Aachen (Aix-la-Chapelle) by the Archbishop of Mainz. At the coronation banquet that followed, the dukes performed court services as chamberlains, marshals, stewards, and cupbearers. The new regime was well characterized by these proceedings. Otto I wanted to be more than a Saxon duke. He attempted to set up a truly centralized monarchical power in the East Frankish realm, the growing Germany. The particularism of the tribes militated against this. Otto's feuds with his brothers developed into a great political struggle that sapped the strength of the kingdom for years. Duke Thankmar soon foundered, but Duke Henry rebelled against his royal brother again and again; he could not forgive him for being the older and much the more gifted. Henry himself was vain and weak and permitted flatterers to push him into active opposition. He had great personal charm, and he did not see, or did not wish to see, that the individual interests of Bavaria, Franconia, Swabia, and Lorraine were exploiting his fraternal envy to their own advantage. Otto bore off the victory, and he was magnanimous toward his misguided brother.

The King allowed Franconia, the Frankish duchy, to lapse, to the gratification of the Saxons. The other duchies he distributed to members of his own family. In Saxony he gave the brave and faithful Hermann Billung the rights of a margrave; a new ducal family with local roots was to spring up here while Otto's line pressed on into a wider world.

Otto continued the struggle with the Slavs in a new way. To the annoyance of the Saxon nobility, who liked to enrich themselves by marauding expeditions into Slavic lands, he undertook to organize the new country politically and religiously, over and above purely military measures. Marches and bishoprics were established. The native Slavic princes were often exterminated with horrible ruthlessness, and German rulership and conversion to Christianity were enforced by discipline and by exploitation of the natives. There was much intermarriage between the two populations, even in the uppermost class. Many a Slavic princess became the wife of a gallant "Junker"—a young noble or younger son.

Otto I had an ambitious spirit that drew Burgundy, France, and Italy into the circle of its plans. For the first time there arose over the German nationality and its sphere of action the concept of a central European power, not in the sense of forcibly Germanizing the country's neighbours—such a method was wholly alien to the spirit of the times—but by the much simpler and more natural means of carrying out an idea of sovereignty. If such an idea were to be realized, then the German Kingdom must above all be safe from its most dangerous eastern neighbours, the Hungarians. They were now threatening the very existence of Otto's growing realm, for German particularism made common cause with these aliens.

The revolt of Otto's brothers was followed by the revolt of the sons of his first marriage to the Anglo-Saxon Edith. Liudolf and Conrad felt themselves somewhat set apart as Anglo-Saxons, and they persecuted their stepmother Adelaide with burning hatred. This second wife was a highly cultivated Burgundian princess, a woman of the world who exerted great influence on Otto by turning him toward universalism. By birth Adelaide was just as Germanic as Edith. The contrast between them was spiritual and political. Against the background of such personal feuds the great essential conflicts of the epoch unfolded. Particularly the eldest son, Duke Liudolf of Swabia, felt that he had been slighted and that his right of succession was obviously threatened, since he had not been born in the purple like Adelaide's son Otto, later Otto II. The danger of the resultant civil war was great, greater than ever before. The fact that the rebels sided with the Hungarians shook the unity and future of Otto's Germany. By a tremendous effort Otto mastered the opposing forces and administered severe discipline. The duchies were distributed anew, and this time Otto I favoured the clerical members of his family, from whom no threat of particularistic or dynastic interests was to be expected. He was now in a position to concentrate all the resources of his centralized government and of his manpower in a great blow against the Hungarians, the brilliant victory of the Battle of the Lech near Augsburg (955). The triumph made Otto's recognition and popularity secure as nothing else had done; henceforth the common people called him "the Great." This battle against the Hungarians was a crucial turning-point. An oppressive fear was lifted from central Europe, and southwestern Germany could now develop freely. The Hungarians, who had to give up their nomadism, were to figure as neighbours and serious participants in all the German-Slavic conflicts of the future.

The civil wars of the Ottonian era were highly personal struggles charged with passion, envy, and the craving for power. Faithlessness, treachery, and hatred gave them a moving human quality in the tragic vein of the *Nibelungenlied*. There was still no collective German national feeling, and as yet there could not be. A very genuine resistance flared up among the tribes against the tutelage and tyranny of the new central power—against Christianity as well as against Cæsarean claims to universal supremacy. The tribes wanted to remain themselves, wanted to go on in their age-old pagan way. They felt themselves living entities, and that was why, over and over, rebellious dukes were able to gather many local followers when they resisted oppression. These circumstances make possible a just interpretation of the revival of the Roman Empire.

THE REVIVAL OF THE EMPIRE

From the point of view of a much later stage of political development, the expeditions of the German kings to Rome and their struggle for the Empire were subjected to repeated and severe criticism. The only appropriate way to judge of these matters is the purely historical method that endeavours to reproduce the conditions of the period faithfully and to understand them. From the end of the East Frankish Carolingian period the Empire and the papacy had been tottering in a lamentable decline. Italy was racked with disorder; Magyars and Saracens infested the unhappy land, which had no means of resisting incursions effectively. Here, in the same way as north of the Alps, separate governments of a local character sprang up. The nobles of Rome, whose inborn Romanism preserved the heritage of late antiquity, made a plaything of the papal crown, while the corruptive influence of adventuresses heightened the general demoralization. The imperial crown passed to the Dukes of Friuli in northern Italy, then to the Dukes of Lower Burgundy. Emperors were held in such slight esteem that Spanish West Gothic and Anglo-Saxon rulers assumed the imperial title without bonds to Rome. The attitude of the East Franks, however, remained decisive for the future. True to ancient traditions, the Swabian and Bavarian nobility had been in the habit of journeying to Italy in order to plunder wherever they could and, if possible, to take advantage of the disorders there to secure power. At that time the bonds between southern and southwestern Germany and northern Italy were much closer than relations between northern and southern Germany. The more developed economic organization and the old cultural bonds worked together in the same direction. The Italian policy was thus no improvisation. It was a continuation of old interests and gave the south

Germans a familiar goal, while it also lured on the north Germans; thus it drew all the German tribes together toward one lofty political purpose.

Upper and Lower Burgundy lay between Italy and the evolving France. The affairs of Burgundy were of interest to the German Kingdom because of the proximity of Lorraine. The co-operation of the Italian and Burgundian ruling houses aroused fears of a resurrection of the buffer state of Carolingian memory, so painfully contrary to the strengthening interests of Germany. These considerations of power politics were reinforced by dynastic circumstances. When the Burgundian Princess Adelaide—the widow of the Italian King Lothair—looked about for a strong protector, she could only turn to King Otto, the most powerful sovereign north of the Alps. Otto's first expedition to Italy was made in 951. Without a formal coronation he called himself King of the Lombards, and having been widowed young himself, he married the beautiful and brilliant Adelaide. For Otto the Italian crown was part of the Carolingian heritage; historical tradition, not opportunism, determined his desire for it. A separate chancery was set up for Italy, for Otto did not dream of fusing his Italian and German domains. Even at this time the Pope offered to crown him as Emperor.

Otto's relations with the papacy disclose the fundamental assumptions of his career. Originally he had been just as cool toward the church as his father before him, but later a change became inevitable. Centralized administration could hardly be built up in Germany on the economic basis of the royal possessions. There were not enough officials; means of transportation were insufficient. But the church was already solidly organized, a strong institution and a unique going concern. Otto had no choice. He had to ally himself with the church: it provided the substitute that was needed for the previous ineffectual temporal administration. And so the Frankish concept of rulership was resuscitated; in the Kingdom of the Franks, too, the king was the supreme lord of the church and of the priesthood. Otto lavished gifts on the church. The cultivated clergy made excellent counsellors and assistants, for even their self-seeking had something more than personal greed in it. When royal property was given to the church it was not quite lost, as it usually was when granted to laymen. The church made the property useful for its own purposes and hence also for the common good. Co-operation was successful as long as the church was loyal. To maintain control of the church became an obsession with the King. He nominated bishops and abbots and invested them with office by the presentation of ring and staff before their consecration by the church. At that time no one regarded this as uncanonical. The bishops were subject to the King's courts. The royal chancery became a seminary for cultivated clergymen of high moral standards who were loyal to the King; such men, along with the women of the princely family, fostered a brilliant intellectual life at court.

But the position of the church also depended on the papacy. Could the German King answer for the domination of the head of Christendom by local Roman and Italian powers or for the influencing of the clergy by these same powers, which made them waver in their relationship to the kingdom? The temporal interests of the papacy called for protection against the Saracens and Byzantium. If the German King did not come to the aid of the papacy, some day a French king would. There had already been a West Frankish emperor (Charles the Bald). It was impossible to hold the Italian Kingdom against the local dynasties unless the imperial crown were won and a western universal authority thereby set up anew in co-operation with the papacy. Only the concept of the Christian mission of the emperorship could provide Otto's central European realm with the inner support that this body politic needed in order to face its neighbours. For example, without the Pope's blessing the newly founded Archbishopric of Magdeburg could not extend its power over the pagan land of the Slavs. Polish and Czech princes would more readily become vassals of an emperor than of a king. The Roman concept survived as a significant political force. Through Christianization and the mission to the pagans the central European imperialistic idea was at work. A just and peaceful kingdom of God on earth was the most welcome form of preparation for eternity. King Otto embodied the world of Carolingian thought. The imperial dignity was by the grace of God —a temporal and a spiritual charge. How could a sovereign such as he, who had become deeply religious, evade this most solemn and profound benediction?

For various reasons the Pope was bound to see some advantage in crowning the German King as emperor. The papacy was in need of temporal territories as a basis for its political and economic existence. The closer the emperor's lands and the more interest he took in acquiring local power in Italy, the more would he be an irritation to the ambitious papacy. An emperor who had to cross the Alps to get to Italy would appear suddenly, but he would disappear as quickly; the papacy could benefit by the authority of such an emperor without suffering constant domination. Here was the first great error in German imperial policy. When Otto had himself crowned, the Pope had to swear never to desert him; in the so-called Ottonian Privilege the Pope's claims to his temporal possessions were guaranteed, but it was prescribed as a condition of the consecration of any future pope that he should swear fealty to the emperor. The Romans gave their oath, not to install any pope without a previous expression of the emperor's will (962); this was later declared uncanonical and hence not binding. Here was the second decisive error in German imperial policy; the arrangement would be meaningless unless the emperor succeeded in permanently dominating both the papacy and the Romans.

More and more Emperor Otto filled in the outlines of the Carolingian style. In the legendary form in which it persisted the image of Charles the Great came to resemble this Saxon prince. Otto I gained the affection of his people through his brilliance, his restlessness, his youthfulness even in riper years—through the leonine force of his wrath, his dignity and obstinacy in negotiation, his tireless energy, and his noble and passionate will. Among the German rulers there were greater soldiers, sharper reckoners, and more careful administrators, but there was hardly another who was able to inspire such immediate confidence in himself and what he stood for.

THE END OF THE OTTOS (973–1002)

Otto's contemporaries may have felt that his political achievements marked the beginning of a great era. But reaction set in at once. The dynasty was secure; Otto II succeeded his father. At the age of seven he was chosen king and crowned, in obvious contradiction of the principle of the election of kings. He received the imperial crown while his father was still alive, and through his marriage to a Byzantine princess, the clever, precocious, and spoiled Theophanu, he secured the recognition of the Empire of the East for the Empire of the West. Otto was of a more deliberate turn of mind than his father, but he lacked the latter's compelling force. The succession, then, went smoothly, but the heritage proved a heavy burden. The southern Italian dynasties of Capua and Benevento and above all the Byzantine sovereignty over Apulia and Calabria had struck even the first Otto as a challenge. Should not all Italy be united as it had been in antiquity? Could there be peaceful rule in northern and southern Italy and a wholesome relationship between emperor and papacy if the entire peninsula were not subject to a single political will? The German rulers strove, then, for a united Italy. But the concept of an Italian state and an Italian culture was to be turned against foreigners, and Italy became for German royalty the land of destiny.

North central Europe could be ruled from Germany. Anyone who possessed all of Italy had a base for dominating the Mediterranean. Where, then, would there be any measure and limits?

If it had been possible to do away entirely with the German tribal duchies and to force the German tribes together into one firmly organized state, Ottonian imperialism might have been successful. Otto II thought it his first duty to curb Bavaria, which had grown beyond all bounds. A new duchy was set off—Carinthia, including the original Carinthia, Styria, Carniola, and in addition the Mark of Verona. The lands of Upper and Lower Austria, also designated as the East Mark, made themselves more and more independent of Bavaria. Here lay the beginnings of Austria's particularism—adherence to Bavaria and opposition to Bavaria being both integral with its history. In 976 the house of Babenberg took over the East Mark, which it held until 1246. For the sake of its own family interests the Saxon imperial house could not tolerate a privileged position for Bavaria and for its dynasty. Breaking up the tribal duchies was thus to the advantage of the supremacy of one house. Otto II had now enough confidence in his own power to interfere in Italy. Here the northern African empire of the Fatimides had established itself and was threatening the Byzantine position in Lower Italy. Even in southern France there was a nest of Arabian robbers. Could Emperor Otto II ally himself with the Mohammedans against Byzantium? This might have been the wisest course, but it was out of the question for the husband of Theophanu. Otto attacked Arabian sea power, but did not receive the support he expected from Byzantium. His connections by marriage brought him nothing but difficulties and annoyance. When the Emperor suffered a severe defeat at Cape Colonne in southern Italy, hostility toward the Germans broke out all over the peninsula. Otto nevertheless put through the election of his little son as German and Italian King in the diet at Verona. But before he could resume his struggle with the Arabs and his negotiations with the Greeks, he died in Rome at the age of twenty-eight (983).

The failure of Emperor Otto II in Italy was the signal for a long-prepared rebellion of the Slavs to break out in eastern Germany. Disunity and mistakes of the German administration had aroused the greatest bitterness in the subjugated Slavic tribes. Markets and monasteries were plundered and destroyed. The conversion of the past two generations was effaced. With this the conciliation policy of the high administrative clergy seemed shattered as well, and again everything was based on brute force, as it had been before.

The high episcopate supported the regency of the Empresses Adelaide and Theophanu for Otto III, and the regime could therefore return successfully to the policy of Otto the Great. The envious Bavarian collateral line of the Liudolfingers was placated. Southern Italy again fell to the Greeks, and internal problems paralysed the striking power of the Arabs. Reason reigned in this period of transition. As yet no decisive loss had been suffered save in the Slavic east. Theophanu was particularly successful. Since she was the sole representative of imperial power in Italy, she took the imperial title. But, precisely because of her personal and intellectual distinction, this Greek princess was never beloved of the Germans. All might have gone smoothly for a long time if Theophanu had not died prematurely, so that the grandmother, the Empress Adelaide, feeble as she had become, was forced to help out again.

At the age of fourteen Otto III began to rule independently (994). He was a precocious youth who had been given the best Greek and Latin education. One of his masters in particular, Bishop Bernward of Hildesheim, a connoisseur of the arts, influenced him profoundly. Bernward embodied the very strict religious tendency that had sprung from the monastery of Cluny, founded in 910. It aimed at a lofty moral standard as well as unconditional subordination of monks to their abbot. Burgundy and Lorraine became the home of this movement. Repression of the laity with its love of life, rational administration, an authoritarian spirit, increase in church property —these were joined, oddly enough, to the idea of pious flight from the world and to solemn religious services celebrated with austere music. About the year 1000 the blissfulness of death was in the air, together with expectancy of the end of the world, and it pushed all worldly interests into the background. The new tendency, proceeding from the monasteries and penetrating the secular clergy, presented itself as the first carrier of the true Christian spirit in everyday life. Instead of the current acceptance of life this movement stood for asceticism and stern discipline. In Italy especially a mystical tendency arose that was positively hostile to all that is mundane. It revived certain trends that were marked in early Christianity and late antiquity: renunciation of the world, mortification of the flesh, a completely revolutionized existence, a new humanity. The passionate Bohemian Adalbert of Prague, who attained the rank of Archbishop of Prague, was active in this movement. He felt for the young Emperor the devotion of an admiring friend. The martyr's death he suffered as a missionary in Prussia only served to increase the fame of this strange and fascinating personality. Another friend of Otto's was the adroit and subtle Frenchman Gerbert, who as Pope Sylvester II was soon urging the new ideas from Peter's chair. Just as the abbot claimed unquestioned superiority over the monks, the bishop over lay authorities, so the Pope now claimed for his spiritual power the rank of the highest universal principle, intrinsically superior to all temporal principles. Otto III desired Rome and the Roman sovereignty; Rome was to be the focus of a revived empire in which Germany would be only one element among many. Emperor and pope figured as joint bearers of the high priest's power, one and indivisible, which was to rule on earth in a realm of peace, justice, and piety, in preparation for the eternal Rome that was Jerusalem and as the realization of the last world empire of Daniel's prophecy.

Emperor Otto no longer wished to be German. He spoke contemptuously of Saxon stupidity. He was completely obsessed by the idea of a resurrected Rome. In enumerating his lands he placed Rome and Italy ahead of Germany and Gaul. In his court he made use of Byzantine customs, titles, and ceremonies. The old and tried leaders of the Ottonian state church regarded all this with much concern. But it would be wrong to see in the Emperor nothing but a dreamer.

He and his friend the Pope were well able to guard their material interests and to act vigorously. Thus the papacy was to be incorporated in the state church, and Otto III rejected the Donation of Constantine as a forgery. The Emperor's decision to grant Poland her independence was also a clever stroke of politics. Poland no longer had to pay tribute. Formally she was still a vassal, but in regard to the church she was released from the guardianship of the Magdeburg Archbishopric. The Polish church organization was given a focus of its own, the Archbishopric of Gnesen, founded in the year 1000. At this time, too, Hungary was recognized as an independent kingdom. Pope Sylvester sent the royal crown to the son-in-law of the Duke of Bavaria, the new King Stephen. This was the first time that the papacy had been instrumental in bringing about a decision in temporal affairs in such a manner. From the point of view of the curia the procedure established a precedent and enhanced its prestige. Stephen's crown and the independent Hungarian Kingdom thus were sacred in a very new and special sense. Now Bohemia too gained practical independence. In this way the German Kingdom lost its influence on the states of eastern Europe. But groups of Germans were active in all of these states as aides, counsellors, and settlers. Rome, the south of Italy, and Lombardy were seething with rebellion against Otto's imperialism, but not even Germany stood solidly behind him. The Ottonian state church mistrusted the universalistic, half-temporal papacy just as much as it did the half-religious emperorship. All the particularistic powers stood with the German church. For the first time something like a national German opposition arose.

Emperor Otto III died unmarried at the age of twenty-two (1002). On his cousin, the last Saxon Emperor Henry II, a difficult task devolved, to which he was scarcely equal. At last it was the turn of the younger line of the Liudolfingers, which for decades had made life so hard for the older line. These Henrys could well have borne collectively the epithet that was attached to one of them, Henry the Wrangler, for passionate rebelliousness was strong in them. But the last Henry was gentle and sensitive, the late flowering of a noble stock. He had something of the decency and dignity of the first Henry; his art of negotiating recalled Otto the Great. He was as well educated as Otto II and was a pious mystic like Otto III. In all things he was a recapitulation, an epilogue. He was sound and persuasive, but not creative. During his rule Germany was never really at peace. The lay princes behaved as they pleased. The fact that more and more their fiefs were becoming hereditary made their position unshakeable. They bragged of their active participation in government, their right to give counsel. The state church helped in the traditional way and guarded public order as well as it could. But Henry II irritated the older school of bishops by his sympathy for the Cluniac Reform. In the new Bishopric of Bamberg the Emperor set up a pious residence for himself at the strategic key point on the line of communication between northern and southern Germany. The missions to the Slavs on the Upper Main were sent out from here, and here Henry and his wife Kunigunde, united in a deep and chaste unconsummated marriage, led a holy life while they still dwelt on earth. They were surrounded by faithful pupils and by the apt scholars of the extremely rich foundation. Such was the refuge of a noble, somewhat weary fighter to whom failures in politics meant little or nothing in the midst of this beautifully fashioned world. For Emperor Henry II, Bamberg became the earthly Rome-Jerusalem.

In Poland, under Duke Boleslav Chrobry (the Bold), a strong state had been formed, which enjoyed the support of the church under conditions similar to those in Germany. Emperor Henry struggled with this Polish Duke for years without being able to break his power. One remarkable circumstance about these battles was the Emperor's treaty with the Lusatians. He gained their allegiance against their cousins the Poles by permitting them to continue to worship their pagan gods. Even this devout sovereign tolerated idolatry if it helped him to exploit the tribal feuds of the Slavs. It was with great difficulty that Henry was able to hold the Counts of Luxemburg, his brothers-in-law, to the Empire. The Burgundian succession was especially important for the future. The eastern boundary was disintegrating; the west seemed to offer compensations of paramount importance to a successful Italian policy.

But in this very Italy the powers of the people were bestirring themselves against alien German domination. The patrician family of the Crescenti dominated Rome and the papacy. The Margrave Arduin of Ivrea acquired the Italian royal crown. As a compatriot he was supported by the cities and the rural nobility, but the bishops pinned their hopes to the Germans. Henry had himself crowned Italian King in Pavia and Emperor in Rome, but even in the course of later expeditions his position in Italy never developed beyond a purely nominal supremacy. New factors of power were taking shape. The maritime cities of Genoa and Pisa assisted the papacy as soon as it decided in favour of a national Italian policy. The papacy found in the Normans a new ally against the Greeks and the Saracens. A first body of troops landed on the return from a pilgrimage to Jerusalem. A larger group of two hundred and fifty knights followed. A new, clearly defined political element became operative in the destinies of central Europe. It was a development of far-reaching consequences. For the moment Henry II silenced the movement of the people in Italy. With the Pope he worked against his own German prelates. But these were only tactical victories. Death saved the Emperor from further serious feuds and painful setbacks (1024).

THE CULTURE OF THE SAXON PERIOD

A springtide light shines from the Germany of the Saxon period. There were few people then, but much land. No one had to go hungry. If a man wanted new land, he cleared a strip of forest and lived on the game. These clearings are the great achievement of the tenth and eleventh centuries. The feudal system spread farther and farther over the mass of the people, and in this early phase it functioned as a form of social progress. The unfree, the poor, the scattered, the earth-bound at last had the chance of contact with higher powers and with it the prospect of security, protection, work, perhaps advancement. In the feudal system three elements were bound up together: the Germanic element of temporary land grants (*beneficia*), the Roman and Frankish form of seignorial right, and finally the Celtic institution of vassalage. A vassal stood in a personal relationship as retainer and liegeman. This relationship imposed on him the obligation of military service, which in turn arose from the private armed forces of the landholders. The military, the government, and the church made use of the feudal system to open up the land and establish a hold over the people. Thus the feudal system changed all public and private life and completely reshaped them. It gave the evolving society of that period its stratified structure. Actually there came to be two Germanys: a devout Roman and Frankish church state and an underlying tameless paganism among the people, deeply rooted in all the non-Frankish tribes. The tensions between these two spheres of power supply the real core of the history of the growing German people.

The lands occupied by the peasantry gradually shrank. Only in the Alps, in the northwestern German marches, and in Westphalia did the peasantry maintain itself as a free class. Where the land was owned by lords, agricultural labour was performed by tenant farmers, who supplied provisions and services that maintained the seignorial court. The crosier—that is, the ecclesiastical lords—had the merited reputation of being easier masters than the temporal lords; and here was one more reason for access of economic and moral power to the church. The clergy acted with great wisdom in the matter of penal justice. The church battled against evil wherever it showed itself and for this purpose upheld the temporal authorities. The spiritual power itself spilled no blood; in supporting the temporal power, it handed offenders over to it for execution.

Fear and repentance noticeably increased the number of donations to the church, sometimes with the aid of pious forgeries. In inclination and practice the older generation of the clergy was very close to the paganism of the people. Among the lower clergy it was still very common for priests to marry. The strong temporal interests of the church forced many of the clergy to perform the services of scribes, local administrators, and treasurers. They best understood these tasks, and they had the spontaneous trust of the laity, which was pulled this way and that by wild and evil selfish passions.

The cities were in part settlements of Roman origin, in part imperial palaces and citadels around which markets had arisen, in part conglomerations of villages that had grown together and won civic rights. Fortification determined the political character of the city. In the same way manors and monasteries in the country were supplied with walls and moats, to which the stone watch-tower of Roman origin was soon added. Under Emperor Otto III more than two hundred new markets were established in Germany. City dwellers were artisans and tradespeople; their not being fully engaged in agriculture defined their position, though naturally it did not prevent them from possessing collective meadowlands or commons or from keeping animals or planting gardens. The city itself was the sphere of civic jurisdiction (*Burgfriede*). In origin this was a purely economic device to guarantee free trade and industry, but it was soon extended to the legal status of citizens in general. Differences in degree of personal freedom, personal and class tensions, would have impeded civic life seriously. City air conferred freedom, because equality of status first made possible the kind of work that was carried on in cities. The cities were immediately subject to king, bishop, or duke; the citizens were answerable to no lords below some such peak of a feudal pyramid. The cities, accorded privileges, became a refuge for economic unfortunates and those who suffered political or religious persecution. Here only personality and ability counted. Membership in a group was broken, only to make way presently for the formation of new groupings.

The evolving German people was full of vigour and the joy of life. The old common law, as laid down by precedent, was still effective. Folk preachers who wandered through the land used old familiar phrases. Minstrels entertained both villagers and courtiers; they went from town to town and sang the old epics, songs full of mockery, playful lies, and riddles—the so-called folksongs, loosely put together and constantly modified. The poetic power of the performer of such songs worked fruitfully with that of his hearers. The church found these productions saucy, immoral, even sinful. All kinds of ancient gods, ghosts, and magical spirits still led their secret pagan life. In the country, sages and wise women gave counsel to the broken, the exiled, the persecuted; they supplied them with potions brewed of herbs and magic fetishes of which the priest must never know. This hoary paganism survived for a long time, furtive but full-blooded, in spite of the efforts of the church to attract and satisfy the people with feast days, relics, and the cult of saints.

The clergy were active as teachers, physicians, poets, artists, and chroniclers of the aristocracy. They founded libraries, instructed high-born ladies, introduced finer breeding and manners in the schoolroom, and managed to stir the hearts of even the rude and obstreperous lords. When a child was born the church saw to it that he received a good Christian name—that is to say, a biblical Latin name. What could anyone do without a good patron saint? The church created saints by the names that were commonest among the people, and the less usual names died out. Monasteries, such as those of St.

Gall and Quedlinburg, played an essential part in shaping the culture of the Saxon period. Even today Hildesheim boasts about its great abbot, Bernward, the holy architect and bronze image-maker. The cultivation of the arts was imitative of the Latin and the antique; it has been misleadingly called Romanic, in contrast to the Greek culture of Byzantium. In many ways this art was genuinely Saxon or Frankish, for the forms of architecture that were taken over received the imprint of popular taste. These structures, crude, heavy, earthy, with the defiant contours to which the masses of stone were shaped, contributed in an essential way to the inception of a consciously German attitude toward life.

Chapter 4

THE SALIC DYNASTY

CONRAD II (1024–39)

THE HISTORY of the German emperors reaches its climax under the Franconian or Salic dynasty. The Salic emperors ascended the throne not as dukes of Franconia—for this duchy, so dangerous to centralization, had been dissolved—but as relatives of the house of Saxony. The right of inheritance had become the most decisive factor. Two cousins, the Dukes Conrad of the female line of the Liudolfingers, were bitter rivals. Not the younger Conrad, who held the greater part of the Franconian family property, but the elder Conrad, of Rhenish Franconia, was chosen. The Saxon nobility had no part in the choice, and the younger Conrad himself was not present at the election after his cousin induced him to withdraw by a promise of substantial compensation.

Conrad II, an impoverished prince, had married the widow of the Duke of Swabia, Gisela, who was too closely related to him to suit the ideas of the church. In his wife's duchy he made his first attempts at power politics without much luck. The beginnings of the new dynasty seemed hardly brilliant, but it was in reality the dawn of a great period. For everything that he achieved Conrad II had only himself to thank. He was always a bit of an upstart, and his shrewdness and persistence won him the place for which his extraordinary gifts fitted him. Amiability was not one of his virtues, and he was forced to be harsh. He was wholly a man of the here and now. Since he had no leanings toward asceticism and mysticism, he was distinctly out of humour with the Cluniac Reform. Conrad was the first East Frankish king whose gifts and whose interest lay wholly in statesmanship. No one who came into personal contact with this brutal nature could love it. His grim humour and coarse, malicious jests found only limited applause. But regarded from his subjects' point of view and in comparison with his predecessors and successors, this prince came very close to greatness. The opposition that arose against him following the election—a commonplace development—was motivated by the envy of the other princes rather than by the old tribal particularism. Times were changing. Duchies had so often passed from hand to hand and from family to family that the new generation of dukes ceased to represent any deep-rooted particularism.

The chief victim of Conrad's vengefulness was his stepson, Duke Ernest of Swabia, a controversial figure whom legend merged with Otto the Great's son Liudolf. Folk poetry could not forget this knightly, charming, but reckless prince. Ernest's claims to sovereignty and his personal happiness were wrecked by the ruthless authority of his stepfather. He came to be the hero of youth, of the little people, of the oppressed with their urge to independence. Ernest was destroyed by the social forces of the times. Despoiled of his Swabian heritage, excommunicated by the church, hunted down and stigmatized, he ended as a rebel and a robber chieftain in the high valleys of the Black Forest.

The opposition of the princes to Conrad was kindled by the question of Burgundy. Conrad's claims to the Burgundian throne were based on the arrangements of the last King of Burgundy, who from his death-bed had sent Conrad the crown. Against the interests of the neighbouring West Frankish Duke of Champagne, Conrad took the country by force. It was not, however, joined to East Francia. The chancery for Burgundy, with an independent office of chancellor, was kept up. A stately kingdom extending from upper Lorraine to the Mediterranean Sea, it was in effect still a land with its own laws and its own boundaries. It suffered from the contrast between Romanized Lower Burgundy or the Kingdom of Arles (including Provence) and the strongly Celto-Germanic Upper Burgundy. The Burgundian crown was the third to be held by the East Frankish Kingdom (1034). The German hold on Burgundy cut off France from Italy. The Alpine passes fell entirely into the hands of the sovereign of central Europe, and holding Burgundy materially aided the Emperor's Italian policy. The magnates of Burgundy were not displeased with a monarchy whose representative could appear only occasionally. The limited crown domains scarcely mattered. The foreign King could not dream of menacing the power and position of the old local aristocracy. Like Lorraine, Burgundy was occupied with the Cluniac Reform; a strengthening of this tendency was something the German Kingdom had to accept along with its new acquisition.

Conrad II did not allow the church to increase its power in any way whatever. He appointed bishops at his own discretion and exacted the usual tribute, which was later so sternly condemned as simony. As far as possible he tried to regain whatever property of the crown had been given away. The royal finances were organized in such a manner that they were independent of the church. The class of royal *ministeriales* was fostered, for in them the King found officials loyally devoted to him and his interests. These people came from a lower social stratum, from the class of the less well-to-do freemen or even from among the unfree. Conrad did more for his lesser vassals than for the great. Their fiefs, too, were now made hereditary, and in this way they rose to power, grew independent of the great feudal lords, and came to have a direct relationship to the monarch. Thus centralization gained ground. Conrad did everything he could to weaken the power of the tribal dukes. With a single exception he gave no duchies to his relatives, whom he preferred to have take the tonsure. Because he knew his own nature, he was suspicious of everyone. His son Henry received Bavaria and Swabia.

The question of the position of the vassals was a determining factor in the Emperor's Italian policy also. The Italian grandees were thoroughly weary of German domination and offered the crown first to the King of France, then to the King of Aquitaine (western France). The latter accepted it on behalf of his son, who, however, soon renounced it. The Italian bishops sided with the German King. Conrad II procured for himself the crowns of Italian King and Roman Emperor. In southern Italy he very wisely contented himself with the homage of Benevento and Capua. Contrary to his custom in Germany, the King rewarded the high dignitaries of the church with substantial gifts. His treatment of the feudal lords there was mild. At that time counts of old family in northern and central Italy held a great deal of land and were very powerful. In token of their lofty influence they called themselves margraves. It was difficult to make headway against them. By giving the lesser vassals (*valvassores*) the right to hand their fiefs down to their sons, Conrad won the aid of this group against the great vassals (*capitanei*). In spite of every kind of resistance and conspiracy the measure was a success. To the ambitious and energetic Norman Rainulf there, Conrad gave the Duchy of Aversa as an *arrière*-fief; in this way he hoped to legitimize the new Norman power in southern Italy and to play it off against the Lombards and the bishops. Conrad had no difficulty with the papacy. He was not at all displeased when the popes were incompetent or led immoral lives. Such matters annoyed the pious reform party, but did not disturb the worldly Emperor in the least.

HENRY III (1039–56). THE CLUNIAC REFORM MOVEMENT

From this very quarter came reaction against the apparently powerful results of the rule of Conrad II (died 1039). His son Henry III was the first East Frankish king to mount the throne without the breaking out of revolts. Dynastic accident gave him almost complete possession of southern Germany. If Conrad II may be compared with Henry, the first king of the Saxon dynasty, then Henry III, the cultivated lover of books and music, suggests the later Ottos. The eastern policy of both the first Salic king and the second shows what a mistake it is to interpret the expansion of Burgundy and Italy as the cause of a weakening in the east. The German kings' claims to imperial power rested on the weakness of the neighbouring West Frankish Kingdom, which was developing into the French Kingdom, on the disintegration of the Slavic tribes, and on the difficult position of the papacy in Italy. The moment a single one of these factors changed, the moment a concentration of power manifested itself in any of these quarters, German hegemony, issuing from domination over central Europe, would be shaken. This had become plain during the rule of the Polish Duke Boleslav Chrobry. He died an independent king, but even his immediate successor was unable to maintain this position and had to pay homage to the Emperor again as a vassal. Even during Conrad's life Upper and Lower Lusatia were annexed to the Empire. The Duke of Moravia and Bohemia also recognized the supremacy of the Emperor. A union of Poland and Bohemia, with their dependencies, would have constituted a real threat to Germany. Serious disturbances in Poland seemed to point to such a development, but Henry III intervened, forced the Duke of Bohemia to give up the major part of his Polish conquests, and made sure of his adherence in the struggle with Hungary, against which Henry III had fought ineffectively when he was still only the heir to the crown.

Three campaigns were needed to install Prince Peter—friendly to the Germans—in Hungary, for a short time at least. Peter was the son of a doge of Venice. He paid homage to the Emperor by presenting him with a golden lance. The Emperor sent this lance to the Pope in Rome in proof of the homage he had received. But the Pope interpreted the act in an unexpected way by taking the lance as a token of homage to himself from the Emperor. The unfortunate King Peter did not profit by German intervention; his eyes were put out, and he was imprisoned by partisans of Hungarian independence. Emperor Henry set up new marches for the defence of the land he had taken. In addition to the enlarged Mark of Austria there were now the Marks of Styria and Carniola, regions with a strongly Slavic, Celtic, and pre-Indo-European population. In the north and northeast also German influence was mounting.

Since the dukes of Saxony of the house of Billung exacted a special tribute from pagan Slavs, they did not favour Christian missions. Old Saxon sympathies for paganism may have reinforced the attitude dictated by economic interest. At this juncture the work was taken up with astonishing energy by the Archbishop of Bremen, Adalbert von Goseck, a descendant of an old noble family, a man of striking and brilliant personality. In him there was incarnated for the first time something of the spirit of Bremen, reaching out into the spaces of the world, as against Saxon localized interests.

This man's aim was to erect a northern patriarchate. He pushed as far as Iceland, Greenland, the Orkneys, and Kurland. Neither the Pope nor the Saxon nobility seemed to regard his plans with enthusiasm, but there was some hope of success; after the death of Canute the Great (1035) the Danish-English northern empire was disintegrating. Conrad II had treated this ruler with circumspection and had won him over by concessions along the northern boundaries. Moreover he had married Henry III to a daughter of Canute's, who died young. Now the coast was clear for new German expansion. Henry III favoured Adalbert wherever he could. He himself was fond of visiting Saxony; he had a new palace built at Goslar and thus worked his way into northern Germany, much to the annoyance of the older lords. The friendly relationship with Denmark and England proved advantageous during disturbances in Lorraine; aided by these allies, who were joined by the King of France, Henry succeeded in forcing the rebellious Duke of Lorraine to obedience, though the powerful position of Flanders, already independent in effect, could not be broken. Threads of understanding were spun across great distances between the opposition party in Lorraine and the Italian feudal lords in their common effort against German power.

Henry's second marriage, to the pious, almost nun-like Burgundian Princess Agnes, laid the court wide open to the reform party. At that time, under the influence of Cluny, the institution of the truce of God had been established in France. The incessant feuds of the lay nobility put such a burden on the church, as well as on the aspiring lower strata, that a truce from Wednesday night until Monday morning seemed a decided advance. Henry interpreted the notion of the truce in his own way. At the Council of Constance in 1043 he granted pardon to all his enemies and caused his vassals to do likewise; he repeated this curious, most earnestly meant attempt several times. What he had in mind was a general peace throughout the Empire. It would have been more practical to content himself with the less pretentious goal of the truce of God. These transactions are characteristic of the monarch. He was of a brooding temperament, genuinely religious, shy, and absorbed in his vaulting dreams. He would have thought it sinful to see his relations to the church as a struggle for power of a temporal nature. Thus it was under him, undisputed and crowned with early success as no other German ruler was, that a great change began.

Henry III did away with simony, though it had nothing in common with heresy or bribery, but was merely a money tribute, a purely administrative device. About its value it was possible to disagree, but the abolition of it represented a great moral triumph and a considerable economic advantage to the dignitaries of the church, beyond any doubt. Henry III, who at the Synod of Sutri had deposed three popes, and who had had himself named as *patricius* of Rome in order to get the papal election entirely into his own hands —this same Henry awarded the papal crown to a Burgundian churchman, who, however, would not accept it without the approval of the Roman clergy and laity. As Pope Leo IX this man laid the cornerstone of a new papacy. He acted with the burning zeal of a reformer, the magic of a born orator, and the keen intelligence of a jurist schooled in canonical law. The college of cardinals was re-formed, the episcopate held to obedience. Numerous synods were convened, and the temporal power of the pope was extended to southern Italy. Whoever possessed southern Italy threatened the part of Italy that was dominated by the Empire and could claim the key position on the Mediterranean. This was the spirit of the future. The monk Hildebrand, who later became Pope Gregory VII, served Pope Leo as subdeacon, and thus in spite of his personal failures the Pope was able to pass his ideas on to his successors. Emperor Henry III not only did nothing to hinder this development, but actually advanced it by his fatalistic negligence. And so this very promising reign ended with disappointments on all sides. Hungary regained her independence. Saxony and Bavaria vied in opposition. Conspira-cies against Henry's rulership and even against his life sprang up. The lay nobility suffered under the economic rise of such towns as Köln (Cologne), Bremen, and Nürnberg, hated the *ministeriales* or retainers, frequently of unfree descent, with whom the King sur-rounded himself, and also hated the high clergy, who wanted to hem in the nobles' rights of feuding and booty. The lay princes also felt themselves personally belittled. The Emperor grew more and more lax. With a premonition of his early end he spent his last years in strengthening the dynastic duchy again in order to assure the suc-cession of his son, who was still a minor. Given to melancholy, feel-ing life as suffering, prepared to do penance and even to mortify the flesh, this conscientious and priest-like monarch was nevertheless capable of exhibiting a blind harshness like that of his father Conrad in the face of criticism and opposition. And so a shadow falls on this pure figure. He died in 1056.

HENRY IV (1056–1106). THE STRUGGLE WITH THE PAPACY

When the three-year-old Henry IV was elected King at Tribur (1053), in accordance with his father's wish, the princes vowed obedience to him on condition that he be a just king. This was un-precedented. It seemed as though the vassals were instinctively on the defensive against a sovereign who even at the age of six was to follow in his father's imperial steps and who was probably the most unhappy of the rulers of Germany. For the second time in a bare hundred years Germany was under a regency. The impractical Empress Agnes and the bishops who advised her proved unequal to their difficult task. After all sorts of quarrels a group of princes kidnapped the young King. The opportunity was to be used to strengthen territorial power. On the other side the great Archbishop Adalbert of Bremen was the strongest representative of the idea of the Empire and of the state church. But the envy of the Saxon dukes and a fresh rebellion of the pagan Slavs brought about his downfall (1066). Adalbert's rival, the wrathful Archbishop of Köln, had a still more unfortunate lot. On one occasion the citizens of Köln simply drove him out of the town.

Henry III may be open to reproach because of his weakness toward the reform movement in the church. The movement was so powerful that in any case it was bound to come into its own soon, especially during the minority of King Henry IV. At first the movement had something non-German about it. Its hierarchical character, the absolutism and strictness of its discipline, its monkish spirit—all these were Latin and Oriental, and they ran counter to the happy, placid, and individualistic tone of the German church. The final success of the movement even in Germany was due to a social factor. The monastery of Hirsau in Swabia, for instance, from which the Hirsau rules spread all over Germany, directed itself decidedly toward the lay world. It founded associations of laymen, ascetic in atmosphere, that spread through the rural districts with amazing rapidity, for this solicitude for the soul was timely and well received. The new inmates of cloisters were drawn from the lower classes. They spoke the language of their class and thus were easily understood. It was the beginning of the first genuine religious movement among the German people. The old cloisters had been strongholds of the nobility, especially of landholders. Now a new demand for equality asserted itself, and the old primitive Christian ideas were applied to recasting social classes. *Ministeriales*—retainers who were not all free men, for the most part townsmen of unfree descent— invaded the monasteries and reorganized them. Whereas the old seignorial class had been of predominantly Germanic character, the class involved here was cross-bred of Celtic, Roman, and pre-Indo-European elements. They were already close in sentiment to the new Western ideas, the realization of which meant a democratization of the church.

The victory of the reform movement carried with it the final Christianizing of the Germans, as far as this could be accomplished, but it destroyed the possibility of a German state church. The truce of God was continually broken by feuds—a matter of grave concern to the devout leaders of reform. Just at this point welcome aid appeared with the crusade movement. Here again was a chance to unite the purified Christian world. A great common task bridged the growing national and social antagonisms; the love of warfare of the new class of knights was given a significant objective, at once Christian and of great political importance.

During the regency of the Empress Agnes Italy was entirely lost. The reform party prevailed in Rome. Its claims were driven farther and farther. One of its representatives, Cardinal Humbert, denounced lay investiture of bishops—that is, their installation by the king—as simony and heresy. This opened a controversy that was to have weighty consequences. The monk Hildebrand, of peasant stock, from the Romagna and therefore regarded as a true Roman, came to exert more and more authoritative influence in Rome. He had now become a deacon, and he had both energy and force of conviction enough to translate Humbert's views into deeds.

The pontificate of Nicholas II (died 1091) was epoch-making for three reasons. The alliance with the Normans was now officially sealed. The Pope himself conveyed Apulia and Calabria, which up to this time had been regarded as imperial fiefs, to the unscrupulous Duke of the Normans, Robert Guiscard, as a papal fief. In Lombardy and above all in Milan a people's movement, called *Pataria* after the rag-market, merged with the religious reform movement. It was directed against the Italian high clergy, who for the most part were still friendly to Germany and loyal to the Emperor. Here, just as in Rome, there was already a feeling of democracy and of Italian nationality. The Pope countenanced these strivings, in which he saw support against the bishops and the Germans. The Lateran Council (1059) was directed against the marriage of the clergy and against lay investiture, but above all it laid down new rules for papal elections. Cardinal bishops alone were to take part, and this meant that the nobility of the city of Rome and the Emperor were excluded. A curial fraud then made all cardinals eligible to participate in the election—even cardinal priests and cardinal deacons. At the Lateran Council the Pope appeared for the first time with the double crown and thus presented himself also as emperor and king. Later a third crown was added to make the papal tiara, presumably to symbolize the three empires of earth, purgatory, and hell. The Roman nobles were much embittered by the papal decree, for the cardinals constituted a new aristocracy of the church that seemed dangerous to them. Accordingly they entered upon a political alliance with the Germans. An anti-pope was set up. Impassioned arguments were put forward on both sides, and the contentions were given complete publicity. The times were full of ferment; a tremor arose in the East and quickened the West. It became quite usual for pious folk to go on pilgrimage to Jerusalem, and these pilgrimages became more and more extensive. The Normans drove the Saracens out of southern Italy and Sicily. The struggle against unbelievers aroused wild enthusiasm, and the crusade idea was again awakened.

When Henry IV came of age he embarked on his reign with high-pitched plans. He was of a fiery nature and had had to endure repression and injustice. Now he stormed ahead with few scruples, with little luck, without any sure instinct for what he was doing. But because he was extraordinarily intelligent he was always able to find a way out of the most impossible situations. The *ministeriales,* the citizens, and the lower clergy were natural allies of the young King. With the assistance of the rising democratic strata, with which he always showed his sympathy, it seemed possible to weaken the power of the princes and to extend the royal rule and establish it firmly. In all this Henry IV was one of the first representatives of royal power who attempted to impose absolute authority on the high nobility. In his personal life he was like any layman; he enjoyed himself in the untroubled manner of a German noble of the period. The story of his first marriage is distasteful from every angle, not only in the eyes of monkish chroniclers. Henry certainly aroused hostility among the classes that had undergone a religious rebirth, and thus he alienated himself from the very groups on which he was politically dependent.

Just as the Saxon rulers had always concerned themselves particularly with rebellious Bavaria, the Salic kings in turn were troubled about Saxony. Emperorship and kingship now took on a south German character. Northern Germany developed almost independently, and the cleavage was never really healed. The situation in Saxony was grave. The missionary work of the great Adalbert fell apart after his death; Hamburg was burned by the Danes, and Christianity died out in the region north of the Elbe (Holstein). The Saxon nobility had seized most of the imperial estates and prerogatives. Henry IV tried to win back what had been lost. But by using inquisitorial methods he contravened ancient Saxon popular justice. The confiscations he ordered, his demands for personal service and for shares of forest and pasture, embittered the free peasants as well as the lesser nobility. The fortresses that Henry set up in Saxony and garrisoned with strangers, *ministeriales* from southern Germany, made him still more hated. To demolish these fortresses was one of the main objects of the great Saxon revolt that now arose against the King. Again a ruler of the Franks was making war on the Saxons; it was to be the last struggle of the kind.

When we read that the Saxons not only tore down the walls of the Harzburg, but also destroyed churches and desecrated Christian graves, this outbreak appears especially significant. The old pagan particularism, rooted in the very earth, rooted in tradition, was defending itself against everything alien, whether royal power or Christian doctrine. King Henry could not relax. And for a time he actually subdued this spirit of paticularism by dividing his adversaries. The Saxon peasants forsook their nobles, and the nobles had to surrender unconditionally. Saxon fiefs, reclaimed by the crown, were assigned to Swabian and Rhenish *ministeriales*.

GREGORY VII (1073–85)

In Rome in the meantime Hildebrand had become Pope. The Roman people proclaimed him; only after that did the cardinals give their approval. In spite of such irregularity King Henry recognized the election when he was notified of it. Gregory VII was the name assumed by Peter's new successor. He took up church reform with great energy. The celibacy of the clergy struck him as a most pressing matter; this annoyed the lower clergy and was not well liked by the bishops. The episcopate found it much easier to deal with married priests, for celibates were apt to be ambitious and to strive for high positions. Gregory's action created bad blood. The Pope even deposed several archbishops and bishops. Thus the quarrel swelled to a struggle over lay investiture. Was the Pope or the temporal ruler to control the bishoprics? Ring and crosier symbolized the offices of teacher and shepherd; investiture, therefore, was a spiritual act, and when it was performed by a layman it became a new form of simony. King Henry was no fonder of the episcopate in itself than of his secular princes; the lower clergy, hostile to both groups, were inclined to help the King. The King would not in any case submit to a non-German power's determining who should and who should not be princes of the German church; it would mean that whoever held the papacy would dominate central Europe and even the entire West. Now the papacy was building up a spiritual and temporal power of its own and undertook to attack traditional practices of the German Kingdom. The new "canonical" law of the church signified its freedom from the imperial authority and thus established the supremacy of the papacy. Ought Henry IV to give in and devote his political gifts to recasting German sovereignty? Should he carry out his absolutist program, reshape German administration and economy, base his authority on the *ministeriales* who had become officials and on taxes collected from the towns, which were the strongest units economically? Should he accordingly leave Italy and Burgundy to themselves and confine himself to the most pressing needs of the growing German nation? Perhaps such a policy of wise self-restraint was in effect impossible to a German king of the eleventh century. Even a ruler as worldly-minded as Henry IV was under the spell of the churchly bond and the sacramental grace of the imperial mission. Therefore he took up the struggle with the papacy, but his weapons were dull; his position in Germany was thoroughly insecure.

Gregory threatened the King with excommunication. The Synod of Worms declared the Pope deposed. Thereupon Gregory excommunicated the King, released his vassals from their oath of fealty, and forbade Henry to continue to rule. It was obvious that the princes of the particularistic opposition in Germany would try to profit by this novel state of affairs. These lords certainly did not think very kindly of church reform with its tinge of democracy, but it was just this that now offered a weapon against the King's claim to power. Henry found a surprising way out of the impasse. He went to Italy, but as a penitent. At Canossa he forced the Pope to undo his excommunication. By personal and moral self-abasement he succeeded in getting the Pope to recognize him as a sovereign again and to resume political relations with him (1077). Pious folk of those times regarded such an act of self-abasement as praiseworthy, and beyond doubt Gregory did not relish his opponent's tactical victory. A king who had been released from excommunication in due form enjoyed the respect of the lower strata in Germany just as much as before. The princes and the nobles reacted differently. The old Germanic sense of self-respect and honour was up in arms against such behaviour in a king, even though shrewdly calculated. The aristocratic laity in particular, who were not too much in favour of the religious reform movement, despised the King because he had turned the ideology of that movement to account politically. On the other hand the power of the papacy was felt as so overwhelming that every layman had to come to terms with it somehow or other. There was something not quite genuine about Henry IV; he lay under the curse that afflicts the man who is too clever, who no longer knows how to act out of naïve instinct, who moves from one small success to another and is more and more amazed to find that real victory remains out of reach. Again and again Henry IV tried to carry it off. There is something affecting about these attempts; as the King grew more mature he gave the best he had with increasing honesty and manliness. But in return he was confronted with growing confusion and resistance, even with the treachery of his nearest and dearest.

In Germany the particularistic opponents of Salic autocracy elected the insignificant, docile Duke Rudolf of Swabia as an anti-king (1077), and the Pope only too gladly encouraged this obvious check to the idea of dynastic succession. A serious civil war began. Henry IV replied by setting up an anti-pope. Excommunications and depositions followed, and civil war fastened on Italy. The Pope summoned his Norman vassals, but they, seizing the opportunity to increase their power, entered Rome as plunderers. Gregory VII did nothing in retaliation, and the Romans never forgave him for it; shorn of power, he died far from home in 1085. But his dream of a universal church supported by strong temporal power of its own in

Italy was to prevail in the future. In character also Pope Gregory was King Henry's opposite; in him the smooth politician encountered the rigour of a strong will. The King was full of ideas and never at a loss for a diplomatic expedient, no matter how shifty. The Pope might indeed take over ideas from others, but he quickened them with the fire and the irresistible impulse of his genius. Henry always weighed many possibilities, and he was always convinced that he was doing the cleverest thing; but the gloom and disharmony of his nature were bewildering even to his friends, who finally all went their own way and left him to himself. Gregory could hardly help despising the King's temperament from his heart, even on personal grounds. The Pope never abandoned his deepest convictions, as the King did under duress. The more Gregory's work was threatened with failure, the more obstinately he clung to the supreme task of his life. As Augustine's follower he fought for the victory of the church, the state of God, over the devil's domain of temporal tyranny. The Pope was inclined to spare even a hateful heretic if he could spite the temporal power by doing so. The Rome idea of Emperor Otto III reappeared in Pope Gregory in a curious mutation: it was now bound up with the concept of feudalism that had overspread the world.

The papacy itself acted in an imperial way and built up a feudal system of its own all over Europe. Many dukes and counts in France and Spain, the Dukes of Bohemia and Poland, the Kings of Hungary and of Croatia-Dalmatia, took an oath of fealty to the Pope or recognized a direct feudal relationship. Duke William of Normandy conquered England with the Pope's sanction. For the European princes this papal sanction was an effective means of evading the much more oppressive feudal supremacy of the Roman Emperor, which existed at least in theory. Gregory VII either did not see this or did not want to see it. He was the first papal absolutist. As St. Peter's representative he regarded himself as the legitimate lord of the earth. King Henry IV did harm to himself and to his cause by his very adroitness. Gregory's cruel and savage nature, his undiplomatic outbreaks and tirades, his bellicosity, his rage and hatred might horrify those about him, but they charged all he did with a current of strength that it was impossible to resist. What could remain of the central European dominion of the German sovereigns? Henry IV had himself crowned by his anti-pope in Rome. He tried to impose the truce of God on the realm. But the country became more and more confused by the civil wars that ravaged it. A new German anti-king came forward. Now the Emperor had to be glad to collect followers wherever he could among the lay princes and in the episcopate, and he made all possible compromises; the Ottonian system was ressurrected, but it was helpful only for a short time. Henry lost Italy. The cities of Lombardy formed an alliance against the alien. And then there was Matilda, the Margravine of Tuscany, Henry's old foe, who hated him even as a man, possibly because she had had designs on him. Now her power was strengthened in an unexpected way, for this pious elderly lady married the seventeen-year-old son of the Swabian Duke Welf. Matilda had made over her estate to the Pope and had received it back from him as a feudal fief. The Emperor regarded the property as belonging to the Empire, and he refused to recognize her manœuvre. Papal interests were now linked with Tuscan and Guelph interests, and there began a struggle that was to last for generations.

Even Henry's son Conrad went over to the papal faction, approved the Tuscan-Guelph affair, and received the Italian crown. The new pope, Urban II, was French; indeed, he had been a monk at Cluny. He stood for the strictest tendency of his order, and he exerted an extensive influence in France and the Romanized borderlands of Germany. It was he who prepared the First Crusade (1096), in which Germany did not take part, isolated and inwardly riven as the country was. She was now overshadowed. All of her neighbours were strengthening themselves and were advocating the new ideas of the time. The German Kingdom experienced only one benefit: many adventurous and quarrelsome elements in the nobility found themselves occupied, and the leaders of the reform movement had a lofty and distant goal to set before their urge to action. Emperor Henry IV honestly tried to achieve the general pacification of the Empire, to which these circumstances were favourable. But even now he had no luck. Again his private life blocked success. His first wife, Bertha, died. At one time he had wanted to get rid of her. Soon after his marriage he publicly declared that he had never touched her, and he thus tried to obtain a divorce. But subsequently he lived with her again. By her he had two sons, Conrad and Henry, who turned against their father and thus avenged their unhappy mother in their own way. The Emperor's second wife was the daughter of the Ukrainian Grand Duke of Kiev, the Princess Praxedis. After a short time this obviously moody and impetuous lady hurled an accusation at the Emperor that gave rise to much scandalmongering: that he had prevailed on her to commit adultery. The Emperor, forced to admit publicly the truth of this dark story, tried to disarm his indignant opponents by penitence and self-abasement, along the lines of the Canossa method. But this time he was less successful. His second son, heir to the throne after Conrad's death, the later Henry V, now sided against his father. He aligned himself with the church, conspired with the Pope and the many discontented princes, betrayed his father shamelessly, and even had him imprisoned. The Emperor escaped and once more tried to save whatever could be saved in the general collapse; it is amazing how even the bitterest experiences could not cripple his resourcefulness and shrewdness. A sudden death, at Liège, put him out of the way at the age of fifty-six (1106).

HENRY V (1106–25). THE CONCORDAT OF WORMS

Henry V is the least likeable of all German rulers. It is true that he grew up under particularly difficult circumstances, but his conduct toward his unhappy father filled even his contemporaries with horror. This last of the Salic kings never became popular, although in those days it was relatively easy to become so through gifts or by favours. Henry was anything but generous; in fact, his most conspicuous trait was his greed for money. He was forced to seek new sources of income to take the place of church revenues, which were sharply reduced since the condemnation of certain dues as simony. He hoped to obtain the means to greater economic freedom from the domestic economy, the Rhenish domains, and city taxes. He even evolved the daring idea of levying a general tax throughout the Empire. Power could not be regained in the east; several campaigns were made without appreciable results. Poland and Hungary became wholly independent, Bohemia with certain qualifications. As the son-in-law of King Henry I of England, Henry was also deeply involved in the affairs of the west. But his attempt to support English claims by marching into France bore no fruit. Never was he able to exercise full royal authority over the German realm itself, for the

KINGDOM OF GERMANY
C. 1097

Denmark

Pomerania

Prussians

Poland

Russia

Kingdom
of
Germany

France

Hungary

Burgundy

Kingdom
of
Italy

Croatia

Serbia

Byzantine
Empire

Two Sicilies

heir of the last of the Billungs, Duke Lothair of Supplinburg, wielded complete and independent power in Saxony. The Archbishopric of Bremen was no longer of any importance; Lothair's power extended as far as Holstein and into Slav territory. Unlike the Saxon opposition, the rising Hohenstaufen family in its Duchy of Swabia was loyal to the King. Officialdom became more and more important in the Empire. Besides the ducal families a new imperial group of princes won recognition and riches as administrators of justice, finance, and military organization; these were the counts palatine, the margraves, burgraves, and landgraves. The kingdom had to acquiesce in this development. The territorial princes were firmly rooted, and they assisted. Germany began to fall apart into a number of relatively small domains. The tribal duchies had been a threat to Ottonian centralization and therefore had been split up and weakened. Now the central power was confronted with a hydra of manifold might in the high aristocracy and its followers, and against this force nothing could be accomplished.

How was the investiture struggle to be settled? The Pope now made a curious proposal that opened up new possibilities. If the Emperor renounced investiture, the bishops would renounce the prerogatives they had assumed; the church would give up its temporal claims and hand back the imperial estates that it had held for centuries. The religious reform movement would have at its disposal a church purged of temporal interests. The German King would take possession of very extensive lands on which to build up a new dynastic power. Neither the episcopate nor the lay princes were interested in a solution of this kind. The plan was dropped, but it may have had a fruitful influence on later rulings about the right to royal prerogatives. After more entanglements—at one time Henry V imprisoned the Pope and his cardinals in Rome—an agreement about investiture was reached in the Concordat of Worms (1122). The King renounced investiture, but in return it was stipulated that the ceremony should take place in his presence or in that of his authorized representative; a certain influence could be brought to bear by this means. The King was to invest the nominees with the prerogatives by a touch of his sceptre; thus a new temporal investiture was created. In Germany this investiture was to precede the consecration in church with ring and crosier; in Italy and Burgundy, to follow it.

The bishops of the papal states were expressly excluded from investiture with the sceptre—a portentous provision indeed. According to the papal interpretation this newly devised mode of investiture with the prerogatives was merely a personal concession to Emperor Henry V. Had it perhaps been conceived as an act that would be performed only once in each bishopric at the installation of a new bishop?

The King's faction sought no less to gain advantage through supple interpretation. They called for a decision in the King's favour whenever there were contested elections, while the concordat provided for an amicable settlement between the archbishop and the other bishops. Only in case such a settlement was not reached was arbitration proposed. The Concordat of Worms signifies an imperial defeat, which, however, was skilfully smoothed over. The episcopate of Italy and Burgundy was now quite lost to temporal influence. In Germany the King could indeed rule out an entirely unsuitable candidate, but the church was in a position to keep any man who might prove disquieting to it out of the bishop's chair, and this doomed the Ottonian state church. The King was now forced to get along with the episcopate as best he could. The bishops were no longer tools of the royal will. The best thing was for the King to treat the bishops as he was already treating the princes: as factors of power to be won over with concessions. The question arose whether the power of the German Kingdom in central Europe could be developed or even maintained under these circumstances.

With the death of the childless Henry V the Salic dynasty came to an unedifying end. After soaring high the monarchy had had to content itself with an indifferent compromise. But German life as a whole had been immeasurably enriched by the experiences of the last two generations. The struggle between Cluniac piety and the old Germanic vigour with roots in the soil ended in a phenomenon that was new and curious from a sociological as well as from a cultural point of view: the rise of the knightly class. This was in fact a phenomenon common to all Europe; it spread through the entire West in more or less the same manner, though there were certain variations, and not all the stages occurred at the same time everywhere. Military organization was no longer based on the individual freeman's ability to bear arms. The German peasant was not willing to leave his land. He was willing to be called up only against alien invaders such as the Hungarians or the Slavs. Feuds with dukes, civil wars with kinsmen, expeditions to Italy, Burgundy, and France— for all such undertakings the kings had to use small armed bands drawn mostly from the unfree classes and made up of mercenaries, for whom war was an occupation that promised a living and possibly advancement and property. The first knights, then, were poor adventurers who lived by taking chances on death. These remained the most numerous. But of course many freemen joined them— relatives of the old nobility, younger sons, illegitimate sons. Service at court and military expeditions brought honour to the *ministeriales* in addition to obvious winnings in land and loot. Social reshuffling opened up great possibilities to enterprising natures. The blessing of the church could not be withheld, because this new stratum also put itself at the service of the concepts of the church—above all, the crusade idea. This class served both the rival powers: temporal rule and the high priesthood, imperialism and sacerdotalism.

From the standpoint of universal history the awakening of the *ecclesia militans* appears as the reply to the holy war of Islam. Charles the Great was the first crusader. The battles in Spain and in Saxony were followed by the spread of militant Christendom in Slavic territory. The Cluniac Reform emphasized the partnership of the cross and the sword. At the beginning of his pontificate even Gregory VII had wanted to unite the church in the West to fight against Islam and to free the Holy Land. Urban II, French by birth, the first true statesman of the reform movement, revived the old idea of reuniting the Western with the Eastern church; he found Constantinople responsive, since the Byzantine Emperor required help against the Seljuks. The substantial success of the First Crusade increased the power of the Pope and of the Byzantine Emperor. The German and Roman Empire was forced into the background. For the first time it found itself unable to maintain its claims to rule central Europe. The world was growing wider. Could the power that had been the strongest in the West fall back and pin itself down to straightening out domestic quarrels? Or was German kingship to embark on a new venture and assume the leadership of the European society of states, knightly in tone, that was being aroused by the crusade idea and was becoming more and more nationally conscious? This was the fateful question of the Hohenstaufen era.

Chapter 5

THE HOHENSTAUFEN ERA

LOTHAIR OF SAXONY (1125-37)

THE HOHENSTAUFENS were an old noble family that had risen from small estates in Lorch and on the Staufen in south-western Germany and received the ducal dignity of Swabia under the Salic dynasty. Emperor Henry V entrusted his nephew Frederick of Swabia with the care of his widow and of the Empire and thus designated him as his successor. The princes of the church, however, did not wish any continuation of the Salic policy. The idea of any limitation whatever on the free right of election was displeasing to most of the temporal princes also. And so, surprisingly enough, the election fell on the deadly enemy of the Salic kings, the elderly Duke Lothair of Saxony-Supplinburg, who had the special advantage of not having a son. He promised to give his daughter and heiress in marriage to the Bavarian Duke, the Guelph Henry the Proud. This was the beginning of the Saxon and Bavarian power of the Guelphs as against the Franconian and Swabian power of the Hohenstaufens. Dynastic and family interests already obscured the broader issues of imperial policy. The secular princes had sufficient power to prevent the establishment of a hereditary dynasty with centralizing ambitions, and the ecclesiastical princes in particular encouraged the cleavage of Germany into two camps, between which the episcopate might successfully mediate.

Lothair, an insignificant and almost foolish personality, never overcame the obstacles presented by his descent and the circumstances of his rise to power. He may be said to have been the first German king to put himself under the Pope's thumb. He sought the Pope's confirmation of his election—an unprecedented procedure. In spite of repeated efforts he was unable to obtain the right of investiture that had been personally granted to his predecessor. At his

54

coronation as Emperor the Concordat of Worms was confirmed by the curia only in the most general terms. The estates of Matilda had been left to the papal government, and the bequest had never been recognized by the Emperor. Now Lothair accepted the property from the Pope as a fief, subject to dues. He also made the greatest concessions in all sorts of important externals. At their meeting in Liège, for instance, he held the Pope's stirrup, as a vassal would for his lord. In a similar manner the Norman Duke Rainulf received Apulia as a fief on the occasion of Lothair's second expedition to Rome, with the Pope holding the point of the flagstaff and the Emperor the end.

The Hohenstaufen family did not want to submit to such a new lord. Civil war ensued. Frederick of Swabia's younger brother Conrad had himself crowned as King in Italy. An agreement was reached only after some years, under the influence of the great Bernard of Clairvaux (1090–1153), who looms larger than all the princes of his time. His sermon in behalf of a peaceful union of all Christendom reconciled even the defiant Italian communities to Lothair and prepared the new crusade, which, in contrast to the first, was to proceed under the leadership of the most eminent princes of the West. Lothair's only real successes were won in the north and in the east. The King of Denmark paid homage as a vassal to the Emperor, and the Germanizing as well as the Christianizing of the east was energetically resumed. In this, Lothair was the precursor of his grandson Henry the Lion. The King of Poland took Rügen and Pomerania as fiefs from the Emperor, paid the arrears of tribute, and in token of submission carried the Emperor's sword on his way to church. The noblemen of Askanien and of Wettin vied in opening up new territory. Priegnitz, Havelland, the Lusatias, the region around Lübeck, and Pomerania were now visited by missionaries. Again the central European basis of the Empire was being widened.

CONRAD III (1137–52). THE CRUSADES

After Lothair's death the same performance was repeated at the new election. The dying Emperor had given the imperial insignia to his son-in-law Henry the Proud, but the lay princes regarded the power of this Duke, who had not only his two duchies, but also the margraviates of Verona and Tuscany, as far too dangerous. In great haste and without regard to proper legal procedure the Archbishop of Trier (Trèves) had the Hohenstaufen Conrad elected; a papal legate crowned him at Aachen. This was the unfortunate beginning of a weak rule.

The irritable Guelph refused to let himself be cheated, and a new civil war broke out. Despite the premature death of Duke Henry the Proud the struggle continued for a long time. The duke's ten-year-old son, Henry the Lion, was now the Guelph heir. The Hohenstaufens were also called Ghibellines, after their family property at Waiblingen on the Rems in Swabia. Thus arose the battle cry: "Here Guelph (Welf), here Ghibelline (Waiblingen)!" At the siege of Weinsberg in Swabia a well-known and well-substantiated episode took place: King Conrad III allowed the women to depart unmolested on condition that they themselves should carry off their own most precious possessions, whereupon they carried away their husbands. The King was amazed, but he did not retract his word in the face of this bold interpretation, and the men were spared.

A treaty with the Guelphs was of no help to the Hohenstaufen King. Guelph power maintained itself and even spread out toward Austria. Political threads were already being spun out toward Hungary and Sicily. Even Conrad's nephew, Duke Frederick of Swabia, the later Emperor Frederick Barbarossa, joined the Guelphs in conspiring against the King. Every foe of Conrad's could count on vigorous support from the Guelph opposition. The feuds spread, and Conrad was never able to master the situation. Like all weak sovereigns, he hoped to propitiate powerful lords by giving them marks of his favour; but this only made him the poorer without any compensating gain of security. Imperial property dwindled, and particularism mounted. Nevertheless Conrad III allowed Bernard of Clairvaux to persuade him to participate in a new crusade. A new and powerful religious movement was reaching out from France and gripping the Rhineland; Conrad's chief counsellor was the Abbot of Stablo and Corvey. The King could not evade the force of the new ideas. But here it became evident how deeply Germany was cloven. The north German princes and lords declared that their interests lay in the German and Slavic east; they did not wish to go to Asia Minor. In this disagreement also the wise Bernard mediated, although he was bitterly disappointed, and he secured the approval of the Pope. While Conrad III crossed the Hungarian border with a fine army, a crusade set forth against the pagan Slavs in the east (1147).

The crusade to the Holy Land ended in utter failure. The expedition to the Wends, however, while it could not be called completely successful, brought an increase of land and influence to the north German lords. The royal central power had to bear the consequences of disintegration. All of King Conrad's enterprises against Iconium, Damascus, and Ascalon were wrecked, and losses were heavy. There was no more military or political unity in Christendom than in Germany or central Europe. King Roger of Sicily found himself aligned with the French and the Guelphs, while Conrad concluded an alliance with the Byzantine Emperor, Manuel, and the Italian maritime cities of Venice and Pisa. Now King Conrad was planning an expedition to Italy; it seemed necessary for several reasons. The papacy was in urgent need of help. The priest Arnold of Brescia had helped foment an uprising in Rome. In this remarkable man old Roman, Italian national, and democratic characteristics were conjoined with Christian ideas of reform. Conrad died in 1152 without achievement in any field—a brave and charming prince, radiant with the grace of courtly culture, but no statesman.

The old core of the German dominions was in process of dissolution. But Henry the Lion and his allies forced the Prince of the Obotrites in Mecklenburg to pay tribute and to accept the Christian faith. Count Albert the Bear of the house of Askanien was given the newly founded Mark of Brandenburg, which he set out energetically to win over to Christianity with the aid of the Premonstrants and the Bishops of Havelberg and Brandenburg. Settlers came from Flanders and Holstein to cultivate the half-empty Slavic east; they rode *nach Ostland,* "toward the eastern lands," as the old folksong has it. Perhaps it was these very successes in colonization that shut the Guelph Henry the Lion out of the new election as Conrad's successor. Hohenstaufen rule had been a decided failure. Things had come to such a pass that the princes preferred a weak monarchy to a strong one. On his death-bed Conrad III generously indicated his nephew Duke Frederick as his successor in lieu of his son, who was still a minor, although Frederick was certainly open to criticism on both personal and political scores. The first Hohenstaufen King hoped that Frederick's gifts would save the realm. In this, at least, he was not mistaken.

FREDERICK BARBAROSSA (1152–90)

Frederick Barbarossa has become the most popular of the German emperors. History and legend have illuminated his figure and made him a symbol of German power and greatness. Even a critical review leaves enough of this tradition standing. He had a most winning personality; he was honest and honourable, well balanced, knightly, versatile—a little overwrought, in fact, like a hero of romance. But he was the knight *par excellence,* the most perfect, the supreme representative of the new class and of its attitude toward life—an attitude at once worldly and devout. He was loyal, a good warrior though not a military genius, a man of order, justice, etiquette. Frederick had nothing of the sombre fire of the Salic rulers; he was cheerful, self-confident, and naïve. His breaches of faith, his violations of oaths, were painful to his own conscience, but his energy and his statesmanlike will never wavered in the face of necessity. Even his statesmanship, however, had certain limitations. He seemed oddly blind to the forces of the future. He had faith in the present, but an inclination to lean on the past. Because he had no real creative power he relied on tradition, and this is also why he clung to the law. He liked to pronounce judgement; he desired justice; he believed in the supreme judicial power of the Emperor more than in anything else. This attitude toward justice carried him easily over failure and compromise.

The new ruler succeeded in establishing peace and order in Germany and central Europe with amazing rapidity. He won over the Guelphs by recognizing Henry the Lion's claims to Bavaria and by endowing Count Welf with Tuscany and Spoleto. Denmark, Burgundy, and Bohemia accepted the King as their supreme feudal lord. The great law about the imperial peace filled a need and was to a certain extent observed. Was Frederick to resume the Italian policy? Conrad III had been the first German ruler since Otto the Great not to have himself crowned Emperor in Italy. It was of course quite possible to abandon Italy and to concentrate German energy on more immediate German tasks. For a variety of reasons the Italian policy had grown more and more difficult to maintain since the time of the

Saxon emperors. Roger, Duke of Sicily and later its first King, "the master of a clear, stern art of rulership," occupied a most important Mediterranean position. He threatened the temporal power of the papacy and buttressed all national and democratic forces in central and northern Italy. Under the influence of the courageous Arnold of Brescia, Rome itself showed the spirit of the old Quirites. She elected a senate and a native-born *patricius*. A new Capitol was built, a romantic duplicate of the old. In northern Italy, Milan, with its urban and republican tendencies, claimed supremacy over the neighbouring towns; such cities as Pavia and Cremona especially, loyal to the Emperor from of old, experienced stern repression. At last, for the first time in Europe, there was something on the order of foreign policy. The states developed personality; now they drew closer to one another, now they drew apart. Frictions, common interests, and friendships sprang up. Alliances shifted. Tensions and mutual advances occupied the diplomacy that was coming into existence. On diplomats' gifts of observation, on their shrewdness and energy, hinged great decisions. The Kingdom of France grew stronger. It mastered its internal problems and developed new goals of power in relation to its neighbours, and a clash with England soon resulted. The relations of these two powers of the West took on importance for every German ruler and equally for the curia in Rome. Imperial and papal claims to power had to adjust themselves to this new situation.

The Pope now sought the help of the German King as steward of the church of Rome. It was impossible for Frederick Barbarossa to turn a deaf ear to such a summons. The spirit of the Carolingians was mighty in him; he later had Charles the Great canonized. His thinking was dominated by revivalist notions at once historical and romantic. He believed that a situation of yesteryear was now repeating itself and that there was a mission to be carried out. Moreover Italy's well-developed economy was the most promising source of ready money for the German Kingdom, and it was likely to remain so. Certainly more was to be got there than from the Slavic east. The German King could not take the responsibility of permitting the papacy to ally itself with Sicily, of possibly letting the rich north Italian cities join such a grouping or of allowing the King of France to make approaches to them. Byzantine advances in southern Italy also had to be reckoned with. Frederick could only

59

be complacent toward friction between the Normans and the Greeks, but an access of fresh power to the Eastern Empire in Italy seemed undesirable as constituting a threat to the papacy and the Western church. The Pope at that time, Adrian IV, the only Englishman who ever reached that eminence, made use of the German King as a temporal aid, though as a true disciple of Gregory VII he had no intention of relinquishing any of the prerogatives of the church, while Frederick was apt to deal high-handedly with the episcopate.

Frederick's first journey to Rome brought him the imperial crown (1155), but nothing else. The cities of northern Italy almost cut off his return to Germany. The Normans remained undisturbed. The Romans were in rebellion. The Pope got the Emperor to hand over Arnold of Brescia, the people's leader, for execution—hardly a creditable proceeding—and even induced the Emperor to hold his stirrup for him, once the act had been explained away as an old custom and a mere ceremonial gesture. On the other hand the concept of the Emperor as a vassal paying homage to the Pope, which stemmed from Lothair's time, now became tenuous; Frederick derived his imperial authority, in the spirit of late antique times, directly from God. The Emperor succeeded in making his position so secure in Germany that he could soon prosecute the Italian policy with greater vigour. Duke Henry the Lion now received Bavaria. The Austrian Mark was separated and made a duchy, and the house of Babenberg was given the right of hereditary succession there, both in the male and in the female line. (Claims to further privileges by this house rested on forged documents of a later period, and such efforts only demonstrate the force of this family's will to independence.) Out of its East Mark it attempted to create an eastern realm with its own interests and alliances, at most linked to Bavaria, but increasingly aloof from the affairs of the Empire at large and oriented toward eastern rather than central Europe. Emperor Frederick took the Silesian duchies from holders too much inclined toward independence and gave them to Polish grandees whom he could trust. Formally Silesia remained part of Poland, but it was more and more drawn toward Germany, and it developed into a particularly responsive and thriving region for settlement.

Like Otto the Great, Frederick gave his policy a special turn by making a Burgundian marriage. The heiress to the Burgundian

Kingdom, Princess Beatrix, was held a prisoner by her uncle, who wanted to keep the country in the power of the native aristocracy. But Emperor Frederick won the Princess, who became his lifelong faithful companion. The old personal union of the Burgundian Kingdom with East Francia was renewed, and local groups of interests had to accommodate themselves to it. The King of France, deeply offended by this development, took occasion to assert his sovereignty and to reject the slightest appearance of submission to an imperial feudal lord (1156).

Cool relations with France were followed by a closer approach to England. In the first stretch of his reign Frederick had the great advantage of being advised by a statesman of the grand style. This chancellor, Count Reinald of Dassel, became Archbishop of Köln (1149–57). His wisdom and energy were responsible for the early successes of the Emperor, who did not keep to the same lines later. The Count succeeded in preventing the dangerous union of the two western powers. He went to England to discuss an alliance. Frederick was in sympathy with the anti-clerical attitude of the English King Henry II. One of the most desirable results of this expedition was the marriage of Frederick's cousin, the Guelph Duke Henry the Lion, to the English Princess Matilda. Frederick and his chancellor did all they could to secure a powerful position in Europe for the Guelph, for only by this means was a successful Italian policy possible. If the Archbishop of Köln had lived longer—he died in 1168 —the wise policy of co-operation with the Guelph and with England would certainly have been continued.

Henry the Lion had good relations with Byzantium also. The part he played was European in scope: he governed as a sort of viceroy in the north, in the east, and in the southeast of Germany. His personality was much drier and harsher than Frederick's; he was without romantic charm, but he was a true ruler. This duke stands out as one of the most significant exponents of absolutist statesmanship through his management of officials and mercenaries, his financing, and his large-scale trade policies. The Christianizing of Rügen, Mecklenburg, and Pomerania was effected under his direction; Kammin was made a bishopric immediately subject to the Pope, and the Cistercian monastery of Oliva was founded. It is true that Henry the Lion's arrogance made many enemies for him; the cities especially feared his heavy hand. But without a substantial show of power toward Denmark and the neighbouring Slavic regions, Frederick Barbarossa's protracted struggles in Italy could not have been sustained.

THE LOMBARD LEAGUE

Emperor Frederick's conflict with the papacy was fanned to flame when Pope Adrian IV called the Emperor his vassal and referred to the imperial crown ambiguously as a papal *beneficium*. The struggle for power of these two universal authorities had the character of a feudal conflict; every contemporary understood the quarrel in exactly that way and took it in bitter earnest. Frederick thought he no longer had any choice but to make his way to Rome through Lombardy; it seemed impossible to dominate the papacy and Italy if the Lombard cities were allowed their autonomy. They had assumed the old royal prerogatives that had once been exercised by bishops and counts, and they governed themselves through their consuls. These cities betokened the triumph of civic and national freedom in Italy. All over Europe civic self-confidence, self-determination, and self-government were directed against the princes and bishops. In Italy this struggle received great national impetus by setting itself squarely against the alien domination of the Germans and the tutelage of central Europe. In the interests of his imperial and royal claims Emperor Frederick tried new means of suppressing this spirit, modern and vigorous as it was even in an economic way. Four doctors of Roman law in Bologna made a list of the royal prerogatives that the Emperor reclaimed except in cases where the cities could give documentary evidence of having acquired them. The Roman concept of rulership and the Lombard royal authority, both resting on feudal law, operated jointly with all the aids of written Roman law and traditional Germanic law to cut off the modernized urban development that was proceeding in such a lively fashion. On their side the cities invoked the hallowed political forms of antiquity to support the natural rights of their mature separate power. Once more Roman republicanism strove against Cæsar. At the same time awakening democracy was striving no less against the feudal system.

The decisions reached at Roncaglia about re-establishing Emperor Frederick's rights as King of Italy were to be enforced by commissions and imperial officers, the rectors or *podestàs*. An extremely bitter struggle began. Cremona and later proud Milan were destroyed. But it was all of no avail. The spirit of the cities would not be put down. The Republic of Venice launched a league for defence. Sicily and the Greek Emperor gave aid; unrest appeared even in towns as friendly to the Emperor as Verona and Padua. The Emperor would never be able to prevail in northern Italy by force.

With the papacy Frederick I had the same sort of experience. After the death of Adrian IV a schism arose. There was a Sicilian party and an imperial one. Alexander III, who was hostile to the Emperor, refused to appear at a synod at Pavia and to submit to the judgement of the orthodox. It had been an axiom with Gregory VII that a pope could not be judged by anyone. The schism clove through the whole West. The Byzantine Emperor planned to unite all of Frederick's enemies in one great group of leagues. The Lombard cities raised their heads again. The League of Verona was enlarged; Alessandria, its capital, was so named in the Pope's honour. Frederick besieged this city in vain. His luck had forsaken him. In the course of his fourth journey to Rome the greater part of his army was wiped out by epidemics.

HENRY THE LION (1129–95)

To collect enough troops for Italian ventures was no longer a simple matter. Frederick had to procure mercenaries at great expense. It was easy for the popular movement in Italy to build up a defence. In 1176, when the Emperor asked for help from Germany, it was refused by Henry the Lion, the most powerful prince of the Empire. According to feudal usage he was not obliged to give aid in Italy; the question involved was not one of feudal law, but purely of politics. The Lion had no fundamental objection to coming to Frederick's aid. He certainly did not disapprove of the Italian policy on principle; he even approved of it in many respects, if only because it spread out political pressure. But he wanted a certain price, the city of Goslar, which had once been his, but which the Emperor had taken from him. Emperor Frederick was unwilling to make such a bargain. He probably did not care particularly about Goslar, and as a rule he put aside purely emotional considerations in spite of possible knightly scruples. What decided him was his distrust of

Henry's power. Henry might make further demands, and the Emperor might conceivably become dependent on him. Subconsciously Frederick no doubt was envious of the Lion, and he could not forgive his cousin for this. Politically Frederick's decision was most unwise, and it had the most portentous consequences. Could he not have taken Goslar away from the Lion a second time? Could he not have penalized him in other ways if necessary? As a statesman he should have found the solution that was most profitable at the moment. Left in the lurch by Henry the Lion, the knightly army of the Emperor was too weak; at Legnano it suffered a severe setback in battle with the Milanese infantry, which outnumbered it very heavily. Now Frederick I began negotiations with Pope Alexander. The Peace of Venice was concluded on reasonably tolerable terms (1178). Frederick was at least allowed to retain the usufructs of Matilda's estates for fifteen years. In return he surrendered the supremacy of the Empire over the papal states. He abandoned the anti-pope he had set up, although doing so meant breaking an oath, and he concluded long truces with the Lombards and with Sicily.

Now at last—if only for a limited period—peace reigned in Italy. The Emperor was free to put Germany into shape. He had been denied victory in Italy; in Germany at least he wanted to be master. Proceedings were begun against Henry the Lion on feudal and other scores. The accused did not respond to any summons. The complaint cited breach of the peace, contempt, and high treason. The instances enumerated were limited to Henry's feuds with his neighbours. The Duke was first banned and then double-banned; he was deprived of his fiefs, and imperial war was declared against him. This was the first high political court action in Germany. With strict observance of legal forms the Emperor and King tore down the overweening power of the greatest prince of the Empire (1181). The true cause of the action, Henry's refusal to supply military aid in Italy, was passed over in utter silence in the court proceedings. Frederick not only destroyed an individual: he balanced his accounts with the tribal duchies. Both of Henry the Lion's duchies, Saxony and Bavaria, were split up. They were, as has been shown, the centres of the most obstinate particularism in Germany. The Archbishop of Köln received the western part of Saxony as the new Duchy of Westphalia;

the eastern part was given to the Count of Anhalt. Bavaria went to Otto, the Count Palatine of Wittelsbach, but Styria was split off and organized as an independent duchy. Of the old tribal duchies only Swabia was now left. The breaking up of Saxony sharpened the contrast between the Rhineland and the east; the whittling down of Bavaria stimulated both Bavarian and Austrian ambition. New frictions were engendered.

Henry the Lion submitted after three years. He got back his allods or private holdings of Brunswick and Lüneburg, the Guelph family property, but he was forced into exile. The Emperor did not permit him to return until 1185. The Lion could never forget his terrible humiliation, and his vengeance had to be reckoned with. The old feud between the Ghibellines and the Guelphs was now utterly irreconcilable. Instead of a normal development that might have led to a northern and a southern kingdom in central Europe, there was nothing but disintegration and confusion. Colonization in the east was arrested, all the lesser lords raised themselves up against the greater, and all the great ones armed themselves against the supreme power with caution and mistrustfulness, mindful of the fate of the Lion. The King of Denmark, Duke Henry's son-in-law, refused to pay homage to the Emperor; wisely, Frederick did not force the issue.

Emperor Frederick Barbarossa was sanguine in disposition. He was apt to celebrate his compromises as victories, and the more he had to yield, the more magnificent was the celebration. The Peace of Constance, which finally brought reconciliation with the Lombards, receded completely from the Roncaglia decisions. The cities were accorded the much-debated prerogatives; the Emperor had to content himself with the investiture of consuls elected by the citizens and with the institution of a court of appeal in issues involving finance and jurisdiction. Whenever the Emperor was in Italy the cities were responsible for his maintenance and transportation—a meagre compensation for the legal claims he had given up (1183). Never before had a German ruler made peace with the Pope and with rebellious vassals. The formality of concluding a peace was in itself evidence that the Emperor now had to deal with powers that aspired to equality with him. The dream of a universal empire melted further and further into thin air. The only thing that still seemed possible was a hegemony in Europe on a basis of shrewd foreign policy and adequate concentration of power.

Frederick Barbarossa now took care of this situation in his own way. His marriage had given him Burgundy; it was a happy marriage and profitable politically. Now he betrothed his son Henry to the heiress of the dangerous Sicilian Kingdom, the aunt of the former King—Princess Constance, who was neither very young nor at all beautiful. This union, obviously a purely political arrangement, spelled the ruin of the house of Hohenstaufen. At the marriage Frederick I gave his son the title of Cæsar (sub-emperor), according to Roman and Byzantine usage. The papacy took the whole procedure as a challenge. Hohenstaufen policy was now to interfere in Italian affairs from the south—that is, from a political sphere that the curia had been accustomed to regard as its own special concern. The reply was not long in coming. Again the Pope conspired with the Lombard cities and the princely German opposition, but Frederick was more or less successful in coping with these difficulties. Thus he was able to take the cross and venture to the Holy Land. He was not to return. While bathing in the Selef, a river of Asia Minor, or perhaps while fording it, he met death, at the right time to save him from hollow success or downright failure (1190).

True to his habit, the Emperor had had a far-reaching program for this long-planned crusade. His program was only partially carried out. Before his departure Frederick I had attempted a reconciliation with Henry the Lion. Once more the two princely cousins came face to face in that very Goslar that had been a bone of contention between them. The Emperor offered his one-time friend a choice: either partial restitution, along with renunciation of the rest of his former fiefs and participation in the crusade, or a new three years' exile. The Emperor did not want to leave his old enemy behind in Germany while he himself went to the East. The Lion was straightforward enough to choose exile; it was easier to return from exile than from a crusade. Not Henry the Lion, not England or France, not even all the Germans he had expected followed the old Emperor to the East as he left behind him a West full of discord. Even so, his army numbered twenty thousand knights, and he won

66

a splendid victory at Iconium. But after his death the enterprise petered out without any notable result.

Frederick Barbarossa was one of those happy temperaments whose failure or defeat we find it hard to credit, since they themselves cannot believe in them. And so this death in a remote land, in the midst of vigorous action that would have been appropriate to a far younger man, was fitting for him in its simple, improbable matter-of-factness. The people had good reason to transfer the emperor legend that grew up around his grandson to him. He was no great, uncanny magician like Emperor Frederick II, but just a brave and gallant knight whose peaceful rule would have been accepted gladly to all eternity.

HENRY VI

To Frederick Barbarossa a choice between a national German policy and imperialistic claims had still been possible. His son Henry VI no longer had this choice from either a political or a personal point of view. He was born to be a harsh absolutist; he strove openly for supremacy over Europe and over more than Europe—that is, for universal power. His reign (1190–7) was too brief to achieve any lasting successes, but it was long enough to make him thoroughly hated even among his kin and his closest followers. No attractive trait is to be found in his character. Even from a point of view of sheer power politics the results of his rash plans must not be overestimated.

At the outset Henry found himself confronted with tremendous difficulties. Henry the Lion broke his oath and reappeared in Germany in order to win back the Duchy of Saxony; he found accomplices of all sorts. The King launched a campaign against this breaker of the peace, but a treaty was soon concluded, though it did not function very long. In Sicily a national party arose against alien German rule. Count Tancred of Lecce, the last King's half-brother, was installed as ruler, to the annoyance of the barons of Apulia, who were supporting another candidate, but to the satisfaction of the Roman curia, which regarded nothing as quite so dangerous as Ghibelline rule in southern Italy. Through his relationship to the Sicilian royal house and through common Norman interests, King

Richard the Lion-hearted of England was deeply involved in all these transactions. With the approval of the curia he made an alliance with Tancred. On his return from the Holy Land he landed in Sicily and for a time thought of settling there permanently. Thus Emperor Henry VI had hard going in Italy. The old quarrels with the Lombards were rekindled. Tancred's position became firm, and he even treacherously took the Empress Constance prisoner—perhaps not without some help from this scheming lady herself.

Henry could secure the imperial crown only by exerting the strongest pressure on the reluctant Pope and by turning over to the Romans the town of Tusculum, which had always been loyal to the emperors. The utter destruction and massacre wrought at this place constituted a strange celebration of the Emperor's Eastertide coronation, and he never lived down the evil reputation that his cynical conduct earned for him. At this time the opposition party of east German princes was joined by the west German opposition that was consolidated under pressure of the murder of the Bishop of Liège, a deed generally attributed to the Emperor. Henry VI did, to be sure, take oath to his own innocence, but he punished the knights who had committed the murder only with exile, and later he rewarded them. Suspicion therefore still clung to him; his contemporaries credited him with having inspired the murder as well as perjured himself. In this unpleasant situation the Emperor had a stroke of luck. He utilized the tension among the western powers to form an alliance with King Philip Augustus of France against England; he undertook to capture the English King, Richard the Lion-hearted, on his return from the East. The plan was carried out. Richard was seized by Duke Leopold of Austria, his personal enemy. Henry made the most of the circumstances; he not only blackmailed King Richard into pledging a large ransom—which was paid off by the English in due order—but also into recognizing the Emperor as feudal overlord of England. He even made use of Richard's person and influence in negotiating with the hostile princes. The marriage of the son of Henry the Lion to the heiress of the Rhenish Palatinate, which was unwelcome to the Emperor, then led to reconciliation with the Guelphs, for whom the prospect of obtaining the Palatinate was a gratifying compensation. What fundamental changes in the work of Frederick Barbarossa! His son now met the old Duke Henry the Lion in person, and the Guelphs were re-established in all their greatness.

Danish plans for conquest now encountered no resistance, for the Emperor did not concern himself about Schleswig and Holstein. Sicily was more important to him. There King Tancred had died. With a large army and supported by the fleets of Genoa and Pisa, Henry conquered the Norman Kingdom, had himself crowned in Palermo, and seized the fabulous treasure of the Normans, which he carried off to the Trifels, a castle in the Rhenish Palatinate. He suppressed the conspiracies of discontented barons and gave his most faithful German *ministeriales* Italian lands as inheritable fiefs, to the indignation of the former holders. Henry's plans expanded in proportion to his success: he wanted to draw both France and Castile into his Empire. He regarded the King of Aragon as his vassal and roused the Genoese against him. Armenia and Cyprus paid homage to the Emperor, and confusion in the Byzantine provinces gave him hopes of still further expansion. He laid claim to the coast of North Africa—to Tunis and Tripoli, which Roger II of Sicily had subdued; and for a time he actually received tribute from North Africa and the Balearic Isles. The Pope, whose feudal claim to Sicily the Emperor absolutely refused to recognize, bowed to so formidable a fullness of imperial power. Henry VI took the cross, and thus it really seemed that Western and Eastern Christendom were to be united once again. The prerequisite to such a union was a guarantee of Hohenstaufen rule in Germany for the future.

Sicily was an absolutely hereditary monarchy. Such an arrangement was no longer possible in Germany. The princes had to be taken into account. But could not the royal office be made hereditary in a single ruling house? By such an expedient Henry hoped to rid himself of Guelph and other rivals. The Emperor was willing to pay a high price. He offered the princes exactly what he himself claimed for the office of king: inheritance of holdings by male and even female descendants and the right to inheritance for collateral lines. As for the ecclesiastical princes, the King would renounce the *spolia* in their favour; these were dues collected at the investiture of an ecclesiastical prince. The Emperor's plan was very tempting, even from the purely selfish point of view of the princes. In spite of all sorts of objections to details it was carried by a majority at the diet of

Würzburg. Now Emperor Henry went to Italy to obtain the Pope's approval. He offered to make the curia financially secure by permanent conveyance of productive beneficia to it, but this offer was not accepted. Henry's plans became more and more high-flown. Even the Byzantine Emperor consented to pay tribute. A crusade was to complete the world monarchy of the Hohenstaufens. But Henry VI died of malaria in Messina (1197). He was only thirty-two years old. Once the Pope in exasperation had called him "the fury of the north wind"; that fury was now spent.

Immediately the alien German government collapsed in Sicily. Emperor Henry VI had suppressed all resistance with cruelty. His own wife, Constance, who was estranged from him, had never been able to refuse her sympathy, even her secret aid, to her compatriots' will to freedom. What would happen now that the hated despot was dead?

A DOUBLE ELECTION (1198). PHILIP OF SWABIA AND OTTO IV

It was soon evident just how weak the foundations of the Hohenstaufen world monarchy really were. If Henry VI had lived longer, this commanding personality might perhaps have been able to attain a certain security, though not without great struggles and sacrifices. Now German destinies took their decisive turn. There was no longer any practical likelihood of universality and centralization. The son of Henry VI, Emperor Frederick II, the most distinguished Hohenstaufen, spent his life fighting for a lost cause.

He was a child when his father died. Was all the cheerless atmosphere of a regency during a ruler's minority to be experienced again, as in the times of Otto III and Henry IV? No one could bear to face the possibility. A wild and evil course of events unrolled. On his death-bed Henry VI had made a political testament that showed how clearly he realized the situation. The Emperor recommended immediate reconciliation with the curia, even at the greatest cost, as the only means of saving the day—even if it meant surrendering Matilda's property and acknowledging the Pope as the feudal lord of Sicily and central Italy. The Emperor's will to this effect disappeared; no one even dreamed of carrying out his instructions, but the development he had outlined proved inevitable. The regent, the Empress Constance, sent all the Germans out of Sicily. The

70

Sicilian national movement was victorious; it recognized the feudal supremacy of the Pope, which was the best protection against the claims of the Germans. In all central and northern Italy the local powers revolted against alien German rule. The idea of central Europe blew up. The Italian cities formed an alliance and laid claim to imperial property. The Roman curia also had a share in the reclamations. A new feeling of unity among the people of Italy gave these events special weight.

A three-year-old king was of no use to Germany. The legitimate election of Frederick II could not be maintained. The opposition of Guelphs and Ghibellines that had been overcome flared up with fresh intensity and led to a double election in 1198. The Ghibelline party elected the youngest brother of Henry VI, Duke Philip of Swabia and Tuscany. The election named an emperor by this title for the first time in German history, and every papal claim to interference was supposed to be silenced therewith once and for all. The Guelph party, headed by the Archbishop of Köln, elected Otto, the younger son of Henry the Lion, as king. He was the favorite of his uncle, Richard the Lion-hearted, who had given him the County of Poitou as a fief. By supporting this Guelph, the King of England wreaked a tardy revenge on the Hohenstaufens; without English subsidies Otto could not have made his way.

A difficult era of civil war now began in Germany. The principal scenes of action were the Rhineland, Thuringia, and Saxony. Both Kings gained adherents by distributing imperial property and sacrificing the prerogatives of the crown. Otto made the beginning. The Archbishop of Köln demanded a reward; *spolia* and royal prerogatives promised rich booty. While England helped the Guelphs, the Ghibellines concluded the customary alliance with the King of France. Through the enmity between England and France the German civil war became significant beyond the boundaries of the country and created a European tension. Flanders too became a battlefield and a prize of war.

The double election in Germany finally gave the papacy the welcome function of arbiter. Innocent III was a distinguished statesman who knew how to interpret law and history. He put the moment to his own uses with diplomatic skill. After well-calculated hesitation he decided in favour of the Guelph, Otto. The Pope, so he

71

explained, had the last word in a divided election; he alone could confer the imperial crown; he was the guardian of the Empire; though the princes could elect a candidate, it was the business of the curia to confirm the choice and to seal it by coronation. Thus the Pope's decision brought up the Ghibelline imperial claim only to refute it. Innocent III recognized Otto as the King who was elected to be Roman Emperor. In return Otto renounced imperial rights in central Italy. His party grew; the Pope emphatically reiterated the right that he claimed to make a decision—it was his responsibility to crown whoever was elected. But soon there was a reaction. Emperor Philip was in mid-career when he was murdered in Bamberg by the Count Palatine Otto of Wittelsbach, who had courted a daughter of Philip's in vain. This Otto believed that Philip had crossed other plans of his for marrying; this was doubtless a mistake, for Philip, who had originally been intended for the church, had the name of being the most knightly and the kindest prince of his time. Poets praised his gentleness and his noble character. This most likable member of the Ghibelline family vanished like a shadow, without effect on German history (1208).

The Guelph, Otto IV, could not take advantage of this unexpected stroke of luck. He submitted to a new election and thus belatedly acknowledged his dead rival. His engagement to the eleven-year-old daughter of Emperor Philip won over to him the powerful Ghibelline *ministeriales*. He punished Philip's murderer and proclaimed a firm new peace in the realm. For a few years all was quiet in Germany. For the sake of his coronation as emperor, Otto IV made important concessions to the Pope. He renounced the rights to the royal prerogatives and the *spolia;* he recognized the papal states established in central Italy by Innocent III; he agreed that the curia should be the unconditional court of appeal in all affairs of the church and conceded complete freedom in church elections. All this testified to the full supremacy of the papacy, preponderant both in temporal power in Italy and in churchly authority throughout all the domains of the Empire. The Concordat of Worms had long ago ceased to exist save in theory; now the Empire gave up even the theory.

Otto IV was crowned in Rome. The coronation was dearly bought. Henry the Lion's son might well have been expected to return at once to Germany, where many great problems awaited him. But this Guelph took over the Ghibelline policy of conquest in an Italy that was consciously becoming more and more Italian. He went back on his promises. He claimed all the old imperial rights in northern and central Italy; he went so far as to attack Sicily, to which the Guelphs did not have even a formal claim. The Pope now banned this Guelph just as he had banned the Ghibellines. With the help of France, Innocent III won over the German princes to young Frederick, the heir to the throne of Sicily, the "boy from Apulia." Again civil war broke out in Germany. True to the Pope's program, Frederick was elected King in Nürnberg. He received Sicily from the Pope as a fief; he allied himself with France, accepted French subsidies, and appeared in Germany as the "Pope's King"—a strange beginning for a great career. In the Golden Bull of Eger, Frederick II formally confirmed all the concessions made by Emperor Otto, and this time the German princes participated by witnessing and sealing the document. Frederick was crowned King in Frankfurt— in the wrong place, by the wrong hand, and with the wrong insignia.

The Battle of Bouvines (1214) brought defeat to the alliance of the Guelphs, the Lower Rhineland, and England against France. Emperor Otto IV no longer had anything to hope for, and he died almost forgotten in 1218. The only Guelph Emperor had gambled away the chances of his house. He did indeed possess the pride and the leonine courage of his ancestors. His impetuousness won friends for him, at least while he was young; from the mature man none could expect moderation in ambition or gracious treatment of inferiors. He always gave an impression of incompleteness. When the charm of youth had passed he was unstable and unpredictable and consequently lonely. If he had been a little wiser, he would have found the fault within himself. But as it was, he spitefully laid the blame on his friends, on the whole world, even on God.

EMPEROR FREDERICK II (1212–50). SICILY. THE CRUSADE

Otto, who came from Lower Saxony, had reached out for Sicily. The idea of a central Europe, of German hegemony, called for a firm hold on all Italy. Frederick the Sicilian moved outward from his native hereditary kingdom. He was in every sense a Norman

73

prince imbued with the Roman spirit. Although he looked like the Ghibellines, he did not have much German blood, and his spirit was not at all German. Earlier emperors had made expeditions to Rome. Frederick now came to Germany as an alien, as patron and tyrant, as pacifier. He undertook his expeditions to Germany because he needed Germany, but the centre of gravity of his world was in Italy. Germany had to content herself with imperial administrators and had reached the point of not even wanting a strong emperor. The papacy's attitude was curious. Rome wished to separate Sicily and Germany. If both were held by one power, the papacy would be caught in a pincers. And so Pope Innocent III exacted the promise that Frederick, once he was crowned, would turn Sicily over to his young son Henry. This was an impossible demand, and the new Pope, Honorius, did not insist on its being carried out. Instead Prince Henry was elected King of Germany. Sicily was Frederick's native soil; it was the centre of power for him. For Sicily's sake Frederick, though in the beginning he was the Pope's creature, was to become involved in an irreconcilable struggle with the curia.

The question of a crusade started the strife. On the occasion of his second and more correct coronation at Aachen, Frederick took the cross (1215). The curia had every reason to press for the fulfilment of this vow. The eastern world had undergone a complete transformation as a result of the so-called Fourth Crusade (1202–14). The business acumen of the Venetians had turned the movement aside toward Byzantium. The Byzantine Empire sank under the Frankish assault, and a Latin Empire arose in the East that had many ramifications. Its Western and feudal organization was grafted on to the utterly different structure of Greek society. The papacy triumphed, and again Western Rome and Eastern Rome seemed to merge. No pope had ever stood forth more impressively than Innocent III at the Lateran Council in 1215; a united and homogeneous Christendom bowed to his temporal and spiritual overlordship. In a spiritual sense Constantine's empire was reconstituted. There was nothing left to desire but the reconquest of the Holy Land: little wonder that the papacy was eager for this. The attack could not be looked for from the Latin Empire, which was wrestling with its own new problems. As for Venice, she was interested in nothing but her rising industrial and colonial power in the eastern Mediterranean. The very gains of the Fourth Crusade seemed to be smothering the crusade idea.

Emperor Frederick really wanted to go on a crusade, but first he had to put his affairs in order. In Sicily he instituted the first modern absolute monarchy. The autocratic spirit of Cluny was here secularized. A carefully graded hierarchy of officials guarded the royal prerogatives and discharged the authority of the crown with unlimited power. Now there was only the King's law, the King's administration. The soldiers were the King's soldiers, and the financiers were equally the King's. Even the most obstreperous barons bowed down as the King's subjects, for only in the King's service could they hope for increased power.

For Henry VI it had still been possible to plan to develop Germany into a hereditary monarchy. Frederick II had to content himself with buying the coronation as king for his young son Henry at the price of far-reaching concessions to the princes of the German church. In 1220 the Emperor spoke of their domains as "territories" for the first time. With a few slight exceptions he gave up the royal jurisdiction over these regions and forbade the building of castles and towns on such properties. At the imperial coronation Frederick had issued a series of laws exempting the clergy from imperial taxes and jurisdiction. In the edict concerning heresy he put his temporal power at the disposal of the church for the persecution of her most dangerous enemies. His relations with the curia, then, were good and remained good for a time, especially since the Pope made an effort to mediate between the Emperor and the Lombard cities. But when Frederick's departure for the Holy Land was postponed because of illness and accidents, Pope Gregory IX excommunicated him, and the conflict between Pope and Emperor blazed up afresh. In spite of his excommunication Frederick II went to the East and by dint of shrewd negotiation accomplished more than any crusader before him. Jerusalem—except for the Mosque of Omar—Bethlehem, Nazareth, and a coastal strip were ceded to him. Frederick, who as son-in-law of the King of Jerusalem had already been calling himself King of Jerusalem, now had himself crowned King, whereupon the Patriarch put the city under interdict because of the presence of the excommunicated Emperor (1229).

The feud between the Emperor and the Pope plunged Germany

and Italy into new civil wars. Gregory was already casting about for an anti-emperor. The Guelph Duke Otto of Lüneburg, nephew of Emperor Otto IV, was not interested, but Louis of Bavaria, who was administering the Empire, started treasonable negotiations. Papal troops were invading Sicily when Frederick, on his return from the East, succeeded by dint of his diplomatic gifts in concluding the compromise peace of San Germano with Gregory. The papal states were given new recognition, but the Pope's demands concerning the position of the Sicilian clergy were only partially granted (1230).

REORGANIZATION IN GERMANY

Fresh disturbance came from the north, from the Lombards and from Germany. During the stern and careful regency of Archbishop Engelbert of Köln for the young King Henry, there had been peace and order. The north German princes won victories over Denmark; for a time King Waldemar II was imprisoned. But after Engelbert was slain as an act of vengeance, confusion again arose. At this time the first federation of cities along the middle Rhine was formed. The common people, abandoned by the lords and pushed about by selfish interests in which they had no share, realized at last that they would never enjoy any degree of security unless they helped themselves to it. They acted on this realization. The political power of Germany, the stem, now rose into its branches. Young King Henry, who had been reigning in Germany independently since 1228, had to buy the friendship of the princes by extensive grants of privileges, most of which his father confirmed. The great Privilege of Worms (1231) accorded the princes jurisdiction over their own territories, including the appointment of judges of the lower courts and determination of the place where court was to be held. The peculiar status of the so-called suburban citizens (*Pfahlbürger*) — citizens who were under the protection and the laws of a city without residing in it — was abolished. For the future the jurisdiction of a town was to be limited to its own precincts; country people were no longer to pay taxes to the cities; the cities were to return fiefs that had been granted by lay or ecclesiastical princes; the princes were to be permitted to fortify their towns and were given the right to build roads and markets; the princes' right of coinage was to have precedence over the Emperor's. In this way rights and claims that had arisen were legally recognized, and the transformation of princely status within the Empire into sovereignty was accomplished. Now for the first time the princes were designated as sovereigns. Simultaneously an imperial decree determined the rights of the diets of the principalities in relation to the princes. The sovereigns could not make new rulings and, in particular, could not impose new taxes without the consent of the diets.

King Henry (VII) was not in favour of the hostile trend of the new order toward the towns. He even joined the Lombards in an intrigue against his imperial father. Was young Henry planning a democratic hereditary kingdom for the German nation? Was he planning to renounce hegemony in central Europe? A new spirit had awakened. It made itself felt in the towns of Italy as well as in those of Germany. It was even alive in small religious groups of a sectarian character that were cruelly persecuted as heretical; pagan beliefs and popular customs that still persisted joined with early Christian anti-clericalism and anti-dogmatism. All this was, of course, an irritation to the sovereignty of the new princedom, which used the crusade idea to stamp out all particularism, every liberal or independent development, all individuality in church affairs or in politics.

Conrad of Marburg had the well-deserved reputation of being the most ruthless judge of heretics. He was a Master of Arts who wormed his way into the court of the Landgrave of Thuringia as a spiritual adviser. Here this narrow-minded, sadistic upstart tyrannized over the virtuous, childlike, touchingly generous Landgravine Elizabeth, who was later sainted. Before the rough force of her husband this gentle soul fled to the sweet serenity of mystic contemplation. But in her fervour she did not recognize the practical goals of a man like Conrad. With the support of the new princely power and of the Dominican Order, this madman raged through the country and left pyres burning in his wake. King Henry was successful in checking the pathological fanaticism of Conrad and his aides. But he could not prevent the terrible destruction of the Stedinger peasantry, whose heresy consisted merely in wanting to live according to their old ways and customs, undisturbed by princes and bishops with their demands for money; pagan superstitions may well have figured in their traditions, but in any case this late group of free Low Saxon peasants became the lamentable victims of a self-constituted crusade.

King Henry's final revolt against his imperial father proved an ill-prepared and poorly organized undertaking. He found faithful followers only in the southwest of Germany, among the Ghibelline *ministeriales* who were dissatisfied with the Italian policy. Discontented bishops joined them. Emperor Frederick's mere appearance in Germany caused the whole movement to collapse. King Henry was taken to Apulia, where he was held captive until he died.

Frederick II now married for a third time. His new wife was the English Princess Elizabeth. This skilfully prepared approach to England was not, however, to indicate a break with the old French allies of the Emperor. Frederick was in dire need of maintaining good relations with both of the Western powers. The great imperial decree of 1235, issued at the Diet of Worms at a happy moment when all was tranquil in the field of foreign politics, is the oldest law of the Empire in the German language. It marks the summit of Frederick's German policy of centralization, order, and reconciliation. Besides regulations about suburban citizens (persons who had acquired civic rights without having permanent residence in the city), guards (for the protection of people attending city fairs), tolls, road building, and coinage, this law was particularly concerned with the public peace. Feuds, or private wars, were to be carried on only in cases of self-defence or where justice had expressly been denied; they were to be formally declared. The Emperor made the chief justiciar his representative as dispenser of justice during his own absence. A codification of the laws of the Empire was promised. Thus a decided centralization of German law was set over against the German tribal and princely particularisms that had to be endured. It was a most promising achievement—a beginning. But the collapse of the Hohenstaufens prevented its being carried further.

Emperor Otto IV, the Guelph, had not been able to resist the temptation of practising Hohenstaufen politics in Italy. Vice versa the Hohenstaufen Frederick II had been utilizing the traditional Guelph policy when he encouraged just as far as possible the spread of the Germans toward the Slavic and Lithuanian east. The Christianizing of Prussia, organized by the leading Cistercian monastery of Oliva near the free town of Danzig, had suffered severe relapses. When a crusade organized by Duke Conrad of Masovia proved unsuccessful, the Duke turned for help to the Grand Master of the Teutonic Order, Hermann von Salza, and offered him the region around Chelmno (Kulm) in return. In the newly founded archbishopric Riga was the see. Soon the Teutonic Order completely withdrew from the East and presently began a magnificent career of colonization near at home. Its knightly and spiritual work was supported by the Order of Brothers of the Sword in Livonia (Livland), as well as by the King of Bohemia. The new land of Prussia, won by the Teutonic Order, never legally belonged to the German Kingdom. But the Bishop of Livonia became a prince of the Empire, and his land was made a mark. Later the Grand Master of the Teutonic Order in person received the rank of a prince of the Empire.

Troubles arose in Austria. The last Babenberg was exiled on account of his participation in King Henry's conspiracy. He had pursued the plan of making one kingdom of his domains: Upper and Lower Austria, Styria, and Carinthia. This kingdom was to be only loosely subordinated to the Empire; the near-by kingdoms of Bohemia and Hungary may have suggested such a plan. Now the Emperor took back the lands as forfeited fiefs. Vienna was given immediacy; that is, it was made directly subject to the Empire. In Vienna, Frederick's nine-year-old son Conrad was elected King. After the death of the last Babenberg Duke (1246) his former lands were put under the administration of captains general by the Emperor.

THE STRUGGLE FOR ITALY

Emperor Frederick II might have forgiven his rebellious son his sympathy for the rising powers of the people in Germany, but never his complicity with the Lombards. The King of Sicily had to have control of the north Italian passes across the Alps if he wished to go to Germany. It was a favourite trick of the Veronese to close the Klausen Pass to the Germans. That was why the Emperor appointed a blood-thirsty *podestà*, Ezzelino da Romano, at this strategic point. In order to bind this man wholly to his interests the Emperor gave him one of his daughters in marriage. In vain Pope Gregory IX tried to mediate between Frederick and the Lombards; the Emperor would not hear of arbitration. Frederick won a brilliant victory at Cortenuova. But Brescia resisted siege, and the other most important

cities, such as Milan, Alessandria, and Bologna, remained unvan-
quished. The Pope felt and acted as an Italian prince. The curia took
offence when the Emperor made his natural son King of Sardinia;
this was the charming Prince Enzio, who had married the heiress to
the Sardinian throne. The Pope regarded this island as his feudal
property. Thus conflicts multiplied. Gregory IX complained bitterly
of the Emperor's inroads, which were also directed against the clergy
and members of religious orders. He mourned the insecurity of conditions in the Holy Land. Could not these matters be adjusted? The
time for quarrels about orthodox principles was past. Under the
Salic dynasty spiritual issues were approached by temporal methods.
Now matters were reversed. The real question concerned Italy. The
King of Sicily was an enemy of the lord of the papal states and of
the Lombards. Frederick, the first person in Italy to be suffused
with the spirit of a new cultural age, was destroyed as a ruler by the
national Italian way of thinking as it progressed.

The new Pope, Innocent IV, was a Fiesco, of the Genoese family
of the Counts of Lavagna. Genoa as well as Venice had shown itself
opposed to Frederick. There were negotiations, but the Emperor rejected the Pope's decision in regard to the Lombards. He feared the
hegemony of the curia in Italy—an intolerable condition for the
King of Sicily. The conflict continued and grew more and more
bitter, secular, and cruel. A bishop who was dying on the rack was
actually denied extreme unction. By now the Emperor had been repeatedly banished and excommunicated by the Pope, finally at the
Council of Lyons (1245). For his part Frederick II protested against
the power that the Pope had assumed in penalizing him. On formal
legal grounds he declared that the verdict pronounced on him was
invalid. He accused the church of utter degeneracy and demanded
that she renounce temporal goods and lands. Thus the struggle
moved on to the fundamental plane of church reform, in prophetic
anticipation of many later dissensions. The conflict now manifested
itself in Germany. Two anti-kings who had been set up there had no
more than local significance. Destiny dealt Emperor Frederick some
severe blows. His officials were all well trained and supervised; the
Chancellor Petrus de Vinea, the most distinguished of the lot, was
convicted of many breaches of trust which had extended over long
years, of embezzlement, and of treacherous double-dealing. The Em-

peror, who was deeply wounded not only as a sovereign but as a man, permitted his erstwhile friend to perish miserably in a dungeon. The people of Bologna imprisoned Frederick's favourite son, King Enzio, the offspring of an adventure with a wonderfully beautiful German girl, and would not release him even for a high ransom. The poor prince and poet, when he tried to flee, was given away by a lock of his blond hair that escaped from the barrel in which he had hidden.

The Emperor was deserted by his soldier's luck. He lost Parma— an important city—and was badly worsted during the siege of this strategic position. He was not yet beaten, but he was no longer able to win a victory anywhere. In 1250 he died suddenly. It had been predicted that death would find him in a city of flowers, and for this reason he had always carefully avoided Florence. But the oracle proved correct. Fate overtook him in the little Apulian town of Fiorentino. Emperor Frederick II is buried in Palermo, whose curious blend of cultures had been the background for his hazardous and precocious development. The sultry atmosphere of this world that was West and East in one would hardly foster a kindly, warmhearted personality. During his entire life Frederick's inclinations and habits tended to the Oriental, for a sultan's mode of living was part of the Sicilian court tradition. Frederick kept a harem. He had eunuchs to guard his three legitimate wives, the last of whom, the English princess, suffered especially from such treatment. The Emperor loved animals, but his elephants, lions, and panthers, which were the terror of northerners, were not merely objects of display in a princely menagerie. Frederick was one who studied and inquired; his book on falconry combines serious sportsmanship with serious science. The attractive picture of him in the Kaisersaal at Frankfurt portrays a huntsman with a falcon.

The Emperor, who spoke many languages, encouraged translation. He drafted plans for buildings and had them executed, collected precious objects, and loved to carry on a subtle conversation with anyone who had something to say. He was free of prejudice like none other in the Middle Ages. He would allow a Jewish or a Saracen physician, for instance, to sit beside him and to drink in his presence. Every question of the times and every timeless question engaged him, but equally no subject, not even a sacred subject, was safe from his mocking tongue. He respected established historical institutions, such as the Christian church—if not quite with love, then with prudence. Frederick composed poems in the Italian vernacular and set them to music himself. To him it was both a mission and a principle of culture to study the antique and to awaken it to new life. He saw himself as the bearer of a sacred majesty, a victor triumphant, a bringer of salvation. The spirit of his political work can hardly be understood without taking into account his Sicilian heritage, the cultural movement in France and northern Italy, and the example of Spain. He gave this work a unique personal character. Seductive, mysterious, dangerous, he strode through his era. He could enrapture and destroy. He dealt with men as though he were a god. He was a magician who dazzled and charmed. For the moment he occupied the emotions, the sympathies, and the imagination of whomever he was with, only to leave behind a strange mixture of feelings—admiration, horror, and hatred. Toward the end of his career the church fought him as the Antichrist, which was indeed a succinct characterization of the cold worldliness of the "Terrible," the cruel and versatile genius, the world ruler with a smile that was like a mask. As a child he was to have received the name of Constantine, the Byzantine Emperor. When he lay dying he had himself swathed in a Franciscan monk's habit—the last half-repentant, half-ironic pose of the unbeliever. He was the son of an unhappy marriage between the harshest and most arrogant of the German Hohenstaufens and a Sicilian princess accursed with ugliness and falsity. He had lived a full enough life according to his own taste to be able to savour the ecstasy of annihilation in renouncing the world with pious weariness.

The death of Frederick II marks the end of Ghibelline world emperorship, based politically on the possession of central Europe. The parts of the imperial domain now went their own ways. Germany was only just saved from the Mongol flood by the brave defence of Wenceslaus, the King of Bohemia, and of Henry, the Duke of Lower Silesia, who fell at Liegnitz (1241).

Now the unfortunate Empire was consumed by constant civil wars. King Conrad IV died (1254) before his time, unable to master the chaos of the imminent interregnum. Jerusalem was lost to the Saracens. The Pope, the maritime cities, and the Lombards ruled northern and central Italy. France, which had long been paralysed by England's continental interests, became stronger in defence. The French Kingdom moved farther and farther toward centralization; the vassals of the crown grumbled but adjusted themselves to the situation; the cities were not permitted to become little republics as in Germany. Royal jurisdiction held together firmly a country fragmented by feudal tenure. Pushing out gradually from the incomparable natural focus of Paris, the French King quietly and patiently built up a politically united France, which shifted her boundaries toward England and Germany more and more to her own advantage. Foreign policy found a new field.

Burgundy broke apart. Duke Charles of Anjou, the brother of King Louis IX of France, who was also called Saint Louis, acquired Provence by marriage. The church liked to flaunt the pious French King in the face of the unholy Frederick II, the heretic, the son of hell. But the King of France was wise enough not to let himself be forced into the role of political opponent of the Hohenstaufens; when he went on his crusades to North Africa he kept within the zone of French interests in the Mediterranean. It was different with his brother. Charles of Anjou accepted the Kingdom of Sicily as a fief from the Pope, and with French funds and French knights he wrested the island from Emperor Frederick's natural son, King Manfred. This campaign, too, went under the name of a crusade. Actually it was the beginning of the struggle of the Germans and the French for the hegemony of central Europe. The passions of the Italian people were not calmed until the entire brood of the Hohenstaufens was destroyed. The last member of this family, Duke Conradin of Swabia, the son of King Conrad IV and grandson of Emperor Frederick II, wanted to seize his heritage of Sicily, which was not, to be sure, above question as a papal fief. He went to the perilous south with insufficient forces. As a rebel and a land-robber he was publicly executed in Naples (1268). The Pope was triumphant. The true sons of the church, the French kings, made no claims to any imperial and universal power. The curia in Rome could therefore rule over Italy as sovereign and over the West as high priest. The end of Hohenstaufen world emperorship marked the beginning of a community of interests between the Pope and France.

Chapter 6

GERMAN CIVILIZATION AT THE

CREST OF THE MIDDLE AGES

THE HISTORY of the Roman Empire and of the East Frankish German Kingdom is a story of disintegration. The union of the three realms of East Francia (Germany), Italy (the part subject to the Lombard crown), and Burgundy had always been to some degree accidental and personal. No statesman was able to weld them into a political whole; no crown lawyer even dreamed of shaping these masses of land into one dominion with the same laws throughout. The idea of a dominant state never became a reality. The popes had the advantage over the emperors, if only through their carefully kept archives and their legally trained councillors who knew how to interpret documents in the Roman manner—that is, the most expedient way. The universal power of the combined Empire and kingdom, its superior dignity, which consisted more in prestige than in the actual power to command, remained rather vague even in comparison with local powers, whose existence rested on grants from the highest quarters. As it worked out, these quarters were put on the defensive and had to make concession after concession.

The East Frankish Kingdom, which was popularly called the German Kingdom, strove in vain for a hereditary rulership. Election within the bounds of the rights of succession remained the rule— that is, election from among the members of the family entitled to the succession—and generally the choice was prompted by the wishes of the dying ruler. Election was an old Germanic concept, whereas a hereditary dynasty was apprehended as Roman-Oriental despotism. Theoretically every freeman had the right to take part in elections, but the election of the king was limited to the aristocracy, if only for expediency's sake. The vote of the mighty was justified by their position as local leaders; it was accepted as the voice of the whole people, and popular acclamation was regarded as a vestige of an original general right of suffrage.

All together the authority of the king was somewhat spasmodic and accidental. The king intervened only when necessary, in contrast to the emperorship of late antiquity, with its tendency to give prohibitive commands through an officialdom thirsting for action. The old German spirit of freedom craved a king and wanted to honour him, but without feeling him too near or too much; it preferred to help itself by means of law and order originating within the community itself.

Beside the secular princes—the lay princes who elected the king— stood the princes of the church, *Pfaffenfürsten*. Gradually a right of preliminary selection developed, for an election was really decided as soon as certain powerful princes expressed their opinion. Out of custom and practice grew this right of preliminary selection, exercised by four secular and three ecclesiastical princes—that is, by the four who held the great offices of the imperial household, which they discharged at the coronation, and by the three arch-chancellors. The four officers were the Count Palatine of the Rhine (seneschal), the King of Bohemia (cupbearer), the Duke of Saxony (marshal), and the Margrave of Brandenburg (chamberlain). The three arch-chancellors were the archbishops of Mainz (for Germany), of Köln (for Italy), and of Trier (for Burgundy, later Gaul—that is, in a specialized sense, the entire left bank of the Rhine). The seven preliminary electors were first designated as electors in 1220, and this was the origin of the electorate. The elections were held at various places; Frankish soil was preferred, and Frankfurt had been customary since the time of the Hohenstaufens. In memory of the coronation of Otto the Great at the grave of Charles the Great, Aachen became the traditional place of coronation.

The king had no fixed residence, but travelled about; he was everywhere and nowhere. Possession of the insignia of the Empire was important for the succession to the throne. Often the successor received them in person when he was designated. The crown, the sceptre, the robe, and the holy lance lent their holder a kind of grace so potent that the electors were reluctant to disregard it. The power of these tangible symbols was often weightier than political calculation and the interests of ambitious individuals. The emperorship was

85

regarded as a divine right. The emperor ruled all Christendom as priestly lord, governor, guardian, propagator of the Christian faith, missionary, and saviour. From the time of Frederick Barbarossa the term "Holy Empire" was current. The emperorship and the papacy were two aspects of one entity; each participated half-way in the divinity of the whole. The imperial coronation was simultaneously a consecration, a feudal procedure, and a sacrament—a single act that raised the bearer of the crown from the level of the rest of humanity to a higher plane. To the elect it would have seemed a mortal sin to attempt to withdraw from this physical and spiritual consecration and elevation.

The Roman concept of empire in antiquity, the sum of traditions from Augustus to Constantine, which was still a living principle to Charles the Great, had begun to fade since the beginning of the eleventh century. Both the Roman universal state and the Roman church had undergone changes. The concept of an imperial world state weakened in proportion to the strengthening of the princes. The cosmopolitan, imperialistic papacy could not take possession of the heritage; its own supernational character had to be spiritualized in order for it to maintain itself as an ecclesiastical power. Emperorship and papacy, in their capacity of great political and spiritual powers, had destroyed each other. As mere institutions they were to survive their actual decay for a long time by dint of the tenacious adaptability that is peculiar to institutions of a sacred character.

Between the king and the people there existed no direct legal or political relationship. The privileged hierarchy of the princes who acted as aides in ruling (*coadjutores imperii*) constituted an agency of mediation. Feudalism, taking precedence over the nobility that came from exercising an office, transformed that nobility completely. A spiritual and temporal state run by officials became a feudal state. On this the new proprietary and territorial powers rested—subordinate to the king and superior to the people, whom they governed. As a result of its military origin the new feudal nobility was organized into army divisions; no fief could be taken from their members. Ecclesiastical princes could be vassals only of a king, but secular princes could receive fiefs from ecclesiastical princes. Lower down in the scale came the high nobility, then the *ministeriales*. Breaking the vassal's oath was punishable by loss of the fief, but only on verdict of the offender's peers. A woman might accept a fief, but she did not participate in the ceremony by which it was conferred on her. Dukes emerged as military leaders of the tribes, counts as judges of certain districts. The territorial powers arose by accumulation of prerogatives and landed property along with different titles. The dukes and the most powerful counts, then, formed the estate of princes of the Empire; the lesser counts ranked between princes and barons. The palsgraves (*Pfalzgrafen*), as representatives of the royal power and stewards of the royal revenues, were a counterbalance to the dukes. The palsgrave of the Rhine—of Lorraine and Franconia—rose to the highest position among the four palsgraves. He became the first secular prince of the Empire, later the regent if the throne were vacant, and supreme judge in suits against the king.

Originally the King of Bohemia had been first in the series of secular princes, but later, because of his Slavic blood, he came after the bearers of the other three high offices. Since 1198 the rulers of Bohemia had regularly borne the title of king, which Emperor Henry IV first granted as a personal privilege. The idea of the Wenceslaus crown arose; it included Bohemia and the neighbouring country of Moravia, later also Silesia and the two Lusatias. This was a unique case of semi-sovereignty, for the King of Bohemia was entirely independent within his own territory, but had accepted his land as a fief from the East Frankish king. Emperor Frederick II limited the Bohemian king's obligation to appear at court to attending it only when it was held in the three cities closest to the kingdom of Bohemia (1212).

Since the death of Frederick Barbarossa neither Poland nor Denmark had been in the Empire. After much vacillation Pope Innocent IV released Hungary from all feudal obligation toward Germany. Many converted Slavic princes became connected with the Empire as vassals. Pomerania, Mecklenburg, and Rügen thus became imperial territory; the Slavic percentage in the population mounted. At the end of the Hohenstaufen era the territory of the German people was clearly staked out for the first time; only then could the integration and unification of the future nation begin. The Germanized West Slavs, who soon lost their Slavic dialects entirely save in a few unimportant sections (the Spreewald and Lusatia), finally became just as good Germans as the Celtic and Roman strains in the

Rhineland. Burgundy dissolved. Purely Romanic Lower Burgundy turned away from Germany completely; Upper Burgundy, which retained its hybrid culture, vacillated politically. The crumbling process affected the entire western boundary of Germany, which adjusted itself to current dynastic and military conditions and not to language or to population factors. Gains in the eastern Slav regions compensated for losses in the west of central Europe. The focus was shifting.

KNIGHTHOOD

The concept of rulership fostered by the feudal system rested largely on technical military grounds. Feudalism really meant the organization of the followers of a ruler and military leader. The military comprised all the vassals. Technical organization, however, changed; armaments became heavy and complicated, and only fully equipped cavalry could decide the issue of a battle. Horsemen were expensive; each of them required long training, mounts, and servants. Anyone who called such a horseman up to service had to have something to offer him. The horseman became a knight. The equipment and maintenance of armies of knights were difficult problems for the royal administration. War, as a calling, fused freemen and unfree *ministeriales* into a new group that, according to the example set in France, developed its own concepts of honour, its own customs, language, and mode of living, all over Europe. Freemen and knights were differentiated in regard to both the property they owned and the respect to which they were entitled. At a relatively early date special merit made it possible for knights who were unfree to rise into the ranks of the free. Sociologically the new stratum of unfree knights and freemen became a homogeneous whole through a common attitude toward life.

There was a sharp line of demarcation at the lower end of the scale. Knights no longer could or wanted to live as peasants, though many *ministeriales* were of peasant descent. Now the peasant was no longer permitted to wear a knight's belt, a prohibition (1186) that closed the knight's estate to this lowly stratum. All at once the free landowner saw himself outstripped in rank by the rise of numerous *ministeriales* who, unlike himself, were eligible to compete in tournaments. Whenever the army of knights was insufficient for purposes of war, the number was eked out with mercenaries. Burghers and peasants stayed at home and tried to keep clear of feuds and military expeditions. The cities, to be sure, were soon to have enough quarrels of their own to cope with. Conditions such as these contributed greatly to marking off the social classes of the realm and estranging them from one another. And so the courtly culture that now developed in Germany was essentially a culture of social classes.

Arabic, Byzantine, and Provençal influences shaped the new class of professional soldiers. The knight from the West, to his amazement, encountered a Saracen knight from whom he learned not only military technique, but also good taste, a new mode of living, and manners. The knight was experienced; that is, he was a well-travelled man who went from adventure to adventure, from one heroic feat to another. He was a fortune-hunter who believed in the power of God and the folly of mankind, who was always fluctuating between the joys of the world and renunciation of the world, between coarse dissipation and lovesick homage to a woman—the lady of his heart to whom he had sworn allegiance. A special language of social rank, a code of the permissible and impermissible, rules for tournaments, and love-service (*Minnedienst*) were developed. From the German point of view all this implied much that was artificial and foreign. Provençal was spoken by cultivated courtiers all over the West and hence in Germany also. Sentimentality and sophistries were the earmarks of this affected mode, which was rejected not only by all those who did not "belong"—the peasants and the craftsmen —but also by many a sturdy nobleman who preferred to use words that came natural to him and who nevertheless thought himself quite as aristocratic as any smooth social climber, if not more so.

The forceful, sturdy German character could not fail to bring forth genuine poetry. Even among the wandering scholars who made their verses in Latin there was a distinguished poet, the Archipoeta. Now Walther von der Vogelweide (died *c.* 1230) gave proof that the Middle High German language also was capable of expressing strength and charm, wit and patriotism, courtship and confession. Many lyric poets grew up around Walther. The Babenberg court in Austria, particularly, became a gathering-place for poets. Two epics, the *Nibelungenlied* and the *Gudrunlied,* were composed around 1200. They reveal the German character as it liked to imagine itself—brave and ready for battle, sturdy and self-confident, torn by passions and responsibilities; and in all this the faithfulness of the vassal to his lord persisted as the noblest virtue. Incidents from the time of the great migrations, historical reminiscences, fancies of wandering minstrels, age-old fairy-tales and legends, all merged in these epics and bore witness to the early development of the German spirit. The knightly epic sprang from northern France. From there the Germans took over the old tales of Charles the Great and his comrades, of Roland's deeds, of Merlin the magician, of King Arthur and his Round Table. Gottfried von Strassburg, charming and liberal, urbane and vivid, vied with Wolfram von Eschenbach, who belonged to the *ministeriales* and was perhaps the most profound and forceful among the poets of courtly culture.

The older German nobility had lived an ample life without too many scruples, respectful toward the church, but with an unburdened and unbroken, naïve, often brutal warrior's attitude toward the demands of the moment. This tradition still made itself felt in the era of courtly poetry that extolled the pleasures and the splendours of living to the full. But a new element was added: the true knight was to practise moderation, he was to control his instincts and his emotions, he was to observe certain forms. Beyond this he was to be generous, compassionate, noble, to eschew faithlessness and fickleness. Humanistic and spiritual elements, then, played a part in the concept of knightliness. The knight was to wear the cross as something more than an external symbol. The greatest cultural achievement of the ascetic clergy was to make the ideal of the crusader spiritual rather than worldly. When the tendencies of the Cluniac Reform weakened in the second half of the twelfth century, new orders were founded: the Cistercians, who distinguished themselves especially by colonizing the Slavic countries; the Premonstrants, who vied with them in clearing forests and extending horticulture, viticulture, and cattle-raising; and finally the two orders of mendicant friars. The Franciscans and Dominicans chose the cities for their sphere.

THE BURGHERS

The knights became the burghers of the open country; the burghers were the knights of the cities. Both classes were new, and their sociological composition was to a considerable extent the same. They altered the character of the older elements of the population. The influence of the knights infiltrated into the upper strata; it infused all seignorial living with its own rhythm and style. A chasm separated this stratum from the lower rural classes, the serfs, the small tenants and other simple freemen. These classes were now drawn together by the fact that they were not knightly; that is, they were held unfit for knightly service in war. That condition held them down socially, whatever their origin. The cities presented a state of affairs in sharp contrast to this. They opened their gates by choice to members of the lower strata. In the cities there was also a strong group that had been free from the beginning: the craftsmen. The craft of the smith, for example, could be practised only by freemen. As soon as the artisan left the household of a lord and began to sell the articles he himself produced, the calling was open to any freeman without diminishment of his status. The city offered the possibility of working independently, of greater personal security, and of greater potential gains; it offered the permanent peace of the castle—civic peace. It was no wonder that people began to desert the country—that those who were not free came swarming into the city, which meant freedom to them.

Germany now became part of the system of international commercial routes. Merchants from southern Germany visited the famous fairs of the French Champagne. Native German fairs such as that of Frankfurt dared to compete with those in foreign countries. South German towns communicated with towns of northern Italy across the Alps. Wares from the Near and Far East reached the Baltic by way of Russia; they came to England and Holland through Italy, Spain, and Portugal. Köln bloomed as a junction for commerce up and down the Rhine; Mainz became important for southwestern Germany, Leipzig for the entire east. People made use of credit; capital was accumulated; a money economy took form, and commercial capitalism in its early stages exchanged and created values.

Since Christians were forbidden by canon law to charge interest, Jews necessarily became the money-lenders. They did not belong to the craft and merchant guilds of the towns. Both in the towns and in the country they regulated their life according to their own religious and social patterns. Ever since late antiquity without interruption Jews had resided in cities along the Rhine; there these oldest inhabitants lived as tolerated aliens, regarded with a blend of suspicion and curiosity. For the most part the church and the nobility got along very well with the Jews. Persecutions were the work of the lower and the middle strata, both of them credulous and intolerant. Now the princes gave the Jews some degree of protection and in return levied dues on them. The Jews grew to fear the open country and moved into the cities, small and large, where they hoped to be able to maintain themselves as a recognized minority. Frederick Barbarossa designated the Jews of Regensburg (Ratisbon) as his servants of the chamber (1182). In the cities the Jews had the opportunity to amass precious metals. They made themselves useful by financing upkeep and armaments. Small wonder that the princes turned to them in their money troubles.

The rate of interest was high; it had to be, considering the great risk incurred by lending capital. The Italian bankers, who were pious Christian folk and knew how to get around the prohibition against taking interest, were reputed to be usurers exactly like the Jews. From time to time the princes took care of themselves by levying special taxes on the Jews or by plundering them. To the classes who were tied to agriculture the preoccupation with money seemed the very work of the devil, and to rob rich Jews or even to kill them was regarded as pleasing to God.

The economic motive seems to predominate in the pogroms of mediæval Germany. Of course the Jews were regarded as the murderers of Christ, as an accursed people, and were accordingly scorned and feared. Of course they were open to suspicion, since they were aliens, with an alien language and alien customs; the indigenous population suspected all aliens of everything infamous, from poisoning wells to spreading pestilences. But these latent prejudices did not prevent Christians from living side by side with Jews for many years in peace and in a naïve friendliness tinged with humour and not always tactful. The religious and social gap was wide. It caused indifference and suspicious rejection. The chief reason for contempt was the Jews' preoccupation with money matters, an activity into which Christian society had forced them by not allowing them to hold land or render military service. Race hatred is a much later phenomenon. The main motive was economic envy. Under one pretext or another the Jews had to suffer for their successes in the financial field.

The king of East Francia had revenues from three sources: property of the state, property of the state church, and property of the state in fiefs. As the king's power disintegrated they all declined. The family ambitions of the German dynasties consisted essentially of attempts to lay a new foundation for rulership, materially reinforced by the king's private property—that is, the family holdings consisting of allods, in contrast to property held in fief. There were no imperial taxes in Germany before the time of Emperor Sigismund.

The splitting up of governmental functions was the real reason for the wealth of the German cities. All these new authorities weighed on those who were ruled and, in one form or another, exacted dues of them. The burghers now opposed the knights both politically and economically. As far as possible the towns freed themselves from the power of rulers and held no immediate sacrifice too high for this end. They became as autonomous as they could in their own economy and administration of justice. The latter they developed from jurisdiction in matters of trade. The development of civic administration of justice went hand in hand with that of a general obligation to aid in defence and to pay taxes. As in Italy, the new privileges of rulership were vested in the city council. This council had all the powers of the former administrators. The cities needed strong organs of government of their own to buttress their thriving economic life. Accordingly they accepted privileges from the king, in return for which they supported with utter conviction his struggle against the bishops. The cities' privileges of self-government are tokens of rebellion against their feudal lords. The first German city to be such in the legal sense of the word was Worms, which drove out its bishop in 1073. Other bishops' cities followed suit.

Cities that had no overlord save the king became the later imperial cities. Cities that were mediate in their relation to the king were forced to leave at least part of their government to a feudal lord; most of them were under lay lords, who were not so easy to satisfy as the bishops. Civic rights were bound up with property-ownership within the city. Anyone who lived on someone else's property was merely an inhabitant, without full civic rights. All city-dwellers had their personal freedom. A feudal lord outside of the city walls lost his rights over any serf who lived inside them for a year. Thus the population of the city had its social gradations. Soon a patrician class developed as capital was accumulated—a class that endeavoured to keep government to itself. The attempt was contested by the craft and merchant guilds; these associations were held together by religious and social factors and were filled with a spirit of brotherly helpfulness.

Worms was the first town to build a city hall. City walls and towers had long been the visible evidence of civic pride and independence. Now the council had its own chapel beside the city hall. The cornerstone of the Cathedral of Köln was laid in 1248. The building of the Cathedral of Strassburg was begun in 1250. The broad stratum of the middle class, so characteristic of the cities, was spiritually uplifted by the sermons of the mendicant friars, by their teachings and their example. Here the poor spoke to the poor, the oppressed to the oppressed. A feeling of social responsibility awoke. The city churches of the Franciscans and Dominicans with their lofty Gothic interiors, the educational institutions, the asylums for foundlings and orphans bear witness to this new attitude of a body of people who, having been stirred, were prepared to make sacrifices.

In Worms, too, the new federation of Rhenish cities was formed in 1254. This comprised all the large cities of the Rhineland, and it also counted many secular and ecclesiastical princes among its members. King William recognized this federation for the public peace, and it became a power in the realm. It almost seemed as though the spirit of self-help were growing out beyond city walls into the region of imperial politics. If the universal powers failed them, then those forces striving toward local freedom had to see to it themselves that peace was maintained. But the federation soon broke up. After the double election of 1257 the princes dropped out of it.

LEGAL RELATIONSHIPS

German royalty had failed in its foreign policy. The long interregnum (1254–73) made a real revival of the emperorship seem unlikely. Count Richard of Cornwall had been elected king because he was a son-in-law of Frederick II, King Alfonso of Castile because he was a grandson of Philip of Swabia. Alfonso never set foot in the German realm. Richard was crowned as king in Köln; he made some journeys into Germany, but never gained any influence there. The interest of both these men centered on Italy. The Hohenstaufen tradition vanished, and the old norms of justice became hollow. The capitularies of Frankish origin were forgotten. The new laws of the realm tended to dissolve rather than to maintain central power.

Prescriptive right—what the English call common law—prevailed. It satisfied local and personal needs; it was flexible and capable of development. Since it furthered the breaking up of classes, it became popular. Frankish law was the king's law; it prevailed in Bavaria and Swabia. Saxony, Thuringia, and East Friesland were governed by Saxon law. Thus in this respect, too, Ghibelline Germany and Guelph Germany stood in opposition to each other. The oldest code of territorial law to be written down was that of the Frisians. The new class of *ministeriales*—not covered by territorial law—demanded a written statement of rights. This was made by noting down legal sentences that would serve as precedents—that is, authoritative interpretations of the current law. The rights of the peasants were specified in special codifications (*Hofrechte*). The oldest are those of Worms and Limburg. Although laws differed in different regions, certain typical characteristics recurred, for similar conditions begot similar laws. The most progressive organization of justice was evolved in the cities. Out of privileges, local rulings, and market regulations was developed a creative justice. The ordinances of the city council arose. These city laws were collected and codified, and when new cities were founded they took over the tried and proved laws of the old. In this way groups of cities came to have the same laws. The city laws of Magdeburg and Lübeck proved particularly fruitful. Since the Empire did not codify the law, this had to be done by private individuals. The oldest and most valuable German code is the Saxon Mirror (*Sachsenspiegel*). It was based on a Latin draft and was written in Low German between 1210 and 1220 by the baron and juryman Eicke von Repgow, who joined the class of the *ministeriales*.

The laws of the Saxon Mirror were valid for northern Germany. For southern Germany the German Mirror and the Swabian Mirror were prepared. During the Hohenstaufen era Roman law began to come in from Italy. A new concept arose, that of imperial law, which comprised both the laws of the Empire and Roman law. It became customary for German law students to go to Bologna to study Roman law. Here they made up a community of their own with stern self-government. Two factors decisively promoted the influence of Roman law. Canon law based on Roman law spread in proportion to the spread of church legislation, and so it became valid for everyday life in Germany to the same extent that the clergy became independent of royal power and placed themselves on a par with the secular princes. The transition to a way of living based on a money economy was in line with the trends of Roman law. The old German law had sprung from primitive agricultural conditions, whereas the *Corpus Juris* was the product of a social culture that had grown up in a money economy.

Chapter 7
THE DYNASTIES OF THE
HABSBURGS, WITTELSBACHS, AND LUXEMBURGS

RUDOLF OF HABSBURG (1273-91)

THE TERRITORIAL princes in Germany were quite content with a foreign emperor who was little more than a shadow to them. Frederick, the Italian, had been succeeded by the English Richard and later by the Spanish Alfonso. King Charles of Naples, whose influence extended into northern Italy, tried to have his nephew, King Philip III of France, elected. Oddly enough it was the papacy that favoured the choice of a German prince. This was because the curia, much concerned with the crusade idea, did not desire the complete disintegration of central Europe. This was the first occasion on which the electors acted as a united group. Their chief aim was to prevent the election of the most powerful prince of the Empire, King Ottokar of Bohemia. They made their own conditions: they wanted confirmation of their privileges, reimbursement for the costs of the election, electoral consent in the disposal of imperial property. Only a comparatively minor lord could stoop to make such bargains.

Such a one was easily found (1273). Count Rudolf of Habsburg came from an old Alsatian dynastic family that had been successful, especially in Switzerland, in combining increasing property with the office of count. The family was of good Ghibelline faith; Rudolf was the godson of Emperor Frederick II. While he could not vie with the ducal families in power, he was by no means just a poor count, but a decidedly modern-minded territorial lord who governed his lands efficiently after the example of the last Ghibelline Emperor, organized his officials, and introduced a tax system that yielded good revenues. Conscientious and sober, careful and calculating, clever and modest—this was Rudolf, and these were the qualities that characterized his rule. He was a good father to his household and to his country; he could be stern when necessary. He arranged profitable marriages for his daughters and looked out for his sons. A promise of marriage even played a part in his election. Rudolf's first task was to come to an understanding with the King of Bohemia, who had shown his defiance by not attending the election. As the grandson of Emperor Philip of Swabia, Ottokar too could invoke Ghibelline tradition. Since Henry the Lion no imperial prince had held such an outstanding position, and now he, the chief beneficiary of the interregnum, was to suffer the fate of the Guelphs.

The Ghibellines had tried to keep the East Mark (Austria), the heritage of the Babenbergs, for their house; but in vain. Ottokar came into possession of it and also acquired the Babenberg allods through his strange marriage with the widow of King Henry (VII), Margaret of Babenberg, who was twice his age. Ottokar was planning on a large scale: he wanted to be feudal lord of Poland and of the newly won lands in the east. Twice he undertook an expedition to the land of the Teutonic Order; it was he who founded Königsberg in Prussia. He also had an eye on Lithuania. He seized Carinthia and Carniola, as well as the free imperial district of Eger, and he even meddled with Hungary. His realm extended from the Riesengebirge to the Adriatic Sea. For the first time the lands that were to become known as Cisleithan Austria in the nineteenth century were united under one rule. Ottokar was a brilliant and energetic sovereign, and he had the quarrelsome nobility well under control. He fostered the advance of the cities, industry, commerce, and mining and brought about a flowering of the arts. Many Germans were attracted to Bohemia. If he could have maintained and developed his rule, Bohemia would probably have been won over to the German language as Silesia was. Bohemia's becoming an ethnical melting-pot would have been most fortunate for all central Europe. But the Slavic factor remained predominant in colonial eastern Germany. If Rudolf of Habsburg had recognized Ottokar's power, Germany would have split into eastern and western halves, and the result would have been eternal unrest. If Ottokar himself had become emperor, he might have been able to break the power of the territorial princes. Now he himself was destroyed.

At first Ottokar was willing to surrender the imperial fiefs he had presumptuously acquired. But war broke out again, and at Dünkrut (1278) he lost both a battle and his life. A great change followed. Rudolf proved moderate in his demands as a victor. He permitted Ottokar's heirs to retain Bohemia, Moravia, and the neighbouring countries—even the Eger district—but he gave his own sons the Austrian domains, and with this he laid the cornerstone for Habsburg power in eastern Germany. A marriage that connected the Habsburgs with the Bohemian ducal family prepared the way for later events. The idea of dynastic power seized on German royalty and never relinquished its hold. The struggle between the interests of the territorial princes, especially of the electors, and the principle of dynastic royal power continued through the next few generations. The electors were willing to recognize a really great dynastic power if their own privileges were not contested. In the end the Habsburgs were to win this contest for power and settlement.

It was easy for Rudolf to arrive at an understanding with the papacy, since he gave it a completely free hand in Italy. Because of this the curia induced King Alfonso of Castile to renounce the German crown, and it ostentatiously recognized Rudolf as Roman King. Neither the electors nor the new King had asked the Pope to confirm the election. But Rudolf wanted the imperial crown. The Pope was willing to grant it on condition of his renewing his promises, which included going on a crusade. Again and again Rudolf pondered a crusade and also an expedition to Rome. For lack of funds neither plan materialized, and he remained an uncrowned Emperor. The truth of the matter was that Rudolf was thrifty to the point of miserliness. If he had really wanted to, he could have got at least as far as Rome. But he did not dream of resuming the Ghibelline policy.

Rudolf had other plans. A union with Hungary seemed desirable to him, and he tried to make a fief of that country, but encountered strong national opposition. It is a notable fact, however, that on the basis of possessing Austrian domains Rudolf took up his enemy Ottokar's plans for expansion. Efforts that he made with regard to Lower Burgundy also failed. For all time to come the double tendency to growth in the southwest and in the southeast remained characteristic of Habsburg policy. The situation in the east brought the dynasty into contact with Hungary, Bohemia, Poland, and the

Ottoman Empire; that in the west gave rise both to co-operation and to friction with Switzerland, Burgundy, Savoy, and France. Already the Babenbergs had thought of founding a kingdom of Austria for themselves. The East Mark and its dependencies were close to ambitious kingdoms of half-alien or entirely alien peoples. In the interests of self-preservation shrewd politics were more necessary here than in any other territory. Under the Habsburgs Austria, turning away from her ever suspicious kindred state of Bavaria, embarked on her special mission: neighbourly co-operation with Bohemia and Hungary.

In the interior Rudolf's main preoccupation was to win back the lost lands of the crown. To this end he revived the office of provincial governor, which had died out in many places; but still he had no great success. In accordance with the obligations he had assumed at his election, he used declarations of assent, the so-called *Willebriefe,* to ensure for himself the necessary concurrence of the electors in matters pertaining to the crown lands. Rudolf tried to draw on the cities for funds; these measures provoked a good deal of civic unrest, in the midst of which the appearance of Tile Kolup, claiming to be the returned Emperor Frederick, had a good deal of effect. Among the many false Fredericks who emerged one after another through the years, this one was the most successful; but in the end he was burned as a heretic.

On the whole, Emperor Rudolf was friendly to the cities. He protected the burghers from their worst foes, the country knights, to whom the public peace was a nuisance and who tried to cope with the unfavourable times by taking toll of overland trade, a practice that soon degenerated into waylayings and highway robberies. Dozens of robber castles were destroyed and their owners punished. But in the imperial cities the Emperor himself made use of castles for collecting taxes. Thus both the new classes of the Hohenstaufen era, the knights and the burghers, suffered. It is not surprising that among the oppressed the memory of the Ghibellines grew into a wistful romantic legend. First it was Frederick II and later Frederick Barbarossa who, in the imagination of the people, became the undying carrier of imperial majesty and who, after long years of waiting in the Kyffhäuser mountain, was expected finally to return.

Northern and northeastern Germany were the parts least influenced by the Habsburg emperorship, for here the idea of federation and co-operation was taken up by the commercial cities of the North Sea and the Baltic. In 1280 Lübeck entered into a federation with Wismar and Riga, and even before that time closer relations had been formed with Hamburg, Bremen, and several Westphalian cities. Common economic interests bred political unity and new standards of justice. The old authorities stood apart from this development, without the will to hinder it or the ability to advance it. Such was the origin of the Hanseatic League.

Rudolf died in Speyer (Spires) and, according to his own wish, was buried beside the Salic kings and the first Hohenstaufen (1291). He came between two eras; when he was dying it was his wish to be counted among the great representatives of the imperial tradition. During his life this businesslike knight with a sense of humour had effected something unprecedented, and he had done it without much ado, simply and efficiently: he had founded a dynasty. Universalism was alien and incomprehensible to him personally. But in its own way his dynasty was again to take up the concept. The Hohenstaufens continued to lead their ghostly lives in the Kyffhäuser. But the mountain never unburdened itself. The dead Rudolf rested in the imperial city of Speyer. His descendants ruled Europe—yes, even the earth.

THE ELECTORS. ADOLF OF NASSAU (1292–8). ALBERT I (1298–1308)

For the time being, Germany's fate depended on the electors, who had one interest in common: not to allow a hereditary right of succession to become established. Hence the saying that for a son to succeed his father was contrary to the old laws. The electors were tacitly agreed that no one among their own number was to be king, for this would have meant debilitation and discord. They made use of a minor lord who grew in power during his kingship. Then, as against this newcomer, another minor lord was set up at the next election. In this way more and more houses were brought forward. The envious competition between older and younger houses held events in Germany to a tiresome and irritating monotony. The electors ruled the best and oldest crown lands. Every new ruling house was driven by this electoral bloc to—so to speak—the very fringes of the realm and was even forced into foreign alliances. This is why Bohemia,

Hungary, and Burgundy now replaced Italy as decisive factors in Germany's destiny. Central Europe was no longer a political entity, but it still constituted a feudal community.

Not Rudolf of Habsburg's son Albert, then, was his immediate successor on the throne, but Count Adolf of Nassau, a puppet of the envious King of Bohemia. Adolf was a petty dynast, fairly well educated, and dowered with a swarm of children on whose account he had to turn soldier to make money. The Count was not troubled by convictions or ideas, but simply continued his *condottiere's* career as king. He gave his electors as many rights and possessions as they demanded; the lion's share went to the Elector of Köln, but after the election he found that in some ways he had been cheated. King Adolf was a businessman, but not a very reliable one. War between England and France offered all sorts of chances for profit. Since France was advancing in Burgundy, Lorraine, and the Netherlands, Adolf came to an agreement with England (1294) whereby he received a subsidy amounting to the not inconsiderable sum of ten thousand pounds sterling. With these funds he mobilized an army, but without any intention of marching against France, for he proceeded to negotiate with the French King and to take money from him also. Understandably, the number of his foes increased. The Bohemian King dropped Adolf and came to an agreement with the Habsburgs. The ecclesiastical electors forsook him. Suit was brought against him. Since he did not appear, the electors deposed him on the grounds of incompetence and failure to abide by the laws of the Empire. The German princes claimed the right to depose a king, to the annoyance of the papal curia, which regarded itself as solely qualified. The day after Adolf's overthrow, Duke Albert of Austria was acclaimed Roman King. The court procedure may not have been quite correct, but from the political point of view Adolf was lost in any case. At least he died the death of an honest soldier in the Battle of Göllheim (1298).

King Albert won immediate success. He too had had to make substantial concessions to the electors; now, as their superior, he imposed restrictions on them. In particular he tried to reduce the excessive tolls levied on Rhine traffic by the ecclesiastical princes, for it was as though thriving commerce were being bled by the "dead hand," and the burghers were very bitter about it.

> ⸙ Had I the tolls on the Rhine,
> If Venice were but mine—

such was the folksong definition of unheard-of wealth. King Albert
gave further proof of his progressive attitude by interceding for more
humane treatment of the Jews. He was energetic in maintaining
good order and the peace of the realm. From the German point of
view it was a great stroke of luck that the Bohemian dynasty of the
Přemyslids, which had united Bohemia, Poland, and Hungary, died
out. A great territorial complex was developing in the east; the mutual dependence of the component parts went far beyond mere dynastic bonds. The last ruler, Wenceslaus III, was murdered. He left
no heir. Albert seized Bohemia and Moravia as fiefs of the Empire
and transferred them to his son Rudolf, who married Wenceslaus's
widow. Eger and Vogtland were also taken back into the Empire.
Albert's foreign policy was mainly based on his alliance with France,
which led to a certain strengthening of German influence in Burgundy. Here, too, a marriage helped hold policy to the direction that
had been chosen.

In the meantime the amicable relationship between France and
the papacy, the result of Ghibelline collapse, had changed to a dangerous tension. The French King also wanted to lord it over his own
clergy. He too refused to put up with interference from the curia.
French influence in Italy was beginning to be just as obnoxious to
the papacy as German influence had once been. Pope Boniface VIII
announced the Pope's claim to universal power with so much
hauteur that the King of France was not the only one to interpret it
as a challenge. Could not Germany ally herself with the curia in this
conflict? At first Boniface had not recognized Albert's kingship and
had refused him the imperial crown; now, reversing himself, he
granted recognition and offered the tempting prospect of the crown,
provided Albert broke his alliance with France. Albert gave ear. For
those parts of the Empire that lay in Italy he promised to appoint an
imperial vicar only with the Pope's consent; he promised also to take
military action against the opponents of the curia. His sons were not
to succeed him except with the Pope's approval. More than this, he
definitely acknowledged that it was the papacy that had conveyed
the Empire to Charles the Great and granted the right of election to

the electors. And Albert was the only king in the history of Germany to take a formal oath to the Pope, which his contemporaries naturally interpreted as a vassal's oath, though certain essential characteristics were lacking. The French policy of expansion in the Netherlands and in Burgundy and the beginning of French pension payments to west German ecclesiastical and secular princes made it easy for Albert to withdraw from France, though he saw to it that no actual break occurred. He still hoped to found a hereditary Habsburg monarchy with the help of the Pope. This idea was the core of all the great and small enterprises of this determined and gifted statesman, whose uncompromising brusqueness sharpened impersonal opposition into personal enmities. He fell in 1308, a victim to the plot of his ill-treated nephew and ward, Duke John, whom history has branded the Parricide.

HENRY VII (1308–13)

King Philip IV of France now felt strong enough to reach out for the royal and imperial crown on behalf of his brother, Duke Charles of Valois. The papacy had moved to Avignon. Royal power had substantially increased in France, and the tradition of Charles the Great was rekindled: was it not possible that, proceeding from the west, an empire might be formed anew that would reach over toward Italy and Germany and do what the German kings had never succeeded in doing completely or lastingly—gain control of the church? In the end, however, the zealous efforts of the Archbishop of Trier succeeded in pushing his brother, Count Henry of Luxemburg, to the centre of the stage. Baldwin himself owed his archbishopric to Henry's help, and he now expressed his brotherly gratitude in this munificent form. Like Adolf of Nassau, Henry was a minor noble, who administered his county on the frontier very soundly. His native tongue was French, and he was a vassal of King Philip of France, who had knighted him. It was therefore reasonable for France to hope that the new German King would not be hostile. Henry sued for the Pope's favour, promised his oath, and asked for the imperial crown; the curia consented. The new ruler maintained as good relations as possible with the princes of the Empire. His most significant achievement was to win over Bohemia. He drove the Habsburgs out of the country, married his son John to the last of the

Přemyslid princesses, and so founded the Luxemburg dynasty in Bohemia. Whoever possessed fortress-like Bohemia ruled eastern Germany; whoever possessed eastern Germany ruled central Europe. The importance of Bohemia from both the strategic point of view and also the economic weighed heavier and heavier in the affairs of Germany. The envious competition of the Habsburgs and the Luxemburgs was largely motivated by the struggle for Bohemia.

But the matter of most importance to Henry was Italian policy. He was the first German King since the interregnum to go south, and he went with the dream of a special imperial mission. At the head of a small force, with only a few Germans among its thirty thousand soldiers—the native tongue of the majority, as of Henry himself, was French—the Luxemburg King appeared in an Italy split into many factions. In the cities, which had matured economically and whose culture was burgeoning, groups were contending under the old party names of Guelphs and Ghibellines. Neither the Pope nor the Anjou power in the Kingdom of Naples could master the great families of the cities. In many places the *signoria* had developed from the office of the *podestà* and the grand vicars of the Hohenstaufen era. Bellicosity, selfish greeds, hate, and cruelty were the order of the day, and many Ghibelline patriots saw the old times of the German emperors in a halo of glory. They acclaimed the new Emperor, Henry VII, as a saviour and a harbinger of peace. The great poet Dante preached the idea of a universal monarchy; he believed in the creative power of peaceful co-operation between pope and emperor. But how could Emperor Henry VII with his weak forces carry out bold plans of significance for world history? He appointed governors in northern Italy. In Milan he received the Iron Crown of the Lombards, but Milan was the very first city to rise against him.

Many cities—both Guelph and Ghibelline—joined together to drive the barbarians out of the country. The Emperor could not continue to be the just and independent judge he had wished to be; he had to assure himself of Ghibelline loyalty while he still could. And now he was involved in violent contention. Florence headed a federation against him; only Pisa kept faith with him. He and the King of Naples became bitter foes in their contention for the Kingdom of Arles (Lower Burgundy). Henry had the King condemned to death on grounds of rebellion and treason; as a result the Pope threatened him with excommunication. Henry won Sicily from the house of Anjou in Naples. He intended to mete out to them the fate of the last Hohenstaufen, Conrad. But death put an end to his momentous plans (1313). He lies buried in Pisa. While it is true that the Salic and Hohenstaufen rulers could hardly avoid prosecuting the traditional Roman policy, Henry of Luxemburg presents a strange instance of romantic dilettantism; he wanted to accomplish what Frederick Barbarossa had accomplished and what King Philip the Fair and his brother Charles would have undertaken with stronger forces if the Frenchman had become king and emperor. Henry's fate was a warning both to the strong French monarchy and to the disintegrated German one.

Around the year 1300 the German people was ethnically and culturally ripe for political unity. It is sad to observe how particularistic forces tore this people asunder. The north and the northeast lived entirely unto themselves, preoccupied with the tensions produced by the rise of the Scandinavian and Slavic countries. It would not have occurred to anyone to choose a north or northeast German prince as king and emperor. King Albert unconcernedly allowed Holstein, Mecklenburg, and Pomerania to be subjected to the feudal lordship of Denmark. Only a dynasty from the west, south, or southeast would receive consideration in connection with the election. The west was the centre of gravity for the group of electors. The three ecclesiastical electors of the Rhineland and the leading secular elector, the Count Palatine of the Rhineland, together constituted a majority. Again and again Saxony attempted opposition in vain; Brandenburg tagged along, weak and dependent. Bohemia had to be reckoned with more than ever. Her relations with all her neighbours, Austria, Saxony, and Bavaria, were charged with increasing friction. When a successor to Henry VII was sought, his son, King John of Bohemia, was quickly disqualified; a vote for him would have been a vote for hereditary succession. The King of France worked on his own son's behalf, with the aid of the Pope, but this too was a vain effort. The Habsburg party backed Frederick the Fair of Habsburg, the Duke of Austria, but the Bohemian and Rhenish group elected the worst foe of the Habsburgs, Duke Louis of Upper

Bavaria. Again Germany fell prey to the misfortune of a double election.

LOUIS THE BAVARIAN (1314–47) AND FREDERICK THE FAIR

Louis is known to history as the Bavarian. He was at least a good Bavarian sovereign. He cannot be called insignificant, but he was sanguine, changeable, and something of a putterer. He was always ready to use petty expedients and to take advantage of the moment by shrewd obsequiousness, and if such a method failed, he tried others with more assiduity than sense of honour. There was no clarity about this reign; yet it is one of the most remarkable of the later Middle Ages, because now, for the first time, powerful forces among the people were stirring in Germany.

Civil war dragged on for years. The Battle of Mühldorf (1322), one of the greatest in the Middle Ages, decided the issue. Frederick the Fair, whom history might also have called the Stupid, was defeated and spent many years imprisoned in the Bavarian fortress of Traussnitz, near Landshut. As was to be expected, Louis exploited the victory to entrench his dynasty. He secured the Mark of Brandenburg for his son and so made certain of an electoral vote for his dynasty. He himself married, for the second time, a young Dutch countess.

When everything seemed most favourable, a new and bitter struggle burst out between Louis and the curia. Louis had sent an imperial governor to Italy to help the Milan dynasty, the Visconti family, but John XXII, the new Pope in Avignon, wanted to recover Italy for the papacy and would not tolerate German influence. By a public proclamation posted on the door of the cathedral in Avignon, the Pope opened his first suit against Louis, whom he accused of daring to assume the titles of king and emperor and of supporting the heretical Visconti; he commanded him to give up his rulership within three months, under threat of excommunication. Louis defended himself. He appealed to the see of Rome, demanded that a council be called, insisted that his election had been legal, and turned from the misguided Pope to one who would be more teachable. In his reply Louis also interceded for the secular clergy, who had much to suffer from the activities of the zealous and successful Minorites. This widened the field of the struggle; the abuses of the church, her internal feuds, and the necessity for reform were brought into question. The Pope now excommunicated the Emperor, claimed the viceregency of the Empire, and began a second suit against Louis. At this point Louis changed policy in his characteristic manner. He allied himself with the Minorites and the radical scholars connected with their movement, for these were the most intransigent and effective critics of the papacy. The Franciscans and the sects scourged both the worldly and luxurious life led by the clergy and the greed of the curia. They appealed from the sophistical lawyer's tricks and the doubtful finances of a papacy glorying in power to the tradition of Christ's poverty and to the force of religious experience as revealed in asceticism and in the teachings of the mystics.

THE MENDICANT FRIARS AND MYSTICISM

The Franciscan Order itself was split into two groups, each of which gave a different interpretation to the absolute rule of poverty. The Pope sided with the more moderate of the two and hence was accused of heresy by the more radical. Such quarrels did signal damage to the respect in which the church was held. Many turned away from the organized church and found peace in direct communication with God, as urged with supreme intensity by the German mystics, especially Master Eckhart. Could the *via antiqua,* the old way as it had been taught by Albertus Magnus, who died in 1283, hold its own against this spiritual passion, the *devotio moderna,* the new nearness to God? The majesty of reason that gave Aristotelian scholasticism its grandeur was thus confronted by the gentle wisdom of mysticism.

Great excitement seized the city folk. For the first time politics and the church effected something like a national movement in Germany, a movement directed against the alien Pope and his patron, the King of France. Imperial cities, nobility, lower clergy, and cathedral chapters sided with the Emperor. Bishops and princes were divided in their interests; so were the monastic orders. Publicists and scholars wielded their weapons in the struggle, above all the great Marsiglio of Padua, who for a time lived at Emperor Louis's court. An entirely new system of church and state organization was built up for the first time in his *Defensor Pacis (Defender of the Peace),* which was completed in 1324. The church and the papacy were to live in apostolic poverty; the state was to take care of their temporal affairs, to administer their properties, to fill vacant positions; the councils were to be the highest authority in all matters related to the church; the community of believers was to be the foundation of the living church; the Scriptures were to be the only source of faith; the Pope was not Peter's successor and could be deposed. Further, there was no world monarchy of emperorship, but the basis of all rule was the sovereignty of the people; the representatives chosen by the people were the lawgivers, and it was for them to appoint officers and elect a monarch, who could also be deposed.

Emperor Louis was very far from taking in the scope of these ideas or underwriting all their consequences. It was enough for him that he had obtained help against the Pope. He was in communication with the leaders of the Ghibelline party in the Italian cities and with the King of Sicily, the foe of Naples. He decided on an expedition to Rome. In Milan he was given the Iron Crown. In Rome he and his Queen were crowned in St. Peter's (1328); four syndics and the prefect of the city, acting as representatives of the Roman people, conferred the crown on him. To quote the poet Uhland (1848), this was the first imperial crown to be anointed with a little democratic oil. The old Pope, John XXII, as avid for deeds as ever, cursed the Emperor, condemned him as a heretic, stripped him of all his offices, and hailed the proceedings against him as a crusade. The Pope offered Lombardy to the King of France as a fief. Emperor Louis, on his part, declared that the Pope had fallen into heresy and that he was deposed, and he took measures to install an anti-pope. The reaction soon came: amid the imprecations of the Romans Louis left the city in company with his new Pope. He found a refuge in Pisa, which had always been faithful to the Emperor. The verdict on John XXII was now reiterated, and the citizens of Pisa executed it in their own way by burning publicly a straw puppet that was supposed to represent him. But John did not yield. He excommunicated the anti-pope together with all of his and the Emperor's followers. Louis's policy in relation to Rome collapsed wholly and lamentably.

SWISS RURAL COMMUNITIES. THE HANSEATIC LEAGUE

The idea of self-determination was springing up everywhere. The Habsburgs in particular were affected by it. Rudolf of Habsburg did not, even when he became Emperor, give up his landgraviate in Switzerland; the Alpine passes were too important to be relinquished. Thus the Swiss rural communities now actually became immediate to the Empire. They were given important privileges as to jurisdiction, and they organized and unified their administration. Even at the time of the interregnum a federation had existed here, as also in other places. The idea of Swiss confederation was taken up by the people of Schwyz. King Adolf of Nassau gave the peasants of Uri and Schwyz a documentary pledge of their immediacy to the Empire. The Luxemburg Emperor Henry VII expanded and confirmed these privileges in a special writ to the people of Unterwalden. The rural communities were to be subject only to an imperial governor. In this way they became more and more independent of Austrian sovereignty and hence were favoured by all the adversaries of the Habsburgs. King Frederick the Fair put the Swiss under the ban of the Empire. But when his brother Duke Leopold wanted to put it into execution, he was defeated at Morgarten (1315). In Brunnen the cantons now renewed the Everlasting League of 1291. Emperor Louis the Bavarian confirmed the old rights with new charters. Later the legend of William Tell shed the magic of myth over the origins of the Swiss Confederation.

Through all the German lands efforts toward peace, order, and the possibility of development were made by the method of confederation. Emperor Louis's laws for the peace of the Empire were well meant: the highways were to be made safe for traffic; unjust tolls were prohibited; robbers and other breakers of the peace were to be arrested and sentenced; common action was to be taken to put down disturbances. This was a landmark on the way to self-help. It accorded with the gathering strength of the popular movement. Federations for maintaining peace sprang up on the Rhine, the Saar, and the Moselle, in Lorraine and the Wetterau. In 1331 twenty-two Swabian towns joined in the first great south German federation to keep the peace; Bavaria and Brandenburg participated. Similar organizations were formed on the Rhine and in Franconia.

Northeastern Germany had entered on the path of federation long ago. Lübeck and her sister cities guarded maritime traffic against Danish aggression, behind which lay the dream of a northern empire. They suppressed piracy in the Baltic and made treaties with

Sweden to serve this purpose. Here in 1344 the name of the German Hanseatic League first appeared in a document. In Bruges the counting-house of the "community of German merchants" was instituted. Three groups of cities of the north and the east were represented here: the Wendish-Saxon, the Westphalian-Prussian, and the Gothic (Swedish)-Livonian. The German spirit of enterprise reached out beyond the limits of the Empire toward regions in the north and east. At first its creative influence was purely economic; later it extended to politics.

THE ELECTORAL CONFERENCE AT RHENSE (1338)

Louis the Bavarian had tried making advances to the Habsburgs even before his expedition to Rome. He abandoned the King of Bohemia and permitted Frederick the Fair a sort of co-regency that was not at all dangerous. Frederick, broken by his long imprisonment, died young (1330). Bohemia and France drew together again. Louis's reply to this pressure on the flank of his Empire was to ally himself with England. His brother-in-law, King Edward III, promised him subsidies amounting to 300,000 gold gulden and in return received the office of imperial vicar over the lands west of the Rhine. Even the electors were seized by the new spirit of federative nationalism. They formed an alliance to maintain the honor of the Empire.

At the conference at Rhense on the Rhine (1338) the electors made a significant declaration. According to tradition the electors transferred the rights and the title of king to the candidate elected, and thereby the rights to imperial rule were also granted; but the title of emperor could be acquired only through coronation by the Pope. In the struggle with the curia, therefore, the electors sided unconditionally with the Emperor. The law that was now proclaimed concerning the election of the emperor went further: whoever had been elected by the majority or by all of the electors was to be regarded as the true emperor and king of the Romans by virtue of this election alone.

Louis was not the man to make the best use of his great position in Europe. He shilly-shallied as to the English-French war; he broke his alliance with England, formed relations with France, and then irritated his English brother-in-law past endurance by his claim to

Holland. The King of Bohemia could not forgive him for the way in which he had added the Tyrol to his possessions. The heiress to the Tyrol, Margaret, was called *Maultasch* (Pocket-mouth) because of her singular ugliness. Like so many women whom nature has neglected, she did not try to conceal her need of fulfilment in life and love. At a session of the diet she publicly accused her first husband, a Luxemburg prince, of impotence and had her marriage with him annulled. Emperor Louis now saw to it that this woman married his son. Machinations of this kind damaged his reputation more and more. The King of Bohemia increasingly overshadowed him. He made an expedition to Italy. There he obtained the *signoria* in several cities; he left his son, Margrave Charles of Moravia, behind as governor of Lombardy. Through his alliance with France and the curia he was able to oppose Louis the Bavarian with a force he could not match. The Pope put a curse on Louis; the electors chose Charles of Moravia. Louis's sudden death on a bear-hunt (1347) spared him further humiliations.

CHARLES IV (1346–78). THE POWER OF BOHEMIA

Now for the first time in many years Germany was again governed by a distinguished and even an extraordinary king. A very successful regime began. Charles IV was perhaps the shrewdest man who ever wore the German crown. He was a curious blend of French, Czech, and German blood. Small and slight in person, he drew attention by his dark beard and the lively glances of his black eyes. He had grown up in the atmosphere of French scholasticism and could interpret the Scriptures in as many different ways as a trained theologian. But for all his academic moralizing he was genuinely religious, lived in devout humility, put clever interpretations on his vivid dreams, read his Book of Hours, and collected relics, happy in edifying solitude. Accustomed as he was to introspection, he wrote his autobiography—an objective and absorbing narrative, a kind of Mirror for Princes, packed with human insight and political wisdom. The grandson of the romanticist, Emperor Henry VII, and son of the knight-errant John, who was a prodigal and a gifted amateur, Charles had been baptized Wenceslaus; now, in honor of the French King Charles VII, he took the great imperial name of Charles, and he was conscious of the universal and sacred challenge inherent in it; but there was still plenty of the Bohemian Wenceslaus left in him. On the ruins of his paternal heritage and in spite of the greedy nobility he created a Bohemian state.

Charles loved his capital, Prague. He built the Hradschin, the Neustadt, the Charles Bridge; he founded the university and endowed it amply. It was the first school for general study to free itself from canonical science and literature. In this German-Slavic institution the four nationalities of Bavaria, Saxony, Bohemia, and Poland were represented. Under fruitful German influence the Czechs were the first of the Slavs to develop a literature of their own. Charles fostered the potentialities of his own people, which he wanted to bring to bear in exchange of ideas and stimulating competition between Germans and Czechs. He took over the tradition established by King Ottokar and handed it down to the Habsburgs: Bohemia as the fortress, the economic and geopolitical focus of central Europe, with its riches in metals, forests, and arable fields, could become the cornerstone for a lasting dynasty and rulership of the Empire, provided Czechs and Germans could be trained to peaceful co-operation. The houses and the monasteries of Prague, among them the Cathedral of St. Vitus, shone with the splendour and fullness of late Gothic architecture. The castle of Karlstein was erected as a sanctuary of rulership by the grace of God, as a storehouse of treasures, of golden secrets; the insignia of the Empire could not have been housed in a worthier shrine. Artists from Germany, Italy, France, and Hungary were represented in the Prague guild of painters who served this proud, wise King.

Charles IV proved a wary financier and a shrewd diplomat. He bought off his rival, the anti-king Günther of Schwarzburg, who was the ineffective candidate of the Wittelsbach party. In a time when money was scarce and much needed Charles always managed to have cash on hand. He worked the silver mines of Bohemia, and he obtained money by encouraging the new Bohemian industries of glass-blowing, dyeing, and pewterware and paper manufacture. He took advantage of every political and economic predicament of his neighbours. From Italy and France he had learned the principles of capitalistic administration and taxation. In brief, he advanced step by step, without any spectacular moves—with infinite deliberation and patience, without sentimentality or illusions. His interests in this world and the next did not interfere with each other, but ran parallel. Charles listened to many people; he would deal with anyone who had something to offer. Whatever action he finally took was based entirely on his own independent decision. His successes pleased him, but never turned his head. Thus he built up dynastic power such as no German king had achieved before him; it spread over Bohemia together with the Eger region, the Vogtland, the Lusatias, the Upper Palatinate, the Mark of Brandenburg, numerous districts in Franconia and along the Main, and Silesia, which the Polish King was forced to renounce; the Piast princes became vassals of Bohemia. Through these lands over which he ruled, Charles controlled the entire Oder, almost the entire Elbe, and the Main. All his competitors—the Luxemburgs, the Wittelsbachs in Bavaria, the Habsburgs in Austria—felt the pressure of this eastern wall. This realm balanced the power of the Rhenish electors. And with this very group the Emperor concluded a treaty of great historical importance in his epoch-making imperial law, the Golden Bull.

THE GOLDEN BULL (1356)

At this time the number of electors was definitely fixed at seven. The Habsburgs had no voice. According to the Wittelsbach family compact one vote was supposed to be exercised alternately by Bavaria and the Palatinate, but now this understanding was honoured only in the breach; the vote was assigned permanently to the Palatinate, and the Wittelsbachs of Bavaria had no say. The slighting of Austria and of Bavaria bore consequences that coloured all of German history. The Archbishop of Mainz was confirmed in the traditional right of summoning the electors and counting the votes; he gave his vote last—and this vote could tip the scales. Trier voted first, Köln second. Among the secular electors the King of Bohemia now again received first place, and he cast his vote first. The lands ruled by the secular electors were declared indivisible and inheritable by the rule of primogeniture. As compared with all the other princes of the Empire, the electors were accorded a position of outstanding power. Their main privileges were monopolies of mining, coinage, and salt works and the revenues derived from protection of the Jews. Furthermore they were given a privilege that had previously been held only by Bohemia: none of their subjects could be summoned before a court anywhere else, while from their own courts no appeal could be taken to other tribunals. In case one of the electoral families died out, its vote was to be reassigned by the Emperor. Only in Bohemia was the old elective right still expressly reserved to the subjects.

The Golden Bull did not deal kindly with the cities. The guilds were dissolved. The formation of leagues of cities was forbidden. *Pfahlbürger* were no longer to be received by the cities—that is, persons who lived in the country, without a permanent residence within the walls. The Church of St. Bartholomew in Frankfurt was designated as the place of election, Aachen as the place of coronation; the first diet was to be held in Nürnberg. The elector of Saxony was made regent in the region that was under Saxon law, the elector of the Palatinate in that of Frankish law. The sovereign position of the electors now seemed secure. Henceforth any one of them might found a hereditary dynasty without jeopardizing the status of the others; this was what the house of Luxemburg did. Under the rules of succession according to relationship the Habsburgs came after them, and they kept the succession until the end of the old Empire. Papal rights were not mentioned at all in the Golden Bull; this was the master stroke of Charles IV. Before his election he had made extensive concessions to the curia. At that time he renounced all rights of the Empire to the papal states, to the County of Venaissin, to Sardinia, Sicily, and Corsica. He recognized the Pope as the final judge in all quarrels with the King of France and promised to enter Rome only on the day of his coronation and to leave it on the self-same day. Only after the Pope's assent might the Emperor claim the right of administration in imperial Italy, but the assent to the election of the Emperor was by no means limited in effect to imperial Italy; instead it had an inclusive general application. The fact that the Golden Bull contained no provisions whatever for the papal assent had the effect of a strenuous attack on old curial claims. On the other hand Charles, who had attained his high position as an enemy of the Ghibellines, did not dream of resuming the old Italian policy. In this respect this Guelph behaved more logically than all the true Guelphs who had preceded him.

THE CENTRE OF GRAVITY SHIFTS TO THE EAST

In Rome, Cola di Rienzi (died 1354) had founded a free state of the people that was intended to revive the old principles of the Roman Republic. The poet Petrarch acclaimed Charles with enthusiasm, but the Emperor would accept no advice either from the humanist or from the tribune. Charles visited Italy as an interested traveller. He had gone to Rome before his coronation in the garb of a pilgrim, and in his official capacity he spent actually only a single day in the Holy City. He did not mix at all in the party strife of Italy. On his second expedition his attitude was fundamentally the same. He would indeed have liked the papacy to return from Avignon to Rome, but he strove for no more than nominal supremacy in Italy. Disagreement with France threatened because of the Kingdom of Arles. Charles was anxious to avoid this. It is true that he had himself crowned there also, but on his visit to Paris in 1378 he transferred the government of the entire Kingdom of Arles to the Dauphin, the heir to the throne of France. With this, although feudal forms were kept up, Burgundy was really handed over to the expanding French kingship. It was one of many decisions that betoken the reduction of the zone of German influence on the western frontier.

Quite in harmony with his dynastic policy, directed as it was toward the east, this Luxemburg Emperor of western descent and with strong French interests continued to find compensation in the east. King Louis of Hungary, of the house of Anjou, at first opposed Charles, but he changed his tactics because he wanted to protect the minor lords of Italy against the Visconti of Milan and because the Turks had seized Adrianople in 1363. This was a serious threat to Hungary too. Charles reached an agreement with that country. Princess Maria, heiress to the throne of Hungary, was affianced to Sigismund, Charles's son. This brought the Balkans, the Adriatic, and the eastern Mediterranean within the horizon of the Luxemburg dynasty. Here, too, he paved the way for the Habsburgs. The power of the Visconti in Milan remained intact; from there so strong a pressure was exerted on the papal states that the papacy did not find the idea of embarking on a new career in Rome in the least attractive. But after the collapse of Rienzi (1354) the Romans wanted a pope again, and it was decidedly in the interests of Germany to remove the curia from French guardianship. The result was the beginning of schism in the West.

Charles held it most important to ensure the succession to his son Wenceslaus during his own lifetime. In order to be quite on the safe side he obtained the assent of both warring Popes; thus the principle laid down in the Golden Bull was abandoned by its inventor for tactical reasons in this case. This one stroke is more characteristic of the Emperor than any other. He was no stickler for principle. At the outset of his rule he made use of the false Waldemar against the Wittelsbachs, although he surely could not have believed in the rights of this Brandenburg pretender (1348); later, in the same unconcerned manner, he betrayed him. Such interludes were not disturbing to the peace of mind of this devout if businesslike Emperor, who made a second Prague of the town of Tangermünde in Brandenburg. Venice and Hamburg, Frankfurt, Prague, and Bruges were to be united with one another in a fruitful give and take. Roads, rivers, and bridges were all to serve the plans of a ruler who, more than any other contemporary prince, saw the larger connections beyond traditional dynastic and feudal alliances.

The Emperor was particularly sympathetic with the Hanseatic League and its interests, although his power did not make it possible for him to give it any real help; or rather he found such leagues of cities so strong that he was not altogether unhappy to see them in difficulties. He was forced in the end to put up with the Swabian League as well. But to offset the Swabian League Charles and his son Wenceslaus founded a league for maintaining peace in Bavaria and Franconia. The author of the Golden Bull was unable to keep the cities from banding together. After the collapse of the Hohenstaufens the rule of Charles IV is the climax and the turning-point in the history of Germany. Germany now had a successful dynasty; she had a constitution; she had abandoned such untenable positions as those in Italy and Burgundy; she was retreating in the west and advancing in the east of Europe. The dream of a central Europe was replaced by dynastic politics in colonized areas.

Chapter 8

THE END OF THE MIDDLE AGES IN GERMANY

ECONOMIC FLOWERING. COLONIZATION IN THE EAST

THE LATE Middle Ages in Germany were no period of decay. It is true that the kingship grew weaker and weaker; the power of the state passed over to the territories. But the German people awakened to a life of abundance and splendour. At this time the cities that had reached economic maturity were building their proud city halls, their walls and towers, and the burghers were setting up their homes and their workshops amid the tangle of streets and alleys. Bridges and castles, parapets and armour, festivals, parades, executions, gay regional costumes, the vivid turns of a speech gaining in expressiveness, the spiritual passion of religious experience and of poetry—all these served to stamp the late Middle Ages with a unique character as something to remember and to cherish. In later times self-confidence looked for support to this era of plenty, of unbroken strength; people gazed back with yearning toward that colourful life of gay and gallant zestfulness. There was much pedantry and narrowness in Germany, but within the self-imposed and obstinately preserved limits there was delight in leading an individual life, there was a capacity for originality, for depth and nuance, there was pride in a personal style of living—in a word, there were all those qualities that are the premise of true creativeness. The great and universal issues were never out of mind or out of sight. It was not for nothing that the bridge tower of the smallest village in the Empire flaunted the imperial eagle.

Only now did the German people take on a national character. Political boundaries became clearer and sharper, and within these boundaries a unity of attitude and emotion developed in spite of territorial disintegration. The German language penetrated to the courts and seats of government. For the first time something like a popular German culture sprang up, nurtured by the rising classes—a secular, lay culture, practical and objective, a culture of burghers.

In the late Middle Ages all Europe experienced an economic flowering for which the burghers were responsible; it had no advantages for the decaying rural nobility. Prosperity made the process of acquiring national character easier, and this process was largely shaped by the burgher class. In France and England the alliance of king and burghers strengthened the monarch's power and paved the way for an absolutistic centralized state. In Germany this possibility was abandoned from the time of Emperor Charles IV. But in the midst of dynastic struggles and civil wars the core of central Europe was still an inexhaustible fountain of strength that could renew itself of its own pressure. While the boundary broke apart in the west and contracted more and more under French impact, colonization in the east was more than indemnifying the Germans for their loss. The agrarian Germany of the early Middle Ages was studded by now with hundreds of prosperous, industrious, and productive towns. These became the economic and political competitors of the territorial princes. A broad new agricultural region was gained in the Slavic east. Internal political friction and fresh economic possibilities took on, because of this, new tensions that were to be of the utmost historical importance.

Colonization of the east proceeded in two ways. Either the German people as such advanced gradually and in increasing numbers —and this frequently happened in the wake of military conquests of new regions—or isolated groups of German pioneers settled at a distance from one another in the heart of alien lands, among peoples who would always remain strange to them. In the first way the Bavarians had been settling the lands of the Danube and the Alpine regions from the eighth century on. This process was extended, by the year 1200, to Holstein, the Mark of Brandenburg as far as the Havel, the greater part of Mecklenburg, the western half of the two Lusatias, the southern part of Bohemia and Moravia, and the lands up to the river March and the Upper Raab, and Drav. All these colonies were in constant contact with the mother country, and their imitation of her was the more spontaneous because she herself also displayed similar ethnical and economic situations involving two or more elements of different origin.

In the second type of colonization conditions were entirely different. Around 1250 the King of Hungary summoned Germans from the Moselle to go to Transylvania (Siebenbürgen). In their new home the settlers were called Saxons. In the same spasmodic fashion merchants, knights, and miners settled in the Baltic region and later in the lands of the Teutonic Order. German minorities came armed with privileges. For the most part they reached the Baltic provinces by water. There was and could be no large agricultural community: the sea, not the land, provided the bridge. Poland was infiltrated in the same manner. After the attack of the Mongols, Polish rulers asked the Germans to come into their country. The Germans came and founded cities with German laws. But purely Slav communities existed alongside the purely German communities. German law, culture, commerce, and industry went farther than the German people. German miners found work as far away as Bosnia. Peasant settlements in the Danubian area remained rarities; the German community of Gottschee in Slovenia is one of these exceptions. German settlers were welcome guests because they developed the eastern lands economically. They adjusted themselves to local Slavic government and became loyal subjects; they had, after all, no choice.

A hybrid type of colonization developed in the lands east of the Elbe, where Slavic princes continued to rule, as it had in eastern Mecklenburg, Pomerania, Silesia, and Moravia. Here the church directed the settlements of knights and peasants. The Slavic element was now treated with the utmost consideration. The German village rose next to the Slavic. With the help of the Germans the princes set up model farms, which were then imitated by the Slavs. Cultural exchange and ethnical mixture were common. Slavic dialects disappeared with few exceptions, but the race persisted, amalgamated by intermarriage.

In Prussia the Teutonic Order developed its own arrogant methods. Here was conquest in the nature of a crusade; the uprisings of the pagan Prussians were suppressed, and such natives as remained were enslaved. At first the order founded manors and only gradually villages and towns. But even the towns were like agricultural communities; their patricians were manorial lords with knightly views and customs. The townsmen were merchants and craftsmen. Most of them owned property outside of the walls and worked their land with serfs. Against the tyranny of the order the landed aristocracy as well as the town patricians developed a circle of local interests, with personal and family ties. They looked for encouragement to the Poles rather than to the harsh monastic order. The defeat of the Teutonic Knights at Tannenberg (1410) was partly due to the particularism of the landed aristocracy, which leaned toward Poland and was united in the League of the Lizards. By the terms of the second Peace of Thorn the King of Poland became feudal lord of the order (1466). Even before this the Poles had begun to immigrate in great numbers, and they noticeably increased the non-German element. In 1515 the grand master of the Teutonic Order was formally released from his ties to the Empire; they had affected him, indeed, only as an individual, not as a representative of the order.

In Bohemia and Moravia the kings as well as the monastic orders warmly encouraged German settlements for economic reasons. Some Germans came directly from the Erzgebirge. Others were brought over in groups from a great distance: from Bavaria, from the Upper Palatinate, even from northern Germany. Some of these groups refused to mix with the Czechs and so invited their marked dislike, an attitude so unusual in these early times that it was conspicuous and was noted by contemporaries. On the whole there was the usual amount of intermarriage among the populations. The majority of the Germans did not arrive as paupers; they brought good farm tools and taught the Slavs how to use them. The head of the settlement had charge of the coveted cash for putting up buildings and securing privileges. The German immigrant wanted to attain to a more independent position than at home, and he generally did. The man who left his native land was not notably considerate of others; he gloried in his own strength. The struggle to get along in the new land was hard and did not allow of gentle manners. The Slavs felt this and had to adjust themselves to it as best they could. The German cities were still able to absorb the overflow of the rural population, especially after wars and epidemics. But the freedom-loving German peasant was more attracted to the eastern lands of the Slavs. The merchant could make more money there, and more quickly, than at home. And this was reason enough for a development that was destined to be the foundation of the most vigorous governments in German history, those of Austria and Prussia.

In the late Middle Ages German colonization of the east was less and less a deliberate conquest, more and more an economic expansion. The Germans took the stage as the technicians, craftsmen, teachers, and organizers of the east. The Letts and Lithuanians, Hungarians, and all the south and west Slavic tribes came to value them as pioneers and leaders in all these fields, although they did not like them. Subsequently the Germans were to play the same role in the development of Russia. The historian needs to regard these events objectively and present them on a basis of factual accuracy. It is just as incorrect to exalt the colonization of the east as a cultural feat as to interpret it as the doom of the non-German tribes involved. At that time and under existing conditions the colonization of the east was a simple matter of course. It comprised a series of uninspired events, and those who participated were moved by very practical considerations. The farther away from the homeland a group of Germans settled, the more easily it could maintain itself in ethnical and cultural purity. In all those regions directly connected with the heart of Germany the overwhelming fact was mixture. In such mixture the German language outstripped the Slavic, while the Slavic manner of thinking and feeling often triumphed over the German. The result was the type of the east German, which predominated in the entire region east of the Elbe, at least among the lower and middle classes.

The contrast between north German and south German was already firmly established by the end of the Middle Ages. Linguistically, culturally, politically, and sociologically there were a northern and a southern Germany. Now the east German factor was added to these two, influenced by both, because both had gone into its making. In Bohemia, Silesia, Moravia, and all the Austrian lands the east German was kin and neighbour to the south German. In the Mark of Brandenburg, east Holstein, Mecklenburg, Pomerania, and Prussia he bore the north German stamp, but had developed more and more along his own lines, and more vigorously and deliberately than in the southeast. The east German colonist was sterner and less liberal than the true German; he had been reared in an atmosphere of conscious authority, and he believed in discipline and commands more than in the old German custom of expressing opinions, voting, self-government, and independence of precedent.

DEVELOPMENT OF THE HANSEATIC LEAGUE. THE CITY MOVEMENT

The Hanseatic League and its history must be considered in the frame of east German colonization. Cities that later belonged to the Hanseatic League played a part in the founding of the new cities in the east. The main artery of German economy ran from north to south; the Rhine linked Flanders and Brabant with the Alpine passes and the way to northern Italy. But the colonization of the east gave the Scandinavian and Baltic markets importance. Norway grew prosperous through her haddock fisheries. German merchants called for the valuable catch in Bergen and distributed it throughout Europe. The herring trade made the Danes masters of the Baltic. The island of Gotland developed into a centre for trade with Russia, especially the fur trade. The land of the Teutonic Order, and soon Poland as well, exported grain to the west, to England and particularly to Flanders. In this way there arose a new traffic between the east and the west that busied many coastal and inland towns. Between Bruges and Novgorod German merchants travelled to and fro. In exchange for their fish they brought home stocks of textiles, metal wares, and weapons, as well as wine and beer. Soon the Dutch joined in the heated competition.

The journey from the North Sea to the Baltic was regarded as difficult and dangerous, and valuable wares were therefore carried by land. In this way Lübeck came to have a key position and headed the league of north German cities. In order to defend its foreign trade this league was soon forced to take measures for self-protection. *Hanse* means "group." Wherever merchants met in foreign countries they banded themselves together, and this was the origin of Hanseatic leagues. By maintaining laws relating to aliens in as favorable a drift as possible these leagues advanced and safeguarded the interests of the guilds with increasing success. At the end of the thirteenth century the many scattered leagues fused into one Hanseatic League for all of Germany. Lübeck became the focus for travellers to Flanders and the east. The city entered the ranks first and foremost against the Scandinavian rulers, who tried to regulate all laws concerning trade from the point of view of their own political interests. It was only natural that the kingdoms of the north should have nothing but suspicion for an international organization under German leadership. They regarded it as a profiteering enterprise that was dangerous politically.

For a while the Hanseatic League had complete control of the Sound, between Sweden and Denmark. A merchant fleet captured Copenhagen, and King Waldemar of Denmark fled from his country. But after the Union of Kalmar, which joined the three Scandinavian kingdoms (1397), the Hanseatic League had to abandon political goals and confine itself to exploiting its economic privileges. For a brief period Mecklenburg threatened to unite with Denmark, which would have put the League into a difficult position. At that time an association of pirates in the service of Mecklenburg made the seas unsafe. The wars of these Vitalian Brothers against the English and the Hanseatic League savoured to contemporaries of a local movement of protest against the encroachments of the rich and of foreigners; after Klaus Störtebecker, the leader and hero, was executed in 1401, he lived on in popular memory as a brave and gallant protector of the weak and exploited.

The Hanseatic League has historical significance for the colonization of the east as well as for the city movement. If we add the church-reform movement to these, we group together the forces that were most potent in the late Middle Ages in Germany, in varying relationships of friction and co-operation. From such soil grew the Germany of the Reformation.

The culture of cities was comparatively new in Germany. The situation was quite different from that in Italy, with its old urban culture and with most of the nobles living in cities. In Germany the increasingly prosperous burgher and the improverished agrarian noble faced each other uncomprehendingly and even with hatred. The German city was a foreign body hedged in with prerogatives, an island surrounded by the carriers of ecclesiastical and secular sovereignty, by the territorial lords. City finances were conducted by an orderly routine. They yielded cash, in sharp contrast to the robber economy of the territorial lords, poor in metal and greedy of security. The light of the city streamed out into the country. The territorial lord reached out toward the cities; he let them feel his heavy hand, built castles in the town, claimed jurisdiction and collected tolls, and kept watch of the market. The *Pfahlbürger* (not true burghers, but suburbanites) were the arch-enemy whom the territorial lords persecuted, for these people evaded their rulership and enjoyed civic rights without surrendering their land. The movement away from the country strengthened the cities and helped them to grow. The most active and productive among the people wanted to be burghers. Now the city dwellers became arrogant. They reached out into the open country; they acquired jurisdiction over territory beyond the city walls (*Bannmeile*), and with it monopoly for their wares in a secure selling area. The steady growth of commerce involved the cities in constant struggles for freedom from tolls and the right to safe conduct. Wealth brought power, but power multiplied dangers. Prerogative opposed prerogative, claim confronted claim. The city leagues created larger spheres of action, but not greater security. Wars on a considerable scale took the place of the usual local feuds.

History has attached the epithet "the Indolent" to the name of King Wenceslaus (1378–1400). He was the gifted, but phlegmatic and unstatesmanlike son of a distinguished father. Under his rule the Empire again lapsed into chaos and disintegration. Up to 1385 the Swabian League, founded in 1376, had come to include forty towns; it extended into the German part of Switzerland. The Alsatian and the Rhenish city leagues were connected with it. The three together formed the great south German league of cities. In northern Germany the Saxon city league was formed. The movement could not be halted; it affected the knights as well. All those social groups that were slighted by the Golden Bull came forward and proved their validity.

The frequent civil conflicts provoked by the ambitious guilds laid a burden on the towns. The old propertied patrician class found it more and more difficult to maintain itself in the face of the prosperous guilds. These patrician families had the traditional right to direct politics. They met the expenses of administration by excise taxes. When this source of revenue did not suffice for increasing armaments and fortifications, the patricians blandly proceeded to new expenditures, to be met by the great mass of the inhabitants. But the guilds rebelled against the patricians' privileges and exploitative policy and demanded a proportionate sharing out of the burden. In many leading cities the guilds staged an insurrection against the patricians, and they usually obtained admission to the council as a result. For a time the weavers' guild had sole sway over Köln, until they were overthrown in the bloody weavers' battle of 1370. In northern Germany the patricians maintained themselves by dint of their extensive wholesale trade, whereas in the industrial cities of the south the guilds came to play an important role in the government. One of the outstanding successes of the city leagues was the Battle of Sempach (1386), in which the Swiss Confederation—recognized by the Emperor in 1297—defeated the Duke of Austria. The Peace of Eger (1389), which was intended to put an end to the great city war, was only a truce of momentary importance. Under the pressure of the territorial princes the cities dissolved their federations, only to recall them to life soon afterward. The rule of King Wenceslaus was incapable of finding a satisfactory permanent solution. The draft of the peace of 1389 was only a weak attempt at remodelling the constitution.

KING WENCESLAUS IS DEPOSED. RUPERT OF THE PALATINATE. EMPEROR SIGISMUND (1410–37)

King Wenceslaus made himself thoroughly hated by instigating the murder of the archiepiscopal vicar general, Johann von Pomuk, who in later legend became a martyr because he refused to reveal what had been said in confession and who as the good Catholic St. John of Nepomuk was contrasted with the heretical John Huss. In relation to foreign policy Wenceslaus, despite his treaty with England (1381), did absolutely nothing to check the French ambition to expand or the dangerous beginnings of a new independent Duchy of Burgundy. King Wenceslaus should have been interested in this development on the western boundary of Germany, if only because Luxemburg, the cradle of his family, had reverted to him. His brother Sigismund, for his share, won the Kingdom of Hungary, but could not obtain command of Poland. The house of Luxemburg was now forced to concern itself with Naples and with the enmity between Genoa and Venice. The dynasty could have become very powerful if it had not been weakened by the mutual envy of the members of the family, who had all been endowed with land. King Sigismund and Margrave Jobst of Moravia joined the enemies of their brother Wenceslaus, and he was imprisoned. This was the first absolute deposition effected by the political will of the electorate. To save at least the position of the dynasty in the Empire, Wenceslaus appointed his brother Sigismund as imperial regent. Another appointment deeply offended the electors and hastened the end: Gian Galeazzo Visconti was made Duke of Milan. This promotion of the Visconti was regarded as a slur on the Empire. The ecclesiastical electors and the Elector Palatine formed a league of princes against Wenceslaus and deposed him (1400).

The only secular elector who had participated in the hardly valid deposition of Wenceslaus was elected. This was Rupert, the Elector Palatine, an honest man, who, however, achieved just as little real success as the first Wittelsbach, Louis the Bavarian. Rupert came to the fore as the candidate of the Rhineland—the old west and south German core of the Empire. His failure proved that genuine imperial power could no longer be erected on this basis. As soon as Rupert believed that southern Germany had been made more or less secure he went to Italy. The new Duke of Milan was on the point of becoming King of Italy, and hence the Pope and the city of Florence, both fearful of such a development, gave Rupert their support. But when he got to Italy obstacles were heaped in his way. Soon out of funds, he was forced to leave this country ingloriously, and he was never able to live down the political effects of his almost ridiculous failure. He tried in vain to prevail against the new city leagues, and he resisted the idea of a church council, which had seized upon all of Western Christendom.

After Rupert's death, in 1410, the house of Luxemburg resumed the lead as a matter of course. Was the new King, Sigismund, the type of person from whom a solution of the most pressing question of the times could be expected, the question of church reform? Sigismund had much of his father Charles's acumen and a goodly portion of his grandfather John's tireless energy and *savoir faire*. As ruler of Hungary he had warred gallantly against the Turks. He was also thoroughly familiar with the insidious ins and outs of Italian politics, for it was in Italy that he had become a master of diplomacy in balancing forces. Dalmatia and Byzantium, crusade and church reform, the liberation of Bohemia and the possibility of reunion with the Greek church—these were the conflicting problems of the life that

Sigismund lived in gay scepticism and splendour. He was an artist in devising irresistible jests, a tireless ladies' man, and well informed even in the methods of theological debate, as was only right and fitting for one who governed church and council. For this Emperor once more re-established the unity of the church.

THE COUNCIL OF CONSTANCE (1414–8). JOHN HUSS

The church schism became more and more intolerable to all believers. Avignon and Rome opposed each other. The city of Rome wanted the papacy back, and all the adversaries of French influence demanded this solution. The struggle had come to an impasse. The demand for a council grew louder and louder. First the cleric Conrad of Gelnhausen, following in the footsteps of the great Marsiglio of Padua, had submitted two opinions to the King of France in which he advocated the view that in the event of a schism — that is, in an emergency that could not be met by the Pope — a council would have to meet even without papal convocation. The notion of the superiority of the council developed and gradually became prevalent. France herself now directed her efforts toward an early conclusion of the struggle. The cardinals were greatly concerned to clarify the situation, and the two groups of cardinals came to an agreement to the effect that their respective Popes should meet personally and that both should retire after a certain period without appointing new cardinals. Since the two Popes did not act in accordance with this resolution, in spite of assurances to the contrary, the two colleges of cardinals agreed to call a general council at Pisa. This council deposed both Popes and elected a new one. But both the previous Popes called councils of their own and refused to accept the decision of Pisa. So now there were three Popes.

Emperor Rupert's most notable achievement was the founding of the University of Heidelberg (1386). It was, indeed, a Heidelberg professor who composed the so-called *Heidelberger Postillen*, a commentary on the points the cardinals wished to bring before the council: The pope derives his power from God; this power is attacked by the revolutionary spirit of France; if the pope is refused obedience, all security and law are at an end; Germany in her political cleavage has need of papal authority to prevent her complete dissolution; the church is in urgent need of reform in regard to morals as well as laws—reform, above all, of the college of cardinals, which has become wholly worldly. Thus, a century before Luther, the very Germans showed how paramount the unity of the church was to them. The idea of calling a council came from France. Now a new council, to be held in Constance, was to make the decision. It was not a German who pleaded the cause of church reform the most zealously there, but a Czech—John Huss.

In the case of this Prague professor and preacher the problem of church reform was bound up with the Bohemian interests of the house of Luxemburg. Huss belonged to that group of religious thinkers who, under the influence of the great Wycliffe of England (died 1384), worked on the Continent to establish St. Augustine and the Bible as the true sources of Christianity. The papacy, the doctrine of the sacraments, the veneration of saints, the cult of relics—all these were attacked, criticized, and condemned in part or reinterpreted. Huss was a cautious disciple of Wycliffe; in the manner of the writers of the Middle Ages he accepted many of his master's teachings literally, but in certain other respects he preferred a more moderate attitude. What to him was most essential was fitting veneration of the sacrament of communion; obedience to the church and the redeeming effect of the sacraments should depend on the personal vocation, the inner merit, of the priest.

Huss also wanted the church to be poor in the apostolic manner. His attacks on prosperous prelates, on clerical hair-splitting in legal issues, on the shrewd financial deals of the church, and on her too comfortable understanding with local aristocratic groups were full of passionate political feeling, for here his Czech nationalism flared up. The spiritual and social contrasts he was concerned with were embittered by quite modern national hatred. Must not the poverty-stricken Czech workman envy the prosperity of the German citizen? Must not the minor Czech noble detest as an intruder the German patrician who was acquiring land? If the church were stripped of her landed property, the native lords of Bohemia could improve their situation without benefit to the German alien. Neither the German nor the Czech higher nobility of Bohemia was greatly concerned with such sentiments. The movement was democratic and radical. The oppressed and the exploited rebelled against the upper stratum; the common people were excited against the Germans by the lesser clergy, who thought that opportunity was knocking for them too. Jerome of Prague, half scholar, half knight, popular with the minor nobles, gave a political cast to the movement, to the annoyance of John Huss; but there could be no turning back. King Wenceslaus had first been friendly and sympathetic toward the Czechs; then he became doubtful and vacillating. Huss attacked dogma and was excommunicated. The reformer, after calling for a general council, left Prague. The Council of Constance summoned him to appear. Huss came.

The council (1414–8) had three problems to consider: ending the schism, reforming the church throughout, and suppressing Wycliffe's heresies. This extraordinary constituent assembly of Western Christianity proved to be a gathering of unexampled size. About seventy-two thousand outsiders are said to have been present in the city of Constance at the same time. More than five hundred ecclesiastical princes and thirty-seven universities—with the University of Paris, zealous for reform, in the lead—were represented. Emperor Sigismund appeared in person. The council disposed of the question of the pope by deposing all three Popes and electing a fourth, who soon won general recognition. John Huss was cross-examined and, after many discreditable public and private attacks, was solemnly sentenced to burn at the stake as a heretic. From the point of view of the church this conclusion was only natural and convenient. The Emperor had given Huss a safe conduct that signified more than a political passport: it implied protection against judgement. According to the current view it was, of course, true that a verdict of heresy pronounced by the highest spiritual authority cancelled all obligations. The Emperor took an attitude of human decency toward the reformer, whose strength of character had impressed him. He tried to save Huss, but could not withstand the pressure of the council. Sigismund was an almost purely political being; anything different could hardly be expected of him.

The council accomplished least in the question of church reform. It drew up new rules for papal elections and the powers of the pope. It was easy to adjust these side-issues; the core of the trouble was not touched here. From this time on, councils were to be convoked regularly, but the concept of the papacy had triumphed once again.

130

THE HUSSITE WARS (1419–36)

The manly courage with which Huss accepted his fate made a deep impression in Bohemia. Four hundred and fifty-one members of the Czech minor nobility drew up a protest at their diet (1415). A revolutionary movement set in, and after the death of Wenceslaus (1419) all Bohemia was in a ferment. For Sigismund, the murderer of John Huss, was now King of Bohemia. In vain the Bohemians cast about for another king.

Various parties had formed among the Bohemian followers of Wycliffe. There were the communistic Adamites, who constituted only a small minority. There were moderates among the nobility and the educated and prosperous bourgeoisie. The chief demand of this group was the lay chalice in communion—the demand, that is, that the laity should partake not only of the bread, but also of the wine. For this reason they were called Calixtines or Utraquists, since they recommended communion in both kinds. And finally there were the radicals under the leadership of the grim one-eyed Ziska. These were called Taborites, after the city of Tabor, which they built for themselves. The Taborites rejected the hierarchy and the traditional forms of worship of the church; they avowed the common priesthood of the laity. Deeply influenced by the Waldensians, the followers of the reformer Peter Waldus in southern France, they denounced worldliness and opulence in religious life with a vehemence coloured by hostility to Mammon everywhere. In Prague, Ziska organized the rule of the common people. Many wealthy burghers emigrated, and for many years Prague was a Hussite—that is, a Czech—city.

Emperor Sigismund proclaimed a crusade against the Hussites. Now the masses came fully into action. Ziska proved himself a great soldier. He organized the people into a mighty force, well armed with scythes and iron-spiked clubs, and in quite the manner of the Swiss peasants this army forced the clumsy knights to flee before it. By maintaining separate communities, one on the battlefield, the other at home, the Hussite leaders successfully carried on war and agriculture at the same time. Bohemia turned into a kind of religious and democratic republic. It was the first time that such forces had played any great part in central Europe. The Hussites even sallied from their fortress of Bohemia to invade neighbouring countries. The name of Procopius, Ziska's successor, became synonymous with terrorism in Austria, Bavaria, the Mark of Meissen, and Silesia. It soon became evident that some settlement must be reached with the rebellious Bohemians by way of a treaty. An inner cleavage in Bohemia made this easier.

The chaos in Bohemia was proof that the papacy did not know how to meet the wish of the times for reform. Pope Martin V convoked a new council at Basel (1431–49). His successor tried in vain to hold another council in Bologna, closer to the sphere of influence of the curia. The Council of Basel did not concur in this papal choice. Papal autocracy had to adjust itself to the conciliar idea. The most eminent spirits of the time met in Basel. Never was the will to reform represented with more earnestness or dignity.

The great German thinker Nicholas of Cusa (died 1464), soon to become a cardinal of the Roman church, presented a far-reaching program of reform. The church and the Empire, papacy and emperorship, were both to be based on new foundations. The temporal parliament corresponded to the church council—both bodies, built up on the principle of the estates, were to serve as controls and counterbalances to the central power. Theology and public law, then, were both concerned in finding a practical solution pointing the way for the future, in contrast to the traditional dogmatism that was the worst foe of vital development. But all these ideas remained academic, for Pope Eugene IV clung to the uncompromising point of view of the curia, with the support of Emperor Sigismund, to whom coronation as emperor was the most pressing matter.

On their side the Bohemians had similar experiences. Their military position was so secure that they could well have been sterner in negotiation. But the conservatives were longing for peace, and the curia appeased them by offering communion in both kinds. The church was able to make this concession the more easily because the lay chalice had been customary up to the thirteenth century; the taint of heresy, therefore, would scarcely attach to it. Civil war now broke out in Bohemia. The Calixtine nobles fought with the Taborites, and Procopius fell. The peace was a compromise: Sigismund was recognized as King, and Prague was assigned an Utraquist Archbishop (1436). Bohemia had won a special position for herself in regard to a state church. Czech influence prevailed over German influence, but the threat of a democratic social revolution was averted. The true religious forces of Hussitism survived in the sect of the Bohemian Brethren, whose kinship with the German mystics and pietists was another factor in preparing the soil for the reform of Christian doctrine in central Europe. These intellectual and spiritual currents were destined to beget new movements.

From the political point of view the peace with the Hussites attested the unqualified victory of the Slavic population. They gathered strength to strike fresh blows in the lands east of the Elbe. The collapse of the Teutonic Order must be considered in a similar connection. Its carefully constructed theocratic state, a model of political and economic military absolutism, was destroyed by Poland because the order had not succeeded in winning over the new forces in the rural nobility, in the towns, and among the common country folk.

REFORM OF THE EMPIRE? THE DYNASTIC POLICY OF THE HABSBURGS

Emperor Sigismund showed a good deal of interest in reforming the Empire and could count on the cities to support him in this enterprise. The electors, to be sure, wished to maintain their position, and they formed a league of their own against the Emperor (1424). The question of reform was discussed at the council of Basel. Sixteen points had been formulated. The most important were improvement in policing, maintenance of the peace within the Empire, division of the Empire into districts, alleviation of economic needs, and reorganization of the mint. The results were negligible, but the ideas were still circulated. As the prosperous burghers accumulated money and property, the poverty in other strata made itself doubly felt. As early as the year 1447 a patrician of Constance left a fortune of over seventy thousand pounds (seven million dollars).

A curious pamphlet on reform was written about 1439 under the impact of manifold abuses: *The Reformation of Emperor Sigismund.* The anonymous author, probably a member of the clergy, demanded secularization of the German ecclesiastical principalities, definite limited income for the clergy, strict discipline in the monasteries, the same payment as far as possible for all secular callings, abolition of serfdom, of guilds, of the power to exile and to issue safe conducts, freedom of immigration in all imperial territories, easier access to civic rights, governmental price-setting for food. Three kinds of reform were combined in this pamphlet: religious, political, and social. The awakening German people was demanding a new German state to realize civil and social justice—in short, what was later called democracy. But there was no one who could fulfil such demands.

After Sigismund's death Frederick I, the Elector of Brandenburg, sought to secure the succession. He had done Sigismund important services in getting him elected. Now this Burgrave of Nürnberg from the house of Hohenzollern, who had quickly consolidated his position in Brandenburg, believed that he was intended for the highest office. Since the time of the Hohenstaufen Emperor Henry VI the Hohenzollerns had been burgraves in Nürnberg. Emperor Charles IV had confirmed their status as princes of the Empire and legally set them on a par with the electors, a proof of the distinguished and influential role this family played in Franconia. The older line had acquired the lands of Ansbach and Bayreuth; the younger had now gone to Brandenburg and was at the start of a great career. Now, at the election of 1438, the Hohenzollerns and the Habsburgs met as rivals for the first time. Sigismund's son-in-law, Albert of Habsburg, was certainly the most powerful prince of the Empire. He combined the claims of the house of Luxemburg with his own. To ignore him would have meant detaching Bohemia and Austria from the Empire. He was therefore elected. Even the Hohenzollern gave him his vote in the end. Thus began the long series of Habsburg kings and emperors, interrupted only once up to the very end of the old Empire.

Much could be expected from the earnestness and energy of Albert II. He set to work at once on reform of the Empire. Then the Turks began to harry Hungary, and in Bohemia the anti-Austrian Taborites turned against the loyal Calixtines and the Catholics and conveyed the crown of Bohemia to the Polish prince Casimir. Slavic society was on the defensive against everything German. Civil war broke out. At this point the forty-two-year-old King Albert died suddenly of dysentery.

The longest rule in the history of Germany now followed the shortest. Duke Frederick of Styria was the natural heir to Habsburg dynastic power. The electors voted for him unanimously. But his regime proved a bitter disappointment, and it was only certain lucky incidents that finally saved Habsburg dynastic power from utter undoing. Frederick III (1440–93) was a gentle and noble character with no fondness for warlike strife, a lover of the arts and sciences with a bent for diplomacy that gave him the chance to exercise his characteristic patience and art of awaiting the right moment. All that happened during his rule, however, occurred in spite of his political views rather than because of them. In his old age he toyed with alchemy and astrology, by which he gained an unwarranted reputation as a philosopher.

The question of church reform ranked first among the tasks that had been undertaken. The Council of Basel, postponed time and again, was deliberately sabotaged by the curia. The electoral princes were at odds, the King weak and interested chiefly in getting himself crowned. One weighty question after another was shelved. In the end Æneas Sylvius Piccolomini, who, having made a swift ascent to the position of Pope, called himself Pius II, scrapped conciliar reform once and for all. He branded as heresy the assumption that councils were superior to the pope. And with this the whole effort died down without appreciable result. Once more the omnipotence of the popes had been re-established.

The Empire now suffered loss after loss. Luxemburg, which Charles IV had most earnestly desired to link forever with the crown of Bohemia, was sold to the French crown, to fall then into the hands of Duke Philip of Burgundy. For Burgundy was arising between France and Germany as a new intermediate realm. Through inheritance, fiefs, and clever treaties the dukes succeeded in piecing together territory that extended from the North Sea to the Jura Mountains and the Alps. It took in the wealthiest and most highly industrialized lands of the Europe of that time, Flanders and Alsace. The Duke of Burgundy, although he was a vassal of the Emperor and of the French King, was very much better off than these neighbours in possessing a united and economically thriving domain. He could well look to the highest dignities and honours.

Frederick III was the last Emperor to be crowned in Rome. But under his ineffective rule both the Empire and the Habsburg dynasty began to crack. The imperial guardian of King Albert's posthumous son did not succeed in making him ruler of Hungary and Bohemia.

The rule of Bohemia was taken over by George Podiebrad, the off-spring of a Hussite family. First he was elected governor, then King, and recognized by the Emperor as an elector. Now Bohemia again had a national government, and the old claims to rulership awoke. King George, in his capacity of master of the fortress of Bohemia, even planned a European federation of states, with a federal court and a federal parliament. Hungary too chose a native son as king— Matthew Corvinus, who exploited the confusion of civil war in Austria by seizing almost all of Upper and Lower Austria, Carinthia, and Styria. He made his residence in Vienna (died 1490). Habsburg fortunes were at their lowest ebb. A new eastern realm arose, but under a non-German dynasty. With French mediation Emperor Frederick III was forced to consent to a peace with the Swiss Confederation, a peace in which he had to abandon all his demands. And so it was in vain that the notoriously brutal mercenaries of the Count of Armagnac, whom the Germans called Armagnaken and from that *arme Gecken,* or "poor fools," had been let loose on unfortunate southern Germany by the King of France with the Emperor's consent.

The collapse of the Hanseatic League and the Teutonic Order resulted in the personal union of the County of Holstein and the Duchy of Schleswig with the Danish crown, on the understanding that feudal relationships were to survive unchanged: the two districts were to remain together and not to be divided. Holstein was still to be part of the Empire, of which Schleswig never had been and never was to be a part. Danish influence, in any case, penetrated far into northern Germany.

In the face of the total ineffectiveness of imperial power the Swabian League was formed in the Empire for the purpose of resisting the encroachments of the house of Wittelsbach (1488). Unlike the old city leagues, it included also princes and knights. The Swabian League maintained peace in southern Germany, but was careful not to become involved in foreign adventures. There was frequent discussion of a plan to depose Emperor Frederick III or to give him a coadjutor with the title of King of the Romans. The Emperor succeeded in having his son Maximilian made King of the Romans, so that if he himself were to be set aside, it would at least be through the agency of his own son. Maximilian brought freshness and vigour to

CENTRAL EUROPE
1490

Norway

Sweden

Denmark

Russia

TO

TO

Lithuania

The
Empire

Poland

France

Savoy

Hungary

Ottoman

Empire

TO *Teutonic Order*

his work. His wife was Princess Mary, the daughter and heiress of Charles the Bold of Burgundy, and with this union circumstances assumed an entirely new shape.

THE NEW BURGUNDY. EMPEROR MAXIMILIAN I (1493–1519)

It was a Habsburg, the ruler of the Austrian Upper Rhine lands, who incited the Swiss Confederation against Charles the Bold, Duke of Burgundy, in the hope of keeping both of his bellicose neighbours occupied. Charles the Bold made a treaty with France and—to his undoing—accepted the challenge of the Swiss. His was a brilliant personality, full of cleverness and charm. His court united in itself all the graces of an over-ripe period of knightly culture, but his clumsy army of pampered knights, unwieldy with baggage trains and hangers-on, was not equal to the compact, relentless attack of the daredevil Swiss infantry. It was evident that the military future lay with a well-organized, well-disciplined, and appropriately equipped army of foot-soldiers. The death of Charles the Bold (1477, in the Battle of Nancy) made Burgundy the focus of central European politics.

Contention arose over the inheritance. France, the Swiss Confederation, the Habsburgs of the Austrian Upper Rhine lands, and of course Mary of Burgundy and her husband, Maximilian, were the claimants. French interests collided with Habsburg interests. This contest between King Maximilian and King Louis XI, which was coloured by their personal differences, was the starting-point of the struggle between the two great dynasties, the Habsburgs and the Valois, that was to determine the destiny of Europe for generations to come. Neither the Hohenstaufens nor the Luxemburgs felt antagonism toward France. The anti-French attitude of the Guelphs and the Wittelsbachs had fluctuated; it had not been based on unshakeable principles or hereditary enmity. Now for the first time, as a result of dynastic rivalry, a bitter and lasting conflict arose between these states.

No wonder the dull old Emperor Frederick gazed on his son Maxmilian with envy, for this prince was haloed with a youthful radiance that delighted all the world. Indefatigably, full of the joy of adventure, like a true champion in the lists, he fought with the cities of Flanders without understanding any too much about their economic power and their significance to the world. For him the proud burghers were cowardly nobodies and treacherous good-for-nothings who needed an energetic master. Maximilian never wearied of the splendours of the richest court of Christendom. He vied with his young wife in the hunt and the dance. He selected the best falcons and greyhounds. Presently he found himself involved in serious dissensions, which were not improved by his increasing financial difficulties. But he made the most of the role of prince consort. He let nothing discourage him. (Once, indeed, the burghers of Bruges captured him and held him for a high ransom.) Maximilian spoke many languages and was skilled in all sorts of arts and accomplishments. In the mountains, where he sometimes lost his way hunting for chamois, he knew all the different minerals. He encouraged, loved, and understood the German painter Albrecht Dürer (1471–1528). His life slipped away while he made plans and drafts. He began too many things at once, would not listen to the warnings of more experienced advisers, and quickly gave up one fantasy for another. And so whatever he did remained unfinished. The true motive that impelled him was, in the spirit of antiquity, the thought of fame after death. He courted the favour of history, of posterity, and did all he could to mould them. He wanted to go down to eternity as a brave and fervent Christian hero, a chevalier *sans peur et sans reproche*.

All this, however, did not prevent the "last knight" from waging his wars with hired infantry and the new paraphernalia of battle. He was fascinated by everything that current technical progress offered, even in mining and coining money. Although no statesman, he was a warm and genuine being; his naïve zest was disarming, and it outshone all his vacillations, whims, and dilettantism. Maximilian tried to fulfil his obligations in the east and west, both intrinsic parts of the heritage of the house of Luxemburg. This central European mission became the fate of the Habsburg dynasty—a fate intertwined with all the interests of Europe and the world. Under Maximilian all the steps were taken that were decisive for this great turn of affairs. He secured the Burgundian heritage and regained the Austrian lands. He married his son Philip to the Spanish heiress Joanna; through a double marriage (treaty of 1515) he prepared the later reunion of the Habsburg hereditary lands with Hungary and Bohemia.

Maximilian's accession to the throne (1493) aroused great expectations. In the foreground was the idea of imperial reform, most pressingly urged by the Elector of Mainz, Count Berthold of Henneberg. In many respects this statesman was Maximilian's opposite both personally and politically. He was neither a rich nor an engaging nature, but self-controlled, objective, and tyrannical, a man who pursued his plans with obstinate vigour and thus far surpassed the incalculable Maximilian as a politician. Berthold's ultimate goal was to create an imperial administration with a committee of the estates to carry on the affairs of government, to preserve the peace, to make alliances, and to levy taxes. Maximilian did not want to be left out so completely, but for the time being he agreed to recognize a diet that was to meet periodically as the executive body. Was this the way to save the Empire from political ruin?

Other points of reform stressed by the Rhenish theorists of empire were concerned with the public peace, the supreme court (*Reichskammergericht*), and a tax called the common penny. The institution of this supreme court was the most important and most permanent innovation. Feuds of all kinds were to be illegal; every crime was to be atoned for and redressed by orderly process of justice. The supreme court was even to be allowed the right to impose banishment from the Empire, albeit in the name of the King. The diet of the Empire was to nominate the members of the court, while the King appointed its president. The imperial tax to support the supreme court and to finance foreign enterprises was intended as a graduated poll tax for every inhabitant over the age of fifteen; every group of twenty-four persons had to pay one gulden.

Emperor Maximilian did everything he could against a reform he regarded as an insurrection by certain privileged groups. But he had great need of the diet, for he was confronted with both the Turkish threat and the epoch-making invasion of Italy by the French King Charles VIII. A modern army of mercenaries could not be organized without money, and money was not forthcoming except on the basis of imperial taxes. In Augsburg (1500), for the sole purpose of furthering his foreign policy, the Emperor approved the standing committee of the estates, the administrative council of twenty (*Reichsregiment*), which was permitted to call itself the regency of the Empire. Since the Elector of Mainz had died, Maximilian could handle the problem of reform in his own way and strip it of its most dangerous implications. In 1508 he assumed the title of Roman Emperor-elect, so that coronation by the Pope appeared superfluous. His later successors did the same, calling themselves emperors immediately after coronation at Aachen. There could have been no more significant indication that a new era had begun. Maximilian's grandson Charles V, in Bologna, was the last Emperor to be crowned by the Pope in person. All the battles in Italy and on the western border that Maximilian tried to fight through by means of imperial funds and troops were simply particular manifestations of dynastic policy. Their universal character rested solely on the universal character of the dynasty, not on an imperial program with universal aims. To the end of his days the Emperor was occupied with projects for marriages and alliances, even with his great adversary France.

THE CIRCLES OF THE EMPIRE

The most significant creation of imperial reform was the division of the Empire into ten districts called circles. They demonstrate the actual extent and character of Germany at the close of the Middle Ages. Originally the Holy Roman Empire and the East Frankish Kingdom had been two entirely distinct entities. Theoretically the Holy Roman Empire included all the known world; it was as universal as the papacy itself. Belonging to the Holy Roman Empire was not the same as belonging to the German land or nationality. From Emperor Sigismund's time on, the old one-headed eagle on the imperial coat of arms was replaced by the double eagle surrounded by a halo; this combined western and eastern form of the armorial bird symbolizes the old universal and sacred character of the Roman imperial idea.

At the end of the Middle Ages the designation "Holy Roman Empire of the German Nation" arose. It shows how both the concepts of the Holy Roman Empire and of the East Frankish or, in effect, German realm were merged. It signified the Empire as represented and borne by the German nation. But this Empire had nothing nationalistic about it. The super-national character of the Empire was always maintained. Burgundy and imperial Italy, lands lying outside the area where German was spoken, were included in the Holy Roman Empire of the German Nation. But political and constitutional development brought it about that the Roman and East Frankish realms—that is, the Empire and the German Kingdom—were more and more identified with each other. It became the* custom to speak of the Emperor and the Empire as of a sort of Janus, analogous to the two eagle heads. The electoral college claimed the right to represent the interests of the Empire.

Imperial reform in Maximilian's time clearly shows the underlying goal. The estates of the Empire demanded their share in the administrative council. When the Emperor definitely freed himself from the necessity of coronation by the Pope and from the political pressure connected with it, the idea of an East Frankish or in effect a German Kingdom faded still further. It had become customary—first under Emperor Henry IV—to call the heir to the throne *Rex Romanorum,* or King of the Romans. Like the Emperor, he was chosen by the electors. The division of the Empire (that is, of the East Frankish Kingdom) into districts, undertaken during Maximilian's rule, was an almost desperate attempt to unify Germany again for military and tax purposes after territorial development had split it asunder.

Two of the ten circles of the Empire comprised the dynastic possessions of the Habsburgs; these were the circles of Austria and Burgundy. Then came the electoral group. The Rhenish circle included the lands of the three ecclesiastical electors and of the Elector Palatine. Here were the roots of the Rhenish notion of the Empire, which, however, was paralysed politically by the endless feuds between Mainz and the Palatinate. The two eastern electorates, Brandenburg and Saxony, made up the Upper Saxon circle. Smaller domains also were taken in by these circles. The names of the old tribal duchies spring to new life in the Bavarian, Swabian, and Franconian circles. The Westphalian, the Lower Saxon, and the Upper Rhenish circles took care of the remaining regions of western Germany. The lands subject to the Wenceslaus crown of Bohemia were not covered in this division into circles, for Bohemia had always held a special position. Though she had her place on the register of the Empire, Bohemia paid no imperial taxes; her kings had had no part in electoral groupings since 1424 and no voice in the election capitulations. The readmission of the Bohemian Elector (1708) proves that since the death of George Podiebrad (1471) Bohemia had been intentionally excluded. The Silesian dukes, whose fiefs were not immediate to the Empire, had never sat in the council of German princes. Prussia—that is, East Prussia—acknowledged Polish feudal overlordship in 1466. The Bishops of Reval, Ösel, and Kurland, who had formerly held the rank of imperial princes, remained untouched by the division of the Empire into circles and thus had nothing more to do with Germany. Kammin was subject to the Pope and did not belong to the Empire any more than the domains of the Teutonic Order. Thus German civilization and German law reached far beyond the political borders of the Empire. In the west the Swiss Confederation succeeded in liberating itself from the Empire; it paid no taxes and did not recognize the imperial supreme court. The Swiss managed their own politics, often in close connection with France. Neither the Wallis (Valais) nor the dukes of Savoy were in the least concerned with the Empire, though they were still inscribed on its register.

There was often some doubt whether individual territories in the west belonged to the Empire or not, because the nobility within the imperial domain frequently entered into a French feudal relation as well. The matter was further confused by marriages across the border and by the inheritances that resulted from them. The French language, which had reached a higher level of development, kept pushing on eastward and helped in the crumbling of boundaries. The territorial diets and the peasants would still often cling to the old German language of the people for a long time, but the knightly class and patricians, canons and jurists, spoke French and soon learned to interpret their special legal connections in the interest of French politics, which pressed toward the Rhine boundary.

Imperial reform proved a failure. In particular the circles, in so far as they had any effect at all, only increased local feuds and thus strengthened particular efforts for power. Anyone who tried to carry on the military and financial business of one of the circles had to reckon with the resistance of the different parts and their banding together obstructively. At the end of the Middle Ages territorial sovereignty was and continued to be the great political pivot of German history.

TERRITORIAL SOVEREIGNTY

In regard to imperial law territorial sovereignty was based on the sovereign's right to exercise supreme jurisdiction—on his powers of life and death. All other rights that split off from the old power of the king and that of the tribal dukes—the levying of tolls, the granting of fiefs, jurisdiction over the church—were bound up with this. Public and private powers were successfully fused, and those who were ruled were simply treated as subjects. The lords had a finger even in the old communal rights of free men in pasture and in woodland. Aristrocratic in their whole form, the ecclesiastical principalities of the Empire were connected with the nobility by countless ties; they became valuable supports for the new class of territorial sovereigns. These sovereigns developed orderly administration. They divided their lands systematically into government districts of different size. The officials lived on their share of the state power and on their fiefs. It was not until money receipts had developed that cash payment became possible out of an accumulation of funds. All sovereigns were deeply in debt. They were forced into exhausting the soil, paying usury, pawning their property and offices. The sovereigns' judicial power was checked by the feudal privilege of everyone to be judged only by his peers.

The sovereign established a privy council made up of his highest officers; he instituted a territorial supreme court that disregarded the possibility of jurisdiction by the diet and supplanted the old division as between the presiding judge and the lay community in doling out justice. This entire development was promoted by Roman law, whose homogeneousness, clarity, and definiteness proved a salvation in the labyrinth of the system of privilege. All scribes and counsellors studied this law at the universities, especially canonical Roman procedure, in accordance with the living doctrine of the post-glossators, the successors of the great Byzantine jurists. Humanism and the imperial supreme court completed the process of Romanizing German law. At first only the superior courts and the city courts were affected. Rural courts clung to the old laws for a long time. The so-called Vehmic courts also continued into the sixteenth century. In contrast to the territorial courts, they were imperial courts in which not only the nobility but the free peasant proprietors, especially those of Westphalia, had full jurisdiction and participated as jurymen. In their heyday the Vehmic courts (the original meaning of *Feme* is "confederacy") helped maintain the public peace and represented a justice that was no respecter of persons. But the arbitrariness of the highest judges (*Stuhlherrn*) of these courts and the rivalry among the presidents (*Freigrafen*) gradually compromised the reputation of this popular institution, invested with all sorts of secret procedure and mummery.

The dualism that cleft the whole of Germany into Emperor and Empire seized on the territorial sovereignties also, and here it served to nip a budding tendency toward absolutism. The estates or diets of the territories represented the interests of distinct classes—knights, prelates, and burghers—as well as those of the whole territory. In contrast to the whims, the prodigality, and the family ties of the sovereign, the diets emphasized what was permanent, what was common to all classes, naturally without forgetting their own liberties and privileges. Thus the growth of territorial sovereignty was furthered by the rivalry of the princes and the diets. The sovereign continued to be dependent on the diet and its consent whenever he required money over and above the customary imposts (*Bede*) and whenever he wanted to levy taxes on the church. The occasion was usually the need of better armaments. New military enterprises and methods exceeded what the knightly class could supply in fulfilment of feudal obligations. All this led to negotiations. The diets stated their conditions. They formed curias according to rank and fought for every fraction of their old traditional rights. The diets were especially powerful in the ecclesiastical principalities, since here there could be no dynasty and for that reason a counterbalance was lacking. In the diets the *Ding,* the old Germanic assembly, lived on, and with it the right of free men to participate in government, a right that had never been abolished; in short, the true concept of a people's state. Clever sovereigns like those of Württemberg knew how to get along with the diets. Others, as in Bavaria, played off the groups within them against one another. The majority of the sovereigns considered life most agreeable without any diets at all. Only in the

Tyrol, in Kempten, in Dithmarschen, and in Holstein did the peasants still persist as a free class with equal civil rights. Stronger and stronger personalities now appear in the history of German sovereignties: Frederick the Victorious, the Elector Palatine, who valiantly defied papal excommunication; the knightly daredevil, Elector Albert Achilles of Brandenburg; the Landshut dukes of the house of Wittelsbach, who in three generations earned themselves the epithet of the Rich. All of these were stalwart, self-confident personalities with a zest for action and battle.

GERMAN HUMANISM

Germany, which had long been a thriving country, now became highly cultured as well. The Italian Renaissance reached across the Alps. Essentially this was a rebirth of the Italian people, an awakening of the burgher's love of freedom, which in its larger aspects was rooted in emphasis on the right to personal life as opposed to the constraints of Empire, church, feudal relationships, and monastic education. The antique had been far less submerged in Italy than elsewhere in the Western world; it had lived on in altered form. Now a new generation was to rediscover it, to disentangle it deliberately from its historical conditions and limitations, and to elevate it to an ideal of human perfection for the newborn national feeling. In Italy these developments were spontaneous. They were bound up with a flowering of art, and they differed in different localities. On the whole they were fruitful and alive beyond anything that was taught or could be learned; they revealed the new creative feeling of culture. In Germany the movement had a much more scholarly character. The early humanists of the mid-fifteenth century were not of independent status, on the whole—travelling scholars who were admitted to patrician circles in the cities and tried to collect an audience among them for ancient writers and their new Italian interpreters. But these German scholastics seldom succeeded in imitating southern spirit and wit, the romantic feeling for form, or the seductive brilliance of a truly critical mind.

Soon, however, humanism in Germany became more clear-cut and more liberal. The philologists were concerned with establishing pure texts, and through the exact wording they arrived at a proper

145

interpretation. The path to the true source led on further, to ethics, history, the natural sciences, and mathematics. The result was a genuine effort to attain to truth, to the values of knowledge, to the meaning of the world for an open, unprejudiced mind. Just as the Italians harked back to ancient Rome and liked to pose as its true heirs and successors, so the patriotic German humanists turned to their country's past.

The *Germania* of Tacitus, discovered in a German monastery, proved a veritable treasure trove for the first Germanic and German romantic movement. This was the beginning of the fatal and inveterate parallelism between the Germanic and the German. It was the beginning also of the exalting of Germanic virtue as against the moral and spiritual corruption of Rome, an appraisal that with Tacitus had had an inner political and pedagogical sense far beyond the actual state of affairs. It was certainly less applicable to the Romans of the Empire than the *soi-disant* successors of Tacitus's idealized Germani could have wished. Wimpfeling proudly attempted a first comprehensive account of German history. There was a general tendency to collect the source material of antiquity, both Roman and mediæval. A plan to bring out a *Germania Illustrata* was partially realized. Nürnberg's glorious past was accorded special and affectionate notice. Collections of German proverbs appeared. Willibald Pirkheimer led the Nürnberg humanists. Conrad Celtes was the most notable proponent of the universalism, of the independent and patriotic trends, that characterized the best adherents of the movement. But the purest and loftiest spirit was the great Erasmus (1465–1536). To him the devout fervour of the late Middle Ages was very real and living, and he was therefore well fitted to make the great attempt of reconciling the new, proud universal education with a very human form of Christianity. Erasmus of Rotterdam was gentle and ironical, full of the true and lasting wisdom that is above and beyond scholarly sophistries. Though he was courted and praised, he never faltered in his modesty, in his sure feeling for what was genuine. And so he stood at the turning-point of his time, too humane to take up arms against the evil world, but so mature in his tolerance that later periods of conflict in matters of faith or conscience must all take account of this unforgettable personality.

RELIGIOUS ABUSES

The humanists either belonged to the ruling class or came to be part of it. These teachers of Greek could become canons or even ambassadors. They made every conversation vivid and spiced everything they wrote. Their influence and their life won the upper class in Germany to an education in Latinity. And even in an increasingly secular-minded age there was soon no other education that counted for anything. It was held in deep reverence, but it widened an already existing chasm. These clever, experienced, travelled, and polished humanists were far removed from the mass of the German people. They had risen out of the mass and wanted to have as little contact with it as possible. Thus it happened that the most gifted sons of the lower class betrayed it. This lower class was suffering; it needed help in both religious and social matters, but who was to give it? All over Europe the beginnings of nationalism affected conditions in religion and the church most powerfully. Was development toward a national church impossible? Such a development was taking place in France at this very time: either the Pope was under supervision at Avignon, or the church became Gallican. In Germany also many an ecclesiastical prince had thought of a national church long ago. But now it was not the emperors or the bishops who upheld the idea. The territorial lords seized on it.

Since the time of the councils the corruption of the church had been ceaselessly bewailed. It became customary to summarize and proclaim these points of complaint (*gravamina*) of the German nation. The well informed lashed out at abuses in appointments, in judicial matters, and in financial management. Mortmain possessions swelled to vast proportions; the weight of the "dead hand" was heavy. Church property had been and continued to be exempt from taxation and was under special jurisdiction; it smothered every kind of free economic competition. There were many who persistently demanded that church property be secularized. But, above all, no German money was to stuff the pockets of the Pope of Rome. This point, as coming under the head of national economy, was certain to be applauded. The irritation every good German felt regarding the Roman church was sharpened by a deep sense of disappointment.

The religious excitement of the masses had never been so strong as it was about 1500. And the traditional organs of the church were not able to withstand the assault. There were pilgrimages and festivals to honor relics; the lay brotherhoods organized processions and worshipped the saints more zealously and ostentatiously than before, but the people wanted something more than the usual sacramental services. The new art of printing, invented by Johannes Gutenberg (c. 1397–1468), had greatly increased literacy and had taught many to think for themselves. In matters regarding the church, too, people wanted to think, to investigate, to learn and to teach, to recognize the truth and to proclaim it. The desire for education underwent here a remarkable democratizing. But all this was not enough. The times were apocalyptic. Spiritual anguish was a grave and pressing reality. A general dissolution was feared. What security was there except the Christian church?

Thus social, humanistic, constitutional, national, dynastic, and religious factors all combined to prepare a great upheaval in Germany. It is called the Reformation.

Chapter 9

THE GERMAN REFORMATION

MARTIN LUTHER (1483–1546)

MARTIN LUTHER was a Thuringian with an admixture of Frankish and Slavic blood. His forebears had all been tenant farmers, always passing the holding on undivided to the youngest son; the other children had to seek their fortunes elsewhere. Hans, the father of the reformer, was employed in the copper mines of the County of Mansfeld. Soon he leased a little foundry and stepped up to the rank of small-scale enterpriser—quite independent—but he remained in the lower middle class into which he had been born. His son Martin grew up in the stern discipline of those times, in simple but not impoverished circumstances. Even as a youth he suffered from life and reality. He had a sensitive spirit that responded to everything gravely and with deep feeling and achieved its poise more and more through religious experience. In this critical period Martin Luther became Germany's great religious genius. All that he did was done from some inner urge, out of ineluctable spiritual necessity. But what he did was also the issue of conflict with his environment, with tradition, with the will and the senses of his own lusty body. Luther never leaned toward cant. In his student days he is described as a gay, merry fellow who could play the lute and wore a sword, a good companion to his friends. Then came the turn and the transformation. He was overwhelmed by disgust with reality, by sorrow for the world, by fear of the hereafter. He vowed to become a monk, and he entered the Augustinian monastery at Erfurt without first obtaining his father's consent, which makes it seem that he must have been fairly certain it would be refused.

Luther was the last great mediæval monk. The German Reformation begins as the late Gothic soul-story of a monk. In the monastery Luther had the leisure to ponder the great tradition. Within himself, with an innate independence and steadfast love of truth, he fought through all over again the long way the church had come: the development from Paul to Thomas Aquinas (died 1274) and then the assault on the mighty doctrinal structure of Thomistic rational metaphysics, from its start with William of Occam (died 1347) and his representation of the exclusive power of faith, of the absolute acceptation of the Bible, and of divine omnipotence. "Reason," so Luther wrote later, "is the devil's whore." Luther made a geniune theological scholar of himself. He rose to a Wittenberg professorship of biblical interpretation, which he held for thirty years. His superiors entrusted him with numerous important offices. He was efficient and helpful in the university and in the monastic community —not as a solitary thinker, but as a highly respected member of the faculty. His outward bearing was firm and self-confident, but within he was still shaken by the growing impossibility of reconciling his soul with God. He journeyed to Rome on business for his order and remained there for four weeks, deeply impressed by all the show of power and not at all shaken in his feelings of loyalty toward the mighty of the church by their obvious abuses.

Through the friendship of his superior, Johann von Staupitz, the provost of the order, Luther became familiar with the noble fruits of universal culture from Christian antiquity to contemporary humanism. All these schools and opinions did not alter Luther's innermost being or exert any decisive influence on his real work. He drew his truth and his faith from the Bible itself; it is the conception of justice at which sinful man must arrive through the inner apprehension of God, made possible by the creative processes of faith. But none is able to apprehend God unless he understands His word. Luther was convinced that he, as a stern and hard proclaimer of the Bible's wisdom, was rediscovering those truths that Augustine and the German mystics had proclaimed before him. Personally Luther remained far too combative a theologian, too passionately intent on the justice of the truth he had arrived at, to pursue mysticism on the level of his predecessors. But he delighted in bringing out a new edition of the little book of an obscure Frankfurt devotee, the *Theologia deutsch,* and found himself and his sense of God in this German teaching. Luther's new interpretation of penance and of the spiritual renewal achieved through penance made this monk and theologian the prophet of the Reformation. And it was the matter of penance that caused the clash with the institutions of the church — the clash that was to have such far-reaching consequences for world history.

THE DISPUTE OVER INDULGENCES

Since the time of Pope Gregory the Great the sacrament of penance had consisted of four stages: repentance, confession, absolution, and atonement. Atonement was made either in this world by suffering temporal punishment, or in purgatory through penalties, also of a temporal nature, intended to purify the soul. But purgatorial penalties could be remitted by the church in view of the wealth of grace accumulated by Christ and the saints. In order to receive this remission the sinner had to fulfil certain obligations. Originally he had to participate in a crusade, but subsequently he was permitted to buy his remission with money. The fear of purgatory led believers to make sacrifices willingly, and the sale of indulgences developed into a flourishing business for the church. Its lower agencies were guilty of all sorts of abuses, such as, for instance, indulgence for the dead, whose wish for atonement was a matter of conjecture, and blanks granting indulgence, which could be filled out anywhere on the payment of certain sums, without inquiry as to whether the sinner had confessed and done penance. In practice these blanks granted indulgence for sins so recently committed that they had not even been confessed.

The Hohenzollern prince Albert of Brandenburg had to pay the curia large sums as a result of his accumulation of high offices in the church; he held three bishoprics. In order to pay these sums he borrowed money from the Fugger banking house and bought indulgences, a not unusual procedure in those times. He entrusted the Dominicans with the sale of these indulgences. The Dominicans' business manager was John Tetzel, a professor of theology who was notorious for his coarse and objectionable methods. Luther did not know the unedifying details, but he resented the fact that, according to the order of Archbishop Albert, indulgences could be bought in the name of the dead even though the beneficiary had shown no readiness to atone. Without consulting anyone Luther decided to declare his view in the usual academic manner by posting his theses in a public place (1517). He invited discussion of ninety-five theses concerning the efficacy of indulgences. Indulgences, Luther was convinced, begot a false form of piety. His statements were coloured by a revolutionary tone. The invisible community of believers took up arms against the visible church, the poverty of the laity against the wealth of the Roman Pope, common sense against theological casuistry.

These theses were the great event of the times. Everyone read them; everyone discussed them. They spread all through Europe. Luther himself was almost frightened, but he bravely took up the fray. He declared that the commands of the church were invalid unless they coincided with the teachings of the Bible. Against the curia he upheld divine truth as the only authoritative power, and he raised the question whether the Pope might not indeed be the Antichrist. The curia knew enough of Luther's teachings to summon him to trial for heresy. Summary proceedings were instituted against him. Luther was branded as a notorious heretic, was asked to recant unconditionally, and in case of refusal was threatened with instant arrest. Luther found the best possible answer. He placed himself under the protection of his territorial lord, Elector Frederick the Wise of Saxony. This was enough to prevent a repetition of the case of John Huss. Territorial interests had been invoked. The Saxon Elector was a devout collector of relics. Only gradually did he become accustomed to the new doctrine, and to the very end he adhered to certain old customs of the church. But this Wittenberg professor was one of his subjects, and he did not give him up. He hated injustice, and he thought that Luther might perhaps be right. And so the hesitant decency of an average man became a factor in history. Connected with this were certain essential premises in European politics.

CHARLES V (1519–56)

The old Emperor Maximilian had made the Sforzas dukes of Milan and in his old age had married the young Princess Bianca Sforza; so important did the position of the house of Habsburg in Italy seem to him—a position that was threatened by France. King Francis I of France defeated the Swiss lansquenets at Marignano (1515) and took Milan. This was the prologue to a new epoch of war that encompassed all of Europe. In vain Maximilian tried to have his grandson Charles elected King of the Romans during his own lifetime. The curia, many of the electors with the Elector of Saxony heading them, and the King of France all feared the superior power of the house of Habsburg. For young Charles was heir to all the domains of Burgundy and Castile, Aragon together with Naples and Sicily, the New World of America, and the Austrian lands. France saw itself caught in a vise, and the Pope found it difficult to maintain his independence as an Italian prince. Thus it was not surprising that all the endangered powers united in order to bestow the imperial crown not on young Charles, but on his rival, Francis of France.

Elector Frederick the Wise appeared as a third aspirant, although he had neither the health nor the energy for such a role. France was not niggardly of pensions, gifts, and bribes; the Rhenish electors were promised cardinals' hats, and the Elector of Brandenburg was won by the tempting offer of becoming governor in Germany for the French King. None the less the awakening national feeling in Germany resented such an arrangement. But the election of Duke Charles of Burgundy proved to be just as fateful from the point of view of national development.

This Burgundian prince, whose native language was French, was a born world sovereign as was none before or afterward. To him Germany was only one country among many. His chief interest was to hold his whole imperium together and to strengthen all the forces that could be of help to him in this—that is, law, treaties, the dynasty, and, of course, the Roman church. Charles could see the German Reformation only as an insurrection, a religious aberration, a political crime. The conflict of the monk and professor, Martin Luther, was not only personally incomprehensible to the world Emperor, but it filled him with horror and loathing. Charles was calm and very cold, knightly but inaccessible, a calculating and watchful connoisseur of human nature. Everything that smacked of the bourgeois, the particularistic, of artistic spontaneity, of independent speculation, was deeply alien to him. He understood the Renaissance just as little as the Reformation, but his imperial power, which he felt as a metaphysical force, could strike a mortal blow at both movements.

The Habsburg party, too, had to pay out vast sums for the election of Charles V: 850,000 gulden, the equivalent of more than ten million dollars. The rich Jakob Fugger of Augsburg supplied the funds. He was the most successful banker of his time, whose mere word commanded confidence. But money was not all that Charles's electors wanted. The capitulation that was entered into by the Empire at the election of 1519 obligated the new Emperor to respect the rights of the estates and of the nation; all governmental action was to be taken with the concurrence of six electors. Only native-born Germans were to hold office at court, no diet was to meet outside the boundaries of the Empire, and no foreign troops were to set foot on German soil without the express consent of the imperial diet. No subject of the Empire was to be exiled without trial. Thus the spirit of territorial princedom protected German national interests in the name of the aristocratic oligarchy. Germany remained an old-fashioned political body based on the principle of the estates, in contrast to the new principle of absolute princely power. The capitulation of the 1519 election was epoch-making; it was the imperial law of the Reformation, and it was only on the basis of its stipulations that Luther's case came to a public hearing before the Emperor and the Empire. Luther's success rested on his alliance with territorial princedom and with the high nobility of the German nation, to whom he expressly addressed a pamphlet. The alien Emperor could not but be an enemy. The German princes stood ready as the natural allies of his cause.

LUTHER'S DOCTRINE. THE DIET OF WORMS (1521)

Luther proclaimed the freedom of a Christian being (1520) and thus established the spiritual bearings of Protestantism. His work called for the self-direction of the soul. But this was only a start. He wanted the true church, a new communion of the faithful. He had attacked the Pope; now he turned against the councils as well and thus really continued the ideas of John Huss, whose writings he knew and referred to. The humanists in particular applauded Luther's criticism of corruption in the church, of her abuses and her frauds.

Ulrich von Hutten now wrote his thunderous indictment of Romanism. He was one of the most curious figures of his time, a man who had freed himself from ancestral traditions and given himself up to the wandering life of a poet and of a contentious, disorderly knight of the Empire. But his high-flown rhetoric was sometimes a little ridiculous and, what was worse, not always above question as to its integrity—as is the way of professional idealists. To Hutten, everything Roman was evil and foreign; sophisticated Roman practices in law and finance were ruinous to good old German usage. To him Hermann, the great Cheruscan who had defeated the Roman Varus in the Teutoburg Forest, personified true German repudiation of Roman trickery. An indomitable champion, Hutten joyfully threw himself into the struggle that the great philologist Reuchlin was waging with the Dominicans; he took delight in showing up the ignorance, the limitations, and the arrogance of these obscurantists. But Hutten's character was flawed. Syphilis, the scourge of the times, early sapped his powers, and the exigencies of living goaded him to confused and contradictory actions. Nevertheless the battles of his best years earned laurels for him. He died in 1523.

Martin Luther utilized the transitional period before Charles V assumed the imperial power to propound his doctrine in his three great writings of 1520. There was no longer to be a rift between priest and layman, for there was to be a general priesthood of believers; the state was to support the church; the offices of priest and judge, working together, were to secure the well-being of the Christian community, and both were vocations; the order of the new Protestant world was to be based on class and faith; every Christian belonged to both spheres of existence, to a temporal class and to sanctity, the idea of faith. Temporal authority must therefore assist in accomplishing sanctification. But Luther was far from meaning to improve the world in any moralistic or idealistic way. He took it as it was. Of course he hoped for reforms, but he did not feel them essential to the religious issue. He needed the authority of the state for carrying through his work, and in return he offered to strengthen the servants of the state in their vocation. He regarded this vocation as work done for all, as a creative activity for the common good. And this he believed to be in accordance with the words of the Bible, which he continued with relentless severity to uphold as the greatest and ultimate source of truth. The minister unto souls helped the temporal ruler; such was the destiny and the limitation of the German Protestantism that was in the making.

A papal bull of 1520 again condemned Luther as a heretic. The strife clamoured for a decision. Luther gave his answer. He burned the papal bull publicly and called for a free council to make decision. Personal negotiations with Luther were fruitless. Emperor Charles, harassed with cares of state in Spain and Italy, wanted to bring the conflict in Germany to some sort of conclusion. This irritating business was developing into a great political movement. All classes were seething with excitement, and each got what it wanted out of Luther's teachings. The estates of the Empire, being against the Emperor, necessarily took sides against Rome. An emperor who would inscribe reform of the church on his banner could now shape all of Germany to his will.

Luther was summoned to the Diet of Worms. It was a great concession on the part of the Emperor to give the German heretic an opportunity to recant in public. But the heretic did not recant. He demanded refutation by argument. He declared that the Pope and the councils had often been in error. He followed his conscience and avowed his doctrine. To the reproach that he was plunging Germany into discord he replied that he could not deprive his native land of his services; strife there must be, for only through strife could truth triumph. Luther was no politician. In the course of repeated debates he declined to make concessions in the spirit of practical compromise. For him his cause was the cause of God and could therefore not be affected by any human agency. But Luther's cause concerned the world also, and so it had to be fought out here and now. The Emperor issued an edict, the Edict of Worms, putting Luther under the imperial ban and ordering the destruction of his writings. But the estates of the Empire did not carry out the provisions of the edict. Luther's elector provided him with the safe shelter of the Wartburg. It became customary in Saxony to take communion in both kinds, and priests began to marry. The reform movement was strong; it would have gone its inevitable way even if Luther had been sacrificed to the ban.

Emperor Charles realized that he was not in a position to exercise his full authority over Germany. The King of France maintained relations with the Spanish political opposition, with rebellious vassals in Burgundy, and with the movement toward independence in Naples and Sicily. From the east the Ottoman Empire threatened the position of the house of Habsburg; Belgrade, the fortress of the Danube, fell. England and the Pope allied themselves with the Emperor. War began as a struggle for hegemony in Europe; with brief interruptions it continued throughout Emperor Charles's tenure. The first great success came in Italy. The Germans and the Spaniards defeated King Francis I of France at Pavia and took him prisoner (1525). But the war proceeded endlessly. From diet to diet only halfway solutions were put together. Meanwhile the reformative teachings spread from one territory to another; all of northern Germany capitulated to them. A special alliance of the Habsburg and Wittelsbach princes with the majority of south German bishops tried to raise a dam across the south. The Reformation had grown to national proportions. Preachers were on the move through the land; people fought for the pamphlets that were being circulated, and the Bible penetrated to the humblest classes. At the Wartburg Martin Luther had been making his translation of the Bible into German; he himself wrote hundreds of pamphlets, and for some time three presses worked for him exclusively. He showed his countrymen that everything can be said in German. He struck off many new words; the glowing language that he wrought and tempered taught a whole generation how to speak and think.

REVOLUTIONARY UPHEAVAL. THE MOVEMENT OF THE KNIGHTS

The Reformation became more and more revolutionary in tone. Here students and journeymen challenged the clergy; there councilmen had to leave their city; in some other place communal taxes were re-allocated. Many monks left the monasteries, and those who remained were threatened in life and limb. Under the fanatical lead of a chronic rebel, Karlstadt, a self-important doctor of theology, furious idol-smashing began. Altars were destroyed, paintings disfigured, images of saints beheaded and otherwise mutilated, banners and candelabra and even crucifixes burned, stained-glass windows shattered; through it all, the mob howled in triumph. In the end a Reformation committee had to be formed to establish order and above all to lay a financial basis for the new church by setting up a "common box"; the funds of monasteries, brotherhoods, benefices, and foundations flowed into this and provided the means for paying ministers and caring for the poor. Unrest continued for a long time.

Luther had to leave the Wartburg and take hold of things again himself. He did not, indeed, approve of self-government for the common people; he was no constitutional or economic organizer. For him the one thing needful was to speak and to write. In these stirring times there were speeches and pamphlets of innumerable kinds, and Luther's attitude consequently led to factionalism and bewilderment in the reform movement.

In Zwickau, for instance, congregations of fanatics were formed under Bohemian influence. The members were mostly poverty-stricken displaced weavers. They could no longer find a niche in an economy that had been given a strong capitalistic turn by flourishing silver mines, and so they were easily touched by millenarian teachings. Here Thomas Müntzer soon took the stage. He was a mystic who regarded Luther's rigid biblical faith with its historical foundations as insufficient for the deepest needs of the soul. Müntzer developed more and more into a radical sectarian, roaming the country as Christ's messenger, founding a secret league of the elect, and proclaiming his Anabaptist tidings with violent fulminations against the authorities as godless beings. This lofty spirit could be satisfied only by complete re-creation of the world. Now destiny swept him into the Peasants' War.

The territorial princes and the cities were the two strongest pillars of public life in Germany at the time. The knights and the peasants kept up a weak defensive stand. No class could ignore the Reformation. The majority of the knights of the Empire retained their immediacy, their direct dependence on the Emperor. Their strength focused in southwestern Germany. By holding close together they tried to keep their footing despite the economic ruin of the nobility. The prosperity of the cities with their money economy, the new methods of territorial rule, did not leave the imperial knights much choice. What were they to do? Plunder the more fortunate classes? Hire out as *condottieri*? Should they let themselves sink to the dependent status of the rural nobility in the different territories, or should they try to lift themselves to the level of the princes? Perhaps the Reformation could be turned to some account by these knights of the Empire, above all through secularization of the ecclesiastical principalities. If these domains became ordinary inheritable property, then the knights, who as a rule dwelt in the ecclesiastical principalities, would have considerable chances of bettering themselves.

Franz von Sickingen became the leader of the imperial knights. One of the most successful infantry captains of his day, he was a blend of unscrupulous energy, naïve imperial patriotism, and heartfelt hatred for the clergy. Sickingen's feud with the Archbishop of Trier was typical: a declining class of the Empire brought old-fashioned blunderbusses to its fight against the modern artillery of the territorial princes. Sickingen's admiring contemporaries even exalted him as the coming emperor. But he died in the midst of these struggles. The knights were actually no better than the rest: they looted and burned just like any of their opponents. Politically Sickingen's only way to success would have been an alliance with the peasants. But he had no use for the riff-raff of the *Bundschuh,* the peasants' confederation. To his last breath he prided himself on his rank. A brave but limited personality, he died in 1523.

THE PEASANTS' WAR (1524-5)

The close of the Middle Ages was agitated by upheavals among the peasants. The territorial lords attacked them; they violated custom and private rights and tried to force the peasants into thorough subjection. The self-government of the villages was drained away; more service was demanded; taxes became more general and more regular. Administrative machinery, as it was modernized, imposed order and discipline. Fraudulent practices were brought into full play even by ecclesiastical princes and feudal lords. The policing of the territorial princes encroached on even the humble customs of everyday life. This excited the most acute bitterness among the peasants. According to legend, the explosion was finally touched off by a lady's making her peasants look for snail shells on which to wind her yarn.

The peasant was fighting for the "old justice." He believed that he was defending the ordinances of God against the whims of man. He despised the modern custom of taking interest, and so he included the Jewish aides of princely administration in his hatred. This anti-capitalistic attitude gave rise to all sorts of radical demands for equality: the abolition of all taxes, equal rights for all in woodland

and pasture, an end to luxury, and day's wages even for clergy and lords.

The *Bundschuh* is the peasant shoe that was tied with leather thongs criss-crossed. Its earliest use as a symbol of the peasants' consolidation and co-operation is traceable to the year 1443. During the following decades a curious interplay of social, political, and religious factors produced a ponderous movement. The peasant believed in the Emperor and the Empire. From the highest powers in Christendom, as old and rooted as himself, he looked for fulfilment of a world mission, the restoration of the old divine justice. The lord of the manor, with his right of judgement, whom the peasant saw before him, was to him the quintessence of impious lawlessness. He could not comprehend the regularly constituted powers of government that intervened between the local ruler and the distant Emperor. As much as he did perceive of them seemed so odious that he could only belabour them. The Reformation now wrought monstrous effects throughout the countryside because it stood up against the authorities of today and of yesterday. Acceptance of Holy Writ as sole guide seemed obvious to the peasants; their life too was to become "evangelical." The reformer Martin Luther was profoundly reverenced. He was of peasant stuff, and country folk trusted his decisions even to the smallest detail.

The Peasants' War started to the southwest of the Black Forest and spread rapidly to the Breisgau and the Markgräflerland. An erstwhile mercenary, Hans Müller of Bulgenbach, was the commander-in-chief. With his red cap and mantle he rode through the country like the king of a coming realm. Anyone who would not join the "Christian Association" fell under the peasant ban, which meant that he could not eat, grind corn, or buy in any community. Religious and legal motives were curiously intermingled. The peasants wanted justice; they wanted to be able to carry on lawsuits; they wanted the Emperor or his representative to rule them, and no one else. The officials of the manorial lords ought either to enjoy the confidence of the people or disappear. All this scarcely looked subversive. Many territorial lords came to definite terms with the peasant swarm.

The same or similar events occurred in Upper Swabia and in Franconia. A Swabian craftsman, Ulrich Schmid, drew up the demands of the peasants with the help of a journeyman furrier who was well versed in the Bible. The result was the Twelve Articles of March, 1525, which were immediately printed and became the manifesto of the peasant movement. Religious demands came first: Communities were to have the right to choose their own priests. A church fund was to be established to pay the clergy, to care for the poor, and to pay the taxes. To be abolished as unbiblical were the tithe on cattle, the *Todfall* (tax paid on the death of a tenant farmer), and serfdom. In connection with restitution of meadows and woodlands as communal property and of fishing and hunting rights a "brotherly" arrangement was suggested with due regard to acquired rights. Required service was to be freshly specified in accordance with ancient precedent, farm rent to be on a fair basis. Obedience to authority was emphasized as the humble duty of every Christian. It might be supposed that this program would seem wholly reasonable to many of the authorities, and a considerable number did indeed undertake negotiations. The majority, however, sensed the underlying revolutionary spirit and resorted to force. The Swabian League called up its troops.

And now the peasants began setting fire to castles and plundering monasteries. In Franconia distinguished members of the ruling class, nobles as well as burghers, joined the peasant cause. One or another would encourage a peasant to refuse to pay his tithe or would denounce the taking of interest as un-Christian usury. Florian Geyer, a wealthy lord of a castle and a proved general, espoused the peasant cause from inner conviction. He took it quietly enough when his own property went up in flames, but even so this apostate to the nobility could never become more than a counsellor who was watched suspiciously. The tragedy of the times is reflected in the division within his character: in order to free the peasants he killed his peers. The nobles' country seats were destroyed simply because the peasants hoped by this means to secure peace on highroads and waterways. Their ultimate aim was the erection of a reformed government, with equal rights for everyone and no privileges for anyone. The concept of the Reformation thus took on a political character. Authority answerable only to the people was to be built up on a democratic foundation.

The cruel murder of the Count of Helfenstein—a magistrate who was hated, with reason—before the eyes of his young wife was fortunately an isolated excess. On the whole the leaders of the warring peasants were reasonable. The best known of the knights who joined the movement was Götz von Berlichingen, a rough and ready daredevil whom the genius of the young Goethe transformed into a noble German patriot. The peasants' program developed further in the course of the struggle. Many an old dream was taken up into it. The "Reformation" of 1525 counted as its chief points a general peace, reorganization of the judicial system with five courts, secularization of ecclesiastical property, abolition of all ground rent, and a uniform system of weights and measures and also of coinage for all Germany. In spite of its weaknesses this was a magnificent draft for reform of the Empire. Who was to carry it out?

Luther's attitude was the deciding factor. The reformer did not wish the ideas of the Reformation to be exploited for worldly purposes. He had admonished the German nobles to be moderate, but to no avail. He had spoken of the obstinacy and the anger of the princes and lords. But in his opinion the shortcomings of the authorities could not justify rebellion. A true Christian must suffer and pray and as a last resort leave the country, but he must never take up arms. Luther's kingdom was not of this world. Lacking political sense, he did not realize that this desire for peace at all costs only served to strengthen the arrogance of those who were in power. Luther wanted to prevent the Reformation from degenerating into revolution; so he forged its alliance with all reactionary forces. After the defeat of the peasants he went out of his way to encourage the victorious territorial lords to take the harshest measures, to strangle the "mad dog," in his pamphlet *Against the Murderous and Rapacious Hordes of the Peasants*. There was horror enough even without this counsel from the reformer. A series of fights occurred. The swarms of peasants could not cope with the princes' armies of mercenaries under superior leadership. At Frankenhausen five thousand peasants were mowed down. Thomas Müntzer was captured and executed with great cruelty (1525). Several times unarmed peasants were slaughtered in spite of their having safe conducts. Hundreds of peasants were tried and condemned to be beheaded or to be mutilated by having their hands chopped off or their eyes put out. In many cases the struggle assumed the form of a crusade against heretics. What was there unjustified in this? If Luther together with the Protestant princes had allied himself with the peasants, the great war that was to be fought a hundred years later for religion and imperial reform would have broken out then and there. Luther sacrificed the peasants and with them the common interests of the Empire, and so a particularistic future was assured to the territorial princes. The Reformation did not unite Germany, nor did it strengthen it. On the contrary, it furthered institutional and social disintegration.

For a long time to come the German peasantry was condemned to the passive role of a lower stratum that vegetated and made no history. With few exceptions its condition had changed only for the worse. Vast sums were squeezed out of the peasants for rebuilding the nobles' country seats that had been destroyed, and forced labour completed the contribution. The peasants were deprived once and for all of the right to carry weapons, and this measure stifled even the memory of former freedom. In Germany the chasm between city and country, between territorial lord and subject, between prince and people yawned deeper than ever. The unfortunate German peasants were now deprived of even their own administration of justice. The old rural community and its collective administration collapsed. With a few exceptions (in the Tyrol and Lower Saxony) the peasantry degenerated into complete personal and material dependence. The peasant bound to his clod became an object of ridicule to the other classes. For he was indeed ignorant, awkward, dirty, and coarse. The enserfment of the rural population is one of the causes of the illiberal way in which German political relationships developed. It was difficult to free the peasants; it was more difficult to give them and their descendants the natural self-confidence of freedom. Luther's individual turn of mind could not grip the masses. His Protestantism was manna for the educated and lost much of its original popular quality. This is one of the reasons for the rapid success of the Counter-Reformation.

THE SWISS REFORMATION

In its very beginnings the Reformation had called forth a Counter-Reformation. By and large the struggle was favourable to Protestantism, but the disintegration that it spread affected it too. In Switzerland a separate evangelical movement arose under the leadership of Ulrich Zwingli. A disciple of Erasmus, thoroughly educated as a humanist and also a devotee of the Bible, he took the political conditions of his native land into his firm, wise hands with the vigour of the free Swiss peasant. This calm, well-poised man had a clear mind. The Swiss now hated the Roman Emperor just as they did the Roman Pope, but their service as mercenaries to the King of France seemed no less an evil to Zwingli. He wanted a truly Swiss church as the helpmate of a truly Swiss policy, independent and self-confident. He had none of Luther's genius, none of his spiritual conflicts, none of his profound and powerful creativeness. He wanted to lead his people back to the simple relationships of the early Christian way of living, to a decent communal life in matters of faith and conscience; and the economic and spiritual premises favoured such a reasonable undertaking. Many city republics of southern Germany, Strassburg in the lead, sympathized with these aims. Luther, however, was suspicious of such rejection of custom and of image-worship as a detestable form of fanaticism. The doctrine of the communion raised the antagonism to bitter hostility and led to an unfortunate break.

Every politically minded person was bound to desire the unity of Protestantism. Philip, the Landgrave of Hesse, hoped to be able to find some common basis, especially since the fight against the Anabaptists drew the two big groups of Protestants together. But the religious discussion arranged by the Landgrave in Marburg did not have the desired results. Zwingli interpreted the communion solely as a commemorative ceremony in which Christ is apprehended by the faith of the soul. Luther, however, insisted that the Saviour was actually present. He wanted to know that the character of the sacrament was preserved in accordance with the Greek text of the miracle-working formula. Historical development argued for Luther, who in this matter did not diverge fundamentally from the Roman concept. But Zwingli claimed for himself the right of timely reinterpretation of tradition and indeed an extension of it. Even on the score of phraseology caution was in order, since Christ had spoken not Greek, but Aramaic—and in Aramaic there is no verb "to be" ("This *is* my body").

164

Agreement between the two groups would have been useful. The fact became another reason for Luther to check a compromise that seemed to him a sacrifice of conscience. Zwingli faced the entire question more objectively and humanly. He regarded Luther's harshness as incompatible with the spirit of love. But Luther acted according to the laws of his work; he would not and could not give up a single essential point.

The cleavage persisted through the centuries. After Zwingli's early death (he fell at Kappel in 1531) his followers united with the Calvinists of Geneva. But the Lutherans hated the German adherents of the Swiss Reformation; they hated the "Reformed" even more bitterly than they did the papists. And this added a new burden to the struggle about the Reformation. For now there was not only the dualism between the Catholics and the Protestants, but the dualism between the Lutherans and the Reformed.

THE WORLD POLICY OF CHARLES V. THE DIET OF AUGSBURG (1530)

All this while Charles V was battling for world emperorship. His ally in this enterprise was the banking house of the Fuggers in Augsburg. Most of the Fuggers' vast resources had come from mining. Silver and copper from the Tyrol and Bohemia made their ascent to unheard-of wealth possible. The Fuggers surpassed even the Medici. They and their business associates collected the dues of the Roman curia. No bishopric was filled without these bankers' having something to say. The other great German firm, the Welsers, kept more to manufacture and trade. They took part in the times' great shift from the Levantine trade to trade with America and India, and so successfully that for a long time they had complete control of the price of spices. They even founded settlements in Venezuela. During the first half of the sixteenth century international commercial capitalism and the money-lending business built up on it were predominantly in German hands.

The movement for imperial reform now affected national economy. Luther himself protested against usury. The diet of the Empire endeavoured to battle against the great trading companies and their monopolistic tendency. A plan to establish customs laws for the Empire was aired by the supreme court and the administrative council; this was a grave threat to the international business of the great trading houses. Two fronts formed: the Reformation, imperial reform, and national economy on one side; on the other, international commercial capital, the curia, and the Emperor. The Habsburgs were always in financial straits; they had need of the great firms. Ferdinand, Charles's brother, now harvested the fruits of the old compact about the inheritance: he became King of Hungary and of Bohemia. But he had to defend his new sovereignty against the Turkish threat. In 1529 Sultan Soliman was before the imperial city of Vienna. In Italy, German mercenaries had stormed Rome with all the concomitant horrors of sack and torture. The French army was pressing Naples hard. Only Genoa's desertion of France made it possible for the Emperor to maintain his position in central Europe.

All these enterprises of the Emperor's devoured tremendous sums of money. The mercenaries repeatedly mutinied because they could not be paid. At the last moment the Fuggers came to the rescue. The Emperor moved from one dilemma to another. The curia resented the Habsburg grip on Italy, but on the other hand the Emperor was the only one from whom they could expect effective opposition to Lutheran heresy. The German territorial lords quarrelled about the Reformation, but formed a solid front against imperial claims. The King of France did not hesitate to ally himself with either Turkish unbelievers or Protestant heretics if he could damage the Emperor by doing so. But this same King of France was also equally ready to incite the pious Duke of Bavaria against the Emperor; he dangled the Roman royal office before him and secured the Pope's help in this subtle intrigue. For Charles, Christian universalism was a sacred fact. He always fought for the unity of the Empire and of faith. For this reason the constantly recurring wars with France were a real cross to him. He was never able to concentrate his great forces effectively. He was always dragging along from truce to truce—from one sham peace, one provisional arrangement, to another. A fresh conflict was for ever calling the impatient Emperor away to the other end of his realm. Once he thought of appealing to the Pope for arbitration. Again, he wanted to challenge King Francis I to a duel; the survivor was then to call a council and lead the armies of Christendom as one against the unbelievers. The Emperor never achieved any finality. His world Empire was to be the foundation of eternal peace, but it was so large that it perpetuated war.

In the meantime the evangelical front of northern Germany was pushing farther and farther south. At the Diet of Speyer (1526) the princes received, by way of a transitional arrangement, the right to reform (*jus reformandi*). Because the followers of the new teachings soon resisted oppression, they were called Protestants. It was not until 1530, in Augsburg, that Charles appeared in person again. He wanted to settle the bad business once and for all as an impartial judge. Was not a reconciliation in the spirit of Erasmus possible? Could one appease the Protestants—as the Hussites had once been appeased—by concessions that would not be too costly? Even among the Protestants some sentiment was setting in this direction.

Philip Melanchthon, Luther's faithful aide, believed in the mildness of Rome and did not wish to break apart the sacred fellowship of the church. This wise student of Aristotle, a successful teacher at the University of Wittenberg and a devout humanist, fathered a thriving school of theology. Even now it would have been possible to come to an agreement with the sensitive, wise, and genuine Melanchthon and his comrades in faith concerning the marriage of priests, the lay chalice, and alteration of the sacrament of the Mass. A German national church similar to the Church of England was rising on the horizon of the future. But Luther had not desired such a solution. He cared more for freedom of conscience than for wise reform of the church. And so the Augsburg Diet ended in dissension. The Lutherans presented their confession of faith, the Augsburg Confession, which has become the basis of their doctrine. Four cities of southern Germany set down their own confessions of faith in agreement with the doctrine of the Reformed. Both views were refuted by the orthodox. The Emperor was willing to mediate; he was ready to submit the matter of the Mass to debate, declared his willingness to safeguard church property, and suggested a world council of the church. But the princes and the curia withstood him. Minds were divided.

Sweden and Denmark, allied with the Duchy of Prussia, which had just been secularized and put under hereditary rulership, now thought it wise to open the doors to the Reformation. Of course the secularization of church property served to strengthen royal power.

Beyond these tangible economic advantages Lutheranism in Scandinavia signified the triumph of German cultural influence and the development of a special northeastern European political entity, which met the north and east German domains in a new fellowship of life. What support Protestantism found in the Scandinavian countries was to be demonstrated most urgently in the Thirty Years' War. The old friction between the Germans of the Empire and the Germans of colonized regions was deepened by the new friction in Germany between northern Protestantism and southern Catholicism. Since in the end extensive regions of northern Germany remained Catholic, while the Reformation penetrated from the Upper Rhine even to the Palatinate and Württemberg, fragmentation was general in this respect too, with a strong tendency of all the estates of the Empire to lean on foreign factors of power. The social revolutionary character of Protestantism was bound to arouse and to consolidate all the conservative powers of the times. This showed itself especially plainly in the fate that befell Anabaptism.

All the responsible leaders of Protestantism criticized and condemned sectarianism, but the evangelical cause still had to reckon with this burden. In 1533 the citizens of Münster drove away their Bishop. In order to gather support the city guilds with their democratic spirit invited Anabaptists from all over northern Germany. Soon Jan Bokelson of Leiden, a journeyman tailor of pleasant appearance and magnetic personality, advanced to a position of leadership. The Anabaptists believed that adults should be baptized. They wanted to return to the apostolic early Christian community. In many parts of southern Germany these groups led a life of pious contemplation, detached from worldly affairs. Others, by urging the radical demands of the craftsman, precipitated many cruel persecutions. Some of the leaders spent their lives in restless wandering, and Anabaptism sprang up in many places.

The times seethed with apocalyptic visions, and now unlucky Münster became the place of fulfilment. The second coming of Christ, supposed to be imminent, sharpened everything. The richer citizens of Münster were driven from the city as godless spirits; their property was retained by the chosen children of Jacob as the illuminati and administered for the public good. The city was converted into a Christian communistic state in which private property, monogamy, and the rest of the traditional order were abolished. A new Jerusalem was to arise. Dazzled by success and weakly succumbing to lordly luxury, the prophet Jan Bokelson stepped forward as Zion's king. Twelve elders, representing the twelve tribes of Israel, were ranged beside him, and apostles fared forth into neighbouring lands. Resistance of any kind was suppressed with violence and bloodshed, polygamy was imposed, terrorism and arbitrariness ruled in the guise of fantastic promises, and splendid processions swept the masses along orgiastically. Now all the princes near by combined with the Elector of Köln, the territorial lord of Münster, against the city and starved it out through treachery (1536). For centuries the bodies of the leaders who had been cruelly tortured to death were kept in iron cages, hung from the steeple of the Lambertus Church as a warning to future generations.

And so Münster again became Catholic. In other ways also Protestantism suffered setbacks. The Protestant Duke Ulrich of Württemberg could return to his country only with the aid of French funds. But Philip the Generous, the Landgrave of Hesse, did much deeper harm to the Protestant cause. He had tired of his wife—a Saxon princess, his equal in rank, who had borne him seven children—because she was aging and sickly. And so he gave himself up to a profligate life, which resulted in syphilis. With his conscience pricking him he fell in love with a young and beautiful lady of the court, whose mother, however, insisted on a legal marriage. The Landgrave wanted a morganatic marriage. Since the reformers feared that Philip might desert the Protestant cause, they countenanced the union with the argument that this custom, practised by the patriarchs, was nowhere forbidden in the Bible. It was true, they said, that the Gospel of Matthew expressly calls for monogamy, but a dispensation could still be claimed, provided the morganatic marriage remained secret. The example of King Henry VIII of England and the Anabaptists made such an impression at that time that individual Protestant theologians were even willing to compromise on polygamy. The upshot of the matter was that under the provisions of the new criminal code of the Empire the Landgrave of Hesse found himself threatened with the heaviest penalties for this double marriage, and he therefore did his best to get along with the Emperor. Protestantism bore the odium of the whole affair.

THE WAR OF SCHMALKALDEN. CHARLES V ABDICATES

Emperor Charles now wanted to assert himself, even by force. The many discussions on religious problems were utterly fruitless. The papacy went its own way. The Council of Trent (1545–63) was preparing to rebuild the edifice of dogma of the Roman church, but it put aside the idea of re-establishing the priestly and military *Respublica Christiana* that was dear to the heart of the Emperor. A reform of the church with the formation of new national churches would not have been contrary to the spirit of the Empire. Since this path was closed, Emperor Charles now took the alternative: he treated the German Protestants as rebels. The Schmalkalden League, formed by the Lutheran princes and towns in 1530, had allowed its best opportunity to slip away unused. Now the Emperor made peace with France and concluded a five-year truce with the Ottoman Empire. The coast was clear.

Charles V promised the Dukes of Saxony and Bavaria electoral rank. Bavaria had remained strictly Catholic, but Duke Maurice of Saxony, who came forward as the antagonist of his cousin the elector, was himself a follower of the new doctrine. His main incentive was boundless egotism. He can scarcely be termed a distinguished diplomat, for he acted harshly and without enough deliberation, certainly uninhibited by any humane considerations or any understanding of world conditions. Immature and incalculable as he was, he played a fateful part in German history; his early death kept him from saving whatever might perhaps still have been saved. The German civil war that now began was soon ended. At Mühlberg (1547) the Elector John Frederick of Saxony lost both his liberty and his electoral rank, which was transferred to Duke Maurice. A military success of the communes of Lower Saxony was of no avail. The Landgrave of Hesse was also captured. Charles V set about reconstructing Germany.

Luther did not live to see this terrible defeat. He died in 1546; he was depressed and for a long time had been ailing, no longer able to defend his work when occasion arose. To the very end his most faithful friend, music, gave him consolation and strength. Martin Butzer,

the best organizer of the evangelical cause, was forced to leave Strassburg and went to England. His was one of the few great political
talents among the Protestants. It was he who originated Protestant
church government, schools, church discipline, and charities. Now
a reactionary movement sprang up among the patricians in many of
the towns of southern Germany, and in country places the feudal
lords rose against the territorial princes. Heavy contributions toward
the maintenance of imperial troops were exacted of the cities. Emperor Charles V carried off the victory, but failed in his reconstruction program. He wanted the estates of the Empire to unite in an
imperial league to carry out the reform. He wanted an imperial
Reformation—the reunion of all Germans in an amended church.
The Catholics rejected this idea. And so there was no choice: till
there should be further decisions from some council, the Augsburg
interim granted the Protestants the lay chalice and priests' marriage,
but in all other respects demanded a return to the old ritual and the
old dogma (1548).

The Habsburg family compact of 1551 irritated all the princes of
the Empire, Catholic and evangelical alike. The Emperor and his
brother Ferdinand agreed in it that Charles's son, Philip of Spain,
was to succeed him as emperor, while Ferdinand's son was merely
to be the King of the Romans. Was Spanish rule to persist in central
Europe? The Germans detested the ceremonious and arrogant behaviour of the Spaniards; nothing, therefore, could be a greater challenge to German feeling or excite it against the Habsburgs more
vehemently. Ferdinand himself obviously resented his brother's
plans. He was accustomed to submit, however. But now the new
Elector of Saxony, Maurice, placed himself at the head of the opposing territorial princes and formed at Chambord a memorable pact
with the bitterest opponent of the Habsburgs, King Henry II of
France. The King of France was made imperial regent over Toul,
Metz, and Verdun, the imperial cities of Lorraine, as well as over
Cambrai in Flanders. In return he promised to pay a monthly subsidy of a thousand kronen (1551). It was in this way that, for the
purpose of making a Spanish emperor impossible, the German territorial princes admitted the King of France into the Empire. Up to
this time the French rulers had not succeeded in obtaining the imperial crown. Now they found a more effective means of weakening

the Habsburg dynasty and extending their own power, and this means was no handicap to German liberty. The disintegration of the western German border had now reached a decisive stage. It would be a mistake to apply modern national standards to these events; most of the inhabitants of the transferred regions spoke French.

The territorial princes desired no foreign emperorship that might perhaps, with the overwhelming military and financial resources of the Spanish monarchy, be able to establish itself as an absolute imperial rule in Germany. This was the great thing. The younger Habsburg line in Vienna hardly constituted any such threat; it was poorer and weaker, and in Bohemia and Hungary it was limited by the diets of these kingdoms. The transfer of the cities in Lorraine was a blow to Habsburg power, because it broke the connection between Burgundy and the Netherlands. Emperor Charles V made one final effort to retake Metz; then he gave up the struggle.

This Emperor had now fared through many lands, over many seas. Wherever he appeared he spread fear and terror. He had often been victorious, but now he saw himself struck down. He had not been able to maintain his Empire as an entity and to hand it on as such. His technical, military, financial, and political failures were due to the vast areas he ruled over and to the contradictory elements of his rule. He abdicated; with solemn ceremonial he laid down all his crowns and withdrew to Spain, where he lived as a great lord in a fine villa near the monastery of San Yuste. Here, in concealment and yet in contact with the world, he awaited death in devout consciousness of having done his work. He left the ordering of German affairs entirely to his brother Ferdinand, who made a preliminary peace at Passau (1552) by abandoning the Emperor's "interim." At the very moment of this Protestant victory its successful front-line champion, Elector Maurice, unexpectedly left the stage. He fell a victim in a feud with the Margrave of Kulmbach (1553).

A religious peace was finally effected in the Diet of Augsburg of 1555, which was not attended by either Emperor or Pope. A treaty was drawn up between King Ferdinand, the leader of the adherents of the old religion, and the Lutherans, the adherents of the Augsburg Confession, under the leadership of electoral Saxony. Anabaptists and the followers of Zwingli and Calvin were not represented. At

Augsburg both religious groups assured themselves of their stability for the time being. The members of the two approved churches were then about evenly matched in numbers, though there were slightly more Catholics because of the many ecclesiastical principalities in the Empire. The territorial states were accorded jurisdiction in matters of religion—that is, the right to determine their own religious adherence. If a subject differed from the prevailing faith for reasons of conscience, he was free to emigrate without losing his property. In the imperial cities only was there parity—that is, equal rights for Catholics and Lutherans. According to a special clause lords of ecclesiastical estates of the Empire who changed their faith were to lose their territories and revenues. This "ecclesiastical reservation" was not recognized by the Lutherans, but was incorporated in the treaty by the King's command. The purpose of the clause was to prevent something that had actually been known to occur: namely, the exploitation of a change of faith by ecclesiastical princes in order to found a dynastic inheritance for their families. To counterbalance this the Protestants were given Ferdinand's secret assurance, not official and not legally binding, that an ecclesiastical territorial lord would not be allowed to oppress his native knights and cities on account of religion. This so-called "eternal" Religious Peace of Augsburg was not a profession of tolerance, but merely a political and legal instrument that laid down as law, in the interest of general peace in Germany, some of the facts of historical development. It was a compromise, with many imperfections and inadequacies. Outwardly the struggle for the new faith was at an end. But it had not yet been inwardly resolved. It was bound to continue.

What Luther had promised, John Calvin from the north of France performed; he welded political and religious factors into a single cogent whole. In Basel he composed the first evangelical doctrinal system. In Geneva he created a theocracy that was clerical, moral, and social, with all the rigidity but all the coerciveness of intolerance. All the elements in France and in Switzerland that had turned to Lutheranism seized now on this new spirit. Issuing from Geneva, a fresh and heartening influence was wafted to the German Reformed, who needed to move onward politically. The Lutheranism recognized by imperial law always contained something quietistic, shrinking from macrocosm to microcosm; the world was after all a vale of tears, and it was the business of the authorities, not of the faithful, to deal with practical problems.

A CULTURAL STANDSTILL

If one compares the Germany of the early Reformation with the Germany of the Religious Peace of Augsburg, it becomes clear that the intellectual flowering of the beginning had not continued. There were no more universal thinkers such as Nicholas of Cusa, whose work in the natural sciences laid the basis for the Polish canon Copernicus. Another kindred spirit was the great Theophrastus Paracelsus (died 1541), who regarded world affairs as a sum of natural processes and wanted to gain the assurance of knowledge only from experience and experiment. Thomas Murner, Geiler von Kaisersberg, Sebastian Brant, and Johannes Fischart vied with one another in poetry. They were all merry and forthright fellows, intrepid fighters, and masters of forceful language. How heartily the excellent Hans Sachs of Nürnberg hailed Luther as "the Wittenberg nightingale"!

At the beginning of the epoch the German churches and the houses of burghers boasted all manner of treasures; wood-carvers and painters, goldsmiths and workers in bronze gave the patricians a sumptuous setting for their self-confident sense of life. For a long time the fine arts had remained on the plane of craftsmanship in Germany, but now Mathias Grünewald, Albrecht Dürer, and Hans Holbein attained the loftiest peaks of immortal creation. Many others came after them: Lucas Cranach, who painted portraits of the heroes of the Reformation, and the sculptors Peter Vischer, Veit Stoss, and Adam Kraft. At the end of the epoch only a faint gleam remained of this serene affirmation of manifold reality, this sensuous and spiritual fulness of living. Everything grew coarser, more commonplace, more sensual. All that was sensitive and personal in the world of the spirit was completely absorbed by the religious struggle. For the best among the people this struggle was a conflict of conscience of the most serious sort, and their whole being was drawn into sympathy with the movement.

The Reformation did not bring the Germans true freedom, but only a self-determined bond. Luther and his followers destroyed a world unity and failed to create what they most longed for: a German unity. Luther's work in morals and education became the premise for further development of Germans, of north Germans and central Germans in particular. The concepts of government, duty, obedience, and vocation, as they evolved from Lutheranism, were not quite the same in Reformed and in Catholic Germany. Certain characteristics of north German, northeast German, and also Swabian state life, government, and thought stem directly from Luther's ideas. The old particularism of the Saxony-Brandenburg electoral group was now appreciably strengthened by the churchly and the ethical. Similar Lutheran influences made themselves felt in the Scandinavian and Baltic countries. Lutheranism, however, never became a world power such as Calvinism. There was no national church in Germany, and for this reason religious momentum reinforced every form of particularism. On the other hand religious cleavage among the German people allowed them to take part in the three great credal spheres of culture in Europe. This wealth of experience compensated to a certain extent for fragmentation.

The Emperor, having permitted Lutheranism to survive, could no longer make an appearance in Rome. No imperial coronation could ever again be effected by the Pope. For the Emperor was the prefect of the church. At the coronation he received the lesser ecclesiastical ordination; the alb was part of his coronation attire. But to the very end of the Holy Roman Empire the Emperor took an oath of obedience and in return received papal confirmation. Thus the old moot bond had shrivelled to a mere gesture. Charles V had to renounce the idea of handing down and perpetuating a world empire. His son Philip did not become emperor, but he never really accepted this fact in his own mind. The Roman church was rejuvenated and tried to regain the ground it had lost. In these attempts Spain and not Austria was the power that aided it. Madrid and Rome formed their alliance that figures in world history. The Counter-Reformation began.

Chapter 10

THE COUNTER-REFORMATION

AND THE THIRTY YEARS' WAR

SPANISH INFLUENCE. THE JESUITS

THE KING of Spain had to leave the imperial office, in the end, to the younger branch of the house of Habsburg, but the world power of Charles V passed to his son Philip, not his brother Ferdinand. Spain's subject lands in Europe now were the Netherlands, the Free County of Burgundy, Milan, Naples, Sicily, and Sardinia. Through his Burgundian heritage the King of Spain formally secured the status of a prince of the Empire; the seventeen provinces of the Netherlands, however, were withdrawn from imperial legislation from 1548. Through her Italian possessions Spain ruled this part of the Roman imperial heritage also. Events in Europe had taken a definite turn toward the West. Spanish power ringed France so closely as to endanger her existence. The Spanish crown, with the vast treasures of precious metals from the American colonial empire, was able to support huge armies and strike out toward the goals of world politics.

The earliest standing army in Western history was the Spanish one in the Netherlands. Formerly the problem had been how to demobilize an army of mercenaries once it had been assembled. An army as a permanent institution was bound to make war itself a permanent institution. The mightier such a professional army grew, the wider the theatre of war could become, and the more sharply it would be affected by the troops economically and sociologically. These facts were realized by the leaders of the Spanish infantry, by men like the iron Duke of Alva and Prince Alexander Farnese, with his clever chess player's strategy. Even recurrent national bankruptcies did not loose the incubus of Spanish world power. Peasants and traders were mired in poverty; the crown remained rich. In this situation the

Austrian line of the Habsburgs was helpless. There were many tensions between the elder and the younger lines, but in general it must be said that the Habsburgs more than any other European dynasty set the interests of their house above everything else. Again and again personal grudges were suppressed. And so the counsel, the diplomacy, and the riches of the Spanish line directed the policies of the Austrian line. Germany did not wish to be ruled by Spaniards. The German princes were in complete accord with the feeling of the people in resisting everything Spanish and in refusing Philip II as emperor. But no one could prevent his becoming the secret emperor of the Counter-Reformation. Germany traced his spirit in the Thirty Years' War.

Spain had been a cradle of crusades. Campaigns against the Moors, the Jews, and the American Indians had been conducted in a crusading spirit. The European crusade against Protestantism issued from Spain. The crusade concept was kept alive constantly in the struggle against the Mohammedans. The constant threat of the Turks had spurred emperors and popes to desperate efforts. Could they not unite Christendom? The Western world had learned much about both fanaticism and organization from the religious wars of Islam. Now the restored Roman church adapted the crusade idea to the destruction of Protestant heresy. In accordance with the pattern of earlier religious wars, the quarrel between creeds deepened into a struggle steeped in bitter hatred, a war of life and death characterized by cruelties utterly alien to the feuds of the Middle Ages. For this new crusade Spain furnished the soldiers, the funds, and a newly formed order that held itself to be the very banner of God and was headed by a general who administered military discipline.

Ignatius Loyola, the founder of the Jesuit Order, had been an officer, and in North Africa he had become acquainted with Mohammedan orders. His Company of Jesus followed only him, the leader. Absolute obedience was demanded of every member, "as though they were corpses." The soldier of Jesus made himself simply a tool for his superiors. Every private concern was laid aside. Spiritual exercises crushed all resistance, and stern selection and constant supervision guarded the hierarchy of offices up to the general of the order in Rome, who recognized none but the Pope as his superior.

The Jesuits were not monks. They did not deny this life. They were practical and versed in worldly matters; they wished to be effective. They studied all the arts and sciences and were found in every sort of calling. They were politicians and wanted to rule. The more polished, the more experienced, the more rationalistic the members of the order were, the more effectively they could serve their great cause, the authority of the Roman world church. Of course the Jesuits were confronted with the envy of the older orders. They had to reckon with resistance from all who were interested in a national church, with all the native and deep-rooted elements that regarded their alien, cosmopolitan proceedings with deep distrust. The spirit of St. Benedict and the spirit of St. Francis stood fast against Loyola, and certainly the learned and politically experienced Dominicans had no wish to be crowded out. But the Jesuits had a very definite advantage in one respect: their temper and their methods were in line with the modern absolutism that was developing. The princes wanted just such officers and diplomats. Here was the combination of intelligence, obedience, and flexibility that the times demanded.

Spanish Jesuit theologians gave the decrees of the Council of Trent their uncompromising tone of hostility toward Protestantism, toward the Germanic spirit of feudal constitutionalism. It was the Jesuits who rejected the bishops' attempts at independence. The supreme power of the Pope was once more established, and the chasm between clergy and laity became too wide to be bridged. The sacrifice of the Mass was to be consummated only by a consecrated priest. A mutual understanding with the general priesthood of the Protestants was henceforth wholly impossible. But many even of the Catholic princes in Germany had regarded the lay chalice, the marriage of priests, and the use of the German language in services as entirely acceptable. The Pope now took over the Inquisition from Spain—that is, the system of clerical jurisdiction over heretics. He sent nuncios or special representatives to supervise the bishops, and from this the diplomatic representation of the curia in foreign countries developed. He started the Index, the register of publications condemned by the church. A real blessing was the abolition of abuses such as the sale of offices and indulgences and the holding of multiple benefices.

Regularity and neatness, discipline and organization were imposed, and the result was a genuine moral and spiritual renewal of the Roman church. But in its teaching the church insisted on its ancient traditions, quite in line with historical development. It affirmed itself as the best and indeed the only source of salvation. The Roman church did not turn back to the teachings of primitive Christianity or to St. Augustine. It had been moulded by Thomas Aquinas, and it held fast by him, true to the spirit of late antiquity and of Oriental despotism. Dissidents were branded as heretics, and for heretics there was nothing but the curse of eternal damnation. Early in his career Loyola showed great interest in Germany, where Catholicism was exposed to special dangers. The defeat of Catholicism in Germany might well be the prologue to catastrophe. Köln had the first German Jesuit college, founded in 1544. Loyola was also responsible for the establishment of the Collegium Germanicum in Rome in 1573 to train fighters against Protestantism in Germany. After the Religious Peace of Augsburg the German bishops took no further part in the sessions at Trent. Everything was tuned to battle.

THE PROGRESS OF PROTESTANTISM. EMPEROR FERDINAND I (1556–64)

Protestantism made significant progress in Germany, where it was helped along by the inadequacy of discipline and education among the Catholic lower clergy. Toward the beginning of the movement the Protestant minister was usually of better character than the Catholic priest. The theological faculties at the universities of Freiburg, Vienna, and Köln were deserted. In Austria the nobility often claimed the *jus reformandi,* the right to reform their territories, though only those lords who were immediate to the Empire were entitled to it. It provided an easy way for the feudal lords to seize the valuable land of churches and monasteries. The canons in the ecclesiastical principalities of the Empire all belonged to the old nobility. In many cases, having taken only minor orders, they remained laymen and defended the interests of their kin, the secular princes, with zeal. The chances of getting hold of a principality were extremely good. Younger aristocrats were chosen as bishops, and immediately secularization of the property set in, a process by which the helpful canons profited.

The power of the territorial dynasties grew, and particularism was strengthened, all in defiance of the ecclesiastical reservation of the Religious Peace of Augsburg. Imperial law suffered serious infringement. That the Protestants did not recognize this reservation was unimportant from the legal point of view. Religious convictions ruptured the strait-jacket of the law, and the Protestants had a good conscience about what they were doing. In this way all the north German bishoprics except Hildesheim were secularized. Either they became independent principalities, or they were combined with other sovereignties already in existence. The movement spread to southern Germany. As early as 1555 all German lands with the exception of Bavaria and Austria were predominantly Protestant. If the Habsburgs and the Wittelsbachs prevented Germany from attaining credal unity, we must interpret it as a belated but terrible revenge taken by the southeast for its neglect by the Empire.

Compared to the world Emperor, Charles V, Emperor Ferdinand I always played the role of the younger who had to do all the dirty work. The everyday affairs that fell to his share were not such as to widen his narrow horizons, and he knew the Empire and its problems too well to entertain great hopes for himself. He was the first Habsburg with a specifically Austrian and no longer central European point of view. At the Council of Trent he won certain special rights for his hereditary dominions, which he was most reluctant to leave—rights that paved the way both religiously and politically for the separation of Austrian dynastic power from the Empire. His main problem was the Turkish peril, which was regularly exploited by the Protestant estates of the Empire to force religious concessions. Since Ferdinand did not wish to avail himself of Spain's help, he decided in 1562 on an eight-year truce with the Ottoman Empire. According to the provisions of this truce, a presentation of thirty thousand ducats was made to Constantinople annually. The financing of this tribute could not indeed be managed without the support of King Philip II of Spain; thus the Spanish crown purchased the chance to conduct its Catholic world politics in western Europe.

The Huguenot wars in France, the revolt in the Spanish Netherlands, and Spain's attack on England are the great chapters in the struggle between the Roman church, as restored by Spain, and Calvinism—a struggle that loosed every force of nation, class, and individual against Catholic imperialism. In all these countries the religious struggle became an affair of the awakening nationality, and the result was that everywhere secular rulership, with a strong national cast, gave rise to a more or less national church, in the face of which those of other faiths played only the part of a tolerated minority. Spain and Italy were, and remained, purely Catholic countries with very slight development of evangelical sects, which in any case lacked political significance. The Council of Trent had a pronounced Romanist bias. Although the Italian Pope did not always see eye to eye with the King of Spain, both Italy and Spain were wholly in accord with the spirit of Trent. On the other side England was dominated by its national church, with a small Roman Catholic minority, and the Scandinavian states were just as Lutheran as Spain and Italy were Catholic. After decades of religious civil war France saved herself by evolving a Roman Catholic state church with strong Gallican tendencies; collective political interests triumphed over Huguenot particularism, and the Huguenots had to resign themselves to being a tolerated, legally recognized, and privileged minority within a state organism.

Many a belligerent German baron took up arms for the Huguenots, who were kindred spirits, but only a few made their fortunes; most of them perished. There was a saying at the time that France was the graveyard of the German nobility. Politically the German princes remained neutral. The period of the Counter-Reformation was uneventful in Germany from a military point of view, but it was filled with individual struggles in both politics and religion. Germany is the only country in Europe that was not strengthened as a nation by the religious schism. Everywhere else the dynasties undertook religious reform and found a solution in a national church. In Germany territorial lords seized on religious reform and gave it a turn that mortally threatened every possibility of developing a national state church and shattered German nationality, indeed the very idea of it.

PROTESTANT FEUDS. EMPEROR MAXIMILIAN II (1564–76)

For a brief period it looked as though Protestantism might win over the major part of Germany. But the chance was wrecked by internal feuds. The Bible was the sole criterion of Protestant doctrine, so that biblical interpretation was crucial. Even on purely scholarly grounds interpretations might differ fundamentally. Differences of opinion of this sort did not remain within the limits of academic dispute. They became questions of conscience and were fought out with passionate intensity. The Protestants no longer acknowledged any Holy Father or any council. In matters of faith the decision lay with the territorial lord, who possessed the highest ecclesiastical authority within his domains. But a territorial lord could err, and different territorial lords could come to very different decisions. Here was a fresh cause for disharmony and pangs of conscience. The "paper pope," the Bible, did not always make for the happiness of the Protestants. Sects multiplied. Theological sophistries were taken too seriously; they were defended with obstinacy and asperity.

Melanchthon had to endure fierce attacks because of his conciliatory spirit. He was willing to put up with certain relatively unimportant Catholic institutions if the solid core of Protestantism found approval. The Lutherans met all Calvinistic influences, and the Calvinists all Lutheran influences, with hatred. In the course of these conflicts such vile language was used and such coarse ideas expressed that a sensitive humanist like Melanchthon was stunned; in 1560 he welcomed death as a release from the "raving of the theologians." And things did not stop at abuse, slander, and setting people by the ears. A pupil of the Nürnberg reformer Osiander, the court preacher Funck, was executed in East Prussia because he taught justification by faith. Lutheranism became a barren creed, academic, quibbling, and alien to the people. German delight in endless pedantic, self-satisfied arguments on theoretical questions passed over from Lutheran theology into all the fields of knowledge and thence into literature and politics.

The most important event in the Protestant camp was that the Elector Palatine went over to the Reformed. The Heidelberg Catechism (1563) is the classical document of German Calvinism; it preserved Luther's deep religious emotion and had something of Melanchthon's noble clarity, while it suppressed the doctrine of predestination. The attitude of the most outstanding elector supported the spread of the Reformed creed in all western Germany. Religious problems revived the old friction between the electoral Palatinate and the electorates of northern and eastern Germany. To electoral Saxony the conversion of the inhabitants of the Palatinate to a heretical sect that was not even recognized by the laws of the Empire was a challenge. All the followers of Melanchthon, the so-called crypto-Calvinists, were ruthlessly persecuted in electoral Saxony. The leaders of the movement were imprisoned for life, and Krakow, the chancellor, was brutally tortured to death. Because German Protestantism was so torn within itself, it never spread to France or to the Netherlands; there Calvinists were active, whereas in Germany Calvinists met with genuine sympathy only among the Reformed. The petty princes in Germany saw the revolutionary character of the rebels as a menace to the dynastic principle that they cherished, for according to the views of some Calvinistic opponents of monarchy it was allowable and even desirable to kill a tyrant.

Emperor Ferdinand's successor, Maximilian II (1564-76), was the only Habsburg who had a certain degree of personal understanding of Protestantism. He had no love for the Spaniards, and he had the less for having lived for a time at the court in Madrid. The old envy toward the mightier senior line stirred in the young archduke. Maximilian read Luther's writings, corresponded with Protestant princes, was disgusted by theological squabbling, and would have liked to be a declared adherent of a true Christian faith based on reconciliation. To the very last he took communion in both forms, and on his deathbed he rejected the Catholic rites. But this amiable gentleman was not cut out for either a statesman or a religious champion.

Maximilian submitted to political necessities. He had hopes of the Spanish inheritance and sent his two sons to Madrid to be educated. The Turkish peril forbade any break with Madrid. There were no military successes, although this time the diet apportioned more funds than ever before. A truce renewed the obligation to pay tribute and again proved the weakness of Habsburg Austria. Ferdinand I had divided the hereditary lands among his sons, and this division hardly heightened the power of resistance. It seemed so much the easier to gain the Emperor's consent for individual "religious concessions," which he granted in the hope of some later unification of faiths. The nobility, favoured in all this, proceeded as if it were immediate to the Empire, for now the Emperor was the territorial lord. In the rural portions of Lower Austria the Augsburg Confession was tacitly tolerated, while in the cities of the territorial lords evangelical services were forbidden. Such half-measures were characteristic of Maximilian II. He was neither a hypocrite nor a professed believer, but a decent man who had got out of his depth.

The Catholic counter-movement savoured this favourable situation to the full. The most promising point of attack among the temporal dominions was Bavaria, whose dukes were the only German princes never to have vacillated in matters of religion. The Jesuits started thriving establishments in Ingolstadt and Regensburg. Bavarian princes were given benefices, and in this way church property was protected from any sort of Protestant secularization. Fulda, Mainz, Jülich, and Cleve were then won back to Catholicism. The Bishop of Würzburg, from the most distinguished noble family of the Spessart Forest region, the Echters of Mespelbrunn, was conspicuous for the energy and efficiency of his rule. A typical representative of the new clerical absolutism, he stands at the head of a whole series of significant Catholic ecclesiastical princes. His program included persecutions of Jews and of witches, but it also provided for the erection of magnificent buildings and the encouragement of every industry. Thus several Wittelsbach princes united numerous ecclesiastical principalities under their crosier, and it became customary to speak of the ecclesiastical realm of the Wittelsbachs on the Rhine and in Westphalia. The Counter-Reformation made use of dynastic interests in this way with increasing success.

For some years (1576–84) Köln was the centre of a struggle invested with romantic charm because of the personalities involved in it. Archbishop Count Truchsess of Waldburg had a mistress, the beautiful canoness Countess Agnes of Mansfeld. The girl's relatives insisted on marriage, and the elector was ready to join the Reformed. He would have preferred to retire to happiness and private life after suitable indemnification. But Protestant interests did not permit him to abdicate, and he had to take up a struggle for which he was not fitted. He tried to transform the archbishopric into a temporal principality for his house. That would have meant a Protestant majority in the board of electors. The succession of the Habsburgs was endangered. Spain regarded Köln as a threat to her fight for the Netherlands. This Köln romance became an affair of world politics. The outcome was that Count Truchsess had to flee to Strassburg with his young wife; there, as a dean of the cathedral, he was to die forgotten. A Wittelsbach prince took over the archbishopric. The war of Köln was the prologue to a far worse war, which was to last thirty years.

EMPEROR RUDOLF II (1576–1612). SECTARIAN DIFFERENCES BECOME ACUTE

The two camps faced each other with mounting bellicosity. There was no imperial authority strong enough to mediate. In Madrid, under his Spanish uncle's influence, Emperor Rudolf II, the son of Maximilian II, had turned out a connoisseur and antiquarian. In the style of the Escorial, he amassed in the Hradschin in his beloved Prague precious things and rarities from all over the world. Spanish etiquette, too, had become part of Emperor Rudolf's existence. In the midst of his treasures he led the life of a lonely misanthrope, and as the years went on his political unfitness only increased. He had to be begged to sign even the most necessary documents. He became more and more irritable and refused to see any strangers at all. His moods grew dangerous, not to say sinister. Servants were the make-shift rulers, and the most important matters of state were decided on the back stairs.

In the face of the Catholic successes electoral Saxony now tried to establish the doctrine of communion in a mild Lutheran form through the so-called Formula of Concord (1580). This formula and other documents were collected in a *Book of Concord* in an effort to settle the sorry doctrinal strife of Protestantism, at least in an external and practical fashion. A reaction toward Lutheranism in the Palatinate appeared to favour this plan. But important princes of the Empire, such as the Landgrave of Hesse, refused to accept the *Book of Concord,* and the Reformed came into power again in the Palatinate. Nevertheless the book was eventually endorsed by fifty-one princes and thirty-five cities. The project of an all-German general conference did not materialize. In any case it would have broken up in disagreement. The Reformed tried to create a counter-concord. It was quite clear that the three parties in the Empire irritated one another increasingly, that all imperial legislation was paralysed by the religious struggles, and that even the diets were unproductive. The brave Elector Casimir of the Palatinate was the only prince of the Empire who saw the danger to the Protestant cause in France and the Netherlands and who tried to save the day by quick action. But of course he was too weak to matter. A fight against Spanish and French Catholic imperialism offered tangible hopes for a time. It would have brought the military issue to a head and taken it out of German territory. But nothing of the sort came to pass.

Conditions in Germany degenerated, because now the Catholic party believed itself strong enough to air the question of the ecclesiastical reservation. In the so-called *Vierklosterstreit* (squabble of the four monasteries) the supreme court decided that the Protestants should no longer be permitted to seize monasteries that were members of the local diet. The reply of the Protestants was the vitiation of all imperial justice: they refused to give up the monasteries they had acquired. At the Diet of Regensburg in 1608 the Protestants even made their aid against the Turks conditional on a reaffirmation of the Religious Peace. Thereupon the Catholic estates of the Empire demanded the restitution of all ecclesiastical property acquired since 1555. At this point the electoral Palatinate, electoral Brandenburg, and several smaller estates of the Empire left the diet. The imperial constitution ceased to function; its central organ had been blasted. In the same year, 1608, the Protestant estates under the leadership of the electoral Palatinate, but without electoral Saxony, formed a Union. The response to this act was the founding of a Catholic League under the leadership of Duke Maximilian of Bavaria. In this way the hereditary feud of the two branches of the Wittelsbach family rose to a level of historical importance. The notion of forming combinations disposed of the little that remained of imperial unity.

Both groups of princes formed contacts with their religious kin in other countries. Schism in Germany grew into conflict on a European scale. Duke Maximilian of Bavaria shone forth as a great administrative talent. Religious questions of conscience did not engage him, and military adventures struck him as uncomfortable. He laboured faithfully for the subjects whom destiny had entrusted to his care. As a pupil of the Jesuits he held unreservedly to the restored Roman church, which represented for him and his princely ambitions the highest fulfilment of self-discipline, energy, and bureaucratic efficiency. The duke kept serenely on his way as a careful, responsible territorial lord. For his family, for his dynasty, he strove toward the highest attainable honour, the electoral dignity, and he carried on the old policy of the electors in the Empire even before he reached his goal. True, he despised the Protestants, but he had no wish for an imperial absolutism of the house of Habsburg.

Just such a motive lay behind the events of the time that had the greatest potentialities. For all of Germany's European neighbours religious conflict had led to a strengthening of dynastic central power and to a foreign policy of expansion. The Polish Kingdom, which had again become Catholic, seized Livonia. The Swedish crown became feudal lord of Estonia, and Denmark laid hands on the islands in the Baltic. Russia was pressing forward behind Poland; Sweden made war on both, and she was soon the greatest power in the Baltic region. The Empire was not concerned in these conflicts, for the formal supremacy of the Roman Emperor over the Baltic region no longer possessed any significance. Electoral Brandenburg accepted the Duchy of Prussia from Poland as a fief (1618).

The struggle for liberty in the Netherlands, too, lay outside the sphere of German history. Relations with Germany had worn thin; these lands were suffering and striving for the right to their own historical destiny. Germany did nothing more for them, and they went their own way. The Spanish world power became used only with great difficulty to the idea of giving up even part of its rebellious provinces. When a pause was finally reached (1609) it really amounted to nothing but a twelve-year truce, which established a boundary between the northern and southern Netherlands corresponding to the military situation at the end of the fighting and therefore essentially fortuitous.

After the Swiss Confederation the Republic of the United Netherlands was the second non-dynastic state to receive at least temporary recognition—a political body consisting of Calvinistic estates, liberal and federal, aristocratic and oligarchic, yet rooted in the people and held together militarily by the hereditary stadholdership of the house of Orange. In the northern Netherlands a Catholic minority could be tolerated. In the southern provinces, which remained with Spain, Protestantism was exterminated among the Flemings as well as the

Walloons. Spanish imperialism was preparing to resume the war with the northern Netherlands, which on their side were doing likewise. The Netherlands were building up their alliance with France and England and contending with Spanish intrigues in western Germany. In the economic field the Republic of the United Netherlands brought on the collapse of German power in world commerce by the interest it took, with its fresh spirit of civilian venture, in the German coasts and rivers. Domestic German trade dwindled, mining and industry declined, and in many regions a return to purely agricultural occupations was made, furthered by the predominance of particularistic and denominational interests.

High tolls imposed by the territorial lords paralysed traffic on the Rhine, and much the same was true of other important German rivers. The administrative apparatus of the Empire was impotent in commercial policy. Would the citizen be able to help himself? Many sons of old merchant families were now becoming courtiers. German finance, once so flourishing, was ruined by the world politics of Spain. The new methods of world commerce did not permit the strengthening of German commercial capital, and merchandising broke down in the Thirty Years' War. Manufacturing became antiquated and inefficient; the increasing influx of goods imported from France gave it the death-blow.

The German dynasties were wholly taken up with themselves— with acquiring property and looking out for their own members. The cities suffered severely because of this; their old institutions became set and inflexible. No one worried about the peasant. This weakening of the Empire was bound to encourage neighbouring countries to meddle in Germany's affairs under cover of religious interests. Just as Holland advanced along the coast of the North Sea and along the Rhine, so Swedish trade expanded in the Baltic. The Habsburg dynastic power took very little interest in these developments. Growing Austria, too, shut herself off from the Empire with her toll policy.

After a long period of confusion France showed herself ready again to engage in European and central European politics. United under her great King Henry IV, she was now about to take up with full vigour the struggle against the Spanish and Roman imperialism

188

of the Habsburg dynasty. Every smaller nation that was endangered, every fellowship of faith that was threatened, could count on the help of France. French foreign policy was the very first, in contrast to Spain's, to break away from sheer sectarianism. This had proved advantageous even to King Francis I. Henry IV and his successors brought the new principle fully into play. They protected Florence and Venice, the Protestant cantons of Switzerland, the independent Netherlands, and the German princes against Madrid and Vienna. In line with old usage they made a pawn of the Ottoman Empire to weaken the Habsburg dynasty's position in the east, and they formed contacts with Sweden, the rising power of the northeast.

Even the assassination of King Henry IV (1610) interrupted this policy only for a short time. France, rejuvenated, manifested new national and universal trends. Henry IV wanted all French-speaking countries for his realm: Savoy, Lorraine, and the Walloon region. Since the French language had become more and more predominant in literature and law from the close of the Middle Ages, the disintegrated western border of Germany was now threatened by a principle of mortal consequence to it. And Henry IV cherished plans on a still greater scale, all of which tended toward French hegemony in Europe, whatever their individual purposes may have been. Thus modern France, with its new national, dynastic, and diplomatic development, entered on the struggle against Habsburg clerical imperialism.

The quarrel over the succession in the regions of Jülich and Cleve on the Lower Rhine promised to be the spark to set off the great explosion. All the possible legitimate heirs were evangelical. A key position of the greatest strategic importance was in question. France, the Netherlands, and the evangelical Union agreed to resist the stationing of Catholic troops here. But now one of the prospective heirs, the Palsgrave of Neuburg, turned Catholic in order to secure the help of the Habsburgs. Immediately the Elector of Brandenburg went over to the Reformed so that he might be more acceptable to the Netherlands. It was natural for the Lutherans to be profoundly disturbed by so many changes in faith. Differences became sharper in all camps. For the time being the fight for the succession ended in a compromise. A provisional division of the inheritance between

Brandenburg and Neuburg was agreed on, and the soldiers who had already been called up were sent home. The impotence of the Empire was disheartening as well as absurd.

TROUBLES IN BOHEMIA. EMPEROR FERDINAND II (1619–37)

The incapacity of Emperor Rudolf II had in the meantime put the hereditary Habsburg lands in a most unfortunate situation. Rudolf voluntarily transferred the rule of Upper and Lower Austria to his brothers. The younger, Archduke Matthias, who survived Ernest, the elder, allowed himself to be played off against the Emperor more and more. The diets of Hungary and Moravia, fearful of the Turks, clamoured for a decision, and the diet of Bohemia also pushed forward. They did not want the Emperor to abdicate, but they forced him into making all manner of concessions. The Utraquists of former days had been given new impetus through the evangelical movement of the Germans. Czechs and German Bohemians were co-operating. In 1609 Emperor Rudolf granted all his Bohemian subjects the famous charter securing freedom of conscience to everyone and according to all the nobility, to the royal cities, and to all subjects living in the crownlands the right to build churches and to hold evangelical services publicly. To guard these rights a committee of so-called *defensores* was appointed and given the privilege of summoning a Protestant parliament whenever it wished.

All this was more than the Protestants in any other country under Catholic rule had been able to attain. Something like a Protestant republic on the order of the United Netherlands was formed within the Kingdom of Bohemia. The struggle of the envious Archdukes was bound to continue even on this account. Rudolf was forced to abdicate in all the hereditary lands (1612); though he was still an Emperor, he had no country. He was deeply embittered; and, at once guilty and guiltless, victim of the fraternal feud in the house of Habsburg, he came to an understanding with the Protestant Union. He even thought of becoming a Calvinist. The Austrian poet Franz Grillparzer has immortalized this tragic figure. The unfortunate Rudolf died before the council of electors that he had summoned to his aid could convene.

Archduke Matthias became Emperor. An elderly, childless man who had grown slow, indifferent, and peace-loving, he tried to circumvent or at least to postpone the impending crash. But his well-meant efforts came too late. The most urgent question was that of the succession. Archduke Ferdinand of Styria, his nephew, had every expectation of inheriting all the scattered Habsburg hereditary lands again as a whole. He was a good-natured, not very clever prince, a pious pupil of the Jesuits, the devoted friend of the very intelligent Duke of Bavaria, and of necessity susceptible to Spanish influence and advice. His rule would be sure to lead to a fanatical religious struggle. Should Bohemia accept such a ruler? The Spanish agent, Count Oñate, who had been ambassador in Vienna for many years and had grown grey with a thousand intrigues, persuaded Archduke Ferdinand to sign a secret treaty (1617). This provided that on assuming his inheritance he would cede to the Spanish crown his possessions in Lombardy, on the Upper Rhine, and in Alsace, with several small regions in Italy. The meaning of this agreement was quite clear. Spain was again playing politics against France; she was trying to build up a Rhenish buffer state from the Netherlands to Milan to squeeze that country. For that purpose Spain was again edging in on German possessions at the western boundary. If France were once shut off from central Europe, it would be easy to destroy Protestantism and the particularism of the German estates simultaneously and to erect the Catholic absolutism of the house of Habsburg on the ruins.

For both religious and ethnical reasons tempers were strained in Bohemia. Local events of minor importance, such as the closing of the Protestant church of Klostergrab by the Archbishop of Prague and the Abbot of Braunau's prohibition against erecting an evangelical church in that place, led to revolution. The Bohemian *defensores* intervened. They called a Protestant assembly and complained that the charter had been violated. Now the Archbishop had the church at Klostergrab torn down, and the imperial councillor Martinitz required Protestants to attend Catholic services under penalty of a fine. Emperor Ferdinand ignored the complaint of the *defensores* and forbade any future Protestant meetings. The Protestant estates brought on the final break. In accordance with an old Bohemian custom two imperial envoys, together with their confidential secretary, were thrown out of the windows of the Hradschin. (None of the three, incidentally, was fatally injured.) A provisional government was set up for Bohemia and an army held in readiness. The house of Habsburg took up the challenge. A small army was marched from the Spanish Netherlands to invade Bohemia. The death of Emperor Matthias increased the gravity of the situation, for now the much-dreaded succession of Emperor Ferdinand II impended. It was not recognized in Bohemia, even though Ferdinand had been "accepted" there as the heir to the crown as early as 1617. The Bohemians protested that Bohemia was an elective kingdom. At a general diet of the Bohemian crownlands Ferdinand was deposed, partly because of his having interfered with feudal privileges and partly because he had recognized a hereditary Spanish right to Bohemia, which was certainly contrary to the constitution. The diet elected Frederick V, the Calvinistic Elector of the Palatinate, almost unanimously.

THE WINTER KING

The Elector of the Palatinate, Frederick, was the charming and knightly husband of an ambitious woman, Elizabeth, the daughter of the first King of Great Britain, James I, a Stuart. The beauty and pride that she inherited from her grandmother, Mary Stuart, proved the glory and the undoing of this princess also. Frederick's father-in-law in London did not wish to become involved in Continental quarrels and advised him not to accept the Bohemian crown. James I was just making approaches to the Spanish world power. His son Charles was about to marry a Spanish princess, and his daughter Elizabeth must simply make the best of the situation. But that was exactly what she did not do.

Frederick, one of the last princes of the German Renaissance, was only moderately gifted, and he needed someone to back him up. To him there was something oppressive in the tradition of Reformed Heidelberg, whose university had proudly and freely kept up its connection with western European Calvinism and whose famous castle, with its different buildings, was a glowing testimony to the Dutch and Italian taste of the epoch. The Palsgrave of the Rhine was the first and most eminent secular prince of the Empire. The Union, which he headed, promised to protect his hereditary lands while he assumed the Bohemian crown. From the point of view of international Calvinism this crown was a mere beginning. This would not be the first time that a reordering of the Empire had issued from Bohemia. Only one answer to the aggressive Habsburg attitude was possible: a Protestant emperorship—the separation, therefore, of universal supremacy from the idea of Rome and the establishment in Germany of a rulership based on social groupings and on a national church, such as the Huguenots had projected in France, such as had been realized in the northern Netherlands, and such as was to be fought for in England. Frederick, to be sure, had nothing of a William of Orange, of a Coligny, or of a Cromwell in him.

Emperor Ferdinand II was in a most unpleasant predicament. The diets of Hungary and Austria made common cause with the Bohemians. Bethlen Gabor, the Prince of Transylvania, in his greed for independence turned against Vienna. But it was possible to build up a Catholic front very quickly. The leader of the Catholic League, the Duke of Bavaria, was won over to the business by dazzling promises, with electoral rank in the lead. The neutrality of electoral Saxony was purchased by the prospect of acquiring Upper and Lower Lusatia. Lutheran envy wished a swift downfall for the Palsgrave. His one brief winter as King of Bohemia gave the unfortunate prince the historical name of the Winter King. It was half with irony and half with pity that Frederick's contemporaries regarded the collapse of a government the effectiveness of which his own healthy instincts had doubted from the very first. The fate of Bohemia was decided by the Battle of the White Mountain (1620), even before negotiations with Denmark and Sweden for assistance could produce results. This engagement was won by Duke Maximilian and his excellent Walloon general, the Count of Tilly, who had been schooled by the Spaniards.

Unhappy Bohemia was terribly punished. The documents left behind by the vanquished government supplied all necessary proofs. Emperor Ferdinand cut the charter to pieces with his own hands. All the Catholic nobles and clergy returned. The *defensores* and their aides were arrested and brought before an extraordinary tribunal. Twenty-seven leaders were executed, and the property of all the rest was confiscated. The Emperor had contracted substantial war debts, and since he wanted to be as independent of Spanish funds as possible, Bohemia had to submit to an unprecedented drain on her finances. The property of all fugitives was seized, and most of the cities were deprived of their revenues. Anyone who had not stepped forward as an adherent of the Emperor was open to suspicion on that score alone. Thus it happened that three fourths of all land changed hands and the population decreased from three million to eight hundred thousand. Fines, obligatory contributions, and currency depreciation ruined the old class of property-owners, while unscrupulous adventurers made their fortunes. Silesia and the two Lusatias escaped punishment because they were occupied by the troops of electoral Saxony.

THE STRUGGLE FOR THE PALATINATE. DENMARK INTERVENES

Duke Maximilian of Bavaria counted on the electoral dignity that had been promised him, and this became one of the reasons for continuing the war. Most of the electors, from a feeling of solidarity, resented the proscription of the Winter King. England and Spain both worked against it. The conveyance of the Rhenish Palatinate to Bavaria appeared undesirable to all the neighbouring countries. Only France supported Maximilian: to her a strong Bavaria was a welcome tool. The Protestant Union was dissolved. A few brave princes and lords nevertheless entered the fray: Margrave George Frederick of Baden-Durlach; Ernest of Mansfeld, an illegitimate scion of the family of the Counts of Mansfeld; and finally the bold Christian of Halberstadt, the administrator of this secularized bishopric, a Brunswick prince of indomitable Guelph initiative who conducted a campaign on behalf of his beautiful cousin the Winter Queen Elizabeth as though it were a tournament, and always wore her left glove on his general's hat. But these hastily assembled Protestant troops were no match for the superior leadership of the Spaniards and of Tilly. The part of the Palatinate on the right bank of the Rhine was taken under Bavarian administration, that on the left bank occupied by Spain. Emperor Ferdinand hit on a temporary solution by conferring the rank of Elector Palatine on Maximilian as an individual, while reserving after the latter's death the agnate rights of the Winter King. But in a secret treaty he promised the Bavarian hereditary electoral rank. Maximilian, in spite of his affability, was a ruthless creditor. He occupied the Austrian hereditary lands as security for his claims. The Emperor found himself having to recognize demands for twelve million gulden damages.

In 1623 the position of the Catholics was excellent. Bethlen Gabor, however, was able to negotiate a tolerable peace. The Spaniards claimed the right of transit through the passes of Grisons, which supplied the only land connection between Spain's Italian possessions and the Austrian hereditary lands. But the war was resumed, with local struggles growing into a general European conflict. The weakness of the Viennese ruling house, with the fact that Madrid had become the centre of European power, made Germany's disintegration into southern, Rhenish, and northeastern groups of states a politically decisive fact; the development in this direction can be traced back to the days of Henry the Lion. This interpretation throws considerable light on the special part played by electoral Saxony and on the reluctance of the Lower Saxon circle to become involved in the turmoils of war.

To the Scandinavian states this situation offered a notable chance of widened power. Economic considerations were as serious here as in the expeditions of the German kings to Rome in the Middle Ages. With a comparatively long period of peace Germany had become a really rich country. The cities were overflowing with goods that had been accumulating for generations. Capital, which found itself increasingly excluded from the new enterprises of world commerce, sought the fields of mining, construction, and the useful arts. The Scandinavian states remained backward by comparison. Just as in former days Italy had drawn the Germans, so Germany, economically prosperous though politically torn asunder, now attracted her northern neighbours as a magnetic field with but slight powers of resistance. The King of Denmark, Christian IV, was a gifted and enterprising prince who had been at odds with the cities of Lower Saxony for years. In his capacity of Count of Holstein, an estate of the Empire, he tried to extend this legitimate connection so as to push into the Empire much as Spain and France were doing. He tried, for instance, to obtain the bishoprics of Bremen and Verden for his son. Secularization here, too, was to be a means of making Denmark's position dominant in the Lower Saxon circle, to the chagrin of his German associates. King Christian was striving for gains such as Sweden was later to carry off on a grander scale. Thus the German border in the north was now crumbling away just as the one in the west did.

Danish plans acquired momentum from the shift in the international situation. Great Britain and Spain broke off relations; the marriage plans of both dynasties missed fire. Charles, the heir to the English throne, married the sister of the King of France. Cardinal Richelieu was raised to the post of French prime minister. France and England made a treaty with Holland that involved subsidies and started negotiations with Denmark, which were concluded at The Hague. England and Holland assumed the obligation to pay subsidies to Denmark, and in return King Christian set up an army. A northern front was thus being erected against the Habsburgs, and France played a deft hand in the game. The Danish King was all the more eager for action because there was bound to be interference from Sweden.

The young King of Sweden, Gustavus Adolphus (1611–32), had successfully maintained himself against Denmark and had won victories in the Baltic countries. He was fighting with the Catholic Poles for supremacy in the Baltic region. His marriage to the sister of Elector George William of Brandenburg was a bond between Gustavus Adolphus and the territorial princes in northeastern Germany. The Duchy of Prussia, which had been connected with Brandenburg since 1618, was a Polish fief. Brandenburg and Sweden regarded Poland as their common enemy, and religious prejudice intensified the antagonism. Electoral Brandenburg, under weak leadership, would have preferred to keep out of all these struggles. Holland and the western powers wanted the help of the two northern kings, but traditional Scandinavian rivalry, with Denmark and Norway on the one hand and Sweden on the other, stood in the way. Gustavus Adolphus demanded compensation and security for himself; he claimed the city of Wismar and the secularized bishopric of Bremen, which Denmark was also eyeing with interest. Gustavus Adolphus then attacked Poland. Even at that time many of the Lower Saxon estates would have preferred Swedish direction to Danish leadership. But now they were past choosing. The Danish King got himself chosen commander in Lower Saxony. Well supplied with Dutch money, the gallant swashbuckler Ernest of Mansfeld also put in an appearance in the north German theatre of war.

WALLENSTEIN (1583–1634)

Once more Emperor Ferdinand found himself in a bad fix. The Spaniards were stepping up their demands; they were asking now for bases in East Friesland and on the Baltic. A plan for a Spanish and German admiralty emerged, for the profitable Baltic trade of the Dutch and the superiority of their fleet could be destroyed only by sea. The Viennese court was oppressed by its dependence on the Catholic League, and more extortions by Bavaria were likely. At this juncture a wealthy Bohemian noble appeared on the scene and offered his aid: Albrecht von Wallenstein.

Wallenstein came from the rural Czech minor nobility. His family was evangelical, but as an adult he was converted to Catholicism under the influence of a trip to Italy. During his entire life religious prejudice was foreign to him. His eminent talent was for mathematical calculations, and he devoted himself to the study of astronomy and astrology, which, in the style of the times, had a scientific as well as a speculative and superstitious character. Then he made a financier and organizer of himself. He exploited the collapse of Bohemia more thoroughly than anyone else. One advantageous marriage had laid the foundation for a princely fortune; a second furnished connections with the upper circles at the Viennese court. His talent for administration and economics could not long remain obscure. As early as 1624 he became a prince of the Empire.

The most important business of the times was now the war. The new standing armies, according to the Spanish mode, consumed enormous sums of money, far in excess of what the ordinary economic arrangements could supply. Setting up a regiment became a speculative affair, for it was a sociological and economic entity in the first place and only secondarily a military and legal one. The practice was for the regiments to live on their pay and to fall back on the country's resources only in emergency; money payment might be made in place of supplying rations for men and horses. Wallenstein introduced a new system. In his view the land should support the army; supplies and pay were therefore secured by forced contributions. Wallenstein's soldiery descended on burgher and peasant households like a swarm of locusts, plundering and enslaving the inhabitants like any foreign invader. They swaggered like lords, with neither shame nor scruple. This system of Wallenstein's had developed in the course of Bohemia's reconversion to Catholicism. Reminiscences of the Roman armies of antiquity may have played a part in it; Wallenstein luxuriated in the imperialist dreams of a Cæsar.

For this military economist his martial state meant power and a future. The larger the army, the better and surer the final gains would be. For the underlying aim of Wallenstein's enterprises was power. He, the last and greatest *condottiere,* wanted to make the leap to a *principe* and absolute rulership. There were enough examples to go by; the times tended to dissolve tradition, and such times and such turns opened up unprecedented prospects to the bold heart and the clever brain. All the military leaders, great and small, were fighting for a cause, but also for themselves. The type of conscientious and selfless officer, such as Tilly, remained an exception. But the most remarkable thing about Wallenstein was that he was not a great general. As a commander he pondered and calculated instead of acting. There was more to this than caution, more than a well-thought-out strategic system: it meant actual weakness. Here is a partial explanation of Wallenstein's dependence on his generals and his desire for peace at any price, his tendency to allay any sort of conflict without coming to grips with the essential problems, simply by a reasonable compromise by which the peacemaker himself stood to gain. Wallenstein's conduct in such matters—springing not from humane considerations but from profoundly selfish motives—provides the key to all the contradictions in his career. The Czech patriots knew very well that he would never honestly promote their cause, and they even called him a scoundrel. To the fanatics who had been educated by the Jesuits this Duke of Friedland seemed too lukewarm, too much the sceptic and too lax toward those of different faith; and the German princes were bound to hate him, because he was eating up their lands and wanted to become even as they—or perhaps rather more than they.

In northern Germany the war took a course that was unfortunate for the Protestant cause. The Danish King and his allies were defeated several times, and with the exception of a few English troops no help came from the powers in the west. The Stuarts were now the occasion of revolutionary stirrings in Great Britain, and leadership against the Counter-Reformation, which would have been so fitting for an Elizabethan England, was to fall to Sweden instead. Denmark withstood naval attack. Plans for a fleet were again brought up. Wallenstein harassed the Hanseatic towns, built ships, got together an imperial squadron at Wismar, and besieged Stralsund. He had taken over the principality of Sagan, and now in 1628 this general of the Baltic and of the North Sea had himself made Duke of Mecklenburg, the native princes of Mecklenburg having first been exiled. He helped the Poles against Sweden, while Gustavus Adolphus, for his part, was making a treaty of aid with Stralsund. It could now only be a question of the precise moment when Sweden would enter the war. Denmark and Sweden, the former enemies, drew together under the pressure of imperial victories. Then Denmark was eliminated by a favourable peace. The imperial troops had occupied Schleswig and Jutland; Stralsund, however, had made a brave stand. In the Peace of Lübeck all of Denmark was returned to King Christian, together with his possessions on the Continent, on the sole condition that he should renounce his policy toward the Lower Saxon bishoprics—that is, the policy of penetrating the Empire.

THE EDICT OF RESTITUTION (1629)

The victorious Counter-Reformation was now prepared to strike a telling blow. Emperor Ferdinand had gone through difficult years. In Upper Austria a serious insurrection of the peasants had broken out (1626), due perhaps primarily to oppression by Bavarian troops of occupation. The people saw themselves confronted by the choice of turning Catholic or emigrating after paying heavy imposts. Ferdinand, who took over the country again after eight years, accorded relief in matters of economics and politics, but remained inflexible on the question of religion. The Elector Maximilian was now indemnified first by the Upper Palatinate on the border of Bavaria and Bohemia and later by the Lower Palatinate on the right bank of the Rhine as well. In the Upper Palatinate the Bavarian ruthlessly insisted on the reinstatement of Catholicism. Here too the alternative was either to turn Catholic or to leave the country.

These successes encouraged the Catholic party to take the portentous step in public law that is known as the Edict of Restitution. The question of secularization had become a rat's nest of dynastic, economic, and social and political problems; imperial and territorial law was woven through it. Emperor Ferdinand's attempt to disentangle the whole business by the simple device of issuing an ordinance was prompted essentially by the pressure of Spain and the Pope. In 1629 the edict went forth: Catholic territorial lords might exile their evangelical subjects; only those who adhered to the original Augsburg Confession were to enjoy religious peace; all church properties that had been seized since 1552 were to be restored. Now there was no evangelical authority left that felt safe. Two archbishops, twelve bishoprics, and over five hundred abbeys were affected. A large number of north German prebends reverted to Catholic possession. Saxony, Brandenburg, and Pomerania were saved only by the appearance of the King of Sweden in Germany. The two north German electors would have liked to remain neutral and to continue negotiations, but matters were coming to a head. On the Catholic side there were many feuds between the Jesuits and the older orders. France stiffened the backbone of the estates of the Empire, evangelical as well as Catholic. A rapprochement between France and Bavaria finally led to the defensive alliance of 1631, in which the nuncio acted as mediator.

The German princes felt their liberty jeopardized by the powerful position of the Emperor. The Edict of Restitution seemed a preliminary to absolutistic imperial rule. What could be expected of further edicts that were already projected? The Emperor showed severity even toward Italy now. The Duchy of Mantua was vacant. The Duke of Nevers was next in succession, but Ferdinand refused to give a fief to this vassal of the French crown, and he granted the property to a distant relative, the Duke of Guastalla. This brought France to the point of making war.

All the rancour that had grown up against the Emperor broke loose at the meeting of the electors in Regensburg. The Emperor wanted his son Ferdinand to be elected King of the Romans, but the electors hedged. Their complaints against Wallenstein's methods of warfare were particularly bitter. A consideration of high politics lay behind this: Wallenstein, upstart though he was, might one day

serve as the Emperor's tool against the princes; this military absolutist might effect political absolutism. That was why Wallenstein
must fall. The Emperor sacrificed the creator of his army. As soon
as he had agreed to do so, his cause was lost. He was now unable to
get anything more, either the election of his son or aid from the
Empire against France. Tilly was made commander-in-chief of the
armies of the Empire and of the Catholic League. The Emperor was
to appoint colonels only with the consent of the general, and he was
not to wage war without the counsel of the electors. Thus the leading territorial princes spoiled the Emperor's greatest triumph. Then,
King Gustavus Adolphus of Sweden landed on the Pomeranian
island of Usedom.

GUSTAVUS ADOLPHUS OF SWEDEN (1611–32)

King Gustavus Adolphus of Sweden was the most powerful and
the most attractive figure of this savage time. In him the north German territorial lords became acquainted with a prince who was just
as good a Lutheran as they themselves, but who nevertheless believed
in a great common Protestant cause. How completely the simplicity
and force of the Swedish King eclipsed the wrangling and greed,
the envy and cowardice, of the petty German dynasts! Emperor
Ferdinand, with all his limitations, possessed the magic of a genuine
conviction. In all questions detached from religion he knew how to
win gratitude through leniency. But in Gustavus Adolphus the same
power of faith was coupled with shrewdness and energy. It is
amazing how this King, still so young, attached the rebellious native
nobility to himself and thus carried through the organization of the
peasant army that won his battles. Not till later did he hire mercenaries—whom he paid out of another's pocket, for Sweden always
remained weak economically, and the religious war became one of
conquest and looting. Gustavus Adolphus was an effective field
commander. He invented new tactics based on the simultaneous use
of various kinds of weapons. A dauntless cavalry leader himself, he
pressed beyond the traditional science of manœuvre, defensive
strategy, and fixed fortifications to a form of war involving movement, tactical originality, swift attack, and decisive concentration.
He hated popery and the Jesuits. The sophistical question whether
he acted from religious or political motives would have seemed sense-

less to him and to his contemporaries. His character and his actions were all of a piece. Rhetoric, cant, and extravagant dreams disgusted him. He was direct and genial, firm and steadfast. His fits of temper were brief; he was not dazzled by his own victories. He had a great task to do; he did not want to waste any time in completing it; and the very fact that it was too great to be completed heightens his significance as a man and a statesman. In the game of European politics he found only one partner worthy of his steel, Cardinal Richelieu of France. At the same historical moment both France and Sweden intervened in the affairs of central Europe. They arrested the triumphal progress of Spain and the Empire and set bounds to it. The future shaping of the Continent and Germany's destiny were already clear.

Gustavus Adolphus protected himself by a six years' truce with Poland. He forced the north German princes into an alliance, but too late to prevent the fall of Magdeburg. The destruction of this old religious and cultural centre of northern Germany roused the Protestants of all nations. Who was to blame for the devastating conflagration cannot be determined. Magdeburg's destiny became symbolic, and that is the reason for its historical importance. The turning-point was reached with the victory over Tilly at Breitenfeld: Gustavus Adolphus was master of northern Germany. Everywhere the evangelicals lifted their heads again. Thousands of volunteers flocked to join the Swedish army, which soon became predominantly German in personnel. The King of Sweden had become a hero and the master of German history as well. He thought to take the future of central Europe into his own hands. There is no doubt as to his ultimate aims. He felt strong enough to complete what the Winter King had vainly attempted in Bohemia and the King of Denmark in Lower Saxony.

Gustavus Adolphus signed "eternal" treaties with the estates of the Empire on the Baltic coast. In this way he fitted them into his political system, which presupposed mastery of the Baltic. With the princes of inland Germany the Swedish King made treaties only for limited periods. Thus he secured military supremacy, which, to be sure, he intended to turn to more permanent uses after the victory at Breitenfeld. Sweden was to stand at the head of the *Corpus Evangelicorum,* the group of Protestant estates at the diet of Regensburg, which co-operated for ecclesiastical purposes; it had therefore to enter the Empire as one of its estates, as Denmark and Spain had done earlier. The King thought he could reach his goal by taking over Pomerania, but the German princes resisted these plans. They were reluctant to sign treaties covering more than a short time. The Elector of Brandenburg suggested the marriage of his son to Christina, the only daughter of the Swedish King. Such a union would have perpetuated the connection of Sweden and northern Germany, and the idea of a Protestant empire, which was the objective of all the plans, might have been realized. The cleavage of Germany and central Europe into an Austrian Catholic empire and a north German Protestant empire would not have been a bad solution from the point of view of world history. Northern Germany would certainly not have become non-German; more likely Sweden would have become Germanized.

Gustavus Adolphus now pressed on southward. He occupied the region along the Main River, made his headquarters in Frankfurt, and won another decisive victory over Tilly at the Lech. Here the old general received a mortal wound (1632). Gustavus Adolphus took Nürnberg and Munich. In the meantime the Saxon and Bohemian emigrants invaded Bohemia.

Who could help in such an alarming situation? Wallenstein was living as a prosperous nobleman in Bohemia, with all possible honours and offices—as a prince of the Empire, even though he had received no fief in the Empire from the Emperor, since the electors had refused to let Mecklenburg be transferred to him. The Emperor not only felt under personal obligation to Wallenstein from of old, but also openly regretted his dismissal on broad human grounds. Wallenstein was a power among powers. He realized the force of his name and of his resources. He wanted to take his revenge on the Elector of Bavaria and the Emperor. When Gustavus Adolphus started negotiations with Wallenstein, he found him approachable. Wallenstein's conduct in this connection can hardly be termed treason, for other princes of the Empire were also negotiating with Sweden. A change of front in their own vital interests was not uncommon among German princes. How often had Maurice, the Elector of Saxony, shifted his allegiance! Even Maximilian of Bavaria proceeded most cautiously; we know of his reinsurance treaty with France, the arch-enemy of the imperial house. Moreover Wallenstein was not born a prince of the Empire, but was made one, and in that age of the divinity of kings and of sacrosanct observances, this fact was one of the underlying causes of his fall. The Emperor needed his services again, and Wallenstein made his conditions—the conditions of a war-lord, not those of a subject accepting a charge. He was given the chief command *in absolutissima forma;* the military counsel to the Viennese court had no power to interfere. All matters concerning the army were under Wallenstein's control in the widest sense, and even Ferdinand's successor was not to appear in the army, lest the corps of officers be disorganized by currying favour. Wallenstein was also given the express right to conduct peace negotiations. His claims for indemnification were drawn up with great exactness: for the time being, the hereditary imperial territory of Glogau; later, some substitute for Mecklenburg and the highest rank in the realm, which could only mean that of an elector. Other important points were that Wallenstein was to have the sole right to confiscate property in conquered lands and the prerogative of taking quarters even in the hereditary territories. Such an arrangement could lead to nothing good.

Even assuming that Wallenstein did everything that was expected of him, the construction and carrying out of these promises meant renewed serious conflict between the Emperor and the electors, and in this conflict either territorial princedom or the emperorship might go under. But if Wallenstein was not victorious? Then the arrangement was fraught with great danger to him personally, for he could not possibly return to private life. The Duke, well aware of all this, dared play for the highest stakes; his ambition conjured up for him the role of peacemaker to Europe. Best of all he would have liked to unite central Europe as an Empire against the Turks: for a prince so successful in war and in peace, no crown was out of reach. He did not doubt that he could have his way with the Emperor and the German territorial princes. Wallenstein knew how the wind set there. And a successful and wealthy war-lord could get along with Sweden and France in one way or another.

The great mistake in Wallenstein's reckoning was in underestimating Spain and her influence in Vienna. The Duke of Friedland's cold and calculating passion was thwarted by many personal and material considerations. But the central reason for his ruin was the fact that his plans conflicted with Spanish world policy. Gustavus Adolphus had first offered him Bohemia as a viceroyalty. But Wallenstein wanted more. He was dreaming of the most splendid electorate, of the palsgraviate on the Rhine as the centre of a Rhenish realm. This project was incompatible with the Spanish conception of a land barrier to connect Milan with the Netherlands. A duchy of Franconia figured in the negotiations with Gustavus Adolphus at Nürnberg, but Wallenstein would never have been content with a territory of second rank. His thoughts were bent on the highest. "Insatiate, he strove on and on," as Schiller says of him.

WALLENSTEIN'S END. THE PEACE OF PRAGUE (1635)

Military events took a momentous and unexpected turn at Lützen. Wallenstein lost the battle, but the King of Sweden lost his life. He fell as a victim of his short-sightedness and his rashness (1632). He had no competent successor, and no one, indeed, could have taken his place, though distinguished military leaders came from his school, and the Chancellor Axel Oxenstierna, who had been his diplomatic adviser through many years, was a true statesman who fought brilliantly and stubbornly for the inheritance of his beloved master. Oxenstierna formed the so-called Heilbronn Alliance with the south German Protestants and thus laid a foundation for the continuation of the struggle. The only possible aim of the regency that ruled for the young Queen Christina, who was a minor, was a peace that offered Sweden adequate compensation for her sacrifices. All other plans had been buried with the dead King.

Wallenstein was now facing the great moment of his life. Personally he had desired peace for a long time. Poor Germany was weary of being always a battlefield. Few judges of the situation still regarded a complete triumph of one party over the other as possible. Why, then, should there not be a compromise? Spain, to be sure, was not yet prepared to yield. She wanted to conquer the Netherlands; she took up the struggle with France; and she encouraged Emperor Ferdinand in his fanatical notion that no peace should be concluded with heretics. At that very moment the Spanish general, Feria, was

marching into the Empire in order to establish a connection between Milan and Flanders. Wallenstein interpreted this action as a
challenge and a breach of faith.

After the death of the Swedish King, Emperor Ferdinand expected decisive action on the part of his generalissimo, but little
enough happened. Regensburg, the fortress on the Danube, was
forced to yield. The Elector of Bavaria realized that he had been
deserted, and his bad conscience suggested that this was the personal
revenge of the Duke of Friedland. Wallenstein indeed was more and
more mistrusted, and his behaviour seemed to justify, and more than
justify, every suspicion. His failure cannot be fully understood without analysing two factors. His health had suffered a severe strain.
His decisions were no longer so clear, purposeful, and cautious as before; furthermore he had alienated the army by stern and not unjustifiable punishment, for disobedience and desertion. From that
time on, the atmosphere around him was heavy with growing dislike and rancour. He was no longer sure of his creature, the army,
and the peace negotiations, of which everyone knew, did not make
him any more popular with the troops, who feared that they would
be discharged without having fulfilled those private expectations
that each was cherishing. The conduct of the war had deteriorated
into a simple matter of acquisitiveness for all concerned, and the
longer it lasted the more senseless a return to a peacetime economy
appeared.

The great leader of hosts, tottering to his doom, was making
desperate efforts to hold his army. Denunciations by two of his generals, forged either at the time or subsequently, refer to this last
period in Pilsen (Bohemia). Treachery on many sides confused the
issue, even in the eyes of his well-wishers. Up to the last the Duke
had friends in Vienna, but Spanish and Jesuit influence finally drove
the reluctant Emperor to branding Wallenstein as a proved traitor
and ordering his arrest and, if necessary, his death. The unfortunate
man became involved in more and more fantastic projects. Only a
very few were still loyal to him. The Emperor's confidential agents
at last decided on murder as the simplest and surest solution—one
that at the same time offered indemnification by Wallenstein's property. He was murdered in 1634.

The historical Wallenstein was neither a German national hero nor a Hussite, neither a criminal nor a lofty tragic character. He was a man of certain specific gifts in one direction only. Lonely all through his life, he acted as though he were under a curse, and conceptions of European scope could not free him from an exaggerated egoism. Ever longing to rise above himself, he grasped at the stars; but Heaven held in readiness for him a death that matched his life in a deeper, more terrible sense than the obvious one—the death of the adventurer.

The imperial party had not been able to profit by the death of Gustavus Adolphus; neither could the Protestants draw any tangible advantage from the fact that Wallenstein was out of the picture. There was much friction between the Swedish generals and the German princely leaders. The imperial army was now under the command of the young King of the Romans, Ferdinand. His path lay open. Now the long-desired union with the Spanish troops took place, and the combined Habsburg armies defeated Duke Bernard of Weimar and the Swedish general, Horn, at Nördlingen. The Heilbronn Alliance, between Sweden and German Protestants, tottered. Joyfully the Saxon Elector, John George, seized the chance to make a separate peace such as Wallenstein had already prepared and arranged with Arnim, the confidential adviser of John George.

The Swedes treated the Calvinists as allies with equal rights, and this served as a stimulus to the Saxon Lutherans to arrive at an understanding with the Emperor. John George, the elector, secured life tenure of the two Lusatias for himself and the Archbishopric of Magdeburg for his son. The year 1627 was adopted as the standard for determining the extent of church property (*annus decretorius*). Although the new ruling was to hold good for only forty years, the imperial Edict of Restitution could be regarded as definitely abandoned. Electoral Saxony, for its part, sacrificed the Reformed and the exiled territorial lords in the Peace of Prague and banded itself with the Emperor for the purpose of driving the Swedes out of the Empire. It remained to be seen whether there was political significance in the underlying idea of the Peace of Prague (1635). That idea was co-operation between the Emperor, who consented to give up certain points of his Counter-Reformation program, and the Elector of Saxony, who wanted to assure the peace and integrity of the Empire on behalf of his position as a Lutheran leader. After much hesitation and bargaining electoral Brandenburg, Hesse, Weimar, Brunswick, and the reinstated Dukes of Mecklenburg participated in the Peace of Prague.

But it was not possible to build up a common front against Sweden. That country, in her usual financial difficulties, insisted on formidable indemnities. The question of how to satisfy Sweden was one of the main causes for the continuation of this miserable war. Oxenstierna's suggestion of eight million gulden as indemnity was rejected, primarily on the advice of electoral Saxony. Duke Bernard of Weimar was also in favour of continuing the war, partly because of his personal ambition, and he arranged an alliance with France. Richelieu now decided to bring his veiled warfare against the Habsburgs into the open. He mediated a new truce with Poland for Sweden, concluded an alliance with Sweden and a treaty calling for subsidies to Duke Bernard, and declared war on Spain (1635). The formal declaration of war against the Emperor was not made until three years later.

FRANCE ENTERS THE WAR (1635)

For a brief period Bernard of Weimar occupied the centre of the stage. The Swedes had promised him the Duchy of Franconia; the French, the Landgraviate of Alsace and the governorship of Haguenau. Thus he inherited something of Wallenstein's plans and opportunities. He could not, of course, compare with the Duke of Friedland, whether as military organizer, as economist, or as conspirator. Exactly like many before and many after him, Bernard, a younger son, lacking means, was out to make his fortune. He was shrewd enough to see that the French wanted to exploit him, and he began to quarrel with his foreign patrons. An early death (1639) spared him disappointments. He would never have become a religious champion or the saviour of his fatherland.

France now took over the Duke's army and began operating in combination with Sweden. Both powers agreed not to make a separate peace. This point was essential; they must act in unison if the peace were to be as profitable as possible. As it was, a compromise was inevitable, for none was strong enough to keep the others from surviving.

The Swedish generals Banér and Torstenson covered themselves with glory. Unhappy Germany had much to suffer for many years to come. The powers involved in the Peace of Prague were also swept into the fury of war again. Sweden even had to defend herself against an attack by the envious Danish King, who, however, was forced to accept humiliating peace terms. This made Sweden the most important power in the Baltic, and her claims on Germany mounted accordingly. France showed a special interest in the border of the Spanish Netherlands, but she cultivated her relations with the petty German dynasts—a rewarding policy. Only belatedly did Sweden and France co-ordinate their military operations against electoral Bavaria. This land, which had been spared so long, had to suffer bitterly, to the sorrow of old Maximilian, its sovereign, who was forced to accept a truce. Now the Swedes marched into Bohemia. The termination of the war had led it back to the country that had cradled it. At this critical moment (1648), after almost four years of negotiations, the Peace of Westphalia was concluded.

In 1637 Ferdinand III had succeeded his father. He was a discreet and skilful prince, unfavourably disposed toward the Spanish influence, critical, and patriotic after his fashion, always with heed to the interests of the Habsburg dynasty. In the diets the wish for peace was voiced more and more loudly. Maximilian, the Elector of Bavaria, served as the leader of a south German and southwest German group of princes, in effect a revival of the league that had been dissolved in 1635. In this quarter arose the threat of some separate understanding with France in case no general peace emerged.

THE PEACE OF WESTPHALIA (1648)

The two chief points considered at the Congress of Münster and Osnabrück were (1) the extension of the Religious Peace of Augsburg, retroactively, to the Reformed, and (2) French and Swedish territorial claims. The result was an amicable compromise. Both sides had in fact been equally winners and losers. The Emperor gave up the Edict of Restitution. As the normal year (*annus decretorius*) for determining the status of church property, 1624 was decided on. This made Catholicism conclusive for the hereditary Habsburg lands and for most of the ecclesiastical principalities of the south and southwest of Germany, while Protestantism won out in northern Germany. In contrast to the Peace of Prague this ruling carried finality. The ecclesiastical reservation was upheld for the future, but with the qualification that family devotions and the education of children in the opposite faith were to be tolerated without jeopardy to civil rights. The ambassadors of electoral Saxony and Saxony-Altenburg protested in vain against the inclusion of the Reformed. Significantly enough, the Emperor refused to recognize the normal year for his hereditary lands. The Silesian Protestants as well as the nobility of Lower Austria were granted small favours. But otherwise people were liable to either ruthless conversion or emigration. These factors contributed essentially to the estrangement between Austria and the rest of Germany. In the future no majority decisions were to be made in the diet in matters of religion; both groups voted as closed corporations. This concession, unendurable from the strict Catholic point of view of the church, called forth the Pope's protest on principle against the settlement.

The normal year named for determining the status of secular property was 1618. The Margraviate of Baden-Durlach, which had been loyal to Sweden to the last, and both Mecklenburg and Württemberg were re-established. In the difficult matter of the Palatinate an agreement was reached that Bavaria was to retain only the Upper Palatinate, while the entire Rhenish Lower Palatinate was restored to the son of the Winter King as a newly created eighth electorate. This arrangement nullified Spanish plans for a barrier of territories along the Rhine.

The satisfaction of Sweden had become the burning problem of central Europe. Sweden was struggling with the perpetual threat of state bankruptcy. Her position as a great power rested on a very weak foundation and required territorial expansion into Germany, both colonial and economic; without it Sweden must relapse into its former position of local importance in the north. With memories of King Gustavus Adolphus, who had fallen in Germany, and the outstanding military achievements of Swedish generals still warm, Sweden became an estate of the Empire and received Hither Pomerania, with Stettin, Wismar, and the territorial bishoprics of Bremen and Verden. Here, too, Denmark saw herself stricken. Northern Germany and Sweden entered on a political life in common. To electoral Brandenburg and the Dukes of Brunswick the proximity of Sweden was oppressive—especially to Brandenburg, which laid claim to all of Pomerania, and which now had to be content with most of Farther Pomerania. It came into crucially dangerous opposition to Sweden. Sweden pressed her German colonial holdings as hard as possible economically; that was her purpose in having them. No repression of German culture occurred; that sort of thing was remote from the spirit of the times. The refreshment of Germanic blood in the Pomeranian population with its strong Slavic admixture meant little. The Swedes were always felt to be foreign masters, but from the local standpoint of Pomerania the sovereignty of electoral Brandenburg was also foreign, and to the subjected rural classes the difference between the two was imperceptible. It was otherwise for Stettin, whose interests were closely bound up with those of the German hinterland. The nobility of Pomerania, too, would in the long run derive more benefits from Brandenburg than from Swedish domination. Thus the makings of future conflicts accumulated.

France had waged war with the house of Habsburg, not with the Empire, whose interests she professed to guard. Accordingly she received the Habsburg possessions in Upper and Lower Alsace, together with the Habsburg protectorates over certain estates of the Empire in Alsace. The Austrian negotiators exaggerated the rights of the Habsburg dynasty in Alsace in order to make the concessions appear as important as possible. A contrast existed between Upper Alsace with its centralized development and Lower Alsace with its federal evolution. France entered the Empire for this position of supremacy in Alsace exactly as she had for the Bishoprics of Metz, Toul, and Verdun, which were now conclusively hers. France even promised to respect the privileges of the Alsatian estates immediate to the Empire. But what could such a promise mean in view of the sharp contrast between the modern rule of aggressive French absolutism and the feudalistic connections within the old Empire, which now saw its alien neighbour powerful and demanding within its boundaries? These boundaries had been mouldering for a long time; now they were altogether dissolved. France was already reaching out across the Rhine. She received the fortress of Breisach and the right to occupy the fortress of Philippsburg in time of war. For the sake of his dignity the French King declared that he did not choose to exercise the privileges that came to him with estates of the Empire.

His doing so might have been interpreted as recognition of the Emperor's sovereign lordship.

The entire settlement had something forced and makeshift about it. Ambiguities both accidental and intentional confused the situation, and clarification in the future seemed inevitable. This desperate compromise peace contained in this respect, too, a fount of fresh dissension. The general spirit of the Peace of Westphalia cannot be better characterized than through its stipulation about the Bishopric of Osnabrück. This bishopric actually was ruled in regular alternation by a Catholic bishop and a Protestant Guelph prince until 1803.

The Peace of Westphalia was a turning-point for the structure of the Empire; its provisions remained the basis of German public law to the end. Imperial absolutism in the style of the Edict of Restitution was made impossible for the future; the territorial princes had carried off the final victory. They were given the right to form alliances among themselves and with foreign powers, provided these alliances did not militate against the Emperor and the Empire, against the public peace and their sworn duty. The deplorable customs of the territorial princes thus received juridical sanction. The limitations imposed had little more than formal significance and were open to any and every interpretation. As for the Emperor, he was utterly dependent on the consent of the electors in matters relating to imperial wars, exile, and alliances and finally in connection with tolls and armaments. Sovereignty, the concept of which dominated the political life of the age, was thus withdrawn from the Emperor and claimed by the territorial princes. The imperial cities now formed their own curia in the diet, alongside the electors and the princes; none of the three curias, all of equal weight, could be outvoted. It remained to be seen how effective such a diet could be.

The Swiss Confederation did not participate in the negotiations of the Peace of Westphalia. Its separate existence, in respect of both public law and international law, was recognized tacitly. The same was true of the northern Netherlands. The war between Spain and the Netherlands had not been concluded, but the war between France and Spain changed the situation completely. The French advance toward the Spanish Netherlands seemed so dangerous to the Republic of the United Netherlands that it now gave its old enemy, Spain, support against France. This development was concluded by

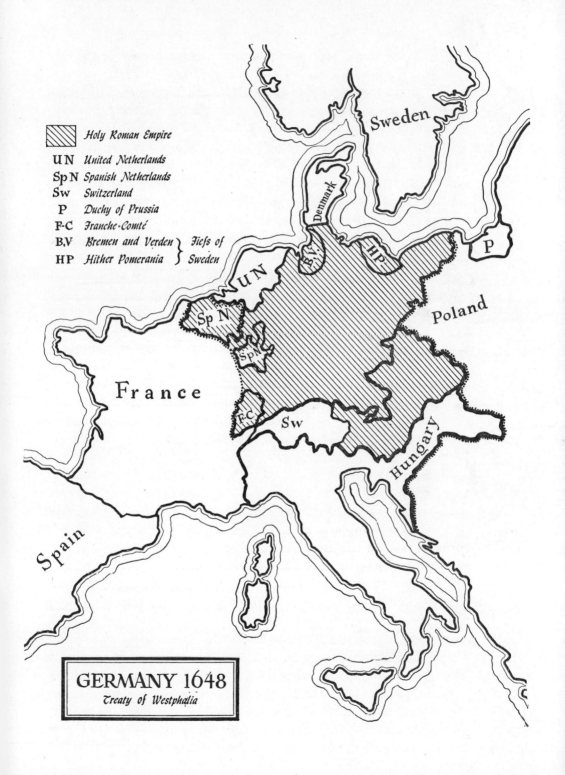

Holy Roman Empire

UN   United Netherlands
SpN   Spanish Netherlands
Sw   Switzerland
P   Duchy of Prussia
F-C   Franche-Comté
B,V   Bremen and Verden } Fiefs of
HP   Hither Pomerania   } Sweden

Sweden

Denmark

B,V

HP

P

UN

Sp N

Poland

Sp N

France

F-C

Sw

Spain

Hungary

GERMANY 1648
Treaty of Westphalia

the Peace of the Pyrenees (1659), which signified the end of Spain as a world power and in particular the end of all her territorial plans in regard to central Europe. In the late Middle Ages the catchword "to go Swiss" became current in Germany. It meant to throw off bonds, to become emancipated, to be liberal. Switzerland, as well as the northern Netherlands, was now just as distinct from the Empire as Denmark or Poland. The dream of the Roman universal empire came to an end with the Peace of Westphalia. Only an estate that had immediate or mediate representation in the diet still belonged to the Empire. It was often asked earlier which territories belonged to the East Frankish—that is, to the German—realm and which, beyond this, belonged to the Roman Empire. Now the Roman Empire had shrunk until it was identical with the German realm. And so it became customary to speak of the "German" Emperor, whereas the heir to the throne was King of the Romans. The Empire had been plundered, crippled, and disfigured, but at least it remained "holy" to the very end.

Many problems were left up in the air by the Peace of Westphalia, either because the negotiators did not perceive them or because they were not equal to dealing with them. It was difficult to settle satisfactorily with the throngs of mercenaries who, for the moment, were not fit for a peaceable life. Sweden received five million gulden for her troops, a sum that was to be collected from among the Catholic and Protestant estates of the Empire; to the recipients it seemed utterly insufficient. What was done with this money hardly quieted the unrest in Sweden, but only served to make that country avid for conquest. She soon made war on Poland. The other belligerents had to devise their own means of getting rid of their soldiery. Groups of mercenaries on the prowl for loot plagued unhappy Germany for years to come.

THE CONSEQUENCES OF THE GREAT WAR

The most significant immediate consequence of the Thirty Years' War was that the religious struggle had led to profound exhaustion. The century was very far from the true ethical and religious tolerance that individual noble spirits had championed in vain. But there was an alternative that seemed possible and within reach: pragmatic tolerance of other beliefs and renunciation of physical force as arbiter between philosophies. Other interests, then, crowded the religious motive out of its place as the basic cause and aim of struggle; it lost its position of primary importance, though it never quite vanished from the political life of Germany and her neighbours. The cleavage in the church now had to be accepted as a fact for all time to come in Germany. Not only did attempts to unite Catholics and Protestants seem senseless in the light of the horrors that had been perpetrated, but even rapprochement between the Lutherans and the Reformed still proved impracticable.

Germany had lost about a third of her population in the war. Exact statistics are available only for certain districts. Extensive regions, such as Carinthia, the Tyrol, Salzburg, Holstein, and parts of Alsace, had been affected only temporarily or not at all. As in most of the wars of olden times, mortality was due more to pestilence and famine than to military operations. All the belligerents did their utmost in oppression and cruelty. The Spaniards employed different methods of abuse from the Swedes, but results were essentially the same. It would be a great error to believe that the German foot-soldiers treated German peasants more gently than foreign infantry did, or that the Germanic Swedes spared their racial kindred, or that the Protestant troops were more humane than the Catholic. The true historical significance of the great war in central Europe cannot be grasped unless it is regarded wholly without national or religious bias, as the first great political and sociological crisis of German nationality. This war deprived the German people of the European leadership that it had managed to maintain, despite signs of stagnation, until the beginning of the seventeenth century.

In order to estimate the consequences of the war in detail, sources of error must be eliminated. It is, for instance, a popular legend that a Franconian decree permitted every man to have two wives, that Catholic priests were expected to marry, that no man was allowed to become a monk before he was sixty. Plaints of depopulation and ravaged countrysides were often exaggerated to hasten official help. But there is still enough horror that can be substantiated by reference to accurate sources. Miles of fields and vineyards were laid waste; in some places the number of families was cut in half or worse; and only a third of the cattle were left. The number of peasants who had no team of their own mounted steadily. In Württemberg, typically enough, the loss of women and children almost equalled that of men. A special set of problems grew up around refugees. For the first time thousands of peaceful citizens had been driven into exile and exposed to misery, exploitation, and devastating disease.

There was less and less respect for property. Police work was as yet rudimentary. The authorities were often helpless to do anything against the formation of robber bands, and delinquents and degenerates took a constantly bolder part in the general looting. Levying contributions, rapine, and simple robbery amounted increasingly to the same thing. The churches were helpless, since they naturally did not want to subject those who had battled for them to hampering restrictions. Education, intellectual work, and art all deteriorated, and the generation that was growing up was exposed to a thousand temptations. Living by instinct and the right of the stronger won a shameful prevalence, and anyone who was not ready to fight his way brutally was beaten before he began. Among the saddest consequences of the Thirty Years' War was the encouragement of certain alarming traits in the character of the German people—in particular the tendency to militaristic violence and contempt for the personal rights and well-being of others.

Instead of surplus population for colonizing enterprises, Germany now had more depopulated areas than any other comparable civilized country in Europe. Her capital had been terribly depleted, and since there were almost no funds for reconstruction the ruins remained. Reserves of precious metals sank low. At that time the best gold- and silverware of the German Renaissance was to be found in rural castles in Sweden. To accumulate new capital was difficult. The arteries of commerce were largely destroyed; even inland communications did not function well and were technically inferior. The mouths of German rivers were in foreign possession. Only overseas colonization could have created new wealth. When Holland was fighting Spain and both powers were adding fuel to the war in central Europe with their subsidies, actually one overseas domain was fighting another; it was a trial of strength between two colonial empires. Germany's money economy had suffered a severe blow. Successful generals and military entrepreneurs bought up land for almost nothing, increased the number of large holdings, and thus contributed to the further paralysis of economic life.

German burgherdom had proudly taken its place side by side with the clergy and the nobility. Since the fifteenth century it had even overtaken these older classes. Its secular view of life agreed with the modern statesmanship of the princes. Throughout Germany the religious conflict was a spur to class interests. Protestantism in itself certainly did not create intellectual freedom, but by critical attacks on the concept of authority it paved the way for it. Politically Protestantism helped the concept of a body politic built up on estates to prevail, although it rendered that concept illiberal intellectually and spiritually. The Empire melted away. The territorial lord had triumphed.

The Emperor and the princes had done everything they could to oppress the free cities. Now these were given equal rights as a group in the diet at the very moment when the war accomplished their economic downfall. From this point on, the political future of Germany rested on the relationship of princes and burghers in the territorial states. The Empire had become brittle form without substance, and the idea of a central Europe slumbered for a long time. In the face of denominationalism and its dogmas true liberation could come only from one of two directions: either from religion or from science. Again and again the Baptists and other religious groups called for a return to the faith of the early Christians. Religious mystics like Angelus Silesius (died 1677) and hymn-writers like Paul Gerhardt (died 1676) tried to bring the religion of love to life again in Christianity. In the field of history a man like Sebastian Franck (died 1543) tried to overcome the prejudices of the church. Philip Melanchthon strove for a natural, undenominational theory of morals. But it was not on German soil that philosophy, natural science, or the new doctrine of natural law ripened into an independent basis for the modern view of life. John Althusius (died 1638), the first man in Germany to defend the theory of the sovereignty of the people, is intellectually akin to the Calvinist pioneers who championed this concept in western Europe and whose ideas formed the basis for the theory of the modern constitutional state. Germany followed her own slow and laborious path, which led away from western Europe. How much superstition still had to be overcome! The cleavage in the church had increased rather than lessened it.

216

Except for religious poetry, the old folk poetry persisted only in a distorted and coarsened form. Grimmelshausen's romance *Simplicius Simplicissimus* gave an affecting picture of the moral and spiritual ravages of war. Humanists and academicians attempted to quicken and to ennoble German literature. Martin Opitz wrote his book on German poetry, and Simon Dach, a native of Königsberg, succeeded in creating a song, "Ännchen von Tharau," that was genuine in its feeling and appealed to every social stratum. The universities were dominated by pedantry and a delight in splitting hairs. Dependence on the church and on the authorities made free research next to impossible. The masses reveled in obscenities, and the taste of academic youth was wholly attuned to vulgarity. The more refined manners that were coming in from the west were either slavishly imitated or enviously rejected as something non-German and suspect. This neap-tide of culture after the end of the Thirty Years' War bequeathed to the future of Germany the fatal belief that everything rough and uncouth was truly German and that even a trace of cosmopolitan culture was to be regarded as treason to one's country.

Chapter 11

THE ORIGIN OF THE TWO GREAT GERMAN POWERS

THE CENTURY of France now followed on that of Spain. Viewed in its bearings on German history, the period of Louis XIV is significant for the rise of Austria and Prussia as a double counterbalance to French claims to European hegemony. The Empire itself was unable to cope with the stern absolutist rule and the more creative culture of France. Not a single purely German territory was highly enough developed to be of itself the carrier of a power that might have equalled this French complex. The upshot of the latest epoch of history was the admission of foreign states into the Empire; Sweden had followed in Denmark's footsteps. Now that France wanted to surpass the achievements of Spain, the most vigorous German territories knew of only one adequate reply: they themselves formed alliances with countries outside Germany. And thus in the final period of its life the Holy Empire again assumed a Roman—that is, a universal—character in new form. The *status quo* was theoretically maintained, but actually it was disturbed by the near-by foreign states. The leading territorial princes in turn reached out across their borders. In this way they fortified their idea of sovereignty, to the damage of imperial authority and to the enhancement of their particular interests.

An Austrian concept of Empire and of state was now developing. Ethnically it was well grounded on the German and Slavic mixture and the Hungarian connection. Dynastically it was shaped by the interests of the Habsburg house; religiously it was characterized by the emphasis on Catholicism. It was fought out strategically in the wars against the Turks, and governmentally it was symbolized by the increasing importance of the court chancery of the hereditary lands as against the imperial chancery. This growing Austria, at once part of Germany and distinct from it, feeling indiscriminately in the manner of a territorial state, imperially, and universally, had long suffered under the guardianship of the Spanish line of the Habsburg house, which had the superiority in respect both to economics and to world policy. Spain's downfall meant Austria's rise. The entire Spanish holdings would have given Austria a commanding position in Europe. The war epoch had made the imperial house well acquainted with the envy of the electors. Even Bavaria, which was under Jesuit influence, placed territorial above religious interests. In all of Catholic Germany electoral Bavaria was the only serious rival of the Habsburgs. She strove for the foremost position within the Empire, but did not aspire beyond it.

The story was different with electoral Brandenburg. The Hohenzollern dynasty had the good fortune, after a series of weak rulers, to produce one of extraordinary gifts in Frederick William, the Great Elector. Two factors gave his political work its character. In 1613 the Hohenzollerns had gone over to Calvinism, but without calling for any change in their subjects' Brandenburg form of Lutheranism. During his years of study in Holland the Great Elector (1640–88) had filled his mind to the brim with the political and economic ethos of western European Calvinism. His methods in all his work were stamped with this unwearying, matter-of-fact, and concentrated spirit. He acted energetically in full confidence of success. As he outgrew the prejudices of denominationalism he shed his other scruples also.

The second important circumstance for the future of electoral Brandenburg was the connection with the Duchy of Prussia that has been mentioned. Brandenburg-Prussia became Poland's and Sweden's competitor in the struggle for the Baltic, and through this friction its government was strengthened and rose beyond the limitations of a merely German principality. Above all, it was now in a position to outstrip its old rival, electoral Saxony. With characteristic self-confidence electoral Saxony took over the direction of the *Corpus Evangelicorum* in the diet, but no palpable profit was drawn from this leadership of the Protestant rebellion, which was recognized by imperial law. While the old Ernestine line in disrupted Thuringia exaggerated German particularism *ad absurdum,* the younger Albertine line did not let its ambition slumber, but secured the Polish crown and, like the rest, built up a realm beyond the borders of the Empire. But this development sharpened the opposition toward Brandenburg-Prussia into hatred.

Thus all the more important east German territories found some sort of compensation for the break-down of the western German border. They were preparing the way for establishing a great power, dynastic and absolutist in character, without regard to internal checks within the Empire. In the course of this process Austria and Brandenburg-Prussia became great European powers with colonial German traits, while electoral Saxony fell behind. Western Germany exhibited only one similar case. The rise of the Guelph house to the electoral dignity in Hanover and then the Hanoverian succession to the British throne caused English political interest in central Europe to persist and to guard against French claims to hegemony. If France was pushing farther and farther into the Empire and exerting influence over individual princes and whole groups of territories, the personal union of England and Hanover raised an effective guard against this intrusion. In the eastern German alliances of German states that had possessions outside of Germany the focus of political activity remained always in the German part. Hanoverian politics, on the contrary, proceeded more and more from London. For a while England played in Lower Saxony a part similar to that of Sweden in its northern German possessions.

Samuel Pufendorf (died 1694), the great teacher of public law, was right in calling the Roman-German imperial constitution a monster, neither monarchical nor aristocratic, composite of all sorts of contradictory governmental elements. The Emperor and the Empire faced each other like partners bargaining jealously. On one side of the scales was a republic based on the estates, on the other an emperorship with antique and Christian traits and universal plans. This balance, however, restrained foreign claims to hegemony, and it held central Europe together in spite of internal dissensions; it did not inhibit the creative power of individual territorial princes, and it did not keep a great new power from springing up on German soil. This preservative and stabilizing influence of the imperial "monster" is not to be underestimated, even though all progressive spirits devoted themselves to the territories.

THE FIRST NORTHERN WAR (1655-60)

Queen Christina, the daughter of Gustavus Adolphus, vainly tried to gain a period of peace for Sweden. It was easier to go on with the war. The queen withdrew, and her cousin Charles X Gustavus brilliantly continued the war with Poland. Electoral Brandenburg was in a most difficult position. The Great Elector was ambitious and enterprising. His chief adviser, Count George Frederick of Waldeck, wanted to win him over to joining Protestant northern Germany to a union of princes against Habsburg politics. But Frederick William had only limited means. He had to get along as best he could, and without tactical manœuvring progress was impossible. At the same time Poland was threatened by Russia and therefore could not defend herself against Swedish aggression. The Swedish King won victories that scholarly flatterers compared with those of Alexander the Great.

The most important move for electoral Brandenburg was to take advantage of the opportunity to shake off Poland's feudal lordship over the Duchy of Prussia. At first the Great Elector tried to do this with the help of the Emperor and the Dutch; then he came to an understanding with Sweden, accepting Prussia from Sweden as a fief at the price of a military alliance. Further acquisitions at Poland's expense were projected; for the first time there was talk of partitioning that country. Russia now invaded the Swedish provinces on the Baltic. In the Treaty of Labiau Frederick William managed to have Prussia conveyed to him as a sovereign possession by the Swedish feudal lord. But Vienna's political shrewdness successfully rescued Poland from her predicament. Brandenburg was approached— the vote of the Elector had great weight in the new imperial election —and the upshot was that now Frederick William took Prussia over from Poland as an inheritable sovereign possession, though, to be sure, on condition of renewed homage. The sudden death of Charles X Gustavus facilitated the conclusion of the Peace of Oliva in 1660 at the ancient monastery near Danzig. The Great Elector did not receive Swedish Hither Pomerania, as he had hoped, but he kept the sovereignty over Prussia that had been so hotly contested. In vain he had presented far-reaching plans at the court of Vienna—plans for creating a German fleet, which he wished to command, and for acquiring colonies in which there should be religious equality. German colonists were streaming to America in increasing numbers, and such ideas were therefore sound; but so much ambition awoke anxiety in the house of Habsburg.

THE FIRST RHENISH CONFEDERATION. THE TURKISH MENACE

At the election of Emperor Leopold I the deep opposition between the Habsburgs and the Bourbons again showed up sharply. Cardinal Mazarin, the leading statesman of France, wanted to prevent the election of a Habsburg; he worked on behalf of the Elector of Bavaria and even held the youthful King Louis XIV in readiness. Emperor Leopold (1658–1705) was elected only because he promised the electors of the Empire not to support Spain in any way in her war against France. From this point the two Habsburg lines took separate paths politically, and the triumph of France over Spain seemed certain. Since 1654 there had been a Catholic alliance of the Rhenish ecclesiastical electors with other west German dynasts. Under French guidance this confederation was widened by the addition of a number of Protestant estates of the Empire. France and Sweden also joined. The purpose was the maintenance of the Peace of Westphalia. More and more minor princes joined this first Rhenish Confederation. Brandenburg was among the last. The confederation lasted till 1668, though it was never very important. French policy soon found more potent means of establishing its influence in the Empire.

One probable cause for the dissolution of the first Rhenish Confederation was the attitude of its members toward the Turkish menace. For the Rhenish confederates and even the French aided the Emperor. In 1606 the Ottoman Empire had recognized the Emperor as the other world ruler, and the humiliating tributes were finally abolished. The Emperor appeased the exacting Prince of Transylvania and so strengthened the eastern position of the house of Habsburg that the Turks did not attack during the whole Thirty Years' War. Quarrels about Transylvania led to renewed intervention by the Emperor as well as the Sultan. The new Kuprili line of grand viziers aimed at renewing the Ottoman Empire by means of foreign policy. In 1663 six thousand men marched into Hungary. The Turkish terror stalked through Slovakia and Moravia, and within Germany, too, special bells again rang through the land to warn of danger from the Turks. These bells had not sounded before since the terrible days of the Reformation. Petitions for immediate help went out to all the courts of Europe. A diet was summoned at Regensburg. After many difficulties it granted aid in the form of fifty *Römermonaten;* according to a ruling of 1521 this meant 128,-000 gulden for every month. A small imperial army took part in the Hungarian campaign. The diet that had been convoked because of the Turkish threat never adjourned, but remained in session until the end of the old Empire. The mediæval assembly of estates developed into a permanent congress of envoys under a name that seemed pathetically absurd to the people of that time: "the everlasting diet." This diet was the scene of struggles over imperial organization for war. Here the German princes, by forming a special association, tried to set aside the prerogatives of the electors and to arrive at a permanent agreement on the imperial election in order to put an end to electoral manœuvring and bargaining.

The diet was now a closed corporation, and thus it remained, without alteration, to the end of the old Empire. It consisted of three deliberative bodies, the so-called benches, which met separately, with occasional joint sessions. On the first bench were the electors, on the second the princes, and on the third representatives from the cities. So many minor and petty estates sat on the bench of the princes that not all could have whole votes; a number of estates might be taken together as a curia, and the vote of the curia would be determined simply by the majority of its members. Representatives of convents, many of them lacking subjects, participated in the curial conferences. Knights who were immediate to the Empire were no longer invited to attend the diet. The minor lords were gathered into four colleges of counts. The right of voting developed in an altogether arbitrary manner. At first it adhered to the person; then it became connected with the particular fief, so that several individual votes might combine in one estate vote. The influence of the electors predominated. As against the east German colonial area, the "old" Empire insisted on its traditional weight. Only those votes actually cast at the diet counted. The diet could appoint committees and deputations. Theoretically it had complete authority over the territories, but in practice this authority was more and more paralysed by the privileges of the territorial lords. An increasing number of questions were regarded as *jura singulorum*—that is, matters in which decisions were valid only when those affected had given their consent. The fate of the imperial diet was the sorriest defeat for the very concept. This experience may well have strengthened German prejudice against all institutions springing from the principle of the estates or diets and against parliamentary government as developed from them.

The combined troops of Europe succeeded in fighting off the Ottoman army. Under the circumstances the Emperor had to be content. The Peace of Vasvar (1664) provided for a twenty years' truce. The Turks retained decisive influence in Transylvania. There were small concessions of land, and the Emperor made the Sultan a "present" of two hundred thousand thalers. Commercial treaties between the two powers were projected. Suspicion of the French allies was the real motive of this peace, which did not at all correspond to the considerable victories of the Christian powers. The necessary breathing-spell had been won, but the final settlement with the Ottoman Empire was still the chief task of Emperor Leopold's regime and influenced all its other measures.

THE FRENCH POLICY OF EXPANSION. THE GREAT ELECTOR

During all his over-long regime (1658–1705) Emperor Leopold remained just as timid and temporizing as at the beginning. One imperative problem did occupy him and his advisers: the impending Spanish succession. King Charles II of Spain was childless. His elder sister had married Louis XIV, his younger sister Emperor Leopold. In spite of the fact that his wife had renounced the succession, the King of France raised claims. But it was a question of foreign policy and of power politics rather than of family rights. The strong French crown was resolved not to suffer any new encirclement by possessions of the house of Habsburg. And this was the root from which a great European war was bound to spring. All the powers were weary of war. Central Europe, in particular, was still suffering from the exhaustion that had come in the wake of the Thirty Years' War, the world war of the religions—the first conflict that can be called a world war. All discerning men were quite agreed that a new catastrophe of such scope must be prevented.

Here was an excellent chance of success for Louis XIV's policy of expansion. He was aiming at local rectifications of boundaries on the basis of claims derived from the original legalistic character borne by his absolutism in the Roman style. For a long time he was astonishingly successful in keeping his opponents apart. The fear of a new general war was greatly in his favour. People thought that it was not inadvisable to allow the King of France to enjoy local gains as long as the chief problem, that of the Spanish succession, could be taken care of by diplomatic means. For decades the diplomats of Europe fought against the spectre of a war of the Spanish succession as if against a decree of the Delphic oracle. Nevertheless this new world war of dynasties finally broke out. As early as 1668 there was a partition treaty; two more were to follow.

This first treaty is of special historical importance because in it Louis XIV countenanced the reunion of Spain and Austria if France were assigned the Spanish dependencies of the southern Netherlands, Franche-Comté, and Naples, with Sicily, as well as the African colonies and the Philippines. This would have taken care of the dominant interest of France, expansion eastward, and would have destroyed the old German boundaries. There was the problem of the separate wars that led up to the great struggle for the Spanish succession. Louis XIV had started to act even before the first treaty. He claimed part of the Spanish Netherlands on the basis of the civil law of old Flanders. Spain bespoke the Empire's help for this threatened imperial area, the Burgundian circle, but the electors refused to interfere, for the King of France had isolated Spain and the Netherlands by separate treaties with the most important of the west German princes. Electoral Mainz, electoral Köln, Münster, and Palatine Neuburg—that is, the most important Rhenish and Westphalian neighbours of France—were that country's allies. Western Europe was preparing to destroy central Europe.

Holland recognized the threat of France most clearly. It was she who initiated the triple alliance of Holland, England, and Sweden, coloured by northern, maritime, and colonial politics, which mediated a tolerable peace for Spain. Austria had not participated in the

225

fight, for she preferred her secret understanding with France through the above-mentioned partition treaty. She had promised Louis XIV to be neutral (1671) and thus made it possible for France to proceed.

France now concluded a series of treaties with German princes. Electoral Brandenburg made a secret alliance for ten years, promised military assistance and co-operation in the renewal of the Rhenish Confederation, and was indemnified by the prospect of receiving the part of Gelderland that had remained Spanish, a yearly endowment of 40,000 thalers, and 150,000 thalers for recruiting purposes. The Elector Palatine married his daughter Elizabeth Charlotte to the Duke of Orléans, the brother of Louis XIV. With the help of pressure from France he had revived the so-called *Wildfangrecht*—the right of a palsgrave to levy taxes on those of illegitimate birth and on aliens to the Empire; he, too, promised neutrality. France made an even better bargain with the Catholic Wittelsbachs in Bavaria. If the question of the Spanish succession should become acute, Bavaria was to prevent the Empire's making war and to refuse passage to Austrian troops. In the event of an imperial election Bavaria's vote was promised to the French King. If he became emperor, the Elector of Bavaria would then become King of the Romans and would receive Austrian land—Bohemia first and foremost, for the Habsburgs were most vulnerable from that quarter. Similar treaties were drawn up with the Rhenish ecclesiastical electors, with Münster, Palatine Neuburg, and the Dukes of Brunswick. Electoral Saxony did not refuse a gift of money from France.

The military and economic superiority of France thus shattered the Empire. The most important princes were all more or less publicly dependent on the French crown. And so for a whole epoch German and French history became intertwined. Louis XIV belongs to German history quite as much as to French; the same was later true of Napoleon I. The King of France was regarded as a hero to be admired, fêted, and imitated. The German ruling class became Gallicized and more and more cut off from the middle and lower classes. For as yet there was no general German sense of nationality; only faint beginnings were making themselves felt here and there. The deep distrust of all that was Spanish was unfavourable for the Vienna house of Habsburg, which along the Rhine and in northern

Germany was felt to be more dangerous than the King of France.

By extremely shrewd use of subsidies and pensions French diplomacy succeeded in breaking up the triple alliance and in isolating Holland completely. But the sudden invasion of Holland quickly altered the international situation. The Great Elector made one of those about-faces that were so typical of him and went over to the Dutch. The Viennese court, vexed by French agitation in Hungary and Poland, came to an agreement with Holland, Brandenburg, and Denmark for the maintenance of the *status quo*. The Great Elector first tried to make a separate treaty with France, but then came to terms with the Emperor after all. Now France set her old friend Sweden against Brandenburg. But Sweden came out badly, for the war spread to the Baltic provinces.

In the meantime a great political change had occurred in Holland. William III of Orange became Stadholder, and the defence of the hard-beset country was successfully organized. With that began the glorious career of the mortal enemy of the French policy of hegemony. At last the Emperor and the Empire also actively entered the war, but the French armies proved the more powerful. At the peace congress of Nymwegen French negotiators succeeded in separating the allies. Holland was the first to make a separate treaty (1678). This principal opponent of Louis XIV had stood her ground brilliantly. The mournful part once again was Spain's; she lost still more places in the Netherlands and Franche-Comté. Evidently the French King was drawing one essential pace nearer to the main goal of the first partition treaty.

No provisions for protecting the rights of the Empire were contained in the peace treaty. For the time being Lorraine remained in French hands, for the Duke refused to accept the conditions made by the French. France renounced the right to occupy Philippsburg, but she received Freiburg, thus reaching beyond the Rhine and gaining a foothold in the Austrian Breisgau. The Emperor also promised not to support those states that were still at war with Sweden. The Elector of Brandenburg, who had changed sides so often, was now left in the lurch by his allies, maliciously rejoicing over his misfortune. After all that had happened he could expect no careful handling from France; he was the very type of the betrayer betrayed. He had won significant successes, beginning with Alsace,

227

where he was first hailed as the Great Elector, and then against the Swedes. The victory over the latter at Fehrbellin (1675) marked the beginning of Brandenburg-Prussia as a great power, though the fact did not become evident until later; for the moment the Elector had to suffer the consequences of his diplomatic methods. In the Treaty of Saint-Germain (1679) Brandenburg received merely a strip of land on the right bank of the Oder, while Sweden gave up her share in the maritime duties of Farther Pomerania.

The Elector had no choice but to return penitently to the French alliance. He accepted 300,000 thalers from Louis XIV as an indemnification for war costs. This was one of the most singular payments of this kind even in the unprejudiced Baroque age—a German prince reimbursed by France for the expenses of a war against France! The so-called "Closer Alliance" of Saint-Germain supplemented this peace treaty. In return for the pledge of security for his possessions, plus an annual payment of 100,000 livres, Elector Frederick William undertook to allow France passage through his lands, to cede his fortresses, to vote for the French candidate in the Polish royal election, and in the imperial election to vote for Louis XIV or for a candidate named by him. With the French subsidies, which increased from year to year, the Elector built a fleet, founded his African trading company, and acquired a base on the coast of Guinea. On the other hand it was only this arrangement with electoral Brandenburg that enabled the King of France to carry through his Chambers of Reunion.

Germany's western border was fully decomposed. Economic life, the technique of administration, and feudal and private law were a chaos of inextricable claims and commitments, to the distress of the inhabitants and the despair of the authorities. The French royal power represented a new dynamic organizing principle that promised tangible advantages to everyone who subscribed to it. The King of France actually belonged to the Empire and aspired to the imperial crown. Foreigners had already worn this crown; the Habsburgs, indeed, were more Spanish than German. From the point of view of etiquette the Emperor possessed the highest rank in all Christendom. In this Baroque epoch, which valued etiquette so highly as the symbol of actual power, the prerogative of the Habsburg dynasty irritated the King of France. France enlarged her possessions in the Empire and clarified her title to them. Behind all this was the military and geopolitical push toward the Rhine boundary, as well as the dynastic and universal will to the imperial crown. From the French point of view the Spanish succession offered prospects of achieving such aims. If Spain were again to unite with Austria, then France would claim the Spanish dependencies and the imperial crown to offset it. This would separate the house of Habsburg and the Empire, to the great satisfaction of many German estates of the Empire, and by no means only those that were Protestant. The Chambers of Reunion also were historically connected with the Spanish succession.

THE CHAMBERS OF REUNION. THE TURKS REACH VIENNA

The French based their policy on legalistic considerations. As early as the reign of Philip the Fair there had been Chambers of Reunion —courts instituted to clarify and settle questions of feudal law. France now demanded that all regions that had ever been in such relations of dependency to lands already surrendered should be reunited with these territories lately acquired by her. The intentional ambiguities of the Peace of Westphalia now bore their logical fruit. All treaties formulated since 1552 were scrutinized, and the whole maze of dietary and feudal privilege had to be subjected to the stern criticism of His Most Christian Majesty's legal advisers trained in Roman law. Decisions were made and carried out summarily. There was no chance for appeals; the imperial supreme court was ignored. An unprecedented political transaction was taking place under the pretext of a legal battle. By 1680 all of Alsace except Strassburg and Mühlhausen had already been assigned to the French crown. Of the Rhenish estates, Saarbrücken and Zweibrücken, several districts of electoral Trier and the electoral Palatinate, castles and abbeys of Luxemburg, and parts of the Bishopric of Liège were affected. The entire western border of Germany was shifting. Many German princes made successful attempts in Paris to obtain special privileges. The effect within the Empire was growing indignation, which reached a climax when Strassburg too, after careful preparation, was taken over by France (1681). Through all the agitation of the times this city had tried to maintain a neutral policy of its own, even toward the Empire itself; now it found itself cut off and deserted. The magistrates and the guilds agreed to yield to superior power. There was no treason; none was needed. The French graciously left the city a certain degree of self-government.

Events such as these hastened the scrapping of the new military organization of the Empire. Estates were differentiated as armed and unarmed. The armed estates—and these were all the larger ones— retained control of their armies. The problem was to organize the smaller estates that could not recruit troops with their own resources, so as to arm the Empire by imperial means. The Emperor made a number of treaties with the princes of the Empire and with Spain and Holland. The King of Sweden was aggrieved because Zweibrücken, his mother-country, had been sacrificed by the Chambers of Reunion; he let himself be won over. The Great Elector, however, obligated himself to the French as an apologist for the Chambers of Reunion.

The deciding factor in the European situation was that the Emperor's twenty-year truce with the Turks was drawing to a close. An extensive movement of Ottoman aggression against the house of Habsburg began, with the encouragement of French diplomacy and actually fomented by the anti-Habsburg party of Hungarian grandees, who were joined by Transylvania with French support. The Turks pushed triumphantly to Vienna. There the commander, Count Rüdiger of Starhemberg, was weak in resources and even by dint of foresight and energy could maintain the defence only briefly. Reinforcements arrived in the very nick of time (1683). Under the banner of the Empire fought many German princes, together with King John III Sobieski of Poland, who had long foreseen what was to come and had tried to form a league against the Turks. True to the tradition of the crusades, the Roman curia had also laboured to the same effect. France, however, utilized the moment when the Habsburgs were under the greatest pressure from the Turkish "watchdog" to invade the Spanish Netherlands anew. The Emperor was unable to wage war on two fronts. Being obliged to follow up his victory over the Turks, he made a twenty years' truce with Louis XIV that left the latter in temporary full possession of his conquests. The war in the east turned into a decided success for the house of Habsburg. Russia, Venice, Sweden, and even Brandenburg came to the aid of the Emperor. Most of Hungary as well as Slavonia and

Transylvania was taken. Hungary renounced her right to elect a king and now recognized the Habsburg hereditary right to the Stephen crown. Archduke Joseph, Emperor Leopold's eldest son, was crowned hereditary King of Hungary. Thus Austria's gradual detachment from the Empire was completed, and the centre of gravity of the Habsburg possessions shifted to the east.

REVOCATION OF THE EDICT OF NANTES. THE LEAGUE OF AUGSBURG (1686)

The new change of front of the Elector of Brandenburg was partially influenced by the revocation of the Edict of Nantes by Louis XIV (1685). The French King believed in his royal prerogative, which included determining the religion he held fit for his subjects. From Richelieu's time the two million Huguenots in France constituted no danger to the French state. The brutal persecutions that now began allowed most of them no choice but to emigrate. The Great Elector replied to the revocation of the Edict of Nantes with the Edict of Potsdam. Twenty thousand refugees found shelter in electoral Brandenburg alone. Erlangen, Kassel, and Friedrichsdorf (in Taunus) were other preferred centres for Huguenot settlements in Germany. The French emigrants introduced their German hosts to the art of velvet- and silk-manufacture and of bookbinding; they diffused acquaintance with foreign tongues, with physical culture, fencing, and dancing. Their personal and commercial trustworthiness quickly earned them wide-spread respect. The intellectual life of Berlin was largely shaped by the French influx. It was just these exiled sons of France who spread her culture through central Europe —the culture, indeed, of the early period of Louis XIV, which in its Protestant variation was moving farther and farther away from the dominant trend in France. Up to the time of the French Revolution French communities in Germany held themselves rather aloof, with their own language and customs, though they were influential and respected. Not till later did they become fully Germanized, and even then many families still clung proudly to their old traditions.

Quite aside from the loss of intelligence and industry, the expulsion of the Huguenots proved to be politically disastrous to Louis XIV. In Sweden and England, in Holland and electoral Brandenburg, the religious refugees strengthened the defensive front against French hegemony. In 1686 the Great Elector formed a twenty years' protective alliance with the Emperor. He now pledged himself to the safeguarding of the Spanish Netherlands and the election of Leopold's eldest son as emperor. The Viennese court wryly assumed the payment to Brandenburg of the subsidies that were due from France. The Great Elector, who died but two years later, faithfully observed the terms of this agreement—the first time he had ever done such a thing.

The "intermittent fever" of which the Elector of Brandenburg was mockingly accused also infected the other German potentates, although not so severely. Under the young and ambitious Max Emanuel electoral Bavaria turned to the Emperor. Max Emanuel made a defensive alliance and married Emperor Leopold's daughter by his first (Spanish) marriage. This union was of the utmost political significance. The Archduchess Maria Antonia renounced her hereditary rights to the Spanish crown in favour of the Emperor and his male descendants, but still claimed the Spanish Netherlands or something of equal value for herself and her heirs. This circumstance offered a possible new solution for the central problem of the times, the future of the Spanish Netherlands. They might become independent under a ruler of their own. Here the future Belgium announced itself.

King Louis XIV sensed the weakening of his position in Europe. He tried in vain to turn the truce into a genuine peace. The Emperor and his allies renewed their Laxenburg Alliance; after 1686 it was called the Augsburg League. The position of the Stuarts in England was becoming more and more precarious; the Glorious Revolution (1688) was to rob France of her ally of many years. Louis tried to take advantage of the last reasonably favourable opportunity to bring about a decision. In 1685, the direct line having died out, the electoral Palatinate fell to the Catholic branch of Palatine Neuburg. Louis XIV promoted the claims of his brother, the husband of the Princess Palatine Elizabeth Charlotte—claims that, under imperial law, could not be made good even for the allodial or private inheritance. A contest about the archiepiscopal election in Köln was the immediate occasion for action. The French candidate was defeated; the Wittelsbach Joseph Clemens carried off the victory, and thus the range of Wittelsbach influence was extended toward the Netherlands. Electoral Köln had been France's most important ally on the

Rhine. Louis XIV had his armies march into western Germany. He hoped to install his candidate in electoral Köln and to gain recognition for the Chambers of Reunion without war. But this time the Emperor did not give in. The territorial princes of northern Germany joined the Augsburg League, and the Empire declared war on France.

It was decisive for the future that the Emperor shelved his religious scruples and for the first time entered on an alliance with the States General of the northern Netherlands. William of Orange and his wife Mary, a Stuart, were reigning in England, which now also joined the great league that had for its aim the re-establishment of the Peace of Westphalia and the Peace of the Pyrenees. Spain and Savoy joined in the following year. France saw herself encircled. Both sides had now deployed their forces for the decisive universal engagement. For the first time something like a popular hatred of the French arose in Germany. The utter devastation of the Rhenish Palatinate by the latest methods of warfare and the destruction, not once but twice, of both the castle and the city of Heidelberg (1693) goaded popular feeling to fury.

Dynastic interests still dominated national feeling. Parts of the land were shifted to this authority and to that without anyone's asking the subjects for their sentiment or opinion. Inquiry was indeed made about church connections, because they were likely to mean something politically, but cultural and linguistic factors were scarcely considered, especially as the lower classes of the people were wholly uneducated. Louis XIV's officials did not dream of Gallicizing the new German subjects of their King. The upper class of the inhabitants knew enough French to carry on the necessary tasks of administration, for French had become the prevalent language of the European upper classes. The most important administrative assignments were collecting taxes and recruiting. The local and private life of the subjects remained essentially undisturbed, if only because there were no officials who could grasp and comprehend it. The state left the care of the common people to the lords and the clergy. This fact must be realized to understand the endless territorial shifts in the period of absolutism. The governing authorities changed, but for the mass of subjects nothing essential was altered. Hence this agitation in Germany over the behaviour of the French in the Rhenish Palatinate is something new and noteworthy. Political aggression and the brutality of modern military methods did not arouse merely the ordinary hatred of foreigners and dread of the horrors of war. Here there was a modern sense of being on guard that rested on the homogeneousness of the people. This feeling ebbed away again. But political nationalism had shown its face.

The Emperor and his allies now saw themselves forced at last to wage war simultaneously on two fronts, in the east and the west. Central Europe was taking up its weapons. The efficient and indefatigable Margrave Louis of Baden distinguished himself so brilliantly in fighting the Turks that the people nicknamed him "Turk Louis." His Oriental trophies can still be seen at Karlsruhe. He was also a notable military organizer for the Empire. In southwestern Germany a special association was formed for supporting troops, even in peace times, as a protective measure against possible attack by France. The Elector Max Emanuel of Bavaria now became Stadholder of the Spanish Netherlands. This was intended to strengthen the defence, and the Elector also hoped to win by this means an advantage in the impending settlement about the succession. In the Empire, Archduke Joseph was elected King of the Romans. The French claims collapsed. But the establishment of a ninth electorate caused a crisis. Duke Ernest Augustus of Hanover had been working for a long while for this highest dignity that a prince of the Empire might attain. The passing of the electoral Palatinate to a Catholic house furthered his plans, since the number of Protestant votes in the electoral college was now reduced to two. All the votes of western Germany were now at the disposal of the Catholics. Ernest Augustus's wife was the daughter of the Winter King and of the Stuart Princess Elizabeth; this was the basis of the Hanoverian dynasty's claims to the throne of Great Britain.

The impending Hanoverian succession became a factor in international politics and effectively strengthened the defensive position of the house of Orange against France. Hanover and its rank in the Empire thus took on an importance that they would not otherwise have had. Ernest Augustus and his wife were energetic, cultivated, clever, and cosmopolitan. Their court became a cultural centre, and expectations of something greater seemed well founded. The Duke was faced with difficulties, for his own younger sons were challenged by their Brunswick cousins for the succession, while the Emperor was tormented with grave religious and political doubts. The Emperor did not accede until the Duke had formed a new party among the princes and thus jeopardized the success of the Empire's war against France (1692). Ernest Augustus was given the ninth electorate and the office of arch-banneret of the Empire. Three Catholic electors and many princes protested, and the princes formed a fresh combination against the electors; the Empire was paralysed. Notwithstanding, the Emperor made a "perpetual union" with electoral Hanover, and so the co-operation of the Habsburgs and the Guelphs, especially in the matter of the Spanish succession, was assured. This connection of the dynasties remained in force for a long time. Hatred of Brandenburg-Prussia was a bond between the interests of Austria and those of Hanover.

Both camps were in a state of exhaustion. A speedy and complete victory for either side was quite unlikely. The real question at issue, that of the Spanish inheritance, could not be decided, for it had not yet come into the open, and the chances of an amicable settlement seemed increasing rather than decreasing. All the requirements for reaching an understanding, for peace, appeared to have been filled. Louis XIV cut off the Duke of Savoy from the coalition by ceding the fortress of Pignerolo to him. Without Savoy it was impossible to wage a successful war in Italy; so the Emperor and Spain made a treaty with France in guarantee of Italian neutrality. The obvious sequel could only be a general peace. Louis XIV had to make great concessions.

At the peace congress at Rijswijk in Holland (1697), King William of Great Britain, who was Prince of Orange, was the strongest diplomatic adversary of France. Louis XIV recognized Joseph Clemens of Wittelsbach as the Elector of Köln and renounced French claims to the Palatinate. Finally he gave up Lorraine as well as all the districts outside of Alsace that had been occupied by decrees of the Chambers of Reunion, including Luxemburg. He ceded Freiburg and Breisach to the Emperor and Kehl to the Empire. Only Alsace, including Strassburg, and Saarlouis remained French. The peace had only one flaw. This was the so-called Rijswijk proviso, according to which, in the areas that had been returned by France, the Catholic faith should be maintained in its existing status—that is, the status established by France. The King of France now held himself to be the heir and the executor of the Spanish Counter-Reformation in contrast to the Habsburg Emperor, who apparently did not hesitate to make alliances with heretics. This motive of militant clericalism became more pronounced with Louis as the decision on the Spanish succession drew nearer.

SAXONY AND POLAND. THE PRUSSIAN KINGDOM

France suffered a new defeat in the Polish royal election (1697). The succession to King John III Sobieski was contested, and there were duplicate elections. Elector Frederick Augustus of Saxony turned Catholic for the sake of the Polish crown. The Prince of Conti, the French candidate, appeared before Danzig with a French fleet, but the Saxon elector was nearer and quicker, and he marched into the kingdom. The personal union with Poland did not change the Lutheran character of electoral Saxony in any way. The Elector continued to preside over the *Corpus Evangelicorum* in the diet. If anything, Saxony was politically more independent than before in regard to the court, which was now Catholic. Culturally the connection, which lasted for two generations, meant a great deal for both sides. The mutual give and take of German and Slavic blood and spirit supplied powerful stimuli. More than ever German politics gravitated eastward.

Electoral Brandenburg was envious of the heightened prestige and power that adhered to electoral Saxony from her connection with Poland. The reversion of the sovereign Duchy of Prussia to Poland, which had already been anticipated as a possibility, now put Brandenburg into an awkward position toward its old rival. There was an urgent desire to clarify the situation of Prussia. Electoral Saxony seemed on the way to becoming one of the great powers of Europe, and Brandenburg did not intend to be left behind. The Great Elector had fought all his life for centralized military and financial organization. He had confirmed all the privileges of the nobles of the Mark of Brandenburg, in particular their manorial rights over the enserfed peasants, in order to secure their consent to military appropriations. The territorial diets resisted stubbornly, especially in Cleve-Mark and in the Duchy of Prussia, where it came to a refusal to pay taxes and ruthless persecution of champions of feudal privilege, such as the assessor Hieronymus Roth of Königsberg. His harsh policy toward all local resistance alone enabled the Great Elector to maintain his army and through the army to play so significant a part in European politics. It is curious that this heavy-handed champion of small-scale absolutism stipulated in his will that his younger sons should be provided with principalities from the hereditary lands. His successor, to be sure, ignored this clause and bought off his stepbrothers, to the anger of his stepmother, who had exerted great influence over the old Elector. The future of Brandenburg-Prussia thus was appreciably endangered by a family feud.

Elector Frederick III was not a very notable personality. He played his distinguished father still another trick, obviously not without a certain satisfaction. In the negotiations with the Emperor the future of the three Silesian duchies of Liegnitz, Brieg, and Wohlau had been seriously disputed. The reigning Piast dukes of these districts had made with the Hohenzollerns a treaty as to mutual succession. But since they were vassals of Bohemia, the Emperor, as King of Bohemia, could take back their lands in the regular way after the Piast family died out. Bohemia had never confirmed the treaty about the inheritance. As arrière-vassals the Piasts were not immediate to the Empire; they were not princes of the Empire at all. Emperor Leopold I, moreover, because of the oath he had taken when he became King of Bohemia, felt it his duty to hold the lands of the Wenceslaus crown intact. And so the Emperor appeased Brandenburg by holding out the expectation of East Friesland and by ceding the district of Schwiebus. But the court at Vienna secured from the electoral prince behind his father's back, a secret promise that this district should be returned. After the Great Elector's death the promise was made good. But now the Brandenburg councillors declared that Silesian claims were again valid. This attitude dumbfounded the Emperor's councillors, for in that case all the change and change-about had been unnecessary. Nothing to any such effect had been contained in the secret treaty, and, besides, East Friesland was by way of indemnification for the claims. Hence the statement of the Brandenburg councillors was not registered. The incident was hardly glorious for either party. This was the peg on which the Silesian wars were hung.

Elector Frederick III proved a lamentably weak ruler. He let him-

237

self be persuaded to imprison and abuse his best minister, Count von Danckelmann, a conscientious public servant and personally distinguished. The extravagance of the electoral court brought the state finances, which up to this time had been admirably administered, into wretched confusion. Intellectual life at least took a turn for the better. The Elector's wife, Sophie Charlotte, transplanted the love of everything great in art and science from her native cultivated Hanover to barbarous Berlin. The philosopher Gottfried Wilhelm Leibniz (died 1716) came to the city to live, and the Academy of Sciences was established according to his plans. The University of Halle was founded (1694); among those who taught there were Samuel Pufendorf, who was soon made court historian of Brandenburg, and the eminent Thomasius. In the theological faculty pietism found a field for creative activity; it was tolerated and even encouraged by the relatively unprejudiced Hohenzollerns.

From the very start Elector Frederick played with the idea of securing a royal crown. All the conditions of the times favoured his plan: the Hanover Electorate, the personal union of electoral Saxony with the kingdom of Poland, and the Emperor's need of pinning down the fickle Hohenzollerns in the matter of the Spanish succession. The Duchy of Prussia had become sovereign. It represented only a part of Prussia; the smaller half had remained Polish, so that if the Duke wanted to become king, he needed the Emperor's recognition and Poland's acquiescence. Now in the coronation treaty the Elector promised military support of the Emperor's claims to the Spanish inheritance. He then crowned himself and his wife in Königsberg (1701); he was sovereign King in Prussia. The Polish diet objected, and the Roman curia refused recognition of the act until 1786. The new King never seriously considered a Hohenzollern conversion to Catholicism on the pattern of electoral Saxony, even though a few Jesuits cherished hope of it and stood ready to assist.

PRINCE EUGENE

At the close of the century the strengthening of the German people in central Europe became a fact of overwhelming significance. The reply to French and Turkish aggression had been given. In the west, Germany had every prospect of self-defence; in the east she waged brilliant offensive warfare. By the terms of the Peace of

Karlowitz the Emperor received all of Hungary, except the Banat of Temesvár, and in addition Transylvania and the major part of Croatia and Slavonia (1699). This triumphant ending of the Turkish wars was largely the work of one personality, who was to decide the military and political destinies of the house of Habsburg for more than a generation—Prince Eugene of Savoy (died 1736).

This prince stood godfather to the new great power, Austria. His twin military and political talents raise him almost to the level of some of the greatest names of modern history, of Frederick the Great and Napoleon. As a younger son of the house of Savoy his prospects were meagre. Physically he was unattractive, even weakly, and he seemed out of place in the elegant French army. At that time the Spanish style still prevailed in Vienna. Etiquette, confessors, and subsidies carried on the traditions of King Philip II of Spain without preserving the scope of his political purposes. Against it worked the French influence, which had been careful to win over such men as the Princes Lobkowitz and Auersperg, the chief councillors of Emperor Leopold. Against both these groups Eugene, an Italian prince with French antecedents, achieved something that was specifically Austrian, German and more than merely German: European, dynastic, Balkan. The new Austrian administration, which undertook to combine the mission of expelling the Turks with the European tasks of the Spanish inheritance, had to develop a superior political reasoning, its own style, its own personnel. Prince Eugene, the most distinguished of the many princely generals of the Turkish wars, had to create an army before he could lead one. He saw to it that his troops had proper food, decent quarters, and sufficient reserves, that they conducted themselves well, and that, if possible, they were given land to settle on in the newly opened east, so that Hungary and the Balkans should become populated by Germans.

Eugene himself was a strange, inhibited personality, lonely and without real human fulfilment, who knew the fate of the oppressed and disinherited; he understood how to encourage his people with a word or a glance, how to prepare them for action. As a general he tried to develop a strategy of annihilation. He liked to outflank the foe by sudden attack. These qualities place him historically between the Swedish Kings Gustavus Adolphus and Charles XII. Himself a calculator and organizer, Prince Eugene was strongly drawn to the natural sciences and the arts, and he showed sound taste and tact in whatever he did. He built the splendid Belvedere in Vienna and filled it with his books, engravings, and rare plants and animals.

THE SPANISH SUCCESSION

Should Austria be forced to fight for the Spanish succession, she was assured of a general. Brandenburg-Prussia as well as Austria ascended to the position of a great power both within Germany and in transcendence of it under the compulsion of foreign policy to finance and mobilize a great army. They thus followed the militarization of the older great powers—of Spain, France, and Sweden, but particularly of the Ottoman Empire and its military state system. Even during the war against the Augsburg League Louis XIV revived the old idea of dividing the Spanish heritage. King William III of Great Britain was decidedly in favour of this plan, since a general peace and the balance of power in Europe, which Holland, in particular, could never forget, could be preserved only by some reasonable partition. The second partition treaty of 1698 recognized the Prince of Bavaria, who was the son of Max Emanuel and the Archduchess Maria Antonia, as the heir to Spain, to the southern Netherlands, and to the colonies. The French Dauphin was to receive Naples and Sicily, as well as Sardinia and border regions in the vicinity of the Pyrenees. The Emperor was to have the Duchy of Milan. The early death of the Prince of Bavaria disposed of this possibility. According to the third partition treaty Archduke Charles, the younger son of Emperor Leopold, was to take the place of the Prince of Bavaria, and the Dauphin was to have Milan also. Spain was not to be joined to Austria, nor the Spanish dependencies to France. Both partition treaties remained agreements between the maritime powers and France. The Emperor did not participate. He was still hoping that the will of the last Spanish King might make him heir to everything.

But here he was doomed to severe disappointment. The national party at the Spanish court was bitterly averse to partition and patriotically held to the idea of a world empire. French diplomacy exploited these sentiments in conference with Charles II, and the Spanish King on his sick-bed made a will in favour of Duke Philip of Anjou, the second son of the Dauphin and the younger grandson of Louis XIV, that made Philip heir to the entire monarchy. At first it seemed that French finesse had been successful. The old Spanish King died; Philip came to Spain and was hailed as King. King Louis XIV was too arrogant to accept any shabby settlement, and now the maritime powers concluded the Grand Alliance with the Emperor. All the partition treaties had been meant to keep the Spanish Netherlands distinct from France. This was a matter that, for Holland and England, touched the quick. Both these maritime powers promised the Emperor the Spanish Netherlands and the Italian possessions, while they intended to compensate themselves with the Spanish colonies. Louis XIV was therefore forced to fight for his claim to European hegemony. In accordance with his former method he acquired an ally of the highest importance in the Empire.

Both the third partition treaty and the Spanish King's will were a great disappointment to the necessitous Max Emanuel, the Elector of Bavaria. He had been loyal and valiantly defended the Emperor's interests against the Turks and in the Netherlands, and he did not want to go empty-handed, especially in view of the successes of electoral Saxony, electoral Hanover, and electoral Brandenburg. He too had set his hope on a kingly crown, but only Louis XIV was prepared to promise him one. Max Emanuel's first step was to assume a position of benevolent neutrality. Then he made an aggressive alliance with France: in return for subsidies he promised to furnish an army of twenty-five thousand men and to join with the French; he was to receive the electoral Palatinate and Palatine Neuburg as a Rhenish kingdom or else the hereditary stadholdership in the Spanish Netherlands. Here again was the old dream of a west German kingdom that Wallenstein too had cherished, the dream of a buffer state composed of Lorraine and Burgundy. Once more the Wittelsbach dynasty rose enviously against the Habsburgs. Max Emanuel's brother, the Elector of Köln, also joined forces with France, which had opposed his election. The Wittelsbachs were heading back to their old course of amicable relations with France.

Strictly speaking, the Austrian line of the Habsburgs had no hereditary rights at all, since Archduke Charles was not the son of Emperor Leopold's first wife, the Spanish Infanta, but of his third wife. But the entire question had long since outgrown the sphere of dynasty and jurisprudence and had entered that of the great problem of European power. If the King of France had either kinsman or friend in the highest seat beyond the chain of the Pyrenees in Spain or beyond the Flemish chain of fortresses in the Netherlands, the way into Germany would lie open to him. He could form a new Rhenish confederation; he could paralyse Holland and endanger England. He would have hegemony in Europe; he might even be said to have the Carolingian world empire.

THE SECOND NORTHERN WAR (1700–21)

While France was fighting for predominance in Europe, Sweden was struggling for its place as a great power in the north. Both of these guarantors of the Peace of Westphalia had to maintain themselves against hostile coalitions. But while France had reached out farther and farther beyond her earlier acquisitions, Sweden had to defend her former gains against envious neighbours. Denmark, Poland, and Russia joined forces against young Charles XII. Sweden's supremacy in the north was insecurely founded. For generations war alone had occupied the nation. There had been no independent economic development, for the country could not rid itself of Dutch middlemen who dominated trade. The constantly recurring threat of state bankruptcy could be averted only by foreign subsidies. The dependencies, or rather the exploitative colonial regions in Germany and along the Baltic coast, only served to occupy and to enrich the satisfied members of the feudal upper class. The country of Sweden itself had small profit from these possessions. Local rights and traditions were suppressed everywhere; every gesture toward independence on the part of the indigenous population was jealously watched. Under Peter the Great, Russia was advancing toward the Baltic with elemental force. Poland regarded herself as an old Baltic power of which advantage had been taken. The Saxon Elector, Augustus the Strong, now furnished her with a king who revolved magnificent projects; a mighty German and Slavic eastern realm was supposed to arise during his rule. Denmark's old envy of Sweden made her an enthusiastic partner of any coalition formed in opposition to Sweden's interests. Prussia and Hanover, neighbours to the Swedish holdings on German soil, manifested deep interest in impending developments in the Swedish colonial possessions.

The Second Northern War (1700–21), which engaged Europe simultaneously with the War of the Spanish Succession and even after this was over, pitted the struggle of the young King Charles XII against an overpowering destiny. The element of destiny, however, lay more in his own character than in external circumstances. Among all the great Swedish kings who became involved in the history of Germany, he was the greatest and the strangest; a military genius, a lovable and magnetic human being, a charming personality, but politically uncreative and without sound instinct for the advantage offered by the moment, without vision, and without flexibility. In spite of all his gifts he was obstinate to the point of self-annihilation, a destructive rather than a constructive force, Sweden's glory and doom. The waning of Sweden's power opened the way to healthy development for northern and northeastern Germany. The dangerous proximity of Russia had, of course, to be taken into account.

THE WORLD WAR OF THE DYNASTIES

Was the situation of the Thirty Years' War to repeat itself? Was Germany again to be the principal theatre of military operations? Perhaps the two great conflicts were growing together, with central Europe as not only a political but also a military focus. The former mutuality of interests between France and Sweden, which might have forced such a development, was not re-established. The estrangement that had originated in the policy of the Chambers of Reunion was sharpened when Charles XII, a good Lutheran, spurned the French King's fanatical zeal for the Counter-Reformation. And so the new world war of the dynasties played itself out on two separate stages. Germany was only partially involved. But German interests in the east as well as in the west were at stake. The new world war was a crisis in the growth of the two German powers, Austria and Prussia. The struggle raged for a long time and proved extremely burdensome. Fighting extended to the East and West Indies and to North America. The contending dynasties invoked the full strength of the peoples. Armies were larger and more mobile. The infantry came to the fore as the new weapon of matured absolutism—the drilled, marching, huge, compact body of subjects. Great manœuvres, daring strategy, surprise, and sudden attacks became commonplace, and losses mounted accordingly. Matériel was rapidly consumed and had to be swiftly replaced. Prince Eugene's generalship was matched and supported by the Englishman John Churchill, the first Duke of

Marlborough. The maritime powers conducted the struggle largely as a naval war. France and Spain were hemmed in, cut off, and exposed to merciless privateering. The struggle overseas was decided long before the fighting on the Continent was concluded. The Great Britain of Queen Anne triumphed on all the seas.

The alliance of France with the Wittelsbachs enabled King Louis XIV to carry the war into southern Germany. Hungary's national insurrection under the leadership of Franz Rákóczy threatened even Lower Austria and Moravia. In the beginning the Emperor's position was therefore decidedly embarrassed. Things were better in Italy, where Prince Eugene was conducting operations. It was possible to alienate the Duke of Savoy from France. The King of Portugal, too, joined the Grand Alliance; he provided a military and political base on the Iberian peninsula. Emperor Leopold conveyed his rights to Spain to his younger son, Archduke Charles, and sent him to Portugal, where the Archduke set out to conquer Spain at the head of an army composed of Portuguese, English, and Dutch troops.

In 1703 the Emperor made a treaty with his two sons regulating the succession: in Spain as well as in the hereditary lands the male line was to have precedence; if the male line died out, the female line was to assume the succession in order of primogeniture. This treaty belongs to the prehistory of the Pragmatic Sanction, for both the elder son, Joseph, and the younger son, Charles, had only daughters as heirs.

The co-operation of the imperial troops with the English and Dutch troops in southern Germany led to the great victory at Höchstädt and Blenheim (Blindheim; 1704). The French and the Bavarians had to fall back behind the Rhine, the two Wittelsbach electors surrendered their lands, and the new Emperor, Joseph I (since 1705), banished both these princes of the Empire, with the consent of the electoral college and after discussion in the diet. They were deprived of all their offices and honours and of princely status in the Empire. The first secular electorate and the Upper Palatinate now reverted to the Elector Palatine. Bavaria was placed under imperial administration, at first with the exception of Munich, the capital, but later including it. The sons of the Elector Max Emanuel were held in Austria, but not in close confinement. The energetic character of these measures was in keeping with popular feeling in the Empire against Wittelsbach high treason. In Bavaria, to be sure, the peasants, who were harshly oppressed by the Austrians, staged repeated insurrections in behalf of the ancestral dynasty.

Emperor Joseph I (1705–11) was a fresh and engaging personality. He was able to carry out essential reforms in the hereditary lands of Austria, but could do little in the Empire. His most important act in this connection was the readmission of Bohemia into the Empire. Bohemia's electoral vote was the only one of which the house of Habsburg was certain. The expansion of Brandenburg-Prussia and Saxony toward the east made it advisable to clarify Bohemia's status. Prussia's claim to Silesia may have been an added impetus. The German and Slavic character of Bohemia reinforced colonial traits in east central Europe. Joseph I improved his brother's prospects of success in Spain by interposing forcibly against Pope Clement XI, who was friendly to France. Austrian and Prussian troops marched into the papal states and threatened to occupy Rome, whereupon the curia recognized Charles as King of Spain and Naples. Since the late Middle Ages no pope had been so ruthlessly dealt with by an emperor. But things were looking bad in Hungary. The patriot rebels formally declared that Emperor Joseph I had forfeited the Stephen crown. Peter the Great, the Czar of Russia, now offered the Emperor an alliance against Hungary, but the Emperor did not dare fall in with the suggestion; it would have meant too great a provocation to Sweden. For the Swedish King, Charles XII, was in Saxony; he had forced the Elector to renounce the Polish crown. Louis XIV tried to win Charles XII over as an ally. Charles, however, contented himself with securing several concessions from the Emperor. Among them were the release of Sweden from its obligation to contribute to the military support of the Empire on account of Swedish holdings in Germany, and also safeguards for the rights of Lutherans in Silesia. If Sweden had turned against Vienna at that time, the house of Habsburg could scarcely have been saved.

On the whole the Grand Alliance made headway in the Netherlands and in Spain in spite of constant rebuffs. In 1709 Louis XIV initiated peace negotiations. He offered to cede Strassburg; he was willing to leave Spain as well as her dependencies to Archduke Charles if his own grandson received Naples and Sicily. The allies now demanded French military assistance to drive King Philip V out of Spain. They were not satisfied with the subsidies Louis had offered. France was exhausted and her old King's spirit broken. He was not willing, however, to promise French help to strike against his own grandson. The blindness of the allies was to be heavily penalized.

THE PEACE TREATIES (1713–4)

In the Northern War a change in favour of Sweden's foes occurred after Charles XII had been defeated in Russia and fled to Turkey. Augustus the Strong, the Elector of Saxony, renewed his claim to the Polish crown. The native Polish King, Stanislaus Leszczynski, withdrew to Pomerania with the Swedes. The maritime powers and the Emperor decided to keep northern Germany neutral, and an army was put in position to guard this neutrality. Only this made it possible to hold Prussia and Hanover to the Grand Alliance. But the sudden death of Emperor Joseph raised an entirely new situation. His heir was his brother, King Charles III of Spain, who was in Barcelona and did not wish to leave. Was the Empire of Charles V to be united again under a Habsburg after all? England now resumed negotiations, in Utrecht, for a separate peace with France on a new basis.

The solution was the old idea of partition (1713). Philip V received Spain and her colonies; all possibility of their connection with France was permanently abjured. Louis XIV recognized the Hanoverian succession in England and promised to reject the Stuarts. He ceded Hudson's Bay, Nova Scotia, Newfoundland, and St. Christopher (St. Kitts) to England. The fortress of Dunkirk was to be demolished. England received Gibraltar and Minorca from Spain and was now the leading colonial power. Holland secured a barrier of fortresses in the southern Netherlands; these lands, like Naples and Sardinia, went to Austria. Emperor Charles VI (King Charles III of Spain), who had to give up Catalonia, did not take part in the peace negotiations, since France did not want to stop at reinstating the Wittelsbachs, but was asking indemnities for them and in addition sought excessive guarantees for her Italian possessions. Prussia came off well: besides universal recognition of the kingdom, she received the principality of Neuchâtel, from the Orange inheritance, and the erstwhile Spanish headquarters of Geldern on the Lower Rhine.

The Duke of Marlborough had been ousted from his command in 1711, and the English army took ship for home. The German mercenaries who were in England's pay continued to fight at least to the conclusion of the separate Peace of Utrecht, but after that the Emperor had to rely on his own forces. He had no choice but to make peace, for the French were winning new victories. The Emperor came to terms with France at Rastatt, and the peace between France and the Empire, at Baden (Aargau, Switzerland, 1714), followed. The Emperor made a thoroughly Austrian peace. He received Milan, Naples, and Sardinia in Italy, the Spanish coastal regions of Tuscany and Mantua, and also the southern Netherlands. But the Empire was left empty-handed. There was no mention at all of Franche-Comté, of Strassburg and Alsace; the French even retained the fortress of Landau, which they had captured during the last year of the war. Not even the Rijswijk proviso as to Catholicism was set aside. The two Wittelsbach electors were again invested with all their rights and possessions, but they received no indemnity. In this point, therefore, the dignity of the Empire was upheld. After this experience no prince of the Empire was ever put under the imperial ban.

The upshot of this world struggle did not appear unfavourable for Germany. It was true that France had guaranteed the boundary of the Pyrenees through Bourbon rule in Spain, but she did have to withdraw from the Netherlands. The maritime powers were obviously determined not to allow this strategic area, full of danger for Holland as well as for Great Britain, to fall into French hands. These possessions, so remote from Austria, involved the Habsburgs in relations with distant foreign powers; for this reason an exchange had been planned from the outset. Elector Max Emanuel, incorrigibly ambitious as he was, did not want to die without a king's crown. He would willingly have given his Bavaria for this Belgium, since the future Belgium was then the Austrian Netherlands. During the entire eighteenth century the idea of such exchange came up again and again. The Austrian Breisgau and the Netherlands forced the house of Habsburg to adopt a Rhenish policy and to maintain good relations with the Rhenish electors and with the Kingdom of

247

Prussia. Prussia had a firm hold on her possessions on the Lower Rhine, and this was to be further strengthened by her prospective acquisition of East Friesland. The obligations arising from the Italian possessions of the Habsburgs presented still graver problems; the Austrians, quite differently from the Spaniards, functioned as strangers in lands that through long experience had become sensitized to alien rule and were approaching an intellectual and political awakening. Manifold perplexities thus lay beneath the brilliant surface of the power of the Austrian house, which once again stressed central Europe. As yet no peace had been concluded with Spain, nor was one arrived at until 1720, with the mediation of the great powers. The Emperor now achieved another success. The arbitrary separation of Naples and Sicily was done away with. The Duke of Savoy had to content himself with poverty-stricken, backward Sardinia, while Austria now took over Sicily. Spain, to be sure, got the reversion of Parma and Piacenza. At the same time Prince Eugene, with the Republic of Venice as his ally, had once more been winning brilliant victories over the Turks. By the Peace of Passarowitz the Ottoman Empire ceded the Banat of Temesvár, northern Serbia with Belgrade, and Little Wallachia to the Emperor (1718). The question of French hegemony was no longer under discussion in Europe. Louis XIV's successors were weak and burdened with the serious financial problems that he passed down to them. The house of Habsburg had every prospect of hegemony in Europe if it were successful in maintaining friendship with the maritime powers and peace within the Empire.

The epoch of world wars at the outset of the eighteenth century ended only with the Second Northern War. It was not surprising that Denmark and Hanover, Sweden's foes, took advantage of the vacillating and finally all but suicidal course of Charles XII. The Russians and the Poles appeared in Hither Pomerania. Prussia started negotiating with Russia in order to assure her claims, and these powers made a treaty of mutual security, with Russia undertaking to see that Prussia should receive Hither Pomerania as far as the Peene River, while Prussia promised the Russians the hitherto Swedish provinces along the Baltic. Prussia would probably not have attained her long-cherished goal without Russia. The Russian policy of expansion, which even extended to Mecklenburg, excited suspicion in the Empire and in England. The Elector of Hanover now ascended the British throne, and this gave his claims greater weight. After the death of Charles XII, Sweden had to make peace; it put an abrupt end to the lofty position she had occupied since the Peace of Westphalia. Russia received the Baltic provinces (1721); Bremen and Verden were assigned to Hanover; Prussia got Hither Pomerania as far as the Peene and the islands of Usedom and Wollin; both Russia and Prussia paid considerable sums to Sweden, which was in financial straits, and this arrangement actually made the peace the more humiliating for Sweden. The only sop to Denmark was the section of Schleswig that belonged to the Duke of Gottorp; this region was united with the principal part of the Duchy of Schleswig and later figured in the struggles over Schleswig as the "Gottorp part" (Peace of Stockholm, 1719–20). Sweden, too, now recognized the Saxon Elector, Augustus the Strong, as King of Poland. Stanislaus Leszczynski was given an annuity and permitted to retain the title of King.

Like France in the west, Sweden in the east was receding into the background. But whereas France was only temporarily weakened, Sweden's period of grandeur was finished. Great Britain and her ally Hanover emerged from the era of world war with the chief gains. The Kingdom of Prussia had improved its position in essential respects; it could not as yet be compared to the universal position of the house of Habsburg, but the suspicious Emperor Charles VI knew better than anyone else that it was necessary to reckon seriously with a state whose huge army enabled it to participate equal-handedly in the great game of European politics. The co-operation of the two great German powers, Austria and Prussia, the pillars of central Europe, had contributed essentially to the favourable conclusion of the period of world war. But in this success the tensions of times to come were rooted.

THE WITTELSBACH "HOUSE ALLIANCE." EMPEROR CHARLES VI (1711–40)

The Wittelsbachs were the only important dynasty in the Empire that had not won some footing across the borders. The fact was a further stimulus to this family of princes that had only just been recalled from banishment. The unwearying Elector Max Emanuel again took part in the Turkish wars and—surprisingly enough—

was able to betroth his son Charles to the younger daughter of Emperor Joseph, while the elder married the heir to the Saxon throne. Both princesses had to renounce their hereditary claims to Austrian lands. This, however, did not prevent the houses of Wittelsbach and Wettin from urging such claims later when the moment offered. Max Emanuel made the so-called Wittelsbach "House Alliance" (1724) with the branch of the electoral Palatinate. Wittelsbach princes ruled most of Catholic Germany. Eleven ecclesiastical principalities were in their hands. It almost looked as if the Wittelsbachs were claiming the core of the old Empire for themselves, after their more fortunate rivals had secured dynastic power outside the Empire. Consequently this house was preparing to contend with the Habsburgs for the imperial crown.

Emperor Charles VI (1711–40) was slow and deliberate, ceremonious in the Spanish fashion. He was never able to forget his best years, spent in Catalonia. At that time he had gathered some knowledge of modern trade possibilities. He had had enough experience with the maritime powers to dislike their position of economic monopoly. The Emperor founded an Oriental trading company in Trieste. Venice watched the rise of a more vigorous rival on the other side of the Adriatic. The Emperor brought the Danube below Vienna into use as far as possible for development toward the east. Thanks to the closing of the Scheldt, Antwerp was dead; Charles VI therefore founded a company in Ostend (1723) for trade with India and Africa. But the envious maritime powers resisted the rise of Ostend; on the basis of provisions of the Peace of Westphalia and that of Utrecht the company was forced to dissolve. Charles did not bear the old imperial name in vain. He wanted to keep up the reunited Habsburg realm as far as possible. The War of the Spanish Succession had been bad enough. Was it not possible to avoid a war for the Austrian succession?

THE PRAGMATIC SANCTION

In 1713 the Emperor issued the Pragmatic Sanction, the solemn statement of a new status of the rights of succession. The new statute about the Habsburg dynasty asserted the indivisibility of the Empire and the right of female succession according to primogeniture, in default of male heirs. The only son of Emperor Charles VI had died soon after he was born. This made his daughter, Maria Theresa, heiress to all his territories. It is easy to understand the Emperor's ambitions from both the political point of view and the human, but from the angle of public law the Pragmatic Sanction was undoubtedly a contradiction of the prior Habsburg treaty concerning the inheritance. It has already been mentioned that the daughters of Emperor Joseph I had renounced their hereditary rights, but now the question arose whether this renunciation was legal, since the Emperor had made his consent to the marriage of his nieces contingent on the recognition of the Pragmatic Sanction. This could be interpreted as putting undue pressure on the young archduchesses, and accordingly their husbands, the Electors of Bavaria and of Saxony, refused to have anything to do with the imperial guarantee of the Pragmatic Sanction in 1737.

The Emperor fought for the Pragmatic Sanction all the rest of his days, and this course brought with it increasing weakness for Austria. First the diets of the various hereditary lands recognized the Sanction. Then began negotiations with all the countries of Europe. The Sanction figured in every treaty concluded by the Emperor. Questions of commercial policy alienated him from the maritime powers. In consequence the political system that had obtained in Europe up to this time was upset. Austria and Spain drew together; Spain recognized the Sanction and the Ostend Company. The maritime powers of England and Holland replied with the Alliance of Herrenhausen, which they formed with France and Prussia in 1725. A new war threatened. The Emperor wished to avoid it. He won over Prussia, which recognized the Sanction. By sacrificing the Ostend Company and making concessions in Italy, he won the consent of England also. A still further decline in Austrian prestige came with the war for the Polish succession that broke out after the death of the King and Elector Augustus the Strong (1733). France sponsored the election of the former King, Stanislaus Leszczynski, who in the interim had become the father-in-law of King Louis XV. The Emperor let himself be won over to the side of the new Saxon Elector, who personally underwrote the Pragmatic Sanction. Russia too worked for the candidate of the Wettin dynasty, but Stanislaus was chosen as the national Polish candidate by an overwhelming majority. France made an alliance with Spain and

Sardinia-Savoy and opened the war by occupying Lorraine and Lombardy. The maritime powers deserted the Emperor. The Empire did indeed declare war on France, but the group of Wittelsbach princes remained neutral, and electoral Bavaria even renewed her treaty of friendship with France. Prussia alone offered the Emperor armed assistance, but he was so suspicious that he accepted only a small contingent. The war was fought in a half-hearted way. Prince Eugene, now an old man, could win no victories on the Rhine, and soon negotiations for peace were opened.

The result was one of the boldest manœuvres of these unscrupulous times. Augustus II, the Elector of Saxony, received the Polish crown against the will of the national majority in that country. He promised to support Count Biron's claims to the Duchy of Kurland, and this decided the Czarina Anna of Russia, who was the Count's highly placed patroness. Stanislaus received the Duchy of Lorraine in place of Poland; the Duke of Lorraine was transplanted to Italy, where he was assigned the Grand Duchy of Tuscany after the death of the last of the Medici. Finally the Emperor ceded Naples, Sicily, and coastal areas of Tuscany to the Spanish Infante, Don Carlos, while some border regions in Lombardy went to the King of Sardinia-Savoy.

What was the political effect of this territorial redistribution? The Emperor and the Empire had suffered an appreciable loss. The Empire had at last forfeited Lorraine, which had long been within the sphere of French power and could no longer act independently; after the death of Stanislaus it would be taken over by the French crown. In Italy the Emperor had to put up with a revival of Spanish influence, represented this time by the Bourbons. The Queen of Spain, Elizabeth Farnese, wife of the melancholy Philip V, had reached the summit of her desires; she combined Italian national ideas with Spanish and Bourbon interests. The house of Habsburg had lost southern Italy. Parma and Piacenza were a modest substitute; soon Tuscany was added to them, since Duke Francis Stephen of Lorraine, the new lord of Tuscany, married Maria Theresa, the Habsburg heiress. The Habsburg dynasty's position of hegemony was weakened still further by the Turkish war of 1737–9.

In 1726 the Emperor had finally made an alliance with Russia, and on the basis of it this advancing power asked help in her war against the Ottoman Empire. Instead of merely sending the auxiliary troops called for by the terms of the treaty, the suspicious Emperor let himself be persuaded to declare war on the Sublime Porte itself. This is the first case of jealous Austrian-Russian co-operation. The war did not go well. The Turks besieged Belgrade. The Empire gave only slight pecuniary help. Emperor Charles VI had to be glad to secure a peace with French mediation, even though he had to renounce almost all the gains of the Peace of Passarowitz—that is, Belgrade, Orsova, and Little Wallachia. The liberation of the southern Slavs and the opening up of the Balkans were abandoned. When Emperor Charles died suddenly in 1740, Austria's domestic politics were disorganized, while her foreign relations were imperilled. She had been unable to maintain her brilliant position of 1720. The Pragmatic Sanction had brought little luck.

KING FREDERICK WILLIAM I (1713–40)

Emperor Charles VI committed his most serious mistake in his treatment of Prussia. King Frederick William I, the successor of her first King, Frederick I, was one of the most remarkable characters in modern German history. Both in personality and in principles he had grown up in sharp contrast to his father, whose weakness and extravagance disgusted him. His clear mind and common sense could not understand anything foreign, high-flown, or pompous and found it almost physically repulsive. These very qualities involved also a lack of interest in high art and deep thinking. Frederick William I was a true east German, akin to the colonial soil on which he dwelt: sturdy and hard, imperious and precise, averse to the intellectualism and refinement that had always thriven in good old Germany. The King positively hated French ways, but even the cultivated and fastidious Hanoverians struck him as questionable, not to speak of the witty Rhinelanders or the elegant Austrians. This coarse-grained King was in sympathy with Russian methods of ruling. Peter the Great and his regime of the knout evoked his admiration. And so under this ruler Prussia turned more or less deliberately away from the west and from the real Germany. Frederick William's greatest virtue was his feeling for the inner organization of his realm. Every last trace of a feudal constitution based on estates, every form of communal independence, was now ruthlessly set aside.

Just because the Prussian states were scattered all over northern Germany, just because there was no community of spirit among them, every vestige of local feeling was held to be dangerous, for it always appeared to take a keener interest in its immediate neighbourhood than in the artificial creation of the entire Prussian state.

This entire state, however, was the King's achievement. From the many odds and ends of his hereditary lands he wrought a homogeneous eastern military despotism that was independent, no longer directed by the subsidies of more fortunate colonial powers, but based on the first and most important institution of the state, the army. Frederick William I created a regular budget, called for exact accounting, and did not merely pay off the debts he had inherited, but left a treasure of seven million thalers. Only personal control by this fanatic for work made such results possible. He himself made all important decisions. Officials were simply appointed on his orders. All the older authorities, the groups of nobles, were demoted to utter insignificance. In an emergency extraordinary commissions quickly created the desired arrangements. It was decisive for Prussia's future that the administration of the domains of the crown, as the main source of direct royal revenues, was combined with the organization of the army. The King unified the separate conflicting agencies of government. He created a single general board for the management of finance, war, and the domains, called for short the General Directory. Here salaried officials who were absolutely honest and reliable worked with careful supervision, under the King's ferule, on the organization of a military state. For Prussia was becoming more and more a military state.

King Frederick William had taken over thirty-eight thousand soldiers from his father; he himself left his son more than double that number of troops. And it was not merely a matter of quantity. This army, technically the foremost of the time, was headed by a homogeneous, highly respected body of officers drawn from the younger sons of the nobility. According to a conservative estimate it consumed two thirds of the entire public revenues. This army alone made the historical alliance between the Hohenzollerns and their rural nobility possible. The elder sons stayed on their estates and belaboured the peasants, while the rest of the family were given posts in the army or in the administration. Each of these groups aided the other in the service of the King. In many ways this petty Prussian nobility was still crude, greedy, and selfish. Now it was adapted to the Prussian state by the discipline of a stern teacher. In the beginning the younger sons had to be virtually forced into joining the ranks of officers. Later the most famous Prussian institution for training officers, the Kadettenhaus in Lichterfelde near Berlin, proudly called itself by that name because of these younger sons or *cadets*.

Whatever there was in Prussia by way of protection for the peasants or of middle-class policy really served the interests of the army and thus of the dynasty and the ruling class. Frederick William I gave refuge to immigrants of many sorts. The Salzburg Protestants who had been driven out by their Archbishop became famous; they found a new home in East Prussia. In his own way the King cared for the elementary schools, but universities and academies could hope for nothing good from him. Construction was practical and cheap; mechanical skill was esteemed. Originality in art or in thinking could not thrive in such a confining atmosphere. The brutality of the King almost destroyed the genius of his own eldest son and did at least cripple it.

Many anecdotes preserve the memory of this soldier King. Some represent him as a blusterer who was really hungering for love, as the fundamentally lonely, unhappy, even miserable being that he really was. To do him justice one must distinguish between his conduct in the later part of his life and in his longer early period. His last years were deeply clouded by his sufferings from gout, of which he died. He was the father of Prussian militarism, and that is why his influence on history was so powerful. This Prussian militarism differs in two respects from all the varieties that preceded and followed it: the army outweighed everything civilian in organizational and economic importance, and the army domineered over the country's whole life with its own ways of living.

In foreign policy King Frederick William was forced into the torturous and only half-comical role of the dolt who is always being outwitted. Everything connected with diplomacy, in the worst sense and also in the best, was foreign to him. It was not hard to take advantage of his peasant-like acquisitiveness. Even his closest political counsellors deceived him and were continually accepting bribes from his adversaries. The question of the Jülich-Cleve succession was a windfall to the imperial court; with it Prussia could be baited. When Prussia demanded a share in the inheritance of the Catholic house of Palatine Neuburg, which was standing on the very verge of extinction, she received the Emperor's guarantee in return for her recognition of the Pragmatic Sanction. But Palatine Neuburg desired recognition of female succession and wanted the entire territory to pass to the Palatine Sulzbach branch of the family. The group of Wittelsbach princes and France supported this proposal, because it would keep the land Catholic and friendly to the French. The old rivalry between the Hohenzollerns and the Hanoverian Guelphs cropped up in this conflict. A double marriage was projected in order to effect a dynastic and political rapprochement. British diplomacy would have liked to take advantage of this opportunity to fit Prussia into the front of the maritime powers, England and Holland, against the Emperor. But after repeated dramatic vacillations the King of Prussia decided to remain true to the Habsburg side. His daughter Wilhelmine did not marry the Prince of Wales; she did not become Queen of England, but only Margravine of Bayreuth. And his son Frederick had to marry the Brunswick grandniece of the Emperor. During his entire rule Frederick William I hoped for some favourable arrangement about the Jülich-Cleve succession, but Vienna kept leading him around by the nose. The maritime powers also were opposed to the expansion of Prussian power on the Lower Rhine. All the interested parties were against this greedy sabre-rattling state. Just before his death the King succeeded in making a secret treaty with France, guaranteeing him the part he claimed. Thus Frederick William I, who prided himself on his German honesty and deep-rooted respect for the Empire, went over to the anti-Habsburg camp. His son made this the substance of his life politically.

THE STRUGGLE BETWEEN PRINCELY ABSOLUTISM AND THE ESTATES

The princes dominated this epoch, and the princes put themselves above everything else. The state of affairs in Germany was exactly what it was elsewhere in Europe. The clerical absolutism of Spain and the legalistic absolutism of France had not been able to vanquish the Empire. Here the old Germanic and primitive German principle of the estates had triumphed—at the top, however, not at the bottom. Germany's old high nobility, represented in the diet of the Empire, flatly refused to accord to the diets in their own territories privileges such as they themselves claimed of the Emperor. The Emperor still had certain rights reserved for himself. The jurisdiction of the supreme court and of the Aulic Council (*Reichshofrat*) was no mean curb on the sovereignty of the territorial princes (*jus territoriale*). The princes did everything to throw off these last shackles on their liberty. The name and the notion of the Empire were narrowed down in the popular mind; they attached to the small territories in the west and the southwest that could form no relations with foreign powers, no hopes of becoming great powers. But a deeper meaning underlay the circumstance that now the native soil of the Salic emperors and the Hohenstaufens perpetuated the honorary name of "Empire" in a curious mutation of the original sense. The princes of the strongest territorial states established indivisible sovereign domains for themselves that were transmitted according to the rule of primogeniture. They organized their own armies and bureaucracies on the great pattern of French Cæsarism.

Prussia executed these tasks with characteristic acuteness. Feudal constitutions based on estates persisted only in Württemberg, electoral Saxony, Mecklenburg, and the Guelph countries. The Habsburg hereditary lands also preserved their local diets. Imperial legislation was now directed against the estates. According to the capitulation of Emperor Leopold I at his election, diets could be held only with the approval of the ruling prince. The princes wished to deprive the diets of the privilege of imposing taxes for the benefit of the Empire, and when the Emperor objected to this encroachment they formed a separate alliance. Thus the princes with constantly increasing success appropriated all the rights of the diets that history had hallowed, without realizing what an absurdity this involved. For their own existence rested on the old dualism that sprang from popular and feudal law. It was a long time before anyone in Germany sought a transformation of the concept of the diets into fruitful parliamentary labour. The rigid frame of the Empire was the despair of many patriotic thinkers. Was not this Holy Roman Empire its own exact opposite—an unholy, very un-Roman constitutional anarchy? A councillor of electoral Saxony who also wrote as a propagandist for Sweden was the first to dispute the Emperor's sovereignty. He called the Empire a sovereign aristocracy of princes and advised the members of it to break away from the house of Habsburg for all time.

In the economic field, too, everything depended on the territorial princes. The new towns and capitals outstripped the old imperial cities. Nürnberg or Frankfurt, indeed, might still preserve its traditional character. Vienna, Berlin, and Dresden were reshaped by their rulers' constructive will. In Dresden a great fire simplified the enterprise, for these lords of the Baroque preferred virgin soil for their creations. Townsfolk were astonished and irritated when, with a certain perversity, Charlottenburg was built next to Berlin, Schönbrunn to Vienna, Nymphenburg and Schleissheim to Munich, Ludwigsburg to Stuttgart, Herrenhausen to Hanover, and Wilhelmshöhe to Kassel. The castle of Heidelberg, which had been destroyed, was not rebuilt. The Elector Palatine of the Rhine, annoyed by the combative Reformed spirit of the university, moved out on to the open plain; Mannheim, rectilinear and well planned, corresponded far better to the dominant feeling of the Baroque period. The same was true of the fan-like city of Karlsruhe, whose founder, a connoisseur of fans, laid it out in the shape of a woman's fan. Bruchsal and Rastatt, but above all the residence of the Prince Bishops of Würzburg, who derived from the Counts of Schönborn, bore testimony to their builders' taste, their pride, sense of spaciousness, and love of fine art. They were rivalled by the settlements of the old landowning orders in Catholic Germany. Monasteries that suggested palaces arose in Göttweig and Melk, in St. Florian and Grüssau.

In front of the palace, in the market-place, or on the most important bridge the princes would set a majestic statue of their most distinguished ancestor. Erected next to the palace, in fulfilment of vows or in token of gratitude for the continuance of the dynasty, rose the court church in the massive Roman style, with domes and columns, portals and statues—splendid and triumphant, compelling awe and, above all, submissiveness. The Theatine Church in Munich and the Charles Church in Vienna were both ecclesiastical and secular palaces; they honoured the Roman faith, but also served

258

Catholic secular majesty. Fortifications, too, figured in the recasting and fresh creation of the Baroque city. Their purpose was to protect the princes against the new technique of attack and to provide shelter for the soldiers. These public works keep the terms "bastion" and "glacis" alive up to our own times.

Rational population policy, manufacturing, military affairs, efficient bureaucracy—all occupied and enlivened the new cities, whose existence revolved around the single centre of the palace. The main concern was to bring as much money as possible into the country. Foreign subsidies were used to set up factories or to build new sections of the city in accordance with a unified plan. The great success of French mercantilism and the position of the States General of the independent Netherlands as a world power were a constant spur to German enterprisers. These gentlemen were particularly fond of soliciting the lesser lords, whose heads could easily be turned by projects involving Africa or the East Indies. This was, moreover, the first time that the idea of economic unification for Germany was agitated. Really sound plans were often wrecked for the commonest of reasons, lack of funds. A canal to connect the Werra and the Main —a genuinely far-sighted idea—was not constructed. Attempts to revive the Hanseatic League failed.

Frankfurt and Breslau maintained themselves as tried and true centres of commerce and fairs. Hamburg, which had been almost wholly spared from the fury of war, throve by dint of its neutral monopolistic position between the envious northern powers of Denmark and Sweden. Here the Dutch founded the first giro-bank on German soil, with a system of credit transfers; it was modelled on the Amsterdam Wisselbank. This constituted Hamburg's real introduction to the money market. Leipzig alone became a trade centre of European scope. Big business, however, still remained the affair of the shrewd and sober Dutch. Their taste in architecture, their way of living, shaped culture in northern Germany and upward along the Rhine. In western Germany French influence predominated; in southern Germany Italian trends contended and merged with the French and penetrated far to the southeast and the east. Thus little room was left for what was properly and originally German.

The Germany of the Baroque period was a receptive and not a creative organism. Every youth of rank signalized his arrival at manhood by making a grand tour, usually to Italy, France, and the Netherlands. No wonder the poor German language, already sufficiently corrupted by the Latin of the humanists, was now further vitiated with Gallicisms. The elegance of foreign education drew the line between classes all the more sharply. As late as the seventeenth century marriages between the nobility and free commoners were regarded as equal; now, however, they became misalliances. The courtiers appropriated to themselves all good breeding, gentility, and polish, every form of cultivation and artistic taste. Nothing was left for the citizen but pedantry and Philistinism.

The courts drained the German land in a deeper sense as well. Everything that was intelligent and graceful was caught up into the circle of court life. Many a lackey ended as a private secretary or even a minister. To be the mistress of some courtier or perhaps of the prince himself meant not only a life of ease, but influence, power, and higher rank. The presence of a prince cast an irresistible spell. People either belonged to his circle or did not count at all. Every honest official, every efficient officer, saw his rise into the noble class as the loftiest goal of his career. Pensions were often carried by court posts and orders. To fall into disfavour with the prince usually spelled economic ruin. And so every successful person felt the need, the moral right, and even the obligation toward his family of looking out for himself. The pursuit of posts and preferments made court life adventurous and attracted many to it. Court society became more and more distinct from the great mass of the German people. It represented a special, sharply defined sociological stratum, claiming for itself cultivation, polish, cosmopolitanism, knowledge of foreign lands, and artistic taste and growing used to regarding the burgher with contempt. The bourgeois came to mean something inferior.

More than elsewhere the aristocratic class in Germany lost vital contact with the people and did not even want to understand the citizen, certainly not the peasant. The members of these middle and lower classes were regarded as creatures living under entirely different conditions. In France there was but a single court, and there these relationships took on a national and imposing character. But when every petty German potentate created a Versailles for himself, complete with theatre, ballet, and harem, when he gathered his subjects from bits of land of widely different sorts and whipped them into an artificial uniformity, when he kept an army with a general for every three hundred men, the result could only be the tragicomic world that German court life presents to the spectator of later times. The sober paternalism of the past was now replaced by silly extravagance, by shameless pleasure in cruelty and excess, which disgusted every decent person. It is true, of course, that many of these courts promoted the arts and sciences successfully. One must not forget what Augustus the Strong, Elector of Saxony and King of Poland, was to his capital city of Dresden, how he tended and cherished it. German princely regimes left to the fatherland more art collections and libraries, more parks and fountains, than are to be found in any other country of Europe. But the long rule of such a variety of princes in the Baroque period laid so great a burden on the mind and the spirit of the German people that long years of self-education were needed to throw it off.

Why did German citizens have such a dull, oppressed look, except perhaps for the leading classes of the great commercial cities? Why did the peasant complain bitterly, cumbered by the continual demands of war, eternally bound to the soil, nameless, speechless, and without a history? Why did he live on so changelessly, far from any possibility of wholesome betterment? Because the princes and the nobility, the dominant class at the courts, in the administration, and in the army, all were interested in keeping conditions exactly as they were.

THE GERMAN ENLIGHTENMENT. RATIONALISM AND THE LIFE OF THE SPIRIT

The Germans became estranged from political labours at this time and acquired the undeserved reputation, gladly disseminated by their rulers, of having no gift for politics. Lutheranism assuredly withdrew its adherents from this wicked world and locked them up as captives in the callings ordained for them by God. But what was done by leaders and states, what came to pass under the seductive guise of reasons of state, was utterly un-Christian. Treaties were made only to be broken, royal marriages were arranged in the interests of territorial aggrandizement, and the more solemnly a future claim was forsworn, the more vigorously it was advanced at the seasonable moment with the support of armed force. Alliances were entered into with the worst enemies of yesteryear, and the most unscrupulous turncoats were loudest in their complaints of the treachery of their partners. Was it surprising that what was best in Germany turned away from these doings as it once had from the sectarian squabbles of zealous theologians?

Pietism, the second German Reformation, opened a welcome refuge to many, but it remained solely a spiritual and religious solution for people who stood apart from active life and who lacked influence. A group like that of the Moravians (*Herrnhuter*), founded by Count Zinzendorf (1727), was not at all hostile to the church. But compared with the stale and sterile dogma of official Lutheranism, it represented a deeper and more sensitive spirit of religious reflection. Here the asceticism of the Middle Ages recurred in personal prayer that strove toward God and away from the Evil One. Here the contemplation of former ages became a penitential struggle that proved the strength of the soul again and again. All this was a very personal matter, not outwardly expressed in any way. But one must not forget that the "silent in the land" were amassing in Germany spiritual treasures that refreshed and warmed the souls of the middle and lower classes and prepared them for deeper intellectual awakening and for creative thought and art. Here were essential impulses toward the rebirth of the German people as a cultural power. Irrationalism, then, co-operated with the rationalism of the new scientific and mathematical thinking to replace the "magic world picture" of tradition with a more appropriate interpretation of life.

The eighteenth century was England's. Revolutionary developments in England brought forward a new concept of state and of society that spread, by way of France, to all Europe. It would be wrong to overemphasize the rationalistic side of the Enlightenment. Nature and Reason were the two ruling principles of the age. It was a question of combining a rational criticism of tradition with a new mental and spiritual attitude in harmony with the eternal powers of historical and physical reality. Gottfried Wilhelm Leibniz with his truly comprehensive genius was the first who tried to express the twofold contribution of nature and reason in his interpretation of the world. Not before Immanuel Kant did this thinker have a successor to equal him, whether in universalism or in depth or in political instinct.

The German professors of the advancing eighteenth century did not attain to the intellectual rank of David Hume or Voltaire. Christian Thomasius (died 1728) was an honest fighter against the superstitions of witchcraft—against bombast, pedantry, the arrogance of Latinists, and the imitation of foreign models. Christian Wolff (died 1754) worked in Halle as a conscientious teacher, training his students in careful, straightforward philosophical thinking. These men were often platitudinous; in their academic and matter-of-fact controversial methods they tended to moralize. Only with difficulty did they and their pupils rise above mental mediocrity. But measured against the dogmatic oppression of the preceding period, their work is in the nature of a purifying process that deserved gratitude and made ready the way for better things. Now many a good German conscience was also shaken by the changes for the worse in the German language, and special societies arose to cure this ill. But it was only in music that the Germany of that age attained true grandeur. It was the good fortune, the grace, probably indeed the salvation of German Protestantism that it created its own church music. Palestrina perfected the Counter-Reformation in the musical expression he gave it, but the evangelical spirit found itself in the hymn, the motet, the Passion, of the masters Heinrich Schütz, Händel, and Johann Sebastian Bach. It will always be a blot on the German name that the fatherland was unable to support an artist such as Händel. He had to find a new home in England, which gave him citizenship, work, and fame.

Chapter 12

FREDERICK THE GREAT AND MARIA THERESA

THE CHARACTER OF GERMAN NATIONAL CULTURE AND OF COLONIAL
GERMANY

THE RISE of the two German great powers, Austria and Prussia, put the final touch to the disintegration of the Holy Roman Empire of the German Nation. The majestic manner of life of former days dragged on for some time like a torn and faded coronation robe. The effective forces in German life no longer had anything to do with the Empire, but were concerned with great powers and small states. Henceforth this contrast ruled the destinies of Germany. Both the great powers achieved and maintained their position only through a development fanning out from central Europe toward the Slavic east. The other estates of the Empire tried to keep pace in cultivating foreign relations, but the core of old German nationality lay here, and it was within the part of the Empire that had remained genuine and uncorrupted that the German spirit awoke to new vigour. It was the beginning of a great flowering in art and philosophy. The fateful question arose to what extent this cultural Germany would be compatible with the colonial Germany that was represented by the two German great powers. Would German culture be able to embrace the organizations of the great powers and to infuse its quality throughout them? Or would the non-German eastern despotic element that stirred within both of the great powers stand in the way of such a reconciliation?

In the same year of 1740 new rulers ascended the thrones of Austria and Prussia. The Archduchess Maria Theresa succeeded her imperial father, and the whole laboriously prepared business of the Pragmatic Sanction collapsed. Again a war of succession broke out, this time the Austrian, and the old European tensions lent it significance—out of all proportion to the actual problem of the succession—as a crisis of destiny.

264

Maria Theresa (born 1717), the last ruler drawn from the old house of Habsburg and the founder of the new line of Habsburg-Lorraine, was, oddly enough, the first member of the house since the Renaissance who showed thoroughly German traits. There was nothing Spanish about her. The Brunswick strain from her mother's side had had good effects. She was warm-hearted and energetic, musical and, full of the joy of living. She was constrained by the rigid convictions of her Catholic faith, but formally rather than in knowledge of life. She was devoted to her husband and unswervingly faithful, bore him sixteen children, and had much to forgive him. When, at the Emperor's death-bed, she encountered his last mistress, she embraced the Princess Lobkowitz with the words: "We have lost much." Politically she rejected any interference by the "co-regent" and left him to his cheerless business interests. During the entire Seven Years' War Emperor Francis I supplied grain to the Prussians. Austria was to reap great benefits from Empress Maria Theresa's indomitable spirit and devotion to her country.

KING FREDERICK'S YOUTH

The new Prussian ruler, King Frederick II (born 1712), was made of quite different stuff. The daughter of the Emperor had been reared in a cheerful domestic atmosphere, untroubled by politics, much learning, or serious quarrels. The conflict between Frederick the Great and his father is one of the most famous examples in the history of feuds between generations. Crown Prince Frederick was unusually gifted. He was an intellectual through and through, consumed with desire for fame as an artist and writer, critical to the point of deadly irony toward everything traditional and sentimental. Fundamentally, then, he was cold and selfish, narcissistically in love with himself, avid for recognition, striving to extract from every indulgence and every refinement a still more exquisite delight, a more unheard-of fulfilment. Frederick William I, the soldier King, could not understand this complex, untransparent, precociously flawed personality, filled with the egoism of the sufferer. Far simpler problems had been too much for him. With all the brutality of the colonial German, of the Borussian Russian, the father now tried to form the son in his own image. His methods were tyranny, threats, and beatings. He destroyed everything that was dear or pleasant to the son and offered him his own world. It had no attractions for the Crown Prince. Frederick's pert cleverness, his disrepectful mockery, was bound to irritate and exasperate his father. Even a better pedagogue would have found this assignment difficult. The quarrel grew worse and worse and ended with Frederick's attempt at flight. The "deserter" had to witness the execution of his best friend and aide, Lieutenant von Katte. The Prince never entirely overcame the spiritual shock of this experience. His unfortunate matrimonial history finally confused his emotional life; thenceforth there was something warped in the soul and character of the Crown Prince. He was virtually forced to pretence and duplicity. His reconciliation with his father always remained superficial, although as a soldier and statesman he knew how to appraise the achievements of the *roi sergeant*. He himself now became the *roi connétable*.

The wit and philosopher learned the art of ruling and commanding. He was born to it. Even in a school less hard he would have learned the tricks of the trade. The magnitude of his later achievement does not justify the violence that was done him in his youth. Not until he came to Rheinsberg did the Crown Prince quite recover. Rheinsberg was a little palace in Brandenburg that he could furnish and decorate to suit his personal taste. There he enjoyed pleasant company, and there he vied with scholarly and much-travelled friends in interpretation of the world. He read prodigiously, he wrote, and here, for the first time, he met the king of the century's writers, the Frenchman Voltaire (died 1778). Among Frederick's youthful writings the *Anti-Machiavelli* is best known. This piece is a criticism of Machiavelli's *Prince*. In it the son describes a new type of ruler, the opposite of the soldier King as represented by his father. He wanted something consciously new—a blend of the prince, such as the Renaissance had brought forth, with the spirit of the philosophers' century; an adaptation of the ruler to the dawning world of liberty, of self-determination, of spiritual independence. In the structure of a mature state comprised of free personalities, there was no place for the prince but that of the highest servant. This wishful dream of the Crown Prince was not original in conception. Frederick never did become a philosopher in his own right, not even in the limited sense of the eighteenth century. The *Anti-Machiavelli* has some air of playful improvisation; it arose from the whim of a

266

prince. The best thing about it is the personal rejection of the paternal tradition. Whatever new contribution Frederick had to make consisted not of shallow moralizing chatter such as was typical of the times, but of his political performance.

The contradiction between the theories in which he delighted and the actualities he was soon to grasp was so obvious that even his contemporaries immediately seized on the apparent explanation: utter cynicism poorly cloaked with hypocrisy. But the problem really lies deeper and concerns a perpetual conflict between the writer and the statesman. Frederick's curious spirit shuttled between the two worlds of action and contemplation. In any case he wanted success, fame, a great name. He wanted to be more than Voltaire and more than Alexander of Macedonia. He compensated for his inadequacy as thinker and poet, a lack of which he was aware in his innermost being, by poised and forceful intervention in the politics of Europe, and he overcame his failures as statesman and general by his historical and poetic reflections. In this way this split personality, this restless, fundamentally unhappy man, tormented with love that was akin to hate, was able to rise up again and again, to find new ways of maintaining himself in the face of an apparently insuperable destiny, and to shape the epoch through the magic force of his name.

THE WAR OF THE AUSTRIAN SUCCESSION (1740–8). SILESIA

When Frederick William I died, he left Prussia a full exchequer and an army of eighty thousand men. The soldier King had built up this force, but he had not known how to use it. In the very first months of his reign Frederick made it quite clear that things would now be different. He intimidated the obstinate Bishop of Liège so much by his harsh procedure that a long-standing quarrel about boundaries was quickly settled. More important events were to follow. Maria Theresa's accession to the throne awoke claims to the succession in half of Europe. Charles Albert, the Elector of Bavaria, invoked not only the family treaty between the Habsburg brothers about the inheritance, but also the will of Emperor Ferdinand III, whose daughter had been Charles Albert's mother. The Archduchess had reserved all rights for herself and her descendants in case the Habsburg male line died out. The Elector of Saxony also had claims. The Spanish Bourbons asserted hereditary claims as the legal successors of the Spanish Habsburgs; here the Austrian succession was connected with the War of the Spanish Succession, the outcome of which had offended Spanish national feeling so deeply. All these circumstances offered France a brilliant opportunity to take revenge at last and to strike the final blow at Austria's already tottering position of hegemony in Europe.

But at this point the Prussian King dumbfounded his contemporaries by the speed and unscrupulousness with which he acted. From a legal point of view Prussia's claims to Silesia were very doubtful, and only certain parts of Silesia were touched by them, as has been said. Frederick blithely ignored these facts. Without attempting negotiations, without declaring war, the King marched into Silesia. Simultaneously he offered Vienna the guarantee of the lands of the Austrian inheritance for Maria Theresa in return for the cession of all of Silesia. Prussia during the rule of her first two kings had had to put up with a great deal from Austria. Now the reckoning was at hand. Maria Theresa rejected the proposal with deep indignation, and war broke out. England tried to mediate. She formed a coalition in favour of Austria; Holland, Russia, and electoral Saxony joined it. Frederick saw himself surrounded and made an alliance with France, in which electoral Bavaria participated. It was agreed that France was to furnish financial and military help; the Elector of Bavaria was to become Emperor, and electoral Köln, electoral Mainz, and electoral Saxony promised him their votes. This Wittelsbach prince achieved the imperial crown as Charles VII. The son of the Elector Max Emanuel, who had once been banned, now defended the imperial concept and the interests of the old core of the Empire against Austria. The painful factor in this strange episode was that without French and Spanish assistance such an attempt could never have been made and that Prussia with her egoistic ambitions to become a great power was the winning partner.

Frederick had considerable military success. He was much gratified that England and Hanover made a treaty of neutrality with France, but the Prussian King did not have any too much confidence in his Bavarian and French allies. He himself wanted to keep Silesia, but a connection between Bavaria and Bohemia seemed most undesirable to him; in his opinion the office of emperor should not serve to make Bavaria a power that might exert pressure on Prussia.

Considerations such as these gave rise to the notorious Treaty of Klein-Schnellendorf (1741), according to which the Prussian King was to receive the fortress of Neisse in return for giving the Austrians free passage to Moravia for the purpose of fighting Bavaria and France, which up to this time had been his allies. But when these countries scored important victories none the less, Frederick abandoned his temporary neutrality and shifted over to the anti-Austrian front again. This interlude was never forgotten. From that time on the Prussian King had the reputation of being an unreliable partner from whom anything might be expected. Austria, at any rate, had every reason to wish this dangerous opponent, with his repeated military successes, out of the running. As a result of English mediation, Frederick was persuaded to sign the separate Peace of Berlin (1742), ratifying the preliminary Peace of Breslau. But his price was high: all of Silesia except Teschen, Troppau, and Jägerndorf, as well as the County of Glatz, fell to Prussia. Prussia was to have full sovereignty, but Silesia continued to be a part of the Empire—that is, a Bohemian fief—a state of affairs that was full of contradictions.

The war situation had become much simpler for Maria Theresa. The War of the Austrian Succession developed into a defensive action against France by the central European powers under the guidance of England. Englishmen, Austrians, Hollanders, and German mercenaries made up the so-called Pragmatic Army, which defeated the French at Dettingen under the personal leadership of the English King George II. Now electoral Saxony again went over to the Pragmatic side. Maria Theresa won Sardinia, Austria's old ally from the War of the Spanish Succession. Peace negotiations bore no results. Austria wanted Bavaria as an indemnity for Silesia. Emperor Charles VII was to be paid off at the expense of France in Alsace and Lorraine. Frederick II, on the other hand, was planning far-reaching secularization of ecclesiastical property. As a perpetual lieutenant-general he wanted to head a neutral army to protect the constitution of the Empire. In Frankfurt he formed a union with several estates of the Empire to protect the position of the Emperor and the Empire. He even planned an association of the circles of the Empire. In vain did the enemy of the Empire pose as its protector. The failure of these plans and Austrian successes on the Rhine again caused the Prussian King to intervene in the war. He invaded Bohemia from three directions in the hope of acquiring parts of that country. But soon the political situation changed completely.

After the death of the Duchess of Châteauroux, King Louis XV's mistress, who had been the main support of the alliance with Prussia, the French prosecuted the war in a lukewarm fashion. The Pragmatic Coalition became more firmly established; Russia's participation was imminent. Emperor Charles VII died suddenly, and at Füssen (1745) Maria Theresa granted his successor in Bavaria a separate peace, which left his native land to him intact in return for his renunciation of all larger claims of inheritance and for his vote in the election of Maria Theresa's husband, Duke Francis of Lorraine, as Emperor. Frederick realized that he stood alone. Maria Theresa regarded him as her worst enemy; she absolutely refused to let him have Silesia; France was tired of the war and was starting negotiations for a separate peace. Frederick won important military victories at Hohenfriedberg and at Soor. Now his gifts as a strategist, part of the Guelph heritage, were developing at an amazing rate. English efforts finally led to a new peace treaty, concluded at Dresden (1745). Frederick had to be content with the mere confirmation of his Silesian conquest, and he recognized Francis I as Emperor. In Germany this was the end of the war. The estates of the Empire that had taken part in the fighting participated in the Dresden Treaty. The War of the Austrian Succession continued for three years longer as a struggle in Italy and Flanders and as a colonial war between England and the French and Spanish Bourbon group. In 1746 Austria made a treaty with Russia for the purpose of holding unreliable Prussia in check. Frederick, on his part, together with the French political group in the Empire succeeded in foiling all plans aimed at an imperial war against France.

Through the Peace of Aachen (1748) Empress Maria Theresa at least obtained universal recognition of the Pragmatic Sanction. She lost only Silesia and certain small areas in Italy. The Austrian power-complex had maintained itself after all, better than the Spanish in its time. The loyalty of the Hungarians and the southern Slavs aided essentially in this. If at this juncture the Ottoman Empire had been in a mood for attack, affairs would probably have taken quite a different course. Prussian pressure had made it impracticable to regain Alsace and Lorraine for Germany, though the dynasty of Lorraine was now so closely connected with that of Austria. Frederick afterward wrote that France needs Alsace just as much as Prussia needs Silesia. Prussia's strength was sufficient also to hinder or to alter any creative imperial policy that might issue from Vienna. Prussia, the robber who had taken Silesia, was and continued to be the archenemy from Maria Theresa's point of view. For the loss of Silesia was far more serious to Austria than the mere loss of one of her hereditary lands. This thriving German and Slavic land in the east, predominantly won over to German culture and splendidly endowed by the late Renaissance, made it possible for Prussia to exert constant pressure on Bohemia, Saxony, and Poland. For electoral Saxony the transfer of Silesia to Prussia meant that her old rival had definitely outstripped her. Austria was crowded out of east central Europe and could no longer maintain a position of hegemony. Thus Silesia had become the land of destiny for both Frederick and Maria Theresa. Both parties could and wanted to regard the decision that had been reached as no more than a truce.

THE INTERNAL REORGANIZATION OF AUSTRIA AND PRUSSIA

The interval before the outbreak of the Seven Years' War gave both of the German great powers an opportunity for internal construction and reconstruction. Maria Theresa had come to realize that the existing disunity of her lands, with the lack of well-ordered traffic, of arrangements for finance, and of administration, had materially impaired the efficiency of the Austrian army. Up to this time the chanceries of Austria and Bohemia had consisted of members of the diets. These chanceries were now replaced by homogeneous, purely bureaucratic boards of directors. Justice and administration were separated. A general Ministry of Justice, which also functioned as the high court of justice, was organized. Maria Theresa, to her great good fortune, secured in Prince Kaunitz a counsellor of high merit. After a successful diplomatic career he received the office of Chancellor in 1753. He became the head of the newly founded chancery of house, court, and state, the Austrian Ministry of the Exterior. This man, who had many personal eccentricities, was the coldest and shrewdest calculator of the times. A council of state was subsequently set over the newly organized agencies.

All these reforms failed to achieve complete centralization in po-

271

litical life. They affected, in fact, only Austria and Bohemia. Hungary and the dependencies always maintained their own political style. Nevertheless the functioning of the collective organism of the monarchy was now substantially improved. Taxes were made uniform and were better distributed. The peasant class was less heavily burdened. A comprehensive customs district was brought into being, taking in all the hereditary lands except the Tyrol, and a system of elementary schools was recognized as a state obligation for the first time in Austria and was founded on a new basis. In so consciously Catholic a state the Protestants and the Jews still suffered from prejudice and even from oppression. But the government itself was out of humour with excessive influence on the part of the Roman church. Church lands and other property were under supervision, and limitations were imposed on clerical jurisdiction. The territorial diets that still existed could not well approve of this increase in central power, but resistance was unthinkable. The Empress, moreover, ruled with a light hand and made it possible for even those who were unconvinced or refractory to co-operate. To the aristocracy in particular so many advantages accrued through the good positions open to them in the new bureaucracy and through the organization of the army that they laid less stress on their feudal privileges. More and more the bearers of distinguished names flocked to Vienna. All these Bohemian, Burgundian, Hungarian, and Italian notables breathed a German atmosphere in the capital, and the court itself emphasized its German character. Spanish etiquette was still practised, but it was changed in many details and even ignored.

The emergence of national Austrian higher and lower nobility contributed materially to Austria's detachment from the Empire. Since the time of Emperor Maximilian I an increasing number of patents of nobility had been issued. The old distinction between lords and knights became blurred. As has been shown, courtiers frequently assumed the rights that went with immediacy to the Empire, so that finally the longed-for admission to the estates of the Empire no longer seemed necessary. The old indigenous local nobility in the dependencies suffered the greatest damage from the events of the Thirty Years' War and the Counter-Reformation. The local nobility that protested either politically or religiously foundered, whereas the loyal Catholic nobles, often newly created at court, in the army, or among officialdom, came forward and aided powerfully in the re-organization of the monarchy.

Many problems were left unsolved. The Empress disliked severity and largely allowed events to take their own course. During her reign Austria was enlivened by tact, gentleness, and humanity, which were handed on to the future. The contrast with Bavaria and Prussia set off the Austrian nationality still farther from the Empire. The emperorship of Francis I, consort and co-regent, the first and only Emperor without possessions of his own in the Empire, could not make headway against the achievements of the Empress, who was, before all, Queen of Bohemia and of Hungary and Archduchess of the hereditary lands.

In Prussia reform ran less gently and smoothly. The first task of King Frederick II was to incorporate into the collective entity of the state the new provinces of Silesia and East Friesland, which he had taken over in 1744 after the old dynasty of local princes had died out. For the period of transition Silesia was given a special administration, which worked directly under the eyes of the King. Difficulties came from the quarter of the Catholic church, which left the Prussian regime as such undisputed, but whose economic and legal privileges were not adaptable to the Prussian system. The Prussian method of recruiting was also a thorn in the side of the Silesians. In the end Frederick, who was without any trace of denominational bias, busied himself skilfully and with success on behalf of the Catholic part of his Silesian subjects. As a gracious gesture of reconciliation the new Catholic church in Berlin was given the name of the patroness of Silesia, St. Hedwig.

In East Friesland the diet fought for its traditional old Germanic position of power, which the new ruler had promised to respect. A clever Prussian member of the administration, however, devised all sorts of trickery and red tape to make the exercise of their rights so distasteful that they perceived they would fare better by voluntarily conforming to the will of Prussia. Frederick made no fundamental changes in the administrative arrangements his father had left him. He elaborated on them, but effected no great alterations. And so a certain discrepancy arose between the departments for the administration of provinces, such as that for Silesia, and special departments, such as that for foreign affairs. The King was awake to these difficulties, and the significance of the royal cabinet and of its head, who made all decisions, increased under these circumstances; in fact it became utterly indispensable. Frederick created a separate department for commerce and industry as well as the Ministry of War.

He was particularly interested in economics. Foreigners such as the Swiss Fäsch advised him in such matters. The introduction of high protective tariffs at the boundaries of the Prussian state was calculated to advance the country's industry at least to the point of meeting domestic needs. Since Prussia was poor in raw materials but rich in boundary lines, this was a decidedly difficult task and involved the state in bitter tariff wars with its neighbours, especially electoral Saxony and Austria. It proved next to impossible to make favourable trade treaties with the greater and more advantageously placed powers of Europe. In the newly acquired city of Emden in East Friesland an Asiatic trading company was formed that made unusually high profits from dealing in Chinese goods. The city was for a time indemnified by this means for what she had lost through Prussian domination.

In instituting very necessary reforms in the administration of justice Frederick had the advice of an expert, the Lord High Chancellor Cocceji. New rules of court procedure were drawn up, and appeals to the law faculties of foreign universities fell off following this. In this respect, too, Prussia was closing herself against influences that came from outside the Empire. Compilation of a new body of common law began. Barbarous methods of questioning witnesses were dropped. In the long run law, economics, and administration all served the army, which was and remained the backbone of the Prussian state. More and more Frederick II thought of himself as the *roi connétable,* who, in contrast to the sergeant's spirit as represented by his father, raised the conduct of war to the status of a lofty intellectual problem. The will to life of an aspiring state like Prussia found its most characteristic expression in gathering together all political and economic forces for military attack. The King's experience of war had taught him needful innovations. He himself worked out modern military rules and instructed his officers in the principles of strategy. He did everything to keep his troops in fighting trim by constant manœuvres and to prepare them for a war of extermination. His instinct told him that he would have to fight again for Silesia.

Frederick had now reached his personal maturity. With wit, mockery, and scepticism he surveyed the world and the seeming senselessness of the forces at play in it. No important matter of state, of art, or of science failed to command his interest. Now, as before, he was eager to exchange ideas with the most distinguished thinkers of his age. He built a great deal and was self-willed even in this; Italian and French elements were often happily adapted to the German style. His little palace of Sans-Souci was set in one of the most delightful spots of the Potsdam landscape. Here Frederick played the flute, enjoyed his collection of paintings, and made verses—and more than one of his poems really came off. He was at his best in writing history, for he knew very well how history is made; he drew on personal recollection and felt himself the peer of his predecessors in this field. From reflecting on history he gathered power and impetus, far more than from the dabbling in philosophy that he indulged in even in his old age. All this carried a non-German character, not only because the King wrote and thought in French, but because this world of his had nothing to do with the best and noblest that was awakening in Germany during his regime. Intellectually Frederick was a follower of the Renaissance and of the *grand siècle* in France —cultivated, European, universal, eclectic, more connoisseur than creator. Not for nothing was he in love with late antiquity. Such was his direction, and it did not point ahead toward the nineteenth century. A melancholy autumnal twilight hangs over Frederick and his work. Women were not wanted at the court of Sans-Souci; the King passed his life in bitterness and constraint, without family happiness. His only warm feeling was for his sister and his valet. Dogs satisfied his need for affection. He was impoverished in the most important part of human life, but this very condition led him to sublimate his manhood creatively in deed and work.

THE SEVEN YEARS' WAR (1756-63)

In these years King Frederick met a strong opponent in foreign policy, one who was superior to the Prussian ruler at least in foresight and tenacity: Prince Kaunitz. As Austrian ambassador to the

Kaunitz

peace conference at Aachen he had come to realize that it was no longer France but the rising Prussia that was the real enemy of the house of Habsburg. To crush Prussia, he reasoned, the traditional alliance with the maritime powers of England and Holland would no longer suffice. A new system would have to be built up. Russia and France must be won over as allies against Prussia. Then Prussia would be encircled, her humiliation inevitable. Russia and France had repeatedly acted in unison with Prussia; as the neighbours of Prussia's immediate neighbours, they were her natural allies. But King Frederick had not been foresighted in his treatment of these two powers. The personal enmity of Empress Elizabeth of Russia, which the Prussian King had carelessly provoked by his slanders, did much to contribute to the renewed alliance between Austria and Russia. Diplomatic relations between Prussia and Russia were broken off before the outbreak of the Seven Years' War. When Prince Kaunitz went to Paris as ambassador he regarded as his principal task the separation of Prussia and France, but nothing definite had occurred when he became chancellor in Vienna in 1753.

France and Prussia were co-operating to prevent Archduke Joseph, eldest son of Empress Maria Theresa, from being elected King of the Romans and Duke Charles of Lorraine, her brother-in-law, from becoming King of Poland, as Russia was planning. Frederick was in bad standing with England. For both England and Holland Prussia's hold on East Friesland was unfavourable from the point of view of trade. And so the Prussian King had every reason to fear that England might join the Russian-Austrian alliance. In 1754 there were new clashes between France and England in North America, and the conflict, which had merely been postponed, called for solution by military means. Frederick advised the French to occupy Hanover, but his counsel was ignored. He himself did not wish by a sudden attack on Hanover to precipitate a European war. Matters then took a surprising turn. The conversion to Catholicism of the hereditary Prince of Hesse-Kassel led to co-operation between Prussia and England and Hanover, as the leading Protestant powers, in the interest of parity—that is, equality of privileges as between denominations. England, in her disappointment over Austria's policy, now tried to persuade Frederick to guarantee Hanover. At first he hesitated, but when he heard that England and Russia had made a subsidy treaty he quickly accepted. He thought that a rapprochement with England might enable him to break the encirclement that threatened him. Thus the Westminster Treaty of January 1756 arose, a convention of neutrality between Prussia and England for the maintenance of peace in Germany and joint armed defence against any disturbance of it by a third power.

The consequences of this treaty were utterly different from what the parties to it had expected. Russia did not desert Austria, and France did not become conciliatory toward England. On the contrary, at this very point Kaunitz was in a position to win the friendship of France. An Austrian-French treaty of neutrality and mutual protection was concluded in May 1756. Russia declared her readiness to join the alliance, and Empress Elizabeth wanted to persuade Poland to join and to proceed to an immediate attack. Kaunitz hesitated. France had to be won over to the idea first by further concessions; part of the Netherlands might be sacrificed to her. The spring of 1757 was set for the attack on Prussia. Electoral Saxony was prepared to help. Her minister, Count Brühl, a spendthrift with a passion for building, was bitterly hostile to the King of Prussia. Frederick now decided to anticipate his foes. He was ready while the coalition forming against him was still in the midst of preparations. From time to time he had played with the idea of taking over electoral Saxony and thus strangling the old enmity forever, but when he struck, in the fateful year of 1756, his action was certainly not determined by a definite plan of conquest. The Westminster Treaty is proof enough that he would have preferred tranquillity. But Frederick's secret service kept him well informed; he had only one choice, either to anticipate his opponents or to be overpowered at some much less favourable moment. This time he tried to clarify the situation by sending an ultimatum to the Empress; he demanded that Austria obligate herself not to attack Prussia either in that year or in the next. The evasive reply was eloquent. Frederick marched into Saxony without warning. The war had come. Frederick's errors in diplomacy had made possible an overwhelming coalition against him. Now it was a question whether he was in a military position to fight off almost certain destruction.

His only palpable prospect consisted in the possibility of winning a decisive victory over the troops of the Empress before her allies could enter the field. A success such as this might have shattered the coalition. But he failed, even though he overpowered the Saxons. The Saxon soldiers were forced to enter the Prussian army, but they deserted during the following years and so did more harm than good. The coalition became threateningly real. The Russian-Austrian treaty of 1757 provided for the payment of a million roubles to the Czarina; East Prussia was to revert to Poland or to go to some archduke as a Polish fief. Now the French-Austrian defensive alliance was transformed into an offensive one: France promised to equip south German troops, to invade western Germany with a French army, and to pay an annual subsidy of twelve million gulden to Austria. Austria was to recover not only Silesia, but also the principality of Krossen; electoral Saxony was to receive Halberstadt and Magdeburg; Sweden, which joined the coalition, was bribed by the prospect of Hither Pomerania; the Prussian possessions on the Rhine and in Westphalia were promised to the Elector Palatine; the Hohenzollerns, accordingly, would have had nothing left but the Mark of Brandenburg. People were already calling Frederick by the mocking name of Marquis de Brandenbourg.

In case of success Austria was willing to cede certain border tracts of the Netherlands to France; the rest of Belgium, however, as well as Luxemburg, was reserved for the Spanish Infante Philip in exchange for Parma and Piacenza. The Empire, too, was now mobilized against Frederick. Under penalty of banishment he was summoned to Vienna to answer for breaking the public peace. He was not actually banished, however, because the *Corpus Evangelicorum* opposed this step. But Frederick's attempt to form a league of princes against the Emperor failed. Austria's proposal for imperial execution was accepted by the diet; even Protestant estates voted for it. An edict of the Emperor made it binding on all the estates of the Empire. The war thus signified a crisis in the Empire. All the old religious tensions sharpened the oppositions. Once more the house of Habsburg wanted to be master in the Empire, master of central Europe, and it tried to break Prussia as a great power. Most of the estates of the Empire concluded subsidy treaties and military conventions with the allied courts of Vienna and Paris. Some few, however, stood by Prussia, England, and Hanover: Hesse-Kassel, Schaumburg, Brunswick, and Gotha; it was thus the old area of Lower Saxony that supported Prussia, the enemy of the Empire, and so in its way carried on mediæval traditions.

Co-operation between England and Prussia was impeded by England's inner political perplexities. The elder Pitt as Prime Minister urged a vigorous prosecution of the war overseas as well as on the Continent. Not until the spring of 1758 was the subsidy treaty made that assured the King of Prussia of aid to the extent of 670,000 pounds sterling annually. Like all other European wars from the beginning of the period of colonization, the Seven Years' War was financed mainly with funds drawn from overseas.

Frederick's invasion of Bohemia, by which he hoped to force a quick decision, was a failure. The Austrians advanced in Silesia and the French in Hanover, while a superior Russian force bore down on East Prussia. Frederick demonstrated his effective generalship by his two victories at Rossbach and Leuthen (1757). The latter in particular was one of his classical strategic achievements. But the fight went on. The push into Moravia was halted. The Russians, who were invading the Mark, could not be destroyed, but they were at least stopped at Zorndorf. Hochkirch, however, proved a serious setback for the King. He was visibly weakening and could no longer dare attempt offensive action on a large scale. There were hardly enough reserves to replace the heavy losses; Prussia had to try to drag the war along, to exhaust and if possible to separate her opponents. It was the beginning of an almost hopeless struggle for the very existence of the Prussian state. In 1759 the King, in the face of a superior Austrian and Russian force, suffered his gravest defeat at Kunersdorf. His downfall seemed at hand, but the victors did not follow up their success. As Frederick himself said, a miracle came to pass. In company with England he now made a peace offer through Holland, but the French would only make a separate agreement with England; no honourable peace was possible for Prussia. Frederick continued to hold out, with brave but apparently hopeless persistence. He won some few successes, none of them decisive, and always there were fresh setbacks. The Austrians advanced toward Saxony and again toward Silesia. The Russians captured Küstrin; East Prussia had paid homage to the Czarina. When Pitt was overthrown the new cabinet that came into power in London leaned toward some sort of agreement with France and Austria. Payment of subsidies to Prussia ceased.

Frederick was forging desperate plans to save himself. He hoped to stir up the Tatars against the Russians, the Turks against the Austrians. And then came the great change. The Czarina Elizabeth died. The coalition broke up. Her successor, Czar Peter III of Russia, immediately concluded a separate peace with Prussia on the *status quo ante,* and he followed this up with a treaty of alliance. Peter was soon overthrown, and the treaty never became effective; but there was peace in the east, and encirclement was a thing of the past. New military successes showed that Prussia could no longer be conquered. Sweden, too, made peace with Frederick II. The estates of the Empire refused to do anything further, and the diet at Regensburg resolved on neutrality for the Empire. England made a favourable separate peace with France; at this time Canada became British (1762). Electoral Saxony, the first victim of the war, finally brought the two great German powers into conference with each other. Austria was isolated and financially exhausted. She could not persuade Prussia into ceding the smallest bit of land. By the Peace of Hubertusburg, a hunting-seat in Saxony, Frederick retained Silesia (1763).

OLD FRITZ

Prussia remained for the future a great power in Germany and equally in eastern Europe. The King of Prussia was now hailed as Frederick the Great by his admiring contemporaries. One man's struggle against destiny had ended in the triumph of a hero. And much is forgiven to a hero. The great coalition had been powerful in diplomacy, military affairs, and economics. Public opinion and an offended sense of what was right had been against Prussia. But the great personality had triumphed.

From time to time Frederick had played with the idea of suicide. He had had to suffer many humiliations. He himself had broken many a treaty, many an alliance; then England left him in the lurch. Only English subsidies had made it possible for him to hold out to the end. For years the King was on the verge of the abyss. As a general, too, he was forced to adapt himself to the most adverse conditions and to bridle the spirit of attack, which seemed too reckless an expenditure of his dwindling troops. The Austrian general Count Daun and Prince Henry, the King's own brother, surpassed the King in his own tactical game of battering the enemy. But in spite of everything Frederick and the Prussian state had maintained themselves. In the history of Germany as a whole this fact meant the perpetuation of the existing dualism of the two great powers; it meant cleavage in central Europe.

In the Thirty Years' War the house of Austria, with the help of Spain, blood kin to it, had tried to establish a Catholic absolutism in Germany. France and Sweden had stood in the way, and the liberty of the German princes had been made secure with foreign help. In the Seven Years' War the house of Austria again made the greatest kind of effort to maintain hegemony in Germany at least—to be the only power in central Europe bearing the character of a great power. This time the old foes of the Habsburgs, France and Sweden, stood at Austria's side; Bourbon Spain helped, and Russia joined in. The great majority of the estates of the Empire wanted the Prussian state, which had so far outflown them, to be humiliated and destroyed. Only the help of England gave Prussia the means of escaping this mortal threat. Prussia's maintenance as a great power is one of the most significant results of the personal union of England and Hanover. The Empire remained what it had been, an accumulation of small states, some of which, roused by the bad example of the most successful estates of the Empire, wanted to be something more. But Prussia, enemy of the Empire and breaker of the peace, did not dream of relinquishing her position in Germany. While she had quite perceptibly crowded Austria out of the Empire, she herself was pushing into it. The Wittelsbach emperorship of Charles VII was an empty episode. The triumph of Frederick the Great in the Seven Years' War made it possible for him to play imperial politics seriously in competition with Austria.

Frederick II returned from the Seven Years' War an old man. In his later days his bent figure, crippled by the gout, was the object of previously unknown popular affection. Legends and anecdotes grew up about the life of Old Fritz. More than ever his days were given up to work. This great power, Prussia, that he had guarded and saved, he must build up yet again from within. Prussia's finances were in better condition than might have been expected, for the King had made the great war pay for itself to some extent by subsidies and contributions and in addition, during the last difficult period, by a reckless currency depreciation, which had caused heavy losses to many private persons. Extensive new settlements grew up in the open country. All in all perhaps three hundred thousand persons immigrated into Prussia during Frederick's rule. The King was not able to decide on the abolition of serfdom, for he felt that the manors must not be deprived of their working forces. The large holdings of the nobility were still the essential basis for the organization of the state in the eastern provinces. Agricultural credit institutions assisted landowners to free themselves of debt and to establish themselves on a sound footing. So far as there was a social policy, it was designed for the landed proprietors and for no one else. The King's rule by cabinet became still more ruthless. The suspicious and unscrupulous monarch intervened wherever he thought it necessary, usually to the advantage of all concerned, but often with disturbing and confusing effect. To improve financial administration Frederick II introduced a system of indirect taxation, according to the French scheme and staffed with French experts. The excessive formality of this system was unsuited to Prussia's still undeveloped money economy and was hated with justice, as the monopolies on tobacco and coffee also were. Such measures seriously damaged the respect in which the King and the administration were held.

Even severe critics must concede that many other measures were beneficial: the encouragement of mining and foundries, the start of shipping trade, from which the Prussian state bank developed, the storing of grain to support prices, and finally the fostering of the silk industry, which was calculated to make the country independent of imported luxuries in spite of climatic conditions. The administration of justice in Prussia kept on developing favourably; new rules of procedure came into use as prologue to the Prussian common law that was promulgated after Frederick's death. The King watched jealously over the impartiality of justice and might intervene himself on its behalf, as in the famous case of the miller Arnold, who maintained that a nobleman's carp pond was drawing off water from his mill. Royal interference was certainly unjustifiable, but it was characteristic of the rough and ready manner in which even Frederick's goodwill expressed itself. The demoniac quality of his nature had changed into a self-surpassing and self-sacrificing performance of duty, but he remained harsh and overbearing in his work for the collective welfare.

In religion and education toleration was practised, though only up to the point of injury to any interests of the state. The King regarded the Jesuits, who had been expelled from other countries, as useful teachers—and also cheap. The low pay of teachers in the primary schools was a severe handicap to the reform of these elementary institutions. At the secondary level the situation was better; classical languages were the basis of the curriculum, in accordance with the King's wish and taste. Large sums brought the Academy of Sciences to bloom; here foreigners dominated. Of the Germans Frederick thought very little; neither the poet Gotthold Ephraim Lessing (died 1781) nor the archæologist Johann Joachim Winckelmann (died 1768) was given even a modest post, for the King had only icy rejection for the striving of the German spirit. Neither had he any regard for the most recent French philosophers. He remained true to his faith in God and Voltaire. But in the case of German literature more was at stake than the discord between the old and new generations. Frederick's taste for Latinity, combined with his dynastic arrogance and his eccentricity, made it almost impossible for him to understand the language of the awakening German bourgeoisie. He had no use for the writings of young Johann Wolfgang Goethe. Frederick himself, however, prophesied that the German spirit would sometime soar!

EMPEROR JOSEPH II (1765-90)

The outcome of the Seven Years' War was the greatest disappointment in Maria Theresa's life. She now devoted herself exclusively to domestic policy, and here there was plenty to heal and to salve. After the premature death of Emperor Francis I she made her eldest son co-regent. Joseph had been unanimously elected King of the Romans after the peace of Hubertusburg, and he was now crowned Emperor. But this son refused to be content with the purely external honours that continued the old Habsburg tradition, though he could not conceal the fact that in the Empire there was nothing left for Austria but to stand resignedly to one side. Strong oppositions existed between mother and son, both in character and in purpose, despite undiminished mutual respect and love. The Empress desired a devout and cautious continuing development of what already existed. Emperor Joseph II shared the views of a clever century. He did not want to lose any time; he wanted to do a complete piece of work; and he had no faith in natural growth. Much that was tyrannical and even something of the revolutionary adhered to the good Emperor Joseph, who spent and sacrificed himself for progress and rationality, who fought with so much fire against prejudice, overbearing conventionality, and class egoism. What Joseph stood for shook Maria Theresa's Austria to the very foundations.

The Emperor himself was a devout Catholic, but he did all he could to make the church fit in with the state as an ineffable but definitely useful instrument. The particularism of the Austrian crown lands seemed to him inadaptable to the ideal of a centralized state with finances thoroughly organized. He believed that the motley mass of colonial districts under imperial and royal rule should be Germanized and thereby disciplined. The concept of absolutism had foundered in the Empire; now this first Emperor of the new house of Habsburg-Lorraine tried to apply it at least to Austria. Admiration of Frederick the Great encouraged this spirit of well-meaning despotism; Emperor Joseph II with his western European and imperial cast of mind was half a foreigner in the east. That her son emulated the wicked Prussian, her lifelong foe, meant new, deep pain for the aging Empress. Joseph's eager enthusiasm, half rigour and half weakness, did not measure up to the Prussian King's cold cleverness and disillusioned knowledge of the world.

THE FIRST PARTITION OF POLAND (1772)

Especially in the matter of foreign policy Emperor Joseph II did not dream of renunciation. He was to be checked again and again. Since the great war King Frederick had been siding with Russia; it was not possible for him to re-establish confidential relations with either England or France. Austria continued to co-operate with the courts of the Catholic Bourbons. A number of marriages arranged by Maria Theresa reinforced this system. The Russian-Prussian defensive alliance of 1764 was aimed at Poland. It succeeded in breaking the connection between Saxony and Poland and in procuring the

Polish throne for the candidate of Catherine II, Stanislaus Ponia-towski. But this national kingship could not quell Poland's inner difficulties. Increasing Russian influence aroused bitter opposition among the Polish nobility; Catholic interests worked against the Greek church, and Austria intervened in favour of the Roman church. A new Russian-Turkish war heartened the Poles to strike against Russia, but they themselves were the sufferers.

At this time occurred two meetings between Frederick the Great and Emperor Joseph II. It was to the interest of both Austria and Prussia that Russia should not grow too strong. The preservation of the Ottoman Empire could be managed most easily by diverting Russia's desire for expansion toward the weakest partner in the game, Poland. Frederick, even before he became king, had given some thought to the possibility of securing Polish Prussia, later known as West Prussia. In his political wills made in 1752 and 1768 he compared the gradual taking over of the Polish regions he desired with the eating of an artichoke. During the negotiations between Russia and Prussia after the Peace of Hubertusburg, West Prussia had been discussed again and again. If there was any one prime mover of the first partition of Poland, it was, then, King Frederick II of Prussia. The fact is not at all changed by Austria's being the first power to occupy part of Poland; this was the Zips, a border region, into which it moved in 1769 in the name and on behalf of Hungary, with the consent of King Stanislaus.

In the hope of averting the European war that now threatened, Russia and Prussia came to an agreement about Polish annexations. Frederick turned the enmity between Austria and Russia to account to increase his share and to close the deal. Catherine II left Moldavia and Wallachia to the Turks and in place of them took Polish Livonia and White Russia. Prussia got Ermland and also West Prussia, with the exception of Danzig and Thorn, and the Bromberg district around the Netze River. Frederick II could now call himself King *of* Prussia instead of King *in* Prussia as heretofore. Maria Theresa objected to the entire transaction on grounds of law and decency, and Kaunitz too was full of grave doubts, though on quite another score. He would have preferred a partition of the European part of the Ottoman Empire, and here again he demonstrated the longer view taken by the misunderstood prophet. Emperor Joseph II, to be sure, thought that one should not allow such an opportunity to slip by.

Austria received an even larger share than Prussia: Polish Zips, Galicia except for Cracow, and finally Bukovina, which Emperor Joseph persuaded the Turks to hand over to him. Austrian Poland, as the Kingdom of Galicia and Lodomeria, was allowed its own diet. The Austrian administration in Lemberg (Lwów) was confronted with urgent problems. Emperor Joseph II himself, whose strongest political implement was his emphasis on Germanism, thus appreciably increased the number of Slavs and eastern Jews in the Empire. The colonial character so peculiar to both the great German powers, Austria and Prussia, was strengthened by the first partition of Poland. As lords of all East and West Prussia, the Hohenzollerns now bore down arrogantly on the rest of Poland. Their partnership with Russia was proving effective, and their position on the Baltic was greatly improved. The non-German features of the Prussian great power increased palpably. In their weakness the Poles could do nothing against the act of violence. Intrigues and bribes played their part, and the Polish diet gave its consent in the hope that this concession would fortify the body of Poland proper. After the conquest of Silesia, with all that ensued, the plundering of Poland now permitted the sheer power politics of the cabinets of Europe to triumph. No one will wish to ignore or to minimize the serious political errors of the Poles. But the suppression of Polish national independence that now began became a veritable doom for further German development. Polish resistance forced the partners in this act, the two great powers of Germany, into a fellowship of guilt with Russia. A front of east European, anti-national, anti-democratic power politics formed.

THE WAR OF THE BAVARIAN SUCCESSION (1778–9)

Immediately after the first partition of Poland the War of the Bavarian Succession offered Emperor Joseph the chance he wanted in order to try to strengthen the German element in the Empire so as to balance the Polish policy to a certain extent. Bavaria had become anything but an agreeable neighbour for Austria. She was closely connected with the Austrian hereditary lands through Catholic faith and kinship. But this very congruity turned these neighbours into jealous rivals. The Wittelsbach ecclesiastical realm, the

Wittelsbach emperorship, had developed out of the common front of the Thirty Years' War, a comradeship-in-arms that had even then been burdened with jealousies. Now Austria had to accommodate itself to Prussia's power. Emperor Joseph was naturally delighted with the chance to dispose of an independent, overblown Bavaria and to expand at the expense of Bavarian territory in southern Germany, a superior compensation for Silesia, in view of the location in the German heartland. With the death of Elector Max Joseph of Bavaria, the Wilhelmine line of the Wittelsbachs died out.

The other branch, headed by the Elector Palatine, Charles Theodore, held rights of succession. But Austria claimed the succession on the grounds of a fief granted by Emperor Sigismund; in addition the Emperor reclaimed the imperial fiefs as well as the Bohemian fiefs in the Upper Palatinate. Elector Charles Theodore had no legitimate children; his heir was the Duke of Zweibrücken. Charles Theodore's personal inclination was to remain in his beautiful, well-kept Mannheim; he was quite willing to recognize the Austrian claims and to make a treaty accordingly. His chief motive in this seems to have been fear of Prussian claims on Jülich and Berg. Austrian troops marched into Bavaria. Then Frederick the Great objected. Both groups armed. Prussia got in touch with all who were interested in the Bavarian succession, but negotiations were fruitless, even when the Hohenzollern dependencies of Ansbach and Bayreuth were offered to the King of Prussia. War broke out (1778), but after some uneventful manœuvring it ended as suddenly as it had begun. Supplies ran short, and so this curious epilogue to great struggles was nicknamed the "Potato War." But many soldiers did die of disease.

At the peace congress in Teschen (1779), with Russia and France participating, Austria was accorded the Quarter of the Inn (the Innviertel), which represented a valuable betterment of her boundaries. Electoral Saxony was indemnified with money, and Prussia with the reversion of Ansbach and Bayreuth. Bavaria and the electoral Palatinate were united under Charles Theodore, so that the number of electoral votes was diminished by one. The house of Zweibrücken was guaranteed the succession. Prussia's political victory was very significant: Austria remained impeded from expanding into the Empire again, and Russia, Prussia's ally, had assumed Sweden's historical role of guarantor of the peace. The guarantee of the peace by France restored that country's old influence in the Empire. Every considerable shift of jurisdiction within the Empire, especially to either of the two great powers of Germany, was now regarded as a European problem.

The Empress Maria Theresa did much to forestall a really serious conflict. At this time she wrote her first personal letter to her great enemy Frederick. Her death (1780) robbed Austria of a firm support. Joseph II now felt that he was entirely his own master. At first he was successful. Even during Maria Theresa's lifetime it had been possible to secure her son, Archduke Maximilian, the position of coadjutor in Köln and Münster, and with this the Wittelsbach rule on the Lower Rhine and in Westphalia came to an end. Austria's new orientation in foreign policy was of the utmost importance. Veering between the Prussians and the Turks, she drew nearer to Russia. Emperor Joseph, who in his spontaneous way liked to arrange personal meetings, conferred with Czarina Catherine and devised a defensive alliance, but soon differences of opinion came up with the development of the question of the Near East. Catherine II contemplated a revival of the Greek emperorship, while Joseph on the contrary promoted Austrian interests in the Balkans. Prussia found herself alone. England was in the midst of her difficult war with her rebellious American colonies. The two Bourbon powers, from motives of envy, were aiding the liberty-loving Americans. Signs of revolutionary turmoil were already appearing in France. Holland also joined the adversaries of England. Britain's position as a great power seemed about to be shattered. England could hardly, therefore, be considered as an ally. Frederick had preferred to show his sympathy with the Americans from the very outset, and he recognized their republic. How, then, was the King of Prussia to create a counterbalance to the advance of Emperor Joseph? The precipitance of the imperial spirit of enterprise was causing unrest everywhere. Joseph II persuaded the Dutch to renounce their right to occupy Belgian frontier fortresses, a privilege that had been accorded to them in the Peace of Utrecht (1712). Since Holland was now working hand in hand with France, the barrier treaty no longer meant very much to her. But more than this, Joseph II demanded the opening of the mouth of the Scheldt. This was wholly justifiable from the standpoint of the trade interests of the Austrian Netherlands, but the matter was a question of life or death for the Dutch economy. The Dutch proved inflexible, and now the Emperor exerted pressure on them by raising territorial claims. For a time there was danger of war, and the Dutch opened the sluices; but France negotiated a peace. The Emperor secured only a trifling rectification of the border and a cash indemnity.

THE LEAGUE OF PRINCES (1785)

The Emperor's attempts to breathe a little more vigour into the imperial authorities, which were tottering with age, were futile. Both the supreme court and the Aulic Council resisted every form of effective supervision. Joseph's fight against the privileges of the ec-clesiastical princes, his abolition of a status of landownership that no longer had any meaning, and his use of ecclesiastical funds for pur-poses of state nettled the bishops and reduced their former tradi-tional sympathies for the house of Austria. There was small prospect of success for further attempts to gather other ecclesiastical principal-ities of the Empire into Austria's hand. But the Emperor caused the greatest excitement by his idea of resuming in a new form his old plans about Bavaria. Joseph offered Belgium and a royal crown to Elector Charles Theodore; Austria was to receive in recompense Bavaria, the Upper Palatinate, and Salzburg, and the Archbishop of Salzburg was to be indemnified with Luxemburg, Limburg, and Namur. Elector Charles Theodore had never felt at home in Munich. He accepted the proposal. But the Duke of Zweibrücken, as heir, was against the idea. Russia was for it; France definitely disapproved. Frederick the Great took advantage of the moment to unite the estates of the Empire that were opposed to Austria in a League of Princes.

The smaller estates had been striving toward union for some time; their point of departure was the old heart of the Empire. The inse-curity of relations to the Empire, the growth of the great powers and of their means of maintaining their position, and the increase in foreign influence all combined to revive the old German idea of comradely co-operation of the weak. France, the patron saint of yes-teryear, now seemed less fitted to play such a role. But Prussia in her isolation pounced on it. Frederick was thinking of something on the order of the Schmalkalden League. The impression made by the proposal for an exchange of Belgium for Bavaria helped Frederick's idea along. Even after Emperor Joseph dropped the exchange, these negotiations continued; their immediate consequence was a league of three electors (Brandenburg-Prussia, Hanover, and Saxony). Then a considerable number of German princes, including Catholic estates of the Empire, entered the widening negotiations for an association (1785). Not only the proposed territorial exchange, but secularization as well was to be prevented. The League of Princes urged the liberty of the estates of the Empire as against the Emperor. The organization brought to Frederick, the erstwhile enemy of the Empire, who looked on the Emperor as a figurehead, enhanced respect as the champion of established law. The effect was to isolate Austria and crowd it out and to destroy the concept of a central Europe. But what actually inspired the movement was the need of Prussia, as a great power, for support by the small estates of the Empire, and from this angle the League of Princes was a presage of Germany's future destiny.

The rising generation in Prussia heaved a sigh of relief at the death of Frederick the Great (1786). His last years had been lonely, peevish, and gloomy. His name and his legacy were to be most significant for the future of Prussia; even while he lived, legend surrounded this strange, uncanny man. As soon as he died a controversy about the significance of his personality and his work set in that has continued well into our own era. All those who perceive the permanent importance to humanity of historical genius that can be fully comprehended only as if it were a work of art must do homage to the old Prussian King.

His unfortunate pupil Emperor Joseph II left the stage only a few years later (1790). In his case the historian finds fewer problems, perhaps too few. The Emperor's lack of spiritual poise, his haste and disharmony, struck everyone who knew him. His personal life was not happy, but withheld fulfilment, and he took refuge in veritable orgies of work to which he was physically unequal. But he did accomplish a few things in Austria that remain unforgotten: reform of the land tax, abolition of serfdom, a trend toward tolerance, and the start of charity organizations. He dreamed of a democratic and social state, but Austria had particularly marked difficulties in developing in this direction, and so nothing came of these beginnings. Justice, thrift, social welfare—these were lofty aims worthy of a great heart, and the lower classes felt the noble uprightness of this ruler, this Emperor of the people, whom they could not forget.

The obstacles were scarcely such as could be surmounted. Not all the peasants achieved the position of hereditary tenant. The very promising land tax was done away with immediately after the Emperor's death; the nobility simply would not tolerate it. The non-Catholic denominations could at least hold services privately and were no longer deprived of any civic rights. The suspension of seven hundred monasteries, which in itself was a blessing, was accompanied by all sorts of destructiveness, harshness, and abuse. Complete freedom from censorship was unknown. The measures of the state church provoked bitter indignation. This was especially true of the Austrian Netherlands. With the clerical opposition was combined that of local diets. The new centralized bureaucracy was regarded as a breach of the constitutional rights of the land, which the Emperor had confirmed by oath. The council of Brabant refused to pay taxes. When, in reply, the Emperor abrogated the Brabant constitution, the old and honoured *Joyeuse Entrée,* revolution broke out, kindled by the example of France close at hand, but led by the clergy. The act of confederation of the united Belgian states, drawn up after the Dutch pattern, gave the new Republic of Belgium its eagerly desired new constitution. Only in Luxemburg did the Austrians still hold fast. Neighbouring Prussia, England, and Holland obligated themselves to respect Belgium's independence by the Treaty of Berlin (1790).

THE AMBITION FOR A NATIONAL CHURCH

Certain efforts in Germany to limit the Pope's absolute power were connected with Joseph's state church. John Nicholas of Hontheim, the suffragan of Trier, published a pamphlet in Latin on reform, under the name of Febronius. The gist of it was that the power of the bishops should be strengthened against Rome; Gallican ideas should now be adapted to German conditions. The Pope had roused the German bishops by sending a nuncio to Munich, and the Emperor interdicted the jurisdiction of the nuncios in Germany. The three ecclesiastical electors and the Archbishop of Salzburg now united in the so-called Agreement of Ems (1786), which stood for a far-reaching program of church reform: discontinuance of all papal exemptions and reservations and of all recourse to Rome and jurisdiction of nuncios, release of all funds destined for Rome, specification of bishops as highest authority for marriage dispensations and in cases of ecclesiastical disagreement, adaptation of church observances to the idea of the time, and finally the holding of a national council in Germany. This sounded very promising, but the Emperor, the secular princes, and the bishops all failed to take part. The four archbishops did not get along with one another, and the storms of revolution threatening from France buried these attempts at reform for the Empire.

The centralization that Joseph had advanced finally became so offensive to the rights and feelings of the Hungarians that they thought of reviving the elective monarchy and began to negotiate with Prussia. But Duke Charles Augustus of Weimar wanted nothing to do with the crown of Hungary, which was to be offered to him. Hungary was also embittered by the burdens imposed on her by the new war against the Turks. Emperor Joseph was carrying on this war rather lucklessly in company with his old ally, Czarina Catherine. His main reason was justifiable in view of failures within the Empire: he did not want Russia to become too powerful in the Near East. But here, too, Prussia and the maritime powers formed an opposition. It even came to an alliance between Prussia and the Turks. Thus Prussia took over the old French policy of playing off the Ottoman Empire against the Emperor. In the midst of these setbacks and complications Emperor Joseph II died (1790). He had tried to combine the revolutionary spirit that was convulsing the times with his absolute dynastic and bureaucratic power, and this attempt wrecked him.

CHARACTER AND ACHIEVEMENT OF THE LESSER PRINCES

The agreement reached at Ems shows what disquiet even the ecclesiastical princes of the Empire were suffering. The times cried out for reform, and the Empire could not fill this pressing need at all. Many observers believed that this spectral Empire was the greatest obstacle to any form of progress in Germany. The German princes had no choice. The conduct and career of the two great German powers proved that there was no longer any security, that everyone must fend for himself, and that the small and the weak must keep on good terms with the mighty. The awakening of the German middle class, the new flexibility and creativeness of the German mind, gave the princes pause, and many of them sought security for their thrones in the very quarter where they had been wont to scent danger, in the awakening and advancement of the lower classes. A man like Margrave Charles Frederick of Baden enjoyed the love and admiration of his subjects for very good reason. He was a tireless reformer, a wise promoter of right living, a kind friend to the poor and needy. He abolished serfdom—and not only on paper—cleaned up the administration, lightened punishments, and insured public safety. If one experiment or another failed, if one aide or another proved humanly disappointing, this noble prince retained his firm faith in goodness and in the possibility of success.

Duke Charles William Ferdinand of Brunswick was also a model ruler. So great was his reputation in Europe that the French reformers wanted him for their king. Charles Augustus, the Duke of Weimar, a mettlesome thoroughbred, a regular fellow, the tireless keynote-sounder for the new generation in Germany, made his little capital the intellectual focus of the fatherland. Even backward Bavaria founded an academy of sciences. Palaces, museums, libraries, botanical gardens, all sprang up in Germany in greater abundance than anywhere else. The origin of the funds for all this was not, indeed, a proper subject of inquiry. The sweat of peasants, of underpaid manual workers, taxes squeezed out of the small citizen, and something even worse was behind it all. This something even worse, this worst of all, was the traffic in soldiers practised by the German princes. Bayreuth and Brunswick, Hesse-Kassel and Württemberg, supplied the Dutch and English with German peasant boys for their colonial wars for good if not excessive payment. Such was Germany's share in colonial policy. With this the petty German princes' right to form alliances reached the summit of its preposterousness.

The most famous subject of Duke Charles Eugene of Württemberg, the poet Friedrich von Schiller, properly denounced his ruler's trade in soldiers for America in his tragedy *Kabale und Liebe*. *The Princes' Mirror* (*Fürstenspiegel*), which Frederick the Great wrote for this relative of his, had little practical effect. The Duke was a notorious profligate and had no desire to change. The Landgrave of Hesse, Louis IX, wasted his time at silly soldier's games while his clever wife, who richly deserved the name of "great" Landgravine, smiled. Two statistical items suffice to demonstrate both the dependence of the German princes on foreign countries and the fruitlessness of their efforts on behalf of the lower classes. In the twenty-two years from 1750 to 1772 the French court paid 137,000,000 francs in subsidies to German potentates. In the ten years from 1756 to 1766, 200,000 German peasant lads emigrated to Russia and America.

Among the German ecclesiastical princes were many friends of reform. Some ceased to attend to their clerical duties, and so the question of a change to temporal rulerships—secularization—came up again and again. The Catholic and imperial sense of life, which previously had prevailed from Salzburg and Passau across Bavaria (Bavaria proper) and Upper Swabia to Freiburg and Constance, became pale and wan. This land of the Upper Danube, famed for its cloisters with onion-shaped domes, nevertheless remained a region of Austrian sympathies and much the same apprehension of life as Emperor Joseph's. Most of the ecclesiastical princes regarded current problems with gentle enlightenment and no militancy at all. Even Protestant scholars were given appointments at the re-established University of Mainz. Under the Stadholder of electoral Mainz, Baron Charles Theodore of Dalberg, Erfurt blossomed as a centre of cultural activity. Destiny had a curious and varied career prepared for this pliant magnate under Napoleon. Göttingen was particularly prominent among the many old and new universities. History and political science were studied there with careful thoroughness, and there the harshest critic of the tyranny of German potentates, August Wilhelm Schlözer, famous in all of Europe, carried on his work. Many an Englishman of rank began his period of Continental study at Göttingen, and many Americans were to follow.

THE SECULARIZATION OF THOUGHT. STORM AND STRESS

The Enlightenment was nothing non-German, but rather a movement that swept over all Europe and that each one of the culturally great nations adapted according to its needs. Essential to its rise was the distaste for religious strife, which was especially marked in Germany, and the rejection of churchly culture that resulted from this.

Theology lost her traditional place of supremacy among the sciences, and philosophy inherited the throne. Tolerance, in the definitive form in which it had developed first in Holland; English deism— that is, unprejudiced, undogmatic, and humanly keyed faith in God; and Voltaire's struggle for liberty, against mental arrogance, pedantry and hypocrisy, all made a deep impression in Germany too; it waked echoes, and it encouraged like-minded thinking and striving. There was an abundance of good material in the fatherland. Gottsched was working in Leipzig in the spirit of Christian Wolff for tolerance, for freedom of thought, for the lifting of every moral constraint.

The Enlightenment was infused with joy of living. It believed in the intrinsic goodness of the human soul and in the possibility of successful education. It distinguished ethics from revealed religion and preached a virtue rooted in nature and corresponding to the facts of nature. Its confidence in human reason sprang from deep feeling, from passionate indignation against whatever was brutal, irrational, base, selfish, and vengeful. The diabolical forces inherent in human nature were only too familiar to this movement; there were enough examples at hand. In the name of a better world, whose realization it firmly believed in, the Enlightenment set out to fight this spirit of negation and destruction. Emotional excitement and the joy of combat were characteristic of the Enlightenment; here it encountered the spiritual side of our human life, exactly as it did the beginnings of a mode of writing history that was purely secular. In a subsequent age opponents of the Enlightenment often chose by preference as the targets for their criticism the representatives of the shallow late period, many of whom doubtless were personifications of tediousness and of brittle self-importance. The best representatives of the early period of the Enlightenment deserve the gratitude of the German spirit. The Enlightenment never lost its pronounced scholarly tone. The much-admired study of mathematics taught it to think; logic led it into ventures to control nature. The Enlightenment discovered secrets; it unveiled the profound eternal laws that govern natural events. On the whole it was cool toward art, and so artists were justified in being critical of it. This is the clue to Gotthold Ephraim Lessing's contention for an æsthetic view of art and of the creative force of the artist.

The Storm and Stress was the first period of purposeful revolutionary thinking in Germany. Its leaders invoked the basic forces of the human soul, the elemental and the subconscious. They interpreted instincts as the actual driving force of human will and action. In history they discovered the effects of temperament, of will, of the soul of peoples and the character of their leaders. All this was intuition, psychology, a convincing power of reanimation, a rich and colourful painting of the past, a description of impressions and circumstances, of experiences and divinings, of destinies and their meaning for mankind. It was at once nature and history, philosophy of life and social reform, overthrow and constructive power, all held together by the emotional will-to-create of the intellect ruled by art. The critical spirit of the Enlightenment with its craving for the new was outstripped by the passionate Storm and Stress that trembled in the words of many minor poets and flamed up in the work of the young Goethe.

GERMAN CLASSICAL IDEALISM. THE EARLY ROMANTIC SCHOOL

At that time Friedrich Schiller inscribed on his play *The Robbers* the motto: *In tyrannos*. He scoriated the conduct of the lesser princes. He understood the fate of the woman who murdered her illegitimate child, and he wrought it into an indictment of the social ruling class. Elsewhere in Germany, too, there was indignation, hatred, and bitter contentiousness. The Rococo with its ruffles and its wigs was dissolving in the passionate love of nature and liberty. But in Germany all this never got beyond a matter of putting it down on paper. Never was there a greater hunger for education than at this time. The generation that was growing up was seized with enormous curiosity. Supermen of genius shook the nerves of their contemporaries. These Titans reached up into the starry world of a new, unheard-of psychic fulfilment. But the end of such excitement was only disgust for an ink-bespattered century.

Dualism and particularism, those old forces of German history, strengthened the resistance of existing social institutions and paralysed every attack. The rising German bourgeoisie had no political organ and no possibility of creating one for itself. And so the whole great impulse ebbed and wasted away, at least in the practical world. Only a supernational universalism could help the Germans; so the revolutionary power of the Storm and Stress was transfigured into love of mankind and into the world citizenship of German idealism. The old traditions of European collectivity, carried by the German spirit, were changed into antiquarian humanism, critical philosophy, comprehension of the world spirit through world literature. The princes and bureaucrats still promoted political and social reform, and honestly enough in their own way. Many were willing to learn and to listen to reason. But they had their own ulterior motives in encouraging the awakening of creative art and thought among the Germans, for the spiritual leaders of the nation could easily be fitted into the cautious reform programs of the high authorities.

The Germans produced poetry; they reflected; they made music. Kant, Goethe, and Mozart demonstrated the possibility of highest perfection. Many groups of minor artists emulated them. Education, taste, and the personal refinements of life were accorded an importance unmatched in public life. Wilhelm von Humboldt, the thinker and statesman, set bounds for the inquisitive and diligent state in a famous pamphlet that was written in his youth, but not published till long after his death (1835). The state, he said in effect, should protect the citizens against thieves and breakers of the peace so that they might devote themselves to the really important things of life. The love of introspection had been prepared in Germany by the spiritual side of religious life. Orthodox Lutheranism indeed had always honoured the authorities as such without daring to criticize or to propose reforms. A quietism innocent of political implications was, then, characteristic of the German. It expressed itself in guilelessness and harmless loyalty and devotion, in a form most welcome to the old authorities. How great was the enthusiasm for the successes of Frederick the Great! What impetus his personality—German to so slight an extent—gave to the groping national consciousness of the bourgeoisie, to whom the decaying Empire and increasingly alien Austria could no longer mean anything!

This German national consciousness, which had formerly been roused by the necessity of fighting off the Turks, now received no spur from politics. For the time being it was directed toward academic and idealistic activities; temporarily it took refuge in history. Johann Gottfried Herder (died 1803) sought to advance the understanding of nationality, the conditions of its existence, the premises of its development as supplied by geographical and ethnical factors; this work, with his sensitive feeling for the destiny of peoples and for universal connections, helped the German to a deeper knowledge of his national self. The Storm and Stress had quieted, and in its final stages the movement rose to the purity of classical idealism. Instructed by Winckelmann, the German mind came to regard the Greek as the standard of all perfection, as the eternal pattern predestined for its own strivings. This æsthetic dogmatism was unhistorical as well as unpolitical. It made possible great works of art, such as Schiller's later dramas and Goethe's *Iphigenie,* but it could not satisfy the Germans' interest in their own destiny; too much yearning, too much force, too much repression, was involved.

Immanuel Kant's philosophy showed how idealism prolonged the Enlightenment and resembled it in universality and didacticism. But his criticism gave new depths and goals to the strivings of the German spirit. Kant and his prophet, Friedrich Schiller, created the concept of the constitutional state as the peak of moral and æsthetic human culture, over and above the ties of class, of nation, of society, and of race. It was a stern and noble doctrine, accomplishing much that Protestantism had attempted. Here was the junction of Kant's ethos, Luther's idea of vocation, and the Prussian view of the state, whose militaristic and selfish character, for the rest, was as alien to true Christianity as to a true philosophy. The constitutional state was a boon to pedagogues and officials. Though it was not always attractive in Prussia, it was on the whole neat and orderly. Not all types of German were satisfied with a fulfilment of this sort. Caught in an avalanche of historical events and excited by the tempest of the French Revolution, the emotional Germans longed above all to know themselves, to know their own past and their mission in the world; they cherished the bonds of home and the age-old customs of their own people.

German romanticism no longer wanted to believe in the unique, in the absolute, in the finality of conceptual knowledge, in the systems and rules, the rhetoric and pose, and the unambiguous clarity of laws, as propounded by rationalism and Hellenism. Romanticism affirmed the artistic itself: change and flux, irony and spontaneity, instincts and dreams, the everlastingness of the world of fairy-tales and magic, the savouring of life, the taste for true values that had sprung from whatever sources, created by a heightened, joyous sense of life. Romanticism reconciled the great contradiction: the decay of traditional labels and connections; sovereignty as against custom, rank, accepted values; the scepticism of sickly degeneration—and belief in the power of the soul and spirit as it appears in religion and among the people, in a growing organism, in tradition and strength sprung from the soil, in personal grace, in genius. Romanticism could produce any kind of thesis and antithesis: an attitude entirely unpolitical, turned away from the world and its doings, dedicated to the reflective and metaphysical, and the exact opposite of this—a pronounced nationalism rooted in the people and inspired by history.

Chapter 13

GERMANY AND THE FRENCH REVOLUTION

THE CONCEPT OF THE CONSTITUTIONAL STATE

EVER SINCE the English Revolution of the seventeenth century the intellectual life of Continental Europe had been preoccupied with the idea of the modern constitutional state. England was the first big country in which an educated bourgeoisie that had become prosperous through work and thrift took its place beside the old ruling feudal classes and exercised political rights in the name of intellectual liberty and of the equal rights of man. English forms of parliamentarism and self-government did have a clearly defined class character from the point of view of social history, because they expressed the will and the interests of the new class that was just coming up at this time and that was destined to affect history. English political ideas and constitutional instrumentalities were arousing the warmest interest on the entire Continent, especially in France. French political literature written by men like Voltaire and Montesquieu accorded the English political system the rank of a classical model; it was lifted out of its historical premises and dogmatized about as a patent solution. Purely national English phenomena, say the life of the parishes within the counties and the position of the gentry, were necessarily lost sight of in all this. Only what seemed of particular importance to the Continent was emphasized: the separation of legislative, judicial, and executive powers, ministerial responsibility, the control of the national finances by representatives of the people, and the imposition of limitations on the prerogatives of the monarch.

So arose the ideology of a liberalism that put its trust in constitutions. In accord with its sources and prevalence this liberalism was a collective European phenomenon. It was something that the entire European continent had to reckon with. In Germany it was diffused

300

in the intellectual and literary form it had assumed in France. The English Revolution had not made any very deep immediate impression on Germany, caught in the chaos of the Thirty Years' War as she was. Now the American Revolution demonstrated the strength of the modern ideas of liberty. France, which was still in the throes of absolutism and feudalism, helped the English colonies in North America to throw off the guardianship of the mother country. Human and civic rights in a community that was economically independent and remarkably autonomous spiritually won the admiration of the world and furnished an example of unforgettable, world-shaking force. England herself, the home of the ideas and of the people involved, had to consider seriously whether a good deal could not be learned from the new, rising libertarian republic. Had not this community new-coined its heritage and filled it with the verve of irresistible youth?

Unfortunately Germany could not take the path to self-liberation on her own momentum. She was a witness and a neighbour of great historical revolutions; voluntarily or involuntarily she herself was swept into the current. More than ever before, German history became the history of central Europe, even the history of the Continent. The German nation found itself first intellectually and artistically. The way thence to political unity, to civic liberty, was difficult for the Germans.

THE INFLUENCE OF THE FRENCH REVOLUTION. FREDERICK WILLIAM II OF PRUSSIA

The French Revolution found warm acceptance among the foremost leaders of German intellectual life. The poets Wieland and Herder, the philosophers Kant and Fichte, Schlözer the teacher of constitutional law, and the historian Johann von Müller welcomed the movement as the final great fulfilment of all the most sacred hopes of the age. In Hamburg, for instance, July 14, 1790, the first anniversary of the storming of the Bastille in Paris, was marked by a public celebration at which the poet Friedrich Klopstock (died 1803) recited a stirring ode. Like the members of all other nations, many Germans hastened to Paris, to the Mecca of freedom and of the new humanity. They gave enthusiastic reports; one of these came from the adventurous, eternally youthful Georg Forster, who had accompanied the English Captain Cook to Australia on his voyage more than half around the world. Such another report came from Eulogius Schneider, the thoroughly benevolent professor from Bonn, who later went to Strassburg and there assisted in conducting a reign of terror that finally proved his own destruction. But in only very few places in Germany was there any readiness for revolutionary activity—in a few imperial cities in the west, in rural Saxony, and in Silesia.

As the movement became radical in France and property and privilege were attacked, the friendly mood in Germany immediately changed. Property-owners became fearful, the revolution excited the lower classes, cruelty and terrorism offended all feelings of decency and loyalty. The Revolution indeed had ceased to be merely a French affair. It had grown into a crusade that threatened the entire existing European order of law and society with destruction. Counter-revolution set in at once. The Englishman Edmund Burke was the first to grasp the deep significance of the epoch and to recommend sweeping counter-measures. His aim was to set up a collective European defensive bloc against revolutionary propaganda, against the spirit of destruction. The gifted publicist Friedrich Gentz (died 1832) translated Burke's writings into German and thus did much to aid in the intellectual defence against revolutionary ideas in central Europe. Although unfortunately he later became a corrupt official in the Austrian administration, he must still be regarded as one of the cleverest and most accomplished writers of his time.

As far as foreign policy was concerned, the first effect of the Revolution was to weaken the position of France as a great power. The two great German powers felt relieved and tried to make the most of the situation. In Prussia Frederick the Great was succeeded by his nephew, Frederick William II (1786–97), a much-discussed figure. His arrangements with his mistresses were too bizarre even for the sophisticated tolerance of the eighteenth century. His worst stroke, no doubt, was the comedy of marriage with beautiful Julia von Voss, whose mother would not sanction anything less. In this disagreeable business a thoroughly ignominious part was taken by the Prussian state church, which agreed to a mock marriage while the Queen was still living, in order to overcome the scruples of the girl and her family. But it would be easy to overlook the weaknesses of this Prussian King's private life if he had ever taken a clear line as statesman. Favourites of dubious and even shady origin were allowed to exert decisive influence. All manner of secret dealings, mystical orders, spirit-conjurings, and self-intoxication with ringing words served to enliven the tedium and nervous laxity of this surfeited circle. The clearness and firmness of the Enlightenment was offensive to the softness of these people. To them good and genuine art or clear, manly thinking or honest faith was a vexation. Strength and depth alike annoyed them, since these qualities were somehow humiliating to them. And so their sensuality and sensationalism strayed this way and that on the perilous edge of vacancy, farce, and vertigo. King Frederick William II had originally been a Freemason, but the moral earnestness and the brotherly and idealistic nature of the order's activity had not appealed to him. Then he joined the Rosicrucians, whose pompous and cabalistic ritual afforded him excitement such as he craved. He could not live without the stimulus of constant change and pleasure. He had neither much time nor much energy left for important affairs of state.

One good side of the new regime was the effort that proceeded from Berlin to get in touch with the great German intellectual movement. The French mode was played out. German authors became members of the Academy of Learning and Sciences; the stage was fondly encouraged. Iffland, the great character actor of the time, was made the manager of the National Theatre in Berlin. Music and the fine arts throve. It was at this time that the Brandenburg Gate, with its imposing elegance, was erected. Gottfried Schadow created his noble sculptures. Chodowiecki, the clever realist of copper engraving, headed the Academy of Arts. But Wöllner, the canting minister charged with oversight of public worship and public instruction, tried to re-establish the old orthodoxy in church and school. His censorship suppressed unwelcome freedom of thought. Even the great philosopher Immanuel Kant had to accept the admonition that he was not to use his philosophy to debase Christianity. The fatal alliance of throne and altar, already rooted in the old Lutheran church government, was now put to a new sort of practical test. Inquiry and intelligence were frowned on; prejudice and platitude were at a premium. A half-lie went farther than the truth; the authorities felt comfortable in an atmosphere of ignorance. Subjects

303

were easy to rule as long as they were kept fed and amused. Examinations became an important means of selection for the career of the servile officialdom. The famous *Abiturientenexamen* was introduced in Prussia; admission to study at the universities was carefully barricaded by this examination. One advance was the completion of the common law that had been begun under Frederick the Great— the Prussian state code, magnanimously conceived and well formulated textually.

EMPEROR LEOPOLD II (1790–2). RAPPROCHEMENT OF AUSTRIA AND PRUSSIA

Prussia's international position gained in importance because Joseph II had left his states in such a chaotic condition. The new Emperor, Leopold II, was a smooth, hardened politician who did what he could to establish order, without any personal sensitiveness, patiently, amiably, and perhaps a trifle contemptuously. The chief exponent of foreign policy in Prussia was Count Hertzberg, a smart fellow, but more suggestive of an apothecary than of a physician. His "great plan" was calculated to take advantage of the favourable moment and to make substantial gains for Prussia. Swedish Hither Pomerania, Danzig, Thorn, the neighbouring Polish regions, and Galicia were to become Prussian. Austria was to be indemnified within the Balkans; she was to take over Moldavia and Wallachia, the principalities on the Danube. Russia was to give Swedish Finland to Sweden and to indemnify herself with the Crimea, Bessarabia, and other parts of the Ottoman Empire. Hertzberg's keen brain had recognized three factors that were bound to play a part in future events: Prussia's impulse toward Poland, Austria's toward the Balkans, and Russia's toward the Black Sea. There was still another point that Hertzberg stressed: Prussia was to approach England again. King Frederick William II intervened in Holland in favour of the hereditary stadholdership against the republican Patriots. England was well pleased with this anti-revolutionary action and formed a triple alliance with Prussia and the Netherlands. Prussia was less successful in her attempt to aid the Bishop of Liège against his revolutionary subjects; she was forced to withdraw without having finished the business. These events had sharpened the antagonism between Austria and Prussia. For a time war threatened. Prussia had at her disposal alliances with Poland and the Turks. Prussian agents were at work in Galicia, Hungary, and Belgium. Austria was at a decided disadvantage everywhere. Emperor Leopold II saw any sort of favourable finish to the Turkish war as his main task. He approached the King of Prussia directly and saved Austria by clever negotiations. The Emperor renounced any gains at the expense of the Ottoman Empire and also the taking over of Bavaria, and Prussia reciprocated by dropping Count Hertzberg's great plan.

Now Leopold II could devote himself to restoring quiet in his lands. He abolished most of Emperor Joseph's reforms. Only the edict of tolerance and the secularization of the monasteries were left standing. The Czechs were allowed a professorship in the Czech language at the University of Prague. Leopold's system was less reactionary in effect than Prussia's at this time. Though censorship and secret police played a part here also, there was a clever ruler, who knew from his experience as Grand Duke of Tuscany how to quell an excited body of subjects with a firm hand. The Hungarians too obtained consent to their patriotic demands. The old constitution came into force again, including the use of Latin as the official language. One of the Emperor's sons was made viceroy of Hungary. The south Hungarian Serbs were recognized as a distinct nation. Transylvania returned to its old threefold division (Hungarian, German, Rumanian) and was given its own chancery. The Austrian Netherlands, however, had to be retaken by force. The attempt of a Belgian national congress to make a Grand Duke of Belgium out of Archduke Charles, Leopold's third son, subsequently famous as a general, came too late. Even an amnesty did not effect a true reconciliation. Belgium continued to be a burden on Austria—though not for long.

The rapprochement between Austria and Prussia that Emperor Leopold II had brought about through dire necessity deepened under the influence of revolutionary events in France. When the French National Assembly abolished privileges and prerogatives, the traditional rights of numerous German princes and other estates of the Empire in Alsace were prejudiced. They asked for imperial intervention in their aid. According to an imperial verdict the French decrees were illegal and invalid. Compromise proposals by the French, which amounted to offers of money indemnification, were flatly rejected by the majority of those involved. Besides, many mem-

305

bers of the French aristocracy of the court had been warmly welcomed into Rhenish Catholic circles. The brothers of the King of France held court in proper style at Coblenz, formed a ministry, and set up troops. This was a challenge to revolutionary France, and even the German hosts did not experience lasting pleasure from their arrogant guests, who would neither adapt themselves to German ways nor make concessions of any kind to the new France. The *émigrés* openly worked for a crusading war against the French Revolution. Their very existence made German-French relations worse than any propaganda could have done. Emperor Leopold II did his utmost to help his sister Marie Antoinette and her husband, the King of France; he played a part in the famous attempted flight (1791), and he wanted to call a European congress to recognize the new French constitution if the King voluntarily approved.

In Poland, too, the French Revolution had strong repercussions. A change in the constitution was supposed to modernize the state and strengthen it; this was precisely what aroused the suspicion of her neighbours. During this entire critical transition period Prussia's attitude was coloured by her desire to expand at the expense of Poland. France was not in a position to champion Poland, and England held back on account of the disturbances in France. It was to be expected that Austria and, above all, Russia would participate in any further partition of Poland. On Prussia's side, then, co-operation with Austria was desirable for a twofold reason: it meant the suppression of Polish independence, and it meant maintenance of the monarchical principle in the face of the Revolution. Ideological considerations were invoked by Russia and Sweden in their anti-French attitude; they, after all, were farthest from the scene of action. The watchword of balance in the north assured calm in the Baltic region. The Declaration of Pillnitz marked a further stage on the way to the Austrian-Prussian alliance of February 1792: united advance of the two great German powers, mutual guarantee of property, assistance in case of attack by France. It was not wholly senseless to speak of French intentions of attacking. The party of the victorious liberal bourgeoisie in France, the Gironde, was in favour of a stronger foreign policy. For reasons of economics and of party it seized on the idea of war, which might have two advantages: occupation for the radical masses that were pressing farther leftward, and consolidation of the achievements of the Revolution through national prestige. Thus two offensives actually fused; intangible and material motives coincided. Young France would not swallow threats, interventions, and humiliations; monarchical Europe wanted to strangle the danger of revolution and if possible to reap profits at the same time. The old conflict for power was kindled by new motives.

OUTBREAK OF THE REVOLUTIONARY WARS. THE DOWNFALL OF POLAND

When France declared war on Austria, a war era that was to last almost twenty-five years began. Germany was to be one of the chief war theatres. Her political future became one of the main problems of the struggle. According to the provisions of their treaty, Prussia immediately joined Austria. The campaign against France, which was utterly isolated politically, was begun in a spirit of complacent optimism. Emperor Leopold II died suddenly. His youthful son, Francis II, was crowned Emperor in Frankfurt (1792) with splendid festivities. There could not have been a better overture for a victorious campaign. But this was the last imperial coronation for the old Holy Roman Empire.

Diplomatic negotiations between the allies concerning the territorial gains that were desired led to no clear results. Prussia wanted to expand along the Lower Rhine, but was thinking even more longingly of Poland. There the Russians were just marching in and overthrowing the liberal May Constitution. Austria was again intent on Bavaria. But Prussia was obstinately averse to surrendering the Franconian parts of it that she had just taken over, and she waved her ally aside to the Upper Rhine—that is, to the old Habsburg area in Alsace, the obvious complement to the possessions in the Austrian Breisgau. So self-confident and arrogant were the two great German powers. In like spirit the war manifesto was worded. The commander-in-chief, wise Duke Charles William Ferdinand of Brunswick, lent his good name to this pronouncement. The allies—so the document ran—wanted to re-establish the legitimate throne and the power of the law in France; all right-minded Frenchmen should therefore join the liberators; if the royal family were molested further, the city of Paris would be threatened with complete destruction. The reply of the French revolutionaries was the overthrow of the kingdom and the proclamation of the republic.

307

Was France really in dissolution? Was she really only waiting for her foreign liberators? The *émigrés* no longer knew the true France. Their guesses and their prophecies were all wrong. The revolutionary spirit rejuvenated France; national passion awoke and showed itself ready for self-sacrifice in order to save the threatened native soil. True, a first spring offensive against Belgium failed. But when the Germans invaded the country and reached the Champagne, they met not merely with a cold reception on the part of the ill-treated population, but also with such energetic military resistance that the Duke of Brunswick decided to give up the idea of attack and to retreat after the cannonading of Valmy (September 1792). His troops were disease-ridden; they had the look of a defeated army when they got back to Germany. The French immediately launched a counter-attack. General Custine appeared on the Rhine. If the French had renounced legitimism for themselves, the play was acted out in reverse order now in Mainz. The city set revolution in motion along the left bank of the Rhine. Members of radical clubs in Mainz summoned a Rhenish conference; it was decided to found a Rhenish free state. But immediately afterward the conquered regions on the left bank of the Rhine were incorporated in the French Republic. Then Austria suffered the terrible blow of French conquest in Belgium; here too the defeated imperialists abandoned the greater part of the neighbouring left bank of the Rhine.

The allies Prussia and Austria were sadly disappointed and began to quarrel. Prussia's first demand, her condition for undertaking another campaign, was additional land in Poland. Since Austria was cool, Prussia and Russia went to work alone. The second partition of Poland took place in 1793. Prussia received Danzig, Thorn, Posen, and Kalisch. Russia secured Lithuania, Podolia, and Volhynia. Austria was furious. Baron Thugut ruthlessly opposed Prussia; his Austrian pride might almost be called nationalistic. Now he took over the conduct of foreign affairs with talent and tireless energy. The French conquered Savoy and Nice and threatened Holland. The old catchword of the natural boundaries of France came up again; the Pyrenees, the Alps, and the Rhine were demanded. The French troops were warmly welcomed by the lower classes everywhere: craftsmen, peasants, and students, all who were young, oppressed, and hungry for life, seized avidly on the temporal gospel of human freedom.

There were adventurers and dreamers, too. Old Europe trembled and tottered, and the Holy Roman Empire creaked on its well-worn hinges. The French plucked property-owners as clean as they could. Nobility, churches, well-to-do citizens—all were bled. The old social order broke down internally and could no longer offer any serious military resistance.

The Empire now formally entered the war against France. Spain and Holland joined the ranks after the execution of the French King. Great Britain followed suit, if only because the Channel coast was threatened. Again and again the magnificent organization of national resistance in France brought forward fresh troops. Young revolutionary leaders spared neither themselves nor their men. They developed new tactics of relentless mass attack with lines of infantry armed with rifles. Constant lack of funds, together with mismanagement and demoralization of the national economy, forced the armies of the Revolution to levy formidable contributions on enemy territory and even to loot and rob. No local victories of the allies could avail against the relentless drive of these powerful masses. Holland fell; it was reorganized as the Batavian Republic. France gained the entire left bank of the Rhine. The members of the Coalition disagreed among themselves. They were casting about for indemnities. Austria and Russia arranged to divide what was left of Poland proper. The Polish patriots could rouse no resistance. Prussia did not want to go empty-handed; she was war-weary, and only considerable subsidies from the maritime powers persuaded her to carry on the war for another year. For the monthly sum of one hundred thousand pounds, with additional funds for armaments and later mustering-out pay, Prussia promised to do battle on whatever field England and Holland designated as preferable. The maritime powers were to dispose of any conquests that might be made. This arrangement was inglorious for Prussia and did not serve to increase her zest for war. The English subsidies failed to arrive as desired.

A wish for peace was astir in the Empire. Attempts to build up a union of German princes in the interest of peace miscarried. In the Diet at Regensburg, however, a motion for peace rolled up a great majority. The Reign of Terror had ended in France. The Thermidorians, the successors of the Jacobins, were more moderate and approachable. To make peace would be to the advantage of the French revolutionary powers and would enhance their prestige, though from the point of view of any counter-revolutionary power the step remained precarious. The deciding factor in Prussian policy was the east. In giving up the Rhine in order to retain Poland, Prussia was acting quite in the spirit of her previous history. Thus the Peace of Basel came into being (1795).

In the public articles Prussia recognized the occupation of the left bank of the Rhine by France for the time being, until some imperial peace should be concluded with Prussian mediation. But in the secret articles Prussia sacrificed her own possessions on the left bank of the Rhine in consideration of suitable indemnity on the right bank. Northern Germany was neutralized by a line of demarcation. But the promised imperial peace did not follow this separate peace. Prussia believed that the outcome of the negotiations at Basel would best safeguard her territorial interests. She was acting as the leading power in northern Germany; it was a presage of the North German Confederation that was to come. Her conduct showed that motives springing from anti-revolutionary feeling and from imperial patriotism were nothing in comparison with her state egoism. Prussia reaped her reward for the Peace of Basel in the third partition of Poland. In spite of Austria's attempts to exclude her this time, she received a really impressive share: Warsaw, Masovia, Bialystok, and part of Podlachia—purely Polish land with a population of a million inhabitants on forty-eight thousand square kilometres (about thirty thousand square miles). For administrative purposes it was organized as New East Prussia and New Silesia. The majority of the inhabitants probably preferred Prussian rule to Russian despotism. More than ever Prussia's centre of gravity shifted eastward. For eleven years she was able to maintain this region as a sort of island of peace in the midst of the European turmoil. Would she be able to preserve this sphere of power?

Austria's share in the third partition of Poland was south central Poland, with the old Polish coronation city of Cracow. Bohemia and Hungary had familiarized the Viennese authorities with lands that functioned as aristocracies, and the Austrians got on better with the Poles than the Prussians or the Russians did. People of mixed German and Slavic blood hailed in the Polish nationality something familiar; Austro-Poles developed into an especially attractive type.

Determined to continue the war against the Revolution, Austria formed an offensive alliance with Russia and England. France made peace and an alliance with Spain and so improved her position. The French government made a series of treaties with Prussia to ensure the neutrality of northern Germany; Prussia was given the right to occupy Hanover. It was not surprising that such obvious friendliness excited the Empire's bitterness against northern Germany and the latter's partnership with the French Jacobins to a dangerous point. Within Austria, also, Baron Thugut was administering a sharp check to Jacobinism. The fortunes of war were changing. In 1796 the French advanced victoriously into southern Germany. Baden, Württemberg, and Saxony made a truce with France and then peace treaties that secured secularized ecclesiastical property for them in indemnification for possessions on the left bank of the Rhine. Thus they followed the much-criticized example of Prussia. Their slight powers of resistance and their greed, under French inspiration, became clearly evident. New Austrian successes, however, especially Archduke Charles's victories at Amberg and Würzburg, caused the south German states to abjure these treaties with France immediately. But the great change came in Italy.

NAPOLEON BONAPARTE. RASTATT

The young French general Napoleon Bonaparte conquered northern and central Italy and advanced into the crown lands of Austria, which was forced to negotiate. Even England was secretly negotiating with France. Czar Paul I, who succeeded Catherine the Great, was not unfriendly. Thugut, the "war baron," had long opposed yielding in any way whatever, but there was no longer any military prospect of winning the war or carrying it on passably. A preliminary peace was made at Leoben and a final peace at Campo Formio (1797) that was even more unfavourable. Napoleon, the master of his era, was showing his claws for the first time. Here too, as at Basel, there were a public treaty and a secret one. Austria ceded Belgium and the Ionian Islands to France and gave her consent to the formation of a Cisalpine Republic taking in all north Italian lands up to the river Adige. Secretly France was accorded the left bank of the Rhine except for electoral Köln and Prussian Cleve. Austria was immediately indemnified with Venice, Dalmatia, and all the islands that up to this time had belonged to the Republic of Venice. In addition it was agreed that she might expect Salzburg and parts of Upper Bavaria as an indemnity for losses on the left bank of the Rhine. Prussia was to be excluded from indemnities as far as possible; that was why Cleve was reserved for her. A peace congress in Rastatt was to bring about the peace of the Empire. The spirit of these peace provisions was the same as at the Peace of Basel. Austria's egoism as a great power outweighed the interests of the Empire. She was giving up her long-standing position on the Rhine and was indemnifying herself at the expense of the weak and outmoded. She was rounding off her domains around the core of the old Habsburg dynastic power, while she abandoned peripheral parts that had become untenable.

The chaotic Empire was torn between the growing power of France in the west and the two German great powers, which had been pushed eastward and were losing more and more of their German character. The Empire's resistance to France was exactly as weak, on both intellectual and economic grounds, as its fear of the two German powers was great, for dynastic reasons. At that time there was no hatred of France within the Empire. On the contrary the rising classes and the commonwealth of German scholars sympathized with the heroic struggle to create a new form of state and to win esteem for the French nation. French was still both the prevailing language of conversation—not only in German court society—and also the medium of instruction among the aspiring citizenry. In the fields of politics, social economy, and polite society the west and the south Germans were ready to learn from French organization, which was both progressive and effective. No one in his right senses wanted to relinquish his German nationality for this. The cosmopolitanism of the time cherished values of whatever origin, but this did not detract from love of real German culture. Of course many shades of feeling could be traced; unfledged dreamers completely surrendered themselves to the world mission of France, but on the whole a soberer tone prevailed in the Empire.

The great German powers, which had become half Slavic, could not look for much affection. They could hardly expect true Germans to warm to those who had left them shabbily in the lurch. If everyone was to think only of himself, then the smaller estates of the Empire were certainly entitled to do just that. No effective political starting-point existed for German national feeling. Finally there was a potent personal force at work: many Germans were enchanted by the figure of Napoleon. He was the answer to the longing for a great man, for the singular and unique—the superman. The Storm and Stress had demanded genius as the salvation of mankind; German classicism had called for one who would execute the will of the world spirit. German romanticism had fought for the idea of a personality that would liberate, that would bring joy, that would clear away what was merely conventional, all that was banal and belonged to the eternal yesteryear—a personality, that is, touched by divine grace. In the eyes of many Germans Napoleon, the master of the epoch, assumed a significance far beyond French nationality. Was he not that world conqueror and world liberator of whom Germany too had need?

The peace congress at Rastatt brought the Empire nothing but bitter disappointments. France simply demanded the left bank of the Rhine. In accordance with their secret agreements with France the two German great powers, Austria and Prussia, surrendered that left bank without a pang. The estates of the Empire that suffered by this action were to be indemnified with secularized church property. Ecclesiastical rule of territory was held to be so far out of tune with the spirit of the times that no objection was forthcoming even from the Catholic princes. Only Austria resisted, for the Emperor's position depended on the ecclesiastical princes. The Empire had not had the strength to effect its own reform. Now it was facing complete reorganization under French leadership. England was the only country that had not participated in the peace negotiations; she was bent now on utilizing Austria's discontent and Russia's anger at French meddling in central Europe to build up a new coalition. The French advanced in the Mediterranean area. In the Rhineland the buffer state of the Cis-Rhenish Republic soon disappeared; the population voluntarily joined with France. The great publicist Joseph Görres, a master of moving eloquence, welcomed with enthusiasm the modern arrangements introduced by France. The oppressed began to breathe more freely. Law and administration were reorganized along clear-

313

cut rational lines. Clerical mismanagement was at an end. Of course many French officials, out for their own advantage, were now oppressing the country.

FRENCH HEGEMONY. THE NEW ORDER IN GERMANY

The outbreak of the war of the second coalition put a sudden end to the peace negotiations at Rastatt. Their close was especially ill-favoured, for Austrian hussars attacked the departing French delegates, and two diplomats were killed (1798). Whatever may have been the motives of those responsible, whoever gave the command, it was a serious breach of international law, and relations between Austria and France long suffered because of it.

Prussia, deaf to all persuasion, did not join the alliance of Great Britain, Russia, and Austria. Since 1797 Prussia had been under the rule of King Frederick William III, a willing but uninspired and clumsy ruler who was markedly inferior to his warm-hearted, artistically gifted wife. Queen Louise took a lively interest in contemporary German literature and music, while the King's preoccupations were limited to the barracks and the ballet—including the ballerinas. Nothing good in the way of politics could be expected from this tiresome and suspicious monarch. Strong personalities upset him; quick decisions embarrassed him. Revolution struck him as a terrible punishment for bad rulers. Reforms of many sorts were started in Prussia, but nothing was carried more than half-way. It is true that the peasants on the royal domains were given their freedom, but the maintenance of the economic and social status of the landowning nobility meant that their peasants could not be touched. The minister Baron vom Stein, who forged ahead energetically, succeeded at least in abolishing domestic duties. The standing army was supplemented by the organization of a national militia, but to unite the two—to modernize the army on a popular basis—would have been thought far too dangerous. Many changes were made in the system of education also, but the spirit that directed them was timid and narrow. Prussia shut herself off from the great events of the times and tried to lock herself into her artificial island of neutrality as long as possible.

At first the new war went well for the allies. General Bonaparte, the coming man of France, was in Egypt. Archduke Charles and the

Russian General Suvarov reaped triumphs. The new-fangled free states in Italy collapsed. An English-Russian expedition appeared in Holland. The south German states made subsidy treaties with England. But soon there were reverses. The undertaking in Holland came to a wretched end. It was impossible to hold Switzerland, and disagreements between Austrian and Russian leaders caused the St. Petersburg government to recall its troops. In the meantime Napoleon Bonaparte returned from the Near East, assumed the chief command in the Italian war theatre, with which he was very familiar, and at Marengo won a brilliant victory over the Austrians. Peace negotiations began, but dragged on without any definite results until a new French victory at Hohenlinden made Austria amenable; young Archduke John was defeated by the French General Moreau. The Peace of Lunéville (1801) was a poor repetition of the Peace of Campo Formio. It was a separate peace of Austria's, in which the Empire necessarily joined. From the political angle the peace signified the incapacity of the imperial states of Austria and of Russia, with their old-fashioned organization, to cope with the technical superiority of modern France, even when they had England's help. The triumph of the foreign policy of the Revolution over the old Europe was complete.

Austria now gave up Italy as far as the river Adige. The Grand Duke of Tuscany was to receive Salzburg; the Duke of Modena, the Breisgau—so the last Rhenish holding of the house of Habsburg-Lorraine fell. All the fortresses on the right bank of the Rhine were to be razed; militarily, this meant that the road into Germany stood open to the French. All questions of indemnity were to be solved in accordance with the principles of the congress at Rastatt—that is, by the secularization of ecclesiastical property and with the active participation of France.

Under the leadership of her First Consul, Bonaparte, France now had undisputed hegemony on the European continent. Napoleon succeeded in making an alliance with Czar Paul of Russia, who had been deeply offended by the English occupation of Malta. Czar Paul made a treaty with the Scandinavian states to ensure their naval neutrality; this was directed against the English trade war. Prussia joined and, under pressure from both France and Russia, sent her troops into electoral Hanover. But the murder of Czar Paul and

Nelson's victory over the Danish fleet in the Sound changed matters. France and England opened peace negotiations, which came to a close in Amiens (1802). The First Consul and the new Czar Alexander I made peace and agreed that the new order in Germany should be supervised by both powers in unison. This was a forerunner of the later partition of Europe between Napoleon and Alexander. The Russian-French scheme became prescriptive for the distribution of lands; the responsible German imperial deputation had to be guided by these principles. The envy between the two German great powers eased the Russian and French moves in the game. The policy of the two flanking powers was to prevent the two German great powers wedged between them from becoming too strong, but to permit the ambitious so-called German middle states to become as strong as possible. This seemed the surest way to keep Germany as a whole from becoming stronger, to prevent her from attaining political unity. France reached her goal by making separate treaties with Prussia, Bavaria, and Württemberg. In the end Austria had to submit, though reluctantly. The Czar favoured his royal relatives, such as the Oldenburgs, in particular. The comprehensive and conclusive instrument of public law for the imperial deputation, the Principal Decree of the Imperial Deputation, bore a name that seemed a veritable monster-word even to the Germans: *Reichsdeputationshauptschluss.* It was dated February 25, 1803.

The map of German lands underwent a complete transformation. One hundred and twelve estates of the Empire disappeared, and about three million persons underwent some shift of allegiance. All the ecclesiastical princes suffered absorption except the Elector of Mainz, who was compensated by territory in Regensburg, and the Grand Master of the Teutonic Order. Even the possessions of abbeys and cloisters that had nothing to do with the estates of the Empire, but were freeholds, were conveyed to the territorial princes. It was a complete clean-up. Many counts and petty princes who had been immediate to the Empire were mediatized; that is, they were subjected to the territorial sovereigns, and their property was no longer subject to imperial constitutional law. The knights of the Empire were not even mentioned, but this did not mean that they were to be spared. They were not represented in the diet, and they were sacrificed to the territorial princes without ceremony. An attempt of the Emperor's to save the knights failed. No more than six of the imperial cities survived. Among the few other important changes that can be mentioned here, Prussia received the bishoprics of Hildesheim and Paderborn, Münster with the eastern portion of the bishopric, the city of Erfurt, and Eichsfeld. Osnabrück fell to electoral Hanover. Bavaria was given the bishoprics of Würzburg, Bamberg, Augsburg, and Freising. Württemberg got the provostship of Ellwangen and also received all the fine Swabian imperial cities. Baden was particularly fortunate, with an indemnity eight times as large as her losses. Hesse-Darmstadt was similarly provided for, though Hesse-Kassel did not come off so well. The two Nassau branches received valuable areas of electoral Mainz and electoral Trier. A group of petty dynasts escaped mediatization; the manner in which they and some of their betters courted French favour was revolting. The Arch-Chancellor, the primate of Germany, though he had not been recognized as such by the Roman curia, was the only ecclesiastical prince of the old Empire to survive the storm; this was Dalberg, the Elector of Mainz, who was given lands in Regensburg. Five new electorates arose. Now the Protestant votes outnumbered the Catholic; there were more Protestant than Catholic estates in the Empire. Emperor Francis II vetoed this arrangement, but no further decision was reached. Had there been another imperial election, the house of Habsburg-Lorraine would have stood no chance. Probably a Guelph would have had a turn. This was one more reason for Austria's cold indifference toward the new order in the Empire.

A territorial transformation should have been effected long before. But the way in which this was now done was a weight on Germany's future rather than a stimulus to it. The carriers of the good old imperial patriotism suffered most. The chief gainers in western and southern Germany, on the other hand, aped the German great powers in developing a shallow localized patriotism of their own. These Lilliputians who had puffed themselves up into secondary states owed their promotion to foreigners, and so to them there was nothing painful in maintaining their foreign connections. The Rhenish electors had always been the warmest adherents of the French. Now France possessed the left bank of the Rhine and with it a large portion of the old electorate. The heirs to the electoral possessions on the right bank of the Rhine became the new friends of France. The second Rhenish Confederation cast its shadow before.

EMPERORSHIP IN FRANCE AND AUSTRIA

The peace between England and France (Amiens, 1802) did not last long. As early as 1803 relations were again broken off, and hostilities began anew. This had an immediate effect on central Europe. The French, on their part, now occupied electoral Hanover and thus violated the neutrality of northern Germany, which Prussia had upheld so long. Prussia should have anticipated the French. She was in a position to do so, and she would have been justified in such an act, but she lacked the courage. A pro-French faction at the Prussian court counselled acceptance of First Consul Bonaparte's repeated proposals for an alliance. Co-operation with France would have been in accordance with the traditions of Frederick the Great and of the Great Elector, but neither could this step be agreed on. In the end a defensive arrangement was made with Russia, with the provision that both countries were to proceed against France in case she encroached further on northern Germany. There was no lack of arbitrary acts and transgressions on the part of France. Worst of all was the arrest in Baden of a French Bourbon prince, the Duke of Enghien, who did not cut a figure in politics and was not in the line of succession; he was shot by the French. Sweden protested vigorously to the Diet at Regensburg. The Emperor of Russia demanded satisfaction as guarantor of the constitution of the Empire; electoral Hanover joined as a matter of course. But Baden urgently begged that matters should be allowed to stand; she was in too great need of French favour.

When Napoleon assumed the title of Emperor of the French, the German princes hastened to congratulate him heartily. Vienna's reaction was to set up an Austrian emperorship. Thus the Habsburg-Lorraine dynastic state, which largely consisted of ancient imperial fiefs, arbitrarily consolidated itself by virtue of a flagrant breach of the public law of the old Empire. The new state stressed its character as a great power that was non-German and outside of Germany. It took leave of the old Empire, whose future seemed so precarious. Whatever happened now, Francis II had made certain of his imperial dignity, in spite of the open contradiction between a Roman and an Austrian imperial crown, which for a brief period were borne by one head. Napoleon had previously given his consent to this Austrian title of emperor and had urged Prussia also to assume imperial dignity—a good enough suggestion from the political point of view—but although public opinion gave it some enthusiastic advocacy, Berlin did not warm to the idea.

England stood quite alone in the fight against Napoleon. She needed allies. The French Emperor was preparing a landing on British soil—one more reason for Pitt's ministry to forge a new coalition on the Continent. After the shooting of the Duke of Enghien Czar Alexander broke off relations with France; he did not recognize Napoleon as Emperor. An English-Russian offensive alliance was signed in April 1805. Russia was to demand the evacuation of northern Germany, Holland, Switzerland, and Italy; if France refused, war was to be begun jointly. The goal of the younger Pitt was the expansion of all the neighbours of France along the Rhine boundary and in Italy and the protection of the Rhine boundary by a strong Prussia; an all-embracing league of states was to fight for these English war aims, which dominated the policy of the next several years and shaped the conclusions of the Congress of Vienna. Austria hesitated for a long while before joining; military and financial conditions were not encouraging. Napoleon's rude goings-on in Italy, culminating in his coronation as King of Italy with the Iron Crown of the Lombards, quite in the style of mediæval emperorship, was so strong a challenge that the party that favoured war came out on top. Austria joined England and Russia in the coalition. Prussia was again courted from two sides. Russia threatened and demanded the right of passage for its troops; Prussia mobilized. France offered a defensive and offensive alliance at the price of Hanover; Prussia declined. Now the French violated Prussian neutrality by entering the Ansbach area. At once there was a strong reaction against France. Russia was accorded the right of passage, and the Czar appeared in Berlin. Prussia and Russia made a treaty for Prussia's armed intervention, but Prussia did not have the courage to act in accordance with this treaty.

Napoleon suddenly abandoned the idea of his long-projected invasion of England. He left his camp at Boulogne, descended on the

Austrians in southern Germany, forced the fortress of Ulm to capitulate, and took Vienna. At Austerlitz (December 1805) he conquered the combined Austrians and Russians. This put Prussia in a very awkward position. Her negotiator, Count Haugwitz, made a treaty for a Prussian and French alliance; Prussia promised to recognize the losses of land that impended for Austria and to accept Hanover as indemnity for her own possessions of Ansbach, Bayreuth, Cleve, and Neuenburg. Even in an era of ferment this treaty was a real scandal. At a time of greatest need the most trusted partner was betraying the Coalition. This infamous Prussian duplicity aroused much bitterness. Czar Alexander departed with his Russians. Emperor Francis held out staunchly against Napoleon's harsh peace conditions. But nothing remained for him but to conclude a separate peace with France (Pressburg, 1805). Austria ceded Venice, Istria, and Dalmatia to Italy and recognized all of Napoleon's dispositions of affairs there; she renounced the bishoprics of Brixen and Trent, which she had only just acquired, and ceded the Tyrol and Vorarlberg to Bavaria. Her Upper Rhine dominions fell to Württemberg and Baden. The Austrian imperial state, which had to pay forty million francs' damages for the war, received Salzburg and Berchtesgaden as its sole compensation. That the Austrian dynasty was now completely shorn of its traditional dominance in Italy, that it was crowded away from the Rhine and out of southern Germany, and that it was almost utterly shut off from the sea—these setbacks were all the more painful because Bavaria, which had always been jealous, might set herself, by virtue of her territorial acquisitions, on a par with the Austrian imperial state. Baden and Württemberg too received their promised reward from the Austrian loot. Emperor Francis had to recognize Bavaria and Württemberg as kingdoms.

THE SECOND RHENISH CONFEDERATION

The Empire was in full disintegration. The power that ranked first in Germany had been humiliated; Prussia, which came second, was shackled by the Treaty of Schönbrunn. Insult was added to injury when the French Emperor encouraged the south German allies to seize the lands of the imperial knights. Napoleon's brother-in-law, General Joachim Murat, received the newly created Grand

Duchy of Berg on the Lower Rhine. Bonds with Napoleon's family served to attach the south German vassals to the interests of France. Dalberg, the primate, even made Napoleon's uncle his coadjutor. What was this Corsican-French prince of the church, Cardinal Fesch, who knew not a word of German, looking for in the old Empire? Napoleon could now proceed to organize the third Germany in his own way—this mere remnant of an Empire that still lingered between the German great powers, with their Slavic elements, and the Rhine. Negotiations about the act constituting the Rhenish Confederation dragged on because the satrap states, headed by Bavaria, were so proud of their newly acquired full sovereignty that they resisted any sort of restriction. A whole series of new mediatizations occurred. Frankfurt became the residence of Dalberg as primate of the Rhenish Confederation; it was soon to be the capital of a new grand duchy under him. French policy had looked toward a collective European act of confederation. Dalberg, the primate, dreamed of a revival of Charles the Great's empire in the form of a confederation. But Napoleon decided on a plan that could be executed more quickly—a plan for a Rhenish Confederation with an initial membership of sixteen states. Every member retained full sovereignty by statute. By becoming members the participating princes abandoned the Empire and recognized the protectorate of the French Emperor over their confederation, which undertook a permanent military alliance with France.

The Rhenish Confederation (1806), which, historically, was the descendant of many German confederations of princes, never got to the point of federal legislation or a federal assembly. Whereas many earlier associations of princes had honestly striven to foster and develop the concept of the Empire, the Rhenish Confederation deliberately dealt the death-blow to the old Holy Roman Empire. France seized on the idea of a central Europe. Emperor Francis II now realized that he had no choice but to renounce the Roman imperial crown. His attempt to use such a renunciation in bargaining for advantages to Austria fell flat. Napoleon declared that he could no longer recognize the body of the old Empire, and with threats of war he forced the Emperor to give up the Roman crown. Vienna had to submit. Francis II declared the Roman emperorship at an end and released all the estates of the old Empire from their obligations (1806). Legally the Emperor doubtless overshot himself in proclaiming the office of chief of the Empire to be extinct and in announcing the death of the Empire as a body politic. But questions of legality no longer signified. The political power-interests of certain estates of the Empire had destroyed its legal foundation. Since the triumph of King Frederick the Great over the concept of the Empire, collapse had been inevitable. The founding of the Empire of Austria, the alliance of the south German princes with Napoleon, their rise in rank, the increases in their domains, their separate alliance under a French protectorate, all were further stages in the process of liquidation.

The old Empire had been a state without boundary markers, a structure with two pinnacles, the Emperor and the diet, whose dealings with each other were conducted by emissaries. It had lacked the most important officials; its military organization had not been thorough-going; it had no economic unity. It had had no system of its own of currency or of weights and measures; there had been an imperial postal system, but it served only the minor estates. Politically the old Empire was smothered in feudalism. In all things it was the direct opposite of Napoleon's proud rising Empire. And yet there were many Germans who mourned its decline. A venerable Christian institution had come to an end. The old Europe, with its feeling for liberty, perished unheroical and uncelebrated, derided indeed by revolutionary democracy with its superiority in technics and organization. The states of the Rhenish Confederation flowered on the ruins of the old Empire, and yet it was in Bavaria that the pamphlet entitled *Germany in the Depths of Her Humiliation* appeared, and the bookseller Palm, a native of the imperial city of Nürnberg, was shot by the French, under martial law, because he had circulated this forbidden publication and refused to disclose its authorship. The old imperial patriotism survived in nooks and corners, in places that had been mediatized and secularized, among the citizens of the imperial cities and in the country, where there were still monasteries, castles, and inns that flaunted the two-headed eagle. Now Napoleon, the iron lord of the era, held sway. He demanded heavy taxes and more and more soldiers, and the well-trained officials of the states that belonged to the Rhenish Confederation hastened to supply what he wanted. When would the enthusiasm for the great man begin to cool? Was not a day to come when a new collective German patriotism would turn again to the imperial idea?

THE COLLAPSE OF PRUSSIA (1806)

The Prussian government did not ratify the Treaty of Schönbrunn, but in February 1806 it concluded a much more onerous treaty with France in Paris. On top of the occupation of electoral Hanover, Prussia was now closing the ports of the North Sea and Lübeck to the English. England had made a tempting offer of subsidies and land, though her government decidedly would not cede Hanover. England now declared war on Prussia. Influential circles at the Prussian court worked hard against the French alliance. The officers' party, under Prince Louis Ferdinand, called for war against Napoleon. Russia was approached behind the back of Count Haugwitz, who was responsible for the alliance with France; Hardenberg was particularly active in the matter. The result was a secret declaration to the effect that Prussia would give the French no help against Russia. In return she received from the Czar a guarantee of her possessions. Mounting encroachments by France gave Prussia sufficient cause for ill humour. Prussia's North German Confederation, which France herself had encouraged as a sort of balance for the Rhenish Confederation and the Austrian Empire, encountered difficulties: France was secretly working against its formation. The arbitrary distribution of German dominions on the Lower Rhine damaged Prussian interests. Napoleon, in his negotiations with England, finally mentioned Hanover; he was, to be sure, planning another indemnity for Prussia. The Prussian government, badly informed and always uncertain, addressed an ultimatum to France that reached that country just as her peace negotiations with Russia foundered. Napoleon saw in all this a decision for a joint attack on France by both powers. He did not even reply to the ultimatum, but took measures to defend himself. The war had come.

Besides Russia, Prussia had only some minor German princes as allies. Within a few weeks the campaign ended in her complete collapse. Her defeat at Jena and Auerstedt was followed by the humiliating capitulations of the most important fortresses. Only at a few points was brave resistance offered. Napoleon occupied the largest part of the monarchy of Prussia and marched into Berlin. It was an unparalleled catastrophe for the old military state. Negotiations for a truce failed. Napoleon, moreover, succeeded in persuading the princes of Saxony and Thuringia to join the Rhenish Confederation on easy terms; electoral Saxony became a kingdom and was thenceforth one of the most loyal allies of the French Emperor. From Berlin, Napoleon had decreed his Continental system against England. Prussia now made peace with England and renounced Hanover in return for subsidies; she also made a military agreement with Sweden and a defensive and offensive alliance with Russia. Austria stuck to her neutrality. Hardenberg, the leading spirit of the resistance policy, now urged the English idea of a collective European league for the liberation of Germany and Italy. It proved impossible to induce the unenthusiastic and vacillating King Frederick William III to give up antiquated cabinet rule, by personal order, and to replace it with a responsible council of ministers, but new men did come forward. The most distinguished of all the reformers, however, Baron Karl vom Stein, so irritated the King with his stormy temperament that he was given a most ungracious discharge. Queen Louise assisted the friends of reform wherever she could, but her opportunities were rather narrowly circumscribed.

In the beginning the war went favourably in East Prussia. The battle at Preussisch Eylau was not decisive, but in the summer of 1807 the Russians suffered a terrible defeat at Friedland. Czar Alexander lost patience. Napoleon handled the situation deftly, while Prussia played a pitiable part in the truce and in the peace negotiations (Tilsit, 1807). For Napoleon the struggle with England was most important of all. He won over the Czar of Russia to the secret Treaty of Tilsit: Alexander promised to break with England if she should reject Russian mediation for peace. The Czar did not need to make any sacrifices whatever; he even accepted Bialystok as his share of the Prussian spoils. Prussia retained only Brandenburg, Pomerania, East and West Prussia with the exception of Danzig, and Silesia. Danzig was again given the status of a free city, as when it had belonged to Poland, but this time it was garrisoned by the French. South Prussia (Posen) and new East Prussia were combined to form the Duchy of Warsaw, which was joined to the new Kingdom of Saxony in a personal union. To the west of the Elbe Napoleon organized the Kingdom of Westphalia, made up of parts of Prussia,

Brunswick, and electoral Hesse. This kingdom, as well as the Duchies of Mecklenburg and Oldenburg, joined the Rhenish Confederation. All these states, Prussia as well, were forced to break off relations with England and to enter the war against her after December 1, 1807. An additional convention, formed at Königsberg, was especially unfavourable to Prussia; since the amount of contributions and war indemnities was not specified, the French could extend their occupation of Prussian territory with impunity and step up their demands on Prussia at will.

With the Peace of Tilsit, Prussia lost its position in Europe as a great power. The purely Polish territory acquired through the third partition of Poland was the least of her losses, for these districts had shown themselves unruly, and they represented an administrative burden not easily managed. But to deprive the Prussian state of its Rhenish and Westphalian lands and even of the Old Mark was equivalent to crowding it out of Germany proper and reducing it to a colonial German, east European secondary state. Electoral Saxony, Prussia's old rival, now set herself on a par with Prussia, with Napoleon's full consent. Prussia's friendship with Russia had been destroyed. Austria, weakened as she was, stood aside in her ill humour. Prussia was again at war with England, this time under compulsion. The situation seemed hopeless. France had long ago exceeded her natural boundaries. The Rhenish Confederation had become a focus of power in central Europe under French leadership. The struggle with England constrained Napoleon to weld the entire Continent into a single domain with unified administration. Even Russia entered the Continental system, into which the Iberian peninsula was also drawn. But it was at this very point that the counter-movement began. Germany and Italy had had to bow to the French Emperor; their peoples had been broken apart and weighed down by foreign government. In Spain, however, the first popular stand was made against the world conqueror. The war in Spain that now started knew no pause until the end of Napoleon's rule.

The states of the Rhenish Confederation felt no desire to change conditions that were highly advantageous, at least to those classes that were having their turn at ruling. Things were different in Austria and Prussia. Stein and the leaders of military reform laboured unceasingly for rebellion and liberation. A compromising letter writ-

325

ten by Stein, which, not without the help of his political enemies, fell into French hands, gave Napoleon a reason for demanding the instant dismissal of his most dangerous adversary. From Madrid he issued a decree of banishment against the Baron (1808). In connection with this affair Prussia had to submit to further humiliations. After much bargaining back and forth the amount to be paid by Prussia was set at the still very considerable sum of one hundred and twenty million francs. France reserved the right to use Prussian territory for military bases. Prussia was permitted to keep not more than forty-two thousand men under arms.

THE SUPPRESSION OF GERMANY

In Erfurt Napoleon had a second meeting with his ally the Czar of Russia. The congress that was held there (1808) was accompanied by splendid festivities and represented the zenith of Napoleon's career, though also its turning-point. The imperator of the west courted the imperator of the east. Central Europe seemed wholly subdued, even though Austria was still free of such limitations on armament as had been imposed on Prussia, and Alexander declined to take steps in this direction. His chief interests were in the east and the Balkans. He demanded the Danubian principalities and Finland, which was allied with Sweden. Napoleon at first was occupied with the idea of compensations; if Russia moved into Moldavia and Wallachia, he wanted to occupy Silesia. But finally he acceded to Russia's demands without making any himself except for help against Austria if she were to declare war on France. Russia's plans for the Balkans were bound to be extremely irritating to Austria; they also drove the Ottoman Empire into the arms of the English. Nevertheless Napoleon now felt himself strong enough to prosecute the Spanish campaign with his full forces.

In Erfurt Talma, the great French actor, played to an audience of kings. Emperor Napoleon received Goethe and invited him to come to Paris to live. The relation of Germany to the French Revolution touched a high point in this encounter. France had set out to make mankind free and happy. The welfare of the struggling lower classes was to be assured by a new regime based on the equality of all citizens, on brotherly helpfulness and freedom of conscience, thought, and opinion. The great Revolution had benefited Germany in many ways. It had cleared away the feudal system with its privileges; it had destroyed antiquated forms of rulership. It had quickened the desire for intellectual independence and for a chance at economic development. It had proved a goad to many German ambitions that could not gain ground by their own power. To this extent the French Revolution was a necessary and creative chapter in German history. But it was also a great burden.

In France the climax of the Revolution had been the erection of a modern despotism whose achievements in the fields of law and administration were flattered by imitation throughout Europe. But this despotism prolonged the traditional foreign policy of the French Kingdom by means of military organization, technics, and leaders of genius, all of which assured dazzling triumphs for many years, but were bound to call forth more and more obstinate and bitter resistance among the victims of these triumphs. There was an intellectual, cultivated, creative Germany that had become aware of its culture, which had become deeper, richer, and finer. But there was no German state, no German realm, that corresponded to this great spiritual achievement in any way whatever. Instead there was a collection of dynastic states under French protectorate. There were remnants of two German great powers that were able to lead only a desperate and suppressed existence. Political equality arose and developed further in Germany also; the struggle to establish the sway of law within the state was carried on successfully. But political freedom scarcely existed except in outward forms. On the contrary, here, too, French despotism found eager imitators, and strict rulership was in high favour. The mass of subjects were restless. They were controlled and registered, taught and disciplined—above all, soundly drilled. The French Revolution had not brought peace to the Germans any more than it had to any other people of Europe. It had conjured up an epoch of war unprecedented in violence, loss of life, wreckage of happiness and well-being, ambition and greed of fame. In the end the suppressed and exploited peoples grew weary of slaughter and the iron rod.

Chapter 14

THE WAR OF LIBERATION AGAINST NAPOLEON

THE FRENCH Emperor was now master of the European continent. He wanted to be master of the world. His fight was a fight against Great Britain. The Britons never again concluded a peace with Napoleon; they were constantly seeking new allies, and they supported every rebellion and every conspiracy against the French Emperor. England maintained her naval supremacy with indomitable courage. From her inviolable insularity she made the plunge to restore freedom to the world. The English resistance meant the ultimate solace and the fairest hope for all patriots among the suppressed peoples. Since the victory of Trafalgar (1805) England had been invincible at sea. But she could never triumph utterly if the European continent did not set new armies on the march against the conqueror. Spain fought stubbornly on against French domination and never let herself be subjugated. France could be attacked most strategically from Spain. The long Peninsular War initiated the great reversal; however, the decision could not come from there.

Central Europe was the centre of Napoleon's rule. Only there could it be broken. What would or could Germany do? Never before in history had all Germany obeyed an alien conqueror. The Revolution of 1789 had ripened the unity and strength of the French nation. But the French nation had utilized this up-swing, under the leadership of Napoleon, only to suppress and exploit all other nations. Just this rule of force matured these backward nations to a new awareness of themselves. Napoleon was the son of the Revolution; he slew the power that bore him, and no atonement was possible. Anyone who wins too many victories ends by believing only in his battalions. The spirit and the will to freedom avenged themselves; they awoke Europe, and its peoples broke the trammels of Cæsarism.

AUSTRIA'S AWAKENING AND DEFEAT

After the Peace of Pressburg (1805), defeated Austria devoted herself to inner reconstruction. No help could be expected from Emperor Francis in this direction; he contributed nothing but obstacles. His pose was that of a good-natured Austrian worthy with a heart of gold, and he had a store of encouraging affability; but his basic views were strictly dynastic, and he scented revolution everywhere —wicked revolution with its abominable demagogic disrespectfulness. He was shrewder and more flexible than the Prussian King, but resembled him in his obstinate haughtiness. Count Philip Stadion, warm-hearted and tireless, became the proponent of Austrian ideas of reform. He realized that no force would serve to strengthen the Austrian imperial state against Napoleon unless it was the awakening of a national patriotism. So Austria began to court Germany once more. This country that, with its Slavic admixture, had moved away from Germany tried now to start a popular movement toward a German unity and thus to shape the German nation constructively. But the non-German components of the people could not be kindled; they were a dead weight that could scarcely be moved. Heinrich von Collin and Georg Fellinger wrote their war-songs at this time. Hormayr struck off inflamed words of hate and of patriotic enthusiasm. Intellectual leaders of the most varied background gathered about the distinguished writer Karoline Pichler. The brothers Friedrich and August Wilhelm Schlegel, the poet Heinrich von Kleist, the publicist Ernst Moritz Arndt, all looked to a rejuvenated Austria for the revival of strong German emperorship. But the contradiction between patriotism toward the Austrian state and German national feeling soon became apparent.

Count Stadion was at least successful in having the various central authorities of the Austrian imperial state merged in one supreme corporate body. This was not yet a compact and vigorous organ of government, for the Emperor and the court would have regarded such an organ with insuperable suspicion. The Emperor's brother, Archduke Charles, who was the military genius of the dynasty, followed the pattern set by the French in dividing his forces into army corps. He organized a reserve and managed by the *Landwehr* law of 1808 to get the principle of the arming of the people applied to all the lands except Hungary. The new Austria, then, was to arise from an army of the people. Napoleon, the military despot, could be conquered only with his own weapons. Attempts to arm all the people had been made in southern Germany as early as 1791–4. A weak point for Austria was her state finances. Archduke Charles needed time and money to organize his militia and to set up his *Landwehr,* but Count Stadion wanted an early decision, because the machine of state could suffer no delay. English subsidies failed to arrive, and it was important to act quickly. Napoleon's main army was tied up in Spain, and such an opportunity ought not to be missed. Even the deliberate, cynical, and wary Count Clemens Metternich, the Austrian ambassador in Paris, advised in favour of war in view of the growing dissatisfaction within France herself.

Austria hoped that help would come to her from all sides, that all the subjugated peoples would arise. A stirring summons to the whole German nationality accompanied the declaration of war on France in April 1809. Only a fraction of Austria's expectations was fulfilled. Russia remained neutral in spite of the agreement of Erfurt. But Italy and southern Germany remained quite calm. The attempted *Putsch* against the Kingdom of Westphalia, undertaken by Colonel Dörnberg, was a failure. The foolhardy enterprise of the Prussian Major Ferdinand von Schill, who made war on Napoleon on his own responsibility, collapsed. Schill himself fell fighting at Stralsund; eleven of his officers were shot in Wesel under martial law. The daredevil Duke Frederick William of Brunswick had better luck; he and his black band fought bravely against Saxony. He forged his way through northern Germany all alone, and from there, with the luck of the foolhardy, he reached England safely. In the course of the war Prussia repeatedly negotiated with Austria, in spite of Russian warnings, but it did not come to intervention. A profound impression was made by the insurrection of the Tyrolese peasants, who wanted to return to their Emperor and drove the Bavarians and French from their country. But Archduke Charles did not use his chances. He hesitated to attack the troops of the Rhenish Confederation that were scattered through Bavaria.

As soon as Napoleon appeared in the war theatre affairs changed. He advanced briskly and forced the Archduke back. He took Regensburg and marched on Vienna. Instead of waging a European war of liberation Austria had to fight for her own survival. At first the war went well. Archduke John defeated Eugène de Beauharnais, the viceroy in Italy; Warsaw fell, and—most important of all—Archduke Charles defeated the French Emperor himself at Aspern (1809). It was the first time Napoleon had lost a battle. Many believed that the tide had at last turned. It was obvious that France no longer had at her disposal the splendid human material of former years. The first symptoms of exhaustion appeared. But at least for a time the military genius of the French Emperor surmounted this difficulty. Viceroy Eugène took revenge. He defeated Archduke John so utterly at the river Raab that John was unable to join the main army under Archduke Charles in time. And so Napoleon won the decisive battle at Wagram.

Reluctantly Emperor Francis had to consent to the Peace of Schönbrunn (1809). It is to his credit that he was most unwilling to give up his faithful Tyrolese. But there was no help for it. The Kingdom of Bavaria now received, in addition to the Tyrol, Salzburg and the region around the Inn River. Western Galicia fell to the Duchy of Warsaw. Russia played the same part as in the Peace of Tilsit: she took over eastern Galicia from Austrian territory, the part that was inhabited by Ukrainians (Ruthenians). But the worst blow was that the imperial state was completely cut off from the sea. All countries on the farther side of the river Save were detached and were placed, as Illyrian provinces, under French military administration, which could now impose the Continental system thoroughly there too. Emperor Francis had to recognize all the rearrangements in Europe, among them the abolition of the Teutonic Order. He had to pay a war indemnity of eighty-five million francs and to cut down his armed forces to one hundred and fifty thousand men. Through these measures Austria was demoted to a second-class power. The war of liberation that she had started against Napoleon ended with her suffering the same fate as Prussia. There were no more German great powers. There was no Germany.

A moving epilogue unfolded in the Tyrol. The Tyrolese peasants clung to their right of forming one class in the provincial diet, to their church traditions, and to their old customs. The rough and tactless behaviour of Bavarian officialdom aroused deep resentment. Andreas Hofer and his comrades accomplished heroic feats even though they had only meagre support. Two battles raged around the Isel Mountain near Innsbruck. In the Peace of Schönbrunn the Tyrolese had been promised amnesty, but certain sections continued the war on their own initiative; they did not want to stand by and see their country distributed piecemeal. Traitors delivered Hofer up to the French, and he was shot in Mantua under martial law (1810). The name of this honest martyr shed its light over all future German wars of liberation against aliens. The southern Tyrol was now given to the Kingdom of Italy, a small part to Illyria. In the course of the following years there were other Tyrolese conspiracies, supported by English funds and aided by Archduke John, who was an English tool and a popular favourite. For a while humiliated Austria could not concern herself with these affairs. She had to make every effort to gain Napoleon's favour by observing all the conditions of the peace. She succeeded in restoring her currency only by feigning state bankruptcy.

THE CONTINENTAL SYSTEM

The son of a Saxon clergyman attempted to murder the French Emperor in Vienna. Did not Napoleon realize that something was afoot in Germany with which even he could not cope? It was difficult indeed to form a clear picture of what was happening. The left bank of the Rhine enjoyed all the advantages of association with a great state organized in a modern fashion. Freedom of trade, a uniform protective tariff, equality before the law, splendid roads, secularization or liquidation of property held by mortmain—these brought an economic upturn with benefit to all who were industrious. Peace with the church and religious tolerance were deeply satisfying. The method of mechanical drill in the schools and universities was less pleasing. The middle class, with its thirst for education, was particularly embittered by the stern censorship and the strangulation of the press. After Austria's overthrow France reached far out across the Rhine into Germany. In connection with the annexation of Holland the entire German part of the North Sea coast became French. Other territorial changes were made within the Rhenish Confederation. The Grand Duchy of Frankfurt received Fulda and Hanau; Napoleon attached great importance to this strategic area, which after the death of Dalberg, the Grand Duke, was to fall to Eugène de Beauharnais. The Kingdom of Westphalia became a model state among the lands of the Rhenish confederates; the Napoleonic Code was introduced, administration was carefully seen to, and a constitution with popular representative bodies crowned the whole. Even beyond the period of Napoleon's great glory this state set an example for Henry the Lion's old Low Saxon territory in spite of the financial frivolity of Napoleon's youngest brother, Jerome, and of his elegant court.

Saxony and Mecklenburg imitated French institutions least. Through all the stormy years they quietly held to the old feudal stratification. But in Württemberg the new-made King brutally cleared away the "old right," as the poet Ludwig Uhland called it. In Bavaria worked the minister Count Maximilian Montgelas, who, like other dignitaries of the Rhenish Confederation, was not native-born; he had been well schooled by the Enlightenment and eagerly busied himself with the severance of feudal and ecclesiastical bonds. The idea of a Bavarian "nation," a Bavarian "empire," was served with bureaucratic calculation by the abolition of serfdom, the intro-duction of special ministries, the training of capable officials, and the establishment of a state church. The most artificial of Napoleon's creations, the Grand Duchy of Baden, a patchwork of the most oddly assorted components, was particularly fortunate in having especially intelligent direction; the spirit of its well-disposed prefects produced admirable results. The states of the Rhenish Confederation had little in common; they eyed each other jealously and courted the favour of the French Emperor as the most important thing in the world. But this sun did not often shine on them; far more frequent was rude intervention, against which they were helpless. To offer opposition might even be dangerous, but nevertheless it was ventured.

One measure was of supreme importance to Napoleon. This was the Continental system, the blockade directed against England. This country, the deadly enemy of the French system, immediately or-ganized the sharpest counter-blockade. In view of the pressing eco-nomic needs of Germany relaxation in some respects appeared nec-essary; it was provided in the form of special licences granted by the French government. Relief was also afforded by smuggling on a grand scale, at which the island of Heligoland distinguished itself. The maritime trade of the Hanseatic cities was crippled. On the other hand the textile industry in Saxony and Alsace flowered. Many large stores of goods were confiscated and often foolishly destroyed. Prussia suffered severe losses. Austria always found a way to keep up her practical connection with England somehow or other; the island of Malta served as the principal warehouse.

THE SPIRIT OF THE GERMAN PEOPLE. ROMANTICISM AT ITS PEAK

Many Germans were now looking back to their own past. Particularly along the Rhine, in the very midst of French domination, groups of warm-hearted men were formed to study the German Middle Ages—their art, their imperial splendour. Every cathedral, every castle ruin, was a living witness to that great legendary time when Germany had assumed the destiny of Europe. The poet-philosopher Friedrich Schlegel, a member of the Köln group, which disclosed the mediæval Köln painters to new appreciation, plunged his circle deep into the intellectual currents of romanticism. F. F. Walraf turned from glorifying the Emperor Napoleon, immersed himself in the atmosphere of the past, and began his collection of old German paintings that was to become so famous. Trier, Bonn, and Heidelberg were drawn into the movement. Joseph Görres turned his back on the Revolution and on everything that smacked of French universalism. He brought the old holy imperial Germany, held together by the Rhine, to life in the consciousness of his contemporaries. To revive this Germany as the bearer of a cultural mission became the yearning dream of the new generation. World citizenship went up in smoke. The French had shaped their power and their political will too distinctly. German self-assertion awoke; it demanded respect and the right to its own life. The spirit of the German people drew strength from history, from prehistoric times and the less remote past; from the landscape, the language, customs, and art; from the deathless vital community of blood and life.

German romanticism pointed the way. Friedrich Wackenroder, a pensive and sensitive thinker, wrote his *Outpourings of an Art-Loving Monk*. Beside a German poetry an equally favoured German school of painting was to stand, equally quickened by the marvellous achievements of the past. Songs of the minnesingers, fairy-tales, legends, epics—everything was collected, interpreted, and imitated.

334

In a state of high excitement that he communicated to his readers Friedrich Schlegel hurled impassioned pamphlets against Napoleon. He refused to be discouraged, and he demanded over and over the restoration of emperorship and Empire as Germans had formerly known them. Adam Müller, who like Friedrich Schlegel had been converted to Catholicism, interpreted the cultural heritage of the Germans with wide knowledge; he preached nationality as a historical experience and the political demand of the morrow; for the Germans also, the necessary goal of popular development was political unity. Even Hamburg, which from of old had been a nucleus of cosmopolitanism, turned sentimental about the fatherland, under the pressure of French domination. As in the other old imperial cities and economic centres of Germany, local patriotic particularism rooted in the soil did not exclude wishes tinctured with universalism for a central European co-operation that should issue from the German nation.

PRUSSIAN REFORMS. BARON VOM STEIN

The transformations in the Prussian state set certain standards for the entire future of Germany. Baron vom Stein looms large at this great crisis. Could Prussia, which had become a colonial German, half-Slavic country, forced now into the modest condition of a secondary state, be won back for Germany and linked creatively to the culture of western Europe? At the same time the states of the Rhenish Confederation were learning a hard lesson. Here in the heartland of the old Empire a momentous process was consummated: a fusion of modern political forms that had proved their effectiveness with German traditions and with national as well as cultural needs. No state that wanted to play any part in the future could shut itself off from modernization.

Baron Heinrich Friedrich Karl vom und zum Stein (1751–1831) now made a mighty effort to find some solution for Prussia that should be at once European, Prussian, and German. This imperial knight belonged to the old nobility of western Germany that had been immediate to the Empire. Growing up in the era of the Enlightenment, he developed in himself the spirit of devotion to nature and dependence on history as a counter-balance to the rationalism that was the main current in contemporary thought. The Lutheran

335

creed in which Stein had been reared accounted for his austerely ethical character and for his passionate delight in clarity and truth, which unfitted him for the intrigues of diplomacy and foreign policy and drew him all the closer to the concept of duty of Kant's Prussia. His personal integrity and his strong and steadfast sense of justice made this true German aristocrat akin in temper to the noblest representatives of German civic liberalism. Thus conservatives and liberals were both justified in a way in claiming the statesman Stein for themselves. Actually he belonged to none but himself. He was always struggling, always learning, a modest man of firm belief, but also a dominant and daring leader who was too strong and upright to be submissive or adaptable.

He was fully familiar with the doctrine of the French physiocrats and with the English Enlightenment. As a true child of the eighteenth century he believed in the possibility of natural and rational reforms, of humanitarian reforms from above in accord with existing authoritarian relationships. He knew the soil and the men who lived on it. He desired prosperity for all of them as their due, and he had little use for a mere counting-house economy or for the soul-destroying drill of the barracks yard. What he strove for was growth in freedom, the regulation of relationships as far as possible by those directly involved in them, and therefore self-government by stouthearted, politically trained, and co-operative citizens who wanted no leading-strings. Stein resented revolution just as much as tyranny. He hated the military arrogance of the Junkers. He was convinced of the rights of the civilian and befriended the little man. Every manly and independent sentiment that sprang from the soil came under his protection. Spying, intrigue, gossip, and greed could not persist in his presence; the selfish and the pushing dreaded the keen glance of his passionate dark eyes. The reason for Stein's extreme contempt for the petty German princes was that their pomp and pretence stood in the way of a strong Germany for the future. Stein, a servant of the Prussian state, became more and more a patriot of the realm (*Reichspatriot*), a new kind of educator of the people. It would be folly to deny that the French Revolution of 1789 influenced his life-work. For this Revolution was the outstanding event of the epoch, and no one engaged in any great project could escape its repercussions. Stein took over a good deal from it without alteration; in other respects he knew very well how to adapt its suggestions to the special circumstances of his setting. The radical, unhistorical, destructive elements of the second period of the French Revolution and the Jacobin movement were always foreign and repulsive to him.

The problem in Prussia was to attune the necessary administrative reforms that were to change and strengthen the state to the humane and moral ideas of German idealistic philosophy. All this was naturally rooted in the collective European efforts at revival. Stein was able to be of practical service to the state for only a brief period. His personal ruin was due to inveterate old-time Prussianism, which strongly withstood real Germanizing. Stein's spirit and ideas, however, continued to make themselves felt, even though they were modified and reshaped. The most distinguished of his associates came from East Prussia; some of them were members of the nobility, others high officials, but all had at some time or other been disciples of Kant. All were sterling liberals with humanitarian leanings. Against these Baron Karl August von Hardenberg, later Prince Hardenberg, represented the opposite tendency of rationalism in administration, a spirit more sceptical and ready to compromise.

Stein's first act was to liberate the peasants by the October Edict of 1807. All peasants were to be just as free as those who lived in the royal domains, but the reform was unfortunately very sketchy. From the legal angle there were now none but free people, and land could be sold at will. The privileges that the nobles derived from their status as landowners were wiped out: no more domestic service by the children of their subjects at the manor house or palace; no more fees for emigration; no more permissions for marriage; no arbitrary decision as to inheritance of a farm on the tenant's death; no more consent of the lord of the manor to the learning of a burgher's trade. Now at last the peasants assumed the citizenship that was arising. They were no longer serfs, no longer bound to the soil. Indeed, the manorial lord was abolished—but he survived. Manorial jurisdiction lasted until 1848 in Prussia, unlimited manorial police power until 1872. Stein tried to strengthen the peasant class economically, but he failed; the superiority of the manorial lords, who were no longer responsible for the welfare of their people, took full effect. The great landowners systematically bought out the peasants cheap. According

337

to the ordinance of 1811 the peasant could become a free owner by giving up a third or a half of his land. This in itself was bad enough, but worse was to come. The manor swallowed the free peasants whenever it could; a proletarian, wholly dependent rural labour force seemed to the large landowners more convenient from both the economic point of view and the social. Thus Germany to the east of the Elbe kept up its colonial, aristocratic, non-German character. The political consequences for the destinies of Germany as a whole were weighty.

Stein's most characteristic work was the municipal ordinance (1808). From this time on, all city dwellers who met a very modest requirement as to minimum income were to be citizens with full rights. All citizens living in a town were allowed to vote. They elected town councillors to represent them, and the councillors in turn elected the magistrates, as executive organ, and the mayor. Cities were given self-government in their domestic economy, taxes, schools, charities, communication systems, and local police. It proved impossible to put through a corresponding rural self-government bill. The municipal ordinance had a wide political bearing. It created islands of liberal citizenship in colonial Prussia; through municipal self-government it educated a new generation of liberals in practical experience. It bridged the gap between this group and the rest of Germany, but it deepened the rift between country and city, manor and town, and it was the seed of the bitter conflict that was to spring up between the later conservative and liberal party groups in Prussia. Prussian townspeople never forgot Baron vom Stein and what he did for them. The old Prussian cities kept his memory green as a symbol of German patriotism and of the striving for liberty. Stein wanted to awaken the lower classes—bourgeoisie and peasantry—and to make them creative members of a state that had been morally renewed. If they and their work could be made fruitful, then the guardianship of an all-wise officialdom would automatically disappear. But Stein did not entirely succeed in recasting the administration for such a purpose. The resistance of absolutism in decline and of the self-confident old bureaucracy was much too great. The state council proposed by Stein did not materialize. But at least specialized government departments were established in the capital and central governments in the provinces, with lord lieutenants (*Oberpräsi-*

denten) as the heads of provincial administration. These agencies of government, functioning in a collegiate way, ought now, according to Stein's ideas, to be integrated by reviving the venerable system of diets. Thus the forces of the people themselves were to be shaped in the gradation of district organization, provincial organization, and the organization of the realm.

HARDENBERG AND HIS OPPONENTS

Stein hoped in this way to develop a political sense in the Prussian people and to give them national form. He wanted to see representatives of distinct groups evolve into responsible associates in the conduct of public affairs. Stein's dismissal in 1808 was final; he never returned to the service of the Prussian state. His best ideas and plans were wrecked against the rigidity of old-style Prussianism. Hardenberg, who followed him in the work of pushing reforms through, made certain of the loyal co-operation of the bureaucracy, which was indeed devoted to him, so that he might achieve something at least. He created the office of chancellor for himself—that is, of prime minister, responsible for everything. He created free trade by introducing a tax on trade that applied equally in city and country. He gave Jews the same rights as all others, both politically and economically. He secularized both Catholic and evangelical church property and planned thorough financial reform. By way of preparation for representation not only of the land, but also of the people, he called an assembly of notables; nothing came of it, however, but a provisional assembly that was in session from 1812 to 1815. The members were elected by the three old classes, with the nobility holding a decided majority over the representatives of the bourgeoisie and peasantry. Modest as these attempts at modernization were, the privileged group fought against them. Old-style Prussians accused Hardenberg of aping the French Revolution. Their bluntest spokesman, Friedrich August Ludwig von der Marwitz, a cavalry general and landed proprietor from the Mark, complained that "honest Brandenburg-Prussia" would be transformed into a "new-fangled Jew state." The leaders of the aristocratic opposition, F. A. L. von der Marwitz and Count Finckenstein, had to be sent to a fortress for a cooling-off period. Thus it went hard with colonial Prussia to join in with the collective cultural development of western Europe, though the old Germany managed it without too many difficulties. Yet Prussia simply could not dispense with alliance to the German spirit in all matters of culture.

Reform of the elementary schools smoothed the way for popular education from the bottom up, according to the fruitful teachings of the Swiss Pestalozzi. Secondary schools undertook to fit the ideals of the antique, Christian ethics, and German classicism into a sort of homogeneous German cultural idealism. As Minister of Education the scholar and statesman Wilhelm von Humboldt worked for reforms in the universities. The University of Berlin was founded with the high-flown intention of creating a seminary for training the new type of German that Prussia needed so badly. The German spirit was free and could not be conquered. No province of life escaped investigation and reshaping by it. German scholarship served truth and truth alone. The spirit of Immanuel Kant pointed the way for it, and all the great thinkers who came after were in a sense his disciples. The problem was how to make the full, deep, mature personal culture of German classicism fruitful in forming German national feeling. The Prussian state needed German intellect; it demanded Prussian fighters to rebuild Prussia as a great power, but they could be won only by arousing self-awareness of the homogeneousness of the German people—and then by putting it to work. This was the deep conflict that the era recognized, without being able to dispose of it completely. Prussia had a German vocation; she could not advance without German idealism, and yet the most powerful social groups in Prussia set their old-style Prussianism above the collective fatherland; they developed a Prussian patriotism at the expense of German patriotism. In the upshot, German idealism held itself to have been exploited by the egoism of this politically conscious Prussianism. Experiences such as these increased the traditional German suspicion of Prussia.

In the bad winter of 1807–8 the philosopher Johann Gottlieb Fichte (died 1814) delivered his *Addresses to the German Nation* in Berlin. Fichte regarded the German character as one of the loftiest and most potent revelations of humanity. Proceeding from a moral basis, through character and conviction, he set to work in the capital of the stricken Prussian state to build up a German national pride and so to give back to this great people its belief in itself and its mis-

340

sion. Fichte's ultimate goal was the perfect state, something absolute even in the actual world. From the reawakened Germany he expected the last, the highest realization. Fichte's ideas mounted to a more and more bold and unhistorical vision of a powerful position in the world for Germany. He called the Germans the primordial people, or simply *the* people, and so this solid, sincere, headstrong man became the mouthpiece for the zealous, fanatical nationalism of many petty spirits.

The activity of the theologian Friedrich Schleiermacher was less alloyed and on a higher plane. He undertook to reconcile the world-renouncing spirituality of the best German Protestants with the life and the demands of the state, and he succeeded. Other outstanding personalities of that early period of the University of Berlin were the jurist Savigny, the philologist Böckh, Niebuhr the historian of antiquity, and Thaer the political economist. The university boasted of the strength of the German scholarly spirit that it represented. But was it not rather a Prussian than a German policy that hid behind this German scholarship? In 1811 the following persons met in the Christian Germanic Club: the poets Heinrich von Kleist and Clemens Brentano; Fichte and Marwitz, the leader of the nobles; the publicist Adam Müller and the young officer of the guards Leopold von Gerlach. No group could have been more typical than this one was of the early stages of a conservative community of interests. These men were anti-Semitic, anti-liberal, and anti-revolutionary. They wanted to strengthen the Prussian spirit, and they used German romanticism as a tool for this purpose. They transfigured very tangible selfish feudal and class interests with the magic of an ideology that was expert in history and exalted the state. At that time several secret societies in Prussia were pursuing similar aims; the Königsberg *Tugendbund* (Society of Virtue, 1808) laboured for the necessary exaltation of the fatherland, with ostensibly liberal ideas. Other groups devoted themselves to fencing and archery as a harmless form of preparation for a serious situation. And the leaders of military reform worked energetically along with these others.

SECRET REARMAMENT

Alongside the municipal ordinance stood military reform as the most successful achievement in the Prussian plan of reconstruction.

Its spiritual fathers were Generals Gerhard von Scharnhorst and Neithardt von Gneisenau, neither of them born in Prussia. The Germany lying outside of Prussia actually contributed very greatly to the rebirth of the Prussian state. After her collapse Prussia was confronted with problems of enormous difficulty. Three thousand officers were discharged at once. A new class of leaders had to be trained. The new army needed theorists, technicians, politicians, and strategists. Armament, education, regulations—everything had to be shaped anew under the effect of the French victory. Many reformers, such as the forthright liberal Hermann von Boyen and the military philosopher Karl von Clausewitz, were closely connected with the movement of German idealism. Others were swashbucklers of the old sort: Gerhard von Blücher and Hans David von Yorck. Scharnhorst brooded over organization and forged out plans. The only creative military thinker who could hold his own with the French Emperor was Gneisenau.

The basic idea of these men was the concept of a "nation in arms" that had been realized for the first time in the French Revolution. A first reserve and a second (*Landwehr*) had been tried out in Austria. But it does not minimize Prussian achievement to put it in the frame of its proper historical connection—quite the contrary. Napoleon could be fought only with his own weapons. His defeat could be brought about only by inspiring the whole people in arms with something that France no longer had: some truly popular political concept. The war of liberation against the French Emperor was not won by means of stronger battalions only. What made the Prussian deed so truly striking and decisive was the fusion of technical reform and reorganization of the army with the political awakening of the people. The old standing army had fallen into disgrace. In the light of history it was quite legitimately regarded as an instrument of the princes' arbitrary rule—one that had been used preferably to suppress free peoples or to attain goals of dynastic ambition that had nothing to do with the nation. Military men added their criticism to that of philosophical and political observers such as Kant, Herder, Fichte, and Möser, and all agreed in condemning the old system.

Scharnhorst, on the other hand, knew Prussia's line of development and character much too well not to want to retain the core of her traditional army organization. So he hit on the curious and brilliant combination of a professional army and a national militia. The army must rest on the nation's spontaneous will to defence; the officers must be popular; anyone with the necessary education who was socially and morally mature should be eligible to become an officer. The old Prussian army had consisted of beaten and belaboured mercenaries and of an officer caste nine tenths of whom had been selected from the nobility and who were usually as arrogant as they were uncultivated. Even Frederick the Great had admitted simple citizens to only the new sections of the troops—the artillery, the hussars, and the engineers. The conceit and the defiant bearing of officers, especially of the younger aristocratic officers, were cause for constant complaint by the more intelligent and better-poised among their fellows. Every self-respecting Prussian citizen avoided both soldiers and officers as much as possible. There was a mental and moral gulf that it was best to leave unbridged. Altering these conditions was hard work and only partly successful.

To begin with, corporal punishment in the army was abolished by order of the King; confinement took its place. Discreditable behaviour might be punished by demotion to the so-called second class. Officers were judged in courts of honour. The officer's career was now to be open also to experienced non-commissioned officers; for the rest, officers were chosen by their professional associates after examination and were then appointed by the King. The feudalistic character of the military class was thus altered somewhat in favour of the rising bourgeoisie. Eligibility as an officer became a class distinction of great social importance in Prussia. An encouraging attitude toward non-commissioned officers who hoped for advancement remained theoretical merely; occasional exceptions did not change the rule.

On these assumptions the army was reorganized into regiments and brigades. The new mode of fighting was introduced, and the new system of defence was made a reality. Though rearmament was forbidden, Prussian armourers' workshops went at full blast, thanks especially to the so-called *Krümpersystem*. The recruits, called crimpers, were given only a brief but intensive training and then made room for others. The number of soldiers prepared in this way was many times what was allowed by treaty. The backbone of the whole reform of the army was general liability to military service, which later became compulsory by law. Everyone who lives within the sphere of a state is its born defender; everyone must stand for the whole to the extent of his physical and mental abilities—and in his own person, not by means of a substitute as in France and the states of the Rhenish Confederation. To produce mass armies that could confront Napoleon's mass armies and to set against Napoleon's tactics of assault and extermination methods equally good was possible only with an army organization that did not spare manpower, because only by staking everything could the highest goal be reached— the goal of military annihilation through a swift, flexible operative strategy that pressed for a decision. An officer corps that could bring forth leaders of the required kind had to be more than merely trained and instructed very thoroughly. What the military academy and the general staff had to offer could be easily assimilated by minds in competition. Something else was needed: a sense of spiritual and emotional community, the friendly unity of comradeship, the character of confederates. It is this that especially characterizes, in a peculiar, often primitive or extravagant manner, the group of reformers and of the later fighters for liberation. No one understood these deep connections so well as the fiery General Neidthardt von Gneisenau; no other so moulded them into the staggering program of the new military, active community of the people, to the considerable alarm of his sober King, who was averse to everything "poetic." Prussia had grown great as a military state; classical Prussian militarism entered on a new era in a changed form. Prussia became a people's state—but only so far as she became a modernized military state. Spiritually she let herself be conquered by Germany, but only on the assumption that she would thus be fitted to lead Germany into the battle for liberation.

BEGINNINGS OF THE NATIONAL MOVEMENT

Napoleon regarded the Prussians with suspicion. Later, on St. Helena, he declared that his greatest mistake had been not to wipe out Prussia completely. The Prussian government, on its part, had to admit that a rising against the French Emperor must end with the triumph of the Prussian state or with its downfall. That was why the King and many of his more cautious counsellors hesitated. The

French had tremendous superiority, and Prussia was exposed to their most immediate and hardest assault. Only a bold and steadfast heart could persist in hoping and believing. Many patriots were tormented by the ambiguity and double-dealing that surrounded them. Heinrich von Kleist, whose drama the *Hermannsschlacht* was an impassioned and even brutal summons to wipe out alien rule, was destroyed by the conflict of his times; he died by his own hand in 1811. The author and agitator Ernst Moritz Arndt (died 1860) was made of sterner stuff. This descendant of serfs in Rügen under Swedish rule knew how to express the need of the Germans, their dreams and their faith, in homely, forceful words that touched the quick. Pithy and straightforward, he was no scholar, thinker, or creative artist, but a master of the word who came to have great influence over public opinion. He fathered the program of a Greater Germany. To include all German-speaking people in one political entity, in a single strong, proud realm—this was a concept so simple and so self-evident in appearance that it required considerable knowledge of history to understand the difficulties of carrying it out and, indeed, the problematical character of the task itself. Arndt, who came from the lower classes, caught the ear of the poor people; their hearts went out to him.

Friedrich Ludwig Jahn (died 1852), a versatile eccentric, had a similar influence on the people, who were now astir. In the difficult period of transition, while military training in Prussia was still limited and subject to inspection, Jahn succeeded in improving the physical condition of the large lower classes by gymnastic exercises of his own invention. He was quite correct in his assumption that city life tended to make the craftsmen, clerks, and shopkeepers soft and effeminate. He pulled them out of stale indoor air and put them in touch with nature again and with the simplest living conditions. In England the contrast between city and country life was never so acute as it had become in Germany, for every social class in England had its own age-old, traditional sports. The German city dweller was a different type, mentally and sociologically, from the German who lived in the country. The new educational idealism was the offspring of the city; it extended to the lower classes of the inhabitants and assimilated them to an academic and literary rhythm of life. The cities were insular in feeling; the politics of their locality meant more to them than the politics of the whole state. Jahn, the inventor of gymnastics, a strange fellow and inconsistent in many ways, had a sound instinct for such matters. He set himself to combat excess in education and in cosmopolitan complacency. The supple cleverness of liberal stay-at-homes filled him with horror. He met the concept of a Gallicized Europe with vehement, primitive hatred. The sturdy crudity of old German times seemed to him a proper counterbalance. And so he set up a new ideal in language, morals, manners, and the concept of the state—the ideal of an intolerant self-assertive German community that would lay great stress on its own past and mode of existence, both historically and romantically. These and related trends gave rise to the popular movement.

Emperor Napoleon held sovereign sway over the continent of Europe, which he had compressed into a single entity. Since his wife Joséphine de Beauharnais had borne him no children, he divorced her and married Archduchess Marie Louise, daughter of the last Emperor of the Holy Roman Empire, who was also the first Emperor of Austria. She bore him the desired heir, to whom he gave the significant title of King of Rome; in the latest period of German history "King of the Romans" had been the title of the Emperor's heir. Here also, then, the old emperorship was again renewed, by a Corsican-French conqueror. The latest and noblest German imperial family, that of Habsburg-Lorraine, allied itself with the new Bonaparte dynasty and thus gave it its blessing and consecration. With this the house of Austria made its essential peace with the new Emperor, and from this time it was interested in the maintenance of the Bonaparte dynasty. The Emperor of Austria himself now headed only a second-class power, but the dynastic connection with France strengthened his influence and gained him new respect. The policies of Kaunitz were revived in a more potent form. After centuries of struggle, the electoral opposition had triumphed in the Empire; the most important dynasties had placed themselves on a par with the rival great powers of Austria and Prussia, only to fall prey, like them, to a new guardian, a new protector—the French Emperor. Central Europe, including Austria and the secretly resistant Prussia, obeyed a single political will, which was bent on destroying England and mastering the Continent—the will of Napoleon. The weak spot in the system was Prussia's growing resistance. But this was not the only weak spot. The struggle in Spain continued with undiminished violence. The decisive factor was the estrangement of France and Russia.

NAPOLEON'S STRUGGLE WITH RUSSIA

Poland and the Balkans made it difficult to be friendly with Austria and Russia at the same time. Czar Alexander I of Russia bore Napoleon a grudge because of his dynastic connection with Austria; the dethronement of his Oldenburg kinsman, too, was bound to offend him. The Continental system ran counter to Russian interests. Even if the Russian government had been better inclined toward it, it could not have enforced the blockade for purely technical reasons. Now it was organizing a growing smuggling trade itself, with better success. A secret treaty with England stopped the decline of the rouble and helped the export trade, which had been upset. This made a break with Napoleon inevitable. Russia and France both prepared for the coming clash. Russia won over Sweden, where the French Marshal Bernadotte, who hated Napoleon, had been made heir to the throne. It was true that Sweden had lost the Grand Duchy of Finland to the Russians; notwithstanding, she promised herself the most profit from siding with her great Russian neighbour.

The attitude of the Scandinavian countries had always been important for northern Germany. Austria was decidedly opposed to helping the Russians—but where did Prussia stand? Scharnhorst and Gneisenau asked the King for an immediate rising against Napoleon. They presented the plan of a people's insurrection. Czar Alexander promised support. Scharnhorst negotiated in St. Petersburg and also in Vienna, but Austria wanted to hold off and to talk Prussia over to neutrality. Even Hardenberg believed that the risk for Prussia was too great. So Prussia put auxiliary troops to the number of twenty thousand at the disposal of the French and renewed her promise to exclude English goods rigorously from the Continent. Prussian patriots were in despair, and many officers took service with Russia or with England. Now Austria also made an agreement with France, and a much more favourable agreement than Prussia. Metternich exacted the promise of Illyria and Silesia; Prussia was to receive a suitable indemnity for Silesia. His explanation to the Czar was that the Austrian auxiliary troops would be only an observation

347

force; Austria hoped to fight on Russia's side for the old order. In this way Metternich was covered in the rear; whatever happened, Austria was to be on the winning side.

Since the spring of 1812 Baron vom Stein had been residing at Czar Alexander's court. Mostly under his influence, the Czar now interpreted the approaching war as the great decisive struggle between the world tyranny of Napoleon and the old dynasties that were freeing and organizing their people for the struggle for national independence. Stein, Arndt, Gneisenau, and many of the other patriots clearly recognized that the awakened peoples would fight for themselves rather than for their dynasts, but that Napoleon's downfall offered the princes the tremendous possibility of winning back their people by modernizing the structure of the state. The turning-point had really come. Russia was Napoleon's military ruin. Europe was ripe for the war of liberation.

UPRISING IN PRUSSIA

The convention that was concluded by General von Yorck, the commanding officer of the Prussian auxiliary troops, with the Russian General Diebitsch in Tauroggen on December 30, 1812, kindled the uprising in Prussia. Yorck was in a difficult military position. He was cut off from his French allies. He could have capitulated if he regarded the struggle as hopeless; but he went beyond this, albeit with a heavy heart. He was an inflexible adherent of the old Prussia and hated reformers; his hope was pinned to a reinvigoration of the Prussian state, and that could not be accomplished unless in alliance with Russia. The Czar assured the Prussian general that Russia would regard the restoration of Prussia as the most important goal in the war for Europe's liberation. So the general decided, entirely on his own responsibility, without any secret orders from his superiors in Berlin or from the King of Prussia, to make an agreement with Russia that the Prussian troops were to occupy the coast between Memel and Tilsit and were to remain neutral. If the agreement were invalidated by the King, the Prussian troops were to be free to leave, but were not to fight against Russia for two months. This agreement gained the Russian troops free passage to East Prussia. Politically the general's action mortally endangered the French and Prussian alliance. According to martial law Yorck was a traitor and his life at

348

forfeit. No one knew it better than he did. With complete awareness and with steadfast purpose he staked all for all.

The historical justification of the convention of Tauroggen lies in the Czar's resolve to conduct the war against Napoleon according to Stein's plan. That the Czar had proved unreliable several times was probably the greatest risk for Yorck as well as for Stein. But this time Alexander I held firm. The Czar's actions were influenced both by Russia's need for expansion toward Poland and by his delight in playing liberator. Stein appeared in East Prussia, temporarily took over the administration of that province, convoked a diet, prepared the organization of the second and of the last reserve, the *Landwehr* and the *Landsturm,* and abolished the Continental system. The King of Prussia found himself in an embarrassing position. He could not countenance General von Yorck's measure from a political, a military, or a human point of view. He never quite forgave him. Frederick William III had no taste for adventure. He put off the break with Napoleon as long as possible, and he negotiated with Austria as to joint action. Prince Metternich had the Austrian auxiliary troops arrange a truce, but he also wished to avoid anything that looked like really cutting loose. The plans that Archduke John and his many friends in the Alpine region were making with England's support were nipped in the bud. In all the provinces of Prussia excitement was mounting. The King betook himself from Berlin to Breslau. Negotiations with Russia finally led to the Treaty of Kalisch. The chief difficulty lay in the future boundaries of Poland. Prussia wanted to restore the boundaries of 1806, but had to be content with Russia's assurance that Prussia would receive appropriate indemnities, would be enlarged, and would be rounded off into one continuous political domain at the expense of any or all parts of northern Germany except Hanover. England's interest in Hanover and Russia's interest in Poland seemed to be sufficiently guarded by this arrangement.

Even before the alliance between Prussia and Russia had been completed, volunteers had been called to form regiments of chasseurs; universal conscription went into effect with the removal of all exemptions, and mobilization followed. After the break with France the King issued the famous "Call to My People." The Iron Cross had been instituted even earlier; the emblem of the order was an adaptation of the cross of the old Teutonic Order—an apt symbol, in accord with the current taste for the romantic and mediæval, for the bond between Prussia and Germany that was to prove so decisive. Volunteers were slow to come forward; mostly they were students who had been fired to enthusiasm by their professors. The *Landwehr* was most popular, because it incorporated the idea of national defence; the line was still regarded with the old-time mistrust. For legal reasons volunteers from parts that were still under French rule were organized into special free corps. The most successful of these corps was that of Major von Lützow; the young poet Theodor Körner, who fell in 1813, and Jahn, the inventor of gymnastics, belonged to it. The financial predicament of the state invited every kind of sacrifice, and during the three years of war voluntary gifts of private property mounted to the astonishing sum of six and a half million thalers. Pamphlets written by Ernst Moritz Arndt and poems by Theodor Körner, Max von Schenkendorf, and Friedrich Stägemann fanned enthusiasm, spurred the spirit of sacrifice, and built up courage. It must be added that they also awakened the hope that this time the longed-for liberation from external pressure would also bring a true inner freedom.

To France, all this was desertion, treachery, and breach of treaty. No Pan-German patriotic movement arose, indeed. Only Mecklenburg-Schwerin joined the alliance of Prussia and Russia. The princes of the Rhenish Confederation still trusted in Napoleon and provided the troops he asked for. Prussia was courting Germany, but the good, sound old Germany refused the eastern liberators. The dynasts' chief interest lay in territorial aggrandizement. Saxony, for example, first let Austria assure her an indemnity for the Duchy of Warsaw and then turned back to Napoleon and delivered the fortress of Torgau up to him. Only Sweden joined the Coalition. She made England promise to give her the Kingdom of Norway, with large subsidies. Prussia's treaty with England was not particularly favourable. Hanover was to acquire Hildesheim and probably East Friesland. Of the two million pounds that England granted the allies for the second half of 1813, Russia received two thirds and Prussia only one third.

Austria now tried to negotiate a compromise peace. She wanted to regain her position as a great power and to end French hegemony, but she did not want the Napoleonic dynasty annihilated. The King of Rome, Napoleon II, as grandson to the emperor, would have become a good confederate of Austria. Metternich offered the French Emperor a reasonable settlement. France was to keep the left bank of the Rhine, but to give up all her possessions on the right bank. Austria's demands for herself were the acquisition of Illyria and liquidation of the Duchy of Warsaw. Napoleon on his part tried to win Austria over by tempting her with Prussian Silesia. Then he began to negotiate directly with the Czar. Russia and Prussia asked for much more than Austria did: the restoration of Spain and Holland and renunciation of Italy. Nevertheless general negotiations were opened, with the Peace Congress of Prague. The truce that existed at least gave both sides time for military preparations. Napoleon was ready in any case to fight once more for what he regarded as his great work. In the end Emperor Francis reluctantly entered the fight against his son-in-law. This was the strongest coalition Napoleon had ever faced. For the first time since 1792 Austria and Prussia were joining forces against France; their disagreement had been one of the principal bases of French hegemony in Europe.

NAPOLEON'S STRUGGLE FOR HIS EMPIRE

Napoleon had the advantage of centralized and proved leadership, but he was handicapped by soldiers who were inferior because of youth and inexperience. The allies most certainly had superiority in both quantity and quality of troops, but they were hampered by frictions that sprang from conflicting views on strategy and aims of policy. Jean Baptiste Jules Bernadotte, the Crown Prince of Sweden, had never been a great general; now he was entertaining the hope of perhaps succeeding Napoleon in France, and for this reason if no other he hung back from the fighting as far as he could. Napoleon lost northern Germany and Silesia in a series of battles and was pushed toward central Germany. The allies managed to come to some sort of agreement concerning their war aims, which even now did not include the reconquest of the left bank of the Rhine. The treaty with Bavaria was a diplomatic coup for Metternich. Negotiations with the southwestern states of Germany had been under way since the spring; now the most finicking monarch in the Rhenish Confederation agreed to desert his benefactor, the French Emperor, in his hour of need. In the Treaty of Ried, October 8, 1813, Bavaria

351

demanded of Austria a guarantee of her sovereignty and of the status of her possessions, which was to be alterable only by exchange for something of equal value. With this, Bavaria left the Rhenish Confederation and joined the Coalition as a partner with equal rights. This treaty was to shape the future of Germany.

For a hundred years the house of Austria had tried to get rid of that annoying neighbour, Bavaria, in some way or other. Now Vienna had to swallow the fact that Bavaria was not only to remain as the nearest south German state, but also by this treaty acquired almost the dimensions of a great power. The way back to the Rhine was thus closed to Austria. The fact that Napoleon's most magnificent satrap state, the Kingdom of Bavaria, was spared established a precedent for the members of the Rhenish Confederation. Finally the recognition of Bavaria meant also a blow to Prussia and to her claims on Ansbach and Bayreuth; if Austria had lost the way back to the Rhine, Prussia had forfeited the bridge to southern Germany. Bavaria became the strongest obstacle to a sound reorganization of Germany and to the building up of a new empire.

Bavaria's desertion of the great Napoleon came even before the Battle of Leipzig. The French Emperor lost this Battle of the Nations, in spite of his brilliant strategy, because the allies succeeded at last in making their superiority in matériel and in reserves fully effective. The Battle of Leipzig (October 16–18, 1813) was Napoleon's last fight on German soil. Now the arrangement of the Rhenish Confederation and the protectorate in central Europe were no longer tenable. The Germany of the right bank of the Rhine was free. The efforts of Napoleon's most recent enemy, Bavaria, failed to prevent the imperial army, in flight, from returning to France.

The princes of the Rhenish Confederation now hastened to follow Bavaria's example. Stein demanded in vain that they be dealt with according to martial law. Only the King of Saxony was imprisoned. Negotiations with the Grand Duke of Frankfurt and with the lesser dynasts were rejected. The Kingdom of Westphalia collapsed. For the time being the masterless countries were made subject to the north German central administration, over which Stein presided. Stein urged that a new German constitution be drawn up, but Metternich would have none of it. The prospects for collective German patriotism were gloomy. For it could not be denied that the destiny of the Germans depended mainly on the dynasties. All the official circles of southern and western Germany were so greatly indebted to the French that they could not be expected to offer really resolute opposition. These regimes, in the fashion of upstarts, were time-servers. Sentiment was divided throughout the mass of the people. Academic circles realized the necessity of the struggle for German freedom and German rights. Ludwig Uhland the Swabian and Friedrich Rückert the Franconian joined the ranks of patriotic poets. But the more sober-minded little man knew that his whole chance of life rested on the modern legislation and administration that had arisen in western Europe; to his mind any change in these foundations was bound to be undesirable. And, finally, the romantic German emperor cult was confronted by a romantic French emperor cult. It was only in northern Germany that Napoleon was thoroughly hated as oppressor and exploiter; in the west and the south admiration for the contemporary Man of Destiny was prevalent, and he was regarded as a hero who belonged to German history also.

The Gallic epoch as a whole signified something quite different in the north from what it did in the south and west of Germany. The arrogance, the caprice, the carelessness, and the mockery of French officers and bureaucrats could not be forgotten. Here were the roots of the so-called hereditary enmity. National circles and those that strove for a Greater Germany cultivated this hatred and used it successfully for their own purposes. Unfortunately it must be admitted that the troops of the Rhenish Confederation often conducted themselves worse than the French in northern Germany. And in the Tyrol the Bavarians in bestial crudity exceeded even the horror of the civil war in Spain. The Napoleonic era produced, even in Germany too, a new sort of civil war. Germans abused Germans, and, notwithstanding academic hopes for emperor and empire, the rift between German strains became all the deeper.

Napoleon had been driven out. He was west of the Rhine. What would happen next? Metternich did not desire his downfall, for he was interested in maintaining a balance of power in Europe. From Frankfurt, the headquarters of the allied monarchs, Metternich against the will of England offered the French Emperor as basis for a general peace the "natural" boundaries of France: the Alps, the Rhine, and the Pyrenees. Napoleon's reply was unsatisfactory. Only in very general terms did he recognize the principle of the independence of all nations. And so the war had to go on.

The Austrian supreme command under Prince Schwarzenberg proved inadequate to the great task in hand. The boldest and most vigorous feats were accomplished by the Prussian leaders. Unquestionably first among these was Blücher, a true military patriarch, simple, strong, and stern. But Gneisenau surpassed all the others in wisdom, in energy, and in technical mastery. He had the profound restlessness of genius that always aspires and never knows content, and this quality made him a leader in the grand style. Among the non-Prussian generals Crown Prince William of Württemberg deserved the richest laurels.

Napoleon proved a veritable artist in generalship: he was inventive, flexible, and tireless. He defied unpropitious circumstances as long as he had any strength or any resources. Once more peace negotiations were started. There was sharp difference of opinion between Metternich and Czar Alexander. As before, Austria did not wish for destruction of France as a great power, because she wanted this power as a counterbalance to Russia. The Czar wanted Bernadotte to rule France and dropped the idea only when Metternich threatened that Austria would leave the Coalition. The Austrian Foreign Minister was at one with England as to the necessity of a single Kingdom of the Netherlands, comprising both Belgium and Holland, in order to make the Channel coast secure. Prince Metternich won Prussia over by promising to let her have all of Saxony.

At the peace congress in Chatillon it was Napoleon who made an offer of "natural" boundaries, but the allies now demanded the boundaries of 1792. The Czar, under Stein's influence, continued to insist that Napoleon be removed and began to suggest the return of the Bourbons. A new treaty welded the Coalition together more closely. The new defensive and offensive alliance was to run for twenty years; its purpose was to put through and to defend the reorganization in Europe even after the conclusion of peace. England promised five million pounds in subsidies for the current year, to be divided among the three other powers. France was to be limited to her "old" boundaries. Germany was to have an association of sovereign princes to guard her independence permanently; dynastic interests strangled the very concept of empire. Napoleon found it impossible to accept the boundaries of 1792. He continued the fight, and now his downfall came speedily. To the very end he was a miracle of buoyancy. Paris capitulated, and the Senate deposed the Emperor. A provisional government was set up to prepare for the return of the Bourbons. Napoleon signed the document of his abdication at Fontainebleau.

THE PEACE TREATIES. THE CONGRESS OF VIENNA (1814–5)

The reorganization of Europe could now begin. After all that had happened Germany's prospects were not of the best. The Allies made a distinction between Napoleon the wicked conqueror and the French nation, whose future under the old dynasty was not to be too heavily handicapped. The German patriots demanded a complete break in the consistent French policy of expansion, which had its roots in French history. Notwithstanding, France not only retained Alsace, but substantially improved the boundaries of 1792, which had been conceded to her. In addition to other areas she received the stretch between Maubeuge and Givet in Flanders and, as her chief gain, the Saar region with Saarlouis and the city of Landau. France was not required to pay any indemnities whatsoever, and she kept most of the art treasures she had carried off from other lands.

This first mild Peace of Paris in 1814 was short-lived. The belief in the possibility of European reconciliation was soon rudely jolted. The wise allied diplomats had forced the war-lord into retirement as Prince of Elba, but Napoleon regarded this state of affairs as merely temporary. While the victors were bargaining for the booty, while the Congress of Vienna was dancing, making love, and intriguing, disagreeing and quarrelling, Napoleon once more returned to France. Once more the tricolor of the great revolution was unfurled; once more Napoleon sounded the call to battle. He relied on his unbroken genius and on the disunity among his opponents. And now he took up the current call for freedom and independence for mature nations. Small wonder that many Frenchmen believed him even after all he had done to them! But England was determined not to tolerate him; so was Prussia; so was Russia. Europe had threatened to disintegrate in the quarrel for loot. But the return of the war-god forced this Europe to union and action. Napoleon lost the Battle of Waterloo (June 18, 1815). The English and the Prussians, his most relentless foes, joined forces to win this victory, which closed a great epoch and determined its meaning. For a long time the Germans called this battle by the name Blücher had given it, the Battle of Belle-Alliance; many good Germans and many good Britons regarded this name of a Belgian inn as a symbol of "fine confederacy"—of the co-operation and exchange of ideas that were necessary for the good of Europe, for the good of the world. The ideas epitomized at Waterloo signified the final reconciliation of central Europe with the west.

The second Peace of Paris, in 1815, set harsher terms than the first, of a year before. France was made to suffer because most of the French had again pledged themselves to Napoleon. Belgium received an improved boundary. Saarlouis and the Saar basin were given to Prussia, while Landau fell to Bavaria. France was to pay the reasonable indemnity of seven hundred million francs. A small district in northeastern France was to be occupied for five years. Most of the art treasures taken by Napoleon were now restored to their earlier locations. The French regarded this second Peace of Paris as an insult to the honour of France. The boundaries of the first Peace of Paris, and beyond these the so-called natural boundaries, became the goal of French foreign policy. Germany had regained only German-speaking districts, but many other German-speaking districts were retained by France. Actually there was no obstacle to a true reconciliation of the two great peoples. France had the enormous advantage of a unified national form. This was the result of the Revolution, and the Napoleonic era had only strengthened French national spirit; it had transformed even French subjects who spoke German, Flemish, Italian, Corsican, or Catalan into convinced Frenchmen.

But how did matters stand with Germany? The spirit of the German people was stirring powerfully. The popular demand of the day was the restoration of emperor and of empire in new and powerful form. The solution was favoured by poets, students who were champions of liberty, inhabitants of free imperial cities, philosophers, merchants, and master craftsmen, but, as usual in the fatherland, they were not at one as to what form it should ultimately take. Baron vom Stein racked his brains to find some way of satisfying all these patriotic wishes. One of his numerous plans provided for the separation of Germany into a north German and a south German empire that should be permanently allied; this plan was based on long-standing tendencies in German evolution that had deep justification. But the really powerful factors of European politics prevented the formation either of strong German imperial unity or indeed of imperial dualism. Russia, Austria, France, and Prussia could none of them find this concentration of central European power compatible with their own interests.

What Metternich wanted was Austria, not a German empire; a self-contained Danubian power was his goal. Quite deliberately he sacrificed outposts, such as the southern Netherlands, that were difficult to hold and the Rhenish possessions and interests of the Habsburg-Lorraine dynasty. It was the Rhine boundary that had made the old opposition between the Habsburgs and the Bourbons so hard to bridge over. Now, however, co-operation with France would be easy and profitable for Austria, for she had to reckon with Prussia and Russia as rivals. Metternich's Austria permitted the secondary states in Germany to become strong. And why not, since the restoration of the emperorship had been abandoned? The old electoral dynasties with their officials and courtiers, which had now grown into kingdoms, were the best allies against a strong empire and against Prussian ambition. The self-contained, powerful Austria of the post-Napoleonic era objected to nothing more strongly than to the idea of nationalism. For anyone who met the demands of German nationalism would also have to reckon with Italian, Czech, Slovak, Slovene, Hungarian, Croatian, Rumanian, Polish, and Ruthenian nationalism. Metternich knew why he had no use for nationalism; for him it was synonymous with revolution. And the Congress of Vienna, with Metternich, the victor over Napoleon, presiding at it, was intended to prepare the counter-revolution in Europe.

Next to Metternich the most outstanding figure in Vienna was the French representative, sly old Talleyrand, who took part in all the important negotiations about territorial readjustments and so established the influence of the new royalist France, which was certainly not responsible for Napoleon's misdeeds. Baron vom Stein was present in Vienna only as a private person. Prussia's interests were represented by Hardenberg and Humboldt, who, however, frequently disagreed in their work together. Czar Alexander personally outshone all the other princes, but he was no match for Prince Metternich in adroitness and practical experience. England's principal representative, on the other hand, Viscount Castlereagh, brought equally brilliant gifts into play. The increasing discrepancy between England and Russian interests, which was to dominate the epoch further, caused a rapprochement between England, Austria, and defeated France that was to have significant results for the outcome of the Congress.

The chief practical point of controversy was the Polish and Saxon question. Czar Alexander favoured a personal union of all of Poland with Russia, and he saw in this a restoration and a liberal reawakening of the Polish nation. Prussia demanded all of Saxony for herself; if there was one state of the Rhenish Confederation that had forfeited the right to its territory, it was certainly the Saxon Kingdom. But Prussia also insisted on the connection that had been promised her between her heartland and East Prussia; this connection involved Polish territory. Austria, too, was disinclined to give up her Polish possessions; she had, moreover, both Catholic and dynastic reasons for wanting Saxony to be at least partially preserved. France and England both sided with Austria, though from different motives; they did not want Russia to grow too strong, nor Saxony, Prussia's old rival, to be quite erased. England in particular was all for a strong position for Prussia on the Rhine, while Prussia herself, as well as Austria, would have preferred one self-contained mass of lands in the eastern part of central Europe. The differences in outlook between the Russian and Prussian group on the one hand and the group of Austria and the western powers on the other immediately led to threats of war and to the danger that the Congress would fall apart. The compromise that was agreed on could hardly give satisfaction even for the moment. Only part of Poland was united with Russia in a personal union, as the Kingdom of Poland— the so-called Congress Poland—with Warsaw as capital. Austria retained her Kingdom of Galicia; Prussia retained West Prussia as well as Danzig and Thorn and the so-called Grand Duchy of Posen; Cracow became a free state under Austrian protection, presumably as a symbol of Polish independence. All the powers that held shares of Poland promised her internal freedom and cultural autonomy.

But no one could feel any doubts whatever that Poland had actually been divided up again, and this partition, like those that had gone before, was nothing but a burden and a stumbling-block for the powers involved.

Prussia now received the greater part of Saxony, but the Kingdom of Saxony persisted, small in extent, but a substantial power economically and intellectually, with Leipzig as the center of the German book business and also with the significant industrial area. Prussia found splendid indemnity in the Rhineland; so-called Rhenish Prussia consisted of hereditary and long-desired lands and also ecclesiastical properties. Together with Westphalia, which had become Prussian, Rhenish Prussia now constituted the western half of the Prussian state, palpably superior to the eastern half in culture, flexibility, and German tradition. At the same historical moment when Austria was withdrawing from Germany proper, Prussia was reluctantly expanding into the best, oldest Germany. In accordance with England's plans Rhenish Prussia, Rhenish Bavaria, and Rhenish Hesse were thus strong along the western German boundary to defend central Europe, with the help of the Kingdom of the Netherlands, against possible new French aggression.

The main part of the Kingdom of Bavaria was separated from the Rhenish Palatinate, just as old Prussia was separated from Rhenish Prussia. Bavaria had tried in vain to acquire the intervening land, with the leading city of Frankfurt. Frankfurt again became a free city and perpetuated its great tradition of being Germany's political focus as the seat of the diet of the German Confederation. Bavaria returned the Tyrol, Salzburg, and the region around the Inn River to Austria and was given splendid indemnity in the shape of Franconia, Swabia, and the Palatinate. Hanover, now a kingdom, was rounded off with the former Prussian districts of East Friesland and Hildesheim—a thorn in Berlin's side. But finally, in the course of these complicated exchanges, Swedish Hither Pomerania fell to Prussia. Bavaria was bitterly disappointed that Baden succeeded in keeping the old Palatine Heidelberg. The fortress of Mainz was also lost to Bavaria; it was given to Hesse-Darmstadt and became a fortress of the German Confederation. Hesse-Darmstadt and the Duchy of Nassau not only maintained themselves but even made gains. As a reward for the patriotism of their dynasties, both the Mecklen-

359

burgs, Oldenburg, and Weimar were raised to grand duchies, while Hesse-Kassel obstinately clung to the title of electorate. In addition to Frankfurt, only Lübeck, Bremen, and Hamburg regained their positions as free cities.

Such, then, was Germany—an association of states under sovereign lords; not as chaotic and senseless as in the period before the French Revolution, but still no empire, still not even a nominal unity; nothing that could possibly be said to correspond to the maturity and the achievements of the German cultural nation.

THE GERMAN CONFEDERATION OF 1815

The diplomats and the reigning heads of Europe gave to the Germans as their future form of state the German Confederation. It had proved impossible to realize an elective emperorship, a division of the realm into administrative districts, or any political and constitutional equality for the two German great powers. There had certainly been no lack of suggestions. But Metternich's idea of a central European defensive confederation had triumphed. Historically this form was the descendant of the Rhenish Confederations, the League of Princes, and other associations of the estates of the Empire; but it added the more recent ideas of Napoleon's new order in Europe and of a European union for peace, such as Kant was the first to demand in his *Perpetual Peace* and many German philosophers and jurists called for after him.

The basic principle of the German Confederation was that all the districts of the old Empire that had still existed in 1806, the year of its dissolution, should be brought together for mutual military support and political co-operation. Both German great powers therefore belonged to the Confederation only on account of their regions that had been estates of the Empire. The history of the old Empire was marked by twin forces: foreign powers broke into imperial affairs, and estates of the Empire broke away from imperial institutional and political bonds. Both these trends appear also in the act constituting the Confederation. The two German great powers had one foot in Germany and the other outside of it; each of them dealt with the Confederation as one power with another. France, Spain, and Sweden, the former interlopers, were now disbarred. But in his capacity of King of Hanover the King of Great Britain had a seat

The
GERMAN
CONFEDERATION
1815

S

H

Li

Lu

The

German

Confederation

France

Kingdom
of
Sardinia

L-V

Italy

Sardinia

The Austrian Empire
including Hungary
outside the German
Confederation

The Prussian
Kingdom outside
the German
Confederation

S   Schleswig
H   Holstein
Li   Limburg
Lu   Luxemburg
L-V Lombardo-Venetian
     Kingdom

and a vote in the Confederation; the King of Denmark belonged to it on account of Holstein, the King of the Netherlands on account of Luxemburg. Thus the Confederation acquired a central European character; one might say that it perpetuated the anti-French comradeship in arms of the War of Liberation, and many hoped that it might develop further along these lines. By the notion of a conservative European association, supernational in character, the German Confederation was linked with the Holy Alliance.

Thirty-nine states were members of the German Confederation, which was indissoluble. Next to external and internal security its aims were to preserve the independence and inviolability of the individual German states. Austria presided over the Federal Diet (*Bundestag*) in Frankfurt. Stein had thought of this corporate body as an association based on the principle of the estates to represent all classes of the German people, and he had devised its name with this in mind. Now the name stood for nothing but a permanent congress of envoys in the old Regensburg style. The whole Act of Confederation bore a magisterial, dynastic character. The famous Article 13, originally formulated in more definite terms, stated rather vaguely that in all states of the Confederation a constitution based on the principle of the territorial diets was to be provided. Bavaria wrecked the proposed federal court of justice. Military regulations were to be drawn up later by agreement.

The ordinary business of the Confederation was transacted by a limited council, in which the eleven greater states had one vote apiece and the others six votes together. The general assembly (*Plenum*), which had sixty-nine votes, dealt only with questions of the most vital importance for the Confederation, such as constitutional changes, declaring war, and concluding peace. On such matters a two-thirds majority was prescribed. The Confederation had the right to send out ambassadors, to declare war, and to make treaties. It was unconstitutional for members to make alliances endangering the safety of the Confederation or of individual states or to engage in separate negotiations in case of war. Compared with the chaotic conditions that had prevailed during the later period of the old Empire, all this meant progress. It seemed as though the German great powers were in assured agreement and as if alliances of ambitious German states with foreign countries for the purpose of self-aggrandizement had been made impossible. But Prussia's position as a great power, the importance of Bavaria and of the other upstart states, Austria's resigned attitude—all these were direct results of the collapse of the Empire, on which the Confederation was based. Herein lay a considerable threat to its future. The Act of Confederation was incorporated in the final act of the Congress of Vienna (1820)—betokening that the various powers of Europe participating in this final act assumed some sort of responsibility for the Confederation. This state of affairs was unpleasantly reminiscent of the intrusion of foreign guarantors in German affairs that had been legally possible since the Peace of Westphalia. Notwithstanding Prussia's objections, England, France, and Russia sent permanent envoys to the federal diet in Frankfurt, which on its side had no diplomatic representation in the capitals of those countries.

This, then, was the result of the great War of Liberation against Napoleon. The Germans suffered the same fate as the Italians and the Poles and other Slavic peoples. Only in spirit was there a unity of the German people. Politically Germany remained cloven. The rising citizenry felt no interest in the reorganization. Dynasties were valued more than tribes, diplomats more than patriots, special interests more than the great collective whole.

Chapter 15

THE GERMAN RESTORATION

THE GERMAN people first became aware of itself as a nation through the German mind and soul. The German language, music, and fine arts were striking realities in German life. Creative work and struggle for spiritual and artistic values gave rise to new groups, bound high-minded people to each other, and helped them to keep their spiritual balance through the difficulties of the times, through persecution, poverty, and even hunger. Spirit made the Germans a far more brave and earnest people than they had ever been before. Because they burned with an immortal spark that was stronger than the cannon of the victor, they were able to defy a destiny that threatened to overwhelm them. Nature and reason had been the two great ideals of the Enlightenment. Proceeding from France, the Revolution had attempted to build up a better world through nature and reason. This world was to be humane; it was to assure a decent, worthy, peaceable existence to all, and therefore even to the upward-striving lower class. The dream of general welfare, of man's humanity to man, of a world made joyous, was to come true. But in pursuit of these aims the great Revolution had failed. It ended in world tyranny, ruin and destruction, and bloodshed without precedent. This experience had transmuted the ideals of nature and reason into those of liberty and nationality. The brotherhood of man had been wrecked by the fresh attempt to set up a world rule. It was necessary to be content with a more modest unity, and within these limits the effort must be made to achieve the good of all. This smaller unity was the nation.

The victor in a great world conflict usually convinces the conquered of the excellence of his state institutions. As long as Napoleon was triumphant the entire Continent aped French administration and French law, either by its own volition or under compulsion. This had occurred in Germany too, of course with the modifications indicated by ethnical or local considerations. Now France, Napoleon, and the Revolution were all overcome. It was England with her unshaken power, her inexhaustible supplies, that had made this victory possible. The armies of the continent of Europe had made their marches because of English subsidies. And it was England that, at the end of the Napoleonic era, had the greatest gains in land and prestige. It was therefore natural that the Continent should take a deep interest in English politics and in England's social institutions, which had made such a victory possible. Only the historically informed knew how much of the English spirit there had been in the French Revolution. Now the revived French monarchy took unto itself a constitution that was regarded as a happy adaptation of the English model to French requirements.

In Germany, too, English institutions were eagerly studied. But it would be a great mistake to suppose that the desire for constitutional conditions that was growing among the leaders of the people meant helpless imitation of foreign institutions. Primordially German were institutions based on the estates or diets; they corresponded to old Germanic customs. Absolutism and the police state were felt to be a foreign phenomenon, at once Oriental and Roman. Territorial estates (*Landstände*) had persisted in individual German countries such as Württemberg and Mecklenburg. The question was whether this old tradition of the estates could be adapted in a parliamentary fashion to the new social stratification. This stratification owed its latest form to the rising bourgeoisie, which was the main carrier of the new culture in Germany. The burgher class attained economic independence through technics and organization; it gained power and influence through its possession of flexible capital, which provided employment. It was natural that this class too should now demand its share in the affairs of state.

LIBERALISM

The burgher class called itself in Germany, as elsewhere, by a party name that had come into use during the Spanish civil war: "liberals." German liberalism is best characterized by its profound contrast with the dynastic authoritarian state. Its aims were not revolutionary, for on the basis of experience, psychology, and historical instinct it believed that destruction was not a necessary premise for reconstruction, but that political and moral progress could be achieved through reform. The style and rhythm of German liberalism was rooted in classical literature and philosophy; it gladly traced its derivation from Kant, Goethe, and Wilhelm von Humboldt. What it fought against stood out plain before all eyes: the privileges of the old ruling class. What it demanded was simple: the participation of the citizens in political responsibility and a guarantee of this in a written constitution.

The demand for its being set down in writing was a most essential point. In England the constitution had evolved without a break and without juristic rigidity; there was no need for it to be written down. Such a development was impossible on the Continent. Subjects were too distrustful; there had been too many revolutions, and historical continuity had long since been shattered. Anyone who wanted to set up a new state had to be quite clear in his own mind about the foundation and plan of construction. So it happened that the struggle of the German bourgeoisie for a free state of the people became primarily a struggle for a written constitution. The majority of Germans who were optimists in this matter hoped to reach their goal by dint of some reasonable agreement, but their hope rested on a dangerous underestimation of the old powers. The deployment of the bourgeoisie for combat was further embarrassed by the explicitly anti-revolutionary attitude of German nationalism. Liberalism and nationalism had both sprung from the soil, but inevitably pulled in different directions. The more liberalism was disappointed by the reactionary attitude of the old powers, the more necessarily it leaned toward the idea of revolution and the more radical it was bound to become. Nationalism in Germany was faced by the same opponents, the egoistic great powers of Austria and Prussia and the touchy particularistic self-consciousness of the individual upstart states; but since nationalism hated everything foreign and credited all sorts of evil to Jews, revolutionaries, and cosmopolitans, it finally tended to fall in with the anti-revolutionary forces.

When the German warriors of liberation came home they found poverty sitting at the hearth. Epidemics and acute famine were racking the country. Foreign oppression now took full effect for the first time. Industries that had sprung up in Germany under the Continental system quickly collapsed for lack of raw materials and also because English goods that had been piling up for want of markets flooded the country. People were supposed to be glad to be allowed to take the products of the great war creditor, England, who was getting repaid for her subsidies; protective measures against this process seemed out of the question for the time being. Hard work awaited everybody. Anyone who had to struggle for the sheer necessities of life as the German of that time did might well lose the enthusiasm and drive of patriotic exaltation. It is wholly understandable that many turned away from public affairs, which were being competently carried on by state officials in any case, and resignedly devoted themselves to immediate duties. Æsthetic and scholarly culture offered the longed-for spiritual relief from the weariness of the petty round.

THE ÆSTHETIC TREND IN GERMAN CULTURE

Goethe dominated the period in the strange and almost uncanny manner of a magician. He had outgrown the bounds of his era and lived only in accordance with his own law, indifferent to malcontents and petitioners. He was master of his work and of his world, familiar with all the primal forces of nature and of cultural evolution. Serene within his orbit as some celestial body of the cosmos, he did not suffer the commonplace, the foolish, or the trivial to penetrate the holy circle of his labours; and thus he completed a wondrous existence, which he enjoyed with all his senses even in his old age, but to which he also brought the ironical wisdom of a wide-ranging sensibility. His contemporaries saw only the mask of the patrician, the connoisseur, the Weimar Minister of State; posterity first came to a true estimation of his legacy.

Not Goethe's writings but rather the efforts of many minor talents that grew up beside him and under his influence were historically characteristic of the epoch. It was a literary age. Versifying and poetic playwriting were part of the paraphernalia of lofty spirituality. But much was written that was noble, fine, and wise. The Swabian school of poets, for instance, derived their power from the simple, genuine everyday conditions in which they worked. Besides honest Uhland there were Gustav Schwab, Justinus Kerner, and Eduard

366

Mörike. No one could tell stories that were so charming and so awesome, so gay and so profound, as that imaginative Swabian Wilhelm Hauff. Adalbert von Chamisso, a French *émigré,* Joseph von Eichendorff the Silesian, and Count August von Platen enriched German lyric poetry with observation of nature, longing for love, delight in aimless wandering, and absorption in history. Sometimes their verses were slight and unpretentious, like folksongs; sometimes, as in Platen's case, they were pensive and artfully wrought into rounded forms. It was a very happy coincidence that at the moment when the German spirit was lyrically creative, German music was ready to supply its verses with melodies. Even the songs of many minor poets were incorporated into the treasury of the German people by Beethoven and Schubert. The older German poetry of Klopstock and Wieland had borne a Protestant character, which was still typical of Schiller and even Kleist. German music was fostered in Catholic Austria more than elsewhere; court and aristocracy encouraged the struggling artists, and Vienna's love of music illuminated all southern Germany even to the Rhine. The less volatile and more critical north followed only gradually. But German philosophy, which, like poetry, was furthered most by Swabians, attained its best and purest in northern Germany. Catholic Germany shut itself against these pagan Greek pursuits. Inversely the fine arts throve in the south and along the Rhine, though in northern Germany as well, particularly in Hamburg, a number of local schools of painting sprang up.

In literature Austria sought her own way. Nikolaus Lenau (died 1850) was one of the most highly gifted of German lyricists. Franz Grillparzer (died 1872) grasped at the highest laurels in the field of drama; few could equal him in his mastery of phrase, but personal circumstances and the atmosphere of the times somewhat inhibited him and kept him from making his work entirely convincing. The regional character of German art is a consequence of the cleavage in religion and also of dynastic particularism. It was natural that the characteristic peculiarities of regional groups should give rise to something equally characteristic and indigenous, but the lack of influential literary periodicals and of theatres that could set standards made it difficult for the artist to reach all of Germany. As patrons the princes were concerned mostly for the glory of their own courts and their own countries. The school of painters that went by the name of Nazarenes attempted to make their work Pan-German, old German, even Roman and universal. This group of artists, awakened and inspired by romanticism, included Friedrich Johann Overbeck, Peter von Cornelius, and Philipp Veit, whose religious and historical frescos competed with the greatest work of the old masters. The Düsseldorf school of painters were simpler and less grave; they were more earthy, more sensuous.

The new humanism of the classicists cultivated a special feeling for sculpture. This was particularly evident in Berlin. Gottfried Schadow and Christian Rauch attempted to reconcile the canons of Greek art with the needs of Prussian realism. Architects also strove to adapt antique forms to northern conditions of life and government. On the other side romanticism emphasized the old German element and produced a new Gothic style. The Biedermeier period (1820–40) characteristically showed the greatest independence and taste in the solution of minor problems such as the furniture of the middle-class living-room: the round table and the massive, dignified desk, the elegant semicircular corner cupboard, the arm-chair with the arching back that invited to well-earned rest. On the walls hung family portraits executed with sound craftsmanship in bright, clear colours and simple lines. It was in such rooms that the cultivated citizens of the time took tea with friends (for those post-war days were too hard for lavish suppers in ancestral style); there people read or made music or conversation. The tone of such gatherings was a trifle affected and *précieux,* but questions of taste and of art, questions humanitarian and cosmopolitan, were taken seriously, as they should be, and everyone who tried to serve beauty and wisdom in his way was welcome and enjoyed the respect proper to his accomplishments and his ambitions.

HISTORY, NATURAL SCIENCE, AND PHILOSOPHY

A generation that had such profound faith in culture was bound to concern itself with every field of life and with every epoch of history. If Goethe took refuge from the confusion of the Napoleonic wars in the serene living from moment to moment of the Persian poet Hafiz, so the host of his disciples emulated this Occidental-Oriental hegira and many another Faustian wandering; there were to be no unexplored regions on the way "from heaven through the world to hell." Schlosser and Rotteck wrote world history from the point of view of a vigorous present, as was right and proper, Niebuhr subjected Roman history to critical penetration that had learned from the labours of archæologists and philologists in the field of the antique. Now the lovers of the German Middle Ages were also constrained to earnest inquiry into sources. Fanciful enthusiasm was no longer enough for political self-consciousness. Here Baron vom Stein came in, helpful as always, calling for the protection of the German cultural inheritance, since the practicalities of the present denied themselves to him more and more. At his suggestion a society for the study of ancient German history was formed; its members' critical selection of mediæval sources, the *Monumenta,* first made it possible to disentangle the history of the German emperors from the overgrowth of story and legend.

The spirit of scientific investigation extended into all neighbouring fields. German philological study broke into bloom under the leadership of the brothers Grimm. Comparative philology opened up entirely new vistas in the earliest periods of cultural evolution. The whole life of the past, its customs and morals, its economy and manner of living, called for explanation and interpretation. Even the science of law was subjected to the historical outlook. Should jurisprudence confine itself to presenting the development of law and its connection with the circumstances of the times, or should it undertake as its most pressing task the summons to legislation in accord with present and future needs? This question was one of the most pressing before the thinkers of the day. How determinedly and zealously in the closing eighteenth century the will to reform had striven to establish itself by legislation! There had been no desire to understand or preserve the old ways; the tablets that had been chipped were blithely shattered, for shining new ones were ready to replace them. Now, under the fullness of historical knowledge, the theoretical formative will of this beginning peacetime slackened wearily. Anton F. J. Thibaut, a professor of law at Heidelberg, called vainly for a great new Pan-German law code to be shaped in the true German spirit. His great colleague Friedrich Karl von Savigny denied that such a thing was possible and buried himself in cautious inquiries into the historical development of law.

Scholarship was at once universal and specialized. The sources to which it returned and the feeling of bygone days that it tried to revivify made equally possible a logical and a sympathetic realization of the past. But these scholars still based their work on accepted premises; they wanted to work the results of their researches into a consistent conception of the world. The fluctuation between tangible particulars and lofty principles made the spirit supple and gave its output the fresh charm of youthful creative energy.

This was also true of the natural sciences. The philosopher Friedrich Wilhelm Schelling (died 1854) indulged in bold and mystical interpretations of nature. Untroubled by them, research probed into natural processes with the conviction that this was the best method of arriving at ultimate knowledge. Karl Ritter (died 1859) was the first to lift geography to the level of a science that confronted reality in a spirit of sober investigation and described it accurately. Wilhelm von Humboldt's elder brother, Alexander, the geographer and globetrotter, was better entitled to speak of the "cosmos" than any of his contemporaries, for he knew the paths that led from microcosm to macrocosm.

The study of philosophy still ruled the curriculum of German upper schools. Much debated was the question as to who should be regarded as the successor of Immanuel Kant. Fichte aroused distrust because he was too easily impressed by the powers of the time and adapted himself to them too readily, which laid him open to error. Schelling was almost tormented by the profusion of his visions; the strength of his emotions and of his will lifted him above the over-refinement of those who knew everything or knew better, but he was unable to organize his wealth of ideas and to mint them into ready coin. Georg F. W. Hegel (died 1831) succeeded once again in forcing the humanities and science, æsthetics and the needs of the state, historical development and eternal values, the German cultural mission and the decree of the world spirit, Prussian authority and Napoleonic universalism, into one comprehensive system that had an answer for every question worth asking. In a masterly way he interpreted revolution and counter-revolution, war as a necessary creator of power and peace as the fruitful interval for the rebirth of strength, action and reaction, tyranny and mass movements, reason and passion, nature and civilization, destruction and reconstruction. His interpretation was profound and gripping, reasonable and exciting, authoritative and stimulating, for he demonstrated that the whole truth did not reside simply in one part or on one side, but in both yes and no, in a thing and its opposite—in totality. Was the victor, the man of power, always in the right according to this system of Hegel's? Not at all, for the rebel of today could be the conqueror of tomorrow if only he had time to wait and power to act. The centuries might learn from Hegel's wisdom; from wave and backwash, from ebb and flow, arose the sea of his world knowledge. This knowledge was soothing to the spirits of those who regarded the world as spectators, but anyone who wanted to get ahead a bit in his own time and age might well be irritated by it. German political thought and German political happenings in the subsequent period were largely shaped and stamped by Hegel. This Germany, unfinished and striving, yearned for unity, for a solution, for a settlement—for the great final synthesis.

METTERNICH

Prince Clemens Metternich (1773–1859) boasted more or less legitimately that he had conquered the great Napoleon. The victor at the Congress of Vienna was in any case the master diplomat of his times. The Restoration in Germany was the period of Metternich's greatest glory. "The Rhine flows in my veins," said the old statesman with wistful pride, and he spent his fairest hours of leisure at the Johannisberg Castle, among the vineyards that produce the best Rhine wine. But the Prince had become a real Austrian, concerned above all with this creation of his, this state of many peoples, the Little Europe of Habsburg-Lorraine, which was an expanded variation of the dream of a central Europe. In his own way and with the poise of a trained scientist Metternich had studied the Emperor Napoleon, the great Revolution, the nationalistic passion of the champions of liberty. He knew that his Austria, the circumscribed imperial state, could have no traffic with these ideas. Could it be that he was still under the influence of his professors, of those well-meaning sages versed in eighteenth-century affairs of state, who had dispensed such edifying oracular wisdom about the republic of Europe and the *Pax Christiana,* the peace of Christendom? An ordered state whose subjects were happy and contented, the carefully cal-

371

culated and preserved balance of political and social forces, were parts of the best inheritance from the Enlightenment. Metternich's playful manner, his gallantries, his readiness to handle easy money, the charm of his conversation even in practical discussions—all this too was of the eighteenth century, in profound contradiction to the ethos of the Wars of Liberation. He rubbed the younger generation quite the wrong way, and this serious younger generation in Germany, Italy, and Poland was destined to pay a bitter penalty for its hatred of Metternich's system. The Prince was a paragon of sobriety. He acted on his convictions unerringly; he was clever and lively, and he felt no need of being swept away by enthusiasms. Thus for a long time he was the master of his epoch. Only at the very end did he become rigid and arrogantly convinced of his infallibility—lacking ideas and even missing fire in foreign policy.

Austria was a thoroughly aristocratic country. Her economy rested on enormous landholdings of the feudal class; intellectually she relied on the unbroken power of the Roman church. The country folk were loyal, faithful to the Emperor and the church; they followed a deeply rooted instinct in clinging to tradition. In the cities a more pliant spirit prevailed, but nowhere, not even in Vienna, had the sense of bonds with the land been lessened at all. The curiosity and the business sense of the Viennese citizens were fully occupied with the court and the assorted high nobility, which resided in the capital, at least in winter. Only scholars and perhaps writers gave vent to criticism. The taste for music gave a lively, charming, almost childlike tone to social and intellectual life; here all classes met as happy connoisseurs. The capacity to enjoy the good things of life blunted the contrasts that existed and robbed judgement of its sting. The great thing here was peace and quiet, and this political hush became almost uncanny as the years went by.

Emperor Francis went on in his old way during the post-war period. He clung obstinately to all that he took for law and order. Officials were well-meaning and for the most part honourable in their work; they did not become rigid and impersonal, and they even participated in the entertaining gossip of the coffee-houses, but in all serious questions of patriarchal state power they were inexorable. Little was done for the army. Finances had been and continued to be a weak point. The house of Rothschild proved helpful.

Industry had to look out for itself. Everything dragged along in the traditional rut without vigour and without ideas. What energy there was was devoted to warding off new thoughts. Roads were built, it is true; the police guarded public safety; customs-houses gathered in as much as possible, and informers served the police with a devotion that was poorly rewarded. But where was any advance being made? Anyone who felt anything different within himself was thrown back wholly on his own resources. In scholarly pursuits only those who cultivated the natural sciences found promotion. Literature served average entertainment; very few were interested in Grillparzer's struggles. In the operetta and the popular play of the little suburban theatre the longing, the disappointment, the humour, and the quiet hopes of honest hard-working people were memorably expressed. The diets of the crown lands were under the influence of the nobility and the clergy; they limited themselves to the discussion of local affairs; their modest counsels were rarely followed and had no wider repercussions. Metternich's handling of Hungarian claims showed how much he feared any form of popular representation. Finally, in 1825, the constitutional diet met, but it closed after two years with nothing decided. During the Restoration period the Austrian imperial state definitely detached itself from Germany spiritually and intellectually. Metternich was thus creating a basis for her domination of Germany, of central Europe, even of the Continent. As long as the imperial state could be forced together in a reactionary way, the system could maintain its prestige. Proceeding from the basis of domestic policy, the Chancellor was working to guard the whole restored world of states. This is the gist of his historical function.

GYMNASTIC SOCIETIES AND STUDENT ORGANIZATIONS

Austria was the presiding power in the diet of the German Confederation. Must Germany submit to the system? During those first years many hoped that the diet would develop successfully to meet the needs of the times. But soon the complete hopelessness of the situation became evident. Only gradually had the War of Liberation against Napoleon grown into a German movement. This movement had been carried on by a minority of the population, but a young and vital minority. The gymnastic societies went to seed the worst

373

of all. After the great victory coarseness and mere brute strength became the fashion; everything alien, everything foreign or cultivated, was attacked in a bullying manner. Vulgar songs and manners satisfied the exaggerated enthusiasm for all that was Teutonic. Many good patriots expressed their disapproval, and the Prussian government took up the feud with satisfaction, since this gave it the opportunity of taking measures against these gymnastic societies, which were politically suspect. The gymnasiums were closed, and many forces of real worth in themselves were paralysed and embittered.

More significant became the founding and the effects of student organizations. Up to this time the life of university students had been crude and schoolboyish. The student clubs (*Landsmannschaften*), from which the later Corps or student organizations emerged, represented the political particularism of the states ruled by princes. The members were bound to dynastic authority through family interests and hopes for a career; they thought and acted accordingly. But now in Jena eleven students, most of whom had fought in the War of Liberation, founded a new association (*Burschenschaft*) in June 1815. They were influenced by the ideas of Fichte, Jahn, and other leaders of the times, as well as by the experiences they had shared in the Lützow volunteer corps. Their aim was the rebirth of Germany as an entity and the revival of the Christian spirit. Their slogan was "Freedom, honor, fatherland," their colours the black, red, and gold that had been worn by the Lützow chasseurs—this combination being formed by putting together the two colours and the hue of the metal used in the old eagle emblem of the Empire; the old Empire had no flag of three colours. This tricolor corresponded to liberal and democratic requirements; it meant faith in a German form of revolution, whose aim it was to free the third estate and to give it equal rights. If there was to be any German tricolor at all, then black, red, and gold, though not in proper sequence, were the symbolic colours that accorded with tradition; the correct order would have been black, gold, and red, since the metal—gold or silver—in such a case should be in the middle.

Very soon two groups formed in the student organization, the stricter Old Germans and the milder Lichtenhainers. In the beginning the association was concerned, not with direct political activity,

374

but mainly with student problems. In line with its program it spread through the entire student body of certain universities, but its activities were limited to Protestant institutions. Thus from the very outset it was anti-Austrian in character and had to look to the predominating Protestant powers for any realization of its ideals. Christian-Germanic ideas were being expressed about this time in a series of journals that drew much attention; the most remarkable of these were edited by the Jena professors Luden and Oken. The Weimar government was tolerant of all such endeavours. That was why, on October 18, 1817, the Wartburg Festival was held on Saxe-Weimar soil, near Eisenach in Thuringia.

Members of the organization and also of gymnastic societies issued invitations to a celebration commemorating the Reformation and the Leipzig Battle of the Nations. Various affairs of the association were to be discussed on this occasion. Twelve universities were represented; all the authorities participated, and the official celebration was solemn and dignified. There was a special divine service and a banquet. But in the evening there followed a kind of political orgy. After the torchlight procession the students, probably at Jahn's suggestion, kindled a great bonfire and burned in it reactionary books that they regarded as non-German, as well as a corporal's stick, a pigtail, and a pair of stays, as symbols of the military authoritarian state. Was this auto-da-fé more than a wild students' prank? The authors affected complained so bitterly that the authorities could not very well ignore the affair. The goings-on showed plainly enough that the association was becoming political. The spirit of Teutonism had seized it and tried to sweep it into a movement that was bound to seem revolutionary to governmental authorities. This impression was deepened when Kotzebue, a Russian councillor of state, was murdered in Mannheim.

Kotzebue was gifted as a playwright, and his comedies pleased the average taste. In his reactionary *Literary Weekly* he struck out against the aims of the student association. Kotzebue was one of the most active agents of the Holy Alliance; the Czar had agents everywhere. Kotzebue's murderer, Karl Ludwig Sand, belonged to the "unconditionals" in Jena, a group within the association that was led by the lecturer Karl Follen. This group wanted to wage political war by means of terrorism—by revolt, murder, and every kind of violence against the established authorities. Though only a small minority, it was very active. Sand's deed was the result of a conspiracy. Other conspiracies and an attempted assassination followed. Sand was publicly executed in Mannheim, but in exclusive circles among the cultivated he was celebrated as a hero of liberty, as patriot and martyr. There was no immediate threat to the government, but the atmosphere had become electric, and disappointment and bitterness mounted in the fatherland; Metternich believed that the time for intervention had come. He invited Prussia and a number of smaller states to conferences in Karlsbad. The result was the Karlsbad Decrees, which were subsequently confirmed by the federal diet at Frankfurt (1819).

PERSECUTION OF POPULAR LEADERS

The universities and the press were taken aback. Authorized agents of the sovereigns were to supervise the universities, regulate discipline and the lecture schedule, and discharge unreliable professors. The *Burschenschaft* and all secret societies were banned; members of them were held unfit for public office. All publications of less than three hundred and twenty pages were subjected to preliminary censorship by the authorities. At Mainz the so-called Black Commission, a central agency of investigation, met to oppose any further revolutionary activities; this was an independent high authority, not under the supervision of the diet. It could call on the governments for what it wanted, order them to make arrests, or make arrests itself. It persecuted all whom it could identify as members of the League of Virtue, of men's and young men's clubs, and above all, of course, of the *Burschenschaft*. This last was officially dissolved in 1819, but was immediately reconstituted as a secret association, which now, under the pressure of persecution, naturally took on a definitely political character. Even mere membership in the *Burschenschaft* meant the loss of freedom for many years. The Black Commission, active until 1829, wrecked the lives of numerous promising young men; many of the best of its victims emigrated to America and attracted others after them. The death penalty, commuted to life imprisonment, was not uncommon.

Metternich crowned his work with the final act of the Congress of Vienna in 1820. It was the issue of convoking for conference at

Vienna the bearers of the seventeen votes of the special committee of the federal diet. Now, for the sake of maintaining internal quiet, the Confederation concentrated on the struggle against revolutionary activities. The leader of the Austrian state was particularly interested in invalidating Article 13 of the Act of Confederation, which he found offensive, concerning constitutions based on the principle of the estates. Now it was decided that the German sovereigns were to remain in possession of unqualified executive power, that no constitution should prevent a prince from fulfilling his obligation toward the Confederation, and that freedom of speech in the parliaments was not to be allowed to endanger the interests of the state or of the Confederation.

PRUSSIAN ADMINISTRATION. THE CUSTOMS UNION

Prince Metternich's master stroke consisted in drawing Prussia completely into the reactionary current. A connection of Prussia with the patriotic movement might have become dangerous to Austria as the presiding power of the Confederation. But Prussia had no thought of such a thing. First of all she had to organize her own territory, so unfavourably situated, and Prussian administration was entirely preoccupied with this task. Prussia had a flourishing educational system, although school laws were blocked by the conflicting interests of state and church. In sum, the Prussian officials handled quite carefully and competently all minor questions that were without political bearing, but the difficulties that attended major problems were apparently beyond solution. The feudalistic elements at court cast the slur of Jacobinism on the bureaucratic liberalism of Prince Hardenberg, while officialdom resisted Stein's ideas of a revival of the old local diets, ideas such as were being agitated by many of his followers. The influence of the aging Prince Hardenberg was declining, thanks partly to distasteful circumstances of his private life.

In Berlin Prince Wittgenstein, the Minister of Public Safety, was a tool ready to Metternich's hand. For years Prussian statesmen were occupied with the promises of King Frederick William III, repeated five times, to give his people a constitution. If a plan for a constitution, such as Hardenberg's, for instance, had been carried out, the serious financial difficulties in particular might have been disposed of. A constitution would have proved invaluable in welding the very diverse Prussian provinces together more quickly, in giving political training to their intelligent and ambitious populations, in making them function. Above all it would have provided a possibility of harmonizing the German national will and Prussian state interests in good season. But the feudalistic element did not permit any summons of the diets, even for advisory purposes. Metternich's warnings against a parliamentary central organ took effect, and sharp reaction set in. A poor substitute was devised in the shape of a council of state as a supreme advisory body, composed of ministers and generals, but especially of the king's confidential agents. The best of the liberals, such as Wilhelm von Humboldt and brave Boyen, now withdrew. The freeing of the peasants was curbed; the municipal ordinance was impaired; the urgently necessary organization of circles—the reform of local administration in the provinces —was wrecked by the resistance of manorial lords, who did not dream of letting the police power slip through their fingers. The eight provincial diets were limited to tedious problems of administration, and publicity as to the debates was forbidden; there was no discussion of politics. The nobility, heavily predominating, allowed no one of any other class to come forward. Such was the pitiful, even ridiculous sum of the speechifying and scribbling of five constitutional commissions.

The Prussian state persecuted demagogues with marked asperity. Ernst Moritz Arndt was admonished; he was forbidden to lecture, and his papers were confiscated. Jahn, the founder of gymnastics, was denounced by a schoolboy and accused of treason; though exonerated, Jahn was kept under surveillance. The police also lent a critical ear to the sermons of the theologian Schleiermacher. Letters, even those of such a man as Stein, were systematically opened and examined. Fichte's *Addresses to the German Nation,* in a new edition, and the writings of Ulrich von Hutten were prohibited. If a teacher or a clergyman was to find a position, the first requisite was that the police should give their approval of his ideas and his con-duct. Printed matter of every description was censored, and publishers whom the authorities disliked were subjected to particularly annoying control.

Not much good could be said of reactionary Prussia; so those who would like to flatter her are forced to concentrate on the Prussian Customs Union. Politically this device has been overestimated. Economically it was an admirable achievement of Prussian officialdom. In the Germany of that period almost three fourths of the population were engaged in agriculture. In the west and in the south, where there were many small and even infinitesimal farms, the great baronies of the mediatized lords constituted a strong aristocratic counterbalance. After the war epoch there was a great increase in population. Industrial centres gradually sprang up; within Prussia they were more especially centered in Silesia, while others appeared on the Lower Rhine, in Westphalia, in Berlin, Magdeburg, and Stettin. Because of the restricted ownership of land and the laggardliness in introducing modern methods, there was a surplus rural population that agriculture could no longer absorb. Industries that grew up in the countryside were therefore particularly successful—the distilleries in Prussia, for example, and the breweries in southern Germany. Oil production, beet sugar refineries, and tobacco products also consumed agricultural raw material and thus gave employment to new generations of country folk.

The manufacture of linen, to which poor mountain regions had always resorted, was crowded out and soon stifled, first by cottage industry and gradually by mechanical development in Silesia, Westphalia, the Wuppertal, and Upper Lusatia. The cotton industry usually established itself in the neighbourhood of the linen industry, and velvet and silk factories followed, especially on the Lower Rhine. Mechanized industries gradually grew up wherever coal and iron were mined. The firm of Krupp was founded in 1819; in 1846 it employed not more than one hundred and forty workers. In 1826 metal workers in Solingen, and two years later silk weavers at Krefeld, protested against low wages. In all these places thousands of children were employed, some of them as little as four years old. In 1816 the rural population in Prussia still made up seventy-eight per cent of the whole, in 1849 still sixty-four per cent. But this agrarian and small-town type of population was not so wholesome as might be supposed, because the number of dependents in the country was increasing too fast. The oversupply of labour caused wages to drop. In 1843 the industrial population was twenty-three per cent of the whole.

379

The industrial middle class did not have an easy time of it in Prussia, that land where everyone was free to exercise a trade. But matters were the same in the lands that still had guild statutes, because only a third of the people who plied a trade still belonged to guilds. The old civically regulated mode of industrial production, providing a sure livelihood, was dissolving. Certain groupings of hand workers became obsolete, say the smiths and hat-makers; others, such as the bakers, the butchers, and the shoemakers, could persist by dint of adaptation to the new forms of technics and business; a third division made the leap into the new era because they absorbed the spirit of commercial speculation and engaged in quantity production, in which the old feeling for craftsmanship and taste had to be abandoned. Only a very few journeymen could now become masters; they were lumped indistinguishably with the untaught and the half-grown, vagabonds, and casual workers. The hopeless journeyman is one of the saddest figures in the German revolutionary movements; here were the beginnings of a German proletariat. Germany was still producing ninety-five per cent of her foodstuffs. Exports of wheat and other agricultural products and of finished silk, linen, and cotton goods supplied the means for the desired imports of raw materials and half-finished or finished manufactured goods.

Only a knowledge of all these factors makes it possible to understand the Prussian Customs Union. Prussia included regions with sixty-seven different tariffs in the old provinces alone, with one hundred and nineteen different currencies. The first step was to abolish all water, inland, and provincial tolls. In spite of opposition from the manufacturers, the principle of "free imports for all future times" was set forth. In 1819 a new tariff for the entire state of Prussia went into effect. Raw materials continued to be admitted free or were only lightly taxed. A modest protective tariff of ten per cent was levied on manufactured articles, twenty per cent on tea, coffee, and other colonial goods. As far as products consumed within the country itself were concerned, only wine, beer, brandy, and tobacco were taxed. Later on, the rates were slightly raised, for iron and metal wares to eighteen per cent, for wine and colonial goods to thirty per cent. The high transit duties deliberately brought pressure to bear on the small states that lay around Prussia. The whole system assured landowners of profitable exports of cheap agricultural products, largely to England; it forced manufacturers to keep wages low in order to meet the competition of foreign goods, again especially those from England. It disposed of the craftsman class and made it possible for individual merchants to accumulate large fortunes. This was entirely in keeping with the aristocratic and reactionary character of the Prussian state.

Austria and the small states scented political danger in the Prussian tariff system, because it put the intermediate countries under constraint and made them powerless in customs policy. Several of the small states ventured on a tariff war; others took to profitable smuggling. Prussia reached an understanding first with several small Thuringian states. The first south German participant in the Prussian system was Hesse-Darmstadt. Bavaria and Württemberg, otherwise constantly involved in neighbourly quarrels, now united for action. Saxony suggested a rival customs union, which materialized with Austria's help as the Middle German Commerical Union, joined by most of the middle German states. Prussia now combined with Bavaria and Württemberg. The middle states were in a quandary. Their union was gradually dissolved in favour of the Prussian Customs Union, which went by the name of the German Customs Union after 1833. The Kingdom of Hanover now formed a separate customs union (*Steuerverein*) with its nearest neighbours, with a friendly relationship to the Prussian system.

The middle states and the small states resisted not only out of envy of Prussia but for substantial economic reasons, particularly the fear that their home industries would be flooded with Prussian manufactures and that consequently the purchasing power of the south German gulden would suffer. Important markets such as Leipzig and great commercial centres like Hamburg and Frankfurt were especially afraid of adverse effects from the Prussian system, which threatened to put the profits of the middlemen into Prussian hands. If in the following period the Customs Union had gone over to protectionism at the right time, Germany's transition to industrialization might have been accomplished under more favourable conditions. This, however, would have brought a readjustment of landownership and agricultural production in Prusssia that would have been unwelcome for both political and social reasons. The Customs

Union certainly did not bring about a political rapprochement between Prussia and the south German states, which, in spite of economic co-operation, sought to go their own way until 1866. The anti-
liberal character of the Customs Union indirectly strengthened all
the aristocratic and feudal forces in the rest of non-Austrian Germany and thus paved the way for later events. Not least among its
effects was the way in which it set the old Prussian views of the
state and of economy above true German interests, which it weaned
from their connections with western Europe.

CONSTITUTIONALISM IN THE "THIRD GERMANY"

Both German great powers persevered in an autocratic attitude
of hostility toward constitutions. A number of south German and
middle German states, however, continued to function on the modern constitutional basis that they had instituted during the Napoleonic era or immediately afterward. None of these constitutions was
democratic. All of them emphasized the prerogatives of the crown;
they accorded overwhelming influence to feudal and ecclesiastical
forces. In spite of the old idea of the estates and the new idea of
liberalism these constitutions functioned primarily by official sanction. But all this did not alter the fact that they did exist. They made
some slight degree of outspokenness and criticism possible, kept at-
tentiveness toward public affairs astir, and spread some information
about political problems. Unfriendly as the touchy authorities
showed themselves toward all parliamentary activities, they were
nevertheless proud of being ahead of the haughty great powers in at
least one respect. Constitutionalism connected southern and central
Germany in some fashion or other with the west—that is, with the
modern concept of the state that had grown out of the French Revolution and that persisted in spite of suppression and persecution.

Out of such sentiments arose the curious notion of a third Germany that should lead its own life alongside the two great powers.
The *Manuscript from South Germany,* a pamphlet by a Kurland
publicist brought out in London in 1820, proposed the union of a
pure and constitutional Germany, exclusive of the half-alien German
great powers, which should be regarded merely as allies. These ideas
were traceable to King William I of Württemberg, who was highly
gifted both politically and militarily.

The idea of a "pure" Germany was very old. It was the natural reply to the egoism of Austria and Prussia as great powers. It turned back to the political significance of the west German electors in the old Empire and to the groupings in the Rhenish Confederation. To brand this tendency offhand as anti-national would be a serious error. In its own way it wanted rather to serve the best unadulterated German interests—of course only so far as they were in harmony with the power politics of the dynasts concerned. The concept of Germany as threefold survived until 1866. Originating in Württemberg, it was later taken up by suspicious Bavaria, which was fond of emphasizing, not wholly without justification, that it was the greatest purely German state, since its entire territory belonged to the German Confederation. Attempts of the southern Germans to invigorate the federal diet and to forge a German policy by means of it quickly ran aground. The diet's transactions were now generally kept secret. Liberal newspapers were suppressed in Swabia. Württemberg, above all, stained its reputation by persecuting the great German patriot Friedrich List, who criticized the officials and their policy of exploitation without restraint. After having been imprisoned in a fortress List went to the United States, where he became one of the leading political economists of his time. On his return to his own country he recommended that an efficient protectionism should be established for Germany as a whole, which would become economically independent and be unified by this means. List committed suicide in 1846.

Bavaria was quickened with new life when King Louis I came to the throne in 1825. He transformed backward Munich, with its breweries, into a brilliant centre of art and scholarship. This monarch was certainly not gifted as a statesman. He was too unpredictable; he undertook too much and behaved like an irritated tyrant whenever he encountered opposition. He was not interested in military matters; so he neglected them. But his warm German sentiment, his love of beauty, his taste for what was genuine, the charm of the simple humanity that hung about him—these qualities awoke sympathy and interest for Bavaria and for Germany in the world at large. King Louis enthusiastically espoused the Greek fight for liberation, and thus he drew near to the forces of freedom of the time, even though he mistrusted real liberalism. It was rare good luck that no military automaton or demagogue-devouring ogre throned it in Munich. The German patriot, when he thought about the future, expected something of this sovereign.

The King's greatest regret was that Heidelberg, Mannheim, and all the old Palatine cradle of his house had been handed over to Baden, and he did everything he could to regain the region. The negotiations in this matter were involved with the curious case of Kaspar Hauser, which aroused feverish excitement at the time. A foundling suddenly appeared in Nürnberg, a boy who had spent many years in a dark prison and who was correspondingly unde-veloped. He quickly acquired a good education and displayed the best of characters. His origin was a mystery, but repeated attempts on his life showed that he must be someone of importance; finally he was murdered. Many indications suggest that Kaspar Hauser was really a prince of Baden, one of the sons of the Grand Duchess Stephanie, Napoleon's adopted daughter, who were supposed to have died young. After Stephanie's time the throne of Baden passed to the collateral line of the Counts of Hochberg. The Bavarian dynasty had hopes of obtaining the Baden Palatinate from the Hochbergs and is therefore supposed to have had a hand in these sinister machina-tions. In any case a tangle of intrigues and crimes, which have never been fully cleared up, surrounded the new dynasty that came into power in Baden in 1830.

THE SMALL STATES

The strange world of German small states fell into several groups. There was the southwest German Rhenish group that centred in Frankfurt, the capital of the German Confederation. The Grand Duchy of Hesse-Darmstadt and the Duchy of Nassau belonged to this group, both of them with western interests. Their political life had a strongly bureaucratic tone, with moderate constitutional tend-encies. The northwest German group was closest to this one geo-graphically. It consisted chiefly of Hesse-Kassel, which suffered from a greedy and irresponsible dynasty; of Hanover, which had been given a scarcely satisfactory constitution by its German chancery in London; and of Oldenburg, Brunswick, and so on. Toward the east there was the Saxon-Thuringian group, which took in the Kingdom of Saxony and Thuringia. The former had been definitely out-stripped by Prussia and was following Austria's course, though not without bitterness. Saxony was on the rise economically and cul-turally, and the Leipzig book trade was flourishing to a degree that would never have been possible under Prussian domination; but her politics were inflexible and stubbornly anti-liberal. Thuringia was the most striking example of German fragmentation. Nowhere were boundaries so completely arbitrary, and as a result there was no such provincial spirit of petty gossip anywhere else. All attempts to or-ganize and simplify this forest of boundary posts in which economic life was almost unbearable met with bitter resistance from purveyors to local interests and from flunkeys. The last group of small states included the two Grand Duchies of Mecklenburg, which were en-tirely surrounded by Prussian territory and were determined to con-tinue in calm dignity as long as they possibly could an existence based on the old estates, suspicious as they were of everything from outside.

The system of small states was the true German destiny in the nineteenth century. Great states, world powers, were now flung across continents and seas; foreign peoples were overpowered, trained, exploited, and developed by their European conquerors. The Germans participated in these processes of world history only as spectators and drew only indirect advantages from them. Anyone who left Germany to go overseas was lost to the German state, which was as yet no more than wishful thinking. The devastating result of the great Napoleonic upheaval was that the best and richest areas of old German territory again fell into a system of small states—no question, this, of a few square miles more or less, but a matter of state of mind. The great conceit of sovereignty that hung over the many petty potentates poisoned German freedom, German nation-ality. In earlier times the single lofty, inviolable majesty of the em-peror had towered above all the Highnesses and Serenities. The longing for emperor and empire that all patriots were now experi-encing was the longing for large, worthy, fitting relationships—for order and clarity within the country, for prestige and power in Eu-rope and the great world.

The best of the Germans were striving for expansion, not only in

385

the world of the spirit, but in that of tangible reality. Were the Germans to forego for ever the chance of moving out into the wide spaces of the world that was the due of Englishmen and Frenchmen, and that Russians were soon also to take? Obviously the prerequisite was to establish a new German empire. The rivalry of the two German great powers stood in the way; no lesser obstacles were the mental attitude, the character, and the conduct of the small states. Everywhere were palaces with lackeys and toadies—everywhere bureaucrats and soldiers, titles and medals, delight in careers and intrigues—everywhere the aping of the great states, in expenditure and speech, in favouritism and arrogance. Industrious folk of the artisan and commercial class were all dependent on the good graces of those above them and on the power of the police. Much ado was made about nothing at all; there was a lot of well-oiled chatter, pedantry of tutors and schoolmasters, clerical and police chicanery. But where was Germany? No other German longed with such bitter intensity as the one who lived within this system of small states for a Germany of the future that should be really great, free, and strong. Was there any other way to it than that of revolution?

The Germans had had ample experience with all manner of reformers. There had been no lack of spirit, of inventiveness, of goodwill. The German character is intrinsically averse to destructiveness. Anyone who wants to build up something new, slowly and soundly, has the immediate sympathy and confidence of the Germans. But what had become of Stein, of Boyen and Humboldt? To suppress, to deaden, to subject to autocratic routine—these had always been the answers to the best proposals. Prince Metternich held sway over Germany, over Europe. In Spain, in Italy, in Greece, new struggles were being kindled for freedom and national independence. Austria, Russia, and Prussia—at first Great Britain as well—held Europe under the dictatorship of counter-revolution. The liberation of the Latin American states and the establishment of a Kingdom of Greece were achieved notwithstanding. England under George Canning warmly encouraged all national movements, while the three eastern powers, Russia, Austria, and Prussia, withstood them in a negative and sullen way. Germany had no voice in all this. But Germany was waiting, full of indignation, full of bitterness and im-

386

patience—waiting for her hour. The counter-revolution had strangled any possibility of reform. Life dragged on languidly, lamely, without warmth. The profoundest philosophy, the noblest music, can assuage a great people only briefly if it feels the stirrings of a mighty future. And this future could only be realized through a German revolution.

Chapter 16

THE FIRST TWO GERMAN REVOLUTIONS

THE PERIOD of the Restoration owed its name to the main work of Karl Ludwig von Haller, a Swiss teacher of public law. He believed that his book entitled *The Restoration of Political Science* marked the end of the revolutionary period. There is no contract between a prince and his people, according to this writer. The people have no constitutional status at all. The prince owns the country as a landowner owns his estate; he does what he pleases with it. If the prince desires, he may let his subjects participate in the labours of politics in whatever way and to whatever extent he sees fit. He himself is responsible only to God. The liberal national state is revolutionary. Only the patrimonial state accords with the will of God and is pleasing to Him.

The July Revolution of 1830 in France was epoch-making because it was a victory for the idea of revolution. Haller and others like him were wrong after all, it seemed. The people had a will; princes had responsibilities; dynasty and citizenry were bound to each other, and this relationship was subject to change and development, to legal determination. A regrouping was in process; new public law was created. God shed His grace even on the nation, and the prince did well to hold fast to the constitution, which prevailed over any personal whim.

France had its tricolor again. Once more there was a French king, but the system of legitimacy had been shattered, historical sequence broken. The primordial force of national determination had again triumphed, and conclusively. The July Revolution convulsed Europe. Belgium declared herself no longer bound to Holland and became an independent state, with Europe's guarantee for her neutrality. Germany thus acquired still another neighbour with a model constitution. The Belgian part of Luxemburg withdrew from the German Confederation; the province of Limburg replaced it, and in the province no one outside of a few aristocratic families took any interest in Germany. The suppressed Poles revolted against Russian despotism, and these events directly affected Prussia and Austria along their most vulnerable border. They applauded the suppression of the insurrection and gladly assisted in it, though they could scarcely approve of all the measures taken by Russia. German friends of freedom were in sympathy with the Polish cause, like all of western Europe. Polish refugees were given help and encouragement; hatred for the powers responsible for the partition of Poland flared up anew, and the rift between the German great powers and the feeling of the German people became deeper. Everyone who subscribed to Russia's barbarous methods was regarded with contempt. And so the tragedy of Poland cast its shadow over purely German affairs.

The July Revolution caused unrest in a whole series of German states. Duke Charles of Brunswick, an arrogant and vicious tyrant, had to flee to England. The arbitrary and senseless actions of this potentate had aroused all classes of the people to anger. His brother William, poised and dignified, succeeded him. In Hesse-Kassel matters came to such a pass that people refused to pay taxes. All social classes called for immediate reform, and it took a quickly organized civic guard to calm the uprising. The Elector accepted his unpleasant son as co-regent and withdrew to Frankfurt with his mistress, the Countess Reichenbach. This excellent land still had much to suffer from the ill humours and the exploitative tricks of its sovereigns. It had the most progressive constitution in Germany, with a parliament of only one house, ministerial responsibility, an oath of allegiance to the constitution for the military, and a state tribunal. This constitution was regarded as a pattern of everything the liberals had been striving for, but precisely for that reason it irritated the wretched dynasty and was thoroughly hated by all reactionary groups.

After various disturbances the Kingdom of Saxony finally adopted a modern constitution with a parliament of two chambers, both of which, however, were built up on the principle of the estates; the second chamber was based on a franchise that made any true representation of the people almost impossible. At least the transition to a constitutional state occurred without major disturbances. Legislation functioned well, but even so there were signs of discontent among the rapidly growing labouring class. Hanover also adopted a new constitution, soon to be the cause of a sensational struggle. In southern Germany it was Baden that gave the strongest evidence of new life. The reactionary limitations and changes in the constitution were done away with, and new laws concerning the press permitted public opinion more open expression than in almost any other German land. Laws on the abolition of forced labour and tithes were put through under the leadership of the liberal professors Karl von Rotteck and Friedrich Welcker, whose names were known to everyone through their successful popular writings on questions of world history and public law. Welcker proposed that the organic development of the German Confederation be promoted by summoning a German parliament.

This gave full publicity to a lofty patriotic goal. Anger at the failure of the German Confederation kept the great conception alive in the national consciousness. The question arose whether the complicated system of the federal diet could not be either quickly abolished by revolutionary methods or forced to function immediately and vigorously. The people's movement was particularly strong in the central Rhenish region, around Frankfurt, in Baden's and Bavaria's parts of the Palatinate. Under the influence of Hesse-Kassel's progressive constitution Hanau was becoming a centre for political writers. In Rhenish Bavaria the laws prevented the desired expansion of newspaper and pamphlet publication; instead people made use of banquets and public assemblies. Considerable funds were collected, and the committees of the champions of freedom, who in many cases had become popular because they were persecuted, believed that the time had come to embark on a larger project. Groups representing different shades of political thought were involved: a good Palatine liberal of the upper class, like Schüler, made common cause with the writer Johann Georg August Wirth, who was in sympathy with the German ideals of the *Burschenschaft,* and with Philipp Jakob Siebenpfeiffer, an administrator who held to the republican ideas of the west.

At the suggestion of these leaders the Hambach National Festival was held on May 27, 1832, the anniversary of Bavaria's constitution, so that it appeared like the loyal celebration of a Bavarian patriotic holiday. Even as a mere problem of physical organization, this festival represented an extraordinary achievement. Twenty-five thousand people came together at this meeting (*Thing*). Every kind of vehicle was brought into use for the conveyance of such masses of people as none had seen since the Napoleonic wars. Representatives of liberal organizations of different political hue from central Germany, Alsace, Baden, and Hesse-Darmstadt came together with the people of the Palatinate. A good German spirit shone through the speeches. The great, strong fatherland was what counted. Many demanded that the princes should be set aside, and some advocated a republican Europe based on popular freedom. Social needs were voiced, and the cry of the oppressed working class was already making itself heard. Nevertheless most of the representatives could not decide for immediate revolution, as had been proposed by isolated individuals; they were content simply with the demonstration of the mobilized people, which they believed would have an effect on the diets and the newspapers in a lawful way.

RENEWED PERSECUTION OF POPULAR LEADERS

Prince Metternich was already preparing counter-measures. He reached an agreement with Prussia on six articles, which were submitted to the federal diet after the Hambach Festival and were promptly accepted. The object was to gag parliamentary activities and journalism in Germany once more. The main points were: no qualification of the full sovereignty of the princes, no refusal or conditional grant of funds by the territorial diets, no legislation by the separate states to the prejudice of the Confederation, which retained the right of control. Then came prohibition of political societies, popular meetings, and the German colours of black, red, and gold. Earlier ordinances against the universities were reiterated, and it was proclaimed that suspicious characters should be kept under surveillance, while political refugees and "criminals" were to be extradited, with military assistance if necessary. The most widely known publicists, such as Karl von Rotteck the historian and Johann Georg August Wirth (died 1848), were forbidden to publish periodicals for an interval of five years. In Baden censorship was reintroduced by force. When the western powers raised objections to these decisions of the federal diet, they were sharply rebuffed.

Prince Metternich would have liked to make war on the successful July Revolution in France, but the deplorable military and financial condition of Austria prevented. Prussian attempts to infuse some life into the federal laws for war failed, mainly because Austria was envious and did not wish to see Prussian influence mount by this means. The success of the July Revolution in France and parliamentary reform in England split Europe visibly into a liberal and an anti-liberal camp. Metternich was unable to proceed to open battle in affairs of foreign policy; there could have been no plainer evidence of the weakness of his system. But he was still strong enough to maintain the counter-revolution in Germany. Again German friends of freedom were gravely threatened. Such was the state of affairs that led to the Frankfurt *Putsch,* an ill-prepared enterprise (April 1833) undertaken by a number of students, Poles, and Frankfurt patriots for the purpose of abolishing the federal diet. They succeeded only in capturing the two detachments of Frankfurt military guards, but they could not hold out against the troops that were called up against them. With malice aforethought the authorities had failed to prevent the outbreak. Now further measures were possible. A central investigating commission was set up again. It consisted of judges who, in contrast to earlier times, could arrange only for investigations in the individual states. They were active until 1842, handling about eighteen hundred cases. Up to 1836 the Supreme Court (*Kammergericht*) in Berlin alone condemned two hundred and four students, among them some who had participated in the Hambach Festival. The commission of investigation communicated the data it gathered to its representatives in foreign countries, so that a watch could easily be kept on political refugees.

Many small states regarded the proceedings of the federal diet as most inconvenient, but who could defend himself against the omnipotence of an anonymous authority that was a cloak for Metternich's knowledge and will? The Hambach Festival had been in effect a motley political Walpurgis night; historically it ranks somewhere between the Wartburg Festival and the later assembly in the Church of St. Paul in Frankfurt. The enthusiasm, boldness, and high hopes raised by the demonstration in Hambach were now followed with fatal speed by harsh suppression. But exactly because of the brute force of this suppression and the full impact of state power the German movement for freedom was consolidated and alerted, and harmless dreamers acquired the technique of successful conspiracy.

Metternich intended to maintain his position at least in central Europe. New conferences of ministers in Vienna concluded with a secret protocol of sixty articles. This was Metternich's German program, of which his contemporaries remained ignorant until ten years later. The fight was against the "party" that tried to obtain constitutions by specious legal methods and claimed executive power by reason of its position in the diets, to the menaced destruction of monarchical power. A federal court of arbitration was set up to settle quarrels between princes and diets; it never had any significance. Objections from the diets were to be disregarded; if these bodies did not accept decisions of the federal diet, they were to be dissolved; they were no longer to have the right to decide on the budget. For soldiers to take an oath to a constitution was now illegal. Censorship was tightened up; the number of daily newspapers was cut down. Matriculations at the universities were supervised; secret societies were again prohibited; lecturers were to exercise their profession subject to ministerial approval and recall. This declaration of war by Metternich against the "anti-monarchical faction"—it is reminiscent of the deliberate cruelty of the Counter-Reformation—remained in force in Germany until 1848.

Federal law now authorized persecution of every description. German champions of freedom were exposed to surveillance, espionage, and sudden arrest. Denunciation and false testimony were the order of the day, and hundreds of people, many wholly innocent, suffered the gravest injury to health, reputation, personal happiness, and advancement. Sovereigns had to accept the Confederation's interference in sentences and pardons. University teachers lost their positions without notice and without compensation. Journeymen, who from the point of view of the authorities were an especially dangerous lot, were annoyed by the police at every step; when their trade took them to foreign parts infected with revolution they were closely watched, and a protracted stay in any suspicious place put them permanently under a cloud. Many of these workers resorted to forged papers; it was good sport to outsmart the shrewd officials.

POLITICAL PARTIES BEGIN TO TAKE FORM

Under the impact of the July Revolution and of all the events connected with it, political party groups began to shape themselves in Germany for the first time. In line with the precedents of German history, this process arose from two impulses. The first was the tradition of German spiritual culture. From the three main currents of the Storm and Stress, classicism, and romanticism were derived the three basic attitudes, social-revolutionary, liberal, and conservative. A fourth party that was highly characteristic, the clerical or Catholic, had its origins in both the liberal and the conservative worlds of thought. Forceful incentives came to it from romanticism, but the principles of freedom were applied to the unfolding of clerical interests.

The second deciding factor for the growth of German parties was the shifting among the social classes, a process that had become very evident after the July Revolution. Up to that time the rural and urban middle class had been strongest numerically; it represented the very heart of the German population. Most of the great masters of German art and thought came from the middle class. At its core were the farmer, who was both peasant and citizen, the master craftsman, the manufacturer, the innkeeper, the tradesman, the official, the pastor and the teacher, the lawyer and the doctor. The circumspect man of the middle class was characterized by economic reliability and independence. He wanted to make an honourable living and to secure reasonable advancement in his chosen field. There was something substantial about him; he was respected; and he wanted all this to remain as it was.

Above itself the middle class saw the feudal nobility and the supplemental military, court, and administrative nobility. It was a caste apparently unshaken, accustomed to rule; they were criticized, but reverenced and frequently envied. Graciously, at their discretion, they elevated the most gifted and adaptable members of the middle class to their own level. Below itself the middle class saw the layer of the economically dependent: auxiliary rural workers of different sorts, shopmen, servants, journeymen. The essential characteristic of

394

PEDIGREE OF PARTY TRENDS IN GERMANY

STORM AND STRESS

Rationalism
Enlightened radicalism
Critical attitude toward all convention and tradition
Ideas of 1789
Social reform or destructive revolution?
Terrorism

CLASSICISM

Humanitarianism
Cosmopolitanism
World citizenship
Confidence in education
Tolerance
Anti-militarism
Historical and philosophical liberalism
Constitutionalism
Evolution, free trade

ROMANTICISM

Teutonism, Pan-Germanism, nationalism
Revival of historical traditions
"Organic" development
Irrationalism
Christianity, pietism
Old-Prussian Junkerism
Statism, authoritarianism
Expansion, protectionism
Anti-Semitism
Power politics

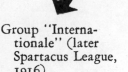

Group "Internationale" (later Spartacus League, 1916)
German Communist Party (1918)

Social Democratic Party (1869)
Revisionists (1891)
Independent Social Democrats (1916–17)
Social Democracy reunified (1922)

Republicans and early Socialists (1848)
Radical liberals (1848)
German Progressive Party (1861)
Secession (1880)
German People's Party (1868)
Deutsch-Freisinnige Partei (1884)
Freisinnige Volks-Partei (1894)
National Social Union (1896)
Progressive People's Party (1910)
Democratic Party (Deutsche Demokratische Partei, 1918)
German State Party (Staatspartei, 1930)

Old liberals (1848)
Conservative Liberals (1858)
National Liberals (1866)
German People's Party (1918)

Centre Party (Clericals; first group, 1851; program, 1861; party, 1871; reorganized, 1918)
Bavarian People's Party (separatist movement, 1918)
Christian Social Party (Austria)

Old conservatives (1848)
Moderate Conservatives (Wochenblatt group, 1851)
Free Conservatives (1866)
German Conservatives (1876)
Anti–Semitic movement (Stöcker, 1878; Christian Social group, 1895)
League of Agriculturists (Bund der Landwirte, 1893)
German Nationalists (German National People's Party, 1918)
Christian (Protestant) Social National Service (1929)
Volkskonservative (1931)

National Socialist Party (1920; former German Worker's Party of 1919)

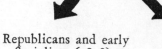

Strongest ideologic trend of the left combines with strongest ideologic trend of the right (Socialism with Nationalism)

Deutsch-Völkische Freiheit-spartei (1922)

National Socialist German Workers' Party (1923)

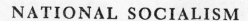

STORM AND STRESS

CLASSICISM

ROMANTICISM

NATIONAL SOCIALISM

this lower layer was that it lacked the means to rise to the middle class, for which it was necessary not only to do something and to know something, but also to have something. By thrift, by marriage, or by scholarships or other such aids, many did ascend into the middle class. Here and there, it is true, one was found to preach an embattled class-consciousness. The Storm and Stress first struck out toward it even before the French Revolution, in a time of social rigidity, but of widely diffused new cultural values; this tension was of the kind that always and everywhere promotes ideas of social revolution. Very little of it could still be detected during the restoration period. Now a new class was forming in Germany, and this subjected the whole social hierarchy to uncontrollable commotion.

A patrician class arose, by virtue of money and of titles. The growing element of academic dignitaries, issuing from the middle class, could no longer be absorbed by the feudal upper class. The princes and their governments had need of this element to organize their new administrations. Government was unthinkable without this patrician officialdom, and the feudal aristocracy was glad to accept intelligent help from this source as long as the best and most lucrative positions were reserved for its own members.

Similar conditions prevailed among the judiciary and the military profession. A patrician class with titles and uniforms or official robes came into being simultaneously with other new callings springing from the middle class: wholesale merchants interested in speculation; the new industrialists and bankers who organized production and commerce on a capitalistic basis, mobilized property and made it fluid and speculative, and thus came to occupy a position of power in the social structure. After the July Revolution the first of the new money patricians appeared prominently in Germany—in the Rhineland and in central Germany. They liked an aristocratic way of life, and many of them penetrated into the aristocracy; they mixed freely with the patricians of title. In the Germany of that time the class struggle manifested itself mostly within this or that layer; the aim was to rise and to adapt oneself to a better manner of living. For the middle class this new development meant the beginning of a disintegration that could not be arrested. The most gifted members of this class struggled upward; the less favoured sank and merged into the serving class. Dependency increased; employees increased in numbers. The struggle for a livelihood grew more acute, and anyone who could not hold his own became proletarianized. Industrial entrepreneurs required many employees, and their profits swelled in inverse proportion to the poor wages they paid.

What did the ideals of culture and the class motive have to do with the appearance of parties? The position taken toward the heritage of the great French Revolution, transmuted by classicism into the nobler form of German liberalism, remained determinative. The anti-liberal elements were Prussian Junkerdom, agrarian feudalism in Austria, and Metternich's police state, along with all who served it and who had interests of their own wrapped up in it. Corresponding strata existed everywhere among the small states. By and large the representatives of a more or less kindly absolutism did not like to rack their brains over the theoretical foundation of their system. They were in power, and they wanted to remain in power. The first deliberately conservative party group was formed in Prussia under the influence of the philosopher Georg Friedrich Wilhelm Hegel. The religious, patriotic views of the Christian-Germanic circle of the period of the Wars of Liberation entered into the anti-liberal, anti-revolutionary ideas of Friedrich Julius Stahl, who taught public law at the University of Berlin. Stahl, a Bavarian of Jewish origin, shrewdly and untiringly whittled out the legal basis for Prussian reaction. Crown Prince Frederick William belonged to these circles. For some time the historian Leopold von Ranke edited a journal in dignified advocacy of authoritarian bonds and a corporative hierarchy of rank. The political weekly of the club of the Wilhelmstrasse expressed itself with less restraint. Hengstenberg's church journal was devoted to the impassioned defence of orthodox Protestantism against liberal criticism.

Old-time Lutheranism, with its contemplative disposition, had been loyal to the state. Now the magisterial character of Protestantism in Prussia was given a special stamp. On the occasion of the tercentenary of the Reformation the King of Prussia effected a consolidation of the Lutheran and the German Reformed churches (1817). This "Union" found small acclaim outside of Prussia. It minimized the genuinely religious factor and turned Protestantism, which was just now attaining greater inner strength, over to an autocratic government, to the prejudice of an independent-minded church. Throne and altar co-operated more and more closely in Prussia; they were in harmony, for the Prussian state church could hardly gird against the government. This Prussian variant of Protestantism accepted many characteristics from Prussian discipline and arrogant harshness, while in return the orthodox gave of their smooth self-righteousness. Rarely had true Christianity been so misunderstood and so abused as in the circles of the conservative party that was being evolved in Prussia. This state church system did indeed have the power to harness Prussian patricians of title to the conservative interests, but it found the undertaking difficult. The cultured liberalism of the high officials and judges resisted with a good deal of energy. The moneyed patricians were easier to approach through their economic interests. This class had every reason to object to being branded as revolutionary; yet it persistently defended reasonable progress and free competition against reactionary interests and advocated a development that would make sense historically.

Liberalism with a basis in history was perhaps best represented by the person and the work of the university professor Friedrich Christoph Dahlmann (died 1860), who was at that time in the front rank as historian and politician. In his principal book, *Politics,* he laid the foundation for German constitutionalism. Hereditary monarchy, ministerial responsibility, the two-chamber system, abolition of censorship, adjustment of state interests to religious freedom — these were the main features of his moderate and always flexible doctrine, which was drawn from practical experience and scholarly knowledge. Historical liberalism took over the German national position of the *Burschenschaft* and allied movements and founded the party of progressive imperial patriotism (*Reichspatriotismus*) as contrasted with the particularism of Austria, Prussia, Bavaria, and elsewhere, which was coloured by the small-scale nationalism of the individual state. The patricians and the upper middle class, as classes, were the most open to these ideas that put trust in reform. But it was just the concept of reform that split the liberals, and this split along party lines furthered the disintegration of the middle class.

After the experiences of the July Revolution in Germany the great mass of the middle class, under the stress of economic effort, had ceased to believe in the possibility of reform. It had lost hope that those in responsible positions would see the light — still more that,

397

even if they did see it, they could bring to bear the goodwill and the ability necessary for the achievement of adequate reform. Spokesmen of this school pointed to revolution as the only possible way; above all they assailed the attitude of the German great powers. Though Dahlmann and that excellent Swabian, Paul Pfizer, fastened their hopes to Prussia, while the historian G. W. Pertz was the first to appreciate the Prussian Customs Union, a violent hatred of Prussia was widely expressed in southern and western Germany. The former imperial cities became centres of an ardent republicanism that preserved the memories of the Hambach Festival; Hambach hats and Hambach beards testified to a state of mind steadfastly bent on radical reconstruction. The great mass of the oppressed, enslaved by hopeless working conditions, were responsive to these trends. The *Hessische Landbote* of the gifted poet Georg Buecher revived social-revolutionary moods of the Storm and Stress. But soon diverse tendencies became apparent even within the parties that were fundamentally revolutionary.

Historical liberalism was confronted with dogmatic liberalism, whose spokesman was Ludwig Börne (died 1837), a Frankfurt Jew highly gifted as a writer; he was a discriminating dramatic critic and a staunch believer in freedom. He and many others regarded the Paris of the July Revolution as the great centre of the collective European movement for freedom, with its goal of liberating all oppressed peoples of Europe and establishing a universal league of youthful states. Representatives of Young Germany now stood beside champions of Young Poland and Young Italy. They, too, were impotent "knights of the spirit," who, in accordance with old German traditions, first fought with their pens the great battle that was looming. Readers of Börne and Heine, of Laube and Gutzkow, of Mundt and Wienbarg, learned from these men that the existing crisis in Germany could only be resolved by building anew from the ground up. Their mockery of German provincialism and credulity, of educational dead weight and prejudices that had taken root, of boot-licking and professional envy, of all this entrenched and even cherished German Philistinism, sprang from honest anger, from a deep love of what was best and most genuine in the German past, from a holy faith in the German revolution of the future, in the political, spiritual, moral, and social revolution of Germany, as a link in the collective European revolution.

The German poet Heinrich Heine, a Jew born in Düsseldorf, cannot be included in the Young German group without some reservation. His real achievement and his claim to immortality belong to a different plane. As a lyric poet he ranks with Goethe and Hölderlin, the Swabian. As a champion of truth and of liberty he became a supremely European figure. Heine's political writings and poems served that great dream of Young Germany in which, in his characteristic way, he both believed and did not believe.

The Teutonist writer Wolfgang Menzel denounced the literary products of Young Germany as dangerous to church, state, and morals, and the federal diet decided to prevent their circulation. Between the young and the old Germany there could be nothing but war.

POLITICAL WRITERS AND POETS

The spirit of the times was shaped by the cities and their attitude of opposition. Urban life gave rise to a new feeling toward the state and society—a feeling that pictured a community of the future modelled on a well-conditioned city, just as the princes and the nobles conceived of the state as a manor, while proletarians saw it as a factory. The struggle for the freedom of the printed and the written word was mainly an urban concern. The police could suppress newspapers, ban novels, and confiscate pamphlets. But people as cultivated and as well versed in literature as the Germans of the cities had become could always find new ways to speak their mind and to express their will to reshape prevailing conditions.

The writers occupied the foreground in the people's will and feeling. Usually the man of letters came from the dwindling middle class. He lived in independence in the garret of one of the new apartment houses, visited the salons of wealthy patrons, and forgathered with kindred spirits in the back rooms of wineshops. The growing cities, with their new human types, their misery, and their gipsy romanticism, occupied the alert minds of these men and women, to whom even everyday affairs were inexhaustible problems for their pens—those accomplished pens that had the double task

of solving eternal problems and earning the day's bread. Not many
went to live in the country, like Levin Schücking the Westphalian
and Berthold Auerbach the Swabian Jew, only to discover even there
the conflicts and cares of the great struggle. Historical novels and
dramas concerned themselves by preference with urban, political, and
social matters. Alongside of eccentrics and recluses, types that were
bound to crop up again and again among a people as mature as the
Germans, a new group of writers now appeared. This consisted of
lyric poets who dealt largely with political subjects and knew how
to cast in unforgettable form the attack on the reaction.

Characteristically it was an Austrian count of a very old family
who first exposed Metternich's system. This was Count Anton
Auersperg, who wrote under the pen-name of Anastasius Grün as a
true friend of the people, an honest and noble personality, a good,
manly German Austrian. He affirmed the new era of labour, of the
masses, even of technics, without reservation. August Heinrich Hoffmann von Fallersleben, on the other hand, was a professor of literature whom the Prussian police state had driven from the lecture plat-
form and who now reciprocated this courtesy with countless melo-
dious verses. He was an itinerant scholar, witty and blunt, cheerful,
and unsurpassable in the heart-warming popular tone. Ferdinand
Freiligrath was a modest employee of the rising class of enterprising
merchants; he was well acquainted with the real world of capitalistic
initiative, and he could feel no fondness for it. This passionate poet
with an amazing command of phrase developed into an ardent republican. He co-operated with the early socialists, prophesied the
awakening of even Russia to freedom, and confessed his faith in the
world mission of America. In him the revolutionary spirit of 1848
found its mightiest herald. But the most gifted among the German
political poets was the Swabian Georg Herwegh, who is almost on a
par with Heine. With eloquent forcefulness that moved all the youth
he declared war on tyrants and Philistines—the struggle of the new
popular party for a great, strong, immortal Germany, for a mighty
republic that, radiating from the centre of Europe, would at last give
this long-suppressed nation the influence intended for it by destiny,
the prestige and world position that were its due. The national quality of German republicanism had a pronounced revolutionary char-

acter. This younger generation knew enough not to expect anything at all any more from the German princes.

LIBERALISM AND DEMOCRACY

The relation of liberalism to democracy in Germany requires some fundamental explanations. Thought and culture predominate in liberalism; in democracy, political convictions and the effort to mould the state. Before the March Revolution of 1848 there was a very broad spread of liberalism in Germany. It might even be said that in the period between 1830 and 1880 no group of any great importance could avoid the sphere of liberal thought. There were a liberalism for princes and a liberalism for officials; there were class liberals and rational liberals, conservative liberals as well as radical liberals. Liberalism occupied so important a place in the life of the nation that everyone had either to make common cause with it in some way or other or to invent an entirely new ideology to justify his rejecting it. This second alternative was chosen by feudal conservatives on the one hand and by socialists and communists on the other. Liberalism came forward as a dominant attitude, with a basis in history and philosophy, that aimed at assuring the individual of his legal and active chances in the face of state and society, groups and vested interests. Nevertheless liberalism employed the slogans and the language of the people; it used simple and striking arguments, for it had to win the uneducated or the half-educated over to convictions that were based on definite knowledge and that served distinct bourgeois class interests. Liberalism deliberately reduced its ideas to the simplest terms. All other parties were to imitate it only too readily in this respect. One cannot say that liberalism leaned more to the right and democracy more to the left; that would be an over-simplification. Their views overlapped. There was a liberalism that inclined leftward and there was a democracy bent on preserving the traditional structure of state and society.

The essential characteristic of democracy was its denial of autocracy. The lines were drawn in this way internationally. At that time opposite poles were represented by the United States of America and Czar Nicholas of Russia. Modern democracy, which has nothing but a name in common with anything in antiquity, has its roots in

401

Christianity, in natural science, and in natural law. The equality of all men before God, the equality of the conditions of life given them by nature, the equality of their forms of social existence before the law—these were convictions held by all citizens of the coming world order as a result of the English, the French, and the American revolutions; unconditional convictions constituting a modern secular religion. The Declaration of Independence of the United States and the French Declaration of the Rights of Man and of the Citizen were regarded as the first striking and triumphant manifestations of the democratic spirit. The more victims of political persecution and economic oppression emigrated from Germany to America, the warmer became German interest in the foundations of American freedom and the more eagerly German specialists in public law and German writers studied the American Constitution, which was bound to be of the greatest significance for the future of Germany, if only because of its federal character.

The ideas of democracy echoed over all the countries of Europe. As previously with absolutism and feudalism, they were altered and adapted to local conditions. In Germany too, even as early as the Storm and Stress, there was a characteristically German democracy. It sprang up along the Rhine and the Main, in Swabia and Lower Saxony, and combined with the old Germanic spirit of fellowship that was still alive there. Anti-democratic were the princes, with their followers, and especially all of eastern colonial Germany with the exception of the progressive strata of the growing cities. The struggle for a democratic way of life sharpened the contrast between the older parts of the country and colonial Germany. Neither the France nor the England of that time was dominated by democratic institutions; these western powers too were still in the throes of gradually adapting the ideal of popular sovereignty to their practical needs, and the Germans watched the process with the liveliest sympathy. The idea of universal suffrage had something terrifying about it for the majority of good liberals; for a long time this point was to mark a parting of the ways.

Universal conscription had put weapons into the hands of even the most modest individual; the elementary schools had spread the minimum of education required for independent thinking and self-direction; newspapers and associations had aroused and shaped the political will. All of these measures had been necessary and had proved effective for fighting the Napoleonic dictatorship. And now was active participation in public affairs to be denied or restricted for the masses who had been stirred up and set in motion by democracy? Dynasties, the military, officialdom, and the church resisted the democratic conception of the state and were criticized accordingly. Many representatives of the old authorities tried to help themselves by concessions to historical liberalism. They identified themselves with its faith in reform and co-operated with it in developing a program of mild concessions that promised to meet specific German requirements. All this was extremely significant. An anti-democratic front was built up that finally forced democratic thought into revolutionary channels and founded the alliance of dogmatic liberalism with the democratic ideology. And so it came about that in Germany everything democratic smacked of radicalism, of foreignness, and of overturn. In many other countries the democratic view of the state gradually came to coincide with the affirmation of the social structure and of the national spirit. But in Germany the selfishness of the old political powers and the credulity of the patricians of money and of title blocked any corresponding process.

SOCIALISM AND COMMUNISM

Still another factor shaped the situation: the beginnings of socialist and communist agitation in Germany. The first great crisis in German industry occurred after 1840. The middle class was changing and was losing its self-reliance and independence, though for a time it was still able to keep its position sociologically. The part of the middle class that was in decline merged with the class of dependents to form a stratum of wage earners, who, so far as they became factory hands, led a poverty-stricken proletarian existence. Even a working day of twelve to fourteen hours brought the merest pittance. Housing and food as a rule were utterly insufficient. Every industrial crisis handed over a fourth or even a third of these workers to relief. The misery of these times is characterized by reduced living standards, fewer marriages and births, more deaths, more emigration, more crime. Now there were German proletarians, and German social contrasts became sharper from year to year. Was there already a German proletariat? The class struggle was still essentially a struggle to rise from below to above. The highest class, which used its social exclusiveness to achieve its political and economic goals, was the feudal aristocracy. Occupational associations, of merchants, employees, farmers, teachers, engineers, were still to come. There were charitable funds for journeymen; according to the Prussian industrial regulations of 1845 factory hands were also to be covered by them, but it was still nothing but organized charity.

Many well-meaning members of the ruling classes racked their brains for the causes of pauperism. There was no lack of suggestions for reform. Harkort, a sterling Westphalian who had practical experience in these matters, was the first to advocate the prohibition of child labour, maximum working hours, suitable housing and food. The teachings of the early French socialists, Saint-Simon, Fourier, and Cabet, were first introduced to Germany through the novels of Young Germany. Then German scholars took up the question; human society, they said, is more important than state constitutions, and equitable distribution of goods is more important than political rights. The idea of ethical progress had been transferred to the political plane, and now it spread to the structure of society, with a more and more temporal, mundane emphasis. Monarchy or republic, suffrage equal or based on class status, autocracy or democracy — all these questions dwindled in importance in the face of the social revolution that was being kindled.

Social revolutionary trends first came up in the Storm and Stress movement, as we have noted. The theme was again sounded in the political and literary writings of the 1830's. The word "socialist" was coined in Germany in 1840. Wilhelm Weitling, a Magdeburg journeyman tailor, was the first to apply socialistic and communistic convictions to political ends. A warm-hearted, sensitive being, he was the illegitimate son of a French officer and a poor girl of Thuringia. In Paris he became a member of the Society of the Just, and from that time on he roamed through Switzerland and Germany as an apostle of communism. He founded societies and published pamphlets and was consistently persecuted by the authorities, who became more and more watchful of his activities. They used *agents provocateurs* against him, confiscated his writings, and arrested his followers.

Socialist and communist teachings found more adherents in the

Rhineland and in Westphalia than in Berlin. Here Karl Grün became known through a number of pamphlets. Moses Hess was probably the first pure communist in Germany. His nickname of "communist rabbi" indicates the vagueness of his illusions, coloured with Messianic fervour. Young Friedrich Engels soon came to the front. He sprang from an old German family of wealthy manufacturers in Barmen—a vigorous and stormy fighter and the author of a sensational book on the condition of the working classes in England. He demonstrated that in this England, the land that was a model of liberal ideology, there was nevertheless so much filth, so much exploitation, so much misery; that the comfort of the upper middle class was bought at such a price. Engels became the active friend and helper of Karl Marx.

The child of a rabbinical family in Trier, Marx began his career as a critic of social conditions on the *Rhenish Gazette* and then went to Paris, where he received the strong impressions that he welded into a system of world historical effect in his very characteristic but equally intolerant and merciless way. Engels always collaborated actively in this creation; he saw to it that the academic, deep-delving dogmatism of Marx was broken down into an inflammatory slogan, a rousing battle-cry, a faith that embraced all mankind, and a decisive will to reorganization by way of revolution. In 1847 the older secret societies were merged into one Communist League. Marx and Engels harshly rejected all rivals and critics and with complete self-confidence assumed the leadership of the movement. Their form of communism was anti-liberal as well as anti-democratic. Autocracy was outstripped in autocratic dogmatism by this, its latest antithesis. Dictatorship, terrorism, class struggle, the annihilation of all that was traditional—these were the principles of the Communist Manifesto, published by Marx and Engels just before the outbreak of the Revolution of 1848. It was a declaration of war on bourgeois society and on its political state, which in Germany was indeed still in the making. The sharp opposition of workers and bourgeoisie corresponded more closely to the advanced relationships that prevailed among the powers to the west than to circumstances in Germany. But the terse, clear argument, the dialectic elegance, and the weight of propaganda in the Manifesto make it a great document for German history too.

405

The division between socialism and communism now became complete and unmistakable. Socialism was ethical; it wanted to improve the world and to develop mankind. In this it resembled the optimism of dogmatic liberalism, though it adhered to a different theory of property, in spite of which the basic principles of democracy could probably be very useful in achieving socialistic goals. The alliance of socialism and democracy was being prepared; it was symbolized in the term "social democracy," first used in France and frequently heard in Germany during the Revolution of 1848. Historical liberalism that was willing to deal with the old powers in Germany was forced more and more toward the right through this development. Opposition to democracy grew more stubborn as democracy became suspect for aiding and abetting socialism. Since the ruling classes were obviously not amenable to reason, the idea of revolution gained ground in Germany. But concerning the aims of revolution there was complete disagreement, and for this reason it failed.

THE COUP D'ÉTAT IN HANOVER (1837)

The man of destiny of the Revolution of 1848 and indeed of the whole epoch was King Frederick William IV of Prussia. Immediately before his long-awaited accession to the throne two events occurred that proved a special spur to the formation of parties that was beginning in Germany. The first affected, not Prussia herself, but a state with whose fate and future Prussian politics were closely connected—Hanover. When Queen Victoria ascended the British throne the long personal union between Great Britain and Hanover came to an end, and English politics was freed of the tedious task of defending the dynastic interests of the English royal family on the Continent. The independent Kingdom of Hanover indicated with a certain degree of obstinacy that London could not prescribe for her. She rather lucklessly attempted a policy that relied on Austria and was directed against Prussia, which surrounded her territory. As far as internal policy was concerned, a constitution that was the well-planned, mature work of official moderate liberalism had been in force since 1833. It left many hopes unfulfilled, but the most important thing, a unified financial administration, seemed guaranteed.

The new King of Hanover, Duke Ernest Augustus of Cumberland, one of Queen Victoria's uncles, was an extreme Tory, bold and blunt, relentless, violent, high-handed, utterly oblivious of the opinions and the welfare of those about him. He had denounced the constitution of 1833 even while he was heir to the throne; now that he was King he did not hold himself to be bound by it, and he declared it invalid. He called a new diet and had the old constitution of 1819 revived with some amendments. Dissatisfaction reached the pitch of complaints to the federal diet and refusal to pay taxes. The breach of Hanover's constitution became a German and even a European event. Were the whims, the tyranny, the greed of a foreign-born potentate to shake a land that was more law-abiding than almost any other in Germany? Was a constitution pronouncedly conservative-liberal in character not to be safe from attack by an autocratic King by the grace of God, who, to make matters worse, talked about his conscience while he broke the law?

Seven professors in Göttingen objected to the King's proceedings. They were immediately discharged and had to leave the country without delay. The next day all Germany knew the names of these martyrs to the law. The most famous among them were the historian Dahlmann, G. G. Gervinus, whose subject was the history of literature, and the philologists and fairy-tale collectors Jakob and Wilhelm Grimm. But still, among all the state servants in the kingdom, among all the teachers of the famous Georgia Augusta University, there were only seven to jeopardize their own existence and that of their families for the sake of justice. Only the faculties of law and philosophy were represented, and besides, all but one of the seven were foreigners—not Hanoverians born. This act had a tremendous effect. Ever since the time of the Enlightenment, Germany, with its zeal for education, had regarded the university professor as a particularly trustworthy guide to a better future. Professors had worked effectively in the south German diets, in the *Burschenschaft* movement, and in political writing after the July Revolution. And now leaders of this class had shown that they could also act and suffer for a sacred conviction. They were not merely respected but idolized. There was a general feeling that the German university was destined to achieve freedom for the nation through the freedom of the spirit.

Historical liberalism and the patricians of title could find no better leaders than professors. But this faith in the professor was quickly shaken by the experiences of 1848.

THE FIRST KULTURKAMPF

The second event that occurred immediately before King Frederick William IV ascended the throne was an ecclesiastical dissension in Köln. A deep religious need was felt after the Wars of Liberation. German philosophy occupied the upper stratum of the cultured and gave them what they wanted. But the intellectual middle class, the common people, whose awareness had increased through education and economic development, either turned to the popular, almost religious belief in political progress or once more called for the comfort and support of the Christian church. The scientific spirit now seized on the traditional teachings of Christianity and treated them as a subject for critical investigation. A book such as the *Life of Christ* by the Swabian theologian David Friedrich Strauss (died 1874) or the sceptical and materialistic writings of Ludwig Feuerbach (died 1872) challenged the devout to self-defence and even counter-attack. Very few realized that independent investigation and the true inner faith of Christianity were not at all mutually exclusive, but activities on entirely different levels of the spirit—that they complemented each other if the underlying attitude and the work were wholly pure and fine. Discussion about the truth and value of Christianity excited and divided opinion and encouraged the formation of parties. The Germans are a religious people; questions of fundamental attitudes toward the world decided their stand on temporal matters both before and after the Reformation. Now all these tensions made themselves fully felt again—even more sharply, indeed, as a result of the spiritual and bodily needs of a mass of people that was growing larger and larger and striving toward new ways of life. It was natural that the Protestant who was a conservative should make common cause with orthodoxy and regard his fight against liberalism as a fight against unbelief also—unbelief or something worse: a half-way variety of Christianity whose adherents were Christians only in name.

The Roman church, on the other hand, was quickened with new life during the period of the Restoration, and this had far-reaching consequences. The re-established Jesuit Order laid stress on papal universalism; it stifled all conciliatory trends toward a national church. In 1815 the curia vainly demanded the restoration of all ecclesiastical principalities in Germany. The future demonstrated that Catholic interests had more favourable prospects without these temporal possessions. There was no concordat of the curia with the German Confederation as such. The Vatican found it more profitable to negotiate with individual states and thereby to satisfy their greed for sovereignty. The south German states knew enough of Catholic affairs to be very cautious notwithstanding. They laid claim to influence over the education of priests, and they held the rulings of bishops and popes to be subject to their approval; they maintained this influence in spite of protests from the Vatican.

Prussia was in a much more difficult position. Her high officials, so competent as a rule, failed in connection with clerical problems. In the Rhineland and in Westphalia there was a Prussian population, of Catholic faith, highly developed intellectually and economically; it regarded the Berlin government with suspicion and arrogance. Rhenish humour and Westphalian law-abiding obstinacy made things hard for the stiff old Prussian officials, accustomed to using a harsh tone of command. The historical, economic, and psychological antagonisms became strongly marked and clear to everyone in connection with ecclesiastical questions.

Two problems were in the foreground. In Bonn a Catholic theologian, Professor Georg Hermes (died 1831), stood for a dignified, scholarly attitude of inquiry, such as the Jesuits found disquieting. His school of thought—Hermesianism—became influential, to the Vatican's displeasure. The question of mixed marriages struck deeper into practical life. According to Prussian law the children followed the religion of the father. The Catholic church, however, insisted that they should be brought up as Catholics; the Council of Trent had even forbidden mixed marriages on principle. Count Ferdinand Augustus von Spiegel, the mild Archbishop of Köln, hit on a tolerable compromise, but his successor, the stubborn Westphalian Baron Clemens Augustus von Droste-Vischering, would not commit himself to it. He made short work of the Hermesianists by forbidding students to attend their lectures, and he insisted on unlimited pledges as to the education of children of mixed marriages.

409

The Prussian government replied to these measures by stern action: the Archbishop was taken to the fortress of Minden as a prisoner. Negotiations in Rome were of no avail. Ecclesiastical strife also spread toward the east. The Archbishop of Posen was set aside and sentenced to confinement in a fortress. The Prince Bishop of Breslau, who endorsed the stand the government had taken, was reprimanded by the Vatican; he resigned his office and later went over to the evangelical church. The effect of these events was tremendous.

Clericalism everywhere in Germany experienced a mighty impetus, heightened, as was to be expected, by the persecutions of this first *Kulturkampf*. Reaction made itself felt everywhere, especially in Bavaria and Austria. Prussia made a bad bargain by finally giving in to the curia on all essential points. A special Catholic department was established in the Prussian Ministry of Ecclesiastical Affairs and Public Instruction (*Kultusministerium*); it was run by Catholic officials. This was an extraordinary concession, wholly without precedent. The general consequences were significant. Prussia had forfeited a good deal of regard and trust in Catholic Germany. The mass of the Catholic population harped on the antagonism already aroused against the Prussian state and intensified it into a political opposition. There was a tendency to support all party activities that were directed against Prussian bureaucracy and militarism; sympathy was felt for Austria and southern Germany, and constitutional security against autocratic interference was demanded for Catholic interests. The prerequisites for a Catholic party were supplied.

FREDERICK WILLIAM IV (1840–61)

The Prussian state had thus failed to reconcile itself with the old, indigenous German elements in a very important province of life. Here lay the problem of the future: Prussia was a Little Germany in the same sense as Austria was a Little Europe. In one way or another Prussia was connected with all the German stocks except the Bavarian. Prussia had again become a great power by associating herself with the ideas of German unity and freedom. It was Prince Metternich's master stroke that for a generation he prevented Prussia from making this association fruitful. Would the new King, Frederick William IV, be able to bring Germany and Prussia together again?

Frederick William IV was psychopathic. He was abnormally normal; his exuberant personality radiated stimulating suggestions, but politically his touch was fatal as a rule. Everything about practical life and everyday affairs bored him. He lived on the glittering vision of the world and of history supplied by the romantic scholarship of his day. Accordingly he regarded the French Revolution as an apocalyptic whore, loathsome both because of its democracy and because of its terrorism. He wanted to set up against this horror something indigenous, sprung of the people—something Christian and at the same time Germanic. Just what it was to be, the King did not know, but he held to his principles all the more obstinately and expatiated on them in speeches and written effusions. His amateurishness revelled in rhetoric and in false starts; he lacked the seriousness, concentration, and composure necessary for creative work. His brilliance overwhelmed his companions with admiration. He relished his position by the grace of God as proof positive of personal superiority. He was sensitive, had good taste, and encouraged artists and scholars as long as they fell in with his principles; naturally he passed over the representatives of advanced thought. The King was devout and even bigoted in his anxious adherence to the prescribed creed; he eagerly busied himself as a church reformer, to whom Protestantism always remained unfortunately foreign. He was no militarist. Conflicts occasioned by foreign policy alarmed and confused him. What he dreamed of was a renewed Holy Alliance, the co-operation of all good men, a universal Europe. In this Christian and peaceful Europe a powerful Germany was to revive the emperorship of the Habsburgs and thus assure the world itself of peace. All this contradicted not only the new forces of the times, liberalism and democracy, but also Prussian traditions. Frederick the Great would have found Prussia's part as German military leader in a renewed Holy Empire rather on the modest side. It was doubtful whether the Austrian imperial state and the petty German princes would be willing to recognize Prussia's claim to even this function.

THE UNITED DIET IN PRUSSIA (1847)

The question of the constitution was the most difficult problem inherited by King Frederick William IV. He had, of course, no thought of a written constitution in the western sense. But to com-

411

bine the provincial diets in a United Diet struck the King as a brilliant solution, in spite of the urgent warnings of Metternich, of Czar Nicholas, and of his own brother Prince William, the heir to his throne. The opposition was insistent—from the Rhineland in a more collective German spirit, but from East Prussia in one that was more specifically Prussian, saturated with the ideas of Kant and Stein; in East Prussia public opinion could be expressed more freely and independently than within the territory of the German Confederation. There were in Prussia notorious cases of suppression of freedom of instruction and of public opinion. Even the sister-in-law of the Prussian Minister of Justice, the famous writer Bettina von Arnim, was sentenced to two months' imprisonment in 1847. This admirable woman had had the works of her husband, the poet Achim von Arnim, published at her own expense and had sold them without the help of bookdealers. Bettina felt warm interest in a question that, as a scandal for Prussia, was occupying the attention of Europe.

This question concerned the miserable condition of the Silesian weavers. Want had been well known among these people from of old. As early as 1793 the weavers had rioted. A destitute class of workers in a cottage industry, they were completely dependent on a form of incipient capitalistic enterprise. As a consequence of closing markets a severe economic crisis occurred in 1842. Entrepreneurs depressed wages as much as they pleased in view of the excess of labour; this finally led to disturbances, and the army took hold. As usual there were many innocent victims. The setting up of factories and the conversion of home workers into factory hands was the only effective salvation for the unfortunate weavers. Strikes in the Rhineland, famines in the eastern provinces, and clashes between soldiers and civilians in Köln and in Königsberg strengthened the impression that antagonisms were becoming sharper in Prussia too, and that revolution would find fertile soil here.

Polish strivings for liberation ended in sensational proceedings in Berlin against the Poles. The principal conspirators were given heavy sentences, but the outbreak of the revolution prevented their being carried out. Public opinion became more and more vocal. Both Johann Jakoby, a Jewish physician in Königsberg, one of the most sincere and penetrating representatives of democratic views, and the old *Oberpräsident* Theodor von Schön, a brave champion of Stein's ideas, had discussed the question of a constitution in detail immediately after the King's accession. But not until 1847 did the long-prepared and much-discussed United Diet convene. The King wanted to summon at regular intervals only committees of the two curias within this assembly, but solely at his own discretion the entire United Diet. This gave the question of periodicity the most pressing importance for the new institution.

The structure of the United Diet was curious. It was made up of representatives of the estates in groups and thus was what the King regarded as old Germanic. This structure was apparently in accordance with history. In reality it was sham Gothic, just as artificial as the Gothic architecture of the period. The United Diet comprised two curias. That of the lords included princes, counts, and barons; the other, representatives of knights, burghers, and peasants. The aristocratic element thus predominated. The primary function of the whole body was to authorize new taxes and loans; the machinery of state, confronted with great new tasks such as the building of railroads, had come to a standstill for lack of funds legally at its disposal. Debts had actually been contracted indirectly—that is, illegally.

At once a strong opposition party arose in the United Diet. It was not satisfied with the King's concessions and demanded its development as a properly chosen and constituted representative assembly. The leaders of the opposition were all men of moderate tendencies. They were Rhenish merchants, like Ludolf Camphausen, David Hansemann, Gustav Mevissen, Hermann von Beckerath, and Karl August Milde, or members of the liberal aristocracy, such as Georg von Vincke, the Auerswald brothers, and Count Maximilian Schwerin. There was no thought of dogmatically progressive or of democratic and socialistic ideas. Nevertheless the King treated the opposition with pronounced disfavour. The honest and serious work that the United Diet was trying to accomplish ended in general ill humour. Important questions, such as the emancipation of the Jews, the income-tax law, the establishment of land-rent banks, and the construction of a railroad to East Prussia, had been expertly discussed, but in practical effect left hanging. The crown had stuck to its principles; experimentation was hardly congenial to it. The mounting excitement in the country proved how deep an impression had been made by the temperate and manly attitude of the opposition.

SECTARIAN MOVEMENT IN GERMAN CATHOLICISM

The United Diet, in its Prussian way, defiantly sided with the diets in southern and central Germany. Was only Austria to stand aloof? Here too there was a strong reaction to events in Prussia; a livelier spirit was astir in the diets of the crown lands. They ventured to attack political problems, and the diet of Lower Austria, in Vienna, took the lead. The gathering of forces for the coming struggle was also effected in societies such as a lawyers' and politicians' reading club in Vienna. Meetings and festivities of such societies became national phenomena. The assembly of Germanists in Frankfurt in 1846 served as the herald of the German parliament that was to come. Regular meetings of leading members of the south German diets were by way of practical preparation for this; Prussian liberals participated and thus came into personal contact with men like Heinrich von Gagern and Karl Mathy. At the Offenburg assembly in 1847 Friedrich Hecker and Gustav von Struve, delegates from Baden, first gave publicity to a comprehensive program, which was decidedly democratic and shot through with socialism. From 1847 on, Gervinus published the *Deutsche Zeitung,* the most dignified organ of the sentiment of German culture that was seeking to found the German state.

The remarkable movement of German Catholicism had an awakening and stimulating effect. It originated as a simple protest against exaggerated Roman ritual, when the Sacred Mantle was exhibited in Trier. But it soon grew into an association of all devout and liberal Catholics who did not want to join in a papal clericalism of international Jesuit stamp. The 1840's were the great age of German Catholicism. For a fleeting moment Johann Ronge, its leader, was hailed as a second Luther, though his personality could exert no such historical force. German Catholicism was significant for two reasons. It promoted interest in the relationship of state and church; it confronted every believer with decisions of conscience and in this way promoted the formation of political parties as well; against its own will it strengthened the cohesion of politically active Catholics.

414

In the second place it gave individuals and groups that were obscure and inhibited the chance to become publicly effective and to help in shaping political sentiment.

The man whose career profited most from German Catholicism was Robert Blum, a Rhinelander, the first German since the peasant wars whose talents made it possible for him to work his way up from the lowest class to a position of leadership in the growing German popular state. He had the look of a peasant or craftsman; he was plain-spoken and good-humoured, proud of being a self-educated man, courageous and alert. He was experienced both as a business-man and as a writer, but most of all he was an excellent speaker. So in spite of all obstacles he won the confidence and admiration of an increasing public, which regarded him as a champion and a believer, as the prophet of Schiller's concept of freedom, as a warm and living member of the German nationality. Did not this guide and leader revive the fighting spirit of Protestantism on the soil of electoral Saxony? And was not this spirit quickened by something like the loyalty and genuineness of an Andreas Hofer?

LOLA MONTEZ

Oddly enough, the German revolutionary movement of 1848 was set off by a romance in Munich, the politically serious side of which belongs to the story of clericalism as it gathered strength in Germany. The aging King Louis I of Bavaria had a Platonic enough friend-ship with the dancer Lola Montez, a very experienced woman who kept beer-loving Munich in constant excitement through her extrav-agant whims and political machinations. The human side of this unfortunate business was not immaterial, for the King was bound to lose face as a jumping-jack in the hands of a seductive adventuress. The court and the burghers of Munich, the ministers and the clergy that stood close to them, had never begrudged their King his pleas-ures. But the conduct of the Countess of Landsfeld—the rank the dancer had attained, not without difficulties—was calculated to arouse the indignation of the most placid and indulgent. It was cer-tainly not Philistinism or fanaticism, but healthy political instinct, that would not sit by complacently while this exotic creature of pleasure jeopardized legitimate demands for reform. Lola Montez, who lived with zest, did not distinguish between libertinism and liberalism. She was not satisfied with exploiting her royal friend, who was befuddled by her charms, but strove to get the political reins into her own hands. The scandal took the most deplorable forms, and the students became involved. The upshot was that the most thoughtful leaders of the reform movement in Bavaria took hold and forced the King to abdicate. The head of the Bavarian upper house, Prince Karl Leiningen, half-brother of Queen Victoria, took the lead in this affair. A temperate form of liberalism, in favour of reform and opposed to autocracy as well as to clericalism, could thrive only in clear air. In public, at least, dynasts had to measure up to the notions of decency of the rising middle class. This was the deeper significance of the Munich episode. Its saddest consequence was the disappearance of King Louis I from the scene of German events.

THE REVOLUTION OF 1848

The Revolution of 1848 shook the entire European continent. What happened in Germany must be considered against a general background, the importance of which should not be underestimated. There was ferment in Hungary and Poland. Insurrections broke out first in Italy, and then the February Revolution in Paris brought about the great explosion. What was taking place in France was only an outward signal for Germany. A series of events now arose from purely German causes, in a purely German manner, predominantly as matters of domestic politics. But their implications for foreign policy proved decisive in the final outcome.

The German Revolution of 1848 proceeded on three levels. In the first place there was a national movement. Its aim was to set up a strong federal German state that should include all German territories and should be under centralized leadership. This concept and the methods by which it was to be realized were of vital importance to all of Europe, to all the neighbours of the German Confederation. The weakness of the core of Europe had been very convenient for all the interested parties who were not German. The western powers, England and France, had joined forces to form a liberal front, involving world policy and colonial policy, that would have economic superiority. Their rising upper middle class aided the rising middle class in all European countries, for both spiritual and economic reasons. The group of eastern powers held the western powers in check through their authoritarian feudal and aristocratic trends, which were anti-liberal both spiritually and economically. These eastern powers were Metternich's Austria, the Russia of Czar Nicholas, and Prussia, which the others took in tow and which no longer had an independent foreign policy of her own. The year 1840 marked the last time that a clash between the western and the eastern group seemed likely. The old hatred of the Germans for the French was rekindled through the conflict between Egypt and the Ottoman Empire. Since that time there had been discord within both groups, and the possibility of reorientation arose.

Metternich's system had incurred the onus of a breach of treaty in annexing the free state of Cracow (1847). When such an action was taken by a power that insisted on the validity of the Vienna treaties, general liquidation and readjustment seemed at hand. The erection of a strong German federal state could hardly count on French sympathy, but might very well enlist that of Great Britain. This problem was bound to revive the old envy between Austria and Prussia, and, as before, Russia could play an important part. If the new German federal state was to include all German territory, the future of the duchies of Schleswig and Holstein would immediately become a pressing point of controversy, involving not only Denmark but also her Scandinavian neighbours and her patrons among the great powers. Many of the peoples of Slavic speech in Austria belonged to the German Confederation; were they to belong to the new German federal state also? Just as the German nation was agitated, so, too, were the Polish and the Italian nations. Not only the Hungarians, but the Slovenes, the Croatians, the Slovaks, the Czechs, and the Serbs came forward with nationalistic claims. The movement of the nations threatened the very life of the Austrian imperial state—could that state withstand it? Here was a problem for central Europe, indeed a Pan-European problem, and its solution depended largely on what shape the German future assumed.

The second problem of the Revolution of 1848 concerned the matter of constitutions. Germany wanted to be, and now was to be, a strong national federal state with an appropriate constitution. But all the individual states were also in need of constitutional reform. Besides the collective German movement there were Austrian, Prus-

417

THE FIRST TWO GERMAN REVOLUTIONS

sian, Bavarian, Württemberg and Baden, and electoral Hessian and Hesse-Darmstadt movements, and so on, even to Hamburg and Frankfurt movements. There was a great German national assembly in Frankfurt, but there was also a Prussian national assembly in Berlin, and there was an Austrian Reichstag—everywhere there were representative assemblies whose business was to draft constitutions. Germany now secured in bewildering excess what hitherto she had lacked. Parliamentarism disintegrated under the impact of the particularism that had become a fixed tradition; it was paralysed by the excess of hopes that were staked on it. The class of princes in Germany grew stronger through this disintegration. Parliamentary bodies took up a heroic struggle against the princes and their agencies of government; in this struggle for power the ideology of constitutionalism might easily be undermined. The foreground of the revolution was entirely occupied by the struggle for a strong national state and for a constitutional guarantee of political life.

But there was also a third level, and what happened here was decisive for the course of events on the other two. In the Frankfurt national assembly and in the parliaments of the individual states the requirements and the wishes of the broad lower stratum in Germany were given only slight attention. The extreme left wing of these bodies consisted of democratic republicans who had no confidence in the satisfactory solution of current problems by negotiated reform legislation; this group was therefore in favour of revolution to the point of wiping out existing public institutions. Socialistic ideas entered into this view. The old social-revolutionary ideas clamoured to be realized. Numerically the republicans of the declining middle class predominated. These were the people who stood behind Hecker, Struve, and Herwegh. The beginning of a German trade-union movement, of an organization of the working classes according to trade and calling, as the printer Stephan Born (died 1898) planned it, was less political in character, but indirectly served to clarify ideas and to produce proletarian class-consciousness. At that time the following of the communists Marx and Engels was very weak. They presented their views, hostile both to parliamentarism and to reform, in the *New Rhenish Gazette,* but for the rest they urged their disciples to take part in democratic and republican associations in order to make these groups radical. The result was bound to be a widening of the chasm between reformists and social revolutionaries, and the counter-revolutionary powers profited by this growing discord.

THE MARCH MOVEMENT

March 1848 was a supreme turning-point for the Germans in the nineteenth century. From then on, people spoke of an ante-March period and a post-March period. The new Germany burst into bloom then like the spring of that great year, which none who experienced it ever forgot. In a speech delivered in the Baden diet on February 12 the delegate Friedrich Bassermann, a bookdealer from Mannheim, called for German unity and for a political confederation patterned after the United States. The keynote was sounded: what Germany needed above all, and needed at once, was a representative assembly of the German Confederation—a German parliament. The movement engaged all the states of western and southern Germany. Those who up to this juncture had been opposition leaders in the diets now organized ministries favourable to reform. But peasant insurrections in the Black Forest and in the Odenwald proved that more was wanted than flags with the black, red, and gold colours, more than civic guards. The princes, the nobles, and the officials were thoroughly hated, and as usual the Jews, because they sustained and profited by the old system, were made scapegoats.

The movement spread to central Germany. The federal diet took action. It abolished censorship; it declared that black, red, and gold, as one-time imperial colours, were the official German symbol; and it invited the various governments to send agents to Frankfurt for the purpose of discussing reform of the Confederation. If at this point Prussia had risen to the opportunity, she could have secured the imperial crown. Metternich's system was tottering toward its end. The old court opposition of the archdukes and of Count Kolowrat, the opposition of the provincial diets, the moderate reform movement among the citizens, and the more intense and insistent attitude of the students, all merged in Vienna into a storm that the old statesman Metternich could not still. He took his departure with some dignity. The arming of the people and freedom of the press were proclaimed. Hungary, Italy, and the Slavs vied with the Viennese in joyful demonstrations; everyone was drafting constitutions, and the Austrian imperial state was in grave danger. Never yet had the natural superiority of the Prussian state been so evident. But a catastrophe occurred in Prussia that was to have great consequences.

King Frederick William IV cherished the idea of waging a variety of defensive war against revolutionary France, but England met such ideas with decided reserve. It would certainly have been most convenient to attack the solution of Prussian difficulties from the angle of foreign policy. But petitions and meetings in Berlin pushed toward a decision in internal politics. There were violent clashes between the people on one side and on the other the police and also the soldiers with whom the capital was flooded—no atmosphere for preserving calm. The Prince of Prussia, the heir to the throne, who later became William I, was among the most ardent advocates of military measures. At the last moment the King reluctantly conceded the immediate convening of the United Diet, freedom of the press, participation in reform of the German Confederation, and the duty of honest constitutionalism in Prussia. A new cabinet was installed—at noon on March 18, which was to become so fateful a day.

Furious street fighting broke out in Berlin and was fanned up by the extremists of both sides. There was only a small group of convinced social revolutionaries in the city. All strata of the population engaged in the battle, which, as nowhere else in all Germany, was an attack of free citizens of the most various political beliefs on militarism, autocracy, and eastern despotism. Berlin was fighting against the non-German colonial spirit, and it was victorious, at least for the moment. From a military point of view the battle was drawn. The troops, of course, had the advantage in the long run, but they had repeatedly faltered. The street fighters put up a brave front; only an extensive military operation could have brought about a clear-cut issue. King Frederick William IV did not desire this; he himself was worn out, and he also thought that it would be poor politics as well as harmful and unnecessary to continue the struggle. To his mind, his dear Berliners had been misguided by foreign agents, and he flattered himself that he could effect a fatherly reconciliation. That was why the troops were withdrawn. The gesture signified the triumph of the revolution. The King saluted the people's dead, and the dignitaries all attended their funeral; Frederick William IV followed the black, red, and gold through the streets of the capital. All the March demands were granted at one stroke. Prussia, it was said, would now be bound up with Germany. This, of course, not only meant that those parts of Prussia that did not belong to the German Confederation would now come under the Confederation's jurisdiction: it meant that Prussia intended to lead the new German federal state.

THE PRELIMINARY PARLIAMENT AND THE NATIONAL ASSEMBLY

The people's movement could not wait for Prussia. There the old authoritarian and militaristic state had been humbled; neither the dynasty nor the nobility would ever be able to forget March 18. Germany was in the lead; Prussia could but follow. The people's movement also ignored the federal diet and the committee of seventeen that it had set up to draft a new German constitution. The method of revolution seemed the only possible way to go about building up anew. The national will was resolved to create its own organs of government. Thus the so-called preliminary parliament met in Frankfurt. This was an assembly of notables from among the political leaders of the old opposition, whose patriotic convictions constituted their sole mandate. Here it was plain from the very outset that the social revolutionaries did not want to work with men of more moderate views.

Friedrich Hecker and his followers wanted more than a constitutional assembly. They demanded a revolutionary popular administration, the overthrow of dynasties, and complete social reorganization. But the majority preferred to guide the revolution back into a new legitimism, that of constitutional reform. They believed in the vitality and in the essential honesty of princely power. Their easy victory on all fronts strengthened their hopes and their self-confidence. Friedrich Hecker tried to impose his views in Frankfurt by fomenting a rising in his homeland of Baden, which, however, quickly collapsed; not even Hecker's brilliant leadership could achieve real success in Baden, which was in a state of social decay and political disintegration. Herwegh's legion of Parisian democrats also fought in vain. The election of delegates to a German parliament proceeded as planned by the committee of fifty that had been appointed by the preliminary parliament. For the first time there was universal and equal suffrage in Germany, although with slight local variations. The result was the national assembly that met in the Church of St. Paul in Frankfurt—the first, the most distinguished, and indeed the one peerless representative assembly of all the German people in history.

The democratic method had won the day, for it united all the real leaders of the nation, the men who ranked highest in a sound sense: officials and jurists in the first place, then professors, landed proprietors, merchants, writers, and officers, with comparatively few representatives of the lower middle class and hardly any of the working class. The choice had not fallen on representatives of political parties, whose existence was largely theoretical because they were not extensively organized; it had gone to men respected in their localities and regions, to those distinguished for intellect, family, merit, or resources. The mature German nation had had to wait a long while for a true modern representative assembly, but now it produced one of the best possible type. And whether this parliament would be successful or unsuccessful was the crux on which the future of the parliamentary principle in Germany hinged. A revolutionary popular administration was obviously not what the majority wanted, but the need for a visible and effective central power in Germany was imperative, for no sort of reform would do the old federal diet any real good. So it happened that the democratically elected national assembly created this Central Power of itself, but chose a prince for its executive. The principle was revolutionary, but the result corresponded to the overwhelming desire to come to an agreement.

Archduke John of Austria, Metternich's old opponent, now chosen as the vicar of the realm (*Reichsverweser*), had played *alter ego* to the weak-minded Emperor Ferdinand in Austria. He first thought to combine the vice-regency of Austria with the administration of Germany, but then found that he must concentrate wholly on Frankfurt. Here he organized a cabinet for the realm, and now the national assembly could proceed with its work of building up a new and free Germany with legal sanction. Committees were appointed for all important matters. The first great subject to come under consideration was the fundamental rights of the German people. The victory of the people's movement was, however, only apparent.

NATIONALIST CLAIMS. SCHLESWIG-HOLSTEIN

Both the social-revolutionary movement and the nationalistic movement continued; neither was pacified by the organization of a parliament, and consequently a counter-revolution set in. Austria, above all, was threatened by nationalism. Hungary broke away; a Slav Congress in Prague proclaimed a war to the knife against the old imperial state; the Ruthenian peasants in Galicia rose against their Polish lords. The national movement in Italy led to war with Sardinia for the Austrian Lombard and Venetian domains. Prussia was menaced by the claims of her own Polish subjects; their demand for a restored Polish state threatened her very life. Czar Nicholas I of Russia mobilized and seemed ready to prevent not only the liberation of Poland, but also the democratization of Prussia. The Prussian Poles, the Czechs in Bohemia, and the Italians in the southern Tyrol did not any of them want to submit to a German parliament and its administration from Frankfurt. The Dutch provinces of Luxemburg and Limburg, which adhered to the German Confederation, offered similar resistance. The possibility of a strong German federal state raised the old border problems again.

The question of Schleswig-Holstein proved to be especially delicate. It became the classic conflict of the century: it involved interests that were bound up with dynasty, foreign policy, international and public law, strategy, democracy, and nationalism. Holstein belonged to the German Confederation; Schleswig did not. Holstein was purely German, Schleswig at least three fourths. The two duchies had always led a joint existence. On historical and legal grounds they wanted to remain together. But in Denmark there was a democratic national movement aimed at forging the various territories under the Danish crown into a modern state. The King whose reign ended in 1847 was the last of his dynasty. The Glücksburg branch that followed in the female line was not entitled to the inheritance of the duchies, particularly not to that of Holstein, so that separation was in the air in any case.

The claims of Danish nationalism evoked lively opposition from German nationalism. Leading scholars of the University of Kiel de-

423

fended the German cause. Indigenous particularism, especially that of the Holstein nobility, set itself against the people's leaders in Copenhagen. But there was a Scandinavian movement that sympathized with Danish claims and, with its Germanic cultural convictions, frowned darkly on the interference of a half-Slavic power such as Prussia. Prussia, however, was the closest powerful neighbour. Her geopolitical and economic interests brought her into close contact with the duchies. The location of these duchies on the North Sea and the Baltic made them strategic points of the utmost importance; thus the whole question swelled into a problem of foreign policy. Russia, the Baltic power, and England, the North Sea power, were both interested in the future of the duchies because Denmark's future hinged on it. Denmark had a fleet at its disposal, but Germany, and more especially Prussia, had none. Prussia eagerly entered into the war that now broke out between Denmark and the German Confederation over the duchies, but this war could be successful only if it was waged on land.

Prussia liked to harp on her national function in the undertaking. She was in fresh contact with the people's movement and was able to outpace Austria, whose interest in this northern problem was naturally slight. But in her foreign policy Prussia collided with England and Russia, the two powers whose friendship Frederick William IV had sought again and again. Whenever the duchies came into question England's sympathies with a strong, liberal German federal state cooled. And France, at the moment, was more than ready to help the Danes as soon as German nationalism demanded increased power. Prussia, then, was fighting for German interests in the Schleswig-Holstein affair. The German national assembly at Frankfurt needed the Prussian sword, but it did not love the Prussian state. For it was not the imperial state of Austria, apparently disintegrating, that presented the most dangerous obstacle to the new German federal state, but the great power of Prussia. And this Prussia was in the process of becoming modernized. She had her own national assembly, a largely democratic body that lacked the brilliance of the Frankfurt parliament but developed a sturdy Prussian patriotism instead. On the other hand Prussian bureaucracy and Prussian militarism were spiritually intact; the Prussian March ministers were utterly unable to liberalize officialdom, and frequent changes in the cabinet did not serve to enhance the reputation of the new system.

The representatives of revolutionary thought were profoundly dissatisfied. They grew tired of the long-winded debates in the Frankfurt parliament. The optimistic alliance of the patricians of title and of money with the old powers had an irritating effect. Labour organizations sprang up; trade unions held congresses. The real needs made themselves felt and could not be allayed by clever speechmaking. Karl Marx's *New Rhenish Gazette,* which the Prussian government wisely countenanced, sneered at the bourgeois belief in progress. The democratic parliaments in Frankfurt and Berlin openly demanded that the revolution should go on and even made preparations for it. The front of the March Revolution was broken. A change set in when Prussia proved unable to carry on a successful war with Denmark and was forced to agree to the inglorious armistice of Malmö in September 1848. The Frankfurt parliament hesitated, but in the end it necessarily fell in line with Prussia, which it needed if it were to fulfill its mission. But what could be expected of a weakened Prussia? It had never been a people's state; it was trustworthy only in military matters, and if it failed in these, not much would be left. A second uprising in Baden, a series of disturbances in western Germany, and street fighting in Frankfurt itself showed that the revolution was still alive. The Central Power in Frankfurt took part in its suppression and thus broke with the revolutionary ideas on which it had itself been built up.

BEGINNING OF THE COUNTER-REVOLUTION

The Austrian army gave the signal for the counter-revolution. The imperial state was still strong and vital among its soldiers. Cracow and Prague, Polish and Czech rebels, all had to submit, and the march went on to Vienna. The Austrian Reichstag had bravely undertaken the enormous task of reoganizing the imperial state along liberal lines. The peasants were freed at last. Among the Catholics a movement had sprung up that tended away from Rome. Economic stress was driving the Vienna intelligentsia more and more toward the left. For a while the archdukes, headed by John and by Stephen, the vice-regent of Hungary, considered a partition of the imperial state, which comprised so many nationalities and which seemed to have lost its vitality. In that event the German territories

425

of Austria would have joined the new German federal state, and in return for this dowry Archduke John would have bespoken the imperial crown of Greater Germany. But Austrian patriots, who believed in their imperial state and flaunted their black and yellow banner, would not hear of this. The imperial court had moved to Innsbruck to escape the mounting disturbances in the capital. Archduchess Sophie shrewdly prepared for the accession to the throne of her son, Francis Joseph. He would be eighteen years old in August 1848, and he could then succeed his uncle, Emperor Ferdinand, who was unfit to reign.

But the October Revolution in Vienna came as a final desperate struggle for the dream of a liberal Greater Germany against the alliance of dynasty, feudalism, clergy, and army. Prince Windischgrätz seized the city. The Catholic Croatians gave eager aid; their loyalty to the Emperor was to be rewarded by their political independence of the Magyars. Prussia too now took courage for the master stroke of counter-revolution. Heinrich von Gagern, first president of the Frankfurt assembly and thus president of the cabinet of the realm, found that the most formidable obstacle blocking the plans of himself and his friends was the Central Power in Frankfurt. That central power was in the hands of the Austrian Archduke, and it was complete with ministers and envoys, laws, even the beginnings of a German navy. Gagern and his friends had been constrained to build up this obstacle themselves, and now they could not surmount it. If Austria wanted to be Greater Austria and nothing else, then Prussia's German vocation was the last and the real hope of the patriots of the German realm (*Reichspatrioten*). In spite of March 18, in spite of the truce of Malmö, it was essential to come to terms with the Prussian King. But Prussia went the way of Austria. The Prussian national assembly was dismissed, with its draft of a constitution, and a relatively sensible new constitution was dictated. The power of the manorial lord and the regiment of the guards was unbroken, and they were prepared to assert themselves still further. General von Wrangel, Minister Otto von Manteuffel, and Count Brandenburg now tried to do in Prussia what Windischgrätz and Schwarzenberg had accomplished in Austria. The King might have played vaguely with the idea of offering Prussia up as a sacrifice in favour of the German realm, but the egoism of the old Prussian state rejected all claims of cultural Germany that appeared politically dis-advantageous to colonial Germany. This rift could not be bridged either then or later.

The counter-revolution was marching on, but the revolution was still alive. A second outbreak was in preparation. Austria, holding her course, downed the "rebels" in Italy and Hungary. The collective state of Austria, which also bore an eastern colonial character, stood in the way of the German national state. Robert Blum was shot in Vienna under martial law in November 1848, and this execution of one of the most distinguished delegates to the Church of St. Paul set Austria off from liberal Germany more than any previous event had ever done.

THE FRANKFURT CONSTITUTION. THE SECOND REVOLUTION

Germany needed a larger and more modern frame of life. Eco-nomics, communications, coinage, law, public opinion—all clam-oured for organization and direction from some more general point of view. How wretched the position of a German in a foreign coun-try was if he did not happen to be a citizen of one of the great powers! Bavaria and all the small states encountered mounting dis-taste among patriots of the larger realm toward all their dynastic state apparatus. The idea of merging all these petty states became urgent. It was no wonder that particularism in its peril clung to existing conditions and did not scorn the expedient, usual among German princes, of exploiting foreign relations with Russia and England. When the assembly in Frankfurt finally completed the draft of the constitution, it could therefore count on its acceptance by all the well-intentioned in spite of certain handicaps. And the Frankfurt constitution was actually accepted by all the parliaments of the individual states except in Austria and Liechtenstein, though in Bavaria it was accepted only by the second chamber, not by the first.

This constitution was a noble achievement. The executive of the realm, its responsible ministry, the Reichstag, and the supreme court demonstrated a unitary spirit. But enough was left to the individual states to constitute a counterbalance. In contrast to the democratic lower house, the upper house was conservative in character and more particularistic. A statement of fundamental rights constituted a magnificent introduction, a monument to German needs and German longing. In this constitution the concept of power was reconciled with liberalism and democracy for the good of an effective national community.

The parliaments of Germany endorsed the constitution in defiance of the counter-revolution, but the King of Prussia declined the imperial crown. He did not want to be emperor of the Germans by the grace of the people. The Prussian government, too, did not care to co-operate with Frankfurt and definitely rejected the Frankfurt constitution, even though it was formulated along dynastic lines and though several objectionable points, such as the imperial delaying veto, had been modified. Prussia was now taking her revenge for March 18. She broke with the revolution and went her own way.

The struggle for a national constitution flared up into the last stirring chapter of the people's movement of 1848–9. It was more than a desperate attempt to complete the work of the Frankfurt national assembly as the majority of the German people wished. Over and above this another enterprise, greater and bolder, was in the making, prompted by the desire to redeem the failures of the March Revolution—in other words, to fight out a second and conclusive revolution. All left-wing groups in Germany joined in a common front for this purpose. Dogmatic liberals, democrats, social revolutionaries, trade unionists, and communists mingled with patriots of the realm of no particular persuasion and with international revolutionaries of entirely different character. The civil war that now broke out was part of the collective European war against the reaction; many personal and material connections ran across boundaries. The participation of the extreme left-wing groups facilitated the propaganda of the counter-revolution; it paralysed the traditional liberals above all, the patricians of money and title who believed in freedom and centralization and were the real leaders of the federal state party (*Bundesstaatspartei*) at the Church of St. Paul. These men could not engage in street fighting, and to their own regret they were forced into a kind of neutrality. In the end they turned to the right and were willing to ally themselves to the old powers if the most imperative concessions with regard to the constitution were only granted. Such was the origin of national liberalism in Germany. Movements for freedom, of various extent, also occurred in

428

Bavaria, Württemberg, Thuringia, and the Rhineland. In Baden, in the Palatinate, and in Saxony there was bitter civil war. The Prussian army struck down the revolutionary administrations, and in its own opinion this supplied moral justification for broaching the problem of the German federal state anew, in its own way.

Externally the revolution in Germany was at an end. But the spirit of the revolution was not dead. The methods used so far had failed; what was defeated was not really the idea but the method of working. Troops marched through the land, parliaments were dissolved, political opponents were shot or discredited by prison terms. Coups d'état by the great had become commonplace, and the less important learned in this school. Bonapartism had revived in France. Louis Napoleon's form of permanent dictatorship was undergoing changes: the authority of the monarch, supported by the army and allied with the financial administration, set the masses into motion directly by means of plebiscites and thus made use of them as a dynamic force, eliminating every kind of rational discussion. Bonapartism was instructive to the great statesman whom Austria now possessed in Prince Felix Schwarzenberg. Greater Austria, reawakened, was deeply wounded by the constitution from the Church of St. Paul, issuing as it did from a Little Germany; she resolved to guard energetically her old preponderance in central Europe. The fortunes of war were with her. She maintained her position of power in Italy and trampled down Hungary with the help of Russia.

THE PRUSSIAN POLICY OF UNION. OLMÜTZ (1850)

When the friend of the Prussian King, the distinguished General Joseph von Radowitz (died 1853), who was a Catholic and a romantic, launched the Union policy that was the meagre aftermath of the revolution, both the sturdy resistance of the revived Austrian imperial state and Russia's unfriendly attitude had to be taken into consideration. What Prussia had in mind was first to make a league with the kingdoms of Saxony and Hanover and then to persuade the other states into joining with them, while with Austria she wanted to form a union that would constitute an indissoluble international bond. The leaders among the Frankfurt advocates of a hereditary emperorship supported this policy by the Declaration of Gotha and were consequently nicknamed Gothaists. During the entire revolutionary period Bavaria's feeble King, Maximilian II, pursued an excessively particularistic policy; the very idea of a Prussian emperor aroused his deep indignation, and he now crisply rejected the plan for union. Since the kingdoms of Hanover and Saxony had taken Bavaria's acquiescence for granted when they promised their co-operation, Prussia's enterprise in reality was already doomed. An independent effort by the middle states to arrive at some tangible goal was also unsuccessful. A Union parliament met in Erfurt; almost half its members were Prussians, the rest largely Gothaists. The discussions here were utterly fruitless.

Prussia's military weakness and her isolation in foreign policy tipped the scales. Calmly and deliberately Prince Schwarzenberg prepared to set up the federal diet in Frankfurt again. There the previous vicar of the realm, Archduke John, steadfastly defied the dramatic changes of the times as a welcome representative of Austrian interests; he played his part reluctantly, but he had no choice but to be loyal. War threatened to break out between Austria and Prussia. Prussia interfered in certain constitutional disturbances in Hesse-Kassel, as a neighbouring country and as the leader in the policy of union. Hesse-Kassel was aligned with Prussia, but she appealed to the federal diet in Frankfurt. Prussia did not recognize this diet, since Austria had summoned it on her own initiative after the time interval agreed on had expired. Prussia was in a most critical situation. In spite of her military successes she had made peace with Denmark on such unambitious terms that none of her justifiable desires had been insisted on, to the indignation of Prussian patriots. Prussia reserved all rights until a final settlement should be laid down. Schleswig and Holstein had separate governments. Schleswig was occupied by Prussian and Swedish troops.

The Prussian King was embarrassed by French overtures: he did not wish to co-operate with the new French President, Louis Napoleon, against Austria. A believer in a Greater Germany such as Frederick William IV was bound to abhor the idea of a German civil war. So he was quite content to arrive at what he regarded as a tolerable agreement with Prince Schwarzenberg in Olmütz. But Olmütz actually signified the abandonment of Prussia's whole policy of union, her return to the federal diet, the settlement of the affairs of Holstein and Hesse-Kassel by the diet and hence under old

Austria's lead—in brief, it meant the end of the last modest hopes of the national revolutionary movement. The Duchies of Schleswig and Holstein were left miserably in the lurch. They continued to fight alone to the bitter end, and many patriots were forced to flee.

The first two German revolutions were without results. It was the counter-revolution that shaped the destiny of Germany. Revolutions that are nipped off do a people no good. The authoritarian state had triumphed; it wrote the history of the times in its own fashion. The Germans were told that their political immaturity was responsible; therefore they should leave the difficult art of ruling to duly appointed experts. It took the Germans a long time to recover from the blow, and in fact they never quite succeeded.

Chapter 17
BISMARCK

SCHWARZENBERG. THE YOUNG EMPEROR FRANCIS JOSEPH

PRINCE FELIX SCHWARZENBERG died in 1852. He was
only fifteen years older than Bismarck, and had he lived longer, he
would have made the Prussian's task difficult. He was far more
Austrian than Metternich, an aristocrat in the grand style, persistent,
dry, and imperious. Although he was not burdened with knowledge,
he was a connoisseur of men and arts. His alert instincts, always on
the watch, responded to the Austrian imperial state and its needs, for
he himself was a living part of this Austria, whose proud history
reinforced his personal arrogance. The concept of popular rights did
not appeal to him; he refused to occupy himself with it. He was a
visionary, almost a genius, who went his way with easy assurance.

Schwarzenberg led Austria back to autocracy. He had, indeed,
pledged himself to constitutionalism. From March 1849 on, Austria,
too, had a constitution, decreed by the monarch, with an upper house
and a lower. This constitution was extended to Hungary, while the
individual crown lands were granted constitutions of their own. But
the system worked badly and seemed to hinder rather than to help
the reorganization of the state. And so Schwarzenberg, as President
of the Ministry, decided on the grave step of having the constitution
abolished by order of the Emperor. Since Emperor Francis Joseph
had never taken an oath to the constitution, he signed the order
with a clear conscience—probably the most serious mistake in a
reign that was rich in error. Austria now became wholly reactionary,
and of the various achievements of the revolutionary year the
liberation of the peasants was almost all that remained. The Catholic
clergy worked successfully hand in hand with the police; it became
still more influential after a concordat with the curia was reached.

For Schwarzenberg all this was merely the beginning. With his

432

gifted Minister of Commerce, Karl Ludwig Baron von Bruck, he worked to extend Austria's political hegemony to economics—in other words, to deprive Prussia of her leadership in commercial policy. Even Metternich had found the Prussian Customs Union irksome; now it seemed that the time had come to set up a controlling central European organization. Austria's financial situation was poor, but her broad agricultural basis made it possible to start industries that could be run cheaply and could easily compete with those of Prussia. The Prussian manorial system was especially threatened by Hungary's low-priced agricultural products. For the Austrian imperial state the revision of its customs system meant an expansion of the economic field under its control and hence the possibility of economic recovery. Bavaria strongly urged Austria's entering the Customs Union, for her interests were similar to Austria's. Prussia fought vehemently for her handiwork, on which her entire political and economic system depended. Protracted conferences finally resulted in a trade treaty between Austria and Prussia. A complete customs agreement was left for the future. Schwarzenberg had no equally gifted successor, and the dream of central European customs unification under Austrian leadership dissolved in air. Prussia was able to retain her Customs Union. Such were the disappointments that initiated the protracted regime of Emperor Francis Joseph.

He had been named for the honest but reactionary Francis and for Joseph, the noble Emperor of the people, and these two names symbolized the dual dynastic tradition of the house of Habsburg-Lorraine. The young monarch was of the uninspired average, very conventional and matter-of-fact—industrious at paper work, a thorough officer who always appeared in uniform, and a good friend to his highly aristocratic companions. There was something joyless about this ruler; he used to call himself ill-starred, and such a spirit may scarcely compel coy fortune. The pride of his ancient house and an unimpeachable Catholicism gave the monarch a bearing that, in the face of all criticism, always won him personal respect and in his later period the reverence of the people as well. He felt himself a German prince, and he conducted his life with Viennese suavity. Toward mounting personal and political misfortune he struck no harsh or violent attitude, but showed such notable composure that in the end his unhappiness seemed an essential part of his being. He never learned to take pleasure in counsellors of brilliant gifts or stormy creativeness; his own egoism and will to power were too far removed from such qualities. He let countless ministers come and go. All that he asked of them was to fulfil faithfully the duties to which they were appointed. It was not surprising that in the face of such restraint the whole machine of state ran down; a really original mind either had no chance at all or was unable to impose itself effectively. Thus the history of Austria under Emperor Francis Joseph was the history of her dissolution.

THE REACTION IN PRUSSIA AND IN THE GERMAN CONFEDERATION

In Prussia, too, there were many who demanded that the constitution be abolished. It was impossible to come to so drastic a decision, but what was actually done was almost worse. A new law establishing indirect election for the lower chamber was decreed by ordinance (May 1849). According to this law the voters were classified according to the amount of taxes they paid; each of three classes, large or small, chose the same number of electors as the others. The electors made the final choice of members of the house. This was the vaunted Prussian three-class system, which remained in force until 1918 — probably the most unfortunate form of suffrage based on taxes that was ever in effect in Germany, even in all Europe. It was decreed that membership in the upper house should be hereditary and for life. This body was called the House of Lords, by analogy with English precedent. Thus the curia of lords of the united diet was resurrected and the curia of the knights merged with it. The King now took an oath to the constitution that had been so thoroughly transformed in a reactionary fashion, although he was reluctant to do so to the very last. His closest personal friends, headed by the brothers Leopold and Ludwig von Gerlach, the general and jurist, continued to regard constitutionalism as a transgression against the true Christian and Germanic spirit. Reaction could now set to work, and there was no lack of either the urge to domination or of pharisaical justice. In spite of the debased suffrage a moderate liberalism still persisted in the second chamber, but it was put to flight by unscrupulous influencing of the elections. The result was that the chamber was made

434

up of heads of districts; it was the so-called *Landratskammer,* consisting mostly of loyal officials.

The most important reactionary measures were the law that destroyed the independence of the courts by providing that judges might be transferred or pensioned off against their will; the law that dealt the death-blow to the freedom of the press by abolishing trial by jury for offences of the press; the law concerning the restoration of entails and the privileges of those who had formerly been immediate to the Empire, a law that gave fresh economic strength to the aristocracy; and the law that established the political and social superiority of the landed proprietors by restoring the old manorial courts and the old provincial diets. Thus the constitutional state created in Prussia by the revolution was systematically dissolved. The spy system throve, and even the Prince of Prussia was secretly watched. Religion was one of the most important subjects taught in the schools, and the teachers in the elementary schools, liberal as a rule, were gagged by the supervision of the clergy. Two sayings of Friedrich Julius Stahl, a professor of constitutional law, characterize the epoch better than anything else: "Scholarship must turn back," and "Authority, not majority."

Similar developments occurred in most of the individual states of Germany. Mecklenburg-Schwerin, Saxony, and Württemberg were again subjected to the old constitutions they had had prior to March. In Hanover a new constitution, patterned on that of 1840, was decreed. In other lands the suffrage laws at least underwent revision. The restored federal diet at Frankfurt appointed a special committee to effect the abolition of all the institutions in the individual states that might prove dangerous to the security of the Confederation. Under pressure of this so-called committee of reaction, the administrations of many of the smaller states decided on reactionary measures, although reluctantly, since they had constituted a sort of refuge for patriotism of the realm when it was persecuted in the revolutionary period. Liberals in Hesse-Kassel staunchly resisted the abolition of the famous liberal constitution of that country, but Austrian and Prussian commissars in combination with the unpopular Minister Hassenpflug finally carried out the work of destruction. The diet abolished the fundamental rights of the German people and discountenanced freedom of the press and of assembly. But the champions of a liberal and nationally unified Germany did not allow themselves to be totally suppressed. By 1853 the versatile Duke Ernest II of Saxe-Coburg-Gotha had founded a literary and political association to promote national spirit and the constitutional concept. It spread over all of Germany. Men such as Gustav Freytag the poet and chronicler of culture and Max Duncker the historian found here a field for their significant contributions.

OTTO VON BISMARCK-SCHÖNHAUSEN, ENVOY TO THE FEDERAL DIET

In July 1851 Otto von Bismarck-Schönhausen (born 1815) was sent to Frankfurt as the Prussian envoy. He had already won a reputation in the united diet, where he had sponsored the autocratic power-state. Early in the revolutionary period he had brooded over counter-revolutionary plans and had been connected with the founding of the feudal journal *Kreuzzeitung*. In 1848 so frank a champion of Prussian Junkerdom could have no mandate. But he appeared as a delegate in the Prussian lower chamber in 1849 and also in Erfurt. He defended the settlement at Olmütz, and thus the Christian-Germanic circle to which he amiably adhered believed it could recommend for Frankfurt no better advocate of Austrian and Prussian authoritarian co-operation than this outsider from the Prussian diplomatic service. But Bismarck was not precisely the man his counter-revolutionary comrades took him for. He was, indeed, a descendant of the ancient nobility of the Old Mark, the scion of a family that had dwelt there longer than the Hohenzollerns and that had not always been on good terms with the dynasty. In the Empire such easterners had been given the somewhat derogatory name of Junkers (*Jungherrn,* young lords), because they had no other title and were not immediate to the Empire, and thus had the appearance of minor nobility. As a matter of fact, here, too, the peculiar spirit of the Mark reigned—a locally, provincially, dynastically coloured sentiment that was just as alien to the old Empire, and even suspicious of it, as it was to the new cultural Germany. Bismarck's father was a true country Junker of this description, simple and capable, attached to his land, in humorous harmony with himself and his world. But his mother's family introduced wholly new traits, for she came of the urban patriciate of title. The Menckens had risen high at the universities and in the service of the state; they were clever and accomplished people. Bismarck's mother had inherited in full measure their ambition, their delight in advancement and in gifted achievement.

Bismarck was educated according to his station in life. He studied at the classical Prussian Gymnasium and later at the University of Göttingen. He was not particularly interested in his studies, but he was very intelligent and quite capable of meeting the test of examinations. He was conspicuous for his Prussian nationalism even in the "Hannovera" student organization that he joined. He entered the service of the Prussian state, but he was not very successful in his work. He found it difficult to adjust himself to the machinery of administration, for he preferred a life without restrictions. He became involved in all sorts of love-affairs, and there were rumours of engagements. He flirted with the Duke of Bedford's niece and actually became betrothed to the daughter of an English clergyman. Finally he took up farming, and that suited him excellently. It was a pleasant thing to be master of one's own ground and not have to consult anyone about anything, to read, to travel, and to lead a gay social life with one's own kind. So the irresponsible young Bismarck lived on his family property in Pomerania and there came to maturity as a man of poise and power.

His searching spirit drew him to all eras and views of the world: Hegel and *Weltschmerz,* Lord Byron and Ludwig Feuerbach, Shakespeare and Heinrich Heine, Goethe and the Bible, and history above all. His varied reading made a thoroughly independent human being of him, and his extraordinary memory would retain all through his life everything he needed. He wrote in a vigorous, vivid, and graceful style tinged with humour, showing keen observation and pleasure in well-turned phrases—unsentimental and unrhetorical, without affectation or artificiality. During the whole of his life he was indifferent to painting and sculpture, but was devoted to music without being a connoisseur, because of a spiritual need of it. Beethoven set forth for him his own struggle, his stresses, and his joy in strife. In an out-of-the-way place in Pomerania he found his future wife, Johanna von Puttkamer, and her pietistic background reconciled him to his inherited Protestant faith, even though he reserved the right to decide for himself all matters relating to God

437

rather than accept the guidance of the church or of religious sects. Bismarck was contented and happy in his marriage to a sensitive and musically gifted woman, who adapted her personality to his life and his work unreservedly, though not without reflection, and who, notwithstanding, had a definite and deep-rooted life of her own. Among the friends of his youth the American John Lothrop Motley, who later became known as diplomat and historian of the Netherlands, meant a great deal to him. As a result of this friendship Bismarck was one of the very few men of his rank and generation who were thoroughly familiar with conditions in England and America and who spoke English fluently. He visited England early in life and was in sympathy with the sports and other habits of the English master class. English aristocrats were the only foreigners whose acquaintance meant anything to him and whose appreciation he valued. The industrial England of the ordinary citizen remained alien to him.

And so the Prussian Junker, who was now to play German politics in Frankfurt along with the autocratic Austria of Prince Schwarzenberg, was in reality far more than a mere party man. His was a rich and forceful personality, with a German and even European culture. He was hard-headed and resourceful in practical affairs. He could show both obstinacy and fine feeling. He could hate, and he could despise, but with very few exceptions he held himself to an exacting code of conduct, at once human and knightly. The most prestigious politicians of the time were Prince Schwarzenberg and Emperor Napoleon III. Young Bismarck was ready to learn from both. Soon it became evident that this champion of the new feudalism had few prejudices and did not put much store in dogma; also that his ready intellectual grasp and his gift of presentation could bend even purely objective issues to his masterful will. Bismarck, the statesman in evolution, proved himself a dangerous fighter even at Frankfurt. He had served the counter-revolution, but he was quite capable of allying himself with the revolution.

THE VICTORY OF MATERIALISM. ECONOMIC LIFE

In a deeper sense the Revolution of 1848 had been a struggle between idealism and materialism. The last great synthesis, evolved by Hegel, was broken. A world of reason could not be brought to pass. Even in the 1840's a realistic view of life was common. Men were turning from pure speculation in favour of history and science. At the Church of St. Paul there had existed, very characteristically, a committee on political economy, side by side with the one on the constitution. The former had been the more modern in many ways; it grappled with and triumphed over the world of matter. Moreover, it cannot be said that the left wing felt no interest in large-scale power politics. In Frankfurt as well as in Berlin there was a movement to organize a people's army, for it was obvious that the old powers could not be cracked as long as they had armies that believed only in them. This was why there were debates over and over again about the troops' being sworn to the constitution. The counter-revolution learned to its sorrow that neither the soldiers nor the authorities could offer a strong enough resistance to the new organs of the people's movement. For this reason the reactionaries tried to make authoritarian energies coalesce in a tighter and more effective way. The police power had much the same relation to the people as a foreign conqueror. The army was now to be a foreign body in the state, a self-contained entity dependent only on the crown. This was the stern view taken by officers, and it was soon expressed in the reform of the Prussian army. Just as the leaders of the people's movement had tried to gain control of the tools of state power, so now the leaders of the counter-revolution laid the spiritual foundation for the political power that they did not wish to let slip through their fingers.

The defeat of the people's movement aggravated the critical situation of Germany's middle class, which was no less the crisis of German liberalism. The victory of brute force over patriotic and human sentiment seemed to confirm the materialistic apprehension of the world that was then, under Darwin's influence, permeating every department of life. The real impulses of history were sheer vitality, instinct, the primitive, self-preservation, blind and unreasoning physical power, the dynamic, the radically evil. Against such forces the very notion of human well-being in this world looked visionary and absurd. The reaction subjected the educated middle class in Germany to a galling suspicion. There were two possible ways of meeting this attitude. Some retreated into resignation and pessimism. The day of Artur Schopenhauer (died 1860) was dawning. His philosophy supplied the appropriate interpretation: blind will was the deepest urge; irrational forces triumphed over the reasonable and the good. A better world was illusion or worse. Later the philosopher Eduard von Hartmann (died 1906) projected this interpretation of earthly dream in his own way, with considerable success. Friedrich Nietzsche was to follow. The effect of this way of thinking was far-reaching. First came a revulsion against political labours and an absorption in artistic and religious studies and sentiments, all of which quickened the German spirit while the authorities and those who felt a vocation for administrative work took care of the business of state. This situation was of decidedly palpable advantage to Bismarck's politics and to the Prussian idea of the state.

The alternative answer that citizens might give to materialism was oriented in exactly the same direction. The afflicted German middle class, well on the way to disintegration, threw itself into economic work with redoubled zeal. Mature capitalism now seized on Germany, too. The construction of railroads, whose high-minded prophet, Friedrich List, had committed suicide in despair at the stupidity of his contemporaries, promoted traffic and trade. Railroads once and for all tore the small German states away from their self-satisfied pastoral tranquillity; they were no respecters of artificial boundaries or dynastic or bureaucratic considerations, and they produced unprecedented psychological changes. Goods and soldiers were shifted hither and thither. Capital circulated freely, accumulated, and brought in good returns. New professions sprang up. The large cities expanded and swallowed up outlying villages. The treasures of the earth could be laid bare and easily and promptly made accessible to industry. The economic imperialism of the Second Empire of Louis Napoleon also made a very deep impression on Germany; new connections were formed, and there was a great deal of imitation. The Viennese lords of finance did not want to be outstripped by the Parisians. Many of the defeated leaders of the German people's movement emigrated to the United States; in that great free country they soon became influential in both economic and intellectual life, and as teachers, musicians, and journalists they had a stimulating effect on education and politics. It was a time of expansion, of invention, of newly discovered forces and values.

The spirit of enterprise that distinguished the Second Empire also roused England and her world empire from self-confident calm.

Russia spread out over Asia and once more knocked at the portals of the longed-for Near East. If Germany had succeeded in becoming a strong national federal state in 1848, she might not have lagged so lamentably behind the world at large in colonial expansion. As it was, Germans helped other nations develop their overseas dominions; in the process the German people enriched itself and others, but no German state was the gainer.

The less dangerous leaders of the people's movement of 1848, who could remain in their own country, turned to economic activity, which alone was still open to them, and they were usually very successful at it. For a long time it was characteristic of life in Germany that the most intelligent members of the rising middle class avoided the service of the state. Many devoted themselves to municipal administration, which was the reason for the excellence of German mayors and aldermen; their administrative methods were so intelligent and progressive that they frequently put the state administration to shame. The great impetus to the economy advanced the culture of the cities, and an odd situation arose: the fatherland was still cloven into halves, one liberal and urban, the other rural and reactionary. "Government" was regarded as a distasteful, suspicious, malignant force that could only oppress and never advance the good life.

The materialistic interpretation of history sponsored by Karl Marx and his fellows did not correspond to the actual course of history. It sprang from impressions of the spirit of the epoch that were especially apprehensible in England, and it gathered irresistible weight as a propagandist and contentious interpretation of the real meaning of the times. The fashionable sciences were political economy, sociology, and biology. The scientific method that had had such overwhelming success in building up a new world picture and in putting it to practical uses was now applied to the study of history. And here, too, this method led to the discovery of laws, to the establishment of facts, and to the revelation of the struggle for existence as an impersonal, almost preordained necessity.

NATURAL SCIENCE. HISTORY. POLITICAL ECONOMY

The academic scholarship of the universities discountenanced ventures of such easy popularity. By preference it broached one new specialized field after another and in this way arrived at generalizations. The book *Tierleben* (*Animal Life*) by A. Brehm combined love of nature with indefatigable delight in new discovery. Rudolf Virchow's studies in pathology opened up new vistas for the physician. The invention of spectrum analysis by Gustav Kirchhoff and Robert Wilhelm Bunsen, the researches in physics that Hermann von Helmholtz and Robert Mayer carried on, and Du Bois-Reymond's work on animal electricity constituted a new knowledge of the conditions of life and made possible technical inventions of revolutionary significance. Barth, Rohlfs, Bastian, and others explored unknown lands. The Geographic Institute, founded by Perthes in 1854, sponsored travels to little-known parts of the earth and thus laid the groundwork for new openings in colonial policy. Psychologists trained in physiology, such as Theodor Fechner, Hermann Lotze, and Wilhelm Wundt, and the racial psychologists Moritz Lazarus and H. Steinthal effected a fusion of natural science and the humanities, a blend that was accurate in method and fruitful in result. The achievements of historical writers demonstrated that it was quite unnecessary for scientific interpreters of the world and of life to invade the province of history with their attempts at salvation. Leopold von Ranke was writing his most mature historical works, inquiring into the bases of English and French political development. Theodor Mommsen's *Roman History* was an unforgettable spur to further research into antiquity, while the Munich Historical Commission supplied German history with a new and living focus; here were gathered comprehensive collections of source material, on which specialized researches and general conclusions could be built up. Austrian scholars were pricked by the Little German trend of much of this work, and the Vienna school began to compete successfully.

The historical spirit gradually penetrated one field of life after another: literature, the fine arts, law, economy, culture, and even philosophy itself. There could have been no more effective reply to Schopenhauer's unhistorical way of thinking than the magnificent attempt to make the development even of philosophical systems the subject of world-wide and world-wise interpretation, as was done by Kuno Fischer, a professor first at Jena and then at Heidelberg. For the many whom the disappointing course of Germany's political history had left bewildered and impatient, Gustav Freytag wrote his *Pictures from the German Past,* graceful but authentic descriptions of German customs and conditions, usages and prejudices, quarrels and hopes, all supported by contemporary sources that the magic of the writer awoke to life.

Karl Marx and his helpers also provoked scholarship into energetic retort by their methods and their choice of material. The development of political economy was inquired into by reference to the sources, and in the process it came about quite naturally that high-sounding systems and programs were explained away by tangible, local, contemporary, and psychological conditions. Scientifically trained political economists, from Wilhelm Roscher to Gustav Schmoller and Adolf Wagner, endeavoured to give a factual account of the relation of politics and economics, and thus they established at least one necessary premise for the solution of current problems. Johann Karl von Rodbertus (died 1873), who was the first to set forth in a consistent and sustained way the concept of obligatory state aid to the workers, was particularly significant in the development of socialism as a creative social device. Opposite him stood the deputy Schulze-Delitzsch (died 1883), whose well-organized co-operative societies successfully supplied the struggling middle classes with credit and thus made their continued independence possible.

LITERATURE. RICHARD WAGNER

In the field of art, too, escape and work were the two leading principles in an age of political reaction. Just as Goethe in the confusion of the Napoleonic era had created a world of his own in his *Westöstlicher Divan,* so now many followed the poet and philosopher of religion Georg Friedrich Daumer in his revival of Hafiz. Friedrich Bodenstedt reaped the fruits of this movement in his somewhat facile imitations of Oriental verse. Emanuel Geibel and Paul Heyse also owed most of their charm and success to exotic subject-matter; the mawkish, feeble creations of Roquette and Brachvogel were stragglers in the train of late romanticism, foreign to the world about them. The need of consolation in an age of epigones gushed forth in the novels of Joseph Viktor von Scheffel. But there were also artists of a new and sturdy cast of mind: Wilhelm Jordan, who made a new alliterative version of the Nibelung saga, Fritz Reuter, a martyr to the persecution of the popular leaders, who gave his beloved Low German dialect its due by using it in his books, and again Gustav Freytag, a disciple of Charles Dickens, whose masterpiece was *Debit and Credit,* a paean to the tireless German merchant. And finally there were the novelists Theodor Storm and Conrad Ferdinand Meyer, and the greatest of them all, Friedrich Hebbel of Ditmarschen and the Swiss Gottfried Keller, who, to be sure, received only belated recognition compared to such popular favourites of the times as Friedrich Spielhagen. Music was still the fondest refuge of the German citizen and proved his consolation through all the disappointments of political life. Felix Mendelssohn and Robert Schumann were succeeded by Johannes Brahms, with greater depth and riches, and many lesser talents lovingly carried on traditional art forms.

Richard Wagner (1813–82), however, as romantic and as revolutionary, seized on German musical creation with all the force and imperiousness of his mind, his genius. Along with the Russian anarchist Bakunin he had fought on the barricades in Dresden in 1849 and had to live in exile for years afterward. His early operas are directly derived, as to both style and taste, from Giacomo Meyerbeer's grand opera, a German form that grew up in competition with the traditional French and Italian forms. Later, Wagner was strongly influenced by Berlioz. The young Wagner was, above all, a master of orchestration and an impresario with an inexhaustible flow of ideas. His energy, his sombre lust for power, and his craving for independence determined his extraordinary career. He was the greatest genius of the theatre in Germany since Friedrich von Schiller. Later on he wrote his own texts in impassioned, exaggerated language not always easily comprehended. His life was full of struggle, devotion, sacrifice, and ecstasy. He hated the uninspired average and the stupidity of habit, and in this respect Wagner's life struggle took on symptomatic significance. In him rebelliousness was joined in an essentially German manner to reflections on the nature of the true German view of the world that should be valid for all humanity. And then the romantic Wagner, who was drunk with history and tended to exaggerate everything to monstrous and Baroque dimensions, came into contact with Schopenhauer's philosophy and was unable to resist its magic, pregnant with destiny. In this era that received its strongest impulses from Bismarck and Karl Marx, in this era of authority with its emphasis on the material of unfolding economic and military power, in this era when science and technics came into their own in spite of the protests of traditionalists, Richard Wagner, sensuous and demonic, became the opponent of all these powers, to which he was nevertheless deeply related—became the herald of the all-embracing work of art that should reflect the new world picture, allaying all want, all conflict.

INTERNATIONAL DEVELOPMENTS AND THE CRIMEAN WAR (1853–5)

During the fifty years of its life the German Confederation ventured to take independent political action in only one instance: the struggle with Denmark for Schleswig-Holstein. For the time being, this spelled its utter ruin. The duchies were sacrificed. In the London Protocol of 1852 the great powers of Europe imposed recognition of the Glücksburg line even for Schleswig-Holstein. The line of Augustenburg dukes, who were entitled to the succession under German law, accepted a compromise, with a large money indemnity for renouncing the succession. Now Denmark had a free hand in the politics of her collective state, and she accorded German interests in the duchies only grudging consideration. The German Confederation had very wisely left the painful winding-up of this affair to the German great powers. It was clear that from the German point of view the question could not be regarded as conclusively solved. The northern border of Germany was thus still exposed to political and popular unrest and insecurity. The same was true of the eastern border. Once again the autocratic powers, Russia, Austria, and Prussia, had succeeded in suppressing a movement for independence among the Poles and the other western Slavic stocks. But Europe still seethed with nationalism. What was good for the German goose must needs be good for the Italian or the Slavic gander. From Italy, therefore, the southern border of Austria was threatened, in the form it had at the time.

The French Second Empire was bringing new pressure to bear on the western border also. Napoleon III revelled in chameleon dreams of expansion. His lively spirit ranged over Belgium and the Palatinate—over the whole left bank of the Rhine, as a matter of fact, especially the Saar region—and then on to Italian border districts in the Alpine area and the Mediterranean. The old French slogan of the boundaries of the first Peace of Paris of 1814 bristled with new meaning. The realm that centered in the Church of St. Paul had in a certain sense carried on the traditions of the third Germany. Now Napoleon III resuscitated the idea of a Rhenish confederation; at the courts of western and southwestern Germany, where he encountered advocacy of Russian interests, his influence was strengthened by his dynastic connections, as became very clear in the course of the Crimean War.

From the end of the reign of Napoleon I up to the first World War most of the great problems of Europe hinged on the eastern question. Czar Nicholas I of Russia, who had some reason to regard himself as the victor over the Revolution of 1848, now thought the time had come to crown his life-work. The events of the revolution had cemented the alliance of autocratic Russia, Austria, and Prussia so firmly that the last two held no threat for Russia; Austria had every reason to be grateful, and Prussia allowed herself to be treated as a sort of vassal. The Czar believed his relations with England to be clear and transparent on the basis of former agreements, while the imperial France of the upstart Louis Napoleon was isolated, so far as foreign policy was concerned. But the Czar's calculations proved mistaken. The western powers, France and England, combined to protect the Turks and took up their fight against Russia. Moreover, the alliance of Russia, Austria, and Prussia broke apart, and the old antagonism between Austria and Russia was rekindled by the eastern question.

Austria regarded herself as a Danubian state. Archduke John, for example, who from living in Styria was well acquainted with the character of the southern Slavs, enthusiastically advocated the Balkan interests of the imperial state. The tradition of Prince Eugene was entwined with the tangible tasks of building up communication systems here and developing an economic policy. Metternich had taken up the cudgels for the Ottoman Empire as being the legitimate ruler of the Christian Balkan Slavs. The prospect of a Russian protectorate over the Balkans was intolerable to Austria. She therefore co-operated diplomatically with the western powers, mobilized her troops at the Russian border, and insisted on the evacuation of Russian troops from the Danubian principalities. The Austrian imperial state and the western powers had a common interest in keeping

446

Moldavia and Wallachia independent of Russia and also in maintaining free shipping on the Danube. They hoped to be able to guard the interests of the Christians under Turkish sovereignty by upholding that sovereignty. This was probably the most serious mistake in the policy of Austria and the western powers. Once the Balkan peoples were touched by nationalism, there could be neither stop nor stay, and the antagonism between Austria and Russia was bound to become more and more pronounced. For this reason Austria's attitude in the Crimean War finally gave the impetus to her own ultimate downfall.

Prussia's stand on these questions was quite different. From the latter part of Frederick the Great's reign she had maintained friendly relations with the Ottoman Empire. In the first war that Nicholas I waged against the Turks (1828) Prussia had played the part of a successful mediator. At that time she felt no pressing interest either in the Balkans or in the Levant; her attitude was therefore shaped by general political considerations. Austria and the western powers urged her to make common cause with them. King Frederick William IV was wavering. The liberal opposition in Prussia was opposed to the Russian policy if only as a matter of principle. The moderate conservatives had founded a journal of their own, the *Prussian Weekly* (*Wochenblatt*); in it a number of well-informed diplomats and high officials were urging a connection with the western powers. The Prince of Prussia, too, approved this policy of the two Counts von der Goltz, Bonin the war minister, Christian J. von Bunsen the Prussian ambassador in London, and Professor Moritz August von Bethmann Hollweg. The strong conservative group around the Prussian King, however, was in favour of co-operation with Russia either through an actual alliance and active participation in the war or at least through friendly neutrality. This policy of the Gerlach brothers and of Edwin von Manteuffel, then a colonel, was strongly supported by Bismarck, the envoy to the German Confederation, who came to Berlin repeatedly to hearten Otto von Manteuffel, the President of the Ministry, in his opposition to the western powers. Bismarck also clashed again and again with the English ambassador in Frankfurt. Thus he came to have the not unjustified reputation of being a Russophile. That Prussia held out against the promises of the western powers was primarily due to Bismarck's energy. The English government never forgot this attitude of Bismarck's and regarded him with suspicion thenceforward; it was convinced that the Crimean War would have ended with decisive victory for the western powers, with the expulsion of Russian despotism from Europe, if Prussia had been willing to join the anti-Russian front in Europe.

The antagonism between Prussia and the west sharpened. Bismarck also had a hand in the alliance that Prussia made with Austria in April 1854 for mutual neutrality. The powers guaranteed the safety of each other's possessions and pledged themselves to guard collective German interests. Bismarck intended to win Austria over to Prussia's pro-Russian policy, but he failed. Nevertheless Austria set great store by the alliance, since she thought that in an emergency she could now count on Prussia's sword to defend her Italian possessions. Prussia, however, did not renew the agreement when it ran out. The German secondary and small states were also afraid of being swept into the war; at the Bamberg Conference they set forth their neutrality. The English government made unsuccessful attempts to enlist German mercenaries in the traditional style.

The Crimean War ended without clean-cut results. In spite of all her military failures, Russia, now under a new Czar, Alexander II, came out well enough. England had had her fill of active participation in the wars of the Continent for a long time. Emperor Napoleon III had done magnificently by himself; the alliance with England had secured the greatest prestige for him, and since he had saved Russia from serious humiliation, it was possible for the two countries to approach each other again. Austria suffered most, since by delivering an ultimatum she had forced Russia to negotiate. Russia was not to forget this cautious and hostile attitude of the Austrian imperial state, which gained nothing from it. Probably Austria, if she had been a little more skilful, could have acquired a protectorate over the Danubian principalities.

Navigation of the Danube had now become free, to the advantage of all southern Germany. Prussia's policy had failed to make any impression; it was only with difficulty that this questionable great power won admittance to the peace conference at Paris, and she played a sorry part there. But Russia's friendship meant much for Prussia's future, and her relations with France were agreeable. Again it was Bismarck who fought all prejudices against the revolutionary upstart Napoleon III and recommended that the countries approach each other in an amicable way. And so the three great Continental military powers, Russia, Prussia, and France, entered on a political collaboration that did not need to consider England and could get the better of all the other European powers. As a result of his experiences in Frankfurt, Bismarck grew more and more embittered against Austria from year to year. His altercations with the Austrian delegates at the federal diet were often petty and venomous; back of them lay the conviction that Austria would never allow Prussia more than a second place in Germany, and this aroused Bismarck, with his Prussian self-confidence, to a state of deep indignation. With his own characteristic genius and cunning he prepared for a great settlement with Austria. For the time being, however, he could only wait.

The rule of his patron, Frederick William IV, came to a sad end. The quarrel concerning the King of Prussia's sovereign rights over the principality of Neuenburg in Switzerland, part of the Orange inheritance, involved Prussia in an absurd conflict with the Swiss Confederation over political principles of a sort. Autocracy and democracy were again snarling at each other, but, thanks to the good services of the French Emperor, the public was spared the spectacle of Swiss soil occupied by the Prussian army. King Frederick William IV retained his cherished right to continue calling himself Prince of Neuenburg, and he released frugal Switzerland from her treaty obligation to pay a money indemnity for his final renunciation. Prussia became a refuge for the leaders of the Neuenburg royalist party. The mounting mental disease of the Prussian King made a proxy necessary, and presently his heir became the regent. This was the beginning of the memorable career of the Prince of Prussia.

WILLIAM I (1861–88). THE NEW ERA

William, no longer in his first youth, was a distinguished-looking officer, still supple and active, as indeed he was even in his old age. The later King and Emperor William I was, above all, a soldier; he remained a soldier to the end of his days. He was not a general, for his intellectual gifts were not above the average. Everything bold or fiery or touched with genius affected him as strange, even when he put up with it with his characteristic self-confidence. He really did know something about training troops and organizing an army; this was the world he lived in. He set down his ideas on these matters, and though he wrote in a long-winded, clumsy style, he said only what he himself really knew and thought, and he stood firm by it. Otherwise he simplified the world to meet his personal requirements. His evangelical Christianity was straightforward and honest, without philosophical scruples and wholly innocent of fanaticism.

According to his philosophy war was part of the natural order of things decreed by God; victories were according to the will of God. This military King of the old military state of Prussia regarded war as an activity of complete propriety; even while he was still heir to the throne he repeatedly proposed resort to arms as a solution to conflicts in foreign policy, though at that time it was a well-known fact that Prussia was not prepared. Any other mode of action would probably have struck him as cowardly. This alone shows how little of a politician he was. He lacked the best qualifications: broad vision, knowledge, and a gift for effecting combinations. During his entire life he depended on his advisers and on his immediate circle in all questions of either foreign or domestic policy. He started on his career as a sober, respectable reactionary, but under the impressions of the year of revolution and of his stay in England, as well as the views of his wife, Augusta, a princess of Weimar who had been reared in the Germany of culture, he was converted to a type of conservatism, friendly to reform, that tried to reconcile whatever was good in the old era with the good in modern demands.

Augusta was cleverer than William. She realized the difficulties inherent in men and in facts better than he. She enjoyed complicated situations and saw through them. She worked unsuccessfully for certain goals, among them the King's abdication and her husband's stepping aside in favour of her son Frederick, a step she suggested several times during the Revolution of 1848. Disappointments merely spurred her on to greater effort. And now that William himself was having his turn at ruling after all, Augusta thought her time had come. William was Prussian; Augusta belonged to the Germany of culture. William was practical and professional; Augusta was idealistic and European, with a strong feeling for peace and liberty. In her something of the cosmopolitan eighteenth century was combined with the romantic trends of the early nineteenth. William's attitude and mode of life were simple and dignified, plain and unpretentious; in Augusta there was a suggestion of preciosity, of the flourishes of the old princely regimes. These human contrasts assumed historical significance because the differences between the royal pair were to culminate in a struggle about the personality and the work of Bismarck.

William, the Prince Regent, initiated the new era by a foreign-policy program that ran counter to the convictions of Bismarck, and the latter soon had to give up his post as envoy to the federal diet in Frankfurt, although he did so against his will. He went into honourable exile in the capacity of minister to St. Petersburg. There this friend of Russia became a true connoisseur of that country and a master of the great business of diplomacy. In the meantime the Prince Regent of Prussia and his staff preferred a co-operation with Austria and England that was directed against France. This was a policy that corresponded to a moderately nationalistic liberal program in internal affairs as well. The new ministers chosen by the Prince Regent were old liberals, faithful to the constitution, such as Baron Robert von Patow, or moderate conservatives, such as the scholarly professor of law Bethmann-Hollweg, or loyal champions of union with Austria, like Alexander von Schleinitz, the most elegant plotter of intrigues at the court of Berlin. Elections were now no longer influenced, and the ministry had an imposing majority of votes. It seemed that Prussia was on the way to becoming a modern constitutional state. She was seeking the road to Germany.

In the meantime Austria's relation to France was growing steadily worse, with Italy as the bone of contention, so that war was inevitable. This put a difficult decision up to the "new era." The reviving people's movement in Germany was in sympathy with Italy's struggle for her national state. The parallel development of the two countries became a favourite point in popular argument. But the imperial state of Austria was still fondly regarded in Catholic southern Germany and along the Rhine; the idea of help from France to tip the scales in Italy offended the national sense of many patriots. The Prince Regent himself would have liked to help the old ally of 1813 against Bonapartism. The methods and the conduct of the state of Sardinia and of King Victor Emmanuel irritated all legitimist court circles. Prussia, then, was prepared to act, but she could ask something for doing so. Austria, however, so far from being cordial, was suspicious. On neither the question of tolls nor that of fortresses of the Confederation did she wish to make the slightest concessions to her competitor Prussia. If Prussia was to fight against Napoleon on the Rhine, the least she could ask for was unlimited command, and this of course meant the beginning of the long-desired military union in the Confederation—the revival, in military form, of the efforts toward union. Emperor Francis Joseph preferred to make a hasty peace rather than commit himself to anything of this sort. Other circumstances influenced his decision: the sorry condition of the Austrian army and the danger of a patriotic uprising in Hungary. But the mainspring of his actions was his envy of Prussia, who had now mobilized her troops and sent them to the Rhine border.

RENEWAL OF THE NATIONAL MOVEMENT. AUSTRIA AS A CONSTITUTIONAL STATE

All the secondary and small states had acclaimed the new era in Prussia. A liberal Prussia could count on the support of patriotic citizens and also on the following of princes who were occupied with the German idea, such as Grand Duke Frederick I of Baden. An awakened and matured people's urgent wish for free national unfolding of its powers was stirringly voiced at meetings and in pamphlets, but especially in associations like the German National Association. Its aims were a unified German central power and a German parliament. Here the most vital and fruitful ideas of 1848 again came to the fore. The National Association openly expressed itself in favour of a Little Germany. Its chairman was Rudolf von Bennigsen, a landed proprietor of Hanover. He was assisted by Johann Miquel, a genius in matters of administration and finance, Franz Duncker, who owned a Berlin newspaper, and Gabriel Riesser of Hamburg, who championed assimilation of the Jews. The National Association made Coburg its headquarters, and Duke Ernest II of Saxe-Coburg-Gotha took it under his protection. Frankfurt had refused to recognize the National Association; in Saxony and Hanover it was subjected to persecution. Nor was the Prussian government cordially disposed toward it. Nothwithstanding, it spread through northern Germany and the Rhineland, while in southern Germany it called forth counter-associations. Its goal in 1862 was the restoration of the 1849 Frankfurt constitution. The Schiller celebration of 1859, the first German gymnastic festival (*Turnfest*) of 1860, which also took place in Coburg, the numerous song festivals and rifle matches, were all manifestations of a national will that would no longer let itself be dammed back. Scientific congresses also tended in the same direction. The delegates of the territorial parliaments even ventured to assemble in order to pledge themselves to the constitution of 1849. The spirit of the Church of St. Paul seemed to have come to life again. But how could all these hopes be realized?

As early as 1859 the ministers of the secondary states drafted a reform program in Würzburg: a unified federal military constitution, a federal court, unified civil and criminal legislation, uniform money and measures and weights. But the great German powers could not agree together. The proposals of the Grand Duke of Baden were too much in the Little German direction to be acceptable in Vienna. Italy was seething with a very strong national revolutionary movement; this was bound to react on defeated Austria, which now had to give up Lombardy. If the imperial state wanted to maintain its position in Germany, it would have to undertake reform no less eagerly than Prussia.

In October 1860 Emperor Francis Joseph issued a decree that restored Hungary's old constitution, promised the crown lands constitutions of their own, and set up a parliament of a hundred members for the collective state. A liberal ministry took over the conduct of public business; it was headed by Anton, Knight of Schmerling, who was well known from the Church of St. Paul in Frankfurt. The February decree of 1861 stated the basic principles of constitutionalism, but the Hungarians wished a purely personal union, and the Poles and the Czechs made national demands of their own and held aloof from parliamentary proceedings. In spite of these great difficulties the budget committee met. The very necessary banking act was adopted. Otherwise the constitutional machinery stalled; nationalist disputes made co-operation impossible. But through her honest efforts toward constitutionalism Austria won many new sympathizers in Germany, and she was able to enlist the majority of the secondary and small states against Prussian aims. The Reform Union of Greater Germany now confronted the National Association. In 1860 the French Emperor received Savoy and Nice in return for his services

453

in helping to establish the Kingdom of Italy. He harped on the right of France to her natural boundaries. The disagreement between the two German great powers improved his prospect of German territorial acquisitions, but his unconcealed designs forced Germany again to unite and to defend herself.

PRUSSIAN MILITARY REFORM. CONFLICT

Austria's liberal policy and her efforts to create a united Germany had all the more hope of success because Prussia's new era was closing with failure and dissatisfaction. After his brother's death in 1861 the Prince Regent at last ascended the throne. William I himself set the royal crown on his head in Königsberg, and by this solemn act he confessed his faith in divine grace and feudalism. Prussia as a great power had in any event already manifested her vigorous will to life, and this played a serious part in the question of military reform. King William as a military expert knew the weaknesses of the Prussian army that had become apparent in 1848 and during various mobilizations. He was troubled on two scores. The levies did not correspond to the great increase in population; universal conscription was no longer carried out, and consequently the first levy of the *Landwehr* was called at once on mobilization. The professional officer had always been suspicious of the *Landwehr's* politics, for it had sided with the opposition, especially along the Rhine.

Every army wants its soldiers to be as young as possible. A plan was therefore conceived to utilize the younger material to the fullest extent and to split up the *Landwehr;* that is, to combine the major part of the first levy of the *Landwehr* with the troops of the line as a reserve. In this way the army was to become a rejuvenated and politically reliable instrument in the hands of the government. The conflict now arising about the army was twofold. So far as military technique was in question, the parliament was perfectly willing to submit to the decisions of military experts. The liberal majority of the lower house, especially the members drawn from the Progressive Party, which had existed since 1861 and had won a great success in the new elections, consisted entirely of Prussian patriots and was completely in sympathy with army reform, which was bound to strengthen Prussia's position in Germany and hence was to the national interest. The majority also realized that not all the technical details could be discussed publicly in the house, since this would mean giving away military secrets about the defence of the country.

It was the other, the political, side of the matter that seemed decisive. The lower house took up the work of the Prussian national assembly of 1848 and wanted to make a modern constitutional state of Prussia. The Prussian army was intended to be an army of the people. The transformation of *Landwehr* regiments into regiments of the line contradicted the spirit of 1813. Possessing budgetary rights, the lower house refused to consider provisional measures. From first to last it was ready and willing to appropriate funds for any necessary technical changes in the army, but it used all the legal means within its power to fight against the separation of the army from the body of the people, the shaping of military power into a tool of reactionary power groups. And that was actually the crux of the matter.

The military party feared the dawn of parliamentarism in Prussia. Its leaders, General E. von Manteuffel (died 1885) and the Minister of War, Albrecht von Roon (died 1879), wished not to join forces with liberalism, powerful as it had become, but to fight against it. They hoped to stifle the new stirrings of a democratic people's movement by means of a counter-revolution, and for this they required troops completely under the control of the crown and the feudal aristocracy. And so the government began to reform the army in defiance of criticism and parliamentary opposition. It slipped from one temporary arrangement into another and carefully kept clear of such possibilities of agreement as existed. Relatively unimportant technical questions were pushed into the foreground in order to make the conflict irreconcilable—for instance, the question of three years' military service, which General von Roon himself regarded as fairly immaterial.

THE FIGHTING MINISTRY (1862). BISMARCK ON TOP

At the bottom of the struggle was the fateful question whether it would be possible to make Prussia German and liberal or whether this great power would hold to the traditional conditions of her growth, a purely Prussian state egoism of autocratic and military stamp. King William I was convinced that he must not yield about military reform. He did not quite see through the secret plans of the

455

reactionary military party. He suffered under the conflict, which shattered the peace of his home, and he even gave some thought to abdication. New conservative ministers met with no success. Roon and his friends recommended a fighting ministry headed by Bismarck. The King rejected the idea, especially as he did not trust either Bismarck personally or his leanings in foreign policy. But Bismarck was finally summoned just the same, and the King remained at his post.

Bismarck enforced the reform of the army against the will of the parliamentary majority. He dispensed with a budget, not caring whether he violated the constitution; he even claimed, with challenging arrogance, that there was an ambiguity in the constitution and that it was the duty of the government to interpret it. He declared that the conflict resolved itself into a question of power and that it would be decided by whoever held the reins in his hand. Here was an event whose importance can scarcely be measured. The Prussian crown denied the constitutional state that was demanded by the Germany of culture; it exercised absolute dictatorship. Neither Bismarck nor Roon hesitated to thunder and sneer in the lower house. Public opinion was shackled by ordinances about the press. Officials were reprimanded, associations dissolved. Town councils that showed liberal tendencies were rebuked by the government. The country was filled with anger, bitterness, and unrest, and Crown Prince Frederick of Prussia himself openly objected to his father's ministry.

FERDINAND LASSALLE

For many years Bismarck had the reputation of being the worst enemy of the liberal citizenry and seemed to cancel out Prussia's German vocation. Two factors soon brought about a surprising turn in events. The first was concerned with party politics. The socialist movement started up again. Karl Marx wrote his great fundamental work, *Capital,* in London. In Paris Proudhon was publishing his most important writings, and Napoleon III gave them some serious thought. The wishes and ambitions of the middle class receded before the elemental needs of the lower classes. How were these masses to be kept occupied, fed, educated, given a place in political life, and how were their desire for acceptance and their right to live to be appeased? Those who thought along socialistic or communistic lines accused capital of ruthless exploitation, and capitalists were terrified by the threat of ineluctable revenge from the miserable. It was only natural that those responsible for their misery should show a willingness to help, if only from an instinct of self-preservation. Sharp criticism was now directed against the bourgeoisie as well, for did they not have just as much pride in social standing, as much selfishness and will to power, as the hated feudal class? Did a liberal ideology make them any more humane, free, or generous toward their dependents? Nowadays the common man was no longer up against the baron, but rather the industrialist and financier. The employee class that was springing up shared in the fate of the proletariat: any attempt to rise was almost hopelessly blocked.

In Germany the genius of Ferdinand Lassalle (1825–64) now seized on the lower classes' need of action. With the sharpest sort of mind and a winning eloquence, Lassalle was a rare blend of intelligence and will. This agitator in the grand style was the offspring of the prosperous Jewish middle class. Fired equally by personal ambition and devotion to a cause, he made himself known to the widest German public as a new power. He believed that neither charity nor economic associations could solve the social question. The workers, as he expounded, must help themselves; they must form a political party of their own and thus secure a voice in affairs of state; they must force the state to recognize them and to co-operate with them. The workers must form their own productive associations and thus gradually become entrepreneurs themselves. That was the only way to escape the iron law by which wages are always kept at a minimum for the barest subsistence, to the advantage of profits for those on top. Lassalle's most striking argument was that only through universal and equal suffrage could the workers become a force in politics. Thus his socialism seized on the basic principle of democracy as a weapon against capitalism. In 1863 the General Association of German Workers was founded in Leipzig, with Lassalle as president.

Bismarck followed these developments closely. Might there be a potential ally here for his struggle with the liberal bourgeoisie? Was this not a welcome counterbalance to the parliamentary ideology of progress? Could there not be co-operation between autocratic dictatorship and the aroused and arising masses? Bismarck, who saw

Lassalle repeatedly, had the greatest respect for his mind and for the ethos of his utterances. The premature death of the agitator put a sudden end to promising possibilities. Later his socialist comrades spoke of him as "Baron Itzig," with a mockery that could not by any stretch of the imagination be set down to mere good-natured teasing. But was it really necessary for Lassalle, like a bourgeois on the rise, to play the part of the knight-errant in the matrimonial and money affairs of Countess Sophie Hatzfeldt? And then there followed that passionate attachment to Helene von Dönniges, the daughter of a well-known Bavarian councillor of state. The beautiful girl went to Lassalle in Switzerland and put herself in his hands; she was engaged to a Rumanian aristocrat. Instead of marrying her at once and thus facing society with an accomplished fact, Lassalle sent her back to her parents, because he thought nothing would do short of a wedding with the usual pomp and the parents' blessing. The Rumanian then challenged him to a duel and shot him. The paradoxical nature of Lassalle's death accorded with the deeper tensions in his life. The German labour movement had been deprived of the man who had "forged its sword." But the masses had become a factor in Prussian and indeed German politics. The Prussian Progressives saw themselves threatened in their struggle against Bismarck's unconstitutional dictatorship by the new mass movement, which was only too delighted to ally itself with state authority against the bourgeoisie. But perhaps the bourgeoisie could steal a march on the lower classes. The possibility was reinforced by a development in foreign policy.

THE BEGINNINGS OF BISMARCK'S FOREIGN POLICY. THE ALVENSLEBEN CONVENTION

Bismarck made a first show of strength in straightening out the affairs of Hesse-Kassel. This state was still embroiled over its liberal constitution of 1831. The mismanagement of the dynasty and of its friends and abettors called for some drastic remedy. The Elector had defied the people's movement within his own domains, as well as the decisions of the federal diet. Bismarck finally succeeded in getting the constitution accepted by threatening to form some connection with the agnates of the Elector—in other words to initiate discussions with the other members of the electoral house with a view to deposing the Elector. Bismarck was without prejudice. In Hesse-

Kassel he acted in defence of just those liberal principles that he opposed in Prussia; such action in this case served to undermine a
dynasty that had earned such contempt as attached to no other in
Germany. Nowhere else had the clear light of the nineteenth century
shone on such a shameless keeping of mistresses. The maddest stroke
of this kind had been the last Elector's paying a cavalry captain,
Lehmann, to give him his wife, who was then made a countess.

Emperor Francis Joseph in the meantime had met with disappointment in Italy, and now, from the vantage point of a liberal Austria,
he tried to gain control of the reform of the German Confederation.
Bismarck worked against him. So the idea of building up a kind of
parliamentary representation in Frankfurt with delegates to the
Confederation was dropped. The assembly of princes at Frankfurt
(1863) was a failure, because, under Bismarck's pressure, the King
of Prussia did not attend—the only German prince who did not.
The discussions among the princes were just as futile as those among
the delegates and ministers.

Immediately after assuming his current post Bismarck had made
the famous remark that the German question could not be solved by
speeches or by majority decisions, but only by blood and iron. Very
early in his career, as early as Frankfurt, he had had in view a forced
settlement between Austria and Prussia as the only decisive method.
But this did not in the least prevent this clever diplomat from going
along with his great Austrian competitor for a considerable period,
if only out of consideration for the feelings of the King and of the
old conservative circles in Prussia, which were profoundly reluctant
to break with their ally of the Wars of Liberation.

The success of the national revolution in Italy spurred the movement among all the Slavic peoples. In 1863 there was a new insurrection in Poland. The minor war that began with the patriots spread
from Congress (Russian) Poland to the regions held by the German
powers. Emperor Napoleon III tried to assist the unfortunate Poles
and initiated diplomatic negotiations with England and Austria that
had the support of other states in Europe. Any substantial help was
out of the question, since Austria, in spite of Slavic sympathies, was
committed to a certain course as one of the partitioning powers,
while England rejected any active interference in Continental affairs.
The alliance of the Crimean War had ceased to function. Bismarck

459

openly sided with Russia; any sort of restoration of Poland seemed intolerable to his Prussian nationalism. Through General Gustav von Alvensleben Prussia concluded a convention with Russia in February 1863, according to which each state could count on the other's assistance in suppressing any insurrection. Military leaders of either country were mutually to be allowed to cross the borders of the other if necessary.

This sacrifice of sovereignty aroused the liveliest protest among representatives of the Prussian people and diplomats of the western powers. The convention went into effect and was acted on, but the Russian military authorities took this as a slur on their prestige and openly expressed their disapproval. Bismarck was perfectly willing to sacrifice the agreement at the earliest possible opportunity; he simply declared that ratification should have been secured. From a long-range point of view this definite diplomatic reverse signified incalculable gain. In the eyes of the King and of the old conservatives Bismarck had been under suspicion as an adherent of Bonapartism; during the brief period of his ambassadorship in Paris his old friendship with Emperor Napoleon III had been still more firmly cemented. But now Bismarck had given proof of his reliability as a counter-revolutionist. And besides this he had won the confidence of the Czar. Only the co-operation of Prussia and Russia made possible the great successes of the coming years. A domestic policy of dictatorship and a foreign policy of friendship with Russia harmonized with each other. Nevertheless Prussia could not decide on an offensive war against Austria and France as proposed by Czar Alexander II of Russia in Berlin. Prussia carried on these wars by herself and wholly on her own account, though she was always sure of Russia's support. Bismarck was not inflexible in his foreign policy. He remained elastic, forestalled any possible coalition among the neighbouring powers, and kept open the chance of forming any alliances he wanted himself. He took advantage of the strong principles of his partners. He had only one aim: the increase of Prussia's power, all the principles of the age notwithstanding.

Bismarck conducted three wars during the first decade that he held office. He regarded war as an indispensable means to reach certain goals, never as either fine or desirable in itself. The short war period was followed by a long period of peace, devoted to the sober consolidation of gains. Bismarck was no world conqueror, but a statesman who knew how to be daring as well as prudent.

WAR FOR SCHLESWIG-HOLSTEIN (1864)

Perhaps Bismarck's most astonishing diplomatic achievement was his solution of the difficult problem of Schleswig-Holstein. The German governments had left the unfortunate duchies in the lurch, but the German people had not forgotten them. The coming German national state must bring even to the duchies the fulfilment of their desires. The Danes stood by the idea of their collective state, and amiable negotiations toward an agreement with the federal diet bore no fruit. The Danish royal decree of March 1863 granted the demands of the Eider Danes; Schleswig was joined to Denmark, so that the Kingdom of Denmark now extended to the little river Eider. Only in Holstein were the estates allowed to participate in legislation. The federal diet demanded that the royal decree be abolished, and it threatened to use force. The kingdoms of Saxony and Hanover were commissioned to enforce the diet's demand. The problem became a European affair when the new Danish King, Christian IX, of the Glücksburg line, ascended the throne and the constitution prepared for the Danish collective state was thereupon promulgated. The Duke of Augustenburg, in spite of his father's explicit renunciation, claimed the hereditary right of succession, and he declared himself ruler of the duchies under the name of Frederick VIII. Although this procedure naturally met with criticism, public opinion in Germany hailed the Duke enthusiastically. Both the Little Germans and the Greater Germans spoke out for him. Princes and representatives of the people, with the Prussians in the lead, saw the cause of the Duke of Augustenburg as the cause of justice and freedom.

Bismarck had long projected the acquisition of the duchies by the Prussian state, but he had to use the greatest caution in pushing this bold idea. The particularistic, the liberal, and the dynastic powers in Germany were opposed to Prussia, which had then reached the peak of her unpopularity. How could Bismarck's plan be carried out? As far as foreign policy was concerned the situation was not bad. During the Revolution of 1848 the three great European neighbouring states, Russia, France, and Great Britain, had co-operated in preventing the problem of the duchies from being solved in line with German desires. Now Bismarck had gained Russia's friendship. The western powers were at odds. Napoleon III bore the English a grudge for their inertia in the matter of Poland, and now he retaliated. Austria, well aware of the greed of the French Emperor, was more willing than formerly to take a lively interest in the duchies, in line with German hopes and duties. For the same reason the secondary states could not hold aloof. England presented the most difficult problem. She became increasingly inimical to Bismarck's policy during the entire period up to the founding of the German Reich. Queen Victoria continued to carry out the ideas of her deceased husband, the Prince Consort, as far as she could: mediation between the two German great powers; preservation of the balance of power between central Europe and the two neighbours, France and Russia; maintenance of existing boundaries, but encouragement of the German national movement. Bismarck, because of his reactionary domestic policy, met with growing suspicion in England. The dynastic connection between the ruling house of Prussia and that of England heightened London's interest and concern, and Prussia was given frequent advice and warning.

What Bismarck did about the duchies led to the verge of an open break with England. Duke Frederick of Augustenburg was related to the English dynasty and was a close friend of the Prussian Crown Prince and his English-born wife; thus English policy was entirely in tune with the general mood of the German people in taking the part of the Duke of Augustenburg. As early as 1848 Palmerston had wanted to detach the Danish-speaking portions of northern Schleswig by a plebiscite and unite them with Denmark. This would have been the most nearly adequate solution for the times, even though it violated historical connections. Bismarck too had once taken up and urged the idea of a plebiscite and of partition along the linguistic dividing line. But he resented English interference as such and replied to threats from England by unflinchingly prosecuting his policy. He was not in the least intimidated, because he was sure that Great Britain was unable to follow up her threats with action. France alone constituted a real danger to Bismarck's policy, but he was certain that Napoleon III would not resort to arms on account of the duchies.

Bismarck involved himself in the most elaborate double-dealing.

462

He prevented Denmark from coming to an understanding with the German Confederation; he saw to it that the secondary states did not take any action; he won Austria over as a collaborator. Thus both the German great powers proceeded jointly against little Denmark, who would have to receive help, or there could be no doubt as to the outcome of the war. The Danes defended themselves bravely, but the German powers had more than merely numerical superiority. For the first time General Helmuth von Moltke, the head of the Prussian general staff, came into the foreground. His well-considered plan of operation was, however, not exactly carried out in every respect. A carefully calculated, powerful Prussian style of warfare was now perfected, warfare without great losses, without noisy heroism, but conducted with the aid of every sort of modern technical aid and with quiet, methodical organization.

Personally Moltke suggested a scholar. He was a supreme master of observation and an enemy of fussiness. As a writer he weighed the value of each word and built his sentences and presented his ideas with the same sense of responsibility with which he led his troops and massed his artillery. Moltke was no politician. He could not organize groups or conceive ambitious plans. His rise was due to his practical achievements, and he had many obstacles to overcome; the arrogance of the guards and the restrictions of the barracks produced petty annoyances of every kind. Many of Moltke's operations were spoiled by the obstinate stupidity of his subordinates. Thus, for instance, the best-known feat of the war against Denmark, the storming of the ramparts of Düppel, was undertaken against his will; if his plan of encirclement had been followed, no great sacrifice of life would have been necessary.

The first peace negotiations in London failed mainly because of the stubbornness of the Danes, who refused to recognize that they were fighting for a lost cause and were still hoping for help from England. But public opinion in England forbade intervention, and the Queen's feeling was the same. Palmerston and Lord Russell, the Foreign Secretary, were not sorry to have to renounce a war that might have netted them a moral victory for their policy of bluffing, but would have ended in military and political defeat. When the Danes triumphed over the Austrian fleet near Heligoland, it became easier for them to make peace. They had to cede the duchies to the two German great powers. But what now was to be done with these lands? If Prussia were to put up with a new small German state at her northern border, she would require certain special strategic guarantees. The Duke of Augustenburg negotiated with Bismarck; even if he had been a great deal cleverer than he was, Bismarck and Prussia were dangerous opponents. In no case would the Duke have had a pleasant time ruling his lands.

The quarrel about the duchies now so poisoned relations between Austria and Prussia that war seemed imminent. The fact that Bismarck transferred the Prussian naval station to Kiel revealed his aims. The old feudal class, the court, and the group around the Crown Prince were deeply averse to war with Austria. The old conservative Prussian spirit had never approved the rising German national movement, but even this ally Bismarck was now ready to mobilize. In his conversations with Lassalle universal and equal suffrage for Prussia had already figured; it symbolized the connection with the idea of revolution and meant a common front of dictatorship and democracy against the bourgeoisie that stood between them. Austria's internal difficulties were so great that she was glad to iron out the quarrel once more.

The Convention of Gastein of 1865 created a provisional arrangement that was very favourable to Prussia. For the time being, Austria assumed the administration of Holstein, Prussia that of Schleswig. But Prussia retained the Kiel naval station and the right to military roads through Holstein, as well as her own postal system there. Besides this, both duchies joined the Prussian Customs Union. Prussia received the small Duchy of Lauenburg, but had to pay an indemnity. She was to be allowed to construct her projected canal across Holstein to connect the North Sea with the Baltic. Duke Frederick of Augustenburg, with whom Bismarck was still negotiating, could no longer hope for anything. Austria had little use for Holstein, which was as good as lost, and immediately tried to exchange it for land in Silesia.

The western powers were not at all satisfied. England felt a growing distaste for this Continental trafficking in territories. Bismarck had to pacify Napoleon III at Biarritz. The French Emperor was not nearly so friendly to Prussian policy as Bismarck had led the old King to believe in order to calm his fears, but was demanding in-

demnities above all, in the interest of his own position and to maintain the balance of power in case of further Prussian increases. King
William had frequently stated in his own precise and unambiguous
manner that France was not to have any German territory. It was
an honourable stand, but it did not lead anywhere. Bismarck struck
a far less rigid attitude. For years he had found ways to put off
Napoleon III with vague promises; he had often pointed him toward
Belgium and Luxemburg and even gave it as his personal opinion
that cession of the Prussian Saar region to France might be discussed. King William, true to the spirit of the Wars of Liberation,
would have liked to confront Bonapartism with his sword drawn.
Bismarck was not held back by any national German sentiment, and
even the old King was horrified at this purely Prussian lack of bias,
which became very evident in the course of Bismarck's further preparations for the settlement with Austria. Prussia forbade agitation for
the Duke of Augustenburg in Schleswig, but Baron Gablenz, the
Austrian governor of Holstein, permitted it. Bismarck demanded
the expulsion of Duke Frederick; Vienna refused. Both powers prepared for war. Moltke suggested that an alliance with Italy was indispensable for military success; Bismarck had already taken the
necessary steps. The aims of the alliance were to be hegemony for
Prussia in northern Germany and the acquisition of Venetia by Italy.
Territory of the German Confederation, such as the Tyrol or Trieste,
could not be promised to Italy.

THE WAR WITH AUSTRIA AND THE GERMAN CONFEDERATION (1866)

Italy presented a revolutionary spectacle. Austria had formed no
sort of diplomatic relations with the kingdom, and many old Prussian conservatives abhorred the idea of any community of interests
with Garibaldi's state. But Bismarck embarked on still more daring
ventures during the crisis of 1866, which offered him the opportunity
of realizing the concept of a "revolution from above" in an astounding sense. Austria was completely encompassed. At this very time,
the beginning of 1866, Prince Charles of Hohenzollern-Sigmaringen
became the ruler of the Danubian principalities, now Rumania,
which had so long been a cause of contention; he reigned first as a
prince, later as the first king. Austria might have secured these valuable lands for herself earlier; their acquisition would have made her

supreme in the Balkans, though at the risk of constant friction with Russia. Now a Hohenzollern occupied the throne of Rumania, and Bismarck expected him not merely to supply auxiliary troops against Austria, but also to stir up the Rumanians who lived in Transylvania. All the nationalities of the Austrian imperial state could count on Bismarck's favour — the Hungarians, the southern Slavs, the Czechs. The ghosts of 1848 were again abroad in Europe.

The outer stress was matched by an inner crisis. The old Prussian King was bound to recoil from the spectacle of the spirits of hell that his minister had conjured up. Never was Bismarck so cordially hated as in those anxious months before the outbreak of war in 1866. Even honourable people approved the idea of an attempt on his life. Proposals for a congress, for disarmament, were in the air. England and Russia pleaded for peace, but without effect, if only because, though England would certainly not march against Austria, Russia might very possibly do so. Bismarck now pushed forward the question of reform of the Confederation as a popular war goal, even ahead of the problem of the duchies. On April 9 Prussia petitioned the federal diet to summon a parliament. The suffrage laws of 1849 were to hold. All the well-known demands of German patriots were again brought up: communications, liberty to emigrate without penalty, and questions of tariff and trade, land and naval armament. It seemed that the man who had suppressed Prussian constitutionalism wished to realize the idea of a German constitution. The secondary states were of two minds. Bismarck made tempting proposals, especially to Bavaria.

The increasing confusion in central Europe gave the French Emperor a long-desired opportunity. The solid, somewhat slow-moving intelligence of Emperor Francis Joseph seemed to offer more than Bismarck's pliability did. Besides, Napoleon made the Austrians believe that Prussia's promises were more binding than they actually were. On June 12, 1866 he made a secret treaty with Austria, according to which Austria obligated herself to cede Venetia to the Kingdom of Italy in any case. France was to receive an indemnity in western Germany, the precise nature of which was to be determined later. The kingdoms of Bavaria, Saxony, and Württemberg were to be enlarged; out of Prussia's province on the Rhine a Rhenish state was to be formed. For herself, Austria claimed Silesia. So, while Bismarck was preparing to shatter the imperial state of Austria from within, Emperor Francis Joseph was planning to demote Prussia to a secondary state such as it had been before the time of Frederick the Great. As against this main goal the sacrifice of German territory to France and the resurrection of the French policy of a Rhenish Confederation meant little to him. Even if Austria had been victorious, she would never have been strong enough to cheat Emperor Napoleon of his share as Bismarck did so successfully. Thus the civil and fratricidal war that now broke out in Germany was again concerned with the hoary war aims of hegemony in Germany and in central Europe.

In those critical weeks before war broke out both of the great German powers were repeatedly guilty of violating federal law, though from a moral point of view it was Prussia that was regarded as the law-breaker and war-monger by Germany and by the world. When Austria induced the Confederation to mobilize the four federal corps of the secondary and small states, Prussia replied that she regarded the Confederation as extinct, but that, true to her proposals for reform, she was willing to form a new confederation. This was the first time that Austria, as the presiding power of the Confederation, had tried to set its legal and military apparatus in motion against a refractory member, and the move caused the collapse of the whole institution. Frederick the Great's Prussian egoism had left the old Empire merely a ceremonial spectre. Bismarck shattered the German Confederation in order to erect a new Empire that was to be the creature of Greater Prussia.

Europe expected a long and bloody war, but after a couple of summer months everything was over. This seven weeks' war of 1866 completed the work of the Seven Years' War very thoroughly. There were three theatres of action. Most of the small states of northern Germany immediately joined forces with Prussia. The middle and south German groups of states resisted Prussian superiority halfheartedly and with insufficient means. The Austrians achieved some notable victories in Italy. But the decision fell in Bohemia. The commander of the Austrian army, General Ludwig von Benedek, thought the situation so hopeless that he favoured an immediate peace offer just before Königgrätz. Even one better acquainted with this Bohemian war theatre could have done little against Prussia.

Benedek was particularly unfortunate in the inefficiency and insubordination of his staff. Emperor Francis Joseph insisted on a military decision, although he was just as little able to win it as anyone else. His sense of honour both as a dynast and as a soldier did not permit him to make peace without a battle, but this same sense of honour caused him no compunction in expecting the defeated General Benedek to sacrifice his good name and the truth. In any case the Emperor and Austria survived, even apart from Germany. The separation that had been so long preparing was now effected with startling rapidity and, it seemed, painlessly. At Königgrätz the Prussian needle-gun, the most advanced offensive weapon of the time, celebrated its first great triumph, and Moltke's superiority made itself felt. The battle, planned as a destructive action, failed of its full effect because of the stupidity of Moltke's subordinates, such as Prince Frederick Charles, a cavalry commander, but not a strategist. Although the enemy was defeated tactically, he was not routed.

Bismarck's most difficult hour had come. His instinctive statesmanship and his genius in solving problems that seemed insurmountable were probably never more striking than in the period before the preliminary Peace of Nikolsburg. Emperor Napoleon III threatened and urged; only physical illness prevented him from interfering at once. Russia, annoyed and envious, called for a congress. Bismarck felt that this attitude was so dangerous to himself that he weighed the possibility of provoking an eruption of the Polish volcano. King William wanted annexations, by way of punishment for all his wicked opponents. Why not deprive the Austrians of a slice of Bohemia, of the German-speaking Sudetenland, and of Eger? Why not take the old Hohenzollern territory of Ansbach and Bayreuth away from Bavaria? The latter plan would have had the advantage of splitting up the most refractory Napoleonic satrap state and also of endowing Prussia with the best land in southern Germany, a step that would perhaps have helped decisively in Germanizing her.

Bismarck was the only one who saw that two things had to be avoided: the deadly enmity of Austria and the instant intervention of the French Emperor. This was why he opposed annexations in Austria and the marching of Prussian troops into Vienna. Perhaps the defeated imperial state of Austria would sometime become an ally again, after all. Bismarck, who had not liked the Prince Consort Albert, nevertheless acted on a wise precept of this statesman who died so prematurely: that one must always avoid humiliating a great power. If Prussia had advanced into south German territory at that time, a general war would probably have broken out in Europe, and through all his life Bismarck feared nothing so much as a coalition of neighbours against central Europe. France and Russia were now establishing relations with each other. Both powers were dangerously interested in the fate of the lesser German dynasties. Only Bismarck's wise readiness to compromise prevented a conjunction of the national revolutionary movement with a general European war. The results were very favourable to Prussia. She acquired all the land lying between the two halves of the state: Hanover, Hesse-Kassel, the Duchy of Nassau, the Landgraviate of Hesse-Homburg, and the free city of Frankfurt, which, unfortunately, suffered very harsh treatment. Bavaria as well as the Grand Duchy of Hesse-Darmstadt had to consent to changes in its boundaries, to Prussia's advantage. All the states north of the Main River, and Hesse-Darmstadt on behalf of its province of Upper Hesse, now joined in a North German Federation under Prussian leadership. Saxony should also have been annexed to it; she was permitted, however, to retain her status, thanks to the strong plea of the Austrian Emperor. The three south German states and the southern part of the Grand Duchy of Hesse-Darmstadt were to form a South German Confederation, but the envy that prevailed between Bavaria and Baden kept this plan from materializing.

Austria, in view of the serious military defeat she had suffered, did not fare badly. When the reckoning was made she had to pay a war indemnity amounting to only twenty million thalers. In land she lost only Venetia and her share in the Duchies of Schleswig and Holstein; she had long ceased to count on them. Austria recognized the North German Federation, but not the Kingdom of Italy. The latter was discontented with her gain and immediately turned her back on Prussia, although it was Prussian victory that had got Italy whatever she did receive. A special article in the treaty between Austria and Prussia, Article 5 of the final Peace of Prague, concerned the Danish-speaking portions of northern Schleswig, whose ultimate state membership was to be decided by a plebiscite. This plebiscite, which

France and also Great Britain urged again and again, was never held, though Bismarck would have been glad to be rid of the obstacle to a reconciliation with the Scandinavians. The main resistance came from the militaristic King William, who from a feeling of false piety did not want to give up the battlefields of the war of 1864 to the Danes.

THE NORTH GERMAN FEDERATION OF 1867. THE REALIGNMENT OF PARTIES

Germany was completely transformed. There was no longer a Greater Germany, but neither had a Little Germany materialized. Greater Prussia asserted herself as a military state that had never hesitated to commit a breach of law. This was a state that had fed on hunger and that therefore had funds at its disposal at the necessary moment, and it did not hesitate to employ daring methods. It was a state of well-disciplined, sober, but ungracious bureaucrats who went about Prussianizing the new territories under its control without inquiring into the wishes of their inhabitants. Prussia annexed the new districts without organizing a plebiscite, for she had no prospect whatever of getting a majority of votes. She constituted an authoritarian state whose class dictatorship, to be sure, availed itself of modern constitutional forms.

The parliament of the North German Federation was elected by the people on a system of universal and equal suffrage. But this democratic Reichstag was counterbalanced by an autocratic organ, the federal council (*Bundesrat*), a corporate body in which the governments were represented in the same way as in the former federal diet, not as a real representation of the people. The distribution of votes in the federal council was also copied from the old federal diet. Prussia had annexed not only the territory, but also the votes of the territory she had conquered in 1866. The executive power in the North German Federation rested with the presidency, which was responsible for the army and navy, diplomacy, and civil service. All the prerogatives of the Prussian crown were extended to the entire territory of the North German Federation. This was the exact opposite of the situation in 1848, when the Frankfurt assembly strove for the integration of Prussia into Germany. Now Berlin insisted that the north German and the middle German states must be Prussian. The constitution of the North German Federation foreshadowed

470

that of Bismarck's future Reich. It was the personal achievement of that great statesman—a veritable masterpiece, considering the time and the circumstances. This special variety of north German constitutionalism was to reconcile the concept of authority with that of majority, and it vigorously opposed the principle of western parliamentarism. Prussia wanted to make use of modern constitutionalism only so far as it would not affect the basic conditions of Prussian life, which were anti-democratic and remained so.

This became clear when the constitutional struggle in Prussia was finally terminated. Many champions of liberalism were constrained to re-examine their position in the light of the imposing successes of the Prussian army. All the groups that adhered to the old liberalism heartily acclaimed the triumphs of the Prussian government and army and were easily won over. But most of the more dogmatic liberals of the Progressive Party demanded a chance for creative participation. Bismarck now very cleverly asked for an indemnity bill, a law providing that the Prussian parliament should later grant the government the funds it had already spent without legal sanction. In this way the appearance of legality was preserved, although politically it was a double triumph for the government. The indemnity bill caused a rift in the Progressive Party. The moderate right wing, under the leadership of Ernst von Forckenbeck and Eduard Lasker, accepted the bill. A little later these men founded the National Liberal Party, which was to take a leading part in building up the new Reich.

Similar reactions appeared among the conservatives. During all these years the Junkers' party had been fighting the aims of the German National Association as well as those of advocates of a Greater Germany. In 1866 this party advocated an understanding with Austria. On grounds of legitimacy it objected to deposing old German dynasties and depriving them of their rights as was being done in connection with the annexations. It wanted Bismarck to use the powerful position that he had occupied since Königgrätz to destroy constitutionalism in Prussia. To these circles the indemnity bill was simply incredible. But the left wing of the conservative party defended Bismarck's policy. This left wing consisted largely of persons who had shared the beliefs of the *Wochenblatt* party from the time of the Crimean War and who therefore represented high officialdom and the nobility apart from the Junkers. They formed a Free Conservative Association and proved faithful helpers of Bismarck in the foundation of the Reich.

In class history the National Liberals and the Free Conservatives largely represented the German patricians of title and money who became powerful in society and politics. They were supported by a broad stratum that emulated them. Bismarck's concept of the Reich contemplated expansion, economic improvement, education and opportunity for many—all in the name of German nationalism. The old dogmatic liberals objected to these aims, because they did not believe that the idea of a constitutional state was adequately realized either in the constitution of the North German Federation or in that of the Reich that followed. The north German Progressives were soon joined by the south German Democrats; the latter were suspicious of Greater Prussia with her pride in authority, which persisted in spite of the constitutional robes with which she adorned herself. This party deplored cleavage from the Austrian Germans as well as the blocking of the needful development toward a western and old Germanic-style free people's state.

What the Catholic party stood for in the growing Reich was an assortment of interests, particularistic and Greater German, liberal and earth-bound. Because of the central seats they occupied in the Prussian lower house, members of this party were called the Centre. Catholic groups were formed first in southern Germany, then (1848) in the Frankfurt parliament and in the Prussian National Assembly. They served predominantly the religious and educational interests of the church in the shaping of the constitution. Since the anti-Jesuit decrees (1852) of Raumer, the Minister of Ecclesiastical Affairs and Public Instruction, the Catholic factions in the Prussian parliament had been acting as a closed group. The annexed territories swelled the Catholics' forces with anti-Prussian elements, and the Catholics also co-operated against the National Liberals with the Guelphs, the Protestant adherents of the Hanover dynasty.

All these parties were predominantly of a middle-class character. Universal suffrage made it necessary for them to recruit support from a wide variety of sources and to formulate their programs in a way that would appeal to the public. The contradiction between democratic institutions and anti-democratic official authority was bound to show up more plainly in the process. Bismarck was well aware of the forces that were struggling upward from below. He had very good reasons for working with the National Liberals; cooperation between the national and the democratic forces in any degree at all was dangerous to the Prussian autocratic state. Such a co-operation had been the dream of Ferdinand Lassalle's life. His successors followed different ideas.

In 1864 Karl Marx and Friedrich Engels founded the International Working Men's Association in London, the so-called First International. The first volume of Marx's *Capital* appeared in 1867, and Marxism began its triumphal progress. For the time being, the German character of Lassalle's General Association of German Workers was preserved by his successors. Wilhelm Liebknecht, who came of an old Hessian Christian middle-class family, was the first to go over to the Marxist organization. August Bebel, the young son of a non-commissioned officer from Köln, was his gifted aide; a Catholic journeyman in the turner's trade, he was a product of working men's educational associations. Bebel was an effective organizer and an eloquent speaker, and he soon became the chairman of the local group in Leipzig. The bourgeois left-wing liberals won much acclaim for their efforts in relation to these ambitions, but they were unable to work them into their political line. Even at the Nürnberg Congress of 1868 it became evident that German workers wanted to present themselves as proletarians, and indeed they had to. A year later the Social Democratic Party was founded in Eisenach. Its program called for universal suffrage throughout Germany, direct legislation by the people, a standard working day, abolition of direct taxes, a progressive income and inheritance tax, state help for productive associations, separation of state and church, a militia instead of a standing army, and a republican form of state.

Germany was entering its capitalistic epoch. From the economic angle the founding of the German Reich was to mean the triumph of the exploiting class and formation of a class-conscious body of labour that presented an increasingly powerful opposition to the militarism of Greater Prussia. The revolutionary idea proved decisive for Bismarck's victory. Now the representatives of the International claimed the revolutionary principle for their own, as adapted to the concept of class struggle.

STRUGGLE WITH NAPOLEON III. LUXEMBURG. AUSTRIA-HUNGARY

For reasons of foreign policy Bismarck had stopped at the Main River. But the extension of the North German Federation to southern Germany seemed only a matter of time and opportunity. Baden was pressing forward, fearful of her neighbours, France and the rest of southern Germany. Hesse-Darmstadt, too, wished to have her situation clarified. But Württemberg and especially Bavaria were blocking the way. For a time Prince Chlodwig Hohenlohe-Schillingsfürst (died 1901), as President of the Ministry in Bavaria, exerted a beneficent influence. This independent and cautious aristocrat effectively encouraged a rapprochement of north and south. Bismarck turned all this to his own uses and awaited his moment. The renewal of the customs treaties in July 1867 was a long step forward, for now a customs parliament convened in Berlin for all of non-Austrian Germany. This body had been constituted according to the election laws of the Reichstag of the North German Federation, and a federal council on tariffs, under the presidency of Prussia, supervised customs legislation. This customs parliament had three sessions up to the founding of the new Reich.

Otto von Bismarck (Count since 1865), President of the Prussian Ministry and now Chancellor of the North German Federation, had won his great triumphs only because of his long years of amity with Napoleon III. Could this confidential relationship be restored? The French Emperor was on the downward curve of his destiny. His failure in Mexico (1867) was a fresh setback to his prestige. He needed success for the sake of domestic calm in France and for the permanence of his dynasty. He believed that he would attain both ends by the long-desired gains on the eastern border of France. Bismarck had pointed out Luxemburg to him, as well as other regions. Now the Emperor very cautiously prepared to acquire this grand duchy, which the impecunious King of the Netherlands was ready to relinquish. At the last moment Bismarck broke up the affair for the French Emperor, for co-operation with the nationalism that was in the ascendant in Germany carried more weight with him than a reconciliation with Napoleon, which perhaps might not have lasted long anyhow.

The little country of Luxemburg was not at all German in sentiment, but it had been the cradle of one of the most illustrious of the old imperial dynasties, and it had a German federal fortress to which Prussia held garrison rights. A conference in London nipped the threat of war. The fortress was razed; the grand duchy was neutralized under collective guarantee by the great powers—a frail enough protection compared with the individual guarantee that each of the great powers had given the Kingdom of Belgium. Napoleon suffered another painful defeat by this compromise about Luxemburg in 1867, but the loss of the fortress of Luxemburg was damaging to the North German Federation, and Bismarck was aware of failure. Neither he nor the French Emperor wanted a repetition. And so the tension in Europe was only apparently relieved. Both opponents were arming and casting about for allies.

In the course of the quarrel over Luxemburg, Bismarck published the secret treaties that constituted a military pact between Prussia and the south German states. The Chancellor also tried to approach Austria, but without success. After 1866 the Austrian imperial state was reorganized as the Austro-Hungarian Dual Monarchy. This unique political creation watched over the destinies of its various peoples up to the time of the first World War under increasing difficulties, but with considerable economic success and with a certain magnanimity. Not federalism, which would have done justice to the Slavs also, but dualism was the rule in the Danubian state. Common to both the Austrian and the Hungarian parts were only foreign policy, army, and finances. There was neither a central government nor a central parliament. But it was provided that delegations from the legislatures of both halves of the Empire were to convene annually. From the very outset the Hungarians had political and economic preponderance; even if they were the weaker section, they exerted a decisive influence over the whole. The western half of the empire was not called Austria officially; the name was not reintroduced until the first World War, and until then the phrase was "the kingdoms and countries represented in the council of the Empire." The two halves were popularly termed Cisleithania and Transleithania, names that had an academic and bureaucratic tinge and were therefore confidence-inspiring. In this way the almost unknown little river Leitha rose to geopolitical importance.

The Dual Monarchy offered its nationalities the possibility of co-operation, of education, of development. Many individuals utilized the economic and intellectual possibilities of this state organization to the full, only to contribute to its subsequent political destruction. Any cocksure journalist could easily prove that the existence of the Dual Monarchy violated the principle of nationalism that was the gospel of the times. Very few indeed realized that the large scale of this structure was able to assure the throng of historically fragmented nationalities in the southeastern colonial region a *modus vivendi* that held promise for the more distant future. Once more German Austria assumed her honourable educational mission; liberal-minded with an academic tinge, under Emperor Francis Joseph, she stood her ground unwearyingly against the increasing Slavic masses. She was superior in organizing, but in vitality she was at a growing disadvantage.

Emperor Francis Joseph had not yet abandoned hope of recapturing the position that had been lost in Germany. He encountered dissatisfaction in Italy and vengefulness in the French Emperor. But the triple alliance that Napoleon desired and laboured for did not materialize; it was blocked by Italy's greed. A substitute was supplied by personal correspondence among the three monarchs. Military conferences were also held. France was apparently resolved to turn on the North German Federation at the first opportunity, even at the risk of war. In case of success she could be sure of allies. Great Britain could no longer be counted among these allies.

The question of what was to be done with the island of Crete, which had a Greek population but was then under Turkish rule, produced a minor crisis in the Near East in 1867. This was the first occasion on which Bismarck worked on intimate terms with England. His old plan of separating the western powers took on plausibility. England tried to assist France, her erstwhile ally, by proposals for frank discussion of current problems and of European disarmament, but flatly rejected active intervention in any European quarrels. Napoleon's cupidity in regard to Belgium, which Bismarck had specifically encouraged, was not calculated to make the English more cordial. A French plan of building railroads in Belgium for the purpose of gaining influence in that country came to nothing; Bismarck's diplomatic counter-offensive could rely on English neutrality. It was in vain that Napoleon III made overtures to St. Petersburg; Russia held to her friendship with Bismarck. The Emperors of France and Austria met in Salzburg. Archduke Albert, who had inherited the military gifts of his illustrious father, Archduke Charles, urged war and drafted bold campaigns, but Austria had not recovered her financial equilibrium and was backward in armaments. Emperor Francis Joseph, after the setbacks he had experienced, wanted to be at least a little more judicious. Spain was now casting about for a new king, and Bismarck went into action.

THE FRANCO-GERMAN WAR (1870–1)

Spain was in hopes of extricating herself from the confusion of civil war and party feuds by means of a new dynasty. Prince Leopold of Hohenzollern-Sigmaringen seemed a suitable candidate. Bismarck liked the idea. Leopold's younger brother, the far more gifted Carol of Rumania, had proved his worth repeatedly as a confidential German agent in the Balkans; it could only be of advantage to have a partner of this sort in western Europe. A more liberal Spain would offset France and the papacy; French troops would be drawn off toward the Pyrenees boundary. So Bismarck backed the candidacy without showing his hand officially. He wanted to make headway with the southern Germans in one way or another. The plan of a united German Reich was brewing, and it excited the suspicion of the French. Either Napoleon would have to put up with the Hohenzollern on the Spanish throne, in which case he would be humiliated again and Bismarck could go on as he pleased; or the candidate would be dropped, and then Bismarck would advance further German demands. From Bismarck's point of view the candidacy was less an end in itself, although as such it was of value, than a means to the loftier essential end of German unification.

The candidacy for the Spanish throne became public prematurely in July 1870 and at once provoked a grave European crisis. Napoleon easily disposed of the candidacy, with the help of England and Russia. But in the flush of triumph the French government overshot the mark in its demands and spoiled its diplomatic victory with threats that Bismarck neither could nor would suffer. Old King William too, who from the very beginning had opposed the proposals for Spain, bore himself with sober dignity in the face of the French demand that he should not merely give a permanent guaran-

477

tee of the complete abandonment of the candidacy, but should write an apologetic letter to this effect to the French Emperor.

Ever since the famous threatening speech made on July 6 by the Duke of Gramont, the foolish French Minister of Foreign Affairs, Bismarck had been determined to break with France. The bungling of French diplomacy, which was usually so suave, put all the trumps into his hand. His masterpiece was the Ems dispatch. Bismarck received from Ems, where King William was staying, a confidential official document crammed with details and awkward and ill organized in style. By compressing it and pointing it up Bismarck turned it into a semi-official newspaper article that burst on the public like a bomb. Two birds were killed with one stone: the public was informed of the very grave situation, and the French government received a blow to which but one reply was possible.

The Franco-Prussian War resulted in an unprecedented triumph for united Germany. All the south German states immediately joined with the North German Federation—even Bavaria, where the discontented clerical party of the patriots was in favour of armed neutrality. The military success of the very first weeks was enough to rob all European neutrals of the slightest desire to come to the aid of France. Napoleon III stood alone. His downfall was swift and sure. France was not prepared for any such war. The Germans had superiority in arms, organization, and leadership. In France, as so often, there was talk of treachery. General indignation cried out for scapegoats, which, since there was no attempt at objective investigation, were easily found. Of course the Germans made mistakes too. Again and again Moltke had to struggle with the obstinacy and the limitations of his subordinates. That was why the great battle of encirclement and annihilation did not materialize either at Wörth or at Gravelotte, or until Sedan. The most distinguished German leaders were the clever visionary and enthusiast Edwin von Manteuffel, the half-academic, brooding August von Göben, who was indifferent to externals, and the wild and daring Bavarian, von der Tann. The achievements of the Prussian Crown Prince, Frederick, were made possible primarily by the careful work of his faithful chief of the general staff, L. von Blumenthal, who came from the old nobility of the Mark of Brandenburg. The gravest difference of opinion in the course of the war arose over the question of the bombardment of

Paris. One group of experts favoured an immediate artillery attack; the other was for starving out the stronghold. Both views were based on purely military considerations; humanitarianism did not enter into the decision.

The capitulation of Napoleon III at Sedan led to the fall of his Empire. Marshal Bazaine, who was besieged in Metz, tried to preserve his army for the Empress Eugénie and to deploy it against the new republic. It was in vain. The national defence of France threw more and more new troops and more and more new leaders into the fray against Germany. Bismarck demanded guarantees for the future: the sacrifice of French fortresses and of French soil. Because of this the people's war was continued, and Adolphe Thiers appealed to the great powers of Europe in the name of France—in vain. England did nothing but furnish a plentiful supply of arms, for which she was severely censured by the German public. Bismarck made the most of this sentiment because he did not desire English intervention in the peace negotiations. The United States supplied as many weapons as England, but without criticism from Germany, for Bismarck was anxious to play off the United States against England. He had consigned the protection of the north Germans in France to the United States, while England looked after the French in Germany.

The darkest hour of the war was in November 1870, when the Germans were in a rather unfavourable strategic position. To make matters worse, Russia, encouraged by Bismarck, had denounced the humiliating Pontus clause in the Peace of Paris (1856), which forbade her to keep warships in the Black Sea. All the signatories of the Peace of Paris were affected. Great Britain and Austria aligned themselves on the French side. For a moment there was danger of what Bismarck had always feared and always avoided, the extension of the war over all Europe. Under pressure from England Bismarck agreed to the calling of a European conference in London. Here the question of the Pontus was reopened and regulated in accordance with Russia's wishes and needs, on condition that no third party should intervene in the Franco-German War.

THE FOUNDING OF THE NEW REICH (1871)

Bismarck succeeded in founding the Reich even before peace was concluded. On January 18, 1871 King William was proclaimed Ger-

man Emperor in the Hall of Mirrors of the palace at Versailles. It
was a simple ceremony, military in tone, with far-reaching consequences for world history. Very few contemporaries knew how distasteful the preliminary negotiations had been. Although Bavaria
certainly wished to continue co-operating with the North German
Federation, she wanted both a narrower and a wider federation; in
other words, she wanted to save as much of her own statehood as
possible, either with or without Württemberg. This Bavarian policy
prevented the joint entrance of the south German states into the
Federation. Tedious special negotiations and a series of separate
treaties were necessary. Württemberg also tried to gain territorial
and other advantages. The final result was so-called reserved rights
for Bavaria and Württemberg in connection with mails, railroads,
financial administration, and army command. In addition Bavaria
was given the right of making her own treaties and received the
permanent vice-presidency of the federal council, as well as assurance
of consent of that council in case of her declaring war, and finally
the right to levy her own taxes on beer and brandy. Baden and
Hesse-Darmstadt entered the Federation without special privileges.

The new Reich had neither a ministry nor an upper house of
princes, counts, and lords. Its highest responsible officer was the
chancellor of the Reich, to whom the secretaries of state were subordinate. It had a democratic Reichstag, but it retained the federal
council (*Bundesrat*), the official body that handled the business of
the Reich in an autocratic manner behind closed doors. For the great
majority of Germans of the time this Reich was not only a satisfactory but an inspiring fulfilment of all their longings. Dynasties and
stocks, particularism and unification, stood side by side. The old
conflicts in German life had not been placated, but the contrasting
elements were bound up together and constrained to co-operate according to Prussia's dictates. The Prussian King had accepted the
title of German Emperor rather ungraciously. His princely instincts
told him that this emperorship was something of a monstrosity, corresponding to romantic needs rather than to political facts. Again
Bismarck had ingeniously combined revolution with counter-revolution. The future would show what Germany could make of Kaiser
and Reich.

THE PEACE OF FRANKFURT (1871). ALSACE-LORRAINE

The Peace of Frankfurt introduced a new epoch in the history of Germany and central Europe. Even if Bismarck had wanted to do otherwise, the army and public opinion would still have made a peace in the style of Nikolsburg (1866) impossible. Germany remembered Louis XIV and Napoleon I. She wanted security. She wanted an end to those claims to hegemony that France had put forth again and again. The cession of three French departments on the Upper Rhine and the Moselle decisively shifted the centre of gravity in Europe. Alsace was predominantly German-speaking, Lorraine partially so, but the majority of even the German-speaking inhabitants shared the western and democratic sentiment of their French compatriots; this was the result of the French Revolution and the Napoleonic era. From of old these lands had been on neighbourly terms with southern Germany, but everything Prussian was entirely alien to them. According to the strategic principles of the times the new western boundary of Germany seemed assured by the possession of the fortresses of Metz and Strassburg. The boundary was fixed in accordance with this view, and to Bismarck's annoyance many French-speaking districts were thus incorporated in Germany. This in itself made adaptation to the new Reich difficult. Historically speaking, Alsace and Lorraine had nothing in common. Both economically and ethnically they were alien to each other. Now that they were combined as a province (*Reichsland*) immediately under the Reich, they entered on a development that was at once spurred and curbed by Berlin. A happier solution would have been to divide this new region among the adjacent lands of Prussia, Bavaria, and Baden.

To forestall intervention by England, Bismarck reduced his demands for war indemnities from six to five billion gold francs in the preliminary peace negotiations. Even this sum, tremendous as it seemed to most Germans, France was able to pay in instalments at short intervals, so that she was soon freed of the German occupation. Both economically and socially France came through the terrible year with amazing resilience. At the last possible moment the Second Empire had tried to save itself by liberal reforms. Now the reply came from the provinces, from clerical and legitimist France, which brutally put down the communistic uprising in Paris and tried to prepare the restoration of the monarchy by drafting a conservative constitution for the Third Republic.

The new German Reich followed these events with attentive reserve. Bismarck did not dream of destroying the great power of France as such. He not only refused to annex French colonies, but later even gave the French every opportunity to build up their own great colonial empire. This allowed his neighbour's national pride its necessary vent and satisfaction. But, even so, French dreams of revenge did not die down; rather they gathered momentum in the great arena of colonial competition. No matter what conditions had been decided on for the peace between Germany and France, a nation accustomed to rule and proud of its army, such as the French nation, could never forget defeat or refrain from arming for retaliation. No military limitations were imposed on France, and so, though the Peace of Frankfurt closed a war epoch, it opened a new epoch of competitive armament.

BISMARCK'S NEW FOREIGN POLICY

The document proclaiming King William Emperor, which Bismarck read on January 18, 1871, contained the statement that the new German Emperor would be "an increaser of the Reich," not by military conquests, but by the goods and gifts of peace. This was a new interpretation of an epithet of the Roman emperorship of the German nation. Bismarck intended these words to mean exactly what they said. In his view Germany was now complete. He wanted to defend the new Reich he had created in its *status quo,* but he did not want to enlarge it. The Germans in Austria, especially in Bohemia, soon developed a new Greater Germany movement in admiring emulation of the Reich and of Prince Bismarck. Bismarck's only reaction to this was to reject it. He believed that the Austrian Germans should stay in their Dual Monarchy and maintain it by their labours. Bismarck sternly refused to jeopardize Germany's relations with Russia by encouraging the Germanizing of the Baltic region. He left Germans who lived in Belgium, Switzerland, the Balkans, or other foreign parts wholly to the governments of those countries. After 1871 he acquired colonies only when occasion

S Schleswig
H Holstein
A·L Alsace-Lorraine
L Luxemburg
B Baden
W Württemberg

BISMARCK'S REICH 1871

- - - Southern Boundary of the North German Confederation

The German Reich of 1871

Prussian annexations in 1866
(Hanover, Hesse, Kassel, Nassau, Frankfurt)

Netherlands

Belgium

France

L

A·L

W

B

Bavaria

Switzerland

Russia

Austria-Hungary
(1867)

Ottoman
Empire

offered, without great eagerness and in the conviction that the life of his Reich in Europe would not be altered by his act. Up to the time of the Franco-German War Bismarck had not hesitated to employ revolutionary methods in his foreign policy, which was ambitious and dynamic. Now it became static and concentrated on defending what had been created, though it remained elastic within the limits of given possibilities. The friendship with France that had endured for years could no longer be kept up in any way. This was a cardinal point. Alone, France was no longer a match for the Reich; she had to cast about for allies. Bismarck tried to cripple all attempts in this direction and to isolate France permanently.

The pivot of Bismarck's policy of alliances was still the friendship with Russia. In 1873 the two states concluded a military convention at St. Petersburg, according to which each was to help the other in case of attack. Austria-Hungary was glad to make overtures to the two other conservative imperial powers. There was an exchange of visits among the sovereigns. In the Convention of Schönbrunn (1873) Russia and the Danubian monarchy pledged themselves to joint political labours; the German Reich entered into the agreement. There was, then, a close understanding between Germany and Russia and a looser one among the three Emperors. Italy soon made advances toward the group, but since at that time she was the only great power maintaining close relations with defeated France, Bismarck mistrusted the rapprochement that would have arisen between Italy and Austria as serving to revive the Catholic triple alliance, with France, that Napoleon III had planned. There would then have been an inauspicious minor encirclement of Germany by France, Italy, and Austria. Besides, Bismarck believed that during the *Kulturkampf* Italy had served the interests of the papacy.

Military circles in Germany were perturbed by the rapid recovery of France. The Peace of Frankfurt was criticized as too mild, and a new war was talked of, to administer a ruthless beating. Bismarck himself probably helped discredit such talk by bringing it out into the open. But the "War in Sight" crisis of 1875, so called after a sensational newspaper article, brought surprises even for the Chancellor of the Reich. France, whether seemingly or actually threatened, enjoyed the strong support of both Great Britain and Russia. For the first time since the Revolution of 1848–9 co-operation between the three great powers of France, Russia, and England showed itself as possible. There was a first feeble suggestion of the great encirclement of 1914, a mere spectre that was soon dispersed in air.

But Bismarck learned two things from this crisis. First, Russia was not reliable. He had to have very serious words with her. The patched-up friendship still held for a time, indeed, but Russia now turned back from Asia to the Near East, and the resumption of an aggressive Russian Balkan policy disturbed the relations of Austria and Russia and thus the relationship of the three Emperors. In the second place, Bismarck realized that he would have to approach England again in order to prevent a revival of the Entente Cordiale. From December 1875 on, Bismarck made overtures to England with the object of turning to account the antagonism between England and Russia regarding Asia and the Near East, as well as that of warning England against possible collaboration between France and Russia. Great Britain's attitude toward Bismarck's approaches was one of polite reserve. At this time the only alliance that might have been a menace to England, a Continental triple alliance of France, Germany, and Russia, seemed beyond the pale of political possibilities. There was every reason to believe that the tension between Germany and France would persist for a long time to come. England was satisfied that this would serve as a sort of guarantee of the balance of power in Europe. But England was in sympathy with the conservative trend of Bismarck's foreign policy toward all the small neighbour states in Europe.

THE CONGRESS OF BERLIN (1878). ALLIANCE WITH
AUSTRIA-HUNGARY (1879)

The insurrection that broke out against the Turks in Herzegovina in 1875, with the subsequent disturbances in Bosnia, introduced a new eastern crisis. The Bulgarians also revolted against their Turkish rulers, and the situation of the Christians in the Balkans urgently called for new adjustments. Bismarck tried to have the three imperial powers undertake mediation. France and Italy were willing to assist. At this point Serbia and Montenegro started warring on the Turks, and now Russia also showed her interest. According to a secret agreement between Russia and the Danubian monarchy, Russia was to receive the part of Bessarabia lost in 1856 and part of

Armenia, while Austria was to take over Bosnia and Herzegovina. Russia grudged Austria this concession and would have liked to strike out at her also, but Bismarck made it clear to the Czar that the destruction of the Danubian monarchy as a great power was undesirable to Germany. This brought about a significant change. Russia's great military success in the Balkans led to the Preliminary Peace of San Stefano, which produced an international crisis. England threatened to take action against Russia. On Bismarck's initiative the matter was settled at the Congress of Berlin in 1878.

Russia and the Balkan powers under her protection had to content themselves with a much more modest prize of victory. Austria-Hungary was accorded the right to occupy and to administer Herzegovina and Bosnia. Emperor Francis Joseph in his time had sacrificed the position of the imperial state in Italy in order to maintain its position in Germany; now he was indemnified for the position he had lost in Germany by this extension of his power to the Balkans, which seemed to fulfil the great long-standing Austrian aims. But the added territory substantially increased the number of Slavic peoples within the pale of the Dual Monarchy, and inner tensions were bound to mount. They were intensified by the friction with Russia, who regarded herself as the protector of all Slavs and was encouraging the claims of the Kingdom of Rumania that were based on the large Rumanian element in the population of Transylvania. Except for Bismarck, Austria's great territorial gain would not have been possible. And so the Balkan crisis ended with emphatic friendship between Austria and Germany, but estrangement between the German Reich and Russia.

Russia interpreted Bismarck's role of "honest broker" at the Congress of Berlin as hypocritical and treacherous. The close collaboration between Austria and Germany became evident when, according to their pact, Article 5 of the Peace of Prague was annulled (1878). This disposed of the plebiscite in northern Schleswig. Denmark was not consulted, and in her weakness she dared not object. Bismarck's ruling idea was to eliminate just as many points of controversy between Austria and Germany as possible and so to pave the way to a permanent alliance, which he even wanted to incorporate in the legislation of the two countries. Thus here, too, fruitful ideas from the Church of St. Paul in 1848 were revived.

485

Old Emperor William resisted strongly, for he wished at any cost to avoid being drawn into conflict with Russia. He was still seeing that country as the Russia of the Wars of Liberation. Bismarck was better acquainted with the new Russia, with its Pan-Slavic ideology and bourgeois desire for expansion, its revolutionary and terroristic mass movements; he, too, was anxious to avoid conflict with it, but he believed that an honest co-operation with imperilled Austria would postpone such a conflict, perhaps even preclude it. And so the Chancellor overrode the objections of Emperor William I and concluded the German alliance with Austria in 1879. The two great powers promised to come to each other's aid with full military strength if either were attacked by Russia; in case of attack by some other power a benevolent neutrality was to be maintained. This agreement was to be communicated to the Czar by way of warning only if Russia's preparations became threatening. This alliance between Austria and Germany marked the attainment of a great aim. The loss of Silesia and the recollection of Olmütz and Königgrätz no longer carried a sting, and the rejection of the imperial crown at Frankfurt (1849) and the annexations of 1866 might now be forgotten. Stein's notion of north German and south German empires had undergone a transformation; yet in a certain sense it had been realized. Central Europe was united, though not as Schwarzenberg had imagined. But Bismarck had now shown more understanding of Austria than any Austrian had ever shown of Prussia. Dynastic authority had achieved both the founding of the Reich and the union of central Europe. The question now was whether complete democratic organization would be effected.

THE CONSOLIDATION OF THE REICH. THE SECOND KULTURKAMPF

The German Reich did not include all the German-speaking people of Europe, nor did all of its citizens regard themselves as German. A motion made by the Polish delegates to the first German Reichstag was characteristic. They did not wish to have Polish-speaking territory incorporated in the Reich, since it had belonged neither to the old Empire nor to the German Confederation. The motion was not carried. But the protesting Poles were followed by the Danish representatives from northern Schleswig and later by the delegates from Alsace-Lorraine. The Guelphs, who were good Germans—as good as the best—persisted in their Hanoverian hostility to the Reich. There was no prospect of an early reconciliation with the Hanoverian dynasty. The interest on the King's confiscated fortune of forty-eight million marks, the so-called Guelph fund, was used for semi-official labours of the press on behalf of Bismarck's policy; it was also helpful in other delicate situations. King Louis II of Bavaria, who was always in need of money, regularly received sums from the Guelph fund and for this reason, which did him little honour, was committed to the policy of the Reich. And so the shining façade of this new Reich concealed tensions and feuds that might menace a favourable continuous development.

For years the strongest party in the Reichstag was that of the National Liberals. It upheld notably the concept of the Reich and the necessity of consolidating this state structure. The Free Conservatives now called themselves the German Reich Party; they were always ready to co-operate with Bismarck. The Progressive Party was still strong enough to be able to help the National Liberals in questions of reform of a more democratic tendency. The opposition, whether conservative, clerical, or socialist, was no match for the National Liberals. The preponderance of the patriotic bourgeois parties was effective in putting through legislation: criminal law and laws concerning court procedure, bankruptcy, and the constitution of the courts. Preparation of a civil code for the entire Reich was undertaken. Laws on the introduction of the gold standard and a unified currency, on the press, and on patents followed. The predominant trend was toward unification and was directed by ideas drawn from western constitutionalism. When the matter of taxes for the Reich was broached, there were difficulties; sharp resistance was immediately met with from the individual states and the feudal classes. Bismarck wanted imperial railroads, but he had to be content with a unified railroad system for only Prussia and Hesse.

The opposition of the Conservatives to Bismarck grew into a bitter personal quarrel over the Arnim scandal. Count Harry von Arnim was a vain, very busy ambitious diplomat who saw himself as a worthy successor to the Chancellor of the Reich himself. Actually highly gifted, this man had excellent connections at court and was also in touch with the French monarchists. Bismarck had always been very sensitive as a leader; he could become utterly ruthless if anyone wanted to succeed him in office, and he destroyed Arnim. The unfortunate and misguided Count was found out in all manner of fumbles, which were interpreted as embezzlement of records, as disloyalty and treason. He fled abroad, was sentenced to imprisonment, and died in voluntary exile. Court society never forgave Bismarck for this brutal persecution of a man who may have been frivolous, but was certainly anything but a criminal.

Vengeance followed. Courtiers, Junkers, the anti-liberal orthodox, anti-Semites, all joined forces and tried to throw suspicion on Bismarck as promoting speculation on the stock exchange and also subversive liberalism. Bismarck's Jewish banker, Gerson Bleichröder, who had been elevated to the nobility, was one of the most prosperous and at the same time one of the most reliable and intelligent leaders of contemporary economic life in Germany. Through his numerous connections, especially with the house of Rothschild, he was able to render eminent service to his master, Prince Bismarck, and to the German Reich. Bleichröder had administered Bismarck's private fortune admirably according to the practices then in vogue and had also advanced the Chancellor's political plans on the stock exchange. The relation of Bismarck to Bleichröder was absolutely above criticism and creditable to both men. But this did not prevent the envious and the intriguing from pointing to Bismarck as having profited from a so-called Bleichröder era, in order to force his resignation. Attacks on Bismarck in the press were heartily approved by a great number of his peers, with whom he now had to break off personal relations.

These unhappy events were closely connected with the so-called promoter crisis. The abundance of money that was pouring in from France gave rise to new capitalistic ventures. New banks that gave promoters financial backing were greedy for profits, but could not match the old private banks in reliability. The public was dazzled by the expansion of German industry and the splendour of political and military success. Many who had accumulated savings and numerous members of the upper classes whose inherited fortunes had shrunk were swept into the whirlpool of speculation without having had any experience of the new business methods. The result was a panic all through Austria and Germany. Eduard Lasker, the National Liberal deputy, made a sensational speech in which he revealed the deplorable connection of well-known aristocrats and high officials with dubious projects. His successful attack, well supported by evidence, was not directed against capitalism as such, but against swindling, bribery, and profiteering in numberless individual cases. For years Eduard Lasker, a distinguished Jewish lawyer (died 1884), had played a leading part in public life. He had the character of an Aristides—a man of great personal integrity, notable for his penetrating mind and his gifts as a writer.

Such events made it very difficult to carry on the business of government. Redistricting, intended to break the power of the Junkers in the rural sections, could be made effective only by creating new peers for the Prussian upper house. The rural nobility realized that Bismarck was sacrificing it to modern constitutionalism and could not forgive him for it. The new Prussian provincial arrangements proceeded according to plan. But the advocates of the old Prussia did not give up the fight. Count Albrecht von Roon, Bismarck's grim old friend who was Minister of War and for some time served as President of the Ministry in Prussia, was the most impressive representative of this theocratic and monarchical anti-parliamentary attitude. Roon quarrelled with Bismarck, grew embittered, and disappeared from public sight; but the obstinate Junkers remained.

Full of significance was the conflict of the Prussian state with the Catholic church, the second *Kulturkampf*. The promulgation of the doctrine of papal infallibility at the Vatican Council in Rome (1870) occasioned the so-called Old Catholic movement in Germany. In 1873 the Old Catholics founded an episcopal church of their own, which was recognized by the German governments with the exception of that of Bavaria, which was bound by its own concordat. The Roman Catholics opposed the Old Catholics; the Prussian state protected the new movement—hence the conflict. The Centre took up the challenge; the natural antagonism of the ultramontane party of Greater Germany to Bismarck's Reich swelled the quarrel to a controversy on the interpretation of the principles of the state and of history. The bourgeois patriots of the Reich, with their liberalism, fought with considerable zest. Conviction clashed with conviction. Protestant Germany had always felt aversion toward everything connected with the Jesuits. Since the question of schools was involved, feeling was intensified by a sense of responsibility for the welfare and education of the rising generation. For Bismarck the authority of the state was the first consideration. The Prussian May laws issued by him in May 1873, 1874, and 1875 provided that the Catholic clergy were to be educated in state institutions and also were to be subject to the jurisdiction of the state. The resistance of the clergy led to confiscation of salaries and the arrest of several bishops and their removal from office. The introduction of civil marriage called forth opposition not only from the Catholics, but also from orthodox Protestants, who now began to side with the persecuted Catholics in increasing numbers. The controversy grew sharper and sharper. Finally all the religious orders were dissolved or banished.

The Pope intervened in person. Emperor William I replied to him with the dignity of a sovereign and an evangelical Christian. Was not the struggle that had been a matter of world history in the Middle Ages now rekindled? Bismarck declared that he would not go "to Canossa." Nevertheless he did just that, though he was not so successful as Emperor Henry IV had been in a like case. The rejuvenated Catholic world church was insuperable. Bismarck had to seek a compromise. He later held the National Liberals and more especially the brave Minister of Ecclesiastical Affairs and of Public Instruction, Dr. Adalbert Falk, responsible for the sharpness of the conflict. In reality it was Bismarck himself who embittered the controversy by making it hinge on basic principles. He applied his methods of foreign policy to his relations with political parties at home, and the outcome could be nothing else than civil war or the defeat of state authority.

SHIFT TO THE RIGHT. PROTECTIVE TARIFF (1879)

The experiences of the *Kulturkampf* cast the first cloud over Bismarck's relations with the National Liberals. He bore them a grudge for taking his part so energetically, but without success. Other forces that coincided with this situation brought about a decisive change in German politics. The economic situation of the Reich was not good. The main reason was the international depression, which could not, of course, be remedied by Germany alone. Compared with the expansion of the rising world powers and with their imperialistic concentration of strength, the German Reich had only just reached a new stage in its development, and again belatedly. Germany quickly became industrialized. The iron and steel industry, in particular, regarded itself as the workshop of the military Reich, whose very existence obviously depended on armaments. "Blood and iron," but iron and coal even more, had made Bismarck's Reich.

The association of German iron and steel industrialists for the first time demanded a protective tariff in 1875. It sounded quite convincing when these circles ascribed the prevailing economic stress to the system of free trade and liberal legislation. For was not the Reich being flooded by manufactures from England and France and by the agricultural products of eastern Europe? For Bismarck two considerations were decisive. He required security for his military budget. It was only with difficulty that the Reichstag had been induced to approve armaments for a seven-year period—that is, until 1881. In the second place he wished the Reich to be financially independent of the individual states.

Both these objectives were in accord with the aims of the National Liberal Party. When in 1877 Bismarck offered the Prussian Ministry of the Interior to the leader of the National Liberals, Rudolf von Bennigsen, the latter presented certain conditions for his acceptance. He asked two additional ministerial posts for party members who were his friends. Bismarck was taken aback. The National Liberals stood for centralization and for the continued consolidation of the Reich. The Chancellor was afraid of taking a road that would lead to parliamentarism in the Reich. He not only was personally hostile to such a development; he also had to consider the resistance of the Emperor, the dynasts, and their courts, as well as the particularism of the individual states. The Junkers, the Prussian ruling class, were bitterly opposed to universal suffrage and liberal legislation. Bismarck, if only for reasons of foreign policy, did not wish to aggravate the antagonisms that already existed. So Germany again turned away from the possibility of democratic development. The German Conservative Party had just been formed. The Prussian Conservatives were therefore ready now to accept the Reich and to co-operate in a positive way—of course on their own terms in whatever had to do with agrarian policy. The Centre, too, included plenty of conservative elements, for the strength of the Centre lay in the fact that it united within itself all bourgeois party tendencies as if in essence.

491

Thus Bismarck had at his dispósal a new grouping to support him in the Reichstag. From the angle of class history it was an alliance of the Junker caste, heavy industry, patricians of money and title who had a religious bias, and all the petty bourgeois for whom liberalism was an evil form of plutocracy.

Bismarck now had a startling experience. His own plans for tax reform were run down to earth and smothered by the protective-tariff movement. He had regarded state revenues from taxes, and especially the tobacco monopoly, as supports for the power of the Reich. But the interested groups placed their own economic security above all considerations of the general welfare. The agrarian party also presented demands for a protective tariff. If industry alone had been protected at this time, the manorial system in eastern Germany, outmoded as it was both technically and in organization, could not have persisted. The existence of the Junker class in Prussia rested on this system, and it was Prussia that actually ruled the Reich. Bismarck had had personal quarrels with most of his peers, but his social and political instinct involuntarily defended the class from which he had sprung. Thus the personal and the objective coincided, and a full turn was completed.

The change to a moderate protective tariff produced a new aristocratic ruling class in Germany. Agrarianism, the armament interests, clericalism, and the authority of the crown combined against liberalism and democracy, against parliamentarism and constitutionalism, behind which, according to the official view, lurked international pacifism and socialistic upset. This conversion of Bismarck's meant the sacrifice of a concept that had originally been essential to him: centralized development of the Reich. The Centre was thoroughly federalist—that is, particularistic. The famous stipulation of its leader, Baron Georg von Franckenstein, called (1879) for some surplus tariff revenues to be returned to the individual states, so that it should be impossible for the Reich to stand on its own feet financially. Bavaria's increasing influence also tended against centralization.

For the most loyal patriots of the Reich, the National Liberals, the change was a blow from which they never quite recovered. The left wing broke with Bismarck and formed a new liberal group, the so-called Secession, under the leadership of Eduard Lasker and

Ludwig Bamberger. Leaders who looked to the future planned to unite all the various scattered liberal elements in a strong new party, but this was never achieved. Liberalism lost more and more of its revolutionary and dynamic character and had to content itself with playing the part of a critical mediator between the new conservative forces on the right and the anti-capitalistic forces on the left.

ANTI-SOCIALIST LAW AND SOCIAL REFORM. ANTI-SEMITISM

Social Democracy was constantly gaining. Since the Congress at Gotha (1875) the international communist movement had been in the lead, although it was emphasized that legal means were to be used to gain its ends. Severe and contemptuous criticism of all patriotic convictions and national institutions, and more especially a mocking attitude toward matters of religious faith, widened the chasm between the socialistic working class and the bourgeoisie, even those parts of the lower middle class that for both economic and sociological reasons belonged to the proletariat rather than to any other class. On occasion the authorities and the courts proceeded against working men's associations. In 1878 two attempts were made on the life of the old Emperor, and the second was successful in wounding him. Although it was not possible to prove that these attacks were connected with Social Democracy, the bourgeoisie regarded them as preparing the way, to a dangerous degree, for socialist or communist revolution. Bismarck took advantage of the excitement among the people to impose an anti-socialist law on the newly elected Reichstag.

This law, repeatedly amended, remained in force until 1890. It prohibited associations, meetings, and publications of Social Democratic or communist tinge; persons who were suspect could be exiled; the distribution of publications could be suppressed and the bearing of weapons prevented. This was the beginning of an unhappy era of persecution. Social Democracy continued to exist, but on an illegal basis. The struggle grew bitterer from year to year. Congresses were held abroad, where it was possible to speak out boldly. A minor state of siege was repeatedly proclaimed. Numerous political suits proved the vitality of the party. Its martyrdom aroused sympathy, and the crude procedure of the reactionary state apparatus did not serve to make Bismarck's system more respected or more popular abroad.

Bismarck had suffered his first defeat in the *Kulturkampf;* the second was on the way.

Was no reconciliation between employers and workers possible? As early as the 1840's conservative state reformers had had more understanding of the problem than most liberals. From 1872 on, the Social Policy Association had been working for some more penetrating apprehension of the economic problem on social and ethical grounds. Gustav Schmoller and Lujo Brentano were the more distinguished of the younger leaders in political economy—the former a keen observer, a wise organizer, and an academic diplomat; the latter a tireless advocate, a fiery speaker, and an enthusiastic reformer who kindled enthusiasm in his public. These professors, well informed about developments in England and often referring to them, worked toward a treatment of economic problems on a basis of historical knowledge, political justice, and human decency. Could not measures of reform, taken in time, effect a balanced economic system of a peaceful and humanitarian sort, that would reconcile the employers' interest in profits with the workers' right to live?

In 1871 the first social policy law went into force—the Employers' Accident Liability Act. In 1876 relief funds were made obligatory. Bismarck now took up this trend of the times and atoned for the persecution of socialists with some magnificent legislation in the field of social policy, first on sickness insurance and then on accident insurance. Further laws for the protection of workers regulated Sabbath rest and restricted the labour of women and children. Unfortunately it cannot be said that this model legislation, imitated by many foreign countries, reconciled the German working classes to Bismarck's Reich. Wages remained low in Germany, and attaining a bourgeois standard of living became constantly more difficult. Emigration, which had risen sharply in southern Germany during the 1870's through flight from compulsory military service imposed by the Prussian system, now reached a new high in the 1880's. The fourth estate in Germany was not satisfied with benevolent social-welfare measures. It demanded living conditions that would open up new prospects and also free political activity.

Bismarck's Reich became more and more a class state. The colonial methods of old Prussia were now adapted to deepening the rift between the new aristocratic class and the new proletariat. And so the political struggles were largely concerned with winning over the unstable, disintegrating middle class, which often tended to the left in feeling, but was constrained toward the right by social and economic considerations. While universal suffrage persisted in the Reich —many, including Bismarck himself, were now saying that its introduction had been a grave mistake—the parties that strove to maintain the existing order were forced to court the favour of the masses. The Centre had no problems of this type. The great majority of devout Catholics followed its banner.

Among the Conservatives anti-Semitism was seen as an effective means of gaining the allegiance of craftsmen and employees, of shopkeepers and minor officials. The Christian Social Working Men's Association, founded in 1878 in Berlin by the court chaplain, Adolf Stöcker, hoped to capture the working class, and to this end it exploited cleverly the irritation caused by the anti-religious attitude of Social Democracy. A petition addressed to Bismarck in 1881 requested restrictions on immigration of foreign Jews and on appointments of Jews as judges and teachers. International anti-Semitic congresses met in Germany in 1882 and 1883. In 1887 the first anti-Semitic delegate appeared in the Reichstag. Anti-Semitism became particularly popular in Pomerania, Saxony, and Hesse. Stöcker was a most eloquent speaker, but a harsh and bold fanatic who had only a very superficial education in history and economics. He was forced to resign his office of court chaplain because of his activities as an agitator, but he remained a member of the Conservative Party until 1896. The anti-Semitic program of 1887 called for delegates of all callings, removal of the Jewish element from the schools, reform of the stock exchange, a new social order corresponding to people's callings, abolition of equal rights for Jews, subjection of German Jews to the laws governing foreigners, and prohibition of the immigration of foreign Jews. Bismarck rejected political anti-Semitism and staunchly maintained his own personal relations with Jews—with his banker, Gerson von Bleichröder, for instance. He declared officially that the government of the Reich would maintain the equality of all religious creeds so far as citizenship was concerned.

495

THE CARTEL. REINSURANCE TREATY. COURTING ENGLAND'S FAVOUR

In the 1880's Bismarck's prestige was definitely on the wane. The old statesman developed an exaggerated belligerence and arrogance. Many of the younger generation turned to him, fascinated by the force of his great nature. But the political quarrels with the growing opposition in the Reichstag became more and more unpleasant. Many plans miscarried. Bismarck grew increasingly sensitive to personal criticism and attacks. He celebrated one last triumph in 1887 when he won the fight for the septennate, the seven-year appropriation for the army. The opposition was not at all anti-militaristic and was ready to grant all demands on the army's account for a period of three years. But Bismarck insisted on seven years, and the so-called Cartel, the alliance of the parties of the right, the Conservatives, the Reich Party, and the National Liberals, overcame the opposition. The rapprochement between right-wing liberalism and the government, together with the reversion of the Centre to the opposition, roused hopes for centralization, which, however, could not be realized; the structure and tendency of the Cartel were far too reactionary.

Bismarck's foreign policy, too, wound up in ambiguities and confusion. To the very end the core of this policy was the alliance with Austria. When Italy joined it in 1882 the Triple Alliance was complete. Italy was annoyed by the French occupation of Tunis, which Bismarck had incited; she also wanted the backing of monarchical powers as against a growing republican and anarchistic movement. Bismarck had as low an estimation of Italy's military prowess as of her faithfulness to treaties if war should befall. Notwithstanding, he valued her co-operation, because within the alliance he hoped to smooth over the differences between Austria and Italy, and also because Italy's membership in the alliance heightened England's interest in it. At Italy's request it was expressly stated in the treaty that the Triple Alliance was not to be regarded as directed against Great Britain. Italy's colonial program and her whole position in the Mediterranean could be advanced only if the friendship with England were maintained. In 1887 the Triple Alliance was renewed in the form of four documents. An essential point was the agreement between Italy and Austria that possible changes in the Balkans in favour of one of these powers should constitute claims to indemnity for the other. The Turkish vilayet of Tripoli was envisioned as a future north African acquisition for Italy. In case of war with France Italy could count on the assistance of the two central European powers, while Austria, in a war with Russia, could expect nothing of Italy but benevolent neutrality.

The history of the Triple Alliance is the history of Italy's land hunger. It was Italian policy to push her partners ahead so as to put them into embarrassing positions. In consequence the Triple Alliance became perhaps the most popular, though by no means the most powerful, of Bismarck's foreign alliances. The agreement between Germany and Austria persisted side by side with the Triple Alliance; to keep up this agreement remained, in consideration of Russia, a matter of prime importance for Germany's position as a great power. In this connection the concept of a central Europe expanded into a program of hegemony.

Bismarck was twice successful in renewing the agreement among the three Emperors, although in weaker form. The way was opened by the death of Prince Gorchakov, who, from being Bismarck's well-wisher, had become his jealous rival, and by the murder of Czar Alexander II. The new Czar, Alexander III, was peace-loving. He was scarcely attracted by Pan-Slavic slogans, and he was little interested in a rapprochement with the French Republic. He was clumsy mentally as well as physically and was most at ease in simple, unambiguous relationships. The increasing English-Russian antagonism in Asia made a discharge of tension in the Balkans desirable. So the three Emperors made a neutrality pact in 1881. If one of the parties to it engaged in war with a fourth power, not excluding the Turks, the other two were to maintain a benevolent neutrality and help to localize the conflict.

In 1884 this agreement was extended for another three years. At that time Prince Alexander of the Hessian collateral line of Battenberg, who was ruling Bulgaria, was striking a decidedly anti-Russian attitude. The Prince, a dark-eyed lady-killer with a handsome beard, was engaged to Princess Victoria, the daughter of the German Crown Prince. Bismarck, holding to his course in spite of such connections, incurred the disfavour of the three Victorias: the Princess herself, her mother the Crown Princess, and her grandmother the Queen of England. The Battenberg Prince finally had to furl his sails before Russian disapproval. The marriage, too, did not come off. A further extension of the neutrality pact of the three Emperors proved impossible (1887) because of disturbances in Bulgaria and increasing tension between Russia and Austria. The successor of the Prince of Battenberg in Bulgaria was Prince Ferdinand, from a collateral line of the house of Coburg that had holdings in Hungary. Austria's sympathy was lukewarm toward him; Russia was entirely negative. For the time being, Germany did not recognize him.

At that time a military group in the Reich under the leadership of the ambitious and scheming Count Alfred Waldersee was demanding a two-front war against France and Russia. The aim was to break French chauvinism, which had flared up under General Boulanger's leadership, and to prostrate Russia, a purpose that would have enjoyed the benevolent neutrality of England. Austria had a secret treaty with Rumania; she hoped to fortify her position in the Balkans and was enthusiastic at the prospect of war. But Bismarck firmly rejected this apparently excellent opportunity to settle accounts with his European neighbours. Emperor William I, who was now a very old man, wished no preventive war. So Bismarck eased the tension with France and made the famous and controversial Reinsurance Treaty with Russia (1887). It provided that Russia should be neutral if France made offensive war against Germany and that Germany should be neutral if Austria attacked Russia. But the true significance of this secret agreement became clear only in the even more secret special agreement appended to the treaty: Germany promised her support in case the Czar should see fit to occupy the entrance to the Black Sea—that is, Constantinople.

The spirit of the Reinsurance Treaty ran counter to the German-Austrian alliance, and the treaty was therefore carefully concealed from Austria. In the second place it was contrary in its after-effects to the agreement concerning the Mediterranean that had been concluded in 1887 with Bismarck's concurrence; according to this Mediterranean agreement England, Austria, and Italy were to maintain the *status quo* against France and against possible attempts by Russia to threaten Constantinople and the Dardanelles. Thus Bismarck was promising Constantinople to the Russians at the moment when his allies, Austria and Italy, were assuring themselves of the aid of the

English fleet for the protection of Constantinople against the Russians. The foreign policy of Bismarck's later period was vague and vacillating, and this became particularly evident in his behaviour toward England. In spite of England's disapproval German enterprise had succeeded in securing for the Reich numerous colonies in Africa and in the Pacific. Bismarck personally wanted to encourage only commercial enterprise, in such a way as to involve the state and its representatives as little as possible. But it was not feasible to carry out this idea in practice.

In 1882 the German Colonization Society was founded. It took in persons who were actively interested in, and also sympathizers with, colonial enterprise. Lüderitz, a Bremen merchant, founded colonies in southwestern Africa in 1884. Karl Peters made his way in eastern Africa with much energy and few scruples. Smaller enterprises followed. Merchants, explorers, adventurers, and imperialists did not always succeed in working together harmoniously.

None of the German colonies was of the first rank. The little Togo region on the coast of western Africa was the most valuable economically. German East Africa offered good prospects. Kamerun, on the other hand, was less desirable, if only because of its unfavourable boundaries. The sandy desert of German southwest Africa was the only region where white settlers could stay permanently, and then not in large numbers and only with the help of state subsidies. After a disagreeable struggle with Spain the Reich had lost the Carolines in the Pacific. A share of New Guinea promised potential gains.

The German Reich had put in a tardy appearance on the colonial stage. Bismarck believed that its position in the heart of Europe was too open to constant danger to make successful overseas colonization on a large scale possible, though the German Reich might indeed have decided to make a perpetual pact with one of the really great world powers. Bismarck presided over the Congo Conference that met in Berlin in 1884, and he self-confidently demonstrated that Germany's power entered into decisions on overseas questions also. But he regarded a conflict about overseas possessions with older colonial powers, above all with Great Britain, as not only undesirable but even senseless, since it would have been contrary to all Germany's real and vital interests. From time to time colonial problems caused friction between Germany and England. Nothing was more important to the old Chancellor than to obviate these tensions and indeed to promote good relations.

During his last years his old plans from the time before the Congress of Berlin again emerged. Every connection between Germany and Russia made England suspicious, but willing to negotiate. Considering the growing unreliability of Russia, an alliance with Great Britain might well be the best guarantee of possessions and of peace that the powers of central Europe could hope for. Austria and especially Hungary were very much in favour of such an alliance. But could it be achieved in a really binding form? Matters of domestic policy were curiously involved in this great problem. In November 1887 Bismarck made his famous written offer of an alliance, not to Gladstone, the Liberal, but to the Conservative Prime Minister, Lord Salisbury. It was without result. On the English side old memories of Bismarck's past must have awakened. England had no confidence in Bismarck's Russophil military autocracy. Through Darmstadt, the Hessian court, the essentials of the Reinsurance Treaty may have been learned in London, or at least the fact that there was such a treaty. At any rate England held back. The future did not belong to Bismarck.

Chapter 18

WILLIAM II AND THE IMPERIALISTIC WORLD WAR

THE POWERFUL form of old Prince Bismarck loomed behind his creation, the German Reich, as a bulwark and a menace. Bismarck wanted this state of his to bear his own stamp and no other. Parties and newspapers that contradicted him were branded as enemies of the Reich, even when their opposition was objective and patriotic, as, for instance, in the case of the progressive delegate Eugen Richter, Bismarck's best-informed critic. Anyone who did not wish to be Bismarck's friend laid himself open to being treated as a foe. In addition to suits for lèse-majesté there were now numerous lèse-Bismarck suits also. None of the adversaries of his domestic policy dared dispute the great statesman's mastery of foreign policy. His influence and the strength of his will were almost as mighty as rumour painted them. He was consulted even in questions that were out of his province, and this made him an all the more conspicuous target for mounting criticism. The public was hardly aware of his many and frequently distinguished collaborators, who were lost in the shadow he cast. But the historian must not forget the names of Rudolf von Delbrück, who was president of the chancery of the Reich for many years, of Heinrich von Stephan, the organizer of the postal system, of Prince Chlodwig Hohenlohe, who was ambassador in Paris and later Stadholder of Alsace-Lorraine, and of many others. Besides these there was the Chancellor's son, Count Herbert Bismarck; many saw in this very able and gifted, though somewhat high-handed man his father's proper successor. He gave striking proof of his outstanding abilities in the course of the negotiations with England during the critical period of colonial acquisitions.

In Bismarck's last period the Reich was a land of elderly gentlemen. Emperor William I died at the age of ninety-one (1888). It was really only during his very last years that his energy slackened. Entirely in sympathy with the new conservative, military trends of the 1880's, he once more felt that he was the patriarchal head of a devout and loyal Prussian community. The clerical and dynastic sympathies of the Empress Augusta, too, were now in sharp contrast to the liberal tendencies of her youth. But Emperor Frederick III, who now ascended the throne, and his wife, Victoria, clung all the more obstinately to their parliamentarian principles, modelled on those of the western powers. Their best friends were adherents of different varieties of liberalism. A whole generation had waited far too long for Frederick's accession to the crown, but an incurable disease now put a swift end to his career. He was not able to do much, but the drift of what he did do was plain enough. The imminent possibility of a redirection of domestic and foreign policy toward western Europe perished with him. Would Germany become truly German? Could she become truly German? In other words, could she be liberated from the Prussian colonial and military autocracy and be harmoniously woven into the collective culture of Europe? This old question of destiny was raised again in altered form by the changed conditions of the whole course of world history.

TECHNICAL DEVELOPMENT. VITALISM. THE CONCEPT OF RACE

The amazing progress in the natural sciences completed the technical organization of life in Germany. The conditions of life, its rhythm, and its tensions rearranged themselves. Machine work destroyed the handicrafts. The new mechanical means of communication regrouped the entire population, created new callings and new communities, made manufactures and raw materials from distant regions available, aroused new and undreamed-of desires, and made them more and more urgent because they could be satisfied only partially and only for the privileged classes. The capitalistic system, which contributed to the triumph of technical development, was itself completed by it. It was a fruitful mutual relationship based on deep spiritual kinship.

Psychologically the mechanization of the world was the most palpable demonstration of Darwinism and of the materialistic interpretation of history. The methods of natural science were now applied to the humanities as well. The idealism of philosophy had been a sort of prerogative of the old form of education, which it had made neither more conducive to happiness nor more practical. The upward-surging masses turned away from the classical German tradition wearily and even with revulsion. In Kant and Goethe they saw representatives of class interests. They wanted more substantial fare. Materialism, as preached by socialists of various shades, proceeded, from the economic approach to an all-embracing view of the world. It was regarded as a sign of strong-mindedness to reject all the political and ecclesiastical rubbish of the past and be devoted to a naïve metaphysics grounded on physical vitality. Ludwig Büchner (died 1899) wrote his successful book on force and matter; the monism of Ernst Häckel (died 1919), with its view of the world as of one substance throughout, was among the last evidences of this drift.

In one way or another all these views sought to further the people's movement. They were deliberately directed toward the left. They justified and affirmed revolution. But just as Hegel's philosophy, in its time, had been grist to the mills of both revolutionists and counter-revolutionists, so now Darwin's biology was the beginning of a new movement toward the right. The French Count Gobineau's book on the inequality of human races (1853–5) met with small favour in the academic world; it was regarded as a somewhat fantastic piece of work by an amateur who had plenty of ideas but was uninstructed both in the facts of the matter and in their critical manipulation. But the effect of the book on certain political groups was all the stronger for those qualities.

The principle of nationality appeared to be scientifically confirmed by the concept of race. It seemed that what was innate prevailed over what was acquired. Heredity turned the scale. Blood determined the destiny and the value of a people. There were superior and inferior races. The characteristics of the superior races adhered to them alone and were to be preserved by keeping the race pure. Only the purest and most superior race could achieve intellectual prowess, political sovereignty, and creation of a true culture. All other races had to give precedence to this one in the struggle for existence and had to be content simply to serve it. Gobineau and his successors in Germany made every effort to prove that this superior race was the Germanic, that Germanic heritage and Germanic leadership had produced everything that was of value in the civilization of Europe. Later this concept of the Germanic was transformed into the notion of a Nordic race.

These doctrines had nothing to do with science. They were not even worth refuting. For the very concept of race was not at all definite. So far as it was to be taken at all seriously, it was concerned only with natural science. The philosophy of race mingled linguistic, ethnical, and sociological factors in a brew of delusions. But the good Germans, who had survived more ethnical admixtures than any other great nation, were elated by this opportunity to see themselves as a noble Germanic or Nordic race. Once this feeling was established, it was easy to build up corollaries concerning the value of their cultural contributions and their right to rule others.

WAGNERIANISM

Gobineau's relations with Richard Wagner gave the first strong impetus to the doctrine of race in Germany. Wagner revived the world of the old Germanic gods and legends with a deliberate purpose. The romantic sense of life of his early years had matured, with the din of battle and the atmosphere of class struggle that accompanied the founding of the Reich, into cultural prophecy of Germanic coloration. Wagner's will to power became quite evident even as early as his rather exaggerated friendship with King Louis II of Bavaria. The all-embracing work of art was still not enough for him; it was only a symbol of something more comprehensive, of a new shaping of the world. Just as Wagner's music combined the sentiment of *Weltschmerz* with a technique that worked through material means and that was akin to the mechanization of existence, so Wagner as reformer of state and of society now undertook to point beyond Bismarck's Reich to a Germanic world mission of the German people. This mission was to be a blend of sovereignty and culture, of ideas and power, in confirmation of racial and creative superiority.

Wagner and the Wagnerians pushed on beyond the limits of the purely musical. They constituted a school of rigid dogma, a propaganda group, in Bayreuth, and they developed into a class of prophets who laboured untiringly as agitators; among them were aristocrats, academicians, and music critics. At first they were no more than a fanatical sect, but their influence extended farther and farther until they were in effect a political and social community, which was the more useful to the aristocratic reconstruction of the 1880's because Wagner in his last work, *Parsifal,* had gone back to the Christian outlook on life. Thus the Christian-Germanic element that had been in evidence at the outset of the century reappeared, in a changed form and with an increased anti-Semitic tendency.

THE HISTORICAL APPROACH AND NATURALISM. FRIEDRICH NIETZSCHE

German feeling for pure music turned from the noisy, vulgar intolerance of the Wagnerians to Johannes Brahms, Hugo Wolf, Anton Bruckner, and later Richard Strauss.

For a long time a historical-minded generation still predominated in German art and literature. They regarded the emotional agitation of late romanticism as the essence of artistic creation and therefore busied themselves in all naïveté with setting a better world, one that was pleasant and charming, alongside of mechanized material reality, by way of solace and uplift. The desire of the newly rich for luxurious comfort lent these efforts a tinge of the exotic, of fulsomeness and sensuousness, such as can be easily detected also in Wagner's music. The novels of Friedrich Spielhagen and Georg Ebers, the stories of Paul Heyse, and even the later works of Gustav Freytag bear witness to this taste, which was reflected in the paintings of Wilhelm von Kaulbach, Piloty, Makart, and the Achenbach brothers. At the same time Adolf Menzel was producing work of a more localized character in Berlin; there were masters of painting in Frankfurt and in southern Germany who not only produced for market but also created a good deal that was able and expert.

The decisive turn against romanticism came from Paris. The collapse of the Second Empire had produced, after a transitional period, an attitude of ruthless irony toward the bourgeois world. The money-mad patriotism that flaunted cupidity and dripped empty slogans, the hypocritical liberalism of the final years of Bonapartist rule, brought art to its senses. And now art demanded the right to exist for its own sake and not for the entertainment of a paunchy bourgeoisie. It claimed significance as the most essential element in life, and it would not be limited to the province of the merely beautiful. Saturated with vigorous life, art claimed all of material and mechanized reality as a subject for serious and relentlessly honest creative work. Only such a cool and detached approach, related to that of the natural sciences, could get the upper hand of reality, make it endurable, and even ennoble it to new and permanent values. This artistic credo worked itself out in state and society as æsthetic anarchism and as complete agnosticism toward every concept of sovereignty.

In Germany, Max Stirner, a curious personality, had put forward views of this kind from a philosophical angle as early as the 1840's. According to him the individual must be wholly cut off from the masses; only the individual had significance. Authority, law, and the state were less than nothing. All that remained was what the strong personality created for himself. Side by side with the artist and the thinker, the man of power took the stage as the new sovereign of the era.

The driving forces of the nineteenth century could not be negated more conclusively. Friedrich Nietzsche (died 1900) now became their greatest foe. The most important influences on Nietzsche's ideas, which he often reshaped spontaneously, were Schopenhauer, the French theory of art for art's sake, Paul de Lagarde, Gobineau, and Richard Wagner. His struggle for truth and his perception of the prerequisites of the beautiful were filled with an earnestness and a sense of responsibility that in themselves were enough to make his personality a field of force of profound creative potency. He attacked militarism and socialism, party factions and journalistic culture, progressive catchwords, the taste of the crowd, and finally the doctrine of Christianity itself with its ethics of pity and its egalitarianism.

On the ruins of tradition he now set about erecting the world of the superman. This superman signified a new human type no less than the sovereign character of individual leaders, and this new world was governed by the highest end-product of biological processes and followed the new aristocratic master morality. By such means slave morality, the spitefulness of the inferior, the grudges of the suffering and the outcast, and the decadence of the uprooted were to be overcome. In such thinking the earlier cult of genius transformed itself into the demand that the world be renewed through an earthly saviour.

The impact of Friedrich Nietzsche's ideas was like that of an earthquake. Their effect increased steadily as the decades passed. A whole generation of young Germans learned from him how to feel, to think, and to write. Vocabulary, turn of phrase, imagery, even the most brittle and fragile ideas, he animated with a breath of fire. Some of the aphorisms of his teaching became common intellectual property, like the phrase "transvaluation of all values." His opposition forced a way for itself because it was impassioned to an unprecedented degree. When he attacked, nothing survived. He was equally relentless whether he was serious or ironical. There was something anarchic about the force of his negation. The rising generation of that period could never forget what Nietzsche had to say about university professors, the organs of the state, the churches, and democratic forms of life. Surely such destructiveness was matched by a noble will to new construction, but this will was millennial, tuned to a thousand-year span. It was prophetic, entirely impractical and unpolitical, and in the end real creativity was denied to Nietzsche. He was too much of a poet to be a philosopher; yet as a poet he bore too heavy a burden of thought. Despair over his sterile isolation made a destroyer of him, and he revelled in mad, bold, reckless critical nihilism. A deep and exquisite sense of form, however, was always with him.

Friedrich Nietzsche, saint and heretic, the eminent prey of misunderstanding and persecution, who fled the world and humankind in order to complete his work, who was overwhelmed with horror of the rising masses and their brutal instincts—this same over-sensitive Nietzsche supplied the mass movement with the sharpest weapons to beat down the whole intellectual heritage, to refute the liberal and humanitarian view of the world that had been the basis of all German culture up to this time. Once that collapsed, then up would rise the primitive. The basest passions would be loosed; the more or less blond beasts would claim the sovereign role of the superman, and, following their example, little supermen would spring up everywhere.

SCANDINAVIAN AND RUSSIAN INFLUENCES

Thus many began to doubt the old standards. All the more serious thinkers were filled with apprehension and disgust at the civilized humanity that was evolving in the great cities. Capitalism proceeded on its magnificent career. Financially and industrially it embraced all seas and continents. In this new unity that was in the making every people could maintain itself only by putting forth all its strength and by availing itself of new methods. A development of this kind might easily prove harmful to the spirit. It was not difficult to criticize, but would it be possible to produce a new type of humanity to guard the things of the spirit and even to carry them farther creatively in an epoch of imperialism?

Socialism in its various aspects now began to take art into its service. The new realism could not be realistic enough. Freed of conventional forms, nature itself, unvarnished, soiled, and base reality, should show men what was actually going on in factories, in the country, among the poor and the wretched, and how every vestige of personal happiness and love was torn and trampled in the harshness of the struggle. Now, as in earlier periods, France exerted an important influence on German literature—from Gustave Flaubert and Guy de Maupassant to Émile Zola.

Scandinavian and Russian influences struck even deeper. Henrik Ibsen exposed the hypocrisy of bourgeois life with the visionary power of a northern seer and the sure taste in art of one who had been schooled in the technique of the theatre of western Europe. Jens Peter Jacobsen the Dane, Björnson and Hamsun in Norway, Strindberg and Selma Lagerlöf in Sweden won over the German public as the decades passed. They formed the taste of the more fastidious lovers of literature, opened up new ethnical and psychological fields, and strengthened the growing Germanic-Nordic self-consciousness. Vague enthusiasms and all sorts of side issues that were no more than half artistic detracted from the worth of these Scandinavian imports.

Russian influence in Germany amounted to much more than a fad. Feodor Dostoievsky and Ivan Turgeniev, Leo Tolstoy and Maxim Gorki made themselves felt far beyond the bounds of the purely æsthetic. The destiny of Russia, which was even then preparing for the revolution, affected the German people more profoundly than any other. For here was a blend of naturalism and faith, of the people's strength and the land's great expanse, of mysticism and vitality, of aristocratic forms of life and the most acute social tension, that provided an exaggerated reflection of Germany's own problems.

Action and reaction of Germany and Russia on each other had never ceased since the conflict between Karl Marx and Mikhail Bakunin. Russian revolutionaries all learned German and studied revolution at the German universities. They had something to learn from Hegel as well as from Lassalle. The great Russian literature, even though it generally devoted itself to purely artistic ends, set the pace for the revolutionary movement. German scholars were more preoccupied with the problems of Russia than scholars anywhere. The psychologist of race may trace this German-Russian interchange back to a joint Slavic heritage; it is true that the Slavic admixture in eastern Germany had always been a link between the German colonial region and the eastern world. In Bohemia and Poland such admixture made relations with the purely Slavic population more difficult, but it eased those with Greater Russia, which was part Tatar. For many generations the German merchant, school teacher, pharmacist, or engineer had helped the Russians, though he had also irritated them by his air of superiority and his pedantry. Now Russia paid back her debt. The great Russian novel pleaded love for Russia, for her suffering people, for her wealth of genius, for her hopeless and desperate strugglings. The German reader was bound to realize why there were terrorism and anarchism in Russia, why the final and most dreadful recourse seemed the only one possible: forcible destruction, ruthless annihilation of all traditional forms of life, nihilism.

In Russia the æsthetic anarchism of the west developed into an attitude that became significant metaphysically and for the history of the world; in this sense Friedrich Nietzsche was subjected to a reinterpretation of staggering irony. Only the most senselessly cruel despotism could change with such suddenness into an equally terroristic dictatorship of the proletariat over state and culture. For many decades intimate relations had obtained between imperial Russia and the Prussian-German state; now the literary and philosophical exchange of ideas between the two peoples supplemented their community of interests in a way that was significant for intellectual history. The more the two regimes drew apart in the course of the following years, the more the exchange of ideas intensified; it proceeded from a general view of the world to the creation of art, from art to social revolution.

509

"MODERN" GERMAN ART

German naturalism dates from the beginning of the 1880's. Struggle against the sweet and banal art of epigones was the motto of the two brothers and critics Heinrich and Julius Hart. Sturdier tones were being sounded. Richard Dehmel, a challenging prophet, revelled in impassioned free rhythms. Otto Julius Bierbaum struck a delightfully impudent note in his verses full of gay Bohemianism. Hermann Sudermann, an East Prussian, put over his effects as a writer of fiction with a sure touch and succeeded in drama by dint of his sensational talents as well as cheap strokes. Max Halbe had better taste, but was less versatile. Detlev von Liliencron was strong and merry, a good comrade who liked a drink or two. He rejected prejudices of any kind and embraced the Bohème of Germany. But throughout all his adventures he remained an excellent officer and a knightly spirit who succeeded in producing many a grave and even solemn strophe; the richness of his nature craved all the form and feeling of the world he loved so much.

German naturalism could not boast of any one very great and compelling artist; so it made the most of what it had: Gerhart Hauptmann (1862–1946), from Silesia, who was a master of word and feeling. He was stirred by predominantly religious impulses, and he was so impressionable that his thought and style were curiously wavering; but he was very human even in his weakness and full of innate kindness. His early success hampered him to a certain extent, but his work, though always controversial, won him more and more followers; and thus he matured into the poet of the epoch of William II—the leading poet of the mounting German opposition.

Theodor Fontane, from the Mark of Brandenburg, was probably the only imaginative writer of the older generation who was accepted by the younger. His Huguenot descent had endowed him with a sensitive feeling for form, which this man of the world utilized in shaping subject-matter drawn from the Mark and more especially from Berlin. Just because he came from the middle class and yet had the advantage of being set off from it through his admixture of French blood, he was well able to describe the Prussian Junker: dry and efficient, unsentimental but soft at the core, very earth-bound and hostile to all that was lofty and far-reaching, brusque and even insolent in manner, egotistic, but rarely base.

Naturalism in Germany took up the old struggle where the Storm and Stress and Young Germany had left it, the struggle against the deathless provincial town and the indestructible bourgeois in the fatherland. Formerly the object of criticism had been the petty prince and his court. But in Bismarck's Reich the princes conducted themselves with great discretion. They were patrons of art and science. Weimar, Meiningen, Darmstadt, and Dessau, in particular, were intellectual centres. After the unfortunate King Louis II of Bavaria, who had lost his mind, was placed under restraint, there were no more scandals involving princes, or if there were, they did not become public property.

Other circles now evoked harsher criticism. There was the wealthy bourgeois, who cherished the hope of invading the aristocracy and the patrician class and filled his ostentatious villas with plush furniture, photographs in gilt frames, and souvenirs of his travels. There was the ambitious career man from the lower middle class, who was employed as an official or in industry, who was always nervously currying favour with the rich and the powerful; he imitated the manners of the ruling class with astonishing facility, was brutal to those beneath him and flattered those above, and often managed to rise well beyond the station he had been born to, thanks to an advantageous marriage. And finally there was the university professor who was all too willing to bow to the interests of the ruling class and to the advantage of the self-confident state, even at the sacrifice of the traditions of freedom of German institutions of higher learning. Such were types of William II's subjects, types that had taken shape in Bismarck's Reich and were now fully developed, to the annoyance of young artists and writers, who heaped mockery on them.

As against this bourgeoisie of the black, white, and red and especially the more and more frequent type of dapper reserve officer and the student who was a member of some influential student organization, Munich became the opposite pole, a focus of originality, of art, of gay and gracious living. Here was a city that combined the small town life and Bohème, piety and tolerance, sensuousness and creativeness, in its own harmonious fashion. There was more asperity about the theatres and newspapers of Berlin, but even there they served as a refreshing offset to authority. In Frankfurt, Hamburg, Düsseldorf, Breslau, and many another sturdy old German city there was still a precious stock of personal independence, self-confidence, mental resilience. Around 1890 there was a better chance than ever before or ever after for a pronounced program of reform and inner reorganization in Germany.

THE YOUNG EMPEROR

At this turning-point the German Reich had the misfortune to acquire an Emperor who did not take the path toward peace, freedom, and social reconciliation. William II (1859–1942) was decidedly talented. He stood out more than any of his royal contemporaries in quickness of apprehension and natural gift for rhetoric. He was bound to be conspicuous in court circles. His well-meaning parents tried to put him in contact with the bourgeois world as far as possible in his school life. But they were disappointed in their expectations. William II always remained a stranger to the industrious working habits of the bourgeois. As the result of an accident at his birth, the Emperor had a withered arm; this fact has been over-exploited by psychologists to build up a theory of a cripple's psychology about the monarch. It is true that the young Prince had to make a special effort to satisfy the usual sports and military requirements. He learned to assume an outward appearance of great energy and discipline, but within himself his powers were not collected at all. Perhaps his technical gift was the greatest of his many talents and interests. From it sprang his rather vain delight in his own drafts and ideas, artistic as well as military.

Since it soon became evident that the young ruler was sensitive to objective criticism, the court forthwith surrounded him with an aura of adulation. He had no real affinity for high art, no ability for scientific investigation, no real Christian goodness. He was content with passing interests in everything new, with pronounced religiosity that did not even hesitate to bespeak for himself the reverence due to a high priest. From such an angle, from an attitude of mysticism and late romanticism, he attacked his vocation of ruler, not in any such theosophic spirit as King Frederick William IV, but as a practical politician. He was both pompous and trivial in his usual manner. The Emperor had an instinct for politics that was always on the alert. He might have been an excellent councillor of embassy under an experienced ambassador, a successful minister of propaganda under an enlightened chancellor. What he needed most—what he never had—was someone in authority over him.

In his youth the Prince was not on good terms with either of his parents. As Emperor he never discussed political problems with his clever mother. He secretly laughed at his many royal uncles and enjoyed acting in direct opposition to their advice in order to prove his intellectual independence. His wife, with whom he led a peaceful life and who bore him numerous children, was so dull and limited that anyone who was familiar with the circumstances could hardly begrudge him his many flights from domestic boredom. William II had the gift of friendship, and some few of his friends, such as Prince Philip Eulenburg, for instance, were even permitted to tell him the truth—in tactful form, of course, adapted to the Emperor's sensitive nerves. But such gentle admonitions had little effect.

All of the Emperor's friends, among them even a Jew, Albert Ballin, had first and foremost to satisfy his craving for entertainment. William II loved jokes, and not always such as were in the best taste. It was characteristic that he clung to the gay immaturity of academic youth and to the tone of the Prussian officers' club far too long. Archæological excavation and magicians' tricks were his favourite occupations; both had technical aspects and the element of surprise, and nothing is more revealing for the psychology of this ruler. In his capacity of statesman, too, he would have liked to dig up old and precious things and to conjure up by magic the wishful dream of a happy future.

The Emperor was neither particularly belligerent nor a master of diplomatic intrigue. He did not know human nature; he himself was fundamentally uncertain, but tried to overcome this feeling by swashbuckling and by luxuriating in all sorts of burlesqued and fantastic uniforms. His naval policy was his most notable achievement, and one that had fatal consequences. William II was in a dilemma. Was he to take up the reform of Germany's domestic policy and carry it through to success, or was he to compete with the older powers, already imperialistic, and establish the German Reich as a new world power from the point of view of both colonies and naval policy? The Emperor did not know very much about the European struggle to produce a new human type; what he did know seemed uncanny to him and called for denial. "Be sure to take a firm stand against modern art for me," he said at a later period to a well-known university professor. If the Emperor had decided to set about the internal reorganization of the Reich, the majority of his generation would gladly have followed him. But only a small minority was willing to work for a world policy, with all its premises and consequences.

Young William II admired Prince Bismarck and confidently regarded himself as the great Chancellor's most distinguished pupil. It was certainly simpler to continue Bismarck's autocratic, militaristic system than the wise and responsible foreign policy behind it. The conflict that blazed forth was something more than the perpetual struggle between the older and the younger generations. Grandfathers and grandsons are apt to agree better than fathers and sons. But Bismarck returned the open admiration of his young sovereign with mixed emotions. He did not like William's constant bustle, and he distrusted his lack of tact, his swollen rhetoric, his tendency to become intoxicated with his own glittering plans. He thought that the Reich was in a grave situation from every point of view, and that at just this moment he was more indispensable than ever. He held to his life-work and wanted to defend it with every ounce of strength as long as he possibly could. But genius was oppressive to the Emperor, as it is to all those who are merely gifted. He wanted to get rid of the old man.

BISMARCK'S DISMISSAL (1890)

These underlying motives became patent through a series of occurrences that belonged to three fields of public life. The Reinsurance Treaty with Russia was due to expire in 1890. Bismarck hoped to renew it. He realized clearly, however, that such an arrangement would be merely an emergency measure. That was why he was so eager to approach England. He was planning to acquire Heligoland. The young Emperor regarded Bismarck's attitude as ambiguous and contradictory; above all he had no confidence in Russia. In his social policy William II was very much under the influence of the Christian Social ideas of the coterie of Count Alfred Waldersee, the future chief of the general staff.

A miners' strike in the Ruhr Valley also served to emphasize the Emperor's opposition to the Chancellor. The Emperor wanted to smooth things over. He was planning extensive social legislation, including full Sabbath rest. But Bismarck refused to make any further concessions. He wanted to fight, and he hoped to get the liberal bourgeoisie alerted about the increasing labour unrest. He did not dream of abolishing the anti-socialist law, but intended rather to institute a new and still harsher law. In this way the problem of social policy was bound up with the third field of conflict, that of domestic policy. Bismarck wanted more than a union of parties, such as had been effected in the Cartel of 1887. He tried to win the Centre over from the opposition and thus to build a broader front against revolution. His plans involved abolishing universal suffrage and making changes in the constitution of the Reich, even at the cost of civil war. Such threats terrified the young Emperor.

The princes belonging to the Reich, his experienced uncle Grand Duke Frederick of Baden above all, sounded warnings. Should this blood-and-iron man really be permitted to destroy the work of a whole generation and to erect a stark autocracy? Repeated conferences between the Emperor and the Chancellor proved so stormy that any fruitful co-operation became inconceivable. Up to this point the Chancellor had had small respect for his young sovereign. Now his feeling turned into bitter hatred. The Emperor, on his part, grew more and more convinced that it was in the interests of the fatherland to remove this dangerous old man. Compromises recommended by more or less honest well-wishers proved impractical. Bismarck's personal wish was that he might continue at least to handle Germany's foreign affairs. He could not realize that his career was really coming to a close. The entire state machinery was at a standstill; if the Reich were to be ruled at all, some clear decision must be reached. The dismissal of Bismarck followed. The old statesman had clung to his office; now he suffered a shock from which he never recovered, in spite of a subsequent formal reconciliation with the monarch. One wonders if William II might not have found some more gracious solution. Certainly he was at a hopeless tactical disadvantage in the face of Bismarck's stubborn suavity.

Bismarck's contemporaries accepted the event as something inevitable, something quite natural. He had made very few friends. The majority of politicians were relieved and hoped better times might be coming. The new course that the Emperor had embarked

515

on was regarded with sympathy on all sides. Many had been oppressed and disappointed; they took new courage. The Emperor may have made mistakes in his handling of Bismarck, but history was ready to approve him if he were successful in putting through his own political program. Bismarck's shadow stood behind him, warning and threatening. The old statesman did not give up the fight. He did not retire like a high official showered with honours and dignities. His revenge took the form of the Bismarck legend, which he and his aides proceeded to spread.

Bismarck had been so great because he had been so flexible. But legend chained him to friendship for Russia as an article of faith and also to antagonism toward England. This represented the exact opposite of the possibilities the Chancellor had been weighing just before he retired. The Bismarck legend developed into an essential factor in the later history of Germany. The true character of his work was recognized only very gradually. The living memories and the views of his contemporaries were buried with them. But as a figure in history Bismarck loomed larger and larger. It grew customary to ask in any difficulty what he would have done. The more unsuccessful the new course proved, the more expressly the dismissal of the Chancellor appeared as the beginning of the end, and the more clamorously the exiled and the outlawed railed against current ineptitude.

THE CAPRIVI ERA (1890–4)

Bismarck's successor was General von Caprivi (1831–99), the best type of clever, respectable, clear-thinking German officer of the general staff. Bismarck himself had had occasion to recommend him, and the Emperor had found him very agreeable as temporary director of the German admiralty. Caprivi was a significant personage whose actions were prompted by purely objective considerations. He fully realized the difficulties of the work he had taken over, and he made an honest effort to improve the situation. His character was, of course, not comparable to Bismarck's, with its versatility and suppleness.

In his foreign policy Caprivi first of all abandoned all thought of renewing the Reinsurance Treaty with Russia, and then the rapprochement between France and Russia, which Bismarck himself had regarded as inevitable, was effected. The treaty Bismarck had prepared with England about Heligoland, on the other hand, was carried through. This island in the North Sea became German and provided an important naval base. Germany sacrificed a considerable part of her prospects for colonies in eastern Africa by ceding Zanzibar for Heligoland. The rapprochement between Germany and England was emphasized to the public in speeches of the Prince of Wales, who later became Edward VII, and of Emperor William. Both expressed the belief that the co-operation of the strongest army and the strongest navy in the world would be a guarantee of peace. This was intended as a warning, especially to Russia, which was hoping to acquire the Dardanelles and had been receiving larger and larger loans from France for armament purposes ever since 1887. For this reason Germany was laying more stress on her friendship with Austria-Hungary and with Italy.

The renewal of the Triple Alliance in the form of a joint pact (1891) obligated Germany to support Italy's claims in the event of changes in Tunis as well as in Tripoli. England's participation in problems relating to the Mediterranean was expressly provided for in the joint treaty. And so the partnership between France and Russia was now openly confronted with the Triple Alliance. The situation in Europe seemed simplified. There was no cause for uneasiness. Germany increased her armaments and felt entirely able to conduct a war on two fronts against Russia and France, should such a necessity arise. Friendship with England was, of course, the essential prerequisite for such a policy. In domestic policy the dispute on the army bill led to a new split among the Liberals. Only a small group under Heinrich Rickert, a newspaper-proprietor of Danzig, recognized the need of enlarging the army, especially because of the final reduction of compulsory military training from three to two years to satisfy an old demand of the Liberals.

Caprivi himself had certain leftist sympathies. The anti-socialist law was not renewed. In 1892 most of the old trade treaties expired. The Social Democrats demanded the abolition of all agrarian tariffs. The Liberals were in favour of a thorough-going reduction of tariffs. The tariffs on cattle, grain, and wood, at least, were to be entirely abolished. Trade and industry energetically called for moderate tariffs, and agreements to this effect were made with Rumania, Russia,

Spain, and Serbia. The question had political significance over and above its economic importance and seemed to open the way to a long-desired reorientation. Bismarck's policy of a protective tariff had served old Prussia, the enemy of parliaments. Caprivi challenged the agrarians on an economic basis. The reply was upheaval.

An agriculturists' league was formed that demanded adequate protection for agriculture and allied occupations, the revision of legislation protecting working men, and supervision of the produce exchange. The league soon became a tool in the hands of Junker proprietors, who wanted to fit all German agriculture into a large-scale agrarian policy and thus prevent any shift to the left. Since Caprivi had the reputation of being the leader of a dangerous program of democratization, his downfall was foreordained. Again Germany stood at a parting of the ways. Agrarian state or industrial state— that was what everyone was talking about.

As the Reich became increasingly industrialized, it became more and more dependent on imports of raw materials and food supplies from abroad. If these supplies could be secured at a low world market price, the old-time manorial estate was doomed. Only peasant farmers would be able to compete. Owing to a shrinking population, estate owners east of the Elbe had to make use of cheap Polish seasonal labour, which asked very little in the way of food and shelter. If the large estates of the Junkers had been converted into peasant holdings and productiveness thus increased, moderate protective tariffs and in consequence easier industrialization would have been possible. The purchasing power of wages had increased, and it had become easier to import raw materials and semi-finished goods. But if domestic policy had been subjected to such a reorganization, the result would have been the introduction of equal suffrage in Prussia and the other states, a parliamentarian regime for the Reich, and democratization of the entire social structure. These changes would have preoccupied Germany for at least a decade. The times were favourable for such a policy; the Triple Alliance on the one hand and England's friendship on the other spelled security for the Reich for an indefinite period. It would have been necessary to shelve imperialistic plans, however. It would have been entirely possible, though not easy, to carry out the armament program even if the

Reich functioned on a democratic basis. For only a minority in Germany was in favour of anything approaching disarmament.

The situation was quite different in the matter of colonial and naval policy. An organization that had been formed in 1891 assumed in 1894 the name of the Pan-German League. It called for the protection of the German people, the support and protection of German national ambitions and the union of all the Germans in the world for these aims, the encouragement of a vigorous German foreign policy in Europe and overseas, and the pushing forward of German colonial policy to practical results. The Reich, in other words, was summoned to enter the theatre of world politics. The members of the Pan-German League were mostly scholars, judges, and teachers, professors of Germanist studies, and also officials, persons interested in heavy industry and in the trade of the Hansa towns, publicists with imaginative gifts, and cosmopolitan travellers —in short, intelligent people who in their own way were trying to cut free of provinciality by taking up the hopes and wishes of earlier patriots. Thus German nationalism received a new impetus from this quarter. Through all sorts of personal cross-connections it cooperated with the agrarian Junkers against democratization, even though the two groups belonged to classes that were alien to each other. The agrarians demanded the protective tariff; the Pan-Germans demanded a world policy. Armaments to the extent necessary for a world policy could be provided only by an autocratic Germany ruled by Greater Prussia. The real connection is found in this circumstance.

PRINCE CHLODWIG HOHENLOHE. THE BEGINNINGS OF WORLD POLICY

At this time the European public was under increasing excitement from anarchistic attacks on the lives of various leaders. After the murder of the French President Carnot (1894) the German Emperor called for a stand against revolution; in doing so he made the very common error of lumping socialists and anarchists together. A number of the princes in Germany were also in favour of harsh measures even at the expense of the constitution of the Reich. Since not a single prince had sworn to support it, this constitution could be changed. Caprivi was on good terms with the Prussian Poles, who were being given better treatment; now the Emperor attacked the Poles too in one of his innumerable speeches. From Prussia and the other states of Germany a tempest arose against the Chancellor that he could not subdue. The dream of a leftward reorganization of the Reich dissolved. Caprivi was dismissed.

His successor, the very old Prince Chlodwig Hohenlohe-Schillingsfürst, followed in Bismarck's tracks, though without making any brilliant strokes. His leanings first became apparent in foreign policy. The new Czar, Nicholas II, had married a princess of Hesse-Darmstadt who was his intellectual superior. From his youth Nicholas had had close personal relations with William II; the latter tried to exploit them politically, and not without success. But the shift of Russian policy toward eastern Asia was to become weightier than this personal factor. Japan's push toward continental eastern Asia also served to focus Russian interests on it. Austria-Hungary, and therefore the German Reich as well, were conscious of the slackening of tensions in the Near East and in the Balkans. William II showed his favour toward Russian policy in eastern Asia in every possible way. When Japan imposed the onerous Preliminary Peace of Shimonoseki on the Chinese, Germany intervened, together with Russia and France. The three Continental powers were successful in this collective intervention, for which Germany was the spokesman, and which took an unnecessarily harsh form. Japan was forced to reduce her demands. Germany had helped Russia. Japan was mortally offended and set about preparing a cold-blooded revenge. But that was still in the future. In the meantime the Emperor's catchword about the yellow peril aggravated existing antagonisms.

A continental triple alliance of the three great military powers had been one of Bismarck's cherished ideas. Shimonoseki seemed to revive it. Germany's relations to France became in general friendlier. As late as 1891 the visit of Emperor Frederick's widow to Paris had called forth stormy demonstrations of vengefulness from the super-patriots, spurred by some young painters whose pictures the Empress had refused to buy. The result was a dangerous political tension. England also resented this ungracious treatment of Queen Victoria's daughter. After Shimonoseki courteous relations between France and Germany were re-established and proved fruitful in a practical way in the handling of African colonial problems. Great

Britain, on the other hand, came up against Russia in Asia and against France in Africa. But when in the spring of 1894 Lord Rosebery, the English Prime Minister, suggested closer co-operation between Germany and England against Russia, Berlin was not interested.

The anti-English trend that now became evident in German foreign policy was advanced primarily by the very able Privy Councillor von Holstein, who became more and more a leader in foreign policy because of his energy and his zest for effecting combinations. Holstein was a monomaniac, infinitely superior to the average diplomat, egoistic and almost abnormally absorbed in his own world of ideas and in his official duties, which so completely sequestered him that in the long run he lost contact with reality and also flexibility of action, the very qualities that had been responsible for Bismarck's greatness. Holstein was personally disagreeable. He delighted in irritating people, casting slurs, and even spreading slanders—in administering every variety of subtle poison; and he was corrupt in money matters. This man, in a position to know the state of international politics better than anyone else, exploited his knowledge in speculations on the stock exchange and thus presented the unusual phenomenon of corruption in Prussian-German officialdom. Curiously enough, Holstein did not become at all rich, but died in relatively modest circumstances; he had at any rate savoured the true gambler's joy, which is simply to gamble. And his fate in matters of foreign policy was the same as in his money ventures; all his diabolical plotting ended in undramatic bankruptcy.

The anti-English attitude had strong support in many substantial circles. In the lead was the Emperor, who wanted to cut free of anything suggestive of English tutelage. Admiration for the English had been inculcated in him by his mother, but now he overcame this feeling by a really very un-English desire to imitate everything English, to compete with the English and outdo them. Society at William's court was emphatically Anglophobe, if only out of opposition to Emperor Frederick's widow. The more the German upper classes were permeated with English sport, English goods, and English modes of life, the more obstinately they dwelt on their political independence of England—above all on the fact that they were the equals of that wealthy cousin whose slightly ironical patronage was like a gag to the German upstart. In William's Germany friendship with England, understanding and admiration for this country and its institutions, was soon regarded as a legacy from the Liberals and was suspect as such. Scholars with a gift for journalism, on the other hand, endeavoured to reveal the true history of British imperialism and of its methods of conquest, but in their perorations revulsion was again oddly mingled with the urge to imitate and compete. Great Britain, the British Empire, apparently could be matched, out-stripped, or defeated only by British methods. This belligerent spirit, which first stirred in the fields of culture and psychology, soon spread to economic and dynastic questions and to foreign policy.

England's South African policy was the first occasion on which the antagonism was clearly expressed. The German government and public opinion were sympathetic to the half-independent Boer republics. The policy of absorption, as represented by Cecil Rhodes, was sharply criticized. Because of German Southwest Africa the Reich had a near neighbour's interest in maintaining the *status quo,* for it would be difficult to hold the German colony in the face of a strong and united South Africa. When Dr. Jameson organized his famous *Putsch* against the Transvaal (1896) the Emperor wanted to intervene at once. He thought of placing the semi-sovereign Trans-vaal under a German protectorate and sending marines there. This would have meant war with England and perhaps with France. The Emperor's counsellors succeeded in pacifying him and limiting his thirst for action to sending a telegram of congratulation to Paul Kruger, the President of the Transvaal. This dispatch was therefore anything but a spontaneous action on the Emperor's part. It was a well-prepared official action to which the Emperor gave his reluctant consent, since it was only the merest shadow of the weighty political step that had been intended. Even this shadow, however, was enough to offend England deeply. Following the Kruger episode, certain English circles were unable to overcome their sensitive suspiciousness of the Kaiser and the Reich. England and Germany were at a part-ing of the ways.

When Lord Salisbury reacted to Turkish atrocities against the Ar-menians by suggesting something like a partition, Germany took her stand by the preservation of the Ottoman Empire; with her partners in the Triple Alliance and also with Russia, she stuck to this attitude even during the war between the Greeks and Turks (1897). Christian and Slavophil circles in the east were consequently forced to seek support among the western powers and in America in their struggle for liberation from Turkish oppression. German imperialism stressed the right of nationality for itself, but denied it to others. Germany's Turkish friendship—a relationship coloured by hostility to England—became a leading point in her world policy.

Baron von Marschall, who had been foreign secretary for a number of years, was sent to Constantinople as ambassador. There he fostered some brilliant enterprises, particularly railroad building. The Anatolian railroad was begun as early as 1888. The Emperor and his wife now made a spectacular trip through the East. The climax came with William's speech in Damascus (1898), in which he proffered himself as protector to three hundred million Mohammedans, to the great annoyance of England and also of Russia, since two hundred and fifty million of this number were actually subjects of those powers. Russia's proposal in 1899 showed her distrust of her German friend: she offered to support Germany's policy in Asia Minor—primarily this meant the projected Bagdad railway—provided that Germany gave her partner a free hand in the Dardanelles. Germany's demand for mutual guarantees of possessions ended all negotiations. Had Russia accepted this condition, she would have had to give up her treaty with France. After this disappointment Russia again directed the greater part of her attention to Asia.

Germany wanted to have a finger in all the pies of world policy, and she developed an excessive activity that made her for the first time generally unpopular. Up to this point the industriousness and reliability of German merchants and settlers had won them goodwill and respect wherever they went. Germans had attained high positions in industry and public life in both the Americas. The German's initiative, his gift for languages, and his intellectual curiosity made him valuable to any colonial community and preferable to the English colonist. Now the German government seized on this situation with purposeful propaganda and undefined schemes for expansion. Substantial aid was expected from the patriotism and self-sacrifice of Germans abroad. The loyalty with which most of them clung to the good old German culture also seemed to offer a guarantee of political enterprise. But every German abroad was a friend of freedom, for usually he was sprung of champions of freedom and martyrs of liberty. Many had accepted Bismarck's Reich, though not without reservations. But now William's imperialism demanded not only a sympathetic attitude, but positively active support. Neither the gestures nor the speeches of the Emperor were such as to win over these colonial Germans, however, for both in their business and in their private lives they suffered to some extent for his arrogant tone.

An episode of the Spanish-American War made itself felt for a long while afterward in the relations of Germany and the United States. Just before the Battle of Manila a squadron of German ships appeared near the Philippines, and a clash with the Americans was prevented only with difficulty. The Americans assumed that the Germans had meant to occupy the islands, and this was probably true. William II was untiring in his efforts to woo the United States. Bygone episodes of history, such as Frederick the Great's friendly attitude, were recalled to aid a rapprochement; the names of Steuben and Carl Schurz were invoked; travelling Americans were made much of at court in Berlin; there was an exchange of professors, and every anti-English sentiment in the United States was encouraged. But Germany did not do the one thing that might have won the friendship of the United States: the Reich did not decide on a liberal domestic policy, which would have had the effect of clarifying and moderating its foreign policy.

THE QUESTION OF AN ALLIANCE BETWEEN GERMANY AND ENGLAND

The Fashoda Crisis (1898), the clash between France and England on the Upper Nile, engendered acute tension between these two powers. The German Reich had never been in so commanding a position. The western powers were at odds. The alliance between France and Russia was practically cancelled by the latter's policy in eastern Asia. England had pressing problems in Asia and Africa and required support and backing. The dream that Bismarck had cherished in his old age seemed on the verge of fulfilment. After his dismissal he had made life hard enough for the young Emperor and his councillors by his criticism and by dogmas drawn from the experiences of his career. Now, immediately after his death (1898), England, which he had wooed in vain, began to court German favour. Joseph Chamberlain, the Secretary of State for the colonies, was bent on an alliance between Germany and England. The old and suspicious Lord Salisbury approved, and his nephew, Arthur Balfour, spoke of the two countries as carrying equal weight. The Angola Treaty of 1898 might easily be a prelude to more important developments. The two powers thereby agreed on a partition of the Portuguese colonies if Portugal, in trying to secure a new loan, should find it necessary to pledge her overseas possessions. England nevertheless made a separate treaty with Portugal only a year later. This treaty, extending the centuries-old relation of friendship between England and Portugal, renewed the territorial guarantee and thus secured Portugal's support against the Boer republics. The menace of a South African war may have justified this treaty, but, whether or no, it made nonsense of the Angola Treaty, England's previous agreement with Germany. The straightening out of disturbances in Samoa was more auspicious. Joint possession by Germany, England, and the United States from 1889 had led to a great deal of contention. Now the group of islands was partitioned, to Germany's advantage.

The disturbances in eastern Asia and the Boxer Rebellion in China, during which Baron von Ketteler, the German minister, was murdered, could not be smoothed over except by joint action of the European powers. In 1898 Germany had leased the Tsingtao district from China for a period of ninety-nine years. And so now she had to play a part in this theatre of world policy, too—more to Russia's pleasure than to Japan's. William II forced Count Alfred Waldersee, his field marshal, into the dubious position of commander-in-chief of the international expedition to China. The Czar was much astonished to discover that the semi-official German press was hailing him as having prompted this appointment. But Waldersee did not appear in China till long after a military decision had been reached. The part of a "world marshal" who really had nothing at all to do was quite in line with the slippery play-acting that characterized his whole career.

In 1900 the Reich made the so-called Yangtze Agreement with England, according to which the principle of the open door was to be observed throughout China. Neither country was to seek territorial advantages, and if a third power attempted to do so, the parties to the agreement were to act jointly to prevent. The way in which the Yangtze Agreement was interpreted was soon to shape relations between Germany and England.

BERNHARD VON BÜLOW. THE NAVAL POLICY

Since 1897 Bernhard von Bülow (1849–1929) had been Foreign Secretary. In 1900 he succeeded the weary Hohenlohe as Chancellor of the Reich. This was the first time that a career diplomat had occupied the highest office in the Reich, and it was as a diplomat that he discharged his office. Bülow had an extraordinary memory, wrote well, and was an impressive speaker who knew how to calculate his effects. Both in literature and in life his taste was epicurean. His subtlety and his naïve delight in flattery and malice were qualities that some students of racial psychology wanted to attribute to a Slavic strain in his heredity. There was certainly no doubt as to his preference for Latin charm and for the forms of the south. He liked to play with ideas and with human beings; there could not be a more gratified or a more contemptuous spectator of the vanities of life. He had no taste for pathos or for lofty trains of thought, and he accepted his imperial master's ideas of a mission as to world policy as an unavoidable evil. He himself had no faith in grandiose words. For him the main thing was to hold on to his cherished post as long as possible, and to this end he studied the Emperor half like a psychiatrist and half like a lion-tamer. For years he was successful in striking the right tone. His Majesty was so charmed that he thought he could not live without this friend. Bülow was always the cooler and cleverer of the two. He knew the Emperor's limitations, but he also recognized his own and masked his lack of real grip with a suave formality. Whenever his actions missed the mark, his unerring memory filled the gap with a striking phrase that somebody else had coined. He smilingly held to his course between Reichstag and bureaucracy, between Emperor and great powers, between parties and press, until his final debacle. His downfall was well deserved on both moral and material grounds.

Admiral Alfred von Tirpitz, Bülow's exact opposite, was Naval Secretary. Like most naval officers, he came from the upper middle class. He was the greatest organizer and most gifted propagandist of William's era. In him the Emperor found the instrument to execute his naval plans, which meant much more to him than just another chapter in the tale of armaments. William II believed in his fleet with fanatical fervour. He agreed with Admiral Mahan, the American writer on naval affairs, in regarding naval power as decisive in the issues of world history. A world policy, he thought, could be pursued only with a great fleet; commerce, German interests abroad, the shaping of the colonial empire—in short, all that was new and strong in the growing world power of Germany—seemed to him to depend on the navy. The colonial-minded elements were the first to support these ambitions, and later commerce and especially heavy industry fell into line.

Stiff opposition had to be overcome in the Reichstag. The old Prussian conservatives regarded the navy with horror, while military circles feared that the army would be neglected. The German Navy League, founded in 1898, became conspicuous with the encouragement of the Reich's navy department. Legislation on account of the navy in 1898 was followed by a further enactment in 1900 that provided for a large fleet of battleships and also for an overseas fleet of cruisers. The only possible purpose of the fleet was to intimidate England; there was no other opponent of the same stature. The Emperor and Tirpitz hoped to build up such a navy that England would hesitate to risk war and would prefer to come to an understanding with Germany under conditions dictated by that country. This notion of risk is the real key to German naval policy; both materially and psychologically it proved itself a grave error.

In November 1899 the British Colonial Secretary, Joseph Chamberlain, had made an address—along lines previously laid down in concert with Bülow—calling for a Germanic triple alliance of Germany, England, and the United States. In spite of the indifferent response Bülow had given then, England now tried to renew discussions. Since Russia was advancing in Manchuria and was thus quite perceptibly jeopardizing English interests in China, statesmen in London were urging joint German-English action in eastern Asia on the basis of the Yangtze Agreement. Some such arrangement might well have been the prelude to greater things. Bülow refused, with the dubious assertion that Manchuria was not covered by the agreement. Bülow never had any luck with the Anglo-Saxons. He was not familiar with their country, their language, or their psychology. At this time and later there were men in the service of Germany who

527

knew England and the United States thoroughly, but they were never allowed to exert substantial influence. This personal factor has to be reckoned with substantially in judging subsequent events and their consequences.

In the matter of China Emperor William proved to have, as he often did, a surer instinct than his advisers. He had communicated England's first proposals to the Russian Czar, who could be serviceable to him with analogous information. Now William II pressed for a clear decision. He was tired of falling between two stools, between England and Russia. But the possibility of an alliance between England and Germany was destroyed by Holstein, who called for the consent of the entire Triple Alliance, the approval of the English Parliament, and, if possible, the inclusion of Japan. Lansdowne, the English Secretary for Foreign Affairs, and his collaborators were deeply in earnest about their proposals, and precisely for that reason they could not accept such conditions. Holstein must have known that it was not the English custom to discuss such diplomatic agreements in Parliament and that for political reasons such discussion was hardly desirable anyhow. Had the Reinsurance Treaty between Germany and Russia been laid before the Reichstag? Had the public been made acquainted with the details of the Triple Alliance treaties? The later Entente between England and France proved how loose the forms of an alliance of the greatest significance in world history could be. As for Austria-Hungary, England had no wish to burden herself with the Danubian monarchy's quarrels over nationalities and with the dangers to foreign policy arising from them. London even wanted Italy, with her incessant claims, treated with caution.

England's relations with Japan were much more cordial than Germany's. It seemed impossible for her to have simultaneous agreements with Germany and Japan. Germany, apparently, was seeking a reconciliation with Japan at the cost of her relations with England, a situation that was not agreeable to either of those powers. The treaty of alliance between England and Japan (1902) actually resulted from the failure of a rapprochement between Germany and England. Holstein did not believe that either a reconciliation between England and France or a slackening of the tensions between England and Russia was possible. He was right on just one point:

that France would never give up the idea of revenge. But here lay the weakness of German world policy. The Reich was striving for expansion, but its real difficulties lay at the western border, close at hand. The colonial empire of France forced that country into a Continental policy that had but a single aim. England and Germany now parted in an atmosphere of irritation and offense. The golden days of William's era were coming to a close.

ESTRANGEMENT FROM ENGLAND. THE AIM OF GERMAN WORLD POLICY. THE PEACE IDEA

William II and his collaborators did not want to dominate the world. They wanted Germany to have her "place in the sun." They did not want a world war, especially not a world war on three fronts, such as broke out in 1914. They wanted peace—armed peace, to be sure, and very heavily armed peace. For they tried to attain their goals by the methods of intimidation, threat, and extortion. Such methods were not new in history. Other powers had employed them. The weakness of German world policy was that it characteristically attempted too much and was not sufficiently unified. What had been achieved in the early years of the reign of William II seemed a little too modest in comparison with the energy expended. Besides the gains in Samoa there were the island groups of the Carolines and the Marianas, Germany's share in the liquidation of Spanish colonial holdings after the Spanish-American War; so that her position in the Pacific was slightly stronger, though her relations with Japan were so much the worse. There neither was nor could be German hegemony in Europe. A fluctuating balance between the Triple Alliance and the Entente had taken the place of Bismarck's system.

In the world at large there were four theatres of German activity. Germany was weakest in eastern Asia and in the Pacific; it would be difficult for her to hold her scattered possessions there in an emergency. The situation in the Near East was better. But best of all was the state of affairs in Africa. In these regions too, however, the Reich came up against its old European rivals, and antagonisms were not only not smoothed over, but actually intensified. Increasing armaments meant increasing danger of war, for armaments in themselves were already part of making war. Again and again German world policy, which emphatically did not desire war, provoked the danger of an outbreak. Threats of war became an indispensable instrument of the diplomacy that preceded the first World War. A great power could give way once; a very strong and self-confident great power might even give way a second time—but certainly not a third.

Was it not possible for the countries of Europe to become mutually reconciled and to co-operate? The pacifist movement that issued from England and the United States sought to apply the idea of justice, the noblest fruit of the English, the American, and the French revolutions, to foreign as well as to domestic policy. It already prevailed in life within the state. The administration of justice, good government, an incorruptible officialdom, control by public opinion, were all taken for granted in the functioning of a modern civilized state; any deficiency showed up at once and demanded immediate correction. But there was an alarming discrepancy between this atmosphere of justice and the anarchy that prevailed in international relations. The continual application of force in the international field threatened to react against the nation and shatter the state itself. International law therefore had to try to develop the idea of justice into an all-embracing principle; in other words, to abolish war as the form of competition and create other means of coming to an understanding in such international quarrels as were bound to arise.

From Immanuel Kant on, German philosophers and jurists had had an important share in developing the concept of peace. Yet this concept could never become popular in Germany, as it did in England and the United States, because the most significant achievements in the history of the German nation were connected with successful wars. The Wars of Liberation against Napoleon and the wars for the establishment of Bismarck's Reich had restored to the German people a form of political life that commanded respect. The militaristic spirit of Greater Prussia resented the demand for disarmament and settlement by arbitration as though it had been a personal insult. The old core of Germany responded to these ideas somewhat more readily. The third of a series of international peace congresses had convened in the Church of St. Paul in Frankfurt in 1850; here the annual loss of productive labour in Europe through compulsory military service was estimated at thirty-six million pounds sterling. All the leaders in the German peace movement came from western Germany: Ludwig Quidde from Bremen, Pastor Otto Umfried from Stuttgart, Walter Schücking from Westphalia.

Socialism in its early stages and left-wing liberalism worked for a new and peaceful Europe, true to the principles of democracy. In the time of Napoleon III and of Bismarck armament limitations proposed by the government and also suggestions for disarmament brought up in parliaments had repeatedly occupied the public mind. In 1889 Baroness Bertha von Suttner, the warm-hearted and indefatigable founder of the Austrian Peace Association, published her novel *Lay Down Your Arms,* which had a world-wide success. A peace association was now founded in Germany also. But though in Austria certain circles among the aristocracy and the big industrialists were glad to advocate the idea of peace and thus strengthened their tendency toward western Europe and against the Triple Alliance, the movement was not able to make any great headway in William's Reich. It was regarded as unpatriotic, as running counter to German history. Its leaders were treated as sectarians and fanatics, eccentrics or even traitors; they were threatened with official and indeed social boycott. When a staunch Prussian used the word "pacifist," it was practically invective. The majority did not take the trouble to inquire into the difference between ethical and religious eschatological ideas and principles of law on one side, and purely economic considerations on the other. From 1872 to 1910 Germany increased her expenditure for armament fivefold. War became a matter of technics and economics that occupied the intelligence of all countries more and more. Constant preparedness dominated the economy of the world and forced even private enterprise to adapt itself to the idea of a war that no one wanted, but that no one was any longer in a position to forestall.

Under the influence of the scholarly labours of Johann von Bloch, a Russian councillor of state, Czar Nicholas II decided in 1898 to make a proclamation that marked an epoch in the history of the peace movement and of international relations. As a result of the manifesto the First Hague Conference convened. Unlike William II, the Russian emperor had a deep personal dislike of war; so far he

531

was acting in good faith, though other factors of course came into play. Russia was struggling against the mounting danger of revolution and was in the midst of a difficult economic transition period. She hoped to solve her problems by opening up Asia, and to embark on this enterprise she needed a peaceful Europe.

Europe had never been more cosmopolitan in sentiment than at this period. Prevailing world policy permitted tensions to slacken on the Continent; if there was ever to be international co-operation, the time was now. But the First Hague Conference did not produce any important results. The Reich was largely responsible for the failure. Russia's proposal to maintain armaments just as they were for five years fell through because of German opposition. Objections from Germany also disposed of the proposal to make obligatory the submission of all controversies of a material nature to a court of arbitration, naturally with the exception of such problems as involved vital national interests and honour. It is true that other states offered objections and were reluctant to yield any part of their freedom to make their own political decisions. But the German Reich seized the centre of the stage with a certain naïve forthrightness and showed its imperialistic ambitions without any thought of disguise. It did not try to conceal its displeasure at the basic principles of the peace movement, and it rejected a freezing of the *status quo* in power and possessions as curtailing its chances of development. No other state so emphatically demonstrated that it regarded the disproportion between its state power and its territorial extent as intolerable. The First Hague Conference revealed the profound rift between the idea of justice and imperialistic dynamics.

At that time no one was threatening the Reich. Even France had half-forgotten her plans for revenge. If France were to develop at all further, she needed allies, and it should have been Germany's concern to prevent such alliances at all costs. Bismarck had aroused the western powers against each other in a masterly way. He had made the most of the antagonism between England and Russia, and he had succeeded in forestalling the rapprochement between Russia and France for a long time. The imperialism of William II now precipitated that great coalition of encirclement whose outlines had first been sketched in 1848, then in 1875. He made a reality of the co-operation of England, France, and Russia, which loomed large in world politics.

THE NEW CLASS STRUCTURE OF THE GERMAN INDUSTRIAL STATE

Germany became a wealthy country. From 1889 to 1900 she increased her exports by one and a half billion marks and her total trade by three and a quarter billion marks. All her foreign trade was carried on under the German flag. The gloomy prophecies of Marxism had not been fulfilled. Some large fortunes had been made, it is true, but also many moderate and small fortunes. There was an increasing tendency to accumulate savings. Even a person of moderate means could hope to acquire capital by his own efficiency and industry. It would have been absurd to speak of the miseries of the working class. Several groups now formed within this class. The skilled worker of the upper stratum, whose wages gradually increased until he was earning a good salary, became more and more bourgeois. He acquired a house and garden, arranged a comfortable life for himself, and spent money on the education of his children. He developed self-confidence and a sense of security that recalled the craftsmen of former days. Craftsmanship itself was by no means completely forgotten; the upper classes demanded workmanship of a quality that restored it to its time-honoured position.

Factories expanded and required an increasing number of hands. Gainful occupations became commonplace among women. Anyone who was clever and ambitious could make his way quickly. Capitalism was on the look-out for ability and offered unusual opportunities to unusual talent. But even those who were merely industrious and capable soon arrived at a substantial bourgeois way of living, for no employee was let go except when it became stringently necessary to reduce running expenses. Employees were animated by the same ideals that were so characteristic of German public officials. There were bank officials and insurance officials; the concept of private officials arose. Great firms trained whole generations of workers and employees; they drew huge profits from the loyalty of these people and from their devoted labours. Each gave a part of his own life to his work.

Classes were being reshuffled again in Germany. The new aristoc-

533

racy was a blend of the feudal class and the upper bourgeoisie. The patricians of title—university professors, judges, high officials—had largely the same interests as this new aristocracy. The middle class became stronger and tried to defend its interests by forming associations for this purpose. All skilled workers were organized into trade unions. The League of Agriculturists had proved how effective this principle could be for a certain class. Other callings followed suit: teachers, authors and journalists, bank officials, physicians and dentists, travelling salesmen, lecturers at universities, and so on. The function of these associations was to deal with questions of salary and wages, standing and rank, training and promotion. As in the unions, so here too the new type of confidential agent, experienced in business matters and organization, came into prominence. Future parliamentarians began their careers in these associations, but at the same time a development was in process against the parliamentary concept. The circle of professional interests pushed forward, and political questions of a more general nature became less important. The change in class structure changed the character of the class struggle, and a reaction was felt in political party life.

MARXISTS AND REVISIONISTS

The Social Democrats were no longer hampered in their rise to power. They had been freed from the anti-socialist law and safeguarded from a renewal of the fight against "revolution" by exceptional laws. Again and again the police tried to suppress the unions and the press, but on the whole unsuccessfully. The old international form of Marxism was now denied by the younger school of the so-called Revisionists. Their spiritual father, Eduard Bernstein, had become acquainted with the Fabians during a visit to England, and he now tried to induce his party to adopt cautious tactics fitted to given conditions. The most intelligent among the younger generation supported him. Since, however, the orthodox Marxists opposed any kind of innovation obstinately and dogmatically, disagreeable disputes became the order of the day. The south German party members were not interested in doctrinal quarrels. They wanted tangible progress. Their leader, a sober Bavarian, Georg von Vollmar, publicly expressed himself in favour of negotiating with parties of sim-

534

ilar interests and with the government. He was also careful to emphasize that German workers were resolved to defend the fatherland in case of attack by a foreign power.

German workers were not an entity politically, spiritually, or sociologically. There was antagonism between trade-unionists and academic intellectuals, between the type of city worker who represented the second or even the third generation of factory workers and the idealist of bourgeois derivation who joined the labour movement partly indeed from conviction, but also because he wanted to achieve political leadership. There were further antagonisms between north Germans and south Germans, west Germans and east Germans, party members who were all for Greater Prussia and others who favoured particularism. All the old antagonisms in German life flared up again in the Social Democratic Party, which spread over the entire country and appealed to the rural population everywhere. There was a very definite sociological distinction between highly trained skilled workers and unskilled occasional workers. Between the two groups stood semi-skilled workers of whom only limited manual dexterity was expected. Qualifications affected wages, and so the working population began again to become a social pyramid whose base consisted of the impoverished proletariat of the great cities, permanently unemployed and condemned to unspeakable living conditions. The social gap between such a member of the fifth estate and a foreman at the Krupp works was much greater than that between such a foreman and the teacher or the pastor who educated his children. When all was said and done, the German bourgeois parties did not have the slightest intention of letting Social Democracy monopolize the working class. The Centre founded its own Christian unions. The progressive Hirsch-Duncker unions persisted, and the anti-Semitic Christian Social unions tried to reconcile the workers to the concept of aggressive nationalism.

Anarchism, syndicalism, and anarcho-syndicalism, new forms of the anti-capitalist movement, never made much headway in Germany. The struggles between Marxists and Revisionists dominated the life of the German Social Democratic Party and were reviewed in periodicals, debates at assemblies, the party press, and particularly

535

party conventions. Personal rivalries, differences in character and temperament, intensified these conflicts, which the great mass of adherents were taught to regard and to tolerate as being purely tactical. The question whether people ought to be preparing for the revolution or taking part in basic reforms was crucial for the future of the party, the future of socialism. On the whole there was no great enthusiasm for revolution, if only because the romanticism of fighting on the barricades as in former times was exploded by the fire-power of a modern military state imperialistically organized. Ever since the collapse of the communist insurrection in Paris in 1871, parties with revolutionary tendencies had been forced to invent more modern methods. Not the Germans but the Russians devised the new mode of revolution. By and large, German Social Democracy was dominated by a spirit of reform. This became apparent in the bills it introduced in the Reichstag—bills for the gradual introduction of the eight-hour day, for free assembly, for the introduction of obligatory arbitration in industry, for the reorganization of the army as a militia. Social Democracy was decidedly against imperialism, which favoured armaments, and the bourgeois world applauded its critical stand on this account.

The method of the general strike came in for much discussion. Party leaders grew more and more dubious and were inclined to give this method grudging recognition as a last resource, to be utilized only if all the representatives elected by the workers agreed to it. From 1904 on, it was customary for Social Democratic factions in the south German legislatures to approve the state budget and come to an agreement with the bourgeois parties at elections. Such a custom could not be established in the Reichstag, for the government of the Reich depended on Prussia, and in Prussia the three-class system of suffrage prevented an influential Social Democratic faction from arising in the lower house. It was hardly astonishing that the Social Democrats agitated most energetically for election reforms in Prussia. But here the party struck rock bottom. In Prussia a Social Democrat could not even be a night watchman. So Germany continued to present the paradoxical spectacle of a country governed in a reactionary spirit and also in a spirit of reform. The coup d'état that Bismarck and others less distinguished than he had contemplated was entirely unnecessary as long as Prussia was ruled by Junkers and members of the conservative student organizations, so that the government of the Reich was conducted in the interests of the aristocratic class.

THE NATIONAL SOCIAL ASSOCIATION OF 1896

In 1893 the anti-Semitic party celebrated its first triumphs. Among the younger followers of Adolf Stöcker, Friedrich Naumann was conspicuous for his gifts as speaker and writer. He was an honest Protestant clergyman and as such refused to participate in the persecution of the Jews. He left the Christian Social party, and in 1896, with a few followers, he founded a National Social Association. The basic idea sounded the keynote of German destiny: external power cannot be maintained unless the great mass of the people are national-minded and take an interest in politics; economic prosperity and social reforms are meaningless unless the lower classes support the state; international communism and revolutionary Marxism, therefore, are undesirable, but German labour is entitled to a larger share in profits; existing property relationships must be fought, and the aim must be to change the traditional state of affairs with the help of trade unions and labour organizations. Naumann sponsored a vigorous foreign-policy program. He was in favour of colonies and of appropriate armaments, but his first demand was equal suffrage for all the parliaments in Germany as the prerequisite for reconciling the masses to the national power-state.

Many of the best among the younger generation became Naumann's enthusiastic adherents. Helmuth von Gerlach, a witty and intrepid journalist, and Hjalmar Schacht, later the president of the Reichsbank, were members of Naumann's group. But he was unsuccessful at the polls and finally joined the Progressive Party, while the left-wing National Social group went over to the Social Democrats. This episode is part of the direct prehistory of Hitler's National Socialism. Historically Friedrich Naumann is intermediate between Lassalle and Hitler. He developed into one of the most effective speakers and journalists of imperial Germany. His book *Democracy and Empire* is a great patriot's impassioned attempt to bring about the reconciliation and co-operation of the most powerful currents of the times: imperialism and mass movement, world politics and social reform, autocracy and democracy.

537

THE POSSIBILITY OF REFORMING THE REICH. THE POWER OF
POLITICAL PARTIES AND ASSOCIATIONS

As the rifts in internal politics widened, the Centre constantly
gained in influence. It regarded itself as the ordained mediator between the Reich and particularism, between the concept of power
and social adjustment. The Reich could not be governed without
the Centre. Bülow's attempt to build up a bloc against the Centre
was no more than a brief interlude. The Centre wanted to dispose of
the last traces of the *Kulturkampf,* such as the vestiges of the law
against the Jesuits. But by and large there was an increasing tendency
to let the religious character of the party drop out of sight. The so-
called Köln faction called for Protestants to be allowed to join and
for the party to co-operate with the Christian Social group; the common interest in Christianity was to be a bulwark against free-
thinkers. The Berlin faction, on the other hand, insisted on the
purely Catholic character of the Centre. This conflict was another
focus for the antagonism between the east and west. In the west the
Rhenish Catholics were so secure socially and culturally that they
would have liked to co-operate with Protestant political parties of
their own bourgeois stamp. But in the east the Catholics were, for the
most part, the lower classes who had to maintain themselves against
the ruling Protestant class, which was in a much higher social and
economic position; the fact of a common creed also made them
sympathize with the Poles, whom the Prussian government through
its policy in the "East Mark" was endeavouring to deprive of their
property and influence, though it achieved the exact opposite.

The distinguishing mark of the National Liberals was their anti-
clericalism. Their approval of Caprivi's system was damped by his
reactionary school policy, with its emphasis on religion. The Reich
always stood first in the minds of the National Liberals, and thus the
party became a faithful adherent of the ambitions that were bound
up with world policy. The right-wing tendency of the National
Liberals became clearer and clearer as their views took on an increasingly materialistic character. They were inclined to make common cause with the Conservatives and the Reich Party, especially
against the Centre. But they were powerless when the Conservatives
united with the clerical party. On the whole the National Liberals

rested on their historical laurels. They were not able to develop constitutionalism toward unification of the Reich. In Catholic centres, such as Köln and Munich, the National Liberal press represented the patriotism of the Reich; in industrial districts, the employers' point of view; in agrarian and feudal areas east of the Elbe, the cultural ideal appropriate there. Toward any subject the position taken was always that of the gentry, of those in power.

In the long run this proved unsatisfactory, and so a National Liberal Youth Association sprang up. These Young Liberals tried to imbue the party with a more vigorous spirit, but they were not particularly successful. Left-wing liberalism also suffered under the double pressure that was exerted from above and below. The brilliant economic development and the strengthening and differentiation of the middle class were in themselves not unfavourable to liberal ideas. This class now lost all revolutionary impulse. How, indeed, could loyal citizens, educated and ambitious, harbour revolutionary thoughts if even the Social Democrats were inclining toward revisionism? Criticism and reform—that was all that was left, and the best that could be hoped was that it might ultimately be of some use. Left-wing liberalism was anti-imperialist as well as anti-socialist. It fought for the principles of democracy and parliamentarism and most of all for a reform of the Prussian system of suffrage. This left-wing party was forced to realize that the rule of the new aristocracy in Prussia-Germany could not be broken by legitimate methods— that is, without war and civil war. If left-wing liberalism was to function in a practical way, the first step was to gather up its offshoots and bind them together. It was too late to realize the old dream of one great powerful liberal party in Germany, but in 1910 all the left-wing liberal groups were consolidated in one Progressive People's Party.

It was important for this group not to permit the National Liberals to outdo it in national spirit and in active patriotism. This kindred liberal party was a bitter rival. Many left-wing liberals were adherents of the peace movement, but the majority decided to support the armament program. This attitude was calculated to win the confidence of the ruling class and to make it readier to accept reform. The desired effect was not achieved, if only because of the growing threat of war. A group of agitators such as the Union to Combat Socialism represented was bound to regard the left-wing liberals as promoters of revolution.

A great statesman could probably have instituted, at the turn of the century, an entirely new course for Germany: in the domestic policy of the Reich, reform in conjunction with left-wing liberalism, the National Liberals, the original National Social group, and the Revisionists; in foreign policy, alliance with England even at the price of war with Russia, which could have been easily won during the Russo-Japanese War and would have led to the liberation of the ethnical minorities in Russia. Such a policy would have been solidly backed by the whole German nation, including the Social Democrats, who were inimical to the Czar. But Germany had no great statesman.

Left-wing liberalism controlled the best German press; thus its influence far exceeded the bounds of party organization. Articles by well-informed critics of world economy, appearing in such newspapers as the *Frankfurter Zeitung,* for instance, had a very decided effect on the course of events—less perhaps on actual affairs than on the boundaries that mark off the possible from the impossible. Such papers and Berlin papers with similar tendencies were read even in palaces and in government offices. They were educational and conciliatory and did much for the enlightenment and cultivation of their friends and their enemies, for the skill with which they were edited promoted emulation; right-wing organs were compelled to vie with this admirable technique of reporting news and presenting opinion. Left-wing liberalism found its greatest difficulty in gaining ground with the masses. It was urban, cultured, and intellectually aristocratic. It had a hard time to influence associations of any kind, but characteristically it founded the Hansa League, an association of commercial capitalists who in 1909 turned against the aggression of heavy industry and its agrarian allies. Thus the aristocratic upper stratum was also becoming differentiated.

The most important factors of public life in Germany were affected. The foreign office sympathized with commercial and finance capitalism, while the navy of the Reich favoured heavy industry. The demagogic way in which the most powerful agrarian interests exploited the League of Agriculturists for the benefit of their own class embittered smaller farmers so greatly that they founded the

German Peasants' League under the guidance of the National Liberals. This organization was particularly successful in Hanover and Württemberg, so that it also helped in the struggle against the egoism of the Prussians east of the Elbe. Agricultural problems, recurrently stringent, led to the enactment of measures to help landed proprietors, especially in connection with tariffs. One of the gravest questions was raised by the labour shortage in the east. Seasonal Polish and Russian labour had to be employed because native workers were tired of inadequate wages and living conditions and made off to the cities. Manorial agriculture could no longer be carried on without state support and assistance in all fields. In spite of all the efforts of the authorities, the tension between the empty colonial east and the old heart of Germany increased.

THE YOUTH MOVEMENT. OPPOSITION OF THE INTELLIGENTSIA

The Germany of William's era liked to make a show of its prosperity. There were frequent celebrations, and innumerable monuments were unveiled. Everyone was expected to feel confidence in the nation and to be in high good humour. The Emperor could not endure pessimists, according to his own much-quoted remark. Exaggeration and distortion in the activities of official Germany offended the good taste of many and were increasingly disturbing to serious patriots. But Germany's innate vigour and the reserves of different sorts that she was then building up enabled her to face with confidence the difficulties that lay ahead. Alongside of this official and semi-official Germany, which was best expressed in the favourite style of architecture of the time, an ostentatious but diluted form of Baroque, stood another Germany. This other Germany, full of dignity, was constituted by the quiet opposition of the intellectuals, by the Youth Movement, by serious devotion to art, by honest and responsible dealing. Germany had at that time an unusually gifted writer of sure judgment who fought for the country's great future on the international stage. This was Maximilian Harden. He gave his journal a name that pointed to a new and better world. *The Future (Zukunft)* was written by one who knew what he was talking about, for those who wished to be informed. Even though Harden's character and literary style became affected and involved in the course of years, he never ceased to be deeply concerned for the

541

cause he championed. He knew how to move the heart, to stimulate the mind, and to rouse enthusiasm.

The founding of the original *Wandervogel* (1898) was significant. The younger generation tried to abolish the hypocrisies of the waning century. They longed to get away from the tawdry *fin-de-siècle* atmosphere into a world of greater reality and purity. Stodgy family life, church services empty of true inner meaning, social conventions, the obsession of living up to one's class, dandyism—the current term then for fashionable snobbery—all the recurrent phenomena of an over-ripe society filled young German spirits with disgust. They sought nature as it really was; a hearty innocent life of wandering about sprang up, far from the health resorts and bathing places popular with good families. The parlour with its false pretensions was outmoded. Boys and girls came together in a natural, healthy, not too delicate fashion that had never quite died out in country places and that now became customary among the sophisticated children of great cities. Folk dances and costumes, folk ways and folksongs, were revived. All manner of romantic yearnings and deliberate defiance were involved, but there was much that was simple and genuine. It was no accident that the Munich journal *Youth* (*Jugend*) flaunted the favourite word of the times on its front page.

An ecstatic feeling of new beginnings pervaded painting, sculpture, and architecture. Talents long unrecognized were at last given their due: Hans Thoma, Arnold Böcklin, Max Liebermann, Max Klinger, Wilhelm Trübner, Ludwig von Hofmann—they differed widely from another, and yet they were held together by the strong will to create art in harmony with a German civilization that gloried in its youth. Many private persons who had good advice now built themselves houses in a simple, straightforward style with a feeling for the laws of space and material. The theatre became more spiritual, more profound, more collective, more effective. Max Reinhardt's premières in Berlin's *Deutsches Theater* were such great events that they were able to eclipse all world politics and even gossip in Berlin, with its faith in art. And Thomas Mann was writing his first novels. He quickly outstripped the older generation, of which the former clergyman Gustav Frenssen was probably the most characteristic representative. But the most gifted of the women poets, Ricarda

Huch, held her place. Frank Wedekind shocked the entire intellectual middle class by the extreme boldness of his bizarre creations; not everyone realized how much sadness and inhibition, how much helplessness and real yearning for truth and genuineness, lived in these overdrawn characters. Heinrich Mann, the elder brother of Thomas Mann, was an accusing prophet, a writer of wrathful satire. It was typical of the era to take refuge in absurdities and improbabilities, as Christian Morgenstern knew how to do with deep humour in his lyrics. Joachim Ringelnatz, Kasimir Edschmid, Karl Sternheim, and Ludwig Thoma followed along the same path. Thoma, in particular, succeeded in creating a warm-blooded, earthy poetry, homely and direct. He was the south German counterpart of certain older Low German writers of popular epics, Klaus Groth and Wilhelm Raabe, and their successor the sensitive Hermann Löns.

Periodicals played a significant part in the life of the times. *Simplizissimus* developed into the most powerful organ of Munich's free culture and of its fanatical struggle for truth as against the sophistication of the Berliners with their rhetoric and poses. The periodical *Hochland,* however, showed that Catholicism in Germany was becoming intellectualized and that an open mind and a fastidious sense of culture could be integrated with kindness and helpful charity.

Stefan George and his circle introduced a new struggle for pure and noble form and for sensitive choice of material. Rainer Maria Rilke became a master of the grave, fastidious, deeply felt poetic language that poets of the rising generation used for the sacred things in which they wanted to believe. Rilke, a Bohemian, was only superficially connected with the Viennese group. In this group Artur Schnitzler felt his way from playful impressionism to a sterner mould. Hugo von Hofmannsthal and many another, such as Karl Schönherr, Anton Wildgans, and R. H. Bartsch, were associated with it. Vienna, Prague, and Munich swarmed with these variegated talents, contending with one another on the whole good-naturedly, whereas in Berlin everything was taken rather harder and more as a matter of principle.

Music was gradually liberated from the spell of Wagnerianism. The opera, the song, and the oratorio again recalled their own style. Taste was improving everywhere. The years just before the first World War were quite rightly regarded as a great period of cul-

543

tural fulfilment. Academies, scientific societies, art associations, museums, and private patrons encouraged struggling talent, with open mind and open hand. The critical evaluation of art and of the theatre and the struggle for the recognition of new intellectual values were taken very seriously, particularly by the many newspapers and periodicals, which thus presented an embarrassment of riches.

AUSTRIA-HUNGARY. PAN-GERMANS AND ANTI-SEMITES

Vienna displayed her own dignified and at the same time brilliant culture in the Hofburg Theatre, in her school of Austrian historians, jurists, psychologists, and political economists. In Austria's domestic policy the struggle among the different nationalities proved too heavy a burden. While the Hungarians lorded it over their Slavic subjects with quite Prussian methods, the German element in Austria found itself in an increasingly hopeless situation. In 1907 universal suffrage was introduced in Austria; this meant the victory of the Slavic population, which predominated numerically. The natural political sequel to universal suffrage would have been to reorganize the Dual Monarchy into a federal state with the same political rights for the Slavic strains as for the German and Hungarian. No one who was familiar with the situation underestimated the difficulties of finding an acceptable solution. The radical groups tended in different directions. To them the Dual Monarchy represented an antiquated structure without any future, which would just manage to last for the lifetime of the old Emperor, Francis Joseph. But even the most impassioned foes of the monarchy could not deny that it was of great service to the economy and to the ethnical weld—which was the exact point at which race fanaticism set in.

The Pan-Germans were particularly active in Bohemia under the gifted leadership of Karl Schönerer. In Vienna Karl Lueger, the mayor, who was popular and apparently harmless, became a champion of anti-Semitism. From 1880 on, the time of the first systematic persecutions of the Jews in Russia, a vicious form of anti-Semitism spread in Rumania, in parts of Poland, and in Austria. While German anti-Semitism claimed to be a way of looking at the world and invoked famous and high-sounding names, Austrian anti-Semitism assumed from the very outset the more brutal aspect of a race war. Many Russian and Polish fugitives entered the country through

Galicia, settled in Vienna's Leopoldstadt, and pressed on to Silesia whenever they had the chance. The anti-Semitic Christian Social group of Austria had strong support in the German Alpine regions, where Slavs, liberals, and Jews were all treated alike; people did not wish to be disturbed in their age-old peasant Catholicism. The Jews who had lived in Bohemia and Moravia from time immemorial had always kept close to the Germans; it would have been impossible to find faithfuller adherents of Emperor Francis Joseph and his government. In Vienna the Jews were the very nucleus of the upper bourgeoisie, loyal to the Emperor; mixed marriages were commoner here than anywhere else. Now the Jews were persecuted from both sides, by the Pan-Germans and by the Slavic nationalists.

The struggle among the nationalities had its effect on foreign relations. English and French scholars investigated the condition of the Slavs in Austria and in the Balkans and aroused sympathy for them in western Europe. Among the Hungarian aristocracy there had always been groups that looked toward western Europe, and especially England. In many cases the old Austrian hatred for the Prussians grew into bitter resentment against all the Germans of the Reich.

There were close connections between the financial circles of Vienna and Paris, and a similar relationship carried over to the theatre and the press. Crown Prince Rudolf was allied to these circles. The unfortunate prince was occupied with serious ideas that were at least partly political. He sought out the company of decided liberals. He was prejudiced against the Triple Alliance and would have preferred both domestic and foreign policy to look toward the west. He disliked military and bureaucratic discipline, and he conducted his private life according to this taste, so that the deepest antagonism arose between him and his sober and pedantic father. The Crown Prince saw himself confronted with a political, physical, and spiritual collapse, and he escaped it probably by the convenient method of suicide. He took a beautiful young girl with him in his rush toward annihilation, the Baroness Mary Vetsera, the last victim of his career of seduction. The frivolity of his whole way of living deprives Rudolf's last act of any tragic dignity. The fury of extermination that possessed this bankrupt drew courage from the sight of the passionate and boundless devotion of the girl, so touching because so innocently guilty.

545

Crown Prince Rudolf's much-discussed end, which was surrounded with an aura of secrecy and gossip, has never been quite satisfactorily explained. The event in itself was damaging to the monarchical concept. Now that a collateral line was to succeed to the throne, a fresh element of insecurity was introduced. The Triple Alliance was poisoned by the growing pressure of its weak member, Italy. The German Reich, to be sure, was not at all displeased by a quarrel between its partners, as serving to strengthen its own position. Official Austria clung firmly to the Triple Alliance. With the despair of the weak she demanded that the other powers engage to strengthen her position in relation to foreign policy; Austria was indeed far behind Germany in military preparedness. The language spoken in the army was an important factor in Austria's situation: it was German. The Hungarians now demanded the use of Hungarian not only in their *Honved* (*Landwehr*), but also in the Hungarian regiments of the line. Few of the Dual Monarchy's army officers knew enough Hungarian to permit of this change. The controversy roused the Croats and the Slovenes as well as the Slavs in the Austrian part of the Danubian Monarchy, who on their own initiative were vehemently battling against German as the language of the army.

Responsible circles in Austria-Hungary were regarding German naval plans with special consternation. A foreign policy of friendship with Great Britain was one of the oldest traditions of the house of Habsburg. There was nothing left for it in an emergency but to rattle the sabre of the German Reich, as Emperor William II once remarked to Archduke Francis Ferdinand, the heir to the throne, with half-humorous reproach.

MOROCCO. CLASH BETWEEN GERMANY AND FRANCE

Twice during the Boer War Russia attempted to initiate joint action by the three great military powers. She tried to apply the successful combination of Shimonoseki to European relationships, against England. Germany replied with the question whether Russia and France were ready for mutual territorial guarantees. Since they were not, the step planned was not taken. France therefore held fast, as before, to the idea of revenge, and the German Reich had to reckon with this circumstance. What virtue was there in a world policy if the western border was not secure? Here lies the origin of the Morocco episode.

Morocco was one of the few overseas points that had so far managed to escape European guardianship. German enthusiasts for colonization called for the taking over of this region. In connection with the negotiations for an alliance between England and Germany, England herself pointed out Morocco to the Germans. France was, indeed, advantageously situated in relation to it as a near neighbour, and old Spanish claims also had to be taken into account. England and Germany were now drifting apart, although it was still possible for them to take joint action, as they did against Venezuela in 1902–3 in defence of business interests that had suffered injury.

Two important regroupings now occurred. The alienation between Germany and England was not well regarded in Italy, which did not want to be forced to oppose her old patron, England. Italy therefore started a rapprochement with France that had been prepared for by the settlement of trade war in 1898. France and Italy made a series of agreements, with England's approval, according to which Italy was given a free hand in Tripoli and recognized in return French rights in Morocco. Zones of influence in the Sudan were also defined. In a separate secret pact between Italy and France (November 1, 1902) Italy promised to maintain neutrality if Germany attacked France or if France was forced to declare war on Germany to defend her honour and her boundaries. This was indubitably a breach of the Triple Alliance treaty, which Italy had only just renewed without amendment.

For many years French statesmen, and especially the shrewd, long-headed Théophile Delcassé, had been trying to effect a rapprochement of the western powers. Either the Fashoda Crisis would repeat itself, and in that case armed conflict would be inevitable, or there would be a thorough clearing of the air, which would renew the Entente Cordiale of the days of Louis Philippe and Napoleon III. From England's point of view rapprochement with France meant two things: it would weaken both the alliance of France with Russia and the Triple Alliance. England's alliance with Japan had already been aimed against Russia. The English now isolated the Russians by drawing France over to their own side. Germany, however, since she did not want to allow herself to be set against Russia, could now be held in check by France. Italy was already drifting away from Germany, and perhaps Austria-Hungary could be won away from her.

The rapprochement between England and France reached a preliminary stage in an arbitration treaty of 1903. This was followed by the important agreement of 1904 concerning Morocco and Egypt, the control of which the two powers mutually guaranteed; a secret article provided for a partition of Morocco between France and Spain, to the exclusion of Germany. Just before the agreement was made the French Foreign Minister, Delcassé, gave the German ambassador some information about the proceedings that was disquieting to Germany. Bülow found in the outbreak of the Russo-Japanese War an excellent opening. The real purpose of what he did was less to guard German business interests in Morocco, even though these were considerable, than to take up again the idea of guarantee. He wanted to break the alliance of the western powers and force France explicitly to abandon her ideas of revenge, agree to a mutual guarantee of possessions, and possibly join a Russo-German alliance.

The guarantee of possessions, as it happened, was the one point on which no French statesman could negotiate without ruining his reputation with his countrymen. Rouvier, the Premier, dropped Delcassé at a dramatic cabinet meeting. He himself would have liked to come to a direct understanding with Germany. At that time Germany could have had a slice of Morocco, a portion of the Congo region, and concessions in the matter of the Bagdad railroad. But she wanted more. Bülow had forced the Emperor to agree to a landing in Tangier in order to demonstrate the independence of the Moroccan government in the eyes of the entire world. From the standpoint of the Reich the Morocco convention (Madrid, 1880) was the legal basis for assuming this, and only a new international conference could make new decisions concerning Morocco. Germany insisted on such a conference; it was held in Algeciras, with only moderately successful results. International supervision was indeed provided for the police organized by France and Spain and also for the bank that was to be established, but in the face of the advantages granted to France and Spain German business interests could have no equal chance in Morocco. Only the surface was saved. Germany had incurred a pressing risk of war. England would probably have assisted France to the utmost of her capacity; now Germany tried to take revenge by the attitude she assumed toward England's proposals. England's suspicion had become insuperable. England and France began to confer on military matters. Holstein was dropped, and it had to be realized that Germany's foreign policy had attained very little by all its great effort.

THE BJÖRKÖ TREATY (1905)

During the Russo-Japanese War the Reich maintained an attitude of benevolent neutrality toward Russia. But the tension between England and Russia almost reached the point of war because of the so-called Dogger Bank affair. Russian men-of-war had shot at British fishing-boats, ostensibly by mistake. The Reich suggested to Russia an alliance against England in which France should join. The opportunity was tempting, particularly since Russia and Austria-Hungary had already come to an understanding about the Balkans, in the Mürzsteg Agreement of 1903. But for the time being, Russia did not agree to the suggestion. In July 1905, however, when the Czar met Emperor William in Björkö, an island in the Baltic Sea, he agreed to a defensive alliance limited to Europe—an alliance that France was to be invited to join. The Czar was prompted by the defeat in eastern Asia and by the menace of the constantly growing revolutionary movement within his country. The proposal, however, was eyed with disfavour by responsible statesmen in Russia as well as in Germany; they rejected this diplomatic action by their sovereigns, because the treaty would have been unsuitable in form as well as in content— indeed, a piece of dilettantism. It had to be dropped. Emperor William was deeply chagrined by this disappointment, which he quite properly interpreted as a personal failure.

His uncle, King Edward VII, was playing a very different part in Europe. The English King put at his country's service all his personal connections and all his masterfulness in dealing with people. He was never out of touch with responsible statesmen, and the best specialists in various fields kept him informed as to what was desirable and possible. It became habitual for German public opinion to lament the wicked encirclement. At that time Germany could not know how far the Emperor and Bülow were responsible for this encirclement through their own behaviour. As soon as England learned even the outlines of the German plan to bring about an anti-English Continental alliance, she gave up all the hopes of a rapprochement with Germany that had been cherished during and after the conference of Algeciras.

The Second Hague Conference was held in an atmosphere weighted with depression and distrust. Germany refused to participate in discussions of disarmament. She was responsible for the failure of the court of arbitration. Her friends in the Balkans, as well as Austria, of course, helped prevent the necessary unanimity. Other powers, too, were not enthusiastic about the idea of a world-wide treaty of arbitration, but again it was Germany that, in the eyes of the world, was principally to blame. England and the United States were deeply disturbed. The reply came promptly: the agreement concerning prizes of war proposed by Germany was accepted, but not ratified. Germany and the United States wished to establish the inviolability of private property in naval warfare. England objected, and the plan fell through.

In 1908 England made her first attempt to discuss mutual limitations on naval armament with Germany. But the Emperor's attitude was one of rude rejection. There was nothing left for England but to continue her Entente policy. Sir Edward Grey, the English Foreign Secretary, and Paul Cambon, the French ambassador in London, corresponded about co-operation between the powers they represented. This historic correspondence was not binding on the English state, but it was binding on the ruling group in England, which at the time was the Liberal Party. Thus the Entente Cordiale developed into a conditional alliance. At the last moment the English Parliament could still decide on some other policy.

Great Britain and Russia also began to draw closer together. In the treaty of 1907 Persia was divided into a northern sphere of influence, for Russia, and a southern sphere, for England. Russia declared her disinterestedness in the future of Afghanistan. English influence spread out from southern Persia to the Euphrates region and to Arabia. Thus it was impossible not to collide with German and Turkish interests in connection with the Bagdad railroad. Even at that time the existence of oil in the Middle East made these lands valuable objects of speculation. When the Arabian independence movement was also taken into consideration, all the world powers had to give thought to this quarter of the globe.

Russia, too, defeated in eastern Asia, turned again to the Near East, In discussions of the Macedonian question England supported Russia's claims. When Edward VII met the Czar in Reval in June 1908 the whole complex of questions relating to Macedonia and the Near East was thoroughly threshed. The diplomatic initiative now fell to Austria-Hungary, since German policy was more or less paralysed and put on the defensive.

THE ANNEXATION CRISIS. BÜLOW'S DOWNFALL (1909)

Baron von Ährenthal, who became Austro-Hungarian Minister for Foreign Affairs in 1906, knew Russia's difficulties and did not fear her striking-power. He and many other Austrian patriots believed that disintegration of the Danubian monarchy could be arrested solely through great collective efforts in the direction of the traditional Austrian Balkan policy. Bosnia and Herzegovina could be developed only by extending railroad connections to Salonika. But an advance of this kind within the Balkans would arouse the envy of Italy, which was already thinking about Albania; it would offend the national feeling of the southern Slavs, with the Serbs as its leading proponents; and it would impinge sharply on Turkish supremacy. The new government of Young Turkey was trying to develop a constitutional state. Would Bosnia and Herzegovina, as Turkish provinces, vote for the new Turkish parliament? What stand would be taken by Bulgaria, which was still, in form, a principality under Turkish suzerainty?

Austria-Hungary and Bulgaria decided to act together. Ferdinand of Bulgaria declared independence and assumed the prerogatives of royalty. The Dual Monarchy annexed Bosnia and Herzegovina. The decisions of the Congress of Berlin of 1878 were flatly violated. An international crisis set in. Ährenthal had prepared the step he took by conferring with Izvolsky, the Russian Foreign Minister, at the Castle of Buchlau in Moravia, the property of Count Leopold Berchtold, the clever, energetic, and ambitious ambassador of Austria-Hungary in St. Petersburg. At this conference it was decided that Russia was to be indemnified by the free passage of Russian warships through the Dardanelles, and Montenegro's position was also to be improved; no decision was reached as to an indemnity for Serbia, which Izvolsky asked for. Izvolsky expected these temporary agreements to be approved by the signatory powers of the decisions of the Congress of Berlin before Austria took action. Ährenthal's performance struck him as precipitate and treacherous. Russia was in a state of high excitement. Serbia was mobilizing; she wanted to fight for a Greater Serbia. The great powers attempted to mediate, but the Danubian monarchy rejected the idea of a congress. Recollections of Algeciras were at work here. In the end a tolerable agreement was reached with the Turks, and Bulgaria's independence was recognized. But the tension between Austria and Serbia persisted.

The German government now took a step that conjured up the threat of war. Bülow let Russia know that she was expected to recognize the Austro-Hungarian annexation in order to pacify stiff-necked Serbia; otherwise the Reich would have to let matters take their own course. In other words Germany was determined to help the Danubian monarchy in case of attack by Russia. The form of the German declaration was extremely courteous, even friendly; perhaps this made it all the bitterer for Russia. It was an ultimatum, and Russia, which had not yet recovered from her war with Japan, drew back. This triumph was Prince Bülow's last achievement in foreign policy. All that had come of his great plans was tension in three directions. He left an evil heritage. But his downfall was largely due to matters connected with domestic policy.

A serious insurrection in German Southwest Africa was brutally put down. On this occasion the Centre uncovered many abuses in German colonial government. The Chancellor broke with the Centre. The elections of 1907 brought victory to a Conservative-Liberal bloc. But the policy of this bloc was fruitful for only a short time. The Conservatives could not decide to grant the taxes essential for carrying through the necessary reforms in the financial administration of the Reich. Resumption of relations with the Centre became inevitable. But it was impossible for Prince Bülow to effect it. His personal relationship with the Emperor, moreover, had been shaken by the unfortunate affair of the *Daily Telegraph* interview.

The distinguished English paper published conversations between the Emperor and an English guest in which William II expressed himself in favour of a rapprochement between the two countries. The

Emperor offered a number of evidences of his friendship for England. One such was that he himself had worked out a plan of campaign during the Boer War, that he had sent this draft to England, and that there had been a remarkable likeness between it and the plan later used with success by Lord Roberts, the British commander-in-chief. A tempest of indignation broke out in Germany. The long-accumulated bitterness about the Emperor's wilful and tactless behaviour was expressed in an almost revolutionary manner. The manuscript of the interview had been read and approved in German authoritative quarters. Prince Bülow had very probably known about it, though in his embarrassment he issued a denial. At bottom he was not sorry that the Emperor was learning a lesson. His defence of his sovereign had a schoolmaster's air about it that William II could not abide and never forgave. The Emperor had a nervous breakdown. He was obliged to promise that he would use more reserve in private conversations, and he kept this promise. After November 1908 he was a changed man. His brisk and jaunty optimism was a thing of the past. The worries of the Reich were shown even in his physical bearing and his facial expression.

BETHMANN HOLLWEG. THE SECOND MOROCCO CRISIS. THE BALKAN WARS

William II took positive pleasure in dismissing Prince Bülow (July 1909). The new Chancellor, Theobald von Bethmann Hollweg, had made a career in government posts. He was a serious and brilliant official who had risen rapidly. Both intellectually and socially he belonged, not to the agrarian Junkers, but to the Free Conservatives, to the cultured patriots who were ready for reform—the successors of the old *Wochenblatt* party, which his grandfather had helped to found. Bethmann and the Emperor had been friends ever since they were students together at Bonn, and it was natural to expect that they would co-operate successfully in mutual good understanding. That their relations did not measure up to these expectations was due to the Chancellor's stiffness and his somewhat monotonous intellectual tone. His conversation was full of profundities; he lacked not only suppleness of mind and a sense of humour, but inspiration and even spontaneity. The Emperor and the Reichstag preferred something more amusing. The philosophical Chancellor became a bird of ill omen for the German Reich.

In domestic policy everything was at cross-purposes. The so-called black-and-blue bloc, the renewed combination of the Conservatives and the Centre, presented the only basis for action that was ready to hand. Social Democracy made huge gains in the elections, and pronounced liberalism became stronger. Was it not possible to venture on a great reform program? Problems of foreign policy, however, overshadowed everything else.

Even Prince Bülow had questioned the navy bills of 1906 and 1907–8 from the point of view of foreign policy, but he had avoided conflict with Tirpitz. The new Chancellor had to undertake this conflict and carry it through, though it was now much more difficult. Competitive naval armaments led to the ultimate estrangement of England and Germany and were one important cause of the imperialistic World War. The second Morocco Crisis showed that the explosion was close at hand. The imperial province of Alsace-Lorraine was still a bone of contention between France and Germany. In an economic way Germany did everything she could for this region. The imperial province was given a constitution of its own, though the hour was late for it. The most salutary policy would have been one of spiritual conquest. But this was out of the question on account of Germany's imperialistic trends, to which the people of the region were opposed for the sake of their self-preservation.

A painful incident in the little town of Zabern in Alsace showed the depth of the antagonism between indigenous particularism and Prussian militarism. This was in the spring of 1913. A half-baked lieutenant struck a shoe-maker with his sword, and the people were aroused against the brutal officer. Instead of allowing him to drop out of the picture the army made an issue of the affair. A state of siege was declared. Respectable citizens were imprisoned. Disturbances, abuses, even revolt occurred. A mere bagatelle provoked a serious political crisis. There was surprised amusement abroad, but many good Germans were not amused. A liberal Germany might well have won the hearts of the people of Alsace-Lorraine, at least of those who spoke German. But Germany's reactionary attitude and her world policy made it impossible to bridge the rift.

In the meantime France was carrying out her self-styled peaceful penetration of Morocco. The purpose of the provisional treaty of 1909 was to re-establish the agreement of Algeciras as the basis for an understanding between France and Germany. When the French occupied Fez, however, that agreement was invalidated. What was to be done? The societies that represented colonial and economic interests brought pressure to bear on the government of the Reich. Bethmann had installed the clever and energetic Swabian Alfred von Kiderlen-Wächter as Foreign Secretary. Kiderlen was the most original diplomat ever to emerge from Bismarck's school. He was outspoken and merry, and it was because of his sharp tongue that he had been kept in inferior posts for so long. But now his chance had come, and he proceeded to act.

The gunboat *Panther* sailed for the port of Agadir in western Morocco. Beyond all doubt Berlin wanted now to get down to business. Germany began negotiations for a settlement with France. For a while a break seemed unavoidable. England sided with the French; on July 21, 1911 Lloyd George, the Chancellor of the Exchequer, made a speech at the Mansion House that had been discussed in advance with other leading members of the cabinet. This speech was an unambiguous warning, even a threat, to Germany. Thus the German Reich could not make demands that were too high if it wanted to avoid war. After many difficulties the two agreements concerning Morocco and the Congo were concluded in October and November 1911. By their terms Germany consented to France's having a free hand in Morocco, though with free trade and free competition reserved for all nations. In return for a narrow strip in the Cameroons the Reich received a large portion of the French Congo colony. This acquisition was the most considerable of William's reign. A new era of colonial co-operation seemed to have begun. The economic value of the new territory might be a matter of disagreement; the material success itself was beyond doubt. These agreements were regarded as the beginning of a fruitful German world policy without war.

A number of obstacles still remained to be disposed of. Italy's attack on Tripoli and her war against the Turks in the autumn of 1911 put Germany in the difficult position of being at once an ally of one party and a friend of the other. Italy's advances in the Mediterranean irritated Austria, which agreed with great reluctance to Italy's temporary occupation of the Dodecanese Islands in the Ægean. In spite of these tensions the German government held to the Triple Alliance

555

and renewed it in 1912 in a more comprehensive form. The allies conferred on military and naval questions, and Italy successfully kept up an appearance of readiness to help. But no unprejudiced observer could doubt that in an emergency she would blithely choose a course favourable to her own interests, without any regard for treaties.

Italy's successes against the Turks heartened the Balkan peoples. Russia, which had been approaching Italy, now definitely turned again to the Balkans and the Near East; the Balkan League against the Turks was formed under her spiritual leadership. This was by way of overture to a crusade of the Christians in the Balkans and the expulsion of the Turks. A reshifting of connections to the disadvantage of the Central Powers appeared inevitable. In the autumn of 1912 the four members of the Balkan League struck. Russia showed her sympathies by rehearsing mobilization. She was supported by a secret agreement with Japan that enabled her to move even her Siberian troops westward; Japan was offered German Kiaochow for her neutrality in case of war. France had tried in vain to prevent the outbreak of war in the Balkans. The success of the Balkan states created a new situation. England and Germany too were doing all they could to localize the conflict. Nothing could have provided a surer proof of the genuine distaste for war that was felt by the great civilized states than this co-operation, which really reduced all the existing tensions.

But the struggle for booty in the Balkans brought new difficulties in its wake. Austria supported Bulgarian interests against Serbia and Rumania. This so embittered Rumania that old King Carol felt forced to declare himself unable to fulfil the obligations of the treaty of alliance with Austria that dated back to Bismarck's time. Nationalism in Rumania evolved a more and more challenging program for a Greater Rumania that aimed at Transylvania, the Banat, and Bukovina. The relations of Austria-Hungary toward Serbia entered an even more perilous phase. The Kingdom of Serbia, which was growing in power, was engaged in a bitter economic struggle with its neighbour Hungary. The idea of a Greater Serbia aroused all the southern Slav subjects of the monarchy against Emperor Francis Joseph. In the autumn of 1913 only an Austro-Hungarian ultimatum could curb Serbia's claims to Albania.

556

COULD THE TENSION BETWEEN GERMANY AND RUSSIA BE REDUCED?

The increasing tension drove the German government to introduce more and more army and navy bills. The citizens of the Reich were expected to make great financial sacrifices; unrest and criticism deepened, but patriotic excitement, ambitions, and expectations mounted at the same time. The German National Defence League now vied with the Navy League, for the army could not be allowed to suffer in comparison with the navy; the fear that such a situation might arise was not unfounded. Responsible men in the Reich did not believe that it would be possible to win a war against the Triple Entente of Russia, France, and Great Britain. If this assumption were correct, then everything must be done to break up the Triple Entente or, if it held together, to maintain peace at any price, for a temporary loss of prestige would be preferable to the loss of a war. Such a policy, however, called not only for unusually brilliant statesmanship, but also for unlimited authority at home. There was no one in Germany who possessed these qualifications.

Bethmann Hollweg made earnest attempts to effect a new rapprochement with Russia. The Russian and German emperors exchanged visits on several occasions and thus continued the relationship that had existed before the German ultimatum during the crisis over Austria's annexation of Bosnia and Herzegovina. A treaty, negotiated in Potsdam and later in St. Petersburg, was signed in the Russian capital in 1911. It dealt with the connection of Persian rail lines under construction with the Bagdad railway, Germany's purely economic interests in Persia, and the recognition of the further interests of Russia in that country. In the Reinsurance Treaty Bismarck had dangled Constantinople before the Russians; it was the very least that Germany would now have had to concede in order to maintain friendly relations with Russia. But the Turkish friendship stood in the way. Could not Germany have sacrificed this friendship? In that case Russia and the Balkan Slavs would have vented their discontents on Austria, and this was a possibility that Germany could not ignore. Every approach to Russia bristled with danger. The only way out was to come to an understanding with Great Britain. Germany was now so strong that France would probably hesitate to proceed against the Reich with Russia alone. Loans and military con-

557

ferences constantly bolstered the co-operation between Russia and France. When France introduced three-year compulsory military service the measure appeared as a preparation for imminent war. But the decision still depended on England. It was hardly likely that England would go to war merely to promote the idea of revenge. Her actions could be determined only by her own closest interests, and the most important of these was the question of the navy.

After the agreement on Morocco and the Congo had been reached, Admiral von Tirpitz asked for a new navy bill to strengthen Germany's prestige, which was alleged to have been injured. In February 1912 Lord Haldane, the English Secretary for War, appeared in Berlin. The visit had been carefully arranged by confidential agents, such as Sir Ernest Cassel in London and Albert Ballin in Hamburg. The purpose of the discussions was to reach an agreement on naval armaments and also a general political understanding. Bethmann and Tirpitz argued bitterly with each other about the supplementary navy bill. Bethmann was willing to sacrifice it, but wanted a neutrality pact with England; the proposed formulation of the pact, however, went too far for the English government. The most practical procedure would have been to come to a disarmament agreement affecting only the navy, but Bethmann could not induce the Emperor to consent to this against the wishes of Tirpitz. An unambiguous renunciation of a naval policy that was hostile to England was the only measure that would have made possible, in case of a Continental war, a further agreement for the English neutrality that was so much desired. There never had been much likelihood of securing English neutrality; at any rate the favourable moment was allowed to slip by. Twice the Emperor offered Admiral von Tirpitz the office of Chancellor of the Reich, and it was unfortunate that the most successful of the ministers did not wish to assume the highest responsibility. Tirpitz preferred to continue his unofficial direction of the affairs of the Reich from his point of vantage in the naval department. Thus he made the difficult tasks of the Chancellor still more difficult; at the same time he shirked responsibility toward the public and toward history. His envious and pompous swashbuckling became fatal to the German people.

Despite disappointments the negotiations between Germany and England went on and produced concrete results in the spring of

1914. Two agreements were drafted, one concerning the future of the Portuguese colonies, the other about further construction of the Bagdad railway system. Those who were in favour of coming to an understanding hoped that the colonial arrangement would further a closer relationship and that on this foundation a naval agreement could then be reached. But the agreements were not put through and published. Russia and France were opposed to them; these powers were working on behalf of an English-Russian naval convention, and they showed government offices in Berlin certain documents dealing with these negotiations in order to make Germany suspicious of England.

The Triple Entente was strong, as became evident in connection with the German General Liman von Sanders. This officer, one of the best drill-masters in the army, was to be made commander of the first Turkish army corps and as such was to supervise the reorganization of the Turkish army. Under pressure from abroad Liman had to give up this command. He remained only an inspector of the army, while an English admiral was entrusted with the command and inspection of the Turkish fleet. Germany swallowed this compromise and gave way. The other side was no less discontented. In the spring of 1914 the German Prince zu Wied took over the new state of Albania as a sovereign principality, but was unable to hold his ground against the machinations that Italy and Greece carried on through Albanian groups. This was still another reverse for the Central Powers.

SARAJEVO. OUTBREAK OF WAR

A German understanding with England was probably still possible at the price of part of the naval program. England was always a hesitant partner in the Triple Entente. She reserved the right of coming to a final decision at the last possible moment. Sir Edward Grey and his close collaborators felt themselves bound by both personal and political obligations, but in the end the decision rested with Parliament and crown. A change of cabinet could mean a change of foreign policy. The English Liberal government thought it was serving peace best by maintaining this attitude. France and Russia were not to be encouraged to strike by being certain of England's sympathy.

The murder in Sarajevo of Archduke Francis Ferdinand, the heir to the Austrian throne, now precipitated an acute international crisis. Was it still possible to avoid catastrophe? The murderers of the unfortunate Archduke and his wife, the Duchess of Hohenberg—the Czech Countess Chotek, who was only his morganatic wife—were Bosnians. They were therefore subjects of Emperor Francis Joseph. In that summer of 1914 it could not be determined whether or to what extent they were connected with official Serbian circles. There was no doubt, however, that they were tools of a patriotic movement for a Greater Serbia. Their victim was one who, stern but sturdy, had always bespoken equal rights for the Slavs of the Danubian monarchy, in his own autocratic way, indeed, but with an honest desire for reform.

Under the direction of Count Leopold Berchtold the Austro-Hungarian foreign office elected to seize this opportunity for settling accounts with a troublesome neighbour. The ultimate aim was a league of Balkan states under the direction of the Central Powers. For the time being, the indignation aroused by the murder paralysed all resistance, but Berchtold allowed the first crucial weeks to slip by before he struck. He made sure of German backing, but he gave his opponents in Russia and France the chance to deliberate and to collect themselves. The result was the famous Austrian ultimatum of July 23, the essentials of which had been previously confided to Berlin. No sovereign state could accept the Austrian demands in their entirety. The clever reply of the Serbian government still allowed of a peaceful solution. The German Emperor and the leading personages of the *Wilhelmstrasse* would have been very much pleased if Austria-Hungary had contented herself with a diplomatic victory. But Berchtold wanted more. He wanted Austrian hegemony in the Balkans, even at the price of war, and he wanted the dismemberment of Serbia. If Serbia had accepted the Austrian note in full, she would have had a civil war on her hands; Russia would have intervened, and the final result would have been much the same. Berchtold thought that it would be possible to wage a localized war with Serbia alone. He wanted this war even at the risk of Russian intervention, but Vienna and Berlin were actually not at all sure that Russia was sufficiently prepared to intervene.

The Central Powers, then, were ready to take the risk. This was their first great error. Russia stood back of Serbia, and Russia was resolved not to bow to an ultimatum a second time. The conflict between Austria and Serbia caused tension between Germany and Russia. The latter aggravated the situation by first mobilizing in great haste on a large scale and then limiting its mobilization. At this point German leadership made its second great error. Partly for considerations of domestic policy, Bethmann Hollweg believed that the controversy with Russia ought to be decided quickly and clearly instead of letting it drag out. He may have feared that Germany might mobilize too late and thus be caught at a military disadvantage. But such fears should not have been decisive, quite aside from the consideration that they were unsupported by facts. At any rate the proposal of the Czar, who was still hanging back, to submit the dispute between Austria and Serbia to the court of arbitration at The Hague was ignored. This made a very bad impression abroad, especially in the United States. Austria-Hungary held her fire with regard to Russia, to let the decision come of itself. But Germany, in straightforward haste, hurled at Russia an ultimatum that had to be answered within a given time; then she declared war.

In the early stages of the war between Austria and Serbia Bethmann Hollweg made desperate attempts to secure French and British neutrality. Everything that years of diplomatic endeavour had failed to accomplish was to be achieved at the last moment. All through this controversy France was working with great skill behind the scenes to hold Russia firmly to the Triple Entente; in the eyes of the world France was only a devoted mediator of peace. When, however, the Germans declared war on Russia, France no longer had any choice. All her responsible statesmen had been awaiting this hour. The great moment for revenge had come. The Reich had technically involved itself with France by an ultimatum and the formal declaration of war.

And now came the third and gravest error of German leadership. As Germany saw it, she had worked with England in a comradely fashion for peace. The colonial agreements had pointed the way to a better future. Hundreds of proofs of friendship had paved the path to the ultimate co-operation of two great nations. Dynastic, economic, psychological, and cultural ties were all opposed to the absurdity of a struggle between two countries that had arrived at historical greatness with mutual helpfulness. That was the German view. England did not, in fact, enter the war because she wanted to destroy a troublesome competitor. She had shown her willingness to allow the Germans their place in the sun. She could feel no fondness for the Emperor's manner, but she had confidence in Bethmann Hollweg, who was indeed the first German statesman in many years to enjoy England's respect. In these last difficult hours England's policy was once more decided by the question of the navy.

If Germany invaded Belgium and overcame France, the German fleet on the Channel coast might well become a threat to England's very life. The leading men in the German government did not recognize the significance of Winston Churchill's and Sir Edward Grey's attitude and clung to the hope that England could be induced to remain neutral. But they failed to do the one thing that might have buttressed this slender possibility: to hold back completely in the west and concentrate on attacking Russia. The German general staff was actually more powerful than any German chancellor, and General von Moltke cautioned the Austrians against Bethmann's earnest warning. Military necessities wiped out diplomatic combinations. The Reich was a military state; in this it obeyed the conditions of its origin and its existence. If England had given Germany a stern and unambiguous warning, could the catastrophe have been averted? Repetitions are annoying. If England had openly threatened the Reich in the style of 1911, Bethmann Hollweg's downfall would probably have followed, and a cabinet under Tirpitz would have taken up the gauntlet.

Germany's violation of Belgian neutrality was a serious breach of international law. It presented the divided English cabinet with a basis in law for its declaration of war, which the majority welcomed. But it did still more: it erased the impression of the murder at Sarajevo from the memory of the world at large and turned sentiment against the Central Powers.

MILITARY AND POLITICAL PROSPECTS OF THE CENTRAL POWERS

Historically the imperialistic World War was the child of German foreign policy, which in turn issued from the imperialistic development of the world at large. The Reich, together with its ally Austria-Hungary, claimed a position of world power. There was no reason why it should not make this claim; other world powers also had had to make a beginning. Imperialistic ambitions were international and employed the same methods everywhere, with slight local and ethnical variations. The problem inherent in Germany's world policy consisted in something different. The Reich was the strongest power on the Continent, but the weakest in relation to the world. It wanted the same respect for its world policy that its superior military and economic strength commanded on the Continent, but this demand was presented to world powers of entirely different extent, entirely different resources and reserves. Germany's modest scattered colonies weakened rather than strengthened her position, since they served to increase her foes, not her means of defence.

Germany immediately lost her acquisitions in eastern Asia and in the Pacific. Japan joined her opponents; ever since the Preliminary Peace of Shimonoseki (1895) she had been awaiting this hour of vengeance. The promising African territories also could not be held; the German colonies there defended themselves valiantly, but it was hopeless to strive against overwhelming superiority, and the cruiser fleet was unable to give any effective help. Nothing was left but the German interests in the Balkans and the Near East. The weakened Turks became Germany's ally, and so did Bulgaria. Both these powers were pursuing their own aims. They expected military and material help and took the time of German experts and advisers without always following their advice. They were both sensitive and selfish. Their claims swelled with every success and wavered with every failure. Rumania and Italy, both old allies of the Central Powers, awaited the course of military events and then joined the stronger and more successful side of the Triple Entente. As far as foreign relations were concerned the situation of the Central Powers grew worse from year to year, and the number of their opponents grew. Germany had to fight out her war for a position of world power on the Continent and with her European resources. But she could not be conquered by the European resources of her opponents. The resources of all the great continents were requisitioned: Africa, Asia, and America united against the Reich and its allies, which were steadily growing weaker. Only a great gift for organization, only the tremendous accumulation of supplies and technical aids during the long period of peace, enabled Germany to sustain her obstinate resistance. The old warlike qualities of the Germans again stood the test. Civilians of all callings, including women, bravely did their share.

Astonishingly enough, the supreme command failed in several decisive situations. In the very beginning the great offensive against France collapsed, not from a lack of troops, but because of inadequate strategy. After tremendous losses the attack on Verdun (1915) ended in German defeat. But the Battle of Tannenberg and the break-through at Gorlice were heroic feats. German striking-power was most effective in the east, against the inadequately organized and poorly led Russian armies, and in the Balkans. In the west the Allies were more than able to hold their defensive positions. Germany was scarcely able to compete with their mass of war equipment, let alone to outstrip it. And the German navy proved a great disappointment. The cruisers were much too weak to protect overseas trade, which was choked off by the British blockade. Submarines alone were able to challenge the blockade and to maintain a kind of counter-blockade. But Tirpitz had been reprehensibly remiss. He had let the construction of U-boats lag in favour of the battle fleet. The Reich had invested more and more funds in the building of dreadnoughts in spite of the warnings of naval experts, particularly Admiral Karl Galster. These dreadnoughts had in the first place made war with England inevitable through the very fact of their existence; in the second place they had worked against the enlargement and equipment of the land army; thirdly they were not able to inflict any notable injury on the English fleet in all the course of the war. The only great naval battle of the World War, the Battle of Jutland, brought no clear-cut decision.

German leadership produced a series of imposing military achievements. These were nowhere more highly acclaimed than in the historical writings of Germany's opponents. The first chief of the general staff, the younger General von Moltke, was rather sickly, a Christian Scientist, and he quickly faded out of the picture. His successor, General Erich von Falkenhayn, had a bold, gambling spirit, but a supple mind and a wealth of ideas. During the difficult final years Hindenburg and Ludendorff bore the full responsibility. Erich Ludendorff, in spite of his indefatigable energy, his power of organization, and his iron will, had not the gifts of a great general, for he lacked the instinct that is constantly on the alert, as well as ingenuity. Hindenburg was underestimated for a long time. He was a powerful, elementally effective figure, and up to his serious illness in October 1917 he kept himself informed on every detail of every event and formulated the final decisions. Even later he still had an unsubtle but sure instinct for what ought to be done. It did not take him long to become accustomed to the great part that destiny and the hero-worship of the public accorded him. He was a grandiose blend of shrewdness and egoism. His massive nature permeated everything about the fatherland. Only those who were closely associated with him knew that he had other qualities: that he was cold and petty, narrow-minded and suspicious.

Germany was quickly cut off from the great world, and so it was easy for emotional propaganda to present a rosy picture of her situation. Anyone who sounded a warning or who was better informed, anyone who ventured to offer loyal criticism, was soon seen as a poor patriot. Military successes in the east made Poland the first focus of weighty plans for the future. The restoration of Poland was a self-evident point in the program of the powers that had been involved in partitioning it. Austria wanted to absorb the Russian Poland established by the Congress of Vienna; that was the Austro-Polish solution. An archduke was to be king, and this Poland was to be very closely bound to the reorganized monarchy. But the Austrian Slavs asserted themselves. Whole Czech regiments went over to the Russians. Their leaders, Masaryk and Beneš, launched from abroad their propaganda for an independent Czechoslovakian state. Official Austria had always had good luck with Poland. Now it was thought that an Austrian Poland might perhaps win over other Slav peoples. Germany, however, did not look kindly on the Austro-Polish solution, because she wanted to retain her own Polish provinces. A weak independent Poland would certainly be more manageable. So finally the Russian part of Poland—Congress Poland—was set up as a kingdom with a hereditary monarchy and a parliamentary constitution. Emperor William II objected to this extraordinary arrangement; a kingdom that was not at once given a king would certainly raise anew all latent territorial claims against the other partition powers and would block every chance of a separate peace with Russia. But in military quarters there was a hope that Poland could provide strong military assistance—a hope that proved completely false.

The Baltic and Lithuanian policy was directly connected with the arrangements for Poland. The sparse German upper stratum in the Baltic provinces that had hitherto been Russian wanted to shake off Russia's yoke once and for all. The oppressed Estonians, Latvians, and Lithuanians supported this ambition, but reserved to themselves the pursuit of their own national goals. The aristocratic element in the Baltic population was connected with the German ruling class through many bonds of spiritual and blood kinship. Most of the barons and the intelligentsia of the cities had only one fervent desire: to lean on Germany. But an eastward German expansion of this kind was bound up with a series of geopolitical and ethnical problems and with questions relating to foreign policy. Was Germany's colonial region to be further increased? Should the Junkers be reinforced anew and the burden of so many aliens be assumed into the bargain? Would not Russia be mortally offended if she were pushed away from the Baltic, and would not the western powers, too, feel resentful?

Thus the war increased Germany's problems. That the situation as a whole was not brilliant was proved by the German peace offer of December 1916. It failed just as earlier attempts had done: the peace feelers of the new Austrian Emperor, Charles, the successor of Francis Joseph, who died in 1916, and the efforts made by the Pope. The obvious peace mediator was Woodrow Wilson, the President of the United States. But Germany's statesmen forfeited his readiness to help by declaring unrestricted submarine warfare, which led to the United States' entering the war. The struggle spread out over all lands and seas. The largest and most populous countries on earth were with the Entente. Power faced power, but ideas also confronted ideas. Germany, along with her flagging allies, was not only fought against, but hated. She was denounced as the matrix of the imperialistic attitude, and a world coalition undertook to fight this autocracy in the name of democracy. The German army and homeland competed to beat off the terrible assault. The collapse of czarism in Russia once more offered the Central Powers the chance to save themselves. The provisional government that was at first established in

Russia tried to continue the war on the side of the Allies. But the Soviet government wanted an immediate peace without territorial annexations. The German supreme command had seen to it that Lenin and his friends, the leaders of Communism, appeared in Russia at the right moment.

An epoch-making occurrence was marching to completion. It was more important and more fraught with consequences than all the events of the war: in Russia the first Communist state arose, detached from the world coalition of democracy. The independent path on which Russia was entering led first toward an understanding with Germany. The Central Powers were dazzled by a tempting possibility. Had not Frederick the Great been able to save himself because of a sudden shift of policy in Russia? If it were possible now to release troops for action in the west by making a cheap peace with Russia and to exploit the economic strength of the east to feed and arm central Europe, then the Central Powers might well be able to weather the attack of their opponents, which was gaining momentum; they might obtain the negotiated peace that many sensible people on the opposing side also desired. Very deplorably, German leadership extorted from Russia as well as from Rumania peace treaties that imposed annexations and indemnities on the defeated, quite in the spirit of traditional European power politics. The treaties of Brest-Litovsk and Bucharest exhibited once again the spirit of autocracy and of militarism. They involuntarily supplied the propaganda of the enemies of the Central Powers with justification. Should and could the imperialistic will of Germany and her allies be fulfilled in the west and overseas?

WAR AIMS. DEFEAT. REVOLUTION

The struggle as to German war aims began immediately after the outbreak of the war. It flared up into a fundamental controversy over the meaning and the value of German world policy. The patriotism of German Social Democracy was beyond question. The German worker did his duty at the front and at home just like any other citizen. War credits were approved by the Social Democratic Party in the Reichstag. The government took a conciliatory attitude. There was peace within. The military authorities permitted socialistic writings to circulate. Socialist provincial and municipal officials were confirmed by the Prussian government for the first time. But presently opposition began to stir in the Social Democratic camp.

Wilhelm Liebknecht, the old champion of Social Democracy, who came of a Christian family of officials in Hesse, had a highly gifted son, Karl Liebknecht, who was a passionate, almost monomaniacal personality. A shrewd jurist, a brilliant speaker, and an unimpeachable moralist, he took over the leadership of the steadfast. They formed a group first called the Internationale and later the Spartacus League, which battled sternly against the patriotism of the majority of the party, which was ready for opportunistic compromise. Liebknecht's group wanted to put a forced end to the war by a general strike and to build up a new international front of the proletariat. Liebknecht and the Polish Jewess Rosa Luxemburg, a woman of great gifts as a speaker and writer, with two other adherents of the group, were in close accord with the leaders of the Russian Revolution and exchanged opinions and plans with them. The brilliant Spartacus letters of Rosa Luxemburg were widely circulated. Karl Liebknecht was drafted for military labour and given a long penitentiary sentence because he continued to agitate against the war. In 1916 a second opposition group was formed under the leadership of Hugo Haase, a deputy from East Prussia. A year later this group named itself the Independent Social Democratic Party of Germany. It stood for the older orthodox Marxism as against the Russian form of Communism preached by the Spartacus League. The so-called Majority Social Democrats had to maintain their revisionism and loyalty against all these new trends. The Independents now voted against the war credits in the Reichstag and denounced any form of annexation in the name of the working people's will to peace.

The struggle over war aims destroyed internal peace. The Pan-Germans and the leading associations of industrialists drew up a sweeping annexation program without respect to either ethnical or linguistic boundaries. Some put forth claims to all of Belgium and large portions of northern France. Others, more modest, saw in the iron regions of Longwy and Briey, together with the coast of Flanders, the minimum that should be called for. By way of basis, recollections of the Holy Roman Empire blended with national and economic considerations to make up an unseemly and ill-assorted whole.

Friedrich Naumann made a deep impression with his revival of the idea of a central Europe. Here too there was a choice of solutions. More moderate circles gathered around Dr. Wilhelm Solf, the experienced and cosmopolitan Colonial Secretary; around the former Colonial Secretary, the leading banker Bernhard Dernburg; and around the historian and publicist Professor Hans Delbrück. These men wanted as little change as possible in European boundaries, which had become an affair of history, but instead a rounding out of Germany's African colonies into a really valuable central African empire. The right-wing parties were all in favour of annexations. The deputy Gustav Stresemann, who was later to choose an entirely different path, distinguished himself among the younger National Liberals in defending this policy.

In the Centre sentiment was divided. The Benjamin of the Reichstag, the ambitious and only too diligent deputy Matthias Erzberger, a petty bourgeois from Swabia, soon dropped the thought of annexations and did battle against Pan-Germanism. He had access to excellent sources of information in the Vatican and thus had a better notion of the grave situation of the Central Powers than most Germans. No one could doubt the patriotism of this indefatigable man. Unfortunately he had less tact than energy. In 1917 Erzberger introduced the peace resolution that was accepted by the majority in the Reichstag. This resolution favoured a dignified negotiated peace while there was still time. This declaration was entirely in keeping with the posture of left-wing liberalism, which had always shown moderation on the question of peace, and it thus proved that since the time of Bismarck insight into questions of foreign policy had moved leftward.

Left-wing liberalism and the Majority Social Democrats believed that the moment had come to reform the Prussian suffrage. The government agreed in theory, but tried by all sorts of shallow pretences to defer reform until after the peace. The question of the Prussian suffrage was no longer purely a constitutional affair. It had grown into a struggle over principles. Economic problems, which were becoming more and more complex, were making the lower classes sensitive and bitter. The refusal of equal suffrage was interpreted as due to arrogance and distrust, and naturally it furthered the work of the revolutionary groups. Bethmann Hollweg had a completely clear picture of the situation, and he wanted to settle the suffrage matter as soon as possible; the Emperor's Easter message of 1917 presented his program. He wished to develop this program into complete "reorientation." But very soon he ceased to be *persona grata* to any party, and he fell in the summer of 1917. His successor, the meritorious official Georg Michaelis, was unable to cope with the growing tension. The third Chancellor in this year was the very elderly Count Georg von Hertling, who had long been an influential professor of Catholic philosophy, a leading member of the right wing of the Centre, and a tried and proved intermediary between the Reich and the Vatican. Hertling attempted to build up a sort of parliamentary regime, but Social Democrats would not enter his cabinet, while the other parties sent their trusted agents.

Germany was disintegrating internally. Complete dissolution was imminent. Would there be a turn for the better if the big spring offensive was successful? The German supreme command concentrated all its strength on this offensive. Because it failed, Germany lost the war; because she lost the war, a new revolution broke out.

Chapter 19

THE THIRD GERMAN REVOLUTION
AND THE WEIMAR REPUBLIC

THERE WERE four causes for the defeat of the Reich in the imperialistic World War. These causes were connected with economics, technics, foreign policy, and strategy. The Reich made the economic experiment of detaching itself from world economy and building up a self-contained war economy in common with its allies. It was necessary to live off the land—its own land—and to fabricate its own domestic raw materials.

Brilliant inventions gave strong support to German defence— above all the process of obtaining nitrogen from the air for agricultural purposes, as a substitute for Chilean nitrates, which could no longer be imported. Wartime economic controls regulated imports and exports; they stretched out food supplies, created substitutes, and fought black markets. More and more new government offices were established in the desperate endeavour to get the economic situation in hand by state instrumentalities. First the *Zentraleinkaufgesellschaft,* a central purchasing board, was established; then the war ministry founded a department for military raw materials. Gradually the government took over grain, cattle-feed, coal, fats, clothing, fruits and vegetables, and housing. State socialism had become a reality for the duration of the war. Everyone who could be of any use was drafted for the service of the fatherland.

But all these efforts proved futile. Failure was not due to the mistakes that were made, both personal and material; errors were unavoidable. The really astonishing thing is that German officialdom, still honest, was able to carry out the undertaking in a way that was on the whole so fair and so effective. The reason for failure lay far deeper. The groundwork was too restricted. The army was eating up the fatherland. No number of well-conducted offices could do anything about the increasing shortages in raw materials and foodstuffs. Neither Rumanian oil nor the agricultural products of the Balkans and the Ukraine gave help enough. People at home were going hungry and ragged. Austria's economic break-down was so marked, even at the beginning of 1917, that the Foreign Minister, Count Ottokar Czernin, drew up an appalling secret report on it for the two Emperors and the Chancellor of the Reich. Through Erzberger this report was known about in wider circles; he committed an indiscretion in the service of the loftier cause of truth.

One of the numerous peace feelers was put out by the brother-in-law of the Austrian Emperor, Prince Sixtus of Parma, an officer in the French army. Through Catholic channels the Emperor let his opponents know that under certain circumstances he would advocate the reunion of Alsace-Lorraine with France. He would not admit to a German that he had mentioned any such concession. The affair ended in suspicion, dissatisfaction, and irritation on all sides. Emperor Charles had the best of intentions, but he was indecisive and open to too many influences.

The peace that the Central Powers made with Russia proved a disappointment, if only because neither Great Russia nor the Ukraine, which had been made independent under German direction, was able to supply a sufficient amount of food or raw materials. The difficulties were technical and also political. None of the Germans who lived on almost nothing but turnips during the winter of 1917–8 ever forgot this terrible experience. The following winter offered no better prospects. The U-boat war and the German blockade had certainly put England too into a serious situation, but the restrictions that became necessary there were not comparable to central Europe's bitter need. Even assuming that England's difficulties might increase, the fact that the United States had entered the war had decidedly improved her outlook. She was saved by supplies from overseas: food, raw materials, munitions, and manpower. Eastern Europe was not able to perform a like service for Germany and her allies. The longer the war lasted, the more evident the superiority of Germany's opponents became. Every added month was bound to make it more and more evident that the war was ending in economic defeat.

572

In the summer of 1918 German soldiers who were undernourished and inadequately armed had to endure the terrible attack of the Americans, who were excellently equipped in every respect. No amount of useful military experience could balance the weight of these basic facts as to matériel. Even in weapons the German command could not maintain the superiority of the early days of the war. The lack of first-class U-boats put an end to the great expectations that had been staked on the German blockade. Gigantic cannon and gas warfare could achieve only local successes and were not effective in the mobile warfare that had again set in. The tank was known to Ludendorff in its full significance; he rejected it. The terror of tank attack broke the German front. This new weapon ushered in the darkest days in the summer of 1918.

As for foreign policy, the expansion of territory under German influence in eastern Europe—namely, the Baltic border states, Finland, and the Ukraine—did not serve to strengthen German resistance. A painful dispute concerning the future of these countries broke out. They expected Germany to give them material help, and this she could not do to the necessary extent. The unfortunate experiences with Poland were repeated in an aggravated form. Germany's allies could not withstand the enemy's attack in spite of the constant support they received, which was very nearly in excess of reasonable needs for self-preservation. In 1916 almost all of Armenia was occupied by the Russians. In 1917 the English took Bagdad, then Jaffa and Jerusalem. The Arabian parts of the Ottoman Empire could not be held; they were looking for liberation and independence. Furthermore the Entente succeeded in shaking the Bulgarian front from the vantage point of Salonika; the break-through in September 1918 cut the main foundation out from under Germany's foreign policy. Even the very last stage on which its world policy had strutted, the Balkans, broke apart. Now the Turks had to be left to their fate; Rumania could no longer be defended. There was no prospect whatever of rebuilding the shattered system of German foreign policy in the face of a world coalition of thirty allied and associated powers. In Bulgaria and among the Turks groups friendly to the Entente tried to come to an understanding with the victors.

Strategically, at the beginning of 1918 the war situation was not yet entirely hopeless for the Central Powers. Peace in the east made it again possible to concentrate troops on other fronts, and the Austrians were holding out bravely against the Italians. Very probably the gravest mistake was the decision of the German supreme command to launch a spring offensive in the west. If the command had focused all possible German strength at the other side's weakest point, which was Italy, a brilliant success might very probably have been won. If the Central Powers had gained possession of northern Italy, the war might still have been kept up for a considerable period, the food situation would have improved, and industrial production would have been strengthened appreciably. In that case the groups within the Entente that favoured a negotiated peace might perhaps have gained the upper hand. In the spring of 1918 the German command overestimated its strength. In line with ancient military tradition it strove for a quick, clear-cut decision. It failed to take in the situation in its entirety, and it was neither flexible nor inventive enough to adapt its tactics to new and unexpected demands. Haughty and stubborn, arrogant and unteachable, Ludendorff wanted to force the great decision. When it came, it was against him, against Germany.

The troops that Germany used in her spring offensive were the best she had at that time, and their morale was intact. As in every army, there were individual traitors, but they did not affect the end result in any important way. This German army in the west had certainly not been undermined by any sort of political agitation. That is why the drives of domestic politics are shut out as a cause of German defeat. There were only four determinative grounds for the defeat, and they are summed up in economics, technics, foreign policy, and strategy.

REVOLUTIONARY AGITATION

After the German peace offer had been rejected in December 1916 the Independent Social Democrats and the Communists developed an increasingly vigorous and successful agitation for immediate peace without victor or vanquished. To this end the slogans and methods of the Russian Revolution were increasingly utilized. Such success was bound to win converts. The agitation aimed at organizing a general strike, paralysing all the ruling powers, and disintegrating the fighting forces. Extensive strikes were called in April

1917 and in January and February 1918, primarily in munitions industries. The revolutionary character of the movement was obvious. Workers' councils were formed. In the summer of 1917 the first plot was laid in the navy. Its aim was to destroy the striking power of the fleet by refusal to obey orders. The leaders were in close contact with influential Independent deputies. In spite of severe punishment the agitation went on. The navy proved particularly responsive because the monotonous and inactive life on board ship, insufficient food, and brutal discipline embittered and demoralized the personnel. When the order to sail came on October 28, 1918 the crews of numerous battleships refused to obey. At the last desperate moment the German fleet was to have been gambled. The prospect of bettering the situation as a whole was very slight, but it was clear that so valuable an instrument could not be allowed to go untried against the prospect of a humiliating peace. And at that moment the navy failed Germany; disturbances broke out, and the assignment could not be fulfilled. This disgraceful experience had no counterpart in the army. Revolutionary agitation was successful in the homeland and even extended to troops behind the lines, but at least up to the middle of August 1918 the front was not touched by them. The impact that rocked the front, both in soul and in body, was the victorious advance of the foe, the increasing hopelessness of resistance. The state of affairs was obvious; the men saw it for themselves without need of propaganda.

THE ARMISTICE (NOVEMBER 11, 1918). THE EMPEROR FLEES

As early as August 14, 1918 the Crown Council in Spa considered the necessity, in view of the gravity of the military situation, of neutral mediation for peace. On September 28 further military reverses led the supreme command to ask the government of the Reich to take immediate steps to secure peace. Hindenburg and Ludendorff frankly asserted that a military victory was no longer possible. At this historical moment Prince Max of Baden, cousin and heir of the ruling Grand Duke of Baden, formed the Reich's first parliamentary government. Prince Max, the new German Chancellor (died 1929), had been soberly advocating a negotiated peace for a long time; he was able to draw on numerous connections and sources of information. This well-intentioned Prince, whose gifts were less creative than receptive, had a better and more exact notion of Germany's condition than almost anyone else. The only question was whether he had enough energy to carry out the ideas of his circle to the best interests of the whole.

The idea of immediate peace overtures was most unwelcome to the new Chancellor. He wanted his new cabinet to have a chance to take hold first and prepare so important a step with due caution. But Hindenburg and Ludendorff were so insistent that he had no choice. And so the famous exchange of messages with President Wilson began, with the new government of the Reich forced to give in to the demands of the enemy step by step. In the middle of October the sudden willingness of the supreme command to fight on after all aroused very natural suspicion in the majority of the cabinet. In the judgement of experts the situation at the front was not really improved in any respect, and to continue fighting could only mean heavier losses, the devastation of German land, and still harsher peace terms. Military collapse had become a matter of fact. German leadership no longer had any strategic openings, but only certain limited tactical possibilities. Deeds of blind heroism could still be performed. Something could still be done to satisfy the sense of honour. But there was no hope of a real turn for the better. It would be useless to sacrifice any more soldiers. American plans to occupy Germany had been worked out. Berlin was to have been bombed in the spring of 1919. General Ludendorff, whose conduct from either the military or the human angle had not been irreproachable, was now dismissed. Field Marshal von Hindenburg, advised by General Wilhelm Gröner, underwrote all the further steps of the government with his name and reputation. Gröner, who had been chief of the military railroad system for many years, gained the reputation later, as chief of the war office, of being a Swabian glutton for work, with unbounded ability and a happy disposition.

The German public was deeply stirred by President Wilson's harsh criticism of the forms of German government in the past and of German methods of conducting war. This was only the introduction to the impending armistice negotiations, and it had repercussions throughout Germany. The Emperor's position had become very shaky. The Majority Social Democrats did not desire revolution for its own sake; they felt certain of attaining all their aims without that desperate remedy. The Independents and the Communists were pushing forward; their leaders, headed by Emil Barth, were not satisfied with the new constitutional guarantees for the life of the German state. The Majority Social Democrats were in a serious dilemma. They believed that just the abdication of the Emperor and of the German princes would clear the way for reorganizing Germany in their revisionist direction. The Independents, however, appealed to the socialist conscience of their colleagues.

Political events now tumbled over each other. The armistice negotiations were held at Compiègne. At the same time many voices urged the Emperor to abdicate. William II was not able to reach a clear-cut decision in good season. Perhaps the crown might have been saved for his grandchild, the eldest son of the Crown Prince. This was what Prince Max had planned, and many Social Democrats would have been willing to accept this solution. William II wanted to remain King of Prussia in any case. Was he perhaps thinking of Prince Max as a stadholder? At any rate William II repeatedly declared that he would not leave his country, but would remain at the head of his army. But in the end he fled to Holland with his immediate retinue. He deserted his people in their utmost need. But what else was he to do? Suicide was out of the question for the Emperor on religious grounds. It was too late for a hero's death, even for one that was prearranged. None of the other German princes felt himself in personal danger from the revolution. All of them stayed in their own lands. The Emperor and the Crown Prince were in a different case.

A flood of hatred was loosed against the ruling class, against arrogant officers, smug officials, insolent and unteachable Junkers and their hangers-on, profiteers, and deliberate deceivers of the public with their rosy accounts of the situation. All these emotions of the oppressed and exploited, the cheated and deceived, came to a head in impassioned demonstrations against outstanding representatives of the old system, such as the Hohenzollerns and their aides, especially Ludendorff and Tirpitz. Was it not sheer mockery that just now universal manhood suffrage had been adopted in Prussia and that under foreign pressure the Emperor was shorn of his uncircumscribed power as supreme war-lord? For four whole weeks imperial Germany was under a parliamentary regime. Now parliamentarism, the constitutional and administrative system of western Europe and America, which good German champions of a democratic Germany had been demanding for decades, must save whatever could be saved in the general collapse.

THE RED REVOLUTION BREAKS OUT

The third German revolution burst forth. Its first visible symptom was the concerted insubordination in the fleet. The mutineers were arrested, and the result was the revolt in Kiel. The government negotiated. There was neither the will nor the power to settle the matter by sheer force. The revolutionary movement spread to Hamburg and Lübeck; the sailors were its carriers. The next stages took it on to Bremen, Hanover, Köln, Brunswick, and Leipzig. Munich was the first city to proclaim the republic. The core of Prussia still resisted. The first triumphs of the revolution were achieved in anti-Prussian regions or in old centres of opposition, such as Holstein, Lower Saxony, and the Rhineland. That the current was setting against old Prussia was clear. Would she defend herself? The government decided against using force. The Chancellor, Prince Max, after all his attempts to save the Hohenzollern dynasty in some way or other had failed, passed the business of government on to the chairman of the Majority Social Democrats, the deputy Friedrich Ebert. Prince Max even gave out the news of the Emperor's abdication before it had been formally declared. It was a bold step, which also was of no avail.

Philipp Scheidemann, the Social Democrat deputy, proclaimed the republic (November 9) from the outer stairs of the Reichstag building—much to the annoyance of Friedrich Ebert. The pressure of the Independents was dangerously strong. The Majority Social Democrats wanted to keep the power in their own hands. Ebert could not be the Chancellor of a democratic monarchy. He and Scheidemann, together with the lawyer Otto Landsberg and three representatives of the Independents, formed the Council of the People's Representatives, a revolutionary executive body with dictatorial power. In the name of this new government, with the express approval of Hindenburg, who had joined the revolution, the armistice committee, headed by the deputy Matthias Erzberger, put their signatures on November 11 to the harsh, only slightly softened conditions imposed by the victors. The war was over. But the revolution that followed on the defeat had only just begun.

The driving power of the German revolution came from the Independents—the old orthodox Marxists—and the new Communist Party of Germany, which had been developed by the Spartacists and represented what may be called the German Leninists. Both parties later broke up into different groups that were mutually antagonistic. The Independents wanted Germany to become a socialist republic governed by trusted agents of the workers and soldiers. They demanded that all bourgeois elements be excluded from the government and that the ministers at the heads of departments be merely technical advisers to those who held positions of responsibility. Thus the party was working toward a dictatorship of councils. It demanded immediate socialization, the transformation of the capitalistic class state into a socialist community; it demanded that the supporters of the old system be set aside and the beginnings of the counter-revolution put down. The resistance of right-wing Social Democrats was to be crushed with revolutionary energy.

The proclamation of the Spartacists on December 4, 1918, which was followed by the founding of the Communist Party of Germany on December 31, went still further. In the burning words of Rosa Luxemburg judgement was pronounced on the Hohenzollerns as the agents of the imperialistic bourgeoisie and the Junkers, and bourgeois class rule was denounced as guilty of the World War; the world had been exploited by international capitalism, whose work had now ended in famine, national bankruptcy, chaos. Further, the world revolution was the only instrument by which a new order of peace, freedom, and true culture could be built up. Its aim was the comradely work of all; the necessary means was proletarian mass action: a great civil war, the greatest in history, would lay the foundation for the dictatorship of the proletariat. The immediate measures called for were: disarming of the police, of officers, of nonproletarian soldiers, of all members of the ruling classes; a workers' militia; a red proletarian guard to protect the revolution; a revolutionary tribunal to pass judgement on those who bore the main guilt of the war and of its protraction; requisitioning of all food; wiping out of individual states, of all parliaments and municipal councils, and election of workers' councils throughout Germany; abolition of

579

all distinctions of rank, order, and title; complete equality of the sexes; a maximum six-hour working day; confiscation of all dynastic and other private fortunes; cancellation of all public debts, including war loans; expropriation of the land of all large and medium-sized agricultural enterprises, of all banks, mines, and big industrial and commercial concerns; socialistic agricultural associations; international brotherhood and the advancement of the world proletariat by revolutionary methods.

THE BOURGEOIS PARTIES COMBAT THE REVOLUTIONARY FORCES

Marxists and Leninists threatened defeated Germany with red revolution. What did the German bourgeoisie do about it? Immediately after the collapse the idea arose of founding one great Democratic Party for all Germany. Those who till then had constituted the Progressive Party and the left wing of the National Liberals collaborated to this effect. The new party advocated maintenance of the principle of private property in independent handicrafts and retail trade; a strong peasant class; socialization only to the extent justified by increased production; abolition of the old authoritarian state; equalizing of class interests; a free people's state; a free people's culture; a national constitutional state with international alliances.

While the old left-wing liberalism subscribed to a republican form of government, the right wing of the National Liberals held to the idea of a people's emperorship as the most appropriate form for the state, in accordance with the history and the character of the German people. This party, which assumed the old and somewhat colourless name of German People's Party, taken over from the old Swabian People's Party, was identified with the principles of democracy and of private enterprise. It demanded a unified state, efficient civil service, and the black, white, and red colours of the Reich.

The Centre too had to adapt itself to the new conditions of the times. It claimed to be a true social and Christian people's party, emphasized democratic principles and the old traditions of culture and politics, but repudiated the sort of socialism that worked against the church and private property. The old aristocratic leaders in the clerical party now either faded into the background or disappeared entirely. The Catholic trade-union organizations exerted the decisive influence. The Centre suffered a severe loss when Bavaria formed her own People's Party, which became a focus for Bavarian Catholics united in hatred of the powerful north, of one-sided Prussian predominance, of the "incapable but obstinate and brutal art of ruling practised in Berlin." Bavaria, so the program of the new party stated, was to belong to the Bavarians. "Berlin must not become Germany, nor Germany Berlin."

The old conservative groups in Germany were the most deeply affected by the overturn of the state. No serious attempt was made to defend the monarchy; these usufructuaries of the dynastic principle allowed the princes and their courts to disappear without lifting a finger. There was no struggle, and there were no martyrs. Nothing else damaged the idea of monarchy so seriously in the old monarchical German fatherland as this astonishing fact. The conservatives were apparently moved by well-grounded fear for their property. In effect they sacrificed the monarchy in defence of private property. They were willing to co-operate in any form of state in which law and order and private property were sovereign. The leading spirits of the various groups of conservatives decided to fuse feudal and bureaucratic with popular and anti-Semitic elements, for if this party trend were to survive, it too must reach out for a broader democratic basis. Its aptly chosen new name, German National People's Party, attracted followers all over the Reich, even in the west and the south, where there had always been an attitude of suspicion toward the old Prussia of the conservatives. The German Fatherland Party and the Association for Ruthless Opposition to England, both typical organizations of the later years of the war, had paved the way effectively for the German National People's Party. Only by sharply whipping up the nationalist instinct could the Junker class hope to secure enough followers to maintain its traditional influence, even if secretly, under the new conditions. Thus the agrarian and anti-Semitic attitude of commercial employees, heavy industry, and the Protestant provinces all joined in a definitely anti-republican and anti-socialist front. Among German Nationalists sympathy for militarism, distrust of an international understanding, and desire for revenge and for a mythical reinterpretation of current events flourished all the more because this party avoided the opportunity for creative co-operation as far as possible. It was most of all this party that believed

and spread the legend of the so-called stab in the back, which propounded the curious idea that the German army had not been defeated on the battlefield, but had been struck down from behind by
the revolution.

CIVIL WAR AND THE NATIONAL ASSEMBLY

Thus new parties sprang up in Germany. It was plain that the
majority of the German nation opposed the Communist revolution.
The wish for a national assembly became more and more urgent.
The governments of the individual states and the majority in the
conference of workers' and soldiers' councils that was meeting in
Berlin demanded that a national assembly be elected for the purpose
of setting up a new order of state and society. To counterbalance the
Council of the People's Representatives an executive committee from
the workers' and soldiers' councils had been formed in Berlin according to Russian precedent; it tried to promote and put through a
Communist revolution. The Russian ambassador was so active in this
enterprise that the German authorities had to turn him away. There
were differences of opinion about the struggle over the system of
councils. The Majority Social Democrats decided the issue. They
now made their memorable pact with the bourgeois parties and the
army. The daily collaboration of Friedrich Ebert and General
Gröner at that time saved Germany from Communism. Now the
Majority Social Democrats did just what the party advocating a
federal state at the Church of St. Paul in 1849 had done, what the
National Liberals in 1867 had done, and what the left-wing liberal
groups later had done on a number of occasions. They shifted to the
right, blocked the course of the revolution, and made their peace
with the strongest powers to preserve the state.

The elections to the National Assembly had been set for January
19, 1919. By way of reply to this move there came an insurrection of
the people's navy division at Christmas. Government troops put
down the revolt. Thereupon the Independents deserted the Council
of the People's Representatives. Karl Liebknecht publicly demanded
the overthrow of the government and the execution of Ebert and
Scheidemann as proved traitors to the people. Georg Ledebour, an
eccentric and intrepid socialist, and Karl Liebknecht organized a
committee of the revolution, which declared the rule of the Council

of the People's Representatives ended. Street fighting broke out in Berlin, but it ended in a few days with the suppression of the Communists. Liebknecht and Rosa Luxemburg were captured and killed by naval officers. Other Communist uprisings occurred in Bremen, Halle, Leipzig, Dresden, Düsseldorf, and Stuttgart. Such were the circumstances under which the elections for the National Assembly took place.

The old Reichstag suffrage had been considerably extended and partially improved by reducing the age limit to twenty years, introducing proportional representation, and giving women the vote. The majority in the new National Assembly was anti-Communist, but also anti-monarchical. Represented in the new government were Democrats, the Centre, and Majority Social Democrats. An emergency constitution was proclaimed, and Ebert assumed the leadership of the Reich as provisional President. Philipp Scheidemann, who had been a cheerful and irrepressible mediator between the Emperor's government and Social Democracy, headed the new cabinet as President of the Ministry of the Reich. And so all was in readiness to set up a new constitutional state, a new order of things.

But the Communist revolution was not at an end. A red army was tyrannizing over the Ruhr region; it was well organized and amply equipped. The government of the Reich found it difficult to cope with this movement. Then a truce afforded a breathing spell, after which the government delivered an ultimatum to the red central council in the Ruhr. The reply was a general strike. Karl Severing, the federal and Prussian commissar of state for Westphalia, an old trade-union organizer of great originality and enormous energy, conducted the negotiations. An agreement was reached, but the Communists did not live up to it. Finally the *Reichswehr* put down the insurrection.

From April 7 to May 1 a Communist republic of people's commissars and councils existed in Munich; it was recognized also in Augsburg. Its rule was fantastic and arbitrary, a strange blend of high idealism and crude terrorism. Volunteers from Württemberg and *Reichswehr* troops succeeded in suppressing the Communist revolution in Bavaria after bloody fighting and deplorable excesses on both sides. In August Bavaria's legal government was able to return to the capital, Munich. Numerous Communist disturbances occurred in the Reich after this time, but the real danger of revolution was out of the way after the summer of 1919.

The National Assembly convened in Weimar. The spirit of Potsdam had been defeated and humiliated; it seemed destroyed for all time. Most of the German people clung to the spirit of Weimar in desperation, yet full of the unshakeable will to survive. For here there was still something left of the German past that yet remained erect, independent of the painful events of the times, and pointed to a happier future. The National Assembly performed two historical acts of far-reaching significance. It accepted the Treaty of Versailles, and it gave the German people the Weimar Constitution.

THE PEACE TREATY OF VERSAILLES

The peace was dictated by the victors, and it could not easily be lightened except in a few points of minor importance. The treaty signified the end of Emperor William's world policy; it stripped Germany of her navy and her overseas possessions. In addition it destroyed the most popular achievement of Bismarck's Reich by detaching from it the imperial province of Alsace-Lorraine. The idea of revenge had triumphed. French foreign policy had reason to rejoice, for it had attained its goal after decades of unremitting toil. Germany accepted the loss of the imperial province with comparative calm. She had had all too sad experiences with these obstinate borderlands, which now went over to the victor with flying banners. Although the German colonies had never been really popular, yet their complete loss, which was bound up with the collapse of the entire position overseas, proved a shattering experience. Even worse, Germany's boundaries were redrawn, more unfavourably than in the year 1815.

Prussia suffered most, since except for a few insignificant groups she lost all her non-German-speaking subjects. The borders affected by the treaty and the plebiscites called for in it were in northern Schleswig, Belgium, and Upper Silesia. In every case the changes were to the Germans' disadvantage. With a few slight exceptions all who belonged to the Weimar Republic came from German stocks, but across the new borders there lived tens of thousands of German-speaking people who were now attached to foreign states. There were substantial German minorities in both Poland and Czechoslo-

NS *North Schleswig*
D   *Danzig*
M   *Memelland*
US *Upper Silesia*
ST *South Tyrol*
S   *Saar*
E   *Eupen and Malmédy*
L   *Luxemburg*

Norway

Sweden

Finland

Soviet Union

Esthonia

Latvia

Lithuania

M

D

East
Prussia

Poland

Denmark

NS

Netherlands

Germany

Belgium

E

L

S

Czechoslovakia

US

France

Switzerland

ST

Austria

Hungary

Italy

Yugoslavia

THE
WEIMAR
REPUBLIC
and her neighbours
1919

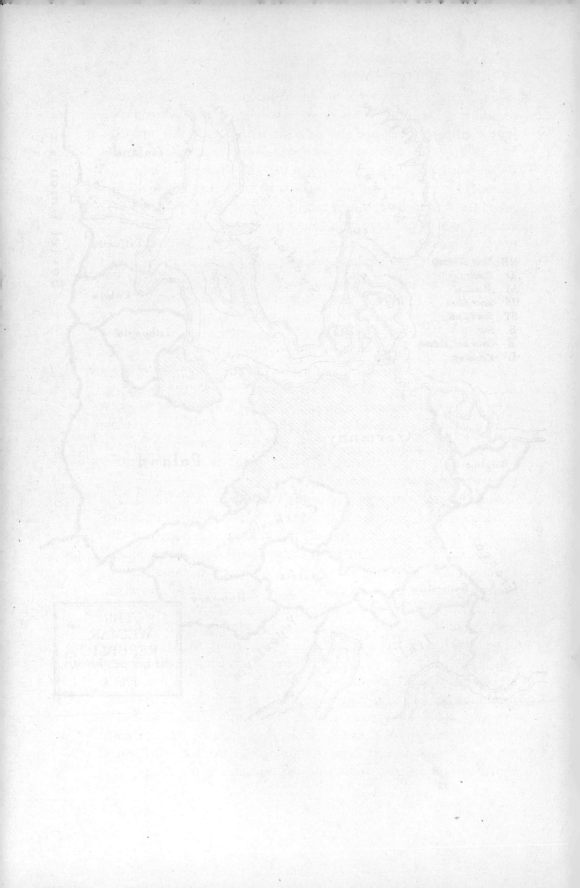

vakia. To right the wrong of the old partitions of Poland it was most certainly a European necessity to restore an independent Polish state. Germany herself had already taken a first step in this direction. But cutting off East Prussia from the main part of the Reich by the Polish Corridor, striking through to the sea, was a serious mistake. German Danzig was now once again a free city. It is true that Poles predominated in the population of the Corridor, but a solution acceptable to all could have been found here by effecting an exchange of population.

The political unity of Germany had been preserved, and this fact was essential for future development. Most Germans came to understand only very slowly that the complete shattering of German unity had been entirely within the possibilities. Very influential Frenchmen believed that the permanent occupation of the left bank of the Rhine was indispensable for the future safety of France. During the following years Rhenish separatists, with French support, made a number of attempts to erect the Rhineland into a buffer state between Germany and France, independent of both Prussia and Bavaria. Thus the old idea of a Rhenish Confederation was revived in a changed form. But the idea of German unity triumphed, and the occupation of the Rhineland by troops of the victorious countries was only temporary.

The demilitarization of the Rhineland had to be accepted. The restrictions as to the future armament of Germany were particularly bitter to a country of great warlike traditions such as Germany had been so far, under the leadership of Greater Prussia. In the classic land of compulsory military service the limitation of the army to a hundred thousand men proved ineffective. The victors had not taken into account that this very army, in which the chances for armament were under supervision, would become the nursery of a new science of war based on exhaustive technical organization. A militia, which was proposed again and again by German left-wing parties, would probably have been adequate for Germany's defensive needs, and it would not have served secret rearmament and the modernization of the army to the same extent. In spite of all controls there was being built up within the Weimar Republic a warrior state whose significance was to be just as great for foreign as for domestic policy. German anti-militarist circles sounded warnings against this impersonal *Blitzkrieg* machine in vain; their well-meant actions only exposed them to the suspicion of being unpatriotic and made them less and less able to further their aim, that of general disarmament throughout Europe.

THE FOUR ERRORS OF THE VICTORIOUS POWERS

Germany had lost the war. It was understandable that the peace terms were harsh. But even from the point of view of the victors several of these terms were also unwise. The Austro-Hungarian monarchy had now become a group of nationalistic states; as a result of the many shifts of population in eastern Europe these states necessarily inherited the mixture of nationalities of the Habsburg Empire without being able to balance this disadvantage by economic organization on a large enough scale. The most unfortunate of these new creations was the republic of Austria. Vienna, the old metropolis, mighty both in the Empire and in the world, had now only a small appendage of Alpine lands, German-speaking throughout, economically dependent on markets and sources of supply in what had become foreign lands. Nothing could seem more natural than to unite this region of the new Austria with the rest of Germany. Probably it could have been done successfully if Germany had acted at once in the general collapse of November 1918. An article in the Weimar Constitution provided for union with German Austria. The victors demanded its invalidation, and they also succeeded in forcing the Viennese government to drop the designation of "German" Austria. Union with Austria would have burdened the Reich with a number of problems that would have not have been easy to solve. Besides, the right-wing north German Protestants were not in favour of the increase that it threatened to effect in the Catholic element with a Slavic strain in Germany. But the majority in the Weimar Republic would have seen in union with Austria, an early *Anschluss,* the fulfilment of old German yearnings and a compensation for other losses.

The second mistake the victors made in the peace they dictated was the provision concerning the surrender and judgement of the so-called war criminals. The left wing in Germany was full of bitterness against those responsible for the war. This emotion might have become very fruitful politically if the demand of the victors had not now made martyrs of these men. A German patriot could condemn certain actions, particularly in Belgium, most severely, but even so he could not think it proper that the more or less guilty should be judged in a foreign court of justice belonging to a former enemy. With even greater strength every sentiment arose against passing sentence on the Emperor and his aides. Even the sternest judge could not say that these men had not acted in good faith for their fatherland. Whatever errors, neglect, or blunders they may have committed were subject to the judgement of history and to none other. There was no court, no judge. The article about war guilt was therefore meaningless; it could not be carried out. If a single article of a treaty cannot be carried out, the whole framework of the treaty begins to crumble.

The third error of the victorious countries concerned the question of reparations. The treaty itself named no fixed amount for the payments, because the statesmen of the Entente were unable to agree on any particular sum. On this point as well as others the English and the Americans tried to mitigate French severity. Lloyd George hoped that later on, when times were quieter, he might be able to settle on some reasonable figure with American help. This hope failed, because the United States did not ratify the treaty and therefore did not participate in subsequent negotiations. Even an inordinately high amount, once decided on, would have been better than the complete indefiniteness that led to years of bickering over German payments. The treaty obligations were couched in such general terms that their interpretation could be argued about end-lessly. A fixed sum would have provided a solid basis and would very probably have made it possible to arrive at tolerable economic and financial results within an endurable length of time.

The fourth error of the victors had to do with the League of Na-tions. The Covenant of the League had been written into the peace treaty. The League was to supervise the plebiscites in the German border regions and assign mandates for the administration of Ger-many's former overseas possessions; it was entrusted with Danzig and the Memel and Saar regions. The philosophical, legal, and po-litical development of the League concept had been materially fur-thered by leaders of German thought. Official Germany now ac-cepted the principles of the west European and American constitutional state, ideologically carried further by the League of Nations. Yet Germany was not a member of the League. She had no chance to express her wishes in a quarter that was concerned with her most vital interests, her whole future position in Europe. Germany was no longer a world power—that was the upshot of her defeat in the imperialistic World War. But she remained a great power in Europe. She had at her disposal the strongest concentration of economic strength, the most priceless cultural treasures, in central Europe. She was surrounded by a number of smaller neighbours to whose welfare she meant much in any event. And this great country, whose best men were labouring for her political rejuvenation and spiritual renewal, now saw herself shut out of the company of the League of Nations. She had to wait at the door until it was seen fit to admit her. This state of affairs had two undesirable results. The League was a sort of bailiff to see that the terms of the treaty were carried out, and all the hatred and bitterness brought forth by the treaty turned against the League with special force, since it not only failed to prevent such conditions of existence for a great people, but even aggravated them.

The peace treaty based the demand for reparations on the statement that Germany and her allies, as the aggressors, had started the war. But the note addressed to the German government in transmitting the treaty went even further and spoke of Germany's sole guilt for the war. It was only natural that the German government and German public opinion, politicians as well as scholars, should resent this superficial disposal of a problem that could be solved only by historical research on the basis of official documents. In the almost endless discussions that followed, moralizing was mingled in a peculiarly painful fashion with legal and political considerations. Many Germans hoped that, if what they called the lie of war guilt were once refuted, the entire peace treaty would collapse. Politically, to be sure, the treaty was not based on more or less controversial interpretations of history, but on the fact of a clear-cut military victory over Germany and her allies.

The peace treaty was accepted only under the greatest pressure. Scheidemann, the President of the Ministry, retired. The Democratic Party left the government coalition. Finally the Centre, primarily under Erzberger's influence, and the Majority Social Democrats were responsible for accepting and signing the treaty. If it had not been accepted, the victorious countries would have been in something of a quandary. They were entirely capable, however, of occupying large areas of Germany and administering them by force, and an improvement in Germany's situation would have been improbable. Possibly the Communist revolution would have blazed up afresh. France would have revived her claims to the left bank of the Rhine. Germany might very easily have been broken apart in the process, and it would have been all the harder to make a fresh start. One thing, however, was certain: the majority in the National Assembly, in spite of all their apologies, had the air of being heavily weighed down by having accepted a peace treaty that not only was spiritually humiliating, but that also could be no more than partially carried out in detail.

THE WEIMAR CONSTITUTION

The spiritual father of the Weimar Constitution was Professor Hugo Preuss, the well-known jurist, but his two main ideas were not realized. He wanted a centralized state, with Prussia dissolved into her historical components and the other individual states developed into bodies capable of administering themselves. The Reich was to make all decisions, even down to municipal elections. This new Reich was to be based in every respect on the national consciousness of a self-directing people; it was to be democratic, centralized, and parliamentarian. A storm of objections arose against this fundamental view of Preuss's, patterned on the institutions of western Europe. It became evident that German particularism had not disappeared with the princes and their courts. A new and extraordinary form of particularism emerged, with separate parliaments, local dignitaries, officials and gentry, coteries and cliques. Although there was hardly an instance in which the individual states still showed the old tribal character, they still laid claim even to these old and venerable interests. The astonishing fact emerged that in so artificial a dynastic structure as Baden, for instance, a new kind of local patriotic spirit had developed; and it now took over the heritage of the lost dynasty with obstinate self-confidence. In Prussia, of course, all the old conservative forces of the east, in the name of true Prussianism, undertook the fight against the break-

ing-up that threatened. The individual states survived, with limited
authority, but with their own parliaments and governments. Half of
all the Prussian votes in the council of the Reich were given to the
provinces and the other half retained by the state government, so
that the Prussian annexations of earlier times were in a sense counterbalanced by giving the annexed territories a sort of autonomy.
The government of the Reich and the Prussian government now
existed side by side in the same capital, Berlin. Both were on
a parliamentary basis and possessed a fully developed bureaucratic
structure, though the Prussian state had no president; it would have
been preposterous to institute such an office in addition to that of the
president of the Reich. The president of the Prussian ministry,
elected by the Prussian parliament, was at the head of affairs for that
part of Germany. There was also a Prussian council of state, which
represented the interests of the provinces; it was modelled on the
council of the Reich. The constitutional setting-off of Prussia from
the Reich, which Bismarck had wisely avoided, led to all sorts of
administrative difficulties. Here indeed was the weakest point in the
new order; do what it would, the council of the Reich was unable
to cope with the difficulty. This council under the Weimar Constitution was a revival of Bismarck's federal council. It did not provide
parliamentary representation like a Senate, but was a bureaucratic
body that naturally leaned toward particularism and red tape. The
democratic principle of referendum was introduced by provisions for
the optional referendum, on the initiative of the voters, and for the
statutory referendum, on the initiative of the government. A temporary dictatorship was provided for extraordinary emergencies (Article 48). The parts of the Weimar Constitution dealing with community life, religion, education, and schools were ample and wisely
formulated. The law in regard to officials was drawn up with special
care. The whole document was only slightly social-minded. It provided for the introduction of workers' councils and emphasized the
freedom to form associations, social welfare, and a minimum of
social rights for workers. The principles of private property and the
right of inheritance were recognized; control of wages, taxation, and
supervision were entrusted to the state; entails were to be done away
with. No one could detect in these cautious measures a revolutionary
attack on the existing order of society or on property ownership.

The Weimar Constitution was therefore thoroughly bourgeois in character. It attempted to set up a German constitutional people's state that would correspond to German needs and wishes. It imitated neither the English nor the French constitution, but was the fruit of old German views of public law and of German political sentiment. It was not the product of an inspired moment and the creative power of a practical statesman, like Bismarck's constitution for the North German Federation. It showed plainly that it had originated in an emergency and both wanted to and had to reckon with a variety of needs and wishes. Even in its final form it was still somewhat patchy, because it arose from the effort to build a dwelling place for the new Germany and to make the start not too difficult for people of any sort of convictions. This very human and tolerant spirit spoke well for the mature academic culture of its authors. The fact that they were thoroughly acquainted with Swiss and American public law and held the movement of the Church of St. Paul in vivid memory enabled them to carry through a labour that will always hold an honourable place in the history of constitutions.

Such was the Little Germany that was to take the place of the former Reich, which had been under the wing of Greater Prussia. This Little Germany, shorn of all alien elements, again made the effort to forge German particularism solidly together at this crucial time when Germany had lost her world position. On the basis of this Little Germany, which was anti-revolutionary but ready for re- form, Prussia, Bavaria, and the smaller states, finally perhaps Austria, were to be won over. Thus at the very instant when it was perfected, the concept of a Little Germany shifted to that of a Greater Ger- many. The most distinguished representatives of the Weimar idea, the leaders of the responsible parties, fought the tradition of a Greater Prussia in order to realize the proud dream of a Greater Germany.

The Centre represented the best old German areas in Westphalia, along the Rhine, and in southern Germany. The Democrats repre- sented the neighbouring Protestant regions, particularly in Swabia and Franconia, and the spirit of the imperial cities. The Majority Social Democrats represented the settled labour force of the great industrial regions and of the large cities; they were strong across all of northern Germany and over to the east. So, oddly enough, the

Reich of the Weimar Republic revived the old Reich that had its roots in western Germany and struggled with the east German colonial regions. The obstinate resistance of Bavarian leaders was also reminiscent of experiences in the Germany of long ago. The Weimar Republic had to deal with twofold opposition — from the right and from the left.

LEFT-WING OPPOSITION

In the very first new Reichstag, elected in 1920, the parties of the Weimar Coalition no longer controlled a majority. This fact gave the German People's Party a key position that ensured its balance of power for the entire following period. The old National Liberals of 1914 would never have gone hand in hand with socialists. The black-white-and-red members of the People's Party now joined with the Weimar parties to form the so-called Great Coalition and thus made further practical co-operation possible. Such a combination served to strengthen the revisionist spirit of the Majority Social Democrats; they drifted farther and farther from Marxism and became a democratic workers' party built up on a trade-union basis. The whole movement was a little dull, stodgy and bureaucratic in style, uninventive and without distinguished leadership, resignedly despairing of the socialization of private enterprise.

The Independent Social Democrats also could not avoid the transformation in the bourgeois direction that current conditions and the tactical situation seemed to call for. In 1922 the great majority of the Independents returned to the parent stock of the old party. Only a small group under Ledebour kept to itself. The Great Coalition did not last long, but minority cabinets of the bourgeois parties that were tolerated and given practical support by the Social Democrats actually played the role of a Great Coalition in disguise.

The proceedings of the Social Democrats can be understood only in the light of their increasing hostility toward the Communists. In 1921 the United Communist Party of Germany, whose ranks were swelled by a number of converts from the Independents, entered the Third International. The new revolts in central Germany that occurred during this year corresponded to Moscow's current program of world revolution. The German opponents of Leninism united to form the Communist Workers' Association, without apparent success. The mounting economic crisis advanced Communist agitation. In Saxony and in the new state of Thuringia, which was made up of several former petty principalities, Communists entered the government and thus worked in official positions for the social revolution. In 1923 new Communist outbreaks had to be forcibly suppressed by the government of the Reich.

This was the last time in the history of the Weimar Republic that Communism had any chance of achieving even local success. During the years of economic prosperity the Communist Party lost so many of its adherents and so much of its significance, while revolutionary enthusiasm lagged to such a degree, that a new group split off and formed the Lenin Association, which conducted its opposition to the main party according to instructions from Moscow. The Weimar Republic felt that it was strong enough to tolerate the activities of this disunited and largely theoretical German Communism, which was doubtless underestimated. Communism very cleverly addressed itself to the young intellectuals, awakened in them a naïve idealism about freedom and culture, condemned all tradition as Philistine and romantic nonsense, and managed to corrode broad strata of liberalism and democracy by propaganda through Communist cells at a personal and all too human level. The actual material superiority of the leadership of the Reich as against Communism rests on the simple fact that the *Reichswehr* could be used against any variety of left-wing opposition without difficulty. Toward right-wing opposition this instrument could not be equally trusted. Thus it was that right-wing opposition grew until it was a menace to the very life of the republic.

RIGHT-WING OPPOSITION. THE KAPP PUTSCH

Right-wing counter-revolution aimed three principal blows at the Weimar Republic: the Kapp *Putsch* (1920), the Munich *Putsch* (1923), and the reorganization of 1933. The first was a purely German Nationalist action; the second rested on a coalition of German Nationalist and National Socialist elements; the third was wholly National Socialist and led to victory. The aim of all these strivings was to destroy the work of the November Revolution. The actions

593

directed against the Weimar Republic deliberately confused the two processes that had gone on in the winter of 1918–9. A democratic reform movement had occurred simultaneously with a Communist revolutionary movement. Only because the democratic reform movement was successful in the face of the collapse of the old powers, and only because it had carried on the struggle against Communism with the full impact of the power of the state, had the traditional social order been preserved. The Weimar Republic had solved a dual problem. It signified a synthesis of revolution and counter-revolution. If anyone is to be credited with having banished the danger of Communism in Germany, it is the leaders of the Weimar Republic. These leaders of civilian life and leaders of the *Reichswehr* joined hands and gave their union full effect. Then what was it that the constantly increasing right-wing opposition really wanted?

The Kapp *Putsch* was a badly prepared enterprise of several reactionary politicians and generals. The leading parts were played by the *Generallandschaftsdirektor* Wolfgang Kapp, a leading German Nationalist and high official of the East Prussian provincial government, the not very intelligent son of the well-known German-American Friedrich Kapp, and by the ambitious desk general Baron von Lüttwitz. The movement was intended to prevent the carrying out of the Treaty of Versailles and to stop disarmament. The leaders had the Crown Prince in mind as a presidential candidate. The legitimate government of the Reich was declared deposed, and Kapp designated himself chancellor of the Reich. In this way or some other the group hoped to bring about the speedy restoration of a black-white-and-red Germany. These adventurers were indifferent to the fact that they were dragging Germany to the very verge of civil war and involving her in international difficulties. Kapp and Lüttwitz even presumed to dissolve legally constituted parliamentary bodies. But the Weimar Republic defended itself bravely. The German National People's Party officially disowned the enterprise. A number of mediators volunteered and tried to prevent bloodshed. The *Putsch* collapsed, and the ringleaders fled. Court examination of eight hundred and fifty officers and officials was soon dropped in most cases. The less important culprits were granted amnesty; the more important were given very light sentences. Lüttwitz later had the impudence to sue for the full payment of his general's pension, including the period covered by the *Putsch*—and he received it.

VEHMIC MURDERS. SECRET ASSOCIATIONS. BAVARIA AS THE NUCLEUS OF THE NEW ORDER

The discharge of the soldiery—the *Soldateska* (mercenaries), as it was called after the Thirty Years' War—was difficult this time too. Not all deserving officers could be taken over into the new Reichswehr. The youngest and most capable were chosen for this distinction. Many others joined the police force, which in this way acquired an undesirable tinge of militarism. Among the many discontented infantry soldiers in the post-war period the most conspicuous were the so-called *Baltikumer,* a group that had served in the Baltic border states. There they had become accustomed to all manner of semi-Russian methods, along with feudal and anti-Semitic sympathies and a rough way of dealing with foreign minorities. These foot-soldiers were well liked in the eastern Prussian provinces, and they volunteered their services at the plebiscites in East Prussia and Upper Silesia. Communists and Poles made work for them. Patriotism, a taste for brawls, a spirit of adventure, and resistance toward the constitutional state all worked together.

Former officers now formed the secret association called Consul, members of which murdered Matthias Erzberger, the Reich minister, in the Black Forest (1921). Erzberger was widely hated for having urged Germany's signing of the peace treaty. As Minister of Finance he had organized a strong financial administration, but he had many foes because of his nepotism and officiousness. A libel suit led to an exposé, and Erzberger resigned his office. His chief enemy was the highly qualified Karl Helfferich, who had been Secretary of State for the treasury for some years during the war. Helfferich came from a patrician family of the Palatinate. His consuming ambition and the supersensitiveness of the disappointed monarchist fanned his hatred for the Swabian upstart who had deftly managed to profit from the revolution. Personal and political motives were curiously blended in the duel between Helfferich and Erzberger, and it was hardly astonishing that many of the younger generation were repelled by all these filthy machinations and base passions. The death of Erzberger meant the loss of one of the most gifted champions of the Weimar Republic, democracy, and international conciliation. He was a victim of the fanaticism of the troopers.

After a scant year, on June 24, 1922, Walther Rathenau, the Minister of Foreign Affairs, was murdered on a street in a Berlin suburb by members of the same circle. Rathenau, who had always proudly avowed the fact of his Jewishness, was one of the most cultivated men of the time. Even in his youth he had been admired and influential. He had come into contact with leaders in economics, literature, and art. In private life he was a connoisseur and a collector. From the beginning of the war he had come into greater and greater prominence, and his activities sprang from a patriotism that was at once aristocratic and progressive. He deserves high credit for his great practical services as Minister of Reconstruction. His suave mastery of phrase and his international connections marked him out for the Ministry of Foreign Affairs, a post that his insatiable personal ambition demanded as his just due. Now this peculiarly strong personality was wiped out of German public life, and the republic had to look to its own safety. None of the dignitaries of the defeated and collapsed monarchy had been harassed or hounded personally; there had been no political prosecution of them, no attempts on their lives. Now assaults on the republicans came crowding on each other. In the course of the year there occurred many less conspicuous Vehmic murders—assassinations popularly described by this phrase in allusion to secret processes of the late Middle Ages. The President of the Reich issued decrees for the protection of the republic. The Reichstag passed a law with the same object; now the authorities could take at least partially effective measures against the sinister machinations of the right wing.

But Bavaria obstinately resisted the emergency decrees. In Bismarck's Reich Bavaria had been forced to keep her displeasure within certain bounds set by Catholic, court, and foreign-policy interests. But Bavarian particularism felt that it could allow itself free rein in the Weimar Republic. The *Forstrat* (Forest Commissioner) Karl Escherich of Munich, a man of considerable local reputation, had formed in 1919 a patriotic association that soon spread over Germany and Austria under the name of Orgesch (Organisation Escherich); its aim was to combat Bolshevism. At first it brought together the most diverse counter-revolutionary elements; certain forms of self-arming and self-defence were tried out in it. The Prussian minister Karl Severing, a Social Democrat, prohibited the Orgesch in Prussia, because he recognized its anti-republican character. Now the organization took a great spurt in Bavaria.

Bavaria regarded herself as the nucleus of a new order in the general German and even central European chaos and again felt a political vocation. Notwithstanding the objections of the authorities of the Reich there were armed citizen guards in Bavaria until an ultimatum from the victorious powers put a stop to them, at least to all appearances. To play the part of the martyr to wicked foreign powers was particularly flattering to Bavarian vanity. Bavaria did not dream of protecting the despised republic; rather she did everything possible to deprive it of all public respect. In lieu of the law for the protection of the republic that she had rejected, Bavaria issued a special decree. An agreement was not reached until after tedious negotiations between Bavaria and the Reich, which were conducted as if between two hostile powers of equal status. Bavaria extorted a series of new advantages in favour of right-wing organizations; they reduced the influence of the Reich to a minimum in her territory. This atmosphere nourished a movement that proceeded from Munich and began its triumphal march through Germany, through Europe, through the world—National Socialism.

THE NATIONAL SOCIALIST GERMAN WORKERS' PARTY

In January 1919 an obscure Munich writer by the name of Harrer founded the German Workers' Party. Member Number 7 was an unemployed Upper Austrian journeyman who had fought in the war on the side of the German Reich, with the rank of corporal. His name was Adolf Hitler. His unusual gifts as a popular speaker gave a strong impulse to the party. There were in fact numerous other groups of similar tendencies. True, the *Deutschvölkische Trutzbund* was dissolved after the murder of Rathenau, but new secret organizations were formed, such as the *Deutsche Kämpferbund,* the *Oberland* group, and the *Reichskriegsflagge* group. All these had in common the struggle against the Weimar Constitution, against the peace treaty which it supported, against parliamentarism and the constitutional state, against centralization, against Berlin, against plutocracy, against the Jews.

In 1922 several deputies left the German National People's Party and founded the *Deutschvölkische Freiheitspartei,* which revived Stöcker's anti-Semitism and had as its goal a class state with a certain socialized trend. The German people was to be reborn with the help of a dictator and by means of power politics. Adolf Hitler now combined his group with this parliamentary representation of political and social anti-Semitism. Since 1921 Hitler had been the chairman of his group and had renamed it the National Socialist Party. The new joint creation was first called the National Socialist Liberation Party and then by its definitive name of National Socialist German Workers' Party. Diagnostic of this development was the fading-out of the idea of freedom and the quickening of the two antagonistic impulses that were quite in the mode of the old National Social Association: nationalism and the class interests of the workers. The mounting success of National Socialism was due to broad developments in Germany in foreign policy and economics.

REPARATIONS. RAPALLO. THE RUHR OCCUPATION

Several conferences were held in the attempt to settle the matter of reparations. Since the United States had not ratified the Treaty of Versailles, she did not take part in these negotiations or form the projected protective alliance with England and France to maintain the new boundaries. As a result the political leaders of France became more and more fearful lest these boundaries be endangered by a strengthened Germany. Thus the question of reparations was bound up with that of security. French policy launched sweeping diplomatic activity in Europe for the purpose of isolating Germany. France drew all the newly formed states—above all Poland, Czechoslovakia, and Yugoslavia—into her circle of interests. Most important of all, of course, was her constant co-operation with Great Britain. During the first few years this worked very well, but it became increasingly difficult because of the harsh methods that France employed, while England neither used nor approved them. As early as 1920 the French occupied the Rhine region as a sanction measure.

New invasion threats forced Germany to further concessions. The Reich had to request a moratorium on several occasions.

The currency depreciation, which was becoming worse, showed how profoundly economic relationships had been upset in central Europe. Germany had no more international credit; she was unable to obtain foreign exchange or other gold values for her payments. A world economic conference in Genoa in 1921 was supposed to straighten out these relationships from the vantage point of a wider view, but it closed without having accomplished anything. Germany, however, demonstrated that she still had backing in the east by the treaty she made with Soviet Russia in Rapallo at that time. The Peace of Versailles had cancelled the treaties made between Germany and Russia during the World War. Now both powers declared all the mutual claims of the past null and void. Russia promised not to indemnify any other state for damages. Diplomatic relations were resumed, and commercial relations were to be regulated in a friendly way on the principle of the most favoured nation. The Treaty of Rapallo initiated a fruitful period of co-operation between Germany and Russia, not only economically but in foreign policy as well—to the annoyance of the western powers and with significant effects at home also. German left-wing opposition detected a contradiction between the Rapallo policy and the suppression of Communist disturbances in Germany, while to the right-wing opposition Rapallo seemed the beginning of Bolshevism in the fatherland.

The only way to stabilize German currency, and thus to make relationships in Europe wholesome, was to define the extent of German reparations as soon as possible. Provisional arrangements, ultimatums, and half-way solutions followed each other in a whirl. There were more and more conferences, discussions, expert opinions, and proposals for a *modus vivendi*. The strife over the policy of fulfilment divided the German people. Some wanted Germany's obligations to be fulfilled up to the limits of possibility; by their goodwill they wanted to show what the objective limits of fulfilment were. Others believed that they could wear down their opponents by mulish failure to fulfil. The peace treaty was in any case a law of the German Reich. Fulfillers and non-fulfillers fell into the way of calling one another law-breakers and traitors to the fatherland.

Wilhelm Cuno, the Chancellor, was very close to the right-wing parties. As director of the Hamburg-America Line he represented big business, and because of his wide experience he was expected to perform the miracle of finding a satisfactory solution—but in vain. It was no longer possible to undo the snarl by sheer goodwill, integrity of purpose, and technical skill. On both sides factors of power politics spoiled the chances of coming to an understanding. Authoritative circles in Germany could not contemplate an economic prejudice to the Reich that might prove mortal; they preferred to drift farther and farther into inflation. But France did not want to be cheated of her claims and was determined to prevent, with all the means at her disposal, any rapid recovery in Germany. Thus there came about the post-war event that was to have the gravest consequences: the occupation of the Ruhr Valley by France and Belgium.

In order to guard their claims, in consideration of non-payment of amounts due, the two powers sent a commission of engineers, with troops for their protection, into the Ruhr Valley. The coal mines there were now worked on the account of these two powers under the supervision of foreigners with bayonets. English crown lawyers termed the proceeding an infraction of the Treaty of Versailles; the English government, however, confined itself to an attitude of neutral reserve. In Germany the event had a concussive impact. After four years of war, after the acceptance of a harsh treaty with some terms that could not possibly be complied with, the Reich had to submit to an act of violence all the more insolent because it employed the means of formal legal proof to hide the real political motives. The French also occupied parts of Baden and Hesse for sanction purposes. The United States expressed her disapproval by withdrawing her army of occupation from the Rhineland. Germany put up a passive resistance in the Ruhr Valley; this cost many lives and damaged the economy to the extent of some four billion gold marks. The international tension was acute, and there were innumerable offers of mediation and attempts at it. The western powers were entangled in heated arguments. By the end of September 1923 German passive resistance had to be given up. This was the darkest hour of the post-war period. Left-wing and right-wing opposition threatened the Weimar Republic. A state of emergency had to be declared. At this time a deputy of the People's Party, Gustav Stresemann (died

1929) came to the fore, first as Chancellor for the Great Coalition, then as Minister of Foreign Affairs.

STRESEMANN. THE CONSEQUENCES OF INFLATION

Gustav Stresemann had always belonged to the left wing of his party. The only reason why the men of the new Democratic Party had not wanted to take him in was that they could not forgive him for having called for annexations during the war. These scruples avenged themselves. Stresemann would have been less of a problem to the party if he had been inside it instead of outside. Only Stresemann gave the German People's Party, the former National Liberals, such driving power that they were able to assert themselves increasingly against the Democrats and even to outstrip them. Stresemann was an indefatigable worker, an incomparably resilient nature, tactically resourceful, a speaker whose power and brilliance sought out difficulties with almost a sportsman's delight, for the sake of surmounting them. Coming of a family in modest circumstances, he had worked his way up as a shrewd businessman and a clever representative of industrial organizations. His wife, well versed in the ways of the world, had assisted his rise. The Weimar Republic was oversupplied with bachelors and widowers or men whose wives did not look beyond their own four walls. Stresemann had a helpmate of unusual social gifts.

Although he was extremely clever, Stresemann always had an easy, jovial air, a trace of the indomitable liveliness of the middle-class Berliner and a trace also of the talented student who disposes of the ultimate riddles of the world over a mug of beer. To the extent that he derived from the movement of the Church of St. Paul, serious literature was an essential need to him; the life of the mind inspired and exalted him. He could not forgo intellectual concerns and returned to them eagerly after the hardest day's work. This explains the remarkable spectacle that was now presented to Germany and the world. Stresemann, who seemed to be merely a hard-headed successful businessman, attained great historical stature. The Benjamin of the old National Liberal Party accomplished what a Bennigsen and a Bassermann had failed to achieve: the conduct of the affairs of the Reich in the spirit of patriotism on behalf of unity. It was vouchsafed to Stresemann to concentrate the inner forces of the nation on new and fruitful work, maintain Germany as a great power in Europe, and regain for the Reich a position that commanded respect abroad.

The inflation assumed the most fantastic forms. The exchange rate shot to astronomical heights. German economic leaders succeeded in making the most valuable German properties invisible and intangible. Wages and salaries did not rise in proportion to the rise in the cost of living. Low production costs made possible the cheap manufacture of goods of permanent value. There was sham prosperity. Heated and ugly contention to guard the last remainder of fortunes confused the people. There was a complete reversal of the nature and the concept of property. Sharp dealers accumulated enormous possessions in a short time. The honest capitalists of yesterday sold off the best they had, dazzled by the seductive power of millions and even billions. From a purely technical point of view stabilization, which finally made the new gold mark equal to a billion paper marks, could have been effected earlier with a more reasonable economic relationship between the new currency and the old. Right-wing and left-wing leaders took the credit of creating the *Rentenmark*.

Inflation had a technical aspect as well as one that bore on foreign policy; the psychological and sociological consequences were even more important. Inflation dealt the pyramid of German society a shock that had not been anticipated by any Marxian or other socialist or communist theories. Imperial Germany had produced a new class structure. Germany had upper, middle, and lower strata of a new sort, and each of these in turn was divided up into classes. Inflation had a crucial effect on all these strata: it split them up. In the top layer the agrarians and the industrial capitalists held firmest; commercial capitalists suffered. The fortunes of stockholders, of younger sons and of women of wealthy families, were largely wiped out. The aristocratic officer and official, the high judge, or the patrician university professor was suddenly impoverished in comparison with his cousin who owned a factory or a large agricultural estate.

In the middle layer there was an analogous situation, but with bitterer consequences. Anyone who ran a store or a workshop could keep afloat. Many medium-sized enterprises were even able to exploit favourable circumstances for expansion and for the technical perfecting of their equipment. But anyone who had made the good conservative investments that every sound bank recommended and with which every reliable legal adviser was accustomed to dealing, anyone who had disposed of older assets in favour of war bonds, saw his modest inherited fortune or the fruit of a lifetime's hard work destroyed at one blow. The big capitalist had regarded war bonds as a sort of inescapable tax; after the loss of the war he wrote off this loss, too, in a businesslike fashion. But the middle-class man, the saver, could not accept the situation so simply. Anyone who was young and had his health could make a new beginning, but the more mature, who suffered personal sorrows in the war, responded to this new affliction with bitterness and indignation. Capital accumulated by saving occasions more apprehensions and worries than speculative capital. Employees, workers, and petty officials were lucky if they had turned their modest hoard into a little house, for the storm of inflation did not touch real estate appreciably. But many such had put their savings into insurance; others of them had laid by a little money to educate their children, or for rainy days of old age or illness, or perhaps even for a trip to a spa, a dowry, or some other good purpose that was in keeping with the bourgeois instincts of the German factory hand. Such savings were all swept away, and whatever was recovered in the revaluation was a mockery except as concerned mortgages. As a result of the splitting-up process all classes in Germany included some who had gained and some who had lost, the fortunate and the unfortunate.

Class hatred and envy now existed at the same social level, within families, and among friends. This situation reacted materially on party life. The déclassés of the upper layer did not wish to become proletarians. They carried their claims on life and their social arrogance with them into an unaccustomed routine of hard labour and irritating struggles. They were in a position similar to that of the soldiers in the post-war period. Was it astonishing that they injected their hatred and disappointment likewise into politics? Who was guilty? Which were the profiteers? It was said that the Jews had suffered very little from the inflation. This was quite untrue. But of course it was true that many Jewish businessmen, just like many Christian businessmen, had taken precautions betimes and thus had limited their losses. Offensive pushing Jews, such as Barnat and Kutisker, did great harm. Nevertheless the most successful profiteer of the day was not a Jew, but Hugo Stinnes (1870–1924). No matter—the déclassés learned to value anti-Semitism as the handiest and simplest lightning-rod. A similar situation existed among the middle and lower layers with some significant differences. Certain of the more modest university teachers turned to Communism; they were impelled at least as much by their general view of the world as by political motives. Young workers gladly turned toward the left. The sober craftsman, in spite of all disappointments, deserted Social Democracy only reluctantly.

The impoverished bourgeois, the unemployed journeyman, the moderately gifted second-rate artist, the small store-keeper who could not compete with the big department stores, the poorly paid schoolmaster or railroad employee who received neither higher pay nor promotion, women employees—who were often the daughters of government officials, clergymen, or physicians and who had to work hard without prospects of marriage—all these found solace and hope in National Socialism.

HITLER'S ATTEMPT TO LAUNCH A NATIONAL REVOLUTION

In the autumn of 1923 Adolf Hitler took advantage of the serious embarrassments of the government of the Reich to attempt a "national revolution" on the night of the 8th of November. All the enemies of the Weimar Republic co-operated in it: the déclassés and the unfortunates, the veterans and the particularists. General Ludendorff, who, under the influence of his fanatical wife, Mathilde von Kemnitz, had stubbornly devoted himself to anti-Christian political labours, represented the extreme nationalist *Völkischen* (members of the *Deutschvölkische Freiheitspartei*), the anti-parliamentary and anti-Semitic group advocating violent power politics. General von Lossow represented the German Nationalists. The government had removed this general from his post as commander of the Bavarian army district for insubordination, but the Bavarian government had made him commander of Bavaria. Gustav von Kahr, the President of the Bavarian Ministry, who was now temporary dictator of Bavaria as general commissar, represented Bavarian particularism. Hitler, finally, typified the proletarianized petty bourgeoisie of National Socialism. The break between Bavaria and the Reich was to be utilized to set up a patriotic directory. The Bavarian government regarded itself as trustee for the German people; it wanted to bind the *Reichswehr* to it and thus to lead the movement to its goal.

In the beer-cellar of the Bürgerbräu in Munich Hitler declared the government of the Reich deposed. But the *Putsch* foundered. Kahr evidently feared that he would not be able to assert Bavaria's particular interests sufficiently against Hitler and Ludendorff. In spite of solemn oaths he left Hitler in the lurch, betrayed the plan, and informed the police; the *Reichswehr* turned against the *Putsch* leaders. The enterprise went dismally awry. The procession of *Putsch* members to the *Feldherrnhalle* was broken up, and more than a dozen of them fell, to become the martyrs of National Socialism. Hitler and Ludendorff had to answer to charges of high treason. Ludendorff was acquitted; Hitler was sentenced to five years' confinement in a fortress—but on probation, so that he was free again after half a year. Kahr and Lossow resigned. Lossow, the audacious conspirator, drew his substantial general's pension for the rest of his days. Kahr, the jovial double-dealer, was murdered by the National Socialists in 1934; revenge did not spare him, though he was a man of more than seventy at the time. In February 1924 the state of siege in Bavaria was lifted. The conflict between Bavaria and the Reich was set aside for the time being. The Weimar Republic dealt thus gently with its mortal enemies. Was it a sign of weakness or of strength? Was it insight or blindness?

REALIGNMENT OF PARTIES. HINDENBURG (1847–1934) ELECTED PRESIDENT OF THE REICH (1925)

The history of the Weimar Republic divides into three periods. That of building up extended to the beginning of 1924; the period of ascendancy lasted until 1930; the period of disintegration ended in 1933. The new German form of state had victoriously maintained itself against Communist and right-wing attacks; it had saved Germany from the threat of ruin. It could now take the path that led to economic reconstruction, to revision of the peace treaty, and to regaining the Reich's position as a European power. All thinking patriots were unanimous as to the necessity of these objectives. But the foes of the Weimar Republic continued their work. They were resolved to prevent at all costs the rebirth of Germany that was in process with the methods of a constitutional state governed by a parliament. The monarchists, the *Völkischen,* the Junkers, the agrarians and big industrialists, the déclassés, the impoverished members of the middle class, the petty bourgeois who had become proletarianized—all these hated the republic. Every one of these groups had its own definite grounds and goals. For the time being, they were united only by their rejection of the republic.

The splitting up of social classes that was effected by the inflation was clearly reflected in the realignment of parties. It happened that the main body of adherents of the Weimar Coalition suffered particularly from the inflation. Many Democrats strayed over to the German People's Party or to Social Democracy. Young Social Democrats became Communists or National Socialists. Conservative Catholics left the Centre; they found kindred spirits among the German Nationalists and met many apostates from the People's Party among them as well. The Democratic Party was especially afflicted by the increase in anti-Semitism, for it had the reputation of being especially popular among the Jews. This was only partially true, however; many orthodox Jews supported the Centre. Groups of highly educated younger Jews were conservatively inclined by reason of cultural considerations and sought connections both intellectual and social with the right wing. Many were members of the German People's Party, and also of the German National People's Party as long as they were tolerated in it. Others, to be sure, swung sharply toward the left. It was characteristic of the German Jews, as a matter of fact, that they participated in the development of all parties and social strata and thus sacrificed the power of resistance that a unified ethnical and religious minority might have had. Zionism had only a few adherents, but those few were zealous. The idea of assimilation was far more prevalent; for both historical and psychological reasons it could not have been otherwise in Germany.

The weakening of the parties of the Weimar Coalition expressed itself in a turn of the government of the Reich toward the right. The Centre was of course able to maintain its traditional key position. It supplied most of the chancellors: Konstantin Fehrenbach, Joseph Wirth, Wilhelm Marx (four times), and finally Heinrich Brüning. The first two represented the patriotism toward the Reich that existed in the southwest of the Alemannic Austrian Breisgau, which was especially important for the Weimar Republic in its quarrels with Bavaria. Fehrenbach was an average provincial lawyer with some business ability, but Joseph Wirth was a brilliant speaker and moreover a first-rate budgetary expert. With an alert instinct for politics he recognized more clearly than anyone else the necessity of fighting the foes of the republic. But his saying, "The foe is on the right," was just what ruled him out of the party reorientation that began in 1924.

In Bismarck's Reich the Junkers had always known how to keep hold of Prussia and thus had controlled the affairs of the Reich. The reverse now came to pass in the Weimar Republic. The new right-wing parties tried to gain the power in the Reich. If this plan had succeeded, the former states (*Länder*), with "red"-ruled Prussia in the van as the greatest, could not have resisted further. The aims of the German Nationalists could be attained only from the vantage point of the Reich. These aims were the restoration of the monarchy, armament, and the paralysing of parliamentarism. The German Nationalists expected the *Völkischen* and the National Socialists to help them toward these ends, and they held out the prospect of reward. But monarchism, and in particular its innermost core the still intact Junker class, wanted to keep the helm.

Friedrich Ebert, the President of the Reich, had never been elected in accordance with the provisions of the constitution. It had seemed preferable to extend his authority by vote of the Reichstag. This first President of the Reich was characterized by tact and dignity, by deliberation and pleasure in ironing out disagreements. His was not a dazzling personality. He performed the duties of his distinguished office as a conscientious observer, joylessly and without illusions, prematurely exhausted by aspersions and calumnies. Ebert died suddenly in February 1925, following an operation. The right-wing opposition saw a great possibility before it. After weighing many pros and cons it selected Field Marshal von Hindenburg as its candidate. No other candidate stood a chance against a name of such almost legendary prestige. Wilhelm Marx, the able Rhenish jurist, who was the choice of the parties of the Weimar Coalition, also suffered for his Catholicism; loyal republicans in Saxony, for instance, turned against him out of misdirected Protestant motives. Hindenburg was regarded as holding the place of the monarchy. Was it to be a liberal popular monarchy, or was right-wing reaction already in preparation? Those who had feudal, militaristic, or armament interests thought their time had come, and they crawled out of hiding. But their expectations were not realized. The situation was much more complicated than they dreamed. In January 1926 for the first time German Nationalist ministers joined a minority cabinet formed by Hans Luther, the Reich Minister of Finance. The episode came to an end as early as October. Foreign policy brought about the change.

THE DAWES PLAN (1924–9)

The dangerous disintegration of European affairs made it impossible for the United States to maintain her policy of isolation. President Coolidge and Charles Evans Hughes, his Secretary of State, sent delegates to a new international conference of experts with which the reparations commission was supposed to come to terms. Several separate committees submitted the results of their investigations. The new plan of settlement that originated in this way was given the name of the American General Charles G. Dawes. The conference, held in London in the summer of 1924, arranged the collective relationships acceptably. The principal matter, as far as Germany was concerned, was the quickest possible evacuation of the Ruhr Valley, for she would not be able to fulfil her obligations in regard to reparations unless her economic unity and productive capacity were restored. The question of evacuation was passably disposed of.

The Dawes plan was a temporary regulation of German payments. It sought to win back international confidence for Germany by having her pay over a number of years certain sums without a definite upper limit, but increasing in proportion to her prosperity. Her capacity was built up on the reorganization of the Reich's railroads into an independent corporation, on bonds to be issued by industry, on traffic and excise taxes, and on a loan. Supervision was to be exercised over the payments by a new bank of issue on the gold basis and by an international committee of transfer. S. Parker Gilbert, an American, was made agent general for German reparations payments.

For a time the Dawes plan, in spite of its obvious weaknesses, helped rehabilitate German economy in its relation to world economy. More important than the actual payments was the central question how long and to what extent such sums could be shifted about without causing general economic demoralization. It was natural for Germany to try to protect herself against such a possibility by increasing imports, by foreign loans of every sort, and by freezing whatever funds she had, in buildings, municipal improvements of many kinds, technical and military advances. Germany took advantage of the international conjuncture that was setting in by getting raw materials cheap. This way of doing was to Germany's interest, for it created an offset to the reparations instalments that went out of the country, and thus it strengthened the economic power of resistance of the Reich. Germany created for herself an impressive new productive apparatus, fully rationalized throughout in a technical way. In spite of the losses and the burdens of the war and the post-war period a prosperous era of productive work set in. The results are visible to this very day. The National Socialists would not have been able to achieve the task of organization they set themselves except for these labours of the Weimar republicans. Roads, housing, factories, and public buildings were constructed, merchant vessels were launched. Defeated Germany succeeded in becoming one of the most productive countries in the world. Under the pressure of necessity, by dint of unexampled concentration of forces and labour, the humiliated Reich was victorious over the victors.

LOCARNO. THE TREATY BETWEEN GERMANY AND RUSSIA

The acceptance of the Dawes plan was the start at further strengthening of German foreign policy. January 10, 1925 was the date set for the evacuation of the Köln zone of occupation. France declared Germany's disarmament inadequate. In case of evacuation, the French argued, an international treaty against Germany would be necessary for the protection of the French border. This marked the resumption of the old French demand for Germany's destruction. The prospect of such a treaty was most unwelcome to Germany, and she succeeded in averting it and concluding a pact in which the Reich participated as a partner on an equal footing.

A whole series of international treaties was made at the Locarno Conference in October 1925. The Rhine Pact provided that the existing boundaries should be inviolable and that the military zone should be maintained according to the conditions of the Treaty of

Versailles. Arbitration treaties were made between Germany on one side and France, Belgium, Czechoslovakia, and Poland on the other. Thus Germany did what the French Republic before 1914 had persistently refused to do: she subscribed to a renewed guarantee of the established boundaries; that is, she again renounced Alsace-Lorraine, and apparently forever. France also made treaties with Poland and Czechoslovakia for mutual help if Germany should violate the Locarno Pact in case of military complications.

The result of the Locarno Conference was a significant slackening of international tensions. The Köln zone was evacuated and the troops in the other occupied zones were reduced. Germany was admitted to the League of Nations and was given a permanent seat in the Council of the League. Further developments were to follow. In his interview with Briand at Thoiry, Stresemann tried to secure the immediate evacuation of the whole Rhineland. There was also a hope that the Reich might be given some colonial mandate. At all events the French troops were withdrawn from the Saar region; only a detachment to guard the railroad was left. Germany also signified, in Geneva, her recognition of the Permanent Court of International Justice for any legal dispute that might arise. Thus the German Reich, whose President was Hindenburg, adapted itself with apparent loyalty to the west European and American world of constitutionalism and faith in treaties. Could not still more happen? Would Germany perhaps join the anti-Bolshevist front of British world policy?

Stresemann, though constantly advised by the British ambassador, Lord d'Abernon, could not have ventured on such a step. Enmity toward Russia meant friendship with Poland, and friendship with Poland meant accepting the German eastern border. Stresemann had to reject an eastern pact with Poland in the Locarno style. Not only would such a pact have drawn down on him the fate of Erzberger and Rathenau; it would also have endangered the new strengthening of the Reich from the angle of domestic politics. And so on April 24, 1926 Stresemann concluded the treaty of amity between Germany and Russia; mutual neutrality was assured in case of attack by a third party, and neither side was to participate in an economic or financial boycott. The parties to the Locarno Treaty were informed of this agreement. It initiated a new period of co-operation between Germany and Russia and carried on the Rapallo policy. The two powers had a great deal to give each other in matters of industry, organization, and armament technics. The ambassador Count Brockdorff-Rantzau (died 1928) did much to advance the rapprochement. Russia assisted the secret rearming of Germany in many ways, and German military leadership showed its appreciation. Old Prussian and Russian sympathies were revived, and the common antagonism to western culture became more pronounced. Stalinism facilitated these developments, for the idea of world revolution was now relegated to the background; the problems of domestic reorganization that were soon summarized in the first Five-Year Plan took precedence, and here German ideas of systematized economy could be of great help.

Thus the Weimar Republic changed into the republic of Herr von Hindenburg. The legendary name of a declared monarchist glossed over many things. Antagonisms became blunted. The form of the state was preserved, and all relationships throughout it assumed a more stable and reliable character of loyalty to authority. The restoration and prosperity of Germany were facts—facts that caused misgivings abroad, especially in France. Stresemann's policy was distrusted by a good many; it seemed vague, perhaps ambiguous. In truth Gustav Stresemann, an opportunist from of old, was clinging to Germany's League of Nations policy with all his waning physical energies. This policy was his last and most honourable faith. For what else was there? What could come of a rapprochement with Italy or from a friendship with Soviet Russia, even under the best conditions? Stresemann looked for nothing good from a new war. Officially Hindenburg's republic desired peace, but the stronger it grew, the more energetically it would have to strive for revision of the peace treaty, for a final settlement of the reparations question, and for the cancellation of intolerable or impracticable peace provisions, as was arranged for in the Versailles Treaty itself.

SETTLEMENT WITH THE PRINCES

Two events showed how far the leaning toward the right wing was taking practical effect. The problem of what to do about the German princes was still unsolved. The Social Democrats and Communists wanted the princes to be expropriated without compensation. Many honest republicans did not wish to go so far, but believed it necessary to confiscate most of the holdings of the princes if the republican form of state were to be maintained and made more secure. This attitude raised a wave of indignation from the right. To these circles it seemed that such a measure would imperil all law and order by assailing private property. In reality it was neither a legal nor an economic problem, but a political question of prime importance.

The princely houses and their adherents were implacable foes of the republic. For the sake of Germany's reputation and in appreciation of the princes' former great achievements, the republic had to assure them of an adequate livelihood, but it could not be expected that the republic would put into the hand of its mortal enemies the means of undermining the existence of the new state. In the early days of the republic they might have been deprived of some of their property by decree. This had not been done, and now it was too late. A demand for a plebiscite on expropriating the princes made itself heard, but quickly died down. A decision had to be put off. The princely houses, as owners of vast estates or partners in Krupp's or other big industrial enterprises, had suffered very little from the inflation. Thus they were in a position to supply backing to the foes of the republic with greater and greater effectiveness. This turned to the advantage of the German Nationalists, but soon to that of the National Socialists as well.

THE DISPUTE ABOUT THE FLAG

One of the oddest and most lamentable tribulations of the Weimar Republic was the dispute over the flag. According to the constitution the colours of the Reich were black, red, and gold. The old tricolor of the movement for German freedom and unity, the flag of the democratic Greater Germany, was thus again honoured officially. The anti-democratic parties, however, had insisted that the merchant flag should remain black, white, and red, though with the colours of the Reich in the upper left corner. This was popularly called the black-red-gold jack—by an error in marine terminology. The colours of the Reich, it was asserted, were difficult to distinguish on the high seas. Other reasons that were given were just as specious. The real reason obviously was right-wing resentment against the black, red, and gold, which carried popular, revolutionary, and south and west German connotations.

In May 1926 Hans Luther, the Chancellor of the Reich, induced the President to issue a decree according to which official quarters in ports overseas were to fly this merchant flag as well as the colours of the Reich. Did the latter really require a kind of supplement to tone it down? Could not the colour symbol of the good old core of Germany show itself without this support from the colonial Germany? The decree was equally assailable from the point of view of international law and from that of political tact. Luther was a rough and ready administrator without the more subtle gifts of the statesman, the type of successful municipal executive who pays no attention to intangibles, simply because he is not in the least aware of them. He lost his post in the dispute about the flag, only to become after a short time ambassador to the United States. Had he proved his fitness for just this ambassadorship? Luther's flag decree was allowed to stand, absurd as it was. Hindenburg's republic leaned more and more toward the black, white, and red. Black, red, and gold began to seem indelicate, as savouring of the street, even the gutter; the old colours conveyed the impression of being somehow western, democratic, and Jewish.

The fear of the increasing influence of right-wing opposition became evident in the Reichstag elections of 1928. Once more the Social Democrats were victorious and formed a new cabinet. Hermann Müller became Chancellor of the Reich for the second time. He was honest and discreet, a practical businessman who knew how to negotiate, but he was colourless and unenthusiastic. In addition his health was seriously damaged, so that he was inadequate to his office. The dearth of vigorous personalities in the Weimar parties is striking. One of their best men was Erich Koch-Weser, the leader of the Democrats, a clever and nimble-witted jurist who was always ready with a jest and a way out of quandaries. Since his party was definitely in decline, however, there was less and less that he could do. If he had concerned himself more with the rising generation, many things might have gone better.

It was characteristic of the chaos prevailing among German parties that the Economy Party (*Wirtschaftspartei*) won such appreciable success. This was a nation-wide party of the German middle class that had originated from local associations of house- and property-owners. It represented the interests of the middle-class elements that had come out of the inflation relatively unscathed. It joined the craftsmen and shop-keepers in opposition to the consumers' co-operatives, which had a socialistic colouring. The Economy Party did not wish to have anything to do with large political questions. It fought against intrusion by the state on the rights of the individual and was ready to support any form of government that promised help in this direction. The party attracted many malcontents and exploited the terror of inflation to its own advantage. The butcher, the baker, the candlestick-maker, all ran after the Economy Party, and the Weimar parties lost many followers to this new form of reaction.

THE KELLOGG PACT AND THE YOUNG PLAN

The slump from post-war prosperity in world economy first became noticeable in Germany in the spring of 1929. The Reich was in financial straits and had to go to the big bankers in search of credit. A loan was attempted. Favourable conditions were offered, but success was slight. Northern and northeastern Germany, where the prevailing crop was rye, grown on moderately good soil, entered on a grave agrarian crisis. The peasants and especially the Junkers could no longer export their products at a profit. Scarcity of labour, wage difficulties, and debts mounted appallingly, and their increase affected the industries dependent on these products.

Banking was in a bad way. Money was scarce. After overproduction there was a sharp decrease in production. Wages were lowered. Unemployment and dumping characterized the grave crisis, which spared no country in Europe. As far as her foreign policy was concerned, Germany had good relations with all the great powers. She had participated as an equal in the negotiation of treaties to abolish war. The result was the Paris Pact of 1928, which became known by the name of the American Secretary of State, Frank B. Kellogg.

Collective sentiment was not unfavourable to a final adjustment of the reparations question, for which Germany was particularly eager in the face of the international crisis that was setting in. Just this economic tension, however, made her opponents more demanding and more sensitive. In June 1929 a new commission of experts, whose chairman was the American Owen Young, submitted a new plan named after him. Germany made the vain attempt to improve her condition in other respects along with regulating reparations. She brought up the questions of doing away with the Polish Corridor and revising the borders of Upper Silesia and suggested the return of the former German colonies. This last measure was proposed in order to improve her productive capacity as well as for other reasons. The other side, however, refused to enter on political discussions of any sort, but kept to the matter of reparations. Even England presented a sterner front than before; her own economic troubles and the severe criticism directed at the ruling Labour Party at home made the English delegates alert to keep Great Britain from suffering in the distribution of reparations. But this posture had the effect of embittering Germany and strengthening hostility toward England in the right-wing opposition. The results for Germany were favourable, measured against former reparations demands; they were, nevertheless, a heavy burden in the face of the economic crisis. All foreign control was removed, and the railroads and industry of the Reich were freed. New factors were introduced by coupling the debts of the Allies to the United States with the reparations payments and by the so-called commercialization—that is, the sale of reparations bonds to private persons and on the open market. For a period of fifty-nine years payments were to be made, increasing gradually for twenty-five years and then declining. A Bank for International Settlements, to which both sides were to contribute working capital, was to handle the payments; it undertook to discharge the last twenty-one instalments from its reserve fund. It was provided that Germany should be allowed to propose postponing some part of the payments if her currency and her economy should become endangered.

On the German side the principal burden of the negotiations had been borne by Hjalmar Schacht, the president of the Reichsbank. For many years he had exerted a decisive influence in the economic life of Germany. Schacht was energetic and obstinate, hard to get along with, but a veritable magician in all matters of finance, never at a loss for a stratagem or evasion; an alchemist, a juggler of credits who possessed astonishing dexterity and inexhaustible imagination. Schacht's inventive mind never took the Young plan seriously. In his eyes this forced settlement was simply the beginning of the end of reparations, and he did everything he could to connect so much malicious manœuvring with the payments that the recipients' pleasure was thoroughly spoiled. The right-wing opposition seized on the matter of reparations and made the government appear a Simple Simon who let himself be taken in by sharpers time and time again. In 1930 Schacht was removed from the presidency of the Reichsbank because of his contentiousness and his domineering. He was now more than willing to furnish material for any attack and even voiced the harshest criticisms in public himself, skilfully glossing over his own responsibility. Hitler restored this ambitious man to the office for which he yearned, and for a long time Schacht (born 1877) craftily supported the moves of the National Socialists.

The Reichstag elections of 1930 brought overwhelming success to National Socialism. Up till then it could still be regarded as simply a sort of sect. Now everyone was forced to recognize it as a political force. The third period in the life of the Weimar Republic began — the period of dissolution.

THE INDIAN SUMMER OF GERMAN CULTURE

Never had there been such passionate devotion to the theatre, such musical fervour, as in this post-war time that was turning into a new pre-war time. In addition to Gerhart Hauptmann with his tireless invention there were now a number of younger talents who had undergone the quickening experience of war and revolution: Georg Kaiser, Ernst Toller, René Schickele, Fritz von Unruh, Bert Brecht. Thomas Mann presented his contemporaries with *The Magic Mountain*, a profound interpretation of their destiny that was a solace and a spur as well. There were many good and average novelists, Agnes Günther, Franz Werfel, Arnold Zweig, Hans Grimm, and Hermann Stehr among the best of these. Both the war generation and the post-war were rich in lyric poets. Rainer Maria Rilke still found imitators and disciples, but a more artless, warm, and tender folklike tone was also cultivated—by Gustav Falke, above all—in accordance with the feeling and taste of the Youth Movement, whose most valuable contribution was the struggle for simplicity and naturalness in the conduct of life as well as in creative art.

There were countless eccentrics and sects in the arts. Beginning

616

with the Berlin Storm Group, more and more new circles sprang up in answer to the inspiration and the challenge of foreign influences. The political excitement and the economic upheavals of these years were reflected with ingenuity and vigour in all manner of bold productions that left good citizens breathless, to the delight of the originators. Perhaps the Bauhaus in Dessau did more than any other group to purify form, refine relationships, clarify and dignify expression, and keep a serious artistic trend from going astray. The atonal tendency in music probably marked the most fundamental break with the past.

The courage with which the Germans preserved and developed their immortal heritage in a period of defeat and overturn, in the midst of humiliation and poverty, evoked the astonishment and admiration of all competent observers. The Weimar Republic laid stress on the connection with Goethe and Beethoven, with Dürer and Veit Stoss. It knew how to commemorate the great men of the past worthily. Its schools were culture-conscious as never before in Germany. The universities were substantially aided. The Emergency Association for German Science and Learning, taking in all older foundations, fostered intellectual work in Germany in a most exemplary way. The work of Schmidt-Ott and Carl Heinrich Becker, the Prussian Ministers of Education, ought always to be remembered. Dozens of experts were engaged in research on the causes and consequences of the war and its military and economic lessons. Publication of the most important documents of foreign policy since the founding of the Reich supplied a great mass of material for historical investigation. It was an important stimulus to intellectual labours and called forth similar undertakings in allied fields. Albert Einstein's theory of relativity and Planck's quantum theory demonstrated that Germany's creative genius still held the lead in the exact sciences.

The interpretation of the world and of the times, the attempt to penetrate to their inmost significance, their true circumstances and conditions of development, gave rise to new and original philosophical and sociological studies. Max Weber and his disciples in Heidelberg astonished their public with the subtlety and vigour of their interpretations. Oswald Spengler was a subject of controversy, but significant because he roused his contemporaries, who were touched to the very soul by his mystical and millennial work *The Decline of the West*. Had the West really come to its end? Could not Germany succeed in preserving it by co-operating with the great civilized nations that were her neighbours? Was it not possible to form a new humanistic intellectual community of peace and culture that should be truly fruitful? Many Germans believed that it was, and they laboured to this end.

It was in vain. The shining and colourful culture of Weimar Germany was an illusion of Indian summer. It might be doubted whether the future would bring the decline of the West. But another decline was a fact. Few were aware of it as yet. The good old Germany was in decline; the age of National Socialism had come.

Chapter 20

NATIONAL SOCIALISM

THE REICHSTAG elections of September 1930 yielded the National Socialists one hundred and seven seats. At a single stroke they had become the second strongest party. During the Locarno period the movement had receded; but then it had sprung into new life. From Bavaria it spread to Swabia and Franconia, from there to Thuringia and Hesse and on to the coast of the North Sea and to Berlin. The world-wide economic crisis and the dispute over the Young plan gave it great impetus. What was to be expected of this party became quite evident from the so-called liberty law submitted to the people in 1929 by the commission of the Reich that was charged with the management of plebiscites. It demanded the immediate cessation of reparations payments and criminal prosecution of the ministers who had been responsible for accepting the Young plan. This affair fell through, but the success of National Socialism in the elections proved the importance of these attacks for the future.

National Socialism exerted growing pressure and became constantly more decisive in Germany's politics. The dilemma of the other parties was acute. In despair the Democratic Party had entered into an alliance with the Order of Young Germans for campaign purposes and thus suddenly invited attention to the interest it took in popular organizations. The move made very little difference. The withering process could not be arrested, and the fact that in the face of bankruptcy the name was changed to "German State Party" only made matters worse. With Stresemann's death in October 1929 the German People's Party lost its most popular leader. During his final severe illness he had withstood his many opponents only with the greatest difficulty. No adequate successor was found for him. The right wing, the big industrialists, steadily lost confidence in the German People's Party. The hour of the German Nationalists had come. But their leader, Alfred Hugenberg, obstinately stuck to it that he would do nothing to preserve the republic, even though it was Hindenburg's republic.

Hugenberg had to suffer the harshest sort of criticism in his own camp. The German Nationalists too were drawn down into the general disintegration. First the *Volkskonservativen,* a democratic popular party, split off under Gottfried Treviranus, a former naval officer who won many personal followers by his freshness and integrity. Then the former anti-Jewish Christian Social group made themselves independent under the curious name of Christian Social National Service. Later a Conservative People's Party and a Christian Nationalist Peasants' Party were formed. Thus Alfred Hugenberg's group of big industrialists was deserted by the young conservatives, by the anti-Semites, by the feudalists, and by the agrarians. Nothing was left except a small but still powerful anti-socialistic and anti-republican bloc, which rejected all proposals to come to an understanding. Hugenberg preferred co-operation with National Socialism to any other sort of alliance, for his object was to destroy the Weimar Republic, trade unions, and parliamentarism. Treviranus' adherents had exceptionally strong support in the so-called Steel Helmets, an association of front-line soldiers that had been formed in 1918 as a patriotic league of veterans. In 1924 a rival association, the Black-Red-Gold Banner of the Reich, was founded; its members were all veterans who championed the Weimar Republic. In the face of increasing confusion among the German Nationalists the black-white-red Steel Helmets successfully preserved the idea of comradely co-operation for a future that, its leaders were convinced, would have need of all able-bodied anti-democratic forces. The Banner of the Reich did much to cement the sense of community between bourgeois and socialistic democratic elements. But only the left wing of the Centre, which had a high regard for trade-unionism, worked with it.

BRÜNING AND RIGHT-WING OPPOSITION

How was the Reich to be ruled now? The President charged Heinrich Brüning (born 1885), chairman of the Centre, with form-

620

ing a new cabinet. Brüning was a Catholic from Westphalia, a highly cultivated man who knew many languages and was steeped in the Low Saxon tradition of the Germanic liberal constitutional state. He was therefore what was formerly called a Conservative Liberal in Germany. He was like a scholar of cloistered, conciliatory habits; his bearing and facial expression were informed with a priestlike wisdom. He had gone along quietly as the budget expert of his party, calm, sober, critical, entirely objective, and fully aware of the unpleasant responsibility imposed by financial problems that were important to the very existence of his country. He had, moreover, been a brave front-line officer who distinguished himself on several occasions and threw himself into every task without sparing himself. To Brüning, Hindenburg, the aged President of the Reich, was always and perhaps too much the honoured field marshal of the World War.

Brüning's cabinet had only a small basis in the Reichstag. A government by a small coalition began. The Centre united with all the bourgeois parties that were close to it and hoped for tolerance from the German Nationalists, who were not included. Thus Hindenburg's republic shamefacedly turned itself into a permanent dictatorship. The famous Article 48 of the Weimar Constitution was subjected to a very broad interpretation. Was there no other solution? The Social Democrats were still the strongest party in the Reich and still predominated in Prussia, the largest state. It is possible to imagine a powerful statesmanlike personality of the left wing who might have taken hold of the country from the vantage point of Prussia and saved the republic. But three factors excluded the practical realization of such a development.

The first was the circumstance that the Social Democrats and the Communists were irreconcilable. In 1929 Severing, the Minister of the Interior, dissolved the Red Front-Line Fighters' Association (*Frontkämpferbund*). No bourgeois statesman was so hated by the Communists as this socialist. Neither the Communists alone nor the Social Democrats alone were strong enough to start a new revolution. The fact that they were divided and were enemies to the death was the strongest card held by the right-wing opposition.

The second factor that prevented any left-wing salvation of the republic was the stand taken by the President of the Reich. As Hindenburg grew older and feebler his immediate circle became proportionately more powerful. His son Oscar was his right hand, naturally enough. But Oscar's companions in the guards and his family and class interests began to insinuate themselves into the affairs of the chancery of the Reich. Like Caprivi, Hindenburg had known no great ambition. His way of life was that of a conscientious officer of old Prussia, happy in his work and uninterested in culture or in making a fortune. In 1927, at the suggestion of his admirers, the Prussian state presented the President with the old Hindenburg family estate of Neudeck, and in 1933 with the crownland of Neudeck and the so-called Prussian Forest, with extraordinary financial privileges. At the close of his life the old field marshal found himself a large land owner in East Prussia, in a feudalistic and agrarian setting where he was involuntarily drawn into this circle of interests and views. The master stroke of the Junkers of old Prussia was this annexation of the President of the Reich.

East Prussia had never belonged to the black-red-gold republic in spirit. Every historical basis was lacking, and geographical detachment by the Polish Corridor did the rest. No other province led so isolated and self-sufficient a life as East Prussia. It was almost a minor realm like the Baltic border states—almost a remote colony. Such was the haven of Hindenburg's old age. Here he took root in his own tough and tenacious way. He loved to dominate, and like Bismarck before him he wanted to die in harness. It might perhaps have been possible to restore the monarchy in these years. Yet whenever the matter was under discussion in the office of the President of the Reich, as seems to have happened fairly often, it was just Hindenburg who voiced the gravest doubts. He had sworn an oath to the republic. Why should he not keep it? He, the elected President, was obviously more popular than any princely candidate. The generals as a group unanimously rejected the idea of a return of William II to the throne. But to pass over the former Emperor in order to install the Crown Prince, who was not at all popular, would violate all legitimistic instincts. And the rest of the confederate princes? Should one decide in favour of a people's monarchy—that is, on recognition of revolutionary premises through a new democratic form—or should one venture a restoration on the basis of historical right?

The third and last factor that made a reorganization proceeding from the left wing impossible was the stand of the *Reichswehr*. Between Oscar von Hindenburg and the most powerful man in the ministry of the *Reichswehr,* General von Schleicher, there was the comradely bond of membership in the third regiment of the guards. Both men agreed on the main point: the *Reichswehr* could not possibly be democratized and turned against right-wing opposition. When General Gröner, with his good republican and democratic views, dissolved the armed guards of National Socialism, the *Schutzstaffeln* (S. S., detachments for protection) and the *Sturmabteilungen* (S. A., storm detachments), because they were a notorious threat to the state, his days as a minister were numbered. A late love-affair of this widower, which rose to a very bourgeois climax with marriage and a nursery, gave his enemies the opportunity of heaping malicious personal abuse on him. His reputation was blackened in the eyes of the President of the Reich, and he dropped from sight, a defenceless victim. Some years later, when he died, the National Socialist government refused him a burial with military honours.

Schleicher was Gröner's successor. His was a character that revelled in bustling and intrigue. He was a desk general, seasoned by every kind of departmental quarrel, and it gave him distinct pleasure to exchange his role of wire-puller for that of a popular hero. Almost every day now there were brawls between National Socialists and Communists that had fatal results. For years Germany experienced a latent civil war. The authoritarian front of the agrarians and big industrialists, of the feudalists and militarists, was more powerful than any group that could have been built up from the left wing. This front of cartels, which was reactionary and tried to effect reconciliation by fiat, claimed the President of the Reich for its own. It also planned to come to an agreement with National Socialism.

In the meantime Chancellor Brüning was honestly endeavouring to save the republic by the technically correct methods of deflation. The situation was bad and grew worse from month to month. Bankruptcies and distraints succeeded one another. Emergency decrees came in a stream. Wages were lowered and new taxes introduced. These dictatorial measures were not sufficient to cope with unemployment. There should have been a slackening of international tension, since the last occupied zone in the Rhineland was evacuated before the time set (June 30, 1930). But such a success was no longer enough in the face of the boundless asperity of nationalistic criticism. Stresemann's successor as Minister of Foreign Affairs, Julius Curtius of the People's Party, now made an attempt to strengthen the position of the Reich in central Europe. Curtius was a more subtle personality than Stresemann, but also less self-assured. He was a clever jurist and a polished man of the world, but he was easily disturbed by attacks and more inclined to dodge an issue than to fight it out to a finish. If his plan had succeeded, Brüning's cabinet would have been much more secure in the face of right-wing opposition.

AUSTRIA. THE CUSTOMS UNION WITH THE REICH

During the post-war period the little Republic of Austria barely managed to maintain its independent existence by dint of great struggle. The dispute over the Burgenland, its most easterly portion, poisoned its relations with Hungary, whose neighbourly help was indispensable if only on economic grounds. The splitting up of the Tyrol, with the suffering of the South Tyrolese German peasants in the Italian province of Upper Adige, was for a long time an obstacle to amicable relations with the enlarged Fascist Italy. Austria's relations with Czechoslovakia were also strained, for Czechoslovakia was suspicious and on the alert against any plan of restoring the Habsburgs. Only through the help of the League of Nations had the Republic of Austria succeeded in putting its economic affairs into some sort of order. The experts of Geneva did some of their best work on this matter. Nevertheless Austria was permanently dependent on the goodwill of her creditors among the western powers.

A number of capable statesmen struggled for an independent future for Austria. Ignaz Seipel the Chancellor in clerical garb, Heinrich Schober the discreet police bureaucrat, Michael Hainisch the sound agriculturist, and finally Engelbert Dollfuss the popular martyr to the concept of Austria, who was both devoted and ambitious—all these did much for their country, whose past had been resplendent, whose present was full of tribulation, whose future was dark. One had to be as brave and as merry as only the Viennese can be in order not to lose heart. The constitution of the Republic of Austria had to be recast several times. The old antagonism between the anti-Semitic and clerical Christian Social group and the Social Democrats was rending the country. The Home Defence Force (*Heimwehr*), nationalistic in colour, was opposed by the republican

Protective League (*Schutzbund*). The bourgeois Greater Germans dwindled away under double pressure. The democratic capital, Vienna, lost contact with the Alpine regions. An increasing majority looked on an *Anschluss* with the Reich as the best ultimate solution, though on the condition that Austria should have the right of self-determination at least as much as Bavaria.

The treaty about the German-Austrian Customs Union, concluded in 1931 by Curtius, the Foreign Minister of the Reich, and Schober, the Austrian Chancellor, was intended as a first step toward economic *Anschluss*. It should have had a favourable effect, especially for Austria. As a result of this arrangement her actual political independence should have been strengthened rather than weakened. But the treaty had to be given up in the face of a tempest of criticism from the western powers—France in particular. The Court of International Justice denounced it. The government was rocked by this defeat. Right-wing opposition now had a new and potent weapon. France paralysed Austria's political economy by withdrawing her credits. Austria's loan-bank, the Austrian Creditverein, collapsed, and the crash was echoed in the Reich. The Nordwolle concern in Bremen, owned by the Lahusen family, suspended payments; the Darmstadt and National Bank closed. Concerns in the Ruhr Valley could maintain themselves only with state assistance. Several large banks also had to ask the Reich for help. Most German firms were unable to realize the foreign credits that were now recalled; the amounts involved were too large and too tightly invested. Exchange of payments was frozen; reparations instalments had become technically impossible. More and more emergency decrees were issued in the Reich and its states (*Länder*). State commissaries were installed everywhere. The American President, Herbert Hoover, suggested that all payments of reparations and war debts be discontinued for a year, and he offered a credit of three hundred million dollars. Responsible European statesmen conferred in person; the French appeared in Berlin, the Germans in Paris. The result was the agreement on a moratorium.

HINDENBURG RE-ELECTED

Possibly the Brüning cabinet ought to have insisted on the German-Austrian Customs Union even at the risk of an international crisis. Such a policy, it is easy to imagine, would necessarily have welded all German parties, from the Social Democrats to the German Nationalists, together into one unified patriotic bloc. The situation was not so simple, however. The Social Democrats and the German Nationalists had nothing in common—less now than ever before; the attempt to overthrow the government of the Social Democrats in Prussia through a plebiscite promoted by the Steel Helmets was proof enough. The German Nationalists were less and less pleased with the Brüning cabinet. The conferences in Harzburg in the autumn of 1931 showed which way the wind was blowing. Hitler and Alfred Hugenberg, Seldte the brandy-manufacturer and leader of the Steel Helmets, and Dr. Hjalmar Schacht formed the so-called Harzburg Front for the purpose of overthrowing the government.

The most curious personality in this coalition was the much-discussed Alfred Hugenberg, who came from one of the best families of Hanover officials. He had begun his career in the civil service, improved his connections by an advantageous marriage, and made himself valuable to Krupp as a shrewd organizer. It was he who built up relations between heavy industry and the press. It gave him personal pleasure to confront the good old German newspapers with a new kind of paper in which, with sophisticated skill, advertising was intertwined with reporting. From the press this dauntless and irrepressible climber pushed into politics, but here his manners of an autocratic magnate only created confusion. This man, unteachable because somewhat of a megalomaniac, who wrought his own party's ruin and gave way to the hangman Hitler, will go down in history as a memorable and melancholy example of the traitor betrayed.

The Banner of the Reich, together with the Free Unions and other republican associations, now united in the so-called Iron Front. This was a defensive organization planned to counterbalance the armed guards of the National Socialists, the German Nationalists, and the Communists. The prætorian spirit gained alarmingly in Germany. Many faithful adherents of the Weimar Republic refused to yield to the double attack from the left and the right wings without a struggle, and from a higher historical point of view it would certainly have been better if they had fought. If one must fall, it is better to fall with a weapon in hand. A state of civil war existed already anyway. It was unfortunate that the great majority of republicans were

626

concentrated in the great cities. They did not understand country people well enough, and it was country needs and forces that largely determined the anti-Weimar front.

Brüning now formed his second cabinet, without Curtius. He himself took the Ministry for Foreign Affairs. New economy measures became necessary. The cancellation of reparations was on the way. Now the long-called-for reform of the Reich seemed overdue, if only for economic reasons. But nothing was done, partly because National Socialism had succeeded in establishing itself in the small states and from them was assaulting Prussia. In the new presidential election Hindenburg was re-elected with more than nineteen million votes. But Adolf Hitler had received over thirteen million. In one way or another this man would have to have his turn in the near future, for even now he was backed by the most powerful forces in Germany. This time it was precisely the old parties of the Weimar Coalition that had voted for Hindenburg, because they hoped that he would maintain the republic—indeed, that he would save it. The German Nationalists gave him their votes for just the opposite reason. Which was right? Brüning now took under consideration various measures that almost bore the character of state socialism—especially labour service, with the introduction of limited compulsory labour service, and the splitting up of unprofitable landed estates. His opponents used this bent to ruin his reputation with the President of the Reich.

At that time a clever politician, Franz von Papen, was making himself *persona grata* in Hindenburg's house. He was also on a friendly footing with Hindenburg's son. Papen was a Catholic aristocrat from western Germany—not a Junker, but a cavalier. His independent means being assured by his marriage and some excellent industrial connections, he was not obliged to build up his career in the usual ways. This elegant raconteur knew how to make himself welcome at the breakfast table of the President of the Reich. He won not only Hindenburg's special confidence, but even a curious variety of senile affection from that rather solitary being. There was at least nothing petty about Papen. Scruples that would have oppressed a Brüning did not touch him in the least. Even while he had been a military attaché in Washington during the World War, he had given proofs of a craftiness surpassed only by his carelessness. As an experienced gentleman jockey he had learned to smile when occasionally he lost a race. He was familiar with many ways and languages, but particularly with the language of his partner of the moment. Even his closest friends could not have said with real assurance whether or not he ever pursued large, serious goals in public life. He had a sound instinct for power and commanded a thousand ruses, wiles, and tricks, all at his finger tips. Nothing ever ruffled him; he was a regular churchgoer—what need to fuss about conscience? This was the man who overthrew Brüning.

THE DICTATORSHIP OF FRANZ VON PAPEN (BORN 1879)

The President of the Reich gave Brüning a short, sharp dismissal. Papen succeeded him. He formed a cabinet of aristocrats and high officials, the majority of whom did not belong to the Reichstag. It was the beginning of open dictatorship for the Gentlemen's Club (*Herrenklub*), the influential Berlin centre of a network of societies that took in anti-democratic worthies of the old ruling class all over the Reich. Papen's first and most important action was to set aside the government of Prussia, where, except for one brief interlude, the left wing under Social Democratic leadership had ruled ever since the November Revolution. Otto Braun, the President of the Ministry, and Severing, the Minister of the Interior, were removed by force. Papen became commissar of the Reich and in this capacity took over the power in Prussia. This was a true coup d'état. Prussia and the Reich were now co-ordinated. The attitude of the *Reichswehr* rendered all resistance useless in the long run; at least that was what most of the left-wing leaders thought. A suit in the supreme court (*Staatsgerichtshof*) came to almost nothing; historical reality did not pause for it.

In June 1932, at the conference that met in Lausanne, the cross of reparations was interred. One last instalment was to be the prerequisite to cancellation. Papen, however, was determined not to make even this payment and openly declared as much with characteristic cynical frankness. Thus he harvested the laurels that were really due to Brüning's wise and persistent negotiations. And now Papen's cabinet, bloated with success, harried their fatherland through two Reichstag elections within half a year. Such a procedure could hardly serve the reputation and the influence of parliamentary institutions. Nor was it intended that it should. The first election

gave the National Socialists two hundred and thirty seats. Thereupon Papen offered their leader, Adolf Hitler, the office of vice-
chancellor, to the dissatisfaction of old Hindenburg, who is said to
have declared in his grim way: "Postmaster general is plenty good
enough for that Bohemian corporal!" But Papen's offer was rejected.
Hitler wanted to be Chancellor of the Reich or nothing at all. The
second Reichstag election, in November 1932, lost the National Socialists thirty-three seats. Many believed the crisis had passed; ebb
was now following on flood tide. Hitler and his followers were in
an embarrassing position. A money shortage threatened. Many party
members were clamouring to be provided for. Where were those
promised fat jobs? Gregor Strasser, a radical Nazi, now began to
negotiate behind Hitler's back for admission to Papen's government.
This insubordination cost him all his party offices; there was no
mercy.

SCHLEICHER'S (1882-1934) REORGANIZATION

In early December 1932, General von Schleicher assumed the task
of forming a new cabinet. This was the last attempt to rule Germany
without National Socialism. Did the fact that the erstwhile minister
of the *Reichswehr* became Chancellor of the Reich mean the much-
discussed dictatorship of the army? Could conservative authority
hold out a hand to the masses for the good of the country, to the
satisfaction of all decent people and the disappointment of demagogues and gangsters? Was this the beginning of a desirable synthesis of Prussianism and socialism? Schleicher took a lively interest
in ideas of state socialism. In consideration of the appalling number
of unemployed—six million—he weighed the introduction of compulsory labour service. He prepared to restore agricultural conditions
to a healthy level, an effort that was indeed overdue. Attempts to
socialize the coal and potash industries were not too encouraging.
Sacrifices had to be made, but one thing was utterly out of the question: a second inflation. It seemed preferable to overpay employees.
Even now a third of the people's income passed through the hands
of the government.

To Schleicher, who was a blend of shrewd bureaucracy and lofty
patriotism, it seemed that the old affinity between Prussia and socialism was to celebrate a creative resurrection. But exactly here was his

misfortune. Since 1930–1 the *Osthilfe* (the Reich's financial assistance to its eastern provinces) had been tiding agriculture east of the Elbe over difficult times. This involved liberating people from their debts, reducing interest, resettlement, and constructing railroads. Large sums had changed hands in the process. Those who were ostensibly in need of assistance had used the money to erect splendid administration buildings and residences, as well as to modernize equipment, machinery, and roads. Left-wing Prussia's administration soon withdrew from the enterprise, but the reactionary government of the Reich went on with it. Schleicher wanted to expose all these abuses. Like Brüning, he was of the opinion that all big estates no longer able to function should be split up for resettlement enterprises and so used for the common good. The Junkers, of course, found this point of view thoroughly distasteful. Agrarian feudalism, after all, counted the President of the Reich as one of its own. The old gentleman was informed that Schleicher was an even worse Bolshevist than the discarded Brüning—the more dangerous because apparently he was bent on reaching his goals through a military dictatorship.

Papen now thought the time ripe. With his mediation authoritarian agrarians and industrialists decided to call on National Socialism for help. The strongest potential in the politics of the time was to be used to free the ruling class from parliamentarism, the tyranny of trade unions, the red peril—from the democratic republic. Hitler was in so difficult a position that he was now ready to accept conditions. When he came into power on January 30, 1933 he actually promised that he would not bring politics into the *Reichswehr* and that he would prepare the way for the restoration of the monarchy. He formed a cabinet in conjunction with the German Nationalists, and he effected a reconciliation with the reluctant President of the Reich on the festive day at Potsdam.

But what was really beginning was something quite different. National Socialism conquered Germany. It was a curious conquest. The decisive actions were planned and executed with a sort of legalistic pedantry. The Reichstag opposition was presented with the choice between a shrewdly concocted, ostensibly legal device, the so-called enabling act, and ruthless terror. Only the Social Democrats voted against the bill. In order to avoid the worse alternative the whole Centre, including Heinrich Brüning, accepted it as inevitable. Through all the years of National Socialism the Weimar Constitution was never abolished. The enabling act and all the ancillary measures adopted in connection with it actually violated the form and spirit of the Weimar Constitution in the most shocking way. The enabling act itself, despite the timely warning of a few courageous men, was exceeded. The hypocritical insistence on formal legitimacy·failed to make the National Socialist movement more tolerable to the victims of its regimentation of German political life.

ADOLF HITLER

The reorganization and co-ordination of January 1933 initiated a new period in German history that was only concluded by Germany's collapse in the second World War. The historian would have good reason for letting the curtain fall. His judgement may lack perspective. But the public knows that there is a fifth act to the play and wants to see what goes on in it. The more closely the story approaches the present, the more impossible it becomes to give a report based on genuine sources. Recapitulation of recent events that still burn in the memory of every reader would be superfluous and unsatisfactory for everybody. But some analysis of National Socialism is in order—for one reason because, in consequence of National Socialism, Germany was put again in the front line of world affairs. It has always been a great and beautiful and famous land. National Socialism has made it the most controversial in the world. Furthermore—and this second reason has the very broadest intellectual and scientific scope—National Socialism recapitulates the entire gamut of German history. All the great problems of Germany's development with which this book is concerned have now been revived. National Socialism is the sum of Germany's past. It became the decisive crisis in the life of the German people, the turn of destiny for central Europe, for the continent, for the inhabited earth.

Only with hesitation can an analysis of the personality of Adolf Hitler be attempted. The majority of the inhabitants of the civilized world loathed this man with daily increasing intensity. The majority of his compatriots admired him and placed him among the greatest carriers of Germany's fame. Many even placed him above all former guides of Germany's destiny. Hitler's idea lives after him and is still in process. Notwithstanding, let us venture an interpretation.

The historian accepts the challenge of Hitler's admirers: what was the significance of the Führer compared with that of his predecessors? Martin Luther belonged to the German people, to the German soil. With matchless courage he fought for his cause, defended his faith, and worked for the truth and the purity of religious conviction, for "the freedom of a Christian." He asked nothing for himself; he left the state and the world to themselves. He made many mistakes, but always with an admirable sincerity. In this vale of tears he wanted to shape life through faith as a preparation for the hereafter, for eternity. He was a hero of the free word, the free deed, and obeyed his conscience only. Martin Luther was the religious genius of the Germans. Adolf Hitler's work has nothing in common with this.

Frederick the Great was hard and clear-headed, bold and shrewd. He triumphed over his contemporaries by the unscrupulousness of his methods, but in taste, culture, and European spirit he was the noblest bloom of his epoch. He was a master of self-irony, a hero of self-sacrificing work, one who did his duty toward the world, one who was cruel to others but even more so to himself. Among the many dynasts of comparatively recent German history Frederick of Prussia was the only genius. Adolf Hitler belonged to an utterly different world.

Immanuel Kant cast German thought into a new mould. His earnestness and profundity shaped knowledge for all coming generations. Cautiously, conscientiously, and relentlessly, untroubled by the times and the affairs of every day, this great architect of the spirit built for German idealism its everlasting mansion. Through Kant justice, freedom, and humaneness have become necessary for the fulfilment of Germany's true destiny. Kant had great and creative successors, but it is he who was the first genius in the field of German philosophy. Adolf Hitler did not show the slightest trace of his spirit.

Johann Wolfgang Goethe, the world-embracing, the unique, penetrator of the secrets of nature, bearer of immortal European art-form, the lonely sage, stands outside every group; any attempt at comparison with him is sheer mockery. But it must not be forgotten that to this day every new generation has groped its way to Goethe; that specifically, the Weimar Republic proclaimed that its cultural labours rested on inspirations drawn from Goethe, that its celebration in 1932 of the centenary of Goethe's death was no mere conventional gesture. Many believed that this celebration set up a program and heralded a hope. Actually it sounded a long farewell. Adolf Hitler never felt even a breath from Goethe's world.

Baron vom Stein was a patriot burning with love for his fatherland, a careful administrator, an indefatigable reformer who was always pressing forward to new objectives, but a hater of rhetoric, precipitateness, ignorant and senseless destruction. Thus he proved a wise guardian for society. He deliberately preserved the state and felt nothing but anger for revolutionary bunglers, for those who stirred up the people, and for nagging doctrinaire critics. He was a man of reason and poise who fostered peaceful evolution and cherished all that was personal and original. He was the genius among German patriots—and the exact opposite of Adolf Hitler in all things.

Otto von Bismarck showed just as few scruples in his choice of methods as Frederick of Prussia. His foreign policy was pliant, flexible, unprejudiced, determined by the egoism of the state. In domestic policy he was violent, class-conscious, authoritarian. But Bismarck had a wonderful instinct for moderation, he had a sense of humour, he was a master of cautious tactics, he spared his defeated opponents, he had the gift of getting the best out of representatives of other classes. He comprised all the best qualities of the German and made them effective. Although not a glib speaker, he uttered unforgettable phrases; he was a great writer with a subtle sense of the meaning and rhythm of his language. Beethoven was his solace, and he was well acquainted with the work of Goethe. The leaders of the Third Reich liked to speak of Bismarck with pitying praise and regarded him as a sort of forerunner who did his job as best he could, and not always even that. For the time being, however, history will have to salute Bismarck as the genius among German statesmen. Adolf Hitler was something quite different.

Hitler's history is the history of his underestimation. Statesmen and professors jeered at this man because of his plebeian speech—his crude, bombastic German, full of clichés. Hitler never forgave the university patricians this hauteur. He answered with hatred the mockery of men who were instinct with culture. It was not without cause that he declined every variety of academic honour. He did not want to accept an honorary doctor's degree from these German institutions of higher learning that were so proud of their prestige.

Hitler's biographers have unearthed every detail of his career. Born in 1889, he was a déclassé of a sort, the son of a lower-middle-class man who had become proletarianized and earned his living as a petty official. He was a failure at architecture. With a vestigial gift for painting, Hitler had to paper rooms because no one wanted to buy his insipid water-colours. He went his half-starved way from one organized charity in Vienna to another, a bitter and restless wanderer. After the World War the discharged lance-corporal was active in Munich as a military spy, and that is how he became connected with politics. This was the beginning of his rise, one of the most curious in modern history. Luck and chance played their usual part, but the essential character of his rise does not depend on these more or less colourful factors. This insignificant man, unattractive and unkempt, had a besetting passion, a will to political power that was strong and unswerving. All his virility, all his urge to live and to work, came to focus in his effectiveness as a speaker, in his mission as a prophet, in his vocation to be the leader of his epoch as its great demagogue.

THE MASTER DEMAGOGUE

There are not many true demagogues in German history. Thomas Müntzer was something of the sort, and so were some leaders in the German Peasants' War; the prophet of Münster, the Anabaptist John of Leiden, reminds one forcibly of Hitler. In more recent times there were Joseph Görres, Friedrich Ludwig Jahn the father of gymnastics, Friedrich Hecker and Robert Blum of the Revolution of 1848, and later Ferdinand Lassalle and the court preacher Stöcker. What all these men have in common is the obsession to influence and to shape the masses, a lack of self-reliance in their ideas, a dependence on advisers, a shiftiness of goals and views, but an unalterable will to hold their place and to celebrate triumphs with the greatest possible publicity. All demagogues repeat themselves incessantly. They require applause as much as actors do; they suffer under the vacillations and tensions of public opinion, but they cannot live without this stimulant. They are moody and sensitive, strong haters and bold liars. They immediately drop friends who dare to criticize, they tolerate no rivals, but they indulge slavishly devoted adherents. Uncreative themselves, they successfully drain creative spirits with skill and cruelty. They are like sponges that must be saturated in order to have something to give out.

Adolf Hitler was the genius among German demagogues. This is his place in history, and this is the cause of Germany's destiny today. He is unrelated to any of the German geniuses of the past, but he joins their ranks. He imitated them all—siphoned off their apprehensions of the world, their religious awakenings, their creative art, their ability to shape social relationships as patriots and statesmen—solely to make himself through all this the presiding genius of a new world under German rulership. Even in the midst of the most dazzling success the demagogue always keeps a trace of the adventurer, not to say the swindler. There is something improbable and unreal in all his radiance. The demagogue, like Shakespeare's weaver, wants to be and play everything, especially the lions—ruler and supreme judge, lawgiver and master economist, diplomat and strategist. He actually feels his way into the most diverse fields of endeavour. He has clever ideas, and his will prods the hesitant and dubious expert into plunging ahead. But there is always a residue of insecurity and uncertainty. The master demagogue is the genius who is condemned to be diabolic. He sets hell in motion against the divine; as the demonic war-lord Lucifer he fights against the disciples of the Prince of Peace. He is—as he was called in late antiquity—the fallen Emperor Saviour. His chthonic, earth-bound realm cannot endure, because it is only of this world. In Wagnerian terms, he is not Lohengrin but Telramund, not Siegfried but Hagen, not Parsifal but Klingsor. He leads the way, not to the Castle of the Grail, but to the twilight of the gods.

Hitler's inner development becomes understandable enough if one considers his relation to two other great leaders of our time, Lenin and Mussolini. The Russian and the Italian arrived before he did, and their creations in state and society excited Hitler's ambition and envy. He admired the work of Lenin, the blood-letting world organizer of a style possible only in Russia, and he hid this admiration under an infuriated persecution of everything communistic. On the other hand he despised Mussolini. In him Hitler saw a Latin comedian who perverted the wealth of ideas that flowed from the north. But practical considerations made it necessary for him to hide this contempt, too, under a front of friendship, of exaggerated good-fellowship. The mass events of our day have given the great demagogue the chance for maximum effectiveness. The more commonplace he is personally, the more trivial and coarse-grained his utterances, the cruder and grosser his dealings, the more will the masses see him as one of themselves; the more certain is he of satisfying their instincts. Germany tried for years to pick a way that would lead between Fascism and Bolshevism to a safe future. Then Hitler snatched at both movements, at once their friend and their foe. He outdid them both by combining them, and he made Germany the centre of a National Socialist world movement.

Without the person of the Führer National Socialism would never have become what it did become. If Hitler had faded out of the picture early in the game, the movement would have gone on, with someone else in the part of the great demagogue. But it would not have been the same thing. Forces that Hitler himself was competent to hold in check would immediately have risen in arms against Rudolf Hess, his faithful poodle who disappeared suddenly to England, or against Hermann Göring, who was waiting for the moment of succession with burning ambition, or against any other of the lesser deities. Hitler, the charismatic leader who wanted to stamp out Marxism, did at least succeed in refuting the Marxian interpretation of history. He proved by his election to grace and success the power of the individual in history. It was not he who had created the ideological premises for National Socialism. He was not in a position to understand them in their full significance. But he was the tool and the vessel of National Socialism. This movement made him the guide of Germany's destiny. He rose with it. He had to fall with it.

National Socialism has four theoretical elements. It accomplished four fundamental triumphs in domestic policy. It had three programs of foreign policy. We must attempt to discuss these eleven points systematically, briefly or in detail according to their relative significance, without trying to recount the events of contemporary history in chronological order, but rather showing in every case the connection between the principle and the personal and the essential objective factors involved. If the method is successful, the result will be a psychological biography of National Socialism such as may not be found elsewhere.

THE THEORETICAL ELEMENTS OF NATIONAL SOCIALISM. ANTI-LIBERALISM

The first element in National Socialism is anti-liberalism. In philosophy the struggle against liberalism in Germany set in with the romantic movement and reached its climax in the work of Schopenhauer and Nietzsche. The concept of the superman in all its variations, of the chosen individual, of the élite summoned to govern — this entire train of thought was familiar before the first World War and found expression in groups that were cultured and conservative or otherwise aristocratic in atmosphere. After the defeat authors like Jung and Moeller van den Bruck, schooled in art and cultural philosophy, took up these ideas and sought to give them a practical application to politics. Their argument ran like this: Germany must be saved; she must regain the greatness that is her due; this cannot be done by way of a parliamentary constitution and a democratic constitutional state; the ideology of a solution of this kind is not in accordance with German tradition and with the habits of the German mind. What Germany needs is a conservative revolution. The elect, the mighty, the representatives of the various strata that created German power and greatness in days gone by, these alone can prepare the revolution in Germany and save true Germanism for the future. Moeller van den Bruck, who came from the Baltic region, was familiar with the works of Feodor Dostoievsky. In them he read of a great people called to a world mission, a people that fulfils its destiny by the spiritual conquest of its vast country, by exploiting its natural resources, by suffering and by shaping its history, by action that spells liberation for itself and for others. Peoples that have lost their power to expand pass over from the dynamic creative process into a static realm of shadows. It was also Moeller van den Bruck who struck off the expression "Third Reich."

The conservative dynamics of the new master class necessarily reached its climax in affirming violence and war, in denying the harmonious co-operation of classes, parties, nations, in denying the ideas of reform, law, and progress that were the very essence of liberalism. There was to be, then, no discussion, no respect for the

637

opinions of one's neighbours, no opportunity to decide by voting, no parliamentary system, no compromise, no equilibrium, no rule of law, no constitutional state, but instead authority, command, terror, and obedience. The National Socialist Party destroyed all political opponents—indeed, all other parties. It set itself up as the super-party, as the order of the elect. Thus it created a sort of dual state. The party's refusal to admit new members immediately after the reorganization of the state indicated the new German superman's desire to be exclusive. The old classes and strata disappeared. Their place was taken by the élite and by the masses under the guidance of the élite.

The new German ruling class consisted of four decidedly anti-liberal groups: the ministerial bureaucracy as the élite of the German civil service; the hierarchy of the Nazi Party, most typically represented by the district leaders of the thirty-three districts (*Gaue*); the industrial leadership; and the agrarian leadership. The ruled classes were organized as the so-called Labour Front, which gradually developed the Labour Law, the Labour Courts, the Honour of Labour —everything being regimented, including leisure itself. The tension between the ruling class and the ruled mounted instead of slackening. The unity of society, one of the great liberal ideas, was intentionally destroyed. Behind the differentiation of wages, one of the great problems of this political system, the old class struggle went on, under new definitions of labour law and labour morale.

ANTI-SEMITISM

The second element in National Socialism is anti-Semitism. It is closely related to anti-liberalism, since many regarded the Jews as the chief carriers of liberal ideas. Anti-Semitism has become the best-known characteristic of National Socialism. The more the movement took on a comprehensive character, the more central became this hostility to the Jews. Wherever there are Jews there has been anti-Semitism. In democratic civilized countries it was usually limited to a social attitude. This was humanly undesirable, but it did not upset the law and order of the state or the structure of society. Russia was the first scene of the pogrom anti-Semitism that spread to Austria and Germany in the watered form of anti-Semitism as scandalmongering propaganda. The Wagnerians gave social anti-Semitism a sort of metaphysical basis. They propagated Count Gobineau's ideas of race through books, periodicals, and associations. Houston Stewart Chamberlain, who was English by birth, but became a naturalized German citizen, was Richard Wagner's son-in-law and a member of the Bayreuth circle. His main work, *The Foundations of the Nineteenth Century,* propounded Richard Wagner's cultural anti-Semitism in a bombastic but at the same time popular manner. Soon it became possible for a Wagnernian to be received in very exclusive homes that were closed to highly educated Jews.

Adolf Hitler, the emotional amateur in art, was a born Wagnerian, and he too was received in good Munich homes on the recommendation of his anti-Semitism, which, to be sure, was of a Viennese rather than of a Bayreuth variety. Hatred of the Jews was among the most profound, one might say sacred convictions of the Führer. He really believed that he could make the world better by destroying those wicked Jews. In Hitler such naïve beliefs were characteristically combined with peasant craftiness and apparent indecision—the simulated indecision that actually veils the pause before the pounce of the beast of prey. As far as the Jews were concerned, he never had a moment of doubt, and the most violent persecutions that his friend Julius Streicher could devise were perfectly satisfactory to him.

The highly cultivated, self-conscious German Jews, the great majority of whom were completely assimilated, were subjected to Russian pogrom methods by National Socialism. They were systematically deprived of their property, their family connections, and the opportunity to practise their professions. Even their religious cult was defiled, in open contradiction to the official axioms stressing race. What happened in concentration camps and prisons and in compulsory transmigrations, the systematic murder of defenceless people, is being fully exposed before impartial tribunals. What has been positively established must fill every honest, decent German with scalding shame. National Socialism worked toward the destruction of Jewry all over the world. Anti-Semitism was proving a secret power that opened doors and broke down barriers everywhere. It is astonishing how easily National Socialism gave a political character to local anti-Semitism of a purely social nature and thus opened the way for nihilistic German propaganda to the most influential groups in every country. Even the second World War could be accounted for as a fight about the Jews.

In Germany anti-Semitism broke out sporadically, but each time with more ferocity. How mild the economic boycott of April 1, 1933 appears in the light of later events! It lasted only a day and damaged so many Aryan businessmen along with the Jewish that they urgently sought a speedy end to it. The law of April 7, 1933 that set out to purge officialdom of Jewish and non-Aryan elements made a profound impression. In 1933 there were about five hundred and seventy thousand Jews in Germany, but over two million non-Aryans. Family trees were subjected to shameful investigation. The existence of even one non-Aryan grandparent was ruinous. Underhand dealings, forgeries, and denials became routine. Individuals who no longer had any personal or spiritual connection with Judaism were branded for all that. Old family ties, happy marriages, and friendships that had gone on from generation to generation were brutally torn apart. Naturally only a small minority stood this crucial test with steadfastness and courage.

At first certain classes of veterans of the first World War were exempt, but very soon no distinctions were made in practice. Jews were treated more and more as second-class citizens. Those of them who had immigrated from eastern Europe were regarded as undesirables and were deprived of their naturalization. It was an overture to what was in store for the German Jews. Jewish books and other publications were in disfavour, and many were burned on a pyre. Thousands of Jews began to arrange to emigrate—at great cost, so that it was possible only under heavy sacrifices. In addition to legal taxes that had to be paid, exploitation and extortion of every variety were practised. Officials and also persons of no authority whatsoever competed in plundering defenceless victims. German authorities called any criticism from abroad uninvited interference and replied to it with infamies. Many Jews committed suicide in order to escape the worst humiliation, that of becoming a burden on friends or relatives abroad. But a very large number of refugees found new homes and by their intelligence and adaptability won the respect of their new compatriots. Unfortunately only a small number of Aryans left Germany. Most German professors and officials acquiesced in the new order. In spite of their political past and their convictions they collaborated with a system whose vileness and criminality they must perfectly have realized.

The first climax in the persecution of the Jews in Germany came in 1938 when one of the younger German diplomats in Paris was murdered by a Polish Jewish refugee. The German government seized this event to loose a storm of brutal persecutions against the Jews. Synagogues were burned. The men were taken off to concentration camps, and emigration was made the condition of release. After the outbreak of the war in 1939, Jews were deported, especially to Poland, which became the centre of infamous wholesale slaughters. Any region that the victorious German troops entered became at once the scene of a persecution of the local Jews that was concerted with the representatives of local anti-Semitism. Under pressure from Germany, Italy, where anti-Semitism had been unknown, took an active part in the persecution of the Jews. The protectorate of Bohemia and Moravia, Hungary, Rumania, the Baltic states, and then even France were drawn into this whirlpool of anti-Semitic madness. The same phenomenon occurred in Norway, Denmark, the Netherlands, Belgium, Luxemburg, Greece, and the Ukraine. German policy reduced the Jews of central Europe and finally almost all European Jewry to a condition of unheard-of misery and persecution and consigned them to inevitable extinction as being active political, intellectual, military participants in the war against Germany. The more critical the position of the German colossus became, the more passionately the leaders grasped at the terrible expedient of handing over the Jews as hostages to National Socialist greed to rob and kill and wipe out.

The climax of the so-called legal measures against the German Jews came in 1940, when they were all shorn of their fortunes and their citizenship. Even the most trusting and loyal elements among the German Jews now realized what was awaiting them. It was they who suffered most both personally and economically, for in the consciousness of their rights and of their good standing they had done nothing at all to protect themselves.

The unexampled crime of Jewish persecutions in Germany must not be allowed to encourage the erroneous assumption that the so-called Aryans had an easy life. Out of seventeen concentration camps

Buchenwald alone was intended expressly for Jews. In all the others there was only a small percentage of Jews. Anyone who was under the least suspicion was in constant danger of sudden arrest. After a year, often even after half a year, the opponents of National Socialism were released. The harsh treatment they received will scar the remainder of their lives. They are mentally and often physically broken. If we put the number of so-called Aryans in concentration camps at three hundred thousand a year, which is conservative, it can be calculated what percentage of the German population was directly or indirectly victimized by the National Socialist reign of terror during more than ten years. There was actually no trade-unionist, no liberal, no pacifist, no religious or intellectual leader of the opposition constituted by the decent people of Germany, who was not affected by this methodical brutality. Circumstantial details of all atrocities have been reliably known ever since 1934.

This achievement, unique of its kind, was mainly the work of one man who looked like a teacher in a girls' school or like a post-office clerk: Heinrich Himmler. "Gentle Heinrich" was a curious product of the times. He came, like many National Socialists, from the petty bourgeoisie. Technically trained and skilled, he was matter-of-fact and uninspired, entirely without interesting characteristics of an extravagant or pathological order. To the outside world he was a quiet, respectable father of a family. He did what he called his duty in a gruesomely oily and slimy manner—a pharisaical hangman, a courteous murderer with an obliging smile.

ANTI-CHRISTIANISM

The third element of National Socialism was anti-Christianism. The official party program indeed avowed Christianity. But the treatment of baptized Jews was in itself the gravest breach of the fundamental principles of Christianity. Immediately after the reorganization of 1933 the evangelical church began to dispute the revision of the constitution; the paragraph about Aryans was to be applied to the church. But a far more serious matter was the party's encouragement of the so-called German Faith Movement (*Deutsche Glaubensbewegung*). From 1921 on, there had been attempts to introduce some national and racial religion. Paul de Lagarde (1827–

642

91) and Alfred Rosenberg (born 1893) supplied a basis of confused and exaggerated fancies for such a religion; its symbol was to be the orb of the sun. Karl Hauer, too, demanded an Aryan religion to supersede Christianity, which was "infected" with Judaism. The year 1934 marked the beginning of a Nordic faith movement that rejected the concepts of salvation and a hereafter. All manner of strange customs and cults developed in connection with it. But the group of the so-called German Christians constituted an even greater threat to Christianity. They fought against Christian world citizenship and against what they denominated the Jewish component in Christian doctrine. Their ideal was a heroic race-conscious devotion; memories of Martin Luther were rightly or wrongly cited to this end. The evangelical church opposed equally these Germanic aberrations and the new paganism; this movement brought together spiritual independents of all sorts in the effort to maintain evangelical freedom against the new state's attempts to interfere in doctrine and constitution.

The Germans have always taken their views of the world seriously. Discussions of metaphysical problems usually started during the lessons preceding confirmation and were continued in the *Prima* (the last year at the Gymnasium) and at the university. The Christian idea of life was revolting to highly regarded influential leaders of National Socialism, and they did not even try to conceal the fact. Julius Streicher, the editor of the anti-Semitic organ *Der Stürmer,* frequently even jeered at the person of the Saviour, Jesus Christ. The Black Corps held the same views, thinly veiled with would-be philosophy. Alfred Rosenberg was emphatically a new-style pagan. It was significant that this very man was the first to receive the German National Prize that Hitler instituted to take the place of the Nobel Prize. Ever since the famous pacifist Karl von Ossietzky, whom the Germans imprisoned and maltreated, had been awarded the Nobel Prize, no German was permitted to receive it.

It goes without saying that the disunity within German Protestantism was anathema to the principles of leadership-conscious National Socialism. But the disagreement between the Reich Ministry of Ecclesiastical Affairs and Public Instruction and the representatives of the churches ended with a compromise only after the outbreak

643

of the war. So long had these Protestant pastors, hardened to disputes, defied the contemptible interference in doctrine and administration.

The Roman Catholic church also suffered bitter disappointments. In the new concordat of July 1933 the curia had promised not to allow any political activity by the clergy. In return for this promise the Catholic Action was to continue as a non-political organization. Catholic schools, youth groups, and cultural associations were also to remain undisturbed. The interpretation of the concordat quite naturally led to endless friction. The Roman church could not acquiesce in the constant attacks on the Old Testament and the crucifix. Catholic press organs and youth associations were exposed to rude interference by the German authorities. In 1937 most of the Catholic schools in Bavaria were taken over by the state. The new, third *Kulturkampf* had broken out. An encyclical of the Pope accused the National Socialist government of violating the concordat. The reply was a bitter attack on the curia's passion for interference. The Pope renewed his complaints in a message to the cardinals in December 1937. More declarations followed. After the outbreak of the war in 1939 the utter credulity of both the German Protestants and the German Catholics and their almost too loyal attitude toward the measures taken by the National Socialist authorities offered no solution to the conflict that still dragged on. The explosion was merely postponed. The form and the spirit in which the war was conducted offended too many faithful German Christians. A religious revival was consummated that could not but lead to a rejection of National Socialist paganism and its dreams of world domination.

Among the Catholic prelates Cardinal Faulhaber in Munich became especially well known for his ruthless criticism of National Socialism. Others were unfortunately all too willing to smooth over the antagonism that existed by supporting the state. The persecution of the Christian churches led to the rise of a silent fellowship among all who professed Christian beliefs; nothing like it had been known in Germany since the Reformation. Count Galen, for example, the Roman Catholic Bishop of Münster, had his parish pray for Martin Niemöller, the Protestant pastor who had been sent to a concentration camp and who courageously refused to make the slightest concession in his fight against official interference with the Protestant dogma. In addition many less religious circles joined the religious opposition for the chance to air their dissatisfaction against National Socialism without immediate personal danger.

ANTI-MARXISM

The fourth element of National Socialism is anti-Marxism. The party laid particular stress on this term, which had been devised by the conservatives, in order to contrast its own good socialism with the wicked socialism of Karl Marx, the Jew, in a clear and edifying manner. In reality true Marxism was not to be found in the revisionism of the German Social Democrats or in Leninism and Stalinism in Moscow. True Marxism existed only among a few of the Independent Social Democrats and in the orthodox element among the German Communists. These were the true disciples of a great dogmatist. Their practical importance dwindled to the vanishing-point. The contention of the National Socialists that Marxism was threatening Germany with revolution in 1933 was therefore utterly unfounded.

No matter how alarming the activities of the German Communists may have been, politically they were isolated and divided among themselves; they no longer constituted an important party numerically. They could not be compared to the *Reichswehr,* the Social Democrats, the Banner of the Reich, and the Steel Helmets. In the years 1918-21, perhaps even up to 1923, it was Social Democracy that neutralized the concrete danger of revolutionary Communism. This circumstance now paralysed any possible resistance to National Socialism. To many observers the most astounding spectacle of the reorganization in 1933 was the meek compliance of the best-known leaders of the Social Democrats, such as Otto Braun and Karl Severing, the unopposed dissolution of the unions, which had become set and semi-official, the collaboration of the press and of associations. Historically all this had deep foundations in the developments of the preceding period.

The shattering of Social Democracy and Communism removed the political groups in Germany that, together with the ineffectual pacifist organizations of the left-wing bourgeoisie, had bravely persisted in the struggle against rearmament. The dispute over the construction of the first pocket battleship showed as early as 1928 how far the idea of rearmament had advanced in Germany. National Socialism now reorganized the entire German economy for military preparedness. This and this alone was the meaning of the tasks that were devised for the unemployed. They were engaged on public works at very low wages in disregard of any minimum wage agreements that the unions had won up to that time. Highways, barracks, fortifications, and concentration camps were built. Cutting through streets and erecting public buildings in Berlin and other large cities served to strengthen the power of the government and hence, indirectly, military preparedness. Heavy industry witnessed a return of prosperity: it was called upon to produce airplanes, cannons, submarines, tanks, and every kind of machine that could be of help in war. Leather, paper, and textile industries flourished correspondingly. Capital for these enterprises was procured by requiring the banks to extend short-term loans and to increase their amount; by raising duties, taxes, and assessments; through so-called voluntary contributions; and finally through trade acceptances that capitalists had to honour whether they wanted to or not. In the one year 1934–5 these trade acceptances alone mounted to two and a half billion reichsmarks. The floating debt was tripled in the first two years of National Socialism; there was a deficit of twenty-one billion reichsmarks.

Most of this income fell to military expenditures. During the first four years of National Socialism rearmament cost thirty-one billion reichsmarks. (These figures are only approximations, since, from 1934 on, no budget was published.) Foreign countries repeatedly refused loans, and thus Germany was thrown back on her domestic market. It could be maintained only by strict isolation from foreign countries and by currency manipulation; the currency was stabilized at home through every sort of compulsory measure, but abroad it was exposed to extremely bold manœuvring. Nearly a thousand ordinances were issued about foreign exchange and related matters; according to a modest estimate the control apparatus consumed two billion reichsmarks annually. Hitler, who knew very little about economic matters, demanded of Schacht that there be neither inflation nor devaluation; otherwise Schacht had a free hand. Without his help the system would not have worked six months.

What was the meaning of this anti-Marxian system? Industrial and agrarian capitalism was creative and therefore was good; finance and trade capitalism was exploitative and hence evil. This was the guiding thought. Private enterprise continued to function; at any rate no one assumed its risks for it. But the tyrannical state supervised every transaction and noted down every profit. Associations, authorities, commissars, and experts of the party and the *Wehrmacht* demanded on patriotic grounds the right to interfere constantly. Wherever profits were made, the buzzards appeared in the name of the good cause, but usually to gorge themselves. A truly planned economy was never achieved. The chaos of schemes and momentary measures was much too great. The old German delight in theorizing triumphed. The bungling and cheating by party favourites so irritated conscientious and responsible men of the old school that Hitler was forced to warn his faithful and impose a council of economic advisers on them. The greatest industrial magnates belonged to it, and so the economy of profits for the individual again came into its own.

The whole picture was confused. There was a state socialism of an improvised, stopgap variety, strongly reminiscent of economic policy in the era of princely absolutism. In olden times the chief gainers had been the princes and their courts. Now the party took their place. Party members were never at a disadvantage. Every agrarian or industrialist who had his wits about him won over party members of long standing as his patrons and rewarded these gentlemen generously for their mediation. The whole thing was a monopolistic racket. The economic tyranny of the party was tempered only by corruption and was sanctified by a patriotic concern for armament. Since there was not enough foreign currency and other gold values to import the necessary raw materials, industry concentrated on substitutes for rubber, gasoline, aluminum, and textiles. Fairly good quality was obtained by such synthetic though still very costly methods.

Agriculture was also to become independent of foreign countries. There were still enough vegetables, potatoes, and sugar beets in Germany, but there was no alternative to importing butter and eggs from abroad. These imports were ruthlessly cut down, for guns were more important than butter, as Göring put it. Wheat and rye production was to be increased, but the program was only partially successful. Imports of cattle feed had to be reduced to three fourths of what they had been, and the number of cattle fell off. The small farmer suffered most from the reorganization; in addition the legislation about inheritance upset the traditional rural organization of labour, based on a family economy. This legislation had the inherently reasonable aim of keeping farms from being split up by constant subdivision. A kind of peasant aristocracy with a minimum amount of land was to be created, such as already existed in some parts of Germany—in the Black Forest district and Lower Saxony. But the younger children, who were now put at a disadvantage, were jealous and objected vehemently. The large estates, on the other hand, were able to exploit most effectively their monopoly position in the production of potatoes and grain. They could be equipped with expensive modern machinery, and thus they profited from the mechanization of agriculture. They alone repaid the considerable investments necessary for high-quantity production. True, the large estates provided land for resettlement projects, but the soil was generally not good, and the majority of the settlers led a meagre existence and either had to ask the help of the state or become dependent on large-scale undertakings. The standard of living in Germany sank from year to year. Quality deteriorated, and general shortages led to illegal trade and price manipulation and even price freezing. An attempt was made to fix prices by fiat, but such a system could not last long. What would happen when the over-expanded apparatus could no longer be supplied with an appropriate flood of raw materials?

In 1933 statistics showed a marked decrease in unemployment in Germany, and even the opponents of National Socialism hailed it as a signal success. But if the impressive figures are examined more closely, several sources of error show up. Many branches of industry were simply forced to employ labour in excess of their actual requirements. Unwanted workers with political records disappeared from the factories, but they were not represented on the lists of the unemployed. Married women were replaced by unmarried women from these lists. The introduction of a forty-hour working week meant that more hands were needed. The voluntary work camps of young people showed that this group was kept busy, but they did not receive full pay. The old trade unions as well as employers' organizations were now dissolved. In their stead the Labour Front, which included all groups, was created: for the first time manual and mental workers, employees in industry, agriculture, and academic professions, found themselves united in one vast organization, which, in line with the Führer principle, was to function without strikes or boycotts, on a basis of mutual confidence and without ugly disputes over wages. The leaders and the led worked together in councils. Trusted agents of this organization, in thirteen districts spread out over Germany, were to handle all problems concerning labour. Economic courts of honour acted as supervisors of the conduct of all concerned. In most cases a return of more than six per cent was practically excluded; any further surplus was to be invested in public projects.

The system was obviously intent on reconciling social expediency with private business interests. In reality the worker was more than ever at the mercy of the employer. Instead of freedom to move about and bargain for himself, he was thrown sugary sops, such as the organization *Kraft durch Freude* (Strength through Joy). But crumbs of culture could not console the more perceptive for the fact that, to the accompaniment of high-sounding slogans, a new form of slave labour had been instituted in Germany and that it had only one serious aim, which remained within reach in spite—or even perhaps because—of the shortage of raw materials and the withering away of export trade, in spite of greater risks and unprofitable over-employment: the aim of military rearmament. The Four-Year Plan proclaimed in 1936 had no point but this. Germany wished to make herself entirely independent of foreign imports. She produced synthetic materials at no matter what cost. Foreign competition was throttled by import duties. Foreign currencies were affected. It was obvious that such developments were to Germany's advantage. The various international crises that arose over Austria and Czechoslovakia were test cases from which many conclusions were drawn. Special assessments on Jews, Catholics, bachelors, and industrial associations enabled the machine to keep running even through critical periods. Innocent-looking social devices, such as the "winter help," actually served the purpose of more and more ruthless extortion and control. The result of all this production, pushed to the utmost, was something that had been unknown in Germany for a

649

long time: a labour shortage, which was now combated by instituting compulsory labour service. From January 1939, when the
Führer issued a decree putting all males over seventeen, except those
in the armed forces, under the supervision of the Storm Troop
leader Lutze, there was actually no male individual whose potential
usefulness for work or war was not well known to the authorities.

The economic system of National Socialism is not to be characterized by so portentous a term as "state socialism." As a matter of
fact, no serious economic term could do justice to that unique combination of dictation as practised by the state, expropriation (or
rather robbery) as practised by the movement, and organized work
as practised by the people. Giant enterprises such as the Hermann
Göring Combine were established—institutions for ruthless individual money-making, and something more: offices, boards co-operating (semi-officially or however seemed convenient) with other
boards; economic states within the state, shaping a new program of
efficiency through the use of price commissions, boards for the ra-
tioning of raw materials, economic general staffs, and federal com-
missioners. Wages, after all, were good enough; private profits were
enormous; a high output was guaranteed. Labour could not protest
against trust-building of this type, which did not lead to autarchy or
self-sufficiency, but attacked the existing monopolies and supremacies
of the world market, emphasizing and heightening the danger of
war. A totalitarian monopolistic economy of a class-stratified society,
operated by class-conscious rulers and obedient masses—this was
National Socialism.

Rearmament, by direct and indirect methods, was the core of the
system. An annually increasing share of the national income and
resources was allocated to weapons and supplies. The nation was
drilled physically and mentally. Air-raid protection and similar
measures made war appear inevitable and self-evident. Every man of
large means had his own interests in the economy of military preparedness and could not wish for a change of the national temper.
The gold supply dwindled; there was iron instead. But war machinery would yield interest only if it were put to use. Besides, not for
another ten years would Germany be able to acquire entirely new
war equipment, such as would be needed in order to keep pace with
technical development. Only a war in the near future could stave

off bankruptcy, chaos, and the collapse of National Socialism. The party transformed Germany into a war factory and barracks. It affirmed war as an integral part of its world philosophy; and from the purely economic point of view it affirmed war as the ultimate big business—the sole and final possibility of striking a balance, of utilizing and cashing in on all the investments that had been made. If the war was successful, it would also be profitable. It would open the way to supplies; it would furnish labour; it would put all sorts of looted values into circulation; it would even bring back gold, which the National Socialist economy maintained was unnecessary.

Wicked Jewish Marxism, which National Socialism had undertaken to suppress, was right in one essential point: the concentration of economic values in the hands of the super-party heightened rather than lowered the tension, and it was leading Germany straight toward a crisis—toward war, revolution, or some catastrophe that combined both.

THE SUCCESSES OF NATIONAL SOCIALISM IN DOMESTIC POLICY.
THE DESTRUCTION OF CULTURE

Anti-liberalism, anti-Semitism, anti-Christianism, and anti-Marxism are the four elements of the National Socialist movement. This movement celebrated four fundamental triumphs in domestic policy. The first was the destruction of Germany's cultural tradition. National Socialism presented itself as a world view made up of exclusive and intolerant dogma. Deliberately and logically it made the claim of totalitarianism. It laid hold of the entire sphere of human interests and activity. There was no legitimate art or science outside of its teachings. The concept of race, the theory of a superior people —these were tenets of faith and as such could not be subjected to critical investigation. Even an attempt in that direction was sufficient to offend the mystical fanaticism that lay behind these ideas. This was the foundation for the state and for society. There was no place for the dubious or the indifferent. Anyone who did not collaborate was an enemy or even a traitor.

Germany's entire past was now re-examined from this explicitly unscientific, consciously anti-scientific position. Anyone who seemed to fit in with the doctrine was made much of—Herder and Fichte, for example. Anyone who could not be dispensed with was reinterpreted and taken over—like Luther and Baron vom Stein. Anyone who was both unadaptable and unnecessary was ignored. Even the enemies of National Socialism who belonged to the past, like Lessing and Wilhelm von Humboldt, were condemned. The same procedure was applied to literature and the fine arts. Liberal, Jewish, Marxian, pacifistic, Masonic, individualistic, and anarchistic tendencies were denounced. Any works that expressed these trends were prohibited, confiscated, and burned, and authors were maltreated, deprived of their rights, driven out, imprisoned, or secretly put out of the way. Institutions of higher learning suffered severe blows. Many scholars of good liberal background did not scorn to adapt themselves to the situation and to reap all the advantages of the removal of so many gifted competitors. There were similar unfortunate incidents in literature, art, and journalism.

German civilization became more and more rigid. The fine arts and literature declined. The level of thought flattened out. Manners became bad; the old German inclination to treat other people in the way of a schoolmaster or a non-commissioned officer triumphed. Brutality and passionate hatred of things not German were considered truly masculine and patriotic. German book production fell sharply. In a country where respect for education had always exceeded respect for money, and faith in officialdom had exceeded even respect for education, National Socialist drill, carried out with traditional thoroughness (*Gründlichkeit*), succeeded in moulding a new type of German citizen.

The triumphant leader of the cultural propaganda of National Socialism was Joseph Goebbels, a Rhinelander of good academic education, whose unusually supple intelligence was probably critical enough toward the assumptions of National Socialism. But his lack of faith and conviction did not prevent him from opening his mouth very wide and uttering his seductive Rhenish nonsense to the whole world. Goebbels's greatest forte lay in attack, in malicious criticism, in mockery of persons and ideas, and in witty arrogance. He failed whenever something positive was called for—a well-thought-out program, confession of active faith. Every real fighter and worker who was giving his sweat and blood was revolted by the silvery gush of talk dispensed by the Minister of Propaganda. Many an honest German yokel would have liked to give this dark and shrivelled

German the good thrashing he had earned a thousand times over for his intrigues and malice, his dissoluteness, baseness, and impudence. This man with the club-foot even forfeited the sympathy that a cripple can usually count on. For he had over-compensated for his infirmity many times by his wild and evil way of living. Goebbels was a cynical comedian who always had a surprise in store, and so he was able to astonish even those who were accustomed to his lies. The manner of his death was brave beyond what was to have been expected of one so vicious.

National Socialist propaganda administered such a stunning blow to German intellectual life that it may be a very long time before it recuperates. Absolutely all cultural influences were pressed into the service of the super-party: institutions of higher learning, the school system, museums, publishing houses, publicity, even lending libraries and literary clubs, the art trade and exhibitions. The aim was to rear a loyal party member and patriot who would be hard and cruel, willing to stake his own life, to fight for the community, and to sacrifice himself if need were. Discipline, order, and authority were the only valid standards. The nation was the highest good on earth. The loftiest achievement of education was to create a community of the people within which the individuals acted on one another and to which each must adjust himself unquestioningly. The military foundation of the concept is obvious; here, too, everything was tuned to war.

A large number of new studies crowded out the old liberal curriculum: the history of prehistoric times, the study of native land and people, the study of race, of geography, of population theory, of geopolitics. Special courses, camps for instruction, associations, students' residences, theatre performances, radio, national celebrations with the most solemn, stiff ceremonials—everything served the new cultural ideal, whose vocabulary and gestures were thus literally hammered into the minds of the people. This new Nazi Germany cut itself off from the cultural sphere of Europe and America with deliberate purpose and with unqualified success. Germany demanded a new form, a new rhythm, a new and more intense feeling of life that regarded itself as absolute and ultimate. Independence of judges, for instance, existed so far as the judges were rooted and grounded in the National Socialist view of the world. Only then might their

653

verdict be regarded as a "service close to the realities of life, performed for the people" (*lebenswirklichkeitsnahe Volksdienstarbeit*). Even the tax laws were to be interpreted in the light of National Socialism. Every scholar who travelled abroad had to report to a representative of the party wherever he went and to report his observations when he returned to his native land. There was no longer any scholarly activity that did not have its aspect of espionage.

Such were the humiliations borne by Germans, members of one of the most cultured and gifted peoples in the world. It was not surprising that hearts grew dulled, that spirits coarsened. What efforts the Weimar Republic had made in behalf of women! They were allowed to hold office; they became deputies; they exercised influence in every significant field. Now all this was reversed. Triumphant men's associations contemptuously thrust women back into their houses. Many of the younger women and even some of the more mature quite liked National Socialism—obviously because party life improved their prospects of marriage.

The party intervened ruthlessly even in the lives of young people. The great true Youth Movement was throttled. A youth leader for the Reich took over its entire conduct and had charge of all youth associations. There was no tolerance for anything individual or personal. There was no love and no respect, no feeling for the seriousness and sensitiveness of young people. Everyone and everything was roughly forced into the same mould. The Germans' old and fine individual culture, which Goethe had celebrated as the greatest good fortune of the children of earth, was systematically and utterly destroyed. What National Socialism required was robots, recruits, policemen, and hangmen. Schiller's concept of freedom collapsed. Goethe's world-wide wisdom, the spirit that he had breathed into nature, lost its meaning. Kant's profound critique and his ethos of reconciling peoples were looked down on, yes, even jeered at. Luther's achievement, the noble passion of Baron vom Stein, Bismarck's perspicacity and controlled power—all this sort of thing was belittled; all these men were now regarded as mere forerunners who should be thankful that they were graciously tolerated by the lackeys of an unenlightened despotism.

It is, however, difficult to accomplish complete destruction. The soul dies harder than the body. Behind locked doors the shades of noble traditional German culture hovered on. In days gone by it had been an emperor who sat waiting in the Kyffhäuser. Now German culture itself had been exiled and was waiting underground, in the very lap of the earth, until the spell should be broken.

For the moment totalitarianism was victorious, or rather the rule of totalitarian terror. Was such stupid barbarism needed to overcome the blow of Versailles? The overbearing, harsh, humourless, brusque manner of the National Socialists represented itself as the outward sign of inward health. Historically the reorganization completed what the Counter-Reformation, absolutism, militarism, and reactionary bureaucracy had tried to do with increasing success. That year of destiny 1933 was only a continuation of former fateful years: 1648, 1715, 1815, 1849, 1866, 1878, 1894. This collective development had just one great goal: the extinction of German freedom.

For many years the cultural sphere of Europe and America had been striving toward a new humanity. National Socialism now isolated Germany from these endeavours. It embarked, moreover, on an endeavour of its own with the purpose of destroying the ideal of humanity.

THE CONQUEST OF PARTICULARISM AND OF DUALISM

Particularism, dualism, and universalism were three age-old burdens in the history of Germany. National Socialism endeavoured to make a decisive change in this respect. The Weimar Constitution was never actually revoked, but its most important sections were abrogated by ordinance. According to the law of January 30, 1934 the government of the Reich had complete freedom to create a new basic law, and the Chancellor of the Reich promulgated such decisions without any participation by the Reichstag or the President. Thus, technically, the reorganization of the Reich had become a very simple affair. The centralized state now took the place of the federal state. All the prerogatives of sovereignty devolved on the Reich. The council of the Reich was dissolved, and the presidents and parliamentary bodies of the states were abolished. In a number of instances states were combined, and the former units survived only as public and legal entities. The dream of particularistic sovereignty was ended. Governors were set over the new groups of states as representatives of the head of the Reich. The plan was to abolish the historical boundaries of the states once and for all and to organize twenty new administrative units. But this was not done, probably because the disputes over old and new district interests (*Gau-Interessen*) made it too difficult to arrive at a final settlement. The government of the Reich appointed the governors. Prussia, however, was an exception. In Prussia the Chancellor of the Reich also held the governorship, but he transferred this post permanently to Hermann Göring, the President of the Prussian Ministry. In the person of Göring Prussian particularism survived to a certain degree—its historical traditions as well as its claim to hegemony.

Göring achieved some popularity in Germany and even abroad, because, among all the psychopaths and cripples, among all the upstarts of National Socialism who wallowed in rhetoric and nursed a thousand grievances, he represented something comparatively healthy. He was as strong as a bear, with sound nerves and senses. He was a scion of the old upper class, an aviator, a soldier and a hunter, a husband and father convinced of his own excellence, a man who could speak German correctly, who cracked broad jokes and treated the exaggerations and eccentricities of his fellow party members with a touch of humour. Being of this type, he reconciled many persons to the party and its activities. But if one probed beneath the surface, it became evident that, next to Hitler, Göring was the most fateful phenomenon. A man of his origin, his past, and his education was bound to see through the emptiness of the National Socialist ideology. But his desire to cut a figure was stronger than his judgement. The mainspring of Göring's existence was boundless cynical personal ambition and, in addition to this, envy of the demoniacal magic of Hitler's personality and of Goebbels's wit and showmanship, envy even of the energy and experience of Wilhelm Frick, for many years Reich Minister of the Interior, and of Heinrich Himmler's talents as an industrious detective and his indefatigable instinct for making combinations.

Göring saw himself—not without justification—as the dunce of this illustrious assembly, and he tried to compensate for his deficiencies by extravagant moods, by the prodigality of a sultan, and by sadistic debauches, brutal rages, and blood-letting. The organization of the *Luftwaffe* was something he could really understand,

and for this many Germans admired him. But he was never a general, not even in the Hitlerian mode of intuition and dilettantism. He was not even particularly enthusiastic about war. For he had a curious lack of personal courage, a love of personal comfort, and finally a passionate wish to survive the Führer in any event and to succeed him as a peace-loving ruler whom all the nations in the world would regard with approval. Göring apparently never believed in the world mission of National Socialism, and thus he saw himself as the obvious mediator, the only man who could still co-operate in one way or another with generals and monarchists, with feudalists and industrialists. That was why, through all his errors and bunglings, he never wavered from his sulky heir apparent's prudent intention of never exposing himself to a single unnecessary risk.

Prussian particularism, then, persisted. It may be asked whether the particularism of the rest of Germany was really dead. Dynastic particularism was replaced by the particularism of the districts (*Gaue*), and this was more or less furthered by the government. The old tribal bonds that had persisted through the Middle Ages were revived. The ministries of the Reich were combined with the Prussian ministries. The rather odd dual system of Berlin authorities disappeared, but with one significant exception: the Prussian financial ministry was allowed to stand, for Göring, the President of the Prussian Ministry, needed a cash-box of his own. The Reichstag was the only remaining parliamentary body in Germany. It consisted of representatives of the one ruling party; it was chosen without an election contest, and it had ceased to function. Witty tongues called it the best-paid male chorus in the world, for it broke its honorific slumbers only to applaud the speeches and acts of the Führer, and it expressed this applause by singing the national anthem and the Horst Wessel song. Horst Wessel was a pimp and a slippery customer altogether, who died obscurely in a street brawl in the Rhineland.

Centralization, then, had almost consumed parliamentarism. State and party grew together indistinguishably. The Weimar Republic had suffered from an excess of parliamentary institutions. Now the opposite condition prevailed. The dualisms between emperor and Reich, between state and church, between kingdom and territorial sovereignty, between Prussia and Austria, between the old core of the

Reich and the colonial region, between Protestants and Catholics, between Lutherans and Reformed, between authority and the people's movement—all these old antagonisms of German life had been vanquished by National Socialism, at least as far as appearances went and at least in accordance with the concept of a centralized totalitarian state.

And what had become of the old universalism? Ethnically the Germans were the most highly composite people in Europe. They occupied the centre of the Continent and had contact and reciprocity with more neighbours than any other nation. Germany had flexible and insecure boundaries. Her neighbours reached across these boundaries into Germany, and German sovereigns reached across them into other lands. These ethnical and geographical conditions were mostly responsible for the universalism, the concept of world domination, that permeated the early Middle Ages. This old universalism was crushed as Germany's European neighbours grew stronger, as they did before the Germans became modernized and unified. And so mediæval universalism shrank to a mere honorary position, to an imperial dignity attuned to peace. It became less and less of a political factor in European events. The old Reich disintegrated. The two great powers of Germany and the many individual states became its heirs. Could and would National Socialism revive universalism in an altered form?

THE METAMORPHOSIS OF UNIVERSALISM

National Socialism revived the concept of universalism by changing traditional citizenship into a nationality minded to live unto itself alone without regard to political, geographical, legal, or historical boundary lines, on the sole basis of the German idea. This nationality of the Germans validated its claims by means of the Germanic, Nordic, and Aryan ideologies. For practical and propagandist purposes these concepts, vague and controversial in themselves, were fused with one another. The universalistic nationality of the Germans was to embrace all who spoke German and also all inhabitants of areas that had once belonged to the Holy Roman Empire and that had been ostensibly or actually lost to the Germans. Even the Flemish- and Dutch-speaking inhabitants of Belgium and the Netherlands were regarded as fellow countrymen—lost, estranged compatriots who must be won back. The concept of a central Europe was no longer enough. Earlier Pan-German theories woke to new and vivid life.

A whole new branch of learning about Germans abroad sprang up and was zealously cultivated. Scholars and publicists took long journeys in order to find German groups in Europe and overseas and set to work on them. The aim was to remind them that they belonged to the German nationality and to develop a corresponding sense of obligation among them. The National Socialist Party was very active in foreign countries for the purpose of binding Germans all over the world together and so serving the economic interests of the Reich and the ultimate and boldest political plans of National Socialism. The old universalism was Germanic and liberal, based on the principle of the estates; it aimed to protect and reconcile the nations; it was Catholic and pacific. The Roman Emperor was thought of as one who would bring both temporal and spiritual salvation and would realize the millennial reign of peace on earth. The new universalism was not only anti-clerical, but un-Christian. It served this mundane existence and nothing else. It attacked foreign nationality only to heighten its own power; it split up and disintegrated what it touched, it thrust and drove forward. It was full of unrest, haste, and greed. It subjugated and suppressed, destroyed and annihilated. Here too were mouthings of a millennium, but the devout concept of imperial world salvation had been transformed into its monstrous opposite: the will to conquest of an unholy leadership, of the Anti-Christ.

The great French historian Hippolyte Taine undertook to interpret the French Revolution of 1789 as the revolt of the Celtic lower stratum against the Germanic upper stratum. For a trained and impartial race psychologist it might be a tempting task to investigate the true relation of National Socialism to the Germanic element. The leaders of the movement would be conspicuous for their strong Celtic or Slavic admixture if for nothing else. The areas where the Germanic element is strongest were the ones that resisted National Socialism longest. The increase in the population of Germany during the last fifty years seems to have brought in general an increase in Celtic and Slavic hybrids. The surplus population in rural districts and small towns is overwhelmingly of this composition, and it was from these sources that the masses in the big new cities were drawn. This was the sub-humanity that furnished the army for the super-party. A psychological factor was also implicated. Countries such as Sweden and Holland, in which the Germanic strain definitely predominates, have utilized the traditional Germanic concept of law and freedom to build up modern democratic institutions. Thus the bitter struggle of National Socialism against everything democratic might well be interpreted as a further sign of its actual estrangement from everything truly Germanic. Nothing is more non-Germanic than eastern despotism; nothing was so alien and revolting to the old Germanic character of the Holy Empire. The despotism of the eastern colonial region was revived by National Socialism; it trampled down the old Germanic concept of freedom. But in order to conceal its alien, non-German, non-Germanic character, this very despotism claimed the Germanic concept as its own and the basis of its system.

THE FOREIGN-POLICY PROGRAMS OF NATIONAL SOCIALISM. THE IDEA OF MILITARY REVENGE

These considerations lead straight to the three foreign-policy programs of National Socialism. The foreign-policy aspects of the movement were not at all unified, and they shifted with the years. Hitler's book, *Mein Kampf,* does indeed posit a series of significant objectives; but it is an error to suppose that the events of 1938–45 were nothing but a faithful realization of the doctrines and the demands stated in this book—an error that does not become truth by frequent repetition. None of the three foreign-policy programs of National Socialism completely obliterated the program that preceded it. They overlapped; they existed side by side; they even conflicted actively. Perhaps this inconsistency was unintentional, but more probably it was deliberately planned in order to obscure the actual goals.

The first foreign-policy program served the cause of military revenge. It was originally propagated by the intellectual leaders of the old Prussian general staff, who were permitted a shamefaced survival by the Weimar Republic to carry on military researches in the archives of the Reich in Potsdam. These clever and highly cultivated men knew exactly why the imperialistic World War had been lost. They smiled at the legend of the stab in the back and were resolved to do better next time. The old muster rolls were carefully preserved in preparation for the time when compulsory military service should be reintroduced. The experiences of the war were systematically recorded, ostensibly for scholarly purposes, but actually for very practical reasons. The old Prussian militaristic spirit was preparing for war, because war was the breath of life to it; it could imagine no future without a victorious war, the personal and historical satisfaction of a new triumph on the battlefield. A new subject for study arose: military science, which was taught at universities even before the reorganization. Periodicals and special investigations discussed the conditions of the future war. The *Luftwaffe,* gas warfare, mechanization—all these problems of technics and organization were pondered and pursued in the upper ranges of the *Reichswehr* ministry. But they were also discussed in semi-scientific and semi-popular writings, such as the books of Ewald Banse, a professor of military science (*Wehrwissenschaften*); so that step by step the public was prepared for the events to come.

What the Prussian militarists wanted above all was revenge on France. The occupation of the Ruhr Valley, the system of French diplomacy that spun its threads all over Europe, had aroused the profound bitterness that is clearly enough expressed in Hitler's book: France is the old hereditary foe; France is said to have the best army in the world; France must be punished. The plan was to isolate France as far as possible, to separate her from her allies on the Continent and even from Great Britain, and to instigate a cleavage in her domestic politics if it were at all feasible. The National Socialist friendship for Italy went back to the days of the Weimar Republic. After the first World War it was not particularly difficult for Germany to approach a disappointed Italy, even though the Weimar patriots did not relish the Southern Tyrol question or, later, Fascism. National Socialism had no trouble whatever in forgetting the unfortunate Tyrolese, and it learned from Fascism only to become its teacher. Italy's friendship was essential for the plan of military revenge, even though her potential military aid would be negligible.

As a consultant in foreign policy Hitler acquired an erstwhile champagne-dealer, Joachim von Ribbentrop, who had lived abroad for many years and who impressed the Führer with his easy command of foreign languages and the elegant manners of the experi-

enced travelling salesman, the lionized dancer of night clubs. Ribbentrop appropriated the noble "von" by having himself adopted
by a distant relative, and he tried to cover up the cheap vulgarity of
his person and his career by malicious bustle. At first he did not
succeed in sowing diplomatic dissension among the western powers,
even though he used the old Bismarckian method of inciting one
against the other for all it was worth.

Hitler's hostility toward Bolshevist Russia appeared deep and irreconcilable. Gradually a possible goal for the first program took
shape as a war on two fronts—a war against the two allied flanking
powers, France and Russia, as well as against their smaller satrap
states, with the assistance of Italy and perhaps even of Great Britain.
The naval agreement of 1935 between Germany and England
seemed very promising. It was a triumph of National Socialism that
England was persuaded to overlook a breach of the peace treaty and
of many other agreements for the sake of reducing the tension with
Nazi Germany. One of the most essential parts of this first program
was a resumption of the old Austrian Balkan policy. Oddly enough,
the domestic policy of National Socialism combined a revival of the
spy system of Metternich's police state with the ideal of the most
Prussian of kings: that is, the ideal of the military state of King
Frederick William I, whose memory was lavishly celebrated in
Germany, and not in vain.

An Austrian program of revenge appeared that fitted in with
Prussia's. Hitler himself always had a suggestion of the old Austrian
border police about him, quite in keeping with the tradition of his
father's calling; he had hated his father, but remained under his
spell. It came natural to the Führer to use police methods with the
minor Slavic nationalities. He regarded Vienna's claim to hegemony
in the Danube basin as a forgone conclusion. His abhorrence of the
Czechs and the Serbs and his sympathy for the Hungarians were in
accordance with the trends of Emperor Francis Joseph's Dual Monarchy. Thus Hitler's Prussian Russophil militarism was linked with
Austrian anti-Russian militarism. The dual nature of German tradition expressed itself in foreign policy. A wishful dream dawned
with the revival of the old Bismarckian idea of a triple alliance, together with good feeling toward Great Britain.

From the angle of foreign policy there were two culminations in the career of the German Führer and Chancellor. The first was the moment when, immediately before the outbreak of war in 1939, he succeeded in separating Russia from the western powers. For many years France and Czechoslovakia had endeavoured to draw Russia into the anti-German front. Great Britain had followed suit with a certain reluctance that was coloured by bourgeois and capitalistic considerations. Now Hitler and Ribbentrop, his Minister for Foreign Affairs, surprised the world with the German-Russian Non-Aggression Pact of August 23, 1939. To thoughtful observers this pact appeared a not too implausible, though temporary, resumption of the former German Rapallo policy.

The second culmination was the moment of the complete military defeat of France. Ever since the end of the first World War France had self-confidently played her part as the greatest military power in Europe. England's hesitant and often dubious foreign policy was dazzled again and again by the splendour of the French military machine. And now this predominance ended in a complete collapse, the underlying causes of which are not yet entirely clear. Hitler had taken his revenge. Even Germans who were not among his adherents acclaimed him now in 1940, particularly in recollection of the Ruhr occupation.

National Socialism had succeeded in separating Russia from the western powers in 1939; now it scored a still more striking achievement: it separated the two western powers from each other. For the time being it put an end to the Entente Cordiale. It isolated England, whose speedy ruin many regarded as entirely possible. Together with its Italian ally, it occupied the larger part, and later all, of France, and it applied the thumb-screws to the weak French government. Finally, with the help of French anti-Semitism and romantic conservatism, it even courted France's friendship, which was necessary for the defeat of England. It seemed as if the economic, spiritual, and moral ruin of one of the most distinguished countries of Europe was at hand.

THE CRUSADE AGAINST BOLSHEVISM

The second foreign-policy program of National Socialism was based on entirely different premises: those of Alfred Rosenberg's idea of a crusade against Bolshevism. The solution of the problems of central Europe that Friedrich Naumann had advocated during the imperialistic World War was now combined with the plan of crowding Russia out of eastern Europe, recommended at that earlier period by the Balts, Theodor Schiemann and Paul Rohrbach. Alfred Rosenberg, the official custodian of the National Socialist view of the world, was also a Balt, and he was filled with the typical bitter hatred of Russian barbarism that made no distinction between Czarism and Bolshevism. At first Hitler was strongly influenced by Rosenberg's views. The Führer's most singular stroke of foreign policy, his ten-year Non-Aggression Pact with Poland (1934), was in line with those views. Rosenberg demanded co-operation with Poland and with the Baltic border states, the separation of the Ukraine, and the liberation of all alien populations, even the independence of Siberia. The ruin of Russia's world empire, with the help of Turkey, Persia, Afghanistan, and Japan, was envisaged.

In 1936 Germany made an agreement with Japan. The western powers were expected to remain neutral. The collapse of Russian imperialism would be advantageous to British imperialism; Germany's eastward expansion would be a relief to France. The French Popular Front was given a clear warning by Germany's and Italy's support of Spanish Fascism. The ultimate aim of Rosenberg's ideas was a Nordic hegemony over Continental Europe for Germany. The national states in the east and the west that were small and therefore only semi-sovereign were to seek the protection of the central European bloc. Here, to be sure, resistance was to be expected, and so particularism was diverted into foreign policy. France and England, those exhausted and petrified creations of democracy, were not looked on as serious adversaries of a concentration of strength that would indubitably open the road to the Orient and Vladivostok.

If National Socialism had co-operated with Poland and Czechoslovakia in a reasonably neighbourly fashion, this program for the east might perhaps have been carried through. Hitler regained the Saar region; he withdrew from the League of Nations; he militarized the Rhineland; he tore up the Locarno Treaties; he achieved the *Anschluss* with Austria. But all these mounting and dazzling triumphs came off within the circle of the concept of a Greater Germany, a circle that the western powers did not intend to disturb, handicapped as they were by their own problems of domestic policy and of defence. But the destruction of Czechoslovakia, which could only be postponed by the negotiations at Munich in the autumn of 1938, the sharp turn of German policy against Poland, and the union of Carpatho-Ukraine with Hungary confronted the western powers with the necessity of fateful decisions.

REVOLUTIONARY WORLD IMPERIALISM

National Socialism had still a third foreign-policy program, it appeared, and this was now ripening toward realization.

Several groups had been constantly urging closer relations with Russia. This program was sponsored by the district leader Erich Koch of Königsberg, in East Prussia, by Professor von Grünberg, the economic planner from the same place, and by the young conservative revolutionaries, but was also promoted by the champions of the second socialist revolution, the true and final one. From General von Seeckt's time the officers of the general staff had been closely connected with Russian officers. In spite of the concept of an anti-Bolshevist crusade, economic relationships had been active ever since Rapallo and the treaty of amity between Germany and Russia in 1926. Hitler never felt at ease toward Russia. His old ambiguous hatred and love for Lenin dazzled and confused him. Some inner voice told him that perhaps the red Czar, Stalin, was the real new ruler of the world and he himself, Hitler, nothing but a bungler. But Russia was the only world power not merely to tolerate but to aid and abet a destruction of Poland. Moreover, for the time being, it was impossible to break up the co-operation of the western powers. These powers were even making overtures to Russia. The great encirclement of 1914 seemed impending. Since the collapse of Czechoslovakia the alliance between France and Russia had slackened. England and Russia had been alienated for a very long time on account of the insuperable distrust of Bolshevism by the English ruling class. National Socialism felt that it had been deceived and misled by England.

Hitler had at first shown little interest in the colonies. But the more successful he was in setting aside the Treaty of Versailles, the more loudly the colonial demand resounded in Germany. The return of any one colony would no longer be enough. National Socialist Germany, swollen with success, had become so hard to please that

665

even all the former German colonies put together would not have satisfied her. The western powers were forced to realize that any concession in the field of colonial policy would mean merely the beginning of wider claims. Public opinion in Germany was already beginning to discuss the future of the Portuguese colonies in Africa and manifested an eloquent interest in the Belgian Congo. But the methods that National Socialism used in dealing with its own countrymen did not serve at all to strengthen confidence in its fitness for colonial policy. The deciding factor was that the western powers, with Britain in the lead, could not expect any assuaging effect from a renewal of German colonial activities, but only excitement and new risks of conflict overseas. This attitude of rejection sharpened Germany's old hatred for England. If National Socialism had to choose between England and Russia, it now chose Russia, but only to be plunged into a new war of two fronts against both. Thus National Socialist Germany grasped at the loftiest reaches of world policy.

According to the teachings of the general and professor Karl Haushofer, whose confused fatalism acted directly on Hitler through Haushofer's pupil Rudolf Hess, Germany was called on to claim the mission of world leadership in the interest of preserving the race. A shadow overhung the old colonial powers—that is the way Haushofer put it in his books, full of magical prescriptions; these powers had become static and sluggish. They were to be replaced by a new master race, by nations active and dynamic. Haushofer had lived in Japan for a number of years and was therefore fairly well acquainted with that country. It seemed to him the very pattern of a nation on the rise, a nation inspired by divine forces and autocratically unified, a nation whose military preparedness and whose policies were directed to a single aim. There had been a good deal of mutual exchange between the Japanese and the Prussian ruling systems. Now, according to Haushofer, the new world rule of the chosen world powers was to be erected on the ruins and shards of small, outmoded state structures. Overpopulation meant danger of national suffocation, as Japan so impressively demonstrated; therefore, with the drive of cosmic destiny as of an inevitable force of nature, the nation's space must be enlarged. A new policy of "inrooting" expansion creates new economic zones, produces new natural growth, builds up new spheres of interest, overcomes all handicaps of space, wins over the like-minded in all parts of the earth, transforms population pressure into a fighting spirit, and through all this creates new imperial power. A class struggle of the nations had begun. The "have-nots" had to attack the "haves"; proletarian imperialism had to overthrow bourgeois imperialism. Anyone who failed to regard the whole earth from the point of view of power politics was lost. This perception lent fresh significance to the idea of the decline of the West. The old saying, "Anyone who thinks only about Europe is wrong," took on a new meaning. For a long time Europe had been living on the labour and the resources of other continents. These continents were now awakening. The political community of Europe was disintegrating. The great nations must maintain themselves. Germany's world mission consisted in preventing the decline of the West by establishing a new order in Europe on the basis of a strong Inner Europe (Haushofer's name for central Europe) and also in transforming this decline into a triumph of Western—i.e., German —leadership.

This was the third program of National Socialism. It was the watchword of a foreign policy based on a metamorphosed universalism. It was the program of revolutionary world imperialism.

THE MEANING OF THE NEW WORLD WAR

Stalin as well as Hitler came from the underdog class, a fact curiously manifested in the revolutionary despotism that at one and the same time made enemies of the two dictators and drew them together. It seemed that they could not live either in lasting hostility or in lasting friendship. It was absurd for a creative statesman to join with the adventurous demagogue; the relationship was ambivalent and must necessarily remain so. That is why they made mutual concessions, only to spy on and attack each other. That is why they broke their pacts. That is why their great struggle for existence, based on apparently irreconcilable views of the world, began churning itself to death with hideous wastage. Hitler promised to make the Soviet state the leading state in Asia with the help of his National Socialist discipline and his magical organizing power; this Soviet state, along with a Europe led by National Socialist Germany, should rule the world. But German foreign policy from Bismarck on showed Stalin how fronts were shifted and allies exploited, how the small was sacrificed to the greater, how risky it was to show one's cards, and how certain goals of growth and security could be pursued with iron persistence, unshaken by the theories of zealous Germanic or Anglo-Saxon ideologues.

Thus the events of the past years that still burn in our souls came to pass. Hitler destroyed unhappy Poland, which was not properly prepared. Stalin was at once ready to participate in a fifth partition of Poland. The Russian dictator also utilized this favourable opportunity to proceed against the Baltic border states, against Finland and Rumania. Old Russian accounts were balanced and new ones opened. Is it possible for a Russian world ruler to renounce Helsinki, Warsaw, and Constantinople? The dynamics of Russia's foreign policy are independent of the social type that heads her government.

Hitler defeated Russia's old ally, France. Just as in 1871, these triumphs produced an anti-German mood in Russia. But there was more to come. Hitler aided his ineffective ally, Italy, against the Greeks. He occupied the Balkan Peninsula and was prepared for the leap to the Near East. Bolshevist Russia had just effected a reconciliation with the Orthodox church. Pan-Slavism, neo-Slavism, and Russian imperialism, welded together by the immortal world mysticism of Dostoievsky, that great prophet, were reawakening. Hitler felt that Russia was a threat to him. He needed support in the east if he wanted to conquer the west. A Russia hostile but defeated seemed to him more desirable than a false friend who was fully prepared. So he attacked Russia. The climax of the war had come. The fact that Russia was kept busy in Europe heightened Japan's readiness to strike. Japan made use of the European situation to push her own program in Asia, and she flung a deadly challenge to the United States. America's entrance into the war gave it its global character.

REVOLUTIONARY ASPECT OF NATIONAL SOCIALISM

The scrapping of political slogans and their revaluation are among the most noteworthy characteristics of our times. National Socialism was strong in giving current concepts a new meaning serviceable to its cause. That is what happened to the concepts of labour, democracy, plebiscites, and self-determination. The use to which the notion of revolution has been put is especially strange. The National Socialist Party seized power by technically legitimate means. It became the greatest political party in Germany. The President of the Reich charged the leader of this party with forming a cabinet. All this was "legal" and "constitutional." But the moment the party was actually in power the picture changed. National Socialism embarked on a series of coups d'état, and in memory of the attempt of 1923 it called them a "national revolution," although this was a misnomer. In reality it was engaging in the systematic counter-revolutionary application of violence, in the reactionary destruction of the traditional form of the state and of society, destruction of the results of the reform movement of 1918–9 in favour of a new anti-democratic permanent dictatorship of a despotic eastern character.

But the revolution did not swallow this mockery. It was not satisfied with this synthetic product. It seethed within Germany as a movement for freedom among those who were stripped of their rights, enslaved, and tortured. And it seethed abroad, though the refugees lacked power and prospects. But even within National Socialism itself the revolutionary idea seized on the radical as well as the conservative wing. Hitler brutally suppressed every variety of opposition; yet it still persisted. When war broke out in 1939 all these movements dropped out of sight. Now even very sceptical German subjects supported the Führer, because, as they saw it, he was defending the fatherland from attack. But the alliance with Russia made the party appear, to the irritation and concern of those who were responsible, more left-wing, more radical, than it wanted to be. Revolutionary methods were applied in the war itself. This war was waged not against foreign armies, but against a strange disintegrating type of state and society. It was as if explosives were deliberately planted in the political way of life of Germany's neighbours.

No one was more amazed at Hitler's co-operation with Russia at the beginning of the war than his ally Japan. Even the great about-face, the break with Russia in 1941, could not re-establish Japan's confidence. There were many similarities in style and method between the revolutionary world imperialism of National Socialist Germany and Japan's idea of dominating Asia; nevertheless an uncomfortable tension existed behind this long-established elective af-

669

finity. The National Socialists would have been well pleased if the Japanese had attacked the Russians in Siberia, and the Japanese would have been just as well pleased if the Germans had succeeded in dealing the United States a mortal blow. Improbable as such eventualities were, time converted the fraternal pact of Germany and Japan into a relationship of reserve and watchful suspicion.

National Socialism wanted this war and prepared for it with every fibre of its being. It was possible for scholars to dispute at length about the origin of the imperialistic World War of 1914, for there it was not easy to measure the relation of cause and effect with perfect accuracy. The new World War was the World War of races. It is simple to state the causes of its outbreak. Its objectives, its historical meaning and importance, are clear. In the name of the race concept National Socialist Germany undertook to become the leading power in the world. A group of powers that believed themselves superior for racial reasons was formed in order to rule the old continents of Europe, Asia, and Africa and to threaten the new continents of America and Australia. One country after another was drawn into this gigantic world conflict. The whole earth was agitated by spiritual, social, and economic mobilization. Germany, together with her vassals and allies, was fighting against everything that was— against everything traditional and, moreover, against all reasonable possibilities of development and reform. Germany was filled with deep resentment, with passionate hatred for the older, wiser, and more fortunate world powers. Her aim was no longer merely, as in the imperialistic World War, to win a "place in the sun." She demanded that all places in the sun be redistributed according to German and Japanese judgement. The war was waged against "democracy" and "plutocracy"—that is to say, against the constitutional state, against humanity, against education, against hard-won values, against the structure of society developed in the course of history, against a healthy further growth of the civilized world. What seemed to be a war of conviction conducted against Bolshevism was actually a war of annihilation against the right of self-determination of the Slavs and the peoples of northern Asia. The domestic policy of National Socialism in destroying civilization had found an outlet in foreign policy. National Socialism and its satellites involved all the regions of the earth that are of any significance to humanity in a whirl of exploitation, propaganda, confusion, butchery. Nietzsche's concept of the superman had engendered the super-party. The super-party was permeated by the will to the super-Reich.

The new World War was the revolutionary world attack of National Socialism, on the dispersion of the values for which humanity has laboured and on the development of those values for the future by wise planning. Thus National Socialism precipitated the greatest crisis in the history of the German people. It produced a new world crisis of the widest possible scope. It unleashed anew all the demoniacal forces of time immemorial. All this proved that it was not National Socialism that was to give lasting shape to the future of Germany, of Europe, of the world.

Chapter 21
THE GERMAN COLLAPSE

THE HOPELESS defeat of National Socialism in the Second World War meant for Germany a collapse without precedent —unconditional surrender, acknowledgement of military annihilation from the highest military authorities of the Reich, the end of any responsible political authority, temporary suspension of the sovereignty of the German nation, the end of an independent foreign policy and of a centralized domestic government, complete occupation by various armies representing different political and economic ideologies. There exists no parallel in modern history.

The previous history of the German nation does, as a matter of fact, include break-downs to a considerable number. When the proudest family of the mediæval emperors, the Hohenstaufens, perished in Italy, there began the *kaiserlose schreckliche Zeit,* the terrible interregnum without an emperor. When the Thirty Years' War at last ended, the Treaty of Westphalia (1648) destroyed the last remnant of a powerful central government in the old Roman Empire, the Kingdom of the Germans became a phantom, the German territories grew almost independent, some of them were given to foreign neighbours, and poverty and distress scourged unhappy peasants and burghers, the victims of religious prejudice and dynastic ambition. When the National Assembly in Frankfurt, at the Church of St. Paul (1849), was shamefully dissolved and persecuted, civil war broke out, the last adherents of democracy and liberalism risked a hopeless fight for the constitution against the Prussian sword of ruthless reaction, and the proverbial "tranquillity of the graveyard," as Schiller had once called it, swallowed up German political aspirations to nation-wide freedom.

But the catastrophe of 1945 exceeded every earlier collapse. Just as, according to our interpretation, National Socialism recapitulated the major issues of German historical evolution in co-ordinating them into a crisis of unique tension, so now all the former debacles of the German past recapitulate themselves in the present distress and constitute a unique picture of historical tragedy *in excelsis*.

The history of the Second World War will sooner or later be written. The outward story is known to all and needs no repetition here. The inside story is known, so far, to very few if known at all. Many of our contemporaries are bound to ask *why* Germany experienced this utter defeat. National Socialism, which promised the nation a definite and dominant world position, has covered the German name with humiliation. Certain groups in Germany, even before the triumph of National Socialism, were pondering a new war. They took up with the Hitlerite movement precisely because it seemed to organize German bellicosity to an admirably efficient degree. Therefore one may say that the idea of a new war made National Socialism politically possible—nay, inevitable. National Socialism flourished by the idea of war. It ruined Germany by its war of aggression fought for German *Lebensraum,* or for the *Grossraum* of the master race, or even for world dominion. For the actual goal was and always remained vague; and the later historian will presumably detect here one disastrous weakness. The foreign policy of National Socialism was confused. Having been lucky enough to make a pact with Russia in the summer of 1939, it had to smash the Western powers as early and as quickly as possible; having been successful enough to beat France in 1940, it had to try to annihilate England, instead of hoping to win over the English by its sudden attack on Bolshevism.

Or did there exist, in spite of the exhaustive preparations for war, some sort of underlying strategical weakness that paralysed the offensives in North Africa, in Crete, in France, even in Russia, in the very hour of culmination? Was the German high command really crippled by the intuitions of the Führer, or did Germany, in the second World War as in the first, suffer from her lack of a transcendent military genius? Some critics will doubtless lay greatest emphasis on the technical aspects of the war and tell us that the Germans overestimated their potential in the air, that the submarines again fell short of what had been expected of them, that the new types of V-bombs were not efficient enough to alter the military situation—

673

that these shortcomings determined the break-down. Or should one attempt an analysis of the vain efforts of the Germans to establish their grandiose European New Order by tyranny and terror alone, without winning any hearts, and under an absurd travesty of their own racial ideology? The Jews were persecuted and liquidated as if they had been a belligerent power, while the equally Semitic Arabs were flattered. The Germanic Dutch, Flemings, and Norwegians were ill-treated, robbed, and tortured, the racially remote Finns, Turks, Hungarians, and Japanese sought after. Or will the more biographically minded critic tell us how the Führer actually coerced the Germans into a national unity of apparently superior strength, how just his magnetic personality held the nation together in spite of setbacks, revolutionary coups and movements, and underground conspiracies, because the army backed him as the source of renewed military glory, because the upper classes supported him out of dread of "radical" National Socialism, because the overwhelming majority of little men believed the propaganda slogans—the slogans that assured them daily that after Hitler nothing but poverty, spoliation, and destruction remained to the fatherland? Was this pitiful wretch Hitler, who toward the end concealed his physical and mental decline, his bad conscience and his utter despair, under more and more trivial and colourless vapourings—was this human wreck indeed to be identified with the German nation, or was Stalin right when he said (in his Order of the Day, February 23, 1942): "History shows that Hitlers come and go, whereas the German people and the German state remain"? And, finally, what would be the attitude of German youth after all these experiences of revolution and war? Would the Hitler Youth eventually become an anti-Hitler Youth? Would they hate and abominate the Führer, his tyranny, his war, his atrocities, his crimes and outrages, and try to create a new life based on a new creed? Would they make the best possible use of each new generation's historical privilege of inaugurating a new world?

Any one of these approaches may be found valuably suggestive, but all of them together yield only a portion of the whole truth. There exists something more basic than the mere events. German destiny has been and is being shaped by the German national character. The dream of National Socialism was the boldest of all German dreams. There were finer, nobler dreams in the German past, but unhappily there is not one to be found that is more typical, more expressive, of the Germans.

From the point of view of a thousand years' unfolding of German history the work and the fate of the man Adolf Hitler are a mere episode, unspeakably revolting and lamentable, freighted with untold consequences for decades to come; a very ugly episode, not to be forgotten for generations, but still an episode. The Germans must find a way to obliterate Hitler and Hitlerism; it is their prime business to do this, and all people of good will must endeavour to help them. Their eventual success will hinge on nothing other than the central qualities of the German national character. The German problem has a crucial importance for the world of today and of tomorrow. We can understand a nation only by studying its history; and the summation of a national history should be an analysis of the national character. Therefore let us conclude our account with such an analysis. It will form a bridge from past to present.

THE GERMAN NATIONAL CHARACTER

The German national character has been widely discussed. We are nevertheless sometimes impelled to wonder if there is any such reality. Voltaire once said that the French own the land, the British the sea, and the Germans the clouds. For a very short time the *Luft-waffe* mastered the clouds in a new and startling sense. Should the Germans now withdraw into their former illusions, and ought their longing for national unity to be renounced as one of the dreams that must remain dreams, in the interest of the self-preservation of more practical neighbours? Is the German national character itself a creature of the clouds?

Everyone who knows Germany is aware how little the sturdy Pomeranian has in common with the lively Rhinelander, or the stiff Hanoverian with the clever Swabian. But coexisting with regional differences, which are more conspicuous than in any comparable country in the world, there is of course something typically and generally German; and it is the product of various geographical, historical, racial, and social factors that will be familiar to readers of this book.

It will be remembered that Germany, the heartland of central Europe, the country of so many rivers and mountains, has been not shaped into a unit by geography, but merely torn asunder. The Rhine country is oriented toward the North Sea, the Danubian region in just the opposite direction—southeastward. The enormous variety of hills and valleys made Thuringia, Württemberg, Hesse, and the Palatinate classic countries of German particularism. German frontiers were "soft," never "natural"; there was a constant vacillation of frontier lines, a monotonous bickering of the larger and smaller rulers over boundaries. German history is full of quarrels without any deeper meaning than the self-interest and greed of innumerable dynasties and towns. Thus a sort of petty self-seeking was developed in the national character—envy, touchiness, jealousy, ambition without generosity. The princes ruined Germany, not only politically and socially, but economically and morally as well. It would be wrong to deny that there were many good princes; some were wise, just, and fair, some were fine soldiers and successful administrators. But there was a majority of rude and petty tyrants who oppressed and exploited the middle class and the peasants. Together with court society and the landed nobility they enjoyed a monopoly of the most shocking arrogance. The princes created in their own image a servile bureaucracy of well-trained, unbribable civil servants, and these also, in their own way, tyrannized over the subjects. The official of this bureaucracy was panoplied in authority, knowledge, power, and a certain remorseless addiction to red tape, all of which contributed to a second very typical component of the German national character: to wit, respect for power, for the authority of the uniform, the title, the office, the inside information.

The dynasties gave free rein to their rivalries; and these were further embittered by the religious cleavage of the German Reformation. Armies and officers, feudal and tribal groups, had no option but to follow their betters. In these old days the neighbour was *ipso facto* the enemy, and the assumption was that a good state must mobilize its power in ample season, because its wicked neighbour would seize upon any moment of weakness to launch a treacherous attack. The result was a further, the third, typical trend in the national character: a chronic distrust of, a sceptical disbelief in, the efficacy of the central and supreme authority—the Emperor of the Holy Roman Empire, the Imperial High Court, or, later, the federal diet at Frankfurt.

676

The fantastic variety of princelings in Germany accentuated the social differences among classes to an almost ludicrous extreme. Even in the period of Bismarck and William II the wives of commoners were not admitted to court society, though the commoners themselves were if they were persons of distinction—high officials or officers, professors, writers, artists. The wives had to stay at home —except the wives and daughters of bourgeois cabinet ministers. The court society of the German princes was passing dull, and only a few centers—Weimar, Gotha, Meiningen, Munich, Darmstadt— at one time or another played stimulating parts in the cultural life of the nation.

The arrogant and prevailingly reactionary attitude of German court society had an enormous influence on the national mind. This is the fourth point of our analysis. The German character developed a kind of touchiness, narrow-mindedness, false pride, and self-righteous ignorance of the actual forces newly at work in the modern world—traits unfortunately typical of the Reich right up to 1914. To be sure, a good deal of criticism arose within Germany herself. The former free cities, the rich bourgeois towns, became foci of loyal opposition, of more or less respectful pressure for reform. Internationally known journals and magazines tried to concentrate the attention of the responsible classes on the complete change in the international situation. Their efforts were largely unavailing.

Serfdom remained an institution in Germany until well into the Napoleonic era, and sundry restrictions upon the peasants' way of living and freedom of contract were even maintained until 1848. Foreigners often overlook the fact that personal liberty and freedom of labour in Germany are very recent achievements. The little man is the great-grandson of a sort of slave. Corresponding to this traditional rural serfdom, a new type of dependency evolved in the industrialized districts, where the old oppression was quickly converted into a new one. If the German of today seems remarkably subservient to authority, it should be remembered that servility is deep in his blood, the lower classes having always been systematically regimented, exploited, tyrannized over, ill-treated, and humiliated. The lower classes were badly off and had but little chance of escaping lifelong poverty, even by dint of industry and skill. Not until after 1880 did capitalism ripen and succeed sufficiently to offer the submerged strata a chance to rise—a tardy development by comparison with England or France. Thus the German middle class was not re-enforced. It was and continued to be politically immature; it disliked any co-operation with the lower tiers of the social pyramid because of their lack of culture; and it preferred (as was always evidenced during the various revolutionary upheavals) to collaborate with the ruling classes, court society, the big landowners, the bureaucracy, and the army. In place of the old economic serfdom a spiritual serfdom developed. Unique in its way, this was a heavy burden upon the future of the nation and a bitter discouragement to all prophets of political democracy and of social reform. It must not be forgotten that there were distinguished Germans who understood the actualities of the modern world and wanted the very best for the future of their nation. But what was their reward? They became suspect; their patriotism was called in question or jeered at; they were vilified as idiots or worse. They were and remained a minority. The overwhelming majority of the nation was infected with this deplorable spirit of serfdom—the only possible explanation of the striking successes attained by the Nazi terrorism. This is our fifth point.

When the political system of 1914 was replaced by the new system of 1919 the change did not turn out to be very fundamental. There were no longer monarchies in the fatherland, but the monarchists were bustling. There was no longer a gigantic army, but the curtailed army of lansquenets and non-commissioned officers was backed by the good old Prussian militarism, which was certainly a civilian affair *par excellence*—a specialized type of enthusiastically bellicose authoritarianism. There were now many larger and smaller parliaments endowed with all the democratic principles and privileges; but precisely this multiplicity of constitutional bodies—a new incarnation of the old German particularism—made the bureaucracy omnipotent. In no period of German history did the civil servant play so distinguished a rôle, in fact, as in the Weimar Republic, especially if he were a party official—one of the innumerable profiteers of the republican period who combined the domineering attitude of former times with the stilted manners of the party careerist. Some of these men were decent and personally blameless, but not one of them was a political fighter and democratic statesman of the first order. They lacked what Bismarck once called the courage of the civilian—a strange phenomenon in a country where the military virtues are part and parcel of character. Precisely in Germany the brave man who stood ready to fight and risk death for a great conviction, as Martin Luther and Baron vom Stein had done, was a comparative rarity.

But the most typical feature of all—the sixth point of our analysis —is only slightly linked with all these phenomena. It has to be explained with special care. Most Germans are enthusiastic experts. They specialize in some separate field of skill, knowledge, practical life, science, or the arts; they fortify their pronounced personal individualism with an exaggerated professionalism. Thus they become creative, each in his own province; but they have to sacrifice something for it, and what is sacrificed has often been their equilibrium as human beings. The number of curious, eccentric, distorted types in Germany is inordinate. These persons are fanatics in their way, and they have responded to fanaticism. A sort of natural sweetness and kindness that one often finds in England, and not only in the "gentleman," is rare in Germany. Even the combination of wit with reasonableness that makes a conversation with Monsieur and Madame Tout-le-monde so delightful in France is exceptional in Germany.

Everyone knows the names of supreme German poets, musicians, scholars, writers. The number of unusually gifted engineers, scientists, medical men, organizers of trade and industry, bankers, inventors, administrators is not less impressive. In some instances one does well to forget the man in the work. The Germans have been accustomed to invest all their tissue, all their capacity, all their creative power in what they call their duty, by which they generally mean something amounting to a mission. They are prepared to neglect almost everything human in order to consummate this ambition. For it they will give up personal comfort, family happiness, even pity and personal solicitude. German greatness of purpose and of achievement is often combined with a certain "romantic" foolhardiness. It makes the German unpredictable and dangerous, and oftentimes uncanny and monomaniacal.

There is, then, a conspicuous lack of balance in the German national character. The tendency to extremes is startling. Provincial

Germans put up with a philistine life of trivial pleasures that is almost pathetic. Cosmopolitan, world-conscious Germans indulge in a sort of barbaric extravagance. If they are poets or musicians, they are sweet and deep and surcharged with genius. If they are rulers, they are likely to become cynical brutes. Power intoxicates them. Harmony in a German is rare. The experience of many centuries of ordeals, bloodshed, destruction; the atrocities of unnumbered wars, of foreign suppression, not to speak of the fury of Spaniards, Swedes, and Frenchmen; the ugly inter-German fratricides of many generations—all these burden their minds and consciences. The bloody struggles between Protestants and Catholics, Austrians and Prussians, western Germans and eastern, were presently replaced by contentions between the *Burschenschaft* and the Corps—that is to say, the adherents of German unity and those of German particularism at the universities. There followed the party strifes between liberals and clericals, conservatives and socialists, reactionaries and progressives. None of these were contests between adversaries who wanted to arrive at an understanding or a compromise: they were bitter battles of annihilation between deadly enemies. One's enemy, in the typical German acceptation, is an infamous fellow: therefore he is called by all sorts of opprobrious names. From the time of Martin Luther the language of objurgation in Germany has been a sort of brutal and hateful explosion justified by the feeling of the unique personal "mission," a feeling oddly compounded of enthusiasm and contempt. It is incumbent on the righteous man to obliterate his wicked opponent. In doing this he is acting, not out of personal resentment, but in defence of a lofty principle, and all softness and fairness must be renounced in favour of something denoted by a very characteristic (and untranslatable) German coinage—*Humanitätsdusel,* an objectionable misapplication of flagrantly sentimental humanitarian theories to practical issues that ought to be decided on their inherent merits.

The psychological consequences are self-evident. Either internal wrangling made the Germans frivolous or ruthless, or else they took refuge in religion, philosophy, mysticism, and the fine arts because the real world seemed too harsh for them.

It is presumably this strange aberration of the German mind that gave the Jews their enormous opportunity in Germany. Their critical and analytical mentality supplemented the German national character in a very salutary way—as long as it was allowed to do so.

In the lower walks of life this curiously emotional self-destructive irrationality of the Germans may impress a foreigner as simply a striking kind of silliness. A German proverb puts it handsomely enough: "Stupidity is a gift of God; it ought not to be abused." To be genuinely unintelligent, to act like a normal healthy animal, is a great privilege of nature, mostly reserved to the so-called lower classes. In the Germans the interesting point is the foolishness of intelligent, well-educated, even widely travelled people. The typical expert, the famous professor, connoisseur, or architect, will astound you with a complete lack of reasonable judgement in most provinces outside his special field, and perhaps even more by the assurance that inspires the opinions he is only too ready to express on these very subjects. The French have an old, not too flattering byword for their neighbours: *bête comme un professeur allemand*. It is possible to think of German high judges, well-known physicists, prominent officials, successful merchants who have expressed opinions on political matters that a British trade-unionist would dismiss as cock-eyed. These Germans were undoubtedly much more gifted than the trade-unionist, they knew much more, they had had infinitely more experience. But they lacked a certain common sense and self-criticism; they were afflicted with the special kind of foolishness and blind fanaticism that we have analysed; they were victims of what we may call, in all sobriety, the blind spot, the queer streak in the German national character.

Only concentrated devotion enables people to do great things. What the Germans have done for the world as masters of the fine arts, music, science, and learning will always be appreciated, and only persons of mean mind would try to belittle it in the hour of the greatest catastrophe of German history. The German-Americans, for that matter, are among the soundest citizens of their great adoptive country, and they have attained extraordinary successes in all provinces of its life. The reason may have been that these immigrants came under the tutelage of a strong constitution and a healthy democratic spirit—privileges which they had missed in the fatherland and which their former fellow countrymen had been unable adequately to create.

On the smaller scale the Germans have governed themselves rather admirably, as, for instance, in the old free towns. The technical aspects of German administration on a larger scale became models for many foreign students. The bigger the German state was, the more authoritarian its system of administration. But the crucial weakness of the Germans was in their foreign policy, which they vitiated with their romanticizing pseudo-philosophy. Bismarck's colossal figure and his Prussianized Little German Reich will remain the classic exception in the unfolding of modern German history. Remember how racially mixed the Germans were. It was precisely their racial medley that prompted the wishful thought of a unique, a united and dominant master race—that supreme aberration of our time which, propagated throughout the world with pig-headed fanaticism, finally collapsed by virtue of its intrinsic senselessness.

Friedrich Nietzsche, the great German thinker whose extravagant spirit was, after all, too noble to be exploited by cheap Nazi propaganda, used to speak of the "good European" who was to be evolved out of the confused variety of national mixtures on the Continent. The German spirit, he thought, would one day play its part in forming an intellectual amalgam out of this chaos. The Nazis led this grand conception off at a new and absurd tangent by organizing a total rebellion not only against rationalism, statism, and political selfishness, but also against everything that bore a trace of the great factors of human progress; against enlightenment, tolerance, peaceful civilization, wise inter- and super-nationalism; against urbane cooperation with all other nations and races. The nation of Goethe's *Faust* and Beethoven's Ninth Symphony, of Immanuel Kant's projection of eternal peace and Hegel's *Phenomenology of the Spirit,* was utterly transformed into a maelstrom of anti-artistic, anti-philosophical, anti-religious vulgarities of which any cultured European must be as utterly ashamed as he is of the worst physical atrocities of the concentration camps. Nazidom undermined all the moral laws governing European civilization. A trivial dogmatism that ignored most of the critical achievements of a century of glorious thought established a kind of secular catechism whose uncompromising bigotry extinguished every heretic. Everything un-German was identified with everything un-National Socialist and was treated with bitter contempt. This glorification and self-adoration of the Nazi

682

super-state mounted in a climax of perversion and self-destruction.

The paramount objective in the foreign policy of any German statesman had to be, as we have shown, to prevent a coalition of Germany's neighbours. Bismarck, who accomplished this very successfully all his life, was haunted by the *cauchemar des coalitions,* as he himself called it—the nightmare of a possible coalition encircling the Reich. The history of the first World War taught a lesson on this score to everybody who could think in a fairly normal way. The man Hitler, who would never have risen to any such eminence as he attained if he had not been a supremely typical embodiment of all six weaknesses of the German national character as here outlined —the man Hitler first protested in his book *Mein Kampf,* an ill-written leading article of some six hundred pages, that any such mistake must and should never be made again in Germany. A few years later this same disastrous, more and more dominant upstart, to the plaudits of an increasing majority of the German nation, was doing everything in his power to organize this identical mistake in a gigantic super-edition. True, National Socialism as an organized party never reached more than roughly one third of the nation before Hitler came to power. A second third, we estimate, always stuck to implacable opposition. But the remaining third, as long as successes kept mounting, lined up behind the triumphant party heroes with flags flying. These facts of German foreign policy in the years 1933–45, more than any other one consideration, corroborate our theory of the essential folly of the Germans, and precisely of the able Germans. To put it plainly, we are not discussing Germany's pathological cases (which of course exist and can only be treated in isolation and with full scientific paraphernalia): rather, we are diagnosing a foolishness within the limits of intellectual and psychic normality—the blindness of exaggerating experts, a professional fanaticism that must always pay with fatal errors for its inhuman over-specialization.

German cartoons used to depict the German as the dumb Michel —the peasant lad who misses every golden opportunity through his lavish abuse of the wonderful gift of stupidity. The episode of National Socialism was, let us hope, the climax, the crowning triumph, and the end of this German folly, and Hitler himself the last as he was the greatest of all the German Michels.

WHITHER?

If a nation can become wise by its hurts, Germany ought to be in future the wisest nation in the world. In former times Europeans were taught to respect Germany as the nation of thinkers and poets; so Mme de Staël interpreted them to the Napoleonic world. Among the British, Carlyle was perhaps the first to try to understand the symptoms of awakening German nationalism, the power politics of the nation of thinkers and poets. In these latter days many of us have experienced the Germans as a nation of brutes and criminals. But consider: not every German of Mme de Staël's day was a poet and thinker, and not every German of ours is a brute and criminal. General judgements on any nation are risky and should be hedged by mature men. But assuredly the visible phenomena are being linked together. Exaggerated romantic nationalism turned great thinkers into foolish politicians. It might be correct to say that there are in Germany more political fools, clowns, charlatans, psychic traumatics, bossy pedants, litigants, grumblers, amateurish conspirators, rebels, inveterate joiners, quacks, and dreamers than in any other great nation—with fewer good orators, reasonable statesmen, leaders of thoughtful opposition, and skilful organizers of public opinion and of social movements.

German historical development has always been dramatic. Complete surprises are still possible and probable. It is a true observation that every German revolution has failed in a deeper sense. But the biography of every great German is essentially the story of a successful personal revolution. Even the revolutionary impulse was here individualized; and this impulse was considered so dangerous that precisely in Germany, the country without successful revolutions, the revolutionary spirit had constantly to be suppressed. Should the revolutionary idea and the revolutionary individuals in Germany one day coincide, there would be revolution of a colossal scope, kindled by a fanatical extremism unparalleled anywhere before.

No reasonable person is going to try to wean the Germans from being German. A German always remains a German, exactly as a Frenchman remains French, an Englishman English. It is part of the wisdom of all good education to take a character as it has been shaped by God and nature. It is possible to reform it, but not to transform it; it is possible to develop the good and suppress the evil,

684

or rather to develop the good *in* the evil, and to modulate the pupil by an appeal to the instincts of self-preservation and sociability.

This is a sad time for everyone who loved the "good old Germany." There will be a new and different Germany. The discarded values of German culture need a new emphasis; they alone can effect a reorientation of the German spirit. No inward regeneration is possible without a ruthless analysis of the German national character. This will be best accomplished by the Germans themselves. Germany must be re-educated, or rather she must be shown how to re-educate herself. Conscientious religious and ethical reformers will once again bring to pass, in the name of human dignity, a redemption of the unhappy, impoverished, hungry, confused German masses. Only a German is able completely to understand his countrymen. He will always love them because he has had to suffer deeply through them.

There is upon Germany something amounting to a blight, a curse. The best Germans have deplored it, and no enemy could say harsher things about the country than some of the Germans themselves have said. They said these things, of course, not for destructive but for creative purposes. To see, now, a whole nation put in the position of a defendant at the bar is a new thing in history, and it is a deeply moving thing to the hearts of those who perceive a meaning in history. It is in the best interests of the German nation itself that the truly guilty be punished, in order that the nation may survive and overcome this terrible crisis and inaugurate a new historical life in conformity with the world conscience, as well as with the most illustrious qualities of the elder Germany herself.

THE ORIGIN OF GERMAN NATIONALITY

768–814   Charles the Great; central European imperialism.
772–814   Saxon wars.
842   Strassburg oaths of grandsons of Charles the Great; Empire broken up.
843   Treaty of Verdun; Empire divided.
870   Treaty of Mersen; revised division of Empire.
876   Death of Louis the German (Germanicus).
899   Death of Emperor Arnulf of Carinthia.
c. 900   *Hildebrandslied, Heliand;* Otfried von Weissenburg; beginnings of German literature.
911   Duke Conrad of Franconia becomes East Frankish King.
918   Death of King Conrad I; collapse of Carolingian centralized administration.

THE SAXON RULERS

919–36   Henry I; tribal duchies versus kingdom.
933   Hungarians defeated at the Unstrut.
936–73   Otto the Great; central European concept revived.
951   Otto marries Adelaide of Burgundy; privileges for the church.
955   Battle of the Lech, defeat for Hungarians.
962   Otto, already King of the Lombards, crowned Emperor.
976–1246   Austria under the Babenbergs.
983   War with Arabs; death of Otto II.
1000   Archbishopric of Gnesen founded.
1002–24   Henry II; war with Poles.

THE SALIC DYNASTY

1024–39   Conrad II; Kingdom of Burgundy acquired; lesser vassals strengthened by making small fiefs inheritable; strong monarchy, without clerical bias.

1039–56 Henry III; conception of supreme ruler as high priest; slackening of temporal authority.

1043–76 Adalbert von Goseck, Archbishop of Bremen.

1056–1106 Henry IV; struggle with papacy; power of princes strengthened.

1077 Emperor and Pope meet at Canossa.

1105 Colonization of eastern Germany begins.

1106–25 Henry V; Concordat of Worms; Emperor forced into concessions to Pope, central monarchy to princes.

THE HOHENSTAUFEN ERA

1115–53 Bernard of Clairvaux.

1125–37 Lothair of Saxony-Supplinburg as Emperor; deference to papacy; crusades.

1137–52 Conrad III; central power weak, particularism strong; mounting conflict between Hohenstaufen and Guelph interests.

1146 Austria set off as duchy.

1149–57 Reinhald of Dassel, Archbishop of Köln.

1152–90 Frederick Barbarossa; personal union with Burgundy; struggles with Lombard cities.

1178 Compromise with Pope and Lombards concluded in Venice.

1181 Suppression of Guelph interests as represented by Henry the Lion.

1190–7 Henry VI; Hohenstaufen dream of world dominion shattered; Teutonic Order founded.

1198–1212 Double election; princes' right of nomination; civil war; national and local powers take precedence of universal and authoritarian factors.

1212–50 Frederick II; temporal as well as spiritual dominion claimed by papacy.

1215 Lateran Council; prestige of Pope Innocent III in former Byzantine Empire as well as in West.

1229 Crusade; Kingdom of Jerusalem.

1230 Teutonic Order receives Prussia as fief from Pope.

1231 Privilege of Worms; Frederick abandons idea of hereditary German monarchy.

1235 Imperial decree issued at Diet of Worms to centralize law in Germany. Absolutism in Kingdom of Sicily.

1236   Empire takes Austria back from Babenberg Dukes.

1237   Struggle with Pope and Lombards; victory for Frederick at Cortenuova.

1241   Mongol invasion; death of Henry the Pious, Duke of Lower Silesia, in Battle of Liegnitz.

1245   Council of Lyons; Frederick finally banished and deposed. Rival kings. Civil war in Germany and Italy.

1246   Death of last Babenberg Duke of Austria.

1250   Hohenstaufen claims to world dominion extinguished; end of German hegemony in central Europe. Community of interests between France and Pope.

GERMAN CIVILIZATION AT THE CREST OF THE MIDDLE AGES

1186   Knight's belt forbidden to peasants.

c. 1200   *Nibelungenlied, Gudrunlied.*

1212   King of Bohemia's obligation to appear at imperial court limited.

1220   Institution of electorates.

c. 1220   Saxon Mirror (*Sachsenspiegel,* law code).

c. 1230   Death of Walther von der Vogelweide.

1235   Landgravine Elizabeth of Thuringia canonized.

c. 1240   Hartmann von Aue, Gottfried von Strassburg, Wolfram von Eschenbach.

1248   Cornerstone of Cathedral of Köln laid.

1250   Cathedral of Strassburg begun.

1254   Federation of Rhenish cities formed in Worms.

THE DYNASTIES OF THE HABSBURGS, WITTELSBACHS, AND LUXEMBURGS

1250   German trade center established in Novgorod.

1273   End of interregnum; election of Rudolf of Habsburg.

1278   Ottokar of Bohemia and his extensive eastern realm collapse; beginning of Habsburg power in eastern central Europe.

1280   Alliance of Lübeck, Riga, and Wismar; origin of Hanseatic League.

1291   Everlasting League of three original Swiss cantons.

1294   King Adolf of Nassau makes subsidy treaty with England for war against France.

1308   Murder of King Albert I. Idea of hereditary Habsburg dynasty in Empire abandoned.

1309   Marienburg becomes residence of grand master of Teutonic Order.

1310   Emperor Henry VII of house of Luxemburg resumes Italian policy. John of Luxemburg marries last Přemyslid princess; Bohemia as citadel of central European power.

1314   Another double election; Louis of Bavaria and Frederick the Fair.

1315   Swiss victory at Morgarten; origin of Swiss Confederation.

1328   Louis of Bavaria crowned Emperor by representatives of city of Rome; Pope excommunicates him and denounces him as heretic.

1337   Alliance of Louis of Bavaria and King Edward III of England.

1338   Electoral conference at Rhense; electors claim right to confer imperial as well as royal prerogatives by their election.

1341   Lübeck as leading power in Hanseatic League; treaty with Denmark.

1346–78 Charles IV; prestige of Bohemia.

1347–51 Black Death. Persecution of Jews.

1348   University of Prague founded.

1354   Fall of Cola di Rienzi and dream of reviving Roman republic.

1356   Golden Bull; number of electors set; Wittelsbachs and Habsburgs slighted.

1364   Emperor Charles IV reaches agreement about succession with Austrian dukes.

1371   Development of royal jurisdiction, especially in Westphalia; Vehmic courts recognized.

1378   Charles IV hands over government of Kingdom of Arles to French Dauphin; German supremacy in Burgundy and imperial Italy reduced to formality.

THE END OF THE MIDDLE AGES IN GERMANY

c. 1250 King of Hungary settles Germans from Moselle region in Transylvania.

1351   Winrich of Kniprode, grand master of Teutonic Order in its most brilliant period.

1370 Weavers' battle in Köln; power exerted by guilds.

1376 Swabian city league formed.

1381 Rhenish city league.

1386 University of Heidelberg founded.

c. 1400 *Theologia deutsch* written by a Frankfurt member of Teutonic Order.

1400 King Wenceslaus deposed by Rhenish group of electors.

1411 Sigismund of Luxemburg, husband of heiress to Hungarian throne, elected Emperor and King.

1414–8 Council of Constance; thoroughgoing church reform discussed; John Huss burned as heretic.

1415 Frederick of Hohenzollern made Elector of Brandenburg.

1419–36 Hussite wars.

1431 Peasant revolt at Worms.

1431–49 Council of Basel; reform program of Cardinal Nicholas of Cusa.

c. 1439 *The Reformation of Emperor Sigismund.*

1443 Luxemburg becomes province of Burgundy.

1452 Frederick III of house of Habsburg; last imperial coronation in Rome.

1453–6 Gutenberg's Bible.

1460 Union of Schleswig and Holstein, with King of Denmark as Duke of both; Holstein remains within Empire, to which Schleswig never belongs; perpetual inseparability of the duchies promised.

1465–1536 Erasmus of Rotterdam.

1466 Second Peace of Thorn; Teutonic Order acknowledges Polish overlordship.

1471–1528 Albrecht Dürer.

1477 Maximilian of Habsburg marries Mary of Burgundy; death of Charles the Bold of Burgundy in battle with Swiss.

1479–1573 Hans Holbein the Younger.

1488 Swabian League, with princes and knights included, resists Wittelsbachs. Movement for reform of Empire, led by Berthold of Henneberg (died 1515), Elector of Mainz; "Rhenish" concept of Empire.

1493–1519 Emperor Maximilian I.

1495 *Ewiger Landfriede;* permanent rule of law established, with jurisdiction of imperial supreme court in all disagreements between estates of Empire.

1499   Independence of Swiss Confederation recognized.

1500   *Reichsregiment,* standing administrative committee of estates, approved.

1508   Maximilian, assuming title of Roman Emperor-elect, does not seek coronation by pope.

1511–20   Reuchlin's dispute with Pfefferkorn. *Epistolae Obscurorum Virorum.*

THE GERMAN REFORMATION

1483–1546   Martin Luther.

1515   King Francis I of France defeats Swiss at Marignano.

1517   Dispute about indulgences; Luther posts his ninety-five theses in Wittenberg. Hans Sachs writes his first carnival play.

1519–56   Charles V (died 1558).

1520   Three writings of Luther on reform.

1521   Diet of Worms. Luther translates Bible.

1522   End of Franz von Sickingen's feud; weakening of imperial knights with increasing ascendancy of princes.

1523   Death of Ulrich von Hutten.

1523   Swiss Reformation; Ulrich Zwingli.

1524–5   Peasants' War; downfall of Thomas Müntzer.

1526   Diet of Speyer; *jus reformandi* conceded to territorial sovereigns; evangelical churches countenanced.

1529   Religious discussion in Marburg between Zwingli and Luther, who proves irreconcilable. Luther's two catechisms. Sultan Soliman before Vienna. King Ferdinand of the Germans becomes King of Bohemia and Hungary.

1530   Diet of Augsburg. Charles V crowned emperor in Bologna. Schmalkalden League of Protestant estates of Empire.

1531   Zwingli falls at Kappel.

1532   Religious Peace of Nürnberg; legal and financial problems raised by Protestantism postponed.

1534   Anabaptists in Münster.

1535   Charles V assaults Tunis.

1537   Jürgen Wullenweber, mayor of Lübeck and its democratic champion, executed as victim of princes' jealousy.

1541 Death of Theophrastus Paracelsus.

1543 Copernicus' book on solar system published.

1546–7 War of Schmalkalden.

1551 Habsburg family compact. Treaty between Protestant princes and King Henry II of France, who becomes imperial regent of Lorraine's three imperial cities; disintegration of western German border. Insurrection and early death (1553) of Elector Maurice of Saxony.

1552 Treaty of Passau; concessions to Protestants.

1555 Religious Peace of Augsburg; concessions to Lutherans, not to Reformed; only subjects in imperial crownlands still not allowed to emigrate; "ecclesiastical reservation": ecclesiastical estates can become evangelical only on giving up territories and revenues; recognition of this clause withheld by Lutherans.

THE COUNTER-REFORMATION AND THE THIRTY YEARS' WAR

1544 First German Jesuit college founded in Köln.

1548 Imperial legislation abandoned for all seventeen provinces of Netherlands.

1560 Death of Philip Melanchthon, Protestant humanist.

1562 Emperor Ferdinand's truce with Ottoman Empire; tribute to be paid the latter. Development of particularistic Austrian interests.

1563 Doctrinal dissensions among Protestants; *Heidelberg Catechism;* Elector Palatine goes over to Reformed. Council of Trent closes; rise of a new Roman Catholicism.

1573 *Collegium Germanicum* founded in Rome to train priests to fight against Reformation in Germany.

1576–84 Religious contention about Köln; defeat for Protestantism.

1580 *Formula of Concord* and *Book of Concord* as bases of Protestant doctrine.

1591 First endeavours toward union of Protestant princes of Empire.

1597–1651 Duke Maximilian of Bavaria (later Elector), spiritual leader of German Counter-Reformation.

1598 Hanseatic *Stahlhof* settlement in London closed.

1608   Protestant Union formed in Empire; opposed (1609) by Catholic League headed by Duke of Bavaria.

1609   Twelve-year truce between Spain and rebellious northern Netherlands. Emperor Rudolf's charter of religious freedom for Bohemia.

1610   Murder of King Henry IV of France. Crisis in struggle over Jülich succession.

1617   Secret treaty between Spain and Austria; Rhenish buffer state against France projected.

1618   Brandenburg receives Duchy of Prussia as fief from Poland. Bohemian estates break with Habsburgs; Frederick, Elector Palatine, elected King of Bohemia; imperial envoys thrown out of the Hradschin in Prague.

1620   Battle of the White Mountain; Bohemia's collapse.

1623   Bavarian-Austrian-Spanish front; struggle against international Protestantism; absolutism as program against concept of estates; Protestantism as allied to liberty of estates.

1625   Wallenstein organizes imperial army. King of Denmark intervenes.

1626   Peasant revolt in Upper Austria.

1628   Wallenstein receives Mecklenburg as fief.

1629   Edict of Restitution; Habsburg Catholic absolutism in central Europe.

1630   War over Mantuan succession; clash of Austrian and French interests after extinction of Gonzaga family. France favours Protestant cause. Electors meet in Regensburg. Wallenstein's downfall; King Gustavus Adolphus of Sweden enters fight.

1631   French-Swedish subsidy treaty.

1632   Wallenstein recalled. Gustavus Adolphus falls at Lützen.

1634   Wallenstein murdered. Battle of Nördlingen.

1635   Peace of Prague concluded separately by electoral Saxony with Emperor; Counter-Reformation recognized in all Habsburg territories; princes of southwestern Germany sacrificed, also Reformed. Heilbronn Alliance between Sweden and southern Germany. Disintegration of Empire. Richelieu takes sides openly and declares war on Spain.

1638   France declares war on Emperor.

1639   Death of Duke Bernard of Weimar. Concept of Upper Rhenish principality abandoned.

694

1648 Peace of Westphalia; 1624 set as *annus decretorius;* Reformed recognized; Sweden becomes estate of Empire; France receives Habsburg lands in Alsace as indemnity. Victory of particularism; concept of German central state founders; German predominance in central Europe collapses.

THE ORIGIN OF THE TWO GREAT GERMAN POWERS

1640–88 Frederick William of Brandenburg, the Great Elector.

1650 Princes of Empire plan to form associations among themselves to counterbalance power of electors; Count George Frederick of Waldeck.—Otto von Guericke; air pump and electrostatic machine.

1654–68 First Rhenish Confederation; France and Sweden participate. Ideal of German liberty.

1659 Peace of the Pyrenees; Spain gives up designs on central Europe.

1660 Peace of Oliva; Duchy of Prussia, held for a while as fief from Sweden, confirmed as sovereign possession of Hohenzollerns.

1663 "Everlasting diet" of Regensburg summoned.

1666 Louis XIV makes separate treaties with west German princes; initiates policy of offensive warfare.

1668 First secret treaty between Austria and France concerning Spanish succession. Treaty between electoral Brandenburg and Louis XIV.

1670 Alliance between France and Bavaria. Louis XIV makes further treaties with German princes.

1673–4 War between Empire and France.

1675 War between Brandenburg and Sweden; victory for former at Fehrbellin.

1679 Treaty of Saint-Germain. Secret alliance and subsidy treaty between France and Brandenburg.

1679–85 Chambers of Reunion; France occupies Strassburg. New military organization of Empire; Emperor forms defensive alliance against France. Turks before Vienna; truce between Emperor and France; Hungary falls to Habsburgs.

1685 Revocation of Edict of Nantes; Huguenots settle in Germany.

1686   League of Augsburg, against France; Bavaria included. Defensive alliance of Emperor with Brandenburg. Struggle over succession in Palatinate; France attacks again.

1692   Ninth electorate established, for Duke Ernest Augustus of Hanover.

1693   Heidelberg destroyed a second time.

1697   Peace of Rijswijk. Prince Eugene defeats Turks at Zenza. Peace of Karlowitz; Habsburgs acquire Hungary except Banat of Temesvár, Transylvania, parts of Croatia and Slavonia. Polish royal election; dynastic connection formed between Saxony and Poland.

1698   Francke Foundation in Halle, stronghold of German pietism.

1698, 1700   Partition treaties on Spanish succession.

1700–21   Second Northern War.

1701   Elector of Brandenburg becomes King *in* Prussia.

1701   House of Hanover secures succession in Great Britain.

1701–15   War of the Spanish Succession.

1703   Emperor Leopold I cedes his rights to Spain to his younger son Charles. Habsburg family compact concerning succession; basis of Pragmatic Sanction.

1704   Prince Eugene and Marlborough triumph at Höchstädt and Blenheim.

1706   Emperor banishes both Wittelsbach electors; Bohemian electorate restored.

1706–7   Charles XII of Sweden in Saxony. Alliance between Sweden and France misfires; Lutherans in Silesia safeguarded.

1707   First steamboat on the Fulda.

1709   Böttger produces first European porcelain in Meissen.

1709–10   Unsuccessful peace negotiations with Louis XIV.

1711   Death of Emperor Joseph I; Charles of Spain succeeds him. Building of the Zwinger in Dresden begun.

1712   Peace of Utrecht concluded separately between France and Great Britain and her allies; British balance-of-power idea triumphs over that of hegemony.

1713   Pragmatic Sanction; indivisibility of Austria; succession in female line by primogeniture.

1713–40   King Frederick William I of Prussia; militarism and bureaucracy.

696

1714   Peace of Rastatt between Emperor and France; Peace of Baden (Switzerland) between Empire and France.

1719–21   Peace treaties ending Northern War; Sweden recedes from eastern and central Europe.

1720   Settlement between Spanish Bourbons and Habsburgs. Brilliant position for Austria.

1723   Charles VI founds Ostend Company for overseas trade.

1723–50   Johann Sebastian Bach in Leipzig.

1724   Wittelsbach "House Alliance"; leading position of this dynasty in Catholic Germany.

1726–8   Rivalry between Austria and Prussia; rapprochement and break between Prussia and Great Britain.

1727   Count Zinzendorf and the Moravians.

1733–8   War of the Polish Succession; Duchy of Lorraine goes to Polish King Stanislaus Leszczynski, to revert to France after his death. Alliance between Austria and Russia.

1737–9   Austrian-Turkish war; heavy losses of territory. Peace of Belgrade.

FREDERICK THE GREAT AND MARIA THERESA

1740   Death of Emperor Charles VI; Habsburg inheritance, Bohemia, and Hungary go to Maria Theresa (died 1780).

1740–5   Emperor Charles VII, of Wittelsbach dynasty. Peace of Füssen between Austria and Bavaria; Austria's dominance in Empire confirmed.

1740–8   War of the Austrian Succession; first and second Silesian Wars. Critical juncture in central Europe; Austrian-Prussian dualism declares itself; tension between older parts of Germany and colonial regions. Peace of Aachen; Austria loses most of Silesia to Prussia.

1740–86   Frederick the Great.

1745   Francis I, Duke of Lorraine, husband of Maria Theresa, becomes Emperor. Construction of château of Sans Souci near Potsdam begun.

1753   Prince Kaunitz becomes Austrian Chancellor.

1756   Westminster Treaty; co-operation of Prussia and Great Britain. Treaty between Austria and France, with Russia participating.

1756–83   Seven Years' War.

1757   Victories for Frederick at Rossbach and Leuthen.

1758   Frederick makes subsidy treaty with England.

1759   English-Prussian peace offer.

1762   Separate peace between Russia and Prussia. English-Spanish-French separate peace (Preliminary Peace of Fontainebleau). Empire declares itself neutral.

1763   Peace of Hubertusburg between Austria, Prussia, and Saxony; Prussia established as European great power.

1764   Alliance between Prussia and Russia.

1765–90   Joseph II as co-regent and Emperor.

1772   Austria acquires Bukovina. First partition of Poland. Frederick assumes title of King *of* Prussia.

1773   Goethe's *Götz von Berlichingen*.

1774   Goethe's *Werther* wins international acclaim.

1776–7   German contingents sent to America to fight against Revolution there; princely traffic in soldiers.

1778–9   War of the Bavarian Succession. Peace of Teschen, with France and Russia as guarantors; Austria's renunciation of Bavaria preserves balance of power between her and Prussia, in accord with general European needs.

1779   Lessing's *Nathan the Wise*.

1781   Kant's *Critique of Pure Reason*. Schiller's *The Robbers*.

1781–2   Serfdom abolished in Austria.

1785   Emperor Joseph's plans for Belgium and Bavaria fail. Frederick's League of Princes.

1786   Agreement of Ems; attempt to strengthen power of German bishops; state church encounters opposition from curia.

1787   Death of Gluck. Mozart's *Don Giovanni*.

GERMANY AND THE FRENCH REVOLUTION

1790   Independence movement in Belgium. Unsuccessful Austrian war against the Turks; Joseph's system of centralization goes under. Tension between Austria and Prussia; Hertzberg's "great plan."

1791   Brandenburg Gate in Berlin completed by Langhans.

1792   Austrian-Prussian alliance; agitation against French Revolution.

1793, 1795   Second and third partitions of Poland.

1794   Prussian civil law codified.

1795   Separate Peace of Basel between France and Prussia, which gives up left bank of Rhine. Kant's treatise *On Perpetual Peace*.

1797   Napoleon Bonaparte victorious. Peace of Campo Formio; Austria surrenders Rhine holdings; attempt at power politics beyond German borders.

1798   Peace Congress of Rastatt ends. War again.—Jenner introduces smallpox vaccination.

1799   Schiller's *Wallenstein*.

1800   Fichte propagandizes for self-sufficient commercial state.

1801   Peace of Lunéville; France triumphs over central Europe.

1803   *Reichsdeputationshauptschluss;* Empire shattered.

1804   Napoleon as French Emperor; in reply Austria sets herself up as an empire, in breach of old imperial law.

1805   Austerlitz. Austria concludes separate peace with France at Pressburg. French-Prussian alliance. Schiller's death; *William Tell* his last drama. Beethoven's *Fidelio*.

1806   Second Rhenish Confederation, under Napoleon's leadership. Holy Roman Empire dissolved. Jena. Humiliation for Prussia.

1808   Baron vom Stein banished. Congress of Erfurt; France and Russia co-operate against England; central Europe subjugated and exploited. Goethe's *Faust I* published.

THE WAR OF LIBERATION AGAINST NAPOLEON

1807–8   Fichte's *Addresses to the German Nation*. Serfdom formally abolished throughout Prussia.

1808   Reform in Austria; Count Philip Stadion; Archduke Charles and people's army. Prussian municipal ordinance.

1809   Napoleon's first defeat, at Aspern; victory at Wagram. Austria's war of liberation fails; her power position broken.

1810   Andreas Hofer, champion of Tyrolese liberty, shot by French in Mantua. University of Berlin founded. Prussia arms secretly; beginning of a national movement; Arndt; Jahn, inventor of gymnastics.

1812   Jews emancipated in Prussia. Napoleon in Russia; Prussia rises against France.

1813 Napoleon rejects negotiated peace; defeat at Leipzig; Rhenish Confederation collapses; French Empire abolished.

1814 First Peace of Paris; Congress of Vienna opened.

1815 Napoleon returns; Waterloo. Second Peace of Paris; European new order; the two great German powers restored; German Confederation takes place of old Empire, and central Europe constitutes a conservative supernational community.

THE GERMAN RESTORATION

1773–1859 Prince Clemens Metternich.

1815 Holy Alliance. *Burschenschaften* (student associations) founded.

1817 Wartburg Festival. Prussian Union (merger of Lutheran and Reformed churches within Prussia).

1819 Karlsbad Decrees; persecution of popular leaders. Single tariff for all Prussia; German customs union planned. Krupp firm founded.

1820 Final act of Congress of Vienna; measures against German freedom. *Manuscript from South Germany;* "pure" and constitutional Germany envisioned as against the two "half-alien" German great powers.

1825 King Louis I of Bavaria ascends throne; Munich becomes art center. Haller's *Restoration of Political Science*. Liebig's chemical laboratory in Giessen. Grillparzer's *König Ottokar*.

1826 Beginning of labour unrest in western Germany. Heine's *Buch der Lieder*.

THE FIRST TWO GERMAN REVOLUTIONS

1830 July Revolution; disturbances in several smaller states. Insurrection in Poland. German Customs Union.

1832 Death of Goethe. Hambach National Festival.

1833 Abortive Frankfurt *Putsch* against federal diet; persecution of demagogues renewed.

1834 Ministers of German states confer in Vienna; program of reaction.

1835 First German railroad, between Nürnberg and Fürth.

1837   Coup d'état in Hanover; seven Göttingen professors pilloried.

1840   First *Kulturkampf* ends. Frederick William IV of Prussia ascends throne.

1842–3 Karl Marx edits *Rhenish Gazette.*

1844   Beginning of German Catholic sectarian movement. Hebbel's *Mary Magdalene.*

1845   Wagner's *Tannhäuser.*

1846   Disturbances among Silesian weavers.

1847   Prussia's United Diet. Offenburg assembly of south German liberals; *Deutsche Zeitung* (Heidelberg) starts publication. Communist League consolidates left-wing associations; Marx and Engels write *Communist Manifesto* in London.

1848–9 Revolutionary movements in central Europe. Metternich's downfall; crisis in Austria. National movement throughout Germany; local reforms. Polish insurrection. War over Schleswig-Holstein. National assembly in Church of St. Paul in Frankfurt; national constitution; champions of Greater Germany and of Little Germany; revolutionary stirrings put down; Frederick William IV rejects imperial crown offered in people's name. Francis Joseph becomes Emperor of Austria.

1849   Prussia's Union policy; conflict between Austria and Prussia.

1850   Ineffective Union parliament at Erfurt. Agreement of Olmütz; Prussia isolated in both domestic and foreign policy. Schleswig and Holstein left in the lurch.

BISMARCK

1815–98 Otto von Bismarck.

1850   Prussian constitution with three-class suffrage sworn to by Frederick William IV; victory of reaction.

1851   Bismarck as Prussian envoy to federal diet (re-established at Frankfurt in 1850).

1852   Death of Prince Felix Schwarzenberg. London Protocol about Schleswig-Holstein succession.

1853   German National Association founded.

1854   Austrian-Prussian treaty during Crimean War for mutual guarantee of possessions.

1855   Gottfried Keller's *Der grüne Heinrich;* Gustav Freytag's *Debit and Credit.*

1858 Prince of Prussia becomes regent; new era opens. Rise of Catholic party, later known as Centre.

1859 Austria's war in Italy; Prussia mobilizes and projects military union in Germany. Fresh German national movement begins.

1860 Bunsen and Kirchhoff establish principles of spectrum analysis.

1861 Progressive Party founded in Prussia.

1862 Conflict in Prussia over military reform; Bismarck's fighting ministry.

1862–88 William I, King of Prussia, later also German Emperor.

1863 Ferdinand Lassalle founds General Association of German Workers. Insurrection in Poland; Alvensleben Convention between Prussia and Russia. Assembly of German princes at Frankfurt; Francis Joseph's attempt at reform of Confederation fails.

1864 The two German great powers make war on Denmark over Schleswig-Holstein; tension between Prussia and England. First International Working Men's Association founded in London.

1865 Convention of Gastein; temporary Austrian-Prussian agreement as to Schleswig-Holstein.

1866 Alliance between Prussia and Italy. Bismarck urges reform of Confederation; breaks with Austria and middle states. Königgrätz. Preliminary Peace of Nikolsburg; Prussian annexations; North German Federation formed. Peace of Prague; France and Russia prevented from interfering. National Liberal Party founded.

1867 Free Conservative Association formed (later, German Reich Party). First session of customs parliament, with all non-Austrian Germany represented. Crisis over Luxemburg; Prussia's secret military treaties with south German states revealed. Austria reorganized as Austro-Hungarian Dual Monarchy. Rapprochement between France, Italy, and Austria. First volume of Marx's *Capital* published.

1868 Wagner's *Meistersinger.*

1869 Social Democratic Party.

1870 Prince Leopold of Hohenzollern-Sigmaringen as candidate for Spanish throne. Bismarck prepares; Napoleon intervenes. Ems dispatch; France declares war. Napoleon captured at Sedan; siege of Paris.

1871   Russia secures conference in London on Pontus clause of Peace of Paris (1856); Bismarck co-operates on condition of nonintervention by other powers in Franco-German War. Peace of Frankfurt. New German Reich, with Alsace-Lorraine as an imperial province. Civil war in France; Third Republic.

1872   Social Policy Association founded.

1873   Entente among emperors of Germany, Austria, and Russia. Reich consolidated. Second *Kulturkampf* begins.

1875   "War in Sight" crisis; hint of great "encirclement" of Germany by France, England, and Russia. Bismarck attempts to approach Great Britain. Gotha program of German Social Democracy.

1878   Congress of Berlin; Bismarck as "honest broker." Attempts on Emperor William's life; anti-socialist law.

1879   German-Austrian alliance. Trend toward protectionism. Reaction against liberalism; beginning of anti-Semitic movement.

1882   Italy joins German-Austrian alliance.

1884   Three Emperors' entente renewed for last time.

1884   Germany acquires colonies; Congo Conference in Berlin.

1887   Agreement concerning Mediterranean between England, Austria, and Italy; Bismarck continues to court English favour. Tension between Germany and Russia; Reinsurance Treaty.

WILLIAM II AND THE IMPERIALISTIC WORLD WAR

1888   Death of William I; Emperor Frederick III succeeds him.

1888–1918   Emperor William II.

1890   Bismarck dismissed. Heligoland-Zanzibar Treaty. Social welfare measures. Anti-socialist law lapses. *Freie Bühne* theatre founded in Berlin.

1892   Protective tariffs reduced; new trade treaties. Agriculturists' League founded (*Bund der Landwirte*). Gerhart Hauptmann's *The Weavers*.

1894   Caprivi discharged; Prince Hohenlohe replaces him as Chancellor. Friendship between William II and Czar Nicholas II. Pan-German League founded.

1895   Shimonoseki; Germany, Russia, and France protest against Japan's peace terms for China.

1896   William II's dispatch to President Kruger of the Transvaal after Jameson's attack. National Social Association; Friedrich Naumann.

1897   Ordinances about languages to be used in Bohemia; struggle between nationalities in Dual Monarchy becomes embittered.

1898   Germany acquires Marianas and Carolines; leases Tsingtao region in China. Emperor William II's speech in Damascus offering protection to all Mohammedans. Policy on Bagdad railway. First navy bill. First Hague Peace Conference. *Wandervogel* founded; start of Youth Movement.

1899–1901   German-English alliance attempted.

1900   Boxer Rebellion; military intervention of great powers in China; Yangtze Agreement between Germany and England. Bernhard von Bülow, Foreign Secretary since 1897, becomes Chancellor. Second navy bill.

1901   Thomas Mann's *Buddenbrooks*.

1902   Secret treaty between Italy and France. Triple Alliance weakens.

1902–3   Joint German-English action against Venezuela.

1903   Mürzsteg Agreement between Russia and Austria-Hungary on the Balkans.

1904   English-French colonial treaty on Morocco and Egypt. Beginning of Germany's Morocco policy.

1905   Landing in Tangier. Draft of Germany's Björkö Treaty with Russia falls through. Plan for a Continental Triple Alliance.

1907   Universal suffrage introduced in Austria. Second Hague Peace Conference. Treaty about Persia between Russia and Great Britain.—Richard Strauss's *Salome*. Albert Einstein's special theory of relativity (general theory, 1915).

1908   *Daily Telegraph* interview; indignation in Germany against William II.

1908–9   Crisis over Austria-Hungary's annexation of Bosnia and Herzegovina; German note to Russia practically an ultimatum.

1909   Prince Bülow gives way to Theobald von Bethmann Hollweg as Chancellor. Provisional treaty with France about Morocco.

1910   Siegmund Freud's fundamental work *Über Psychoanalyse*.

1910–1   German-Russian Treaties of Potsdam and St. Petersburg.

1911   Second Morocco crisis; German gunboat sent to Agadir; Lloyd George's Mansion House speech; agreements on Morocco and the Congo. Italy occupies Dodecanese Islands and attacks Tripoli. Triple Alliance further weakened.

1912   Balkan War. Secret Russo-Japanese agreement. Tension between Austria and Rumania. France and England secretly exchange notes on co-operation. Negotiations for German-English rapprochement; Lord Haldane discusses naval question in Berlin.

1913   Austrian ultimatum to Serbia about Albania. Zabern affair.

1914   Crisis precipitated by General Liman von Sanders in Turkish army reorganization. Prince zu Wied becomes ruler of Albania. Tension mounts between Germany and Russia. German-English colonial treaty drafted. Heir to Austrian throne murdered in Sarajevo; Austrian ultimatum to Serbia; Russia mobilizes; England attempts mediation; German ultimatum to Russia, with time limit; France appears passive. Outbreak of war; invasion of Belgium; first Battle of the Marne; Russians kept out of Germany; cruiser fleet unable to defend German colonies. Japan seizes Kiaochow; Bulgaria and the Ottoman Empire side with Germany.

1915   German conquest of Poland and Baltic region; defeat at Verdun. Italy takes sides with Entente; Treaty of London.

1916   U-boat warfare. Battle of the Somme; Battle of Jutland. Rumania occupied. Francis Joseph succeeded by Emperor Charles. German peace overtures; Wilson as mediator.

1917   Unrestricted submarine warfare; break between Germany and the United States. Revolution in Russia; Kerensky regime overthrown; Bolshevism. Separate German peace treaties: Brest-Litovsk, with Russia; Bucharest, with Rumania. English-Japanese treaty on German colonies.

1918   German offensive in France fails; counter-offensive. Wilson's Fourteen Points and other utterances. Collapse of Germany and her allies; German demand for immediate peace; William II flees; German Republic proclaimed. "Steel Helmets," nationalistic and monarchistic veterans' organization, formed.

THE THIRD GERMAN REVOLUTION AND THE WEIMAR REPUBLIC

1919 National Assembly; Weimar Constitution. Treaties of Versailles (with Germany) and Saint-Germain (with Austria). Republic of Austria. New German parties; threat of communism; government by red commissars in Munich.

1920 French sanctions in Rhineland. Kapp *Putsch*. Communist disturbances in central Germany.

1921 United Communist Party of Germany joins Third International. London ultimatum on reparations. Erzberger murdered. International economic conference in Genoa. Rapallo Treaty with Russia. German Workers' Party of Munich and *Deutsch-völkische Freiheitspartei* merge as National Socialist German Workers' Party under leadership of Adolf Hitler.

1922 Rathenau murdered.

1923 French and Belgian troops occupy Ruhr Valley; action denounced in authoritative English quarters as breach of Versailles Treaty. Passive resistance; policy of fulfillment. Gustav Stresemann becomes Chancellor. End of inflation. Last important Communist outbreaks put down; reactionary *Putsch* attempted in Küstrin; Hitler's Munich beer-cellar *Putsch*.

1924 French-Czechoslovak alliance. Conflict between Bavaria and Reich smoothed over. Dawes plan. Stresemann becomes Foreign Minister. *Reichsbanner Schwarz-Rot-Gold* founded. Thomas Mann's *Magic Mountain*.

1925 Death of President Ebert; Hindenburg elected. Locarno Conference; Rhineland treaties. Germany admitted to League of Nations.

1926 German-Russian treaty of amity. Disputes about expropriation of princes; about flag. Mounting right-wing opposition; old parties in disintegration.

1927 International economic conference at Geneva.

1928 Germany caught by international economic crisis. Young plan; attempt to wind up reparations question.

1929 Stresemann's death. Severing dissolves *Rotfrontkämpferbund*.

1930 Schacht dismissed as president of *Reichsbank*.

NATIONAL SOCIALISM

1930   First Brüning cabinet. September election; Nazis become second strongest party in Germany.

1931   German-Austrian Customs Union crisis. Foreign Minister Curtius dismissed; second Brüning cabinet.

1932   Hindenburg re-elected President; Hitler rolls up more than 13,000,000 votes, 36.8 per cent of electorate. Legislation and administration by frequent decrees. Gröner, dropped as *Reichswehrminister* after dissolving S.A., remains as Minister of Interior. Heinrich Brüning dismissed with entire cabinet; Franz von Papen becomes Chancellor, General von Schleicher *Reichswehrminister*. Coup d'état in Prussia; Socialist ministers ousted. Reichstag dissolved; Nazis, electing 230 delegates, are strongest party; Göring becomes president of Reichstag. Second Reichstag election (November); Nazis lose 2,000,000 votes and 34 delegates. Schleicher becomes Chancellor. Gregor Strasser demoted by Nazi party.

1933   Papen, Thyssen, Hugenberg, and the *Landbund,* an agrarian organization, combine against Schleicher. Hitler becomes Chancellor (January 30); first cabinet includes three Nazis, nine non-Nazis. Persecution of German Communists; Reichstag fire; election (March) under conditions of terror. First boycott of Jewish shops (April 1). Enabling Act endorsed by Reichstag; later extended illegally. Stalin renews with Hitler regime Berlin treaty of 1926 and arbitration treaty of 1929. Concentration camps become permanent institution all over Germany. All German parties except Nazis dissolved; only Nazi candidates permitted in November election. Co-ordination measures; totalitarianism; dictatorship organized; General Economic Council formed. Germany withdraws from disarmament conference and League of Nations.

1934   Hitler's blood purge; 1186 victims murdered. Severe persecution of Jews, liberals, Marxists, and Freemasons. Göring creates *Luftwaffe*. German-Polish non-aggression treaty. Assassination of Dollfuss, Austrian Chancellor; death of Hindenburg.

1935   New commercial treaty with Russia. Army enlarged to 300,-000; conscription re-instituted by Hitler. Saar plebiscite yields overwhelming majority for reunion with Reich. Anglo-German naval agreement.

1936　Unilateral abolition of Locarno pact by Hitler; Rhineland remilitarized; lengthy negotiations fail to produce new treaty. Carl von Ossietzky (1887–1938), leading German pacifist and political martyr to Nazi persecution, awarded Nobel Peace Prize. German-Japanese Anti-Comintern Pact.

1937　Heinrich Himmler's terroristic program laid before officers of *Wehrmacht;* Nazification of army started. Italy joins German-Japanese Anti-Comintern Pact.—Thomas Mann's historic letter to faculty of University of Bonn.

1938　Austria taken over by German Nazis; Hitler in Vienna. Crisis precipitated about Sudeten Germans; Hitler visited by British Prime Minister Neville Chamberlain; Munich conference; Reich takes over German-speaking parts of Bohemia; bad boundaries for reorganized Czechoslovak Republic. Minor German diplomat murdered in Paris; acute persecution of Jews in Germany. Franco-German agreement guaranteeing common frontiers.

1939　Hitler breaks all agreements about Bohemia; Prague occupied; German protectorate imposed on Czechs; special status for Slovakia. Germany occupies Memelland. British and French guarantees to Poland, Rumania, and Greece. Polish crisis; fresh appeasement of Germany. New German military alliance treaties concluded with Italy and Japan. Berlin-Moscow agreement; new partition of Poland. Hitler invades Poland in spite of warnings, without declaration of war; Britain and France declare war on Germany; complete collapse of Polish military resistance. Russia attacks Finland.

1940　Finland gives way to Russia, with territorial sacrifices. Nazis invade Norway and Denmark, occupy the Netherlands, attack Luxemburg, Belgium, and France; *Blitzkrieg*. British army escapes to England through Dunkirk. Italy declares war on France and Great Britain; French resistance to Nazis breaks down; German-French armistice; Germans occupy northern France; Free French movement inaugurated in London by General de Gaulle. Pact of Berlin. German air attacks on England; war in North Africa. Conscription adopted in United States. Italy attacks Greece.

1941   President Roosevelt proclaims Four Freedoms. Hungary, Rumania, Slovakia, Finland, and Bulgaria join Axis. Nazis occupy Yugoslavia, Rumania, and Greece. Rudolf Hess flies to Britain. Tension between Soviet Union and Germany; German attack on Russia. Atlantic Charter proclaimed by President Roosevelt and Prime Minister Winston Churchill; United States extends lend-lease aid to Russia. Japan attacks United States navy at Pearl Harbor; Germany and Italy declare war on United States; United States declares war on Germany and Italy.

1942   United Nations Pact. Field Marshal Rommel drives toward Egypt. German occupation extended throughout France. Allied armies land in North Africa. Allied aircraft begin destroying most of Germany's large cities. Siege of Leningrad; attack on Moscow; defense of Stalingrad marks turning point of war.

1943   Casablanca conference. Allied armies land in Sicily; Mussolini overthrown; Italy capitulates. Cairo conference. Stalin, Roosevelt, and Churchill meet in Teheran. Allied armies land in France; liberation of Paris; American troops take Aachen, their first German city. Free German Committee in Russia. Marshal von Rundstedt leads German counteroffensive in the Ardennes. Germans give up Rome. Goerdeler-Witzleben attempt on Hitler's life, third most serious conspiracy against him, fails. New purge and terrorism.

1944   Russian forces reach Warsaw. Yalta conference. Allies cross the Rhine. American forces conquer Bavaria and reach the Elbe. The Russians near the Oder.

1945   Death of Hitler and of Himmler. Admiral Doenitz as successor to the Führer. Russians take Berlin. German forces capitulate in Italy, Netherlands, Norway, and northern Germany; final German surrender accepted at American and Russian headquarters. Allied military occupation of Germany; British, American, French, and Russian zones set up; Russian rule in northern East Prussia, Polish rule in southern East Prussia, part of Pomerania, Posen, and Silesia; temporary suspension of German sovereignty. Potsdam conference. Nürnberg trial of Nazi war criminals begins. Expulsion of Germans from Alsace-Lorraine, Poland, Hungary, Slovakia, Bohemia, Yugoslavia, Transylvania.

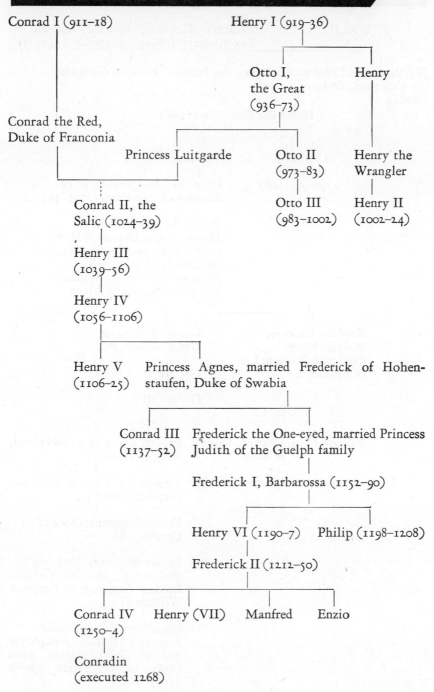

Conrad I (911–18)   Henry I (919–36)

                                   Otto I,   Henry
                                   the Great
                                   (936–73)

Conrad the Red,
Duke of Franconia

          Princess Luitgarde   Otto II   Henry the
                                 (973–83)   Wrangler

Conrad II, the   Otto III   Henry II
Salic (1024–39)   (983–1002)   (1002–24)

Henry III
(1039–56)

Henry IV
(1056–1106)

Henry V   Princess Agnes, married Frederick of Hohen-
(1106–25)   staufen, Duke of Swabia

     Conrad III   Frederick the One-eyed, married Princess
     (1137–52)   Judith of the Guelph family

          Frederick I, Barbarossa (1152–90)

          Henry VI (1190–7)   Philip (1198–1208)

          Frederick II (1212–50)

Conrad IV   Henry (VII)   Manfred   Enzio
(1250–4)

Conradin
(executed 1268)

Otto von Northeim, grandson of Henry
the Wrangler (of Saxon imperial house)

Welf II   Princess Richensa, married Lothair of
Saxony-Supplinburg, Emperor (1125–37)

Judith, married Frederick   Henry the Proud   Princess Gertrude
the One-eyed, Duke of
Swabia

Henry the Lion (died 1195)

Otto IV,   William
Emperor
(1198–1218)   Otto the Child, first Duke of
Brunswick-Lüneburg (1235–52)

Ernest Augustus, Duke of
Hanover, first Elector of Han-
over (1692), married Sophie,
daughter of Frederick V,
Elector Palatine, the Winter
King, and Elizabeth Stuart

Sophie Charlotte,   George I, King of
married King   Great Britain, etc.
Frederick William I
of Prussia   George II

George III

William IV...Edward, Duke...Ernest, Duke of Cumberland,
         of Kent   King of Hanover

Queen Victoria   George V, King of Hanover
(deposed 1866)

Ernest Augustus, Duke of
Cumberland

Ernest Augustus, Duke of
Brunswick, married Victoria
Louise, daughter of Emperor
William II

Hereditary Prince Ernest
Augustus, Prince of Hanover
and of Great Britain, etc.,
Duke of Brunswick (born
1914)

Otto of Wittelsbach,
Count Palatine of Bavaria

Otto, Duke of Bavaria (1180–1183)

Louis the Bavarian,   Rudolf, Elector Palatine
Emperor (1314–47)

Maximilian (1597–1651),
first Elector of Bavaria, married daughter
of Emperor Ferdinand II, Princess Marianne

Maximilian Emanuel (1679–1726)   Joseph Clemens, Elector
                                             of Köln
Charles Albert (1726–45; as
Emperor, Charles VII, 1742–5)

Maximilian Joseph (died 1777), succeeded
by Palatine line of Wittelsbach

Maximilian I Joseph (1795–1825), Elector
of Bavaria, first King of Bavaria

Louis I (1825–48)

Maximilian II (1848–64)   Luitpold, Regent of
                                             Bavaria (1886–1912)

Louis II   Otto   Louis III, Regent and
(1864–86)   (1886–1916)   later King of Bavaria
                                             (1912–18, died 1921)

                                             Rupert, Crown Prince
                                             (born 1869)

                                             Prince Albert (born 1905)

713

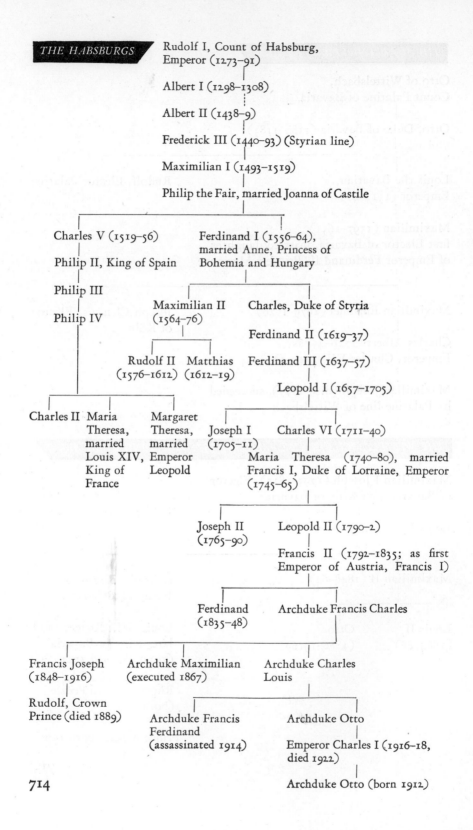

THE HABSBURGS

Rudolf I, Count of Habsburg, Emperor (1273–91)

Albert I (1298–1308)

Albert II (1438–9)

Frederick III (1440–93) (Styrian line)

Maximilian I (1493–1519)

Philip the Fair, married Joanna of Castile

Charles V (1519–56)

Philip II, King of Spain

Philip III

Philip IV

Ferdinand I (1556–64), married Anne, Princess of Bohemia and Hungary

Maximilian II (1564–76)

Charles, Duke of Styria

Ferdinand II (1619–37)

Rudolf II (1576–1612)   Matthias (1612–19)

Ferdinand III (1637–57)

Leopold I (1657–1705)

Charles II   Maria Theresa, married Louis XIV, King of France

Margaret Theresa, married Emperor Leopold

Joseph I (1705–11)

Charles VI (1711–40)

Maria Theresa (1740–80), married Francis I, Duke of Lorraine, Emperor (1745–65)

Joseph II (1765–90)

Leopold II (1790–2)

Francis II (1792–1835; as first Emperor of Austria, Francis I)

Ferdinand (1835–48)

Archduke Francis Charles

Francis Joseph (1848–1916)

Rudolf, Crown Prince (died 1889)

Archduke Maximilian (executed 1867)

Archduke Charles Louis

Archduke Francis Ferdinand (assassinated 1914)

Archduke Otto

Emperor Charles I (1916–18, died 1922)

Archduke Otto (born 1912)

714

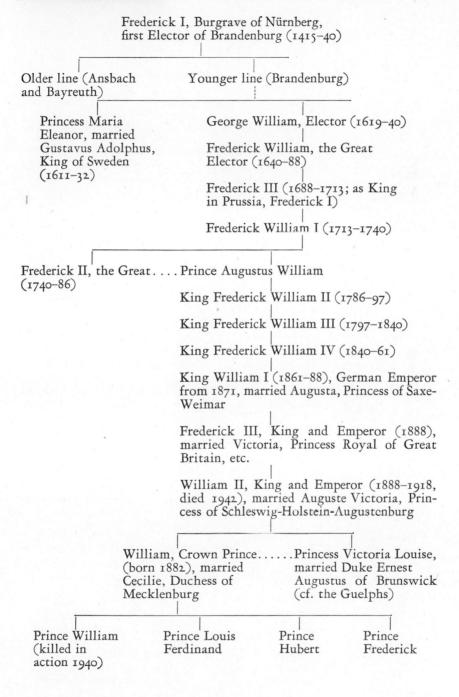

Frederick I, Burgrave of Nürnberg,
first Elector of Brandenburg (1415–40)

Older line (Ansbach
and Bayreuth)

Younger line (Brandenburg)

Princess Maria
Eleanor, married
Gustavus Adolphus,
King of Sweden
(1611–32)

George William, Elector (1619–40)

Frederick William, the Great
Elector (1640–88)

Frederick III (1688–1713; as King
in Prussia, Frederick I)

Frederick William I (1713–1740)

Frederick II, the Great.... Prince Augustus William
(1740–86)

King Frederick William II (1786–97)

King Frederick William III (1797–1840)

King Frederick William IV (1840–61)

King William I (1861–88), German Emperor
from 1871, married Augusta, Princess of Saxe-
Weimar

Frederick III, King and Emperor (1888),
married Victoria, Princess Royal of Great
Britain, etc.

William II, King and Emperor (1888–1918,
died 1942), married Auguste Victoria, Princess of Schleswig-Holstein-Augustenburg

William, Crown Prince......Princess Victoria Louise,
(born 1882), married   married Duke Ernest
Cecilie, Duchess of   Augustus of Brunswick
Mecklenburg   (cf. the Guelphs)

Prince William   Prince Louis   Prince   Prince
(killed in   Ferdinand   Hubert   Frederick
action 1940)

715

BIBLIOGRAPHICAL NOTE, READING LIST, AND INDEX

SOME BOOKS IN ENGLISH ON GERMAN HISTORY

As SUPPLEMENTARY literature I shall suggest only a scattering of titles in English. For the serious student there is no escape from the classic bibliography of the subject, the famous Dahlmann-Waitz reference work published in German only, *Quellenkunde der deutschen Geschichte* (two volumes, K. F. Koehler, Leipzig, 1931–2), which is as complete as any bibliography can be. No later book of the sort exists in German, and there is nothing equivalent in English.

Of my own sixteen monographs on German history, only one is included in the lists given here, for only one has been translated into English. This is perhaps the place to set forth briefly my qualifications for laying the present book before the English-speaking public at a crucial time. I was dismissed from my two offices as professor and archivist in Berlin and Potsdam in 1933, after Hitler came to power, on the ground of my being "a politically unreliable civil servant," a characterization that, from such a source, I accepted as honourable. I was known as a reform-minded progressive liberal who denounced German rearmament as a provocation to war and anti-Semitism as an international scourge. I had served at the front in the first World War; was a Protestant of purely "Aryan" descent; was neither a Social Democrat nor a Communist; and was never a member of the Reichstag, though I was known politically through my articles in independent democratic newspapers. In spite of all this I suffered the typical personal history of such cases: my telephone conversations and correspondence were under surveillance, my name blacklisted to keep me from publishing a word, and my books withdrawn from the market.

I left Germany in July 1933. Later that year I went to the University of London to lecture, and beginning in 1939 I lectured at many American institutions of learning. I returned to Germany only in the summer of 1945, in an official capacity for the American government. My lectures at the University of London formed the basis of *The German People*.

A writer is inevitably influenced by the political and intellectual atmosphere that surrounds him, and his conclusions must be weighed in its light. Hence two listings of books in English on German history are offered below: works by German or German-born authors and works by writers of American and British nationality. Subdivisions correspond to periods of historical thought. Practically all the books mentioned were published since the turn of the century; they are arranged chronologically according to year of publication. American editions are cited for most titles; those preceded by an asterisk are London issues unless otherwise specified.

I. BOOKS BY GERMAN OR GERMAN-BORN AUTHORS

Which German books on German history have been translated into English, which books not—and why—would be a fascinating study to everyone interested in international intellectual relations. Heinrich von Sybel's old-fashioned semi-official account of the founding of the German Reich was translated immediately after publication, though it was regarded by Germans at the time as dull and rather mediocre. On the other hand such a brilliant piece of historical writing as Treitschke's *German History* waited many years and was not laid before English readers until the first World War, when it became interesting to them as a demonstration of the aggressive Prussian spirit. Heinrich Friedjung's classic *Struggle for Supremacy in Germany,* whose publication was a major event of scholarship before the first World War, suffered a similar fate; it was not translated until the Nazi era, when German-Austrian relations made its subject timely. Heinrich von Srbik's masterly biography of Prince Metternich has never been Englished at all; neither have the indispensable writings of Erich Marcks and Friedrich Meinecke. Of the many works of Hermann Oncken only one has appeared in English; the choice, from obvious political considerations, fell on his book on Napoleon III and the Rhine, which is a respectable source on the Rhenish question. But the biography of the German socialist leader Ferdinand Lassalle, an excellent book that might well have become a best-seller, has never been brought out by an English or American publisher.

Memoirs of leading German statesmen and generals naturally aroused great interest abroad and were translated, for these names were familiar from the headlines—Bismarck, Prince Hohenlohe-Schillingsfürst, Prince Bülow, Bethmann Hollweg, Waldersee, Tirpitz, Ludendorff, Prince Max of Baden, Stresemann. Such books have always had a better chance of translation than those of the most distinguished scholars or even of a great historical writer such as Ricarda Huch.

What was translated was decided by business and political factors in the English- and German-speaking realms. On the whole it may be said that during times of good relations, about 1900, for instance, or after Locarno, the wave of interest swelled, while it receded during periods of estrangement, especially whenever British friendliness toward Germany waned. Another consideration was that historical writing was progressing among the British and also, with marked fresh vigour, among the Americans; English-speaking experts were now expected to know German well enough to read German books in the original. The general public was turning away from matters German, partly under the spell of more exotic and less hackneyed parts of the globe. But when estrangement from Germany culminated in a grave political crisis, indifference evaporated, and an urgent need for information about the political climate in what was soon to be an enemy country raised the demand for books by Germans to an all-time high.

The considerations that controlled the publication of translations have had the unfortunate result that the English-speaking countries became familiar primarily with nationalistic German writings inspired by Prussian expansionism, while the German Catholic, liberal, and socialist approaches remained little known. American and British scholars, of course, were acquainted with these less frightful trends in German scholarship, but the average reader of translations neither was nor could be completely informed as to German thought, but was given instead an unfortunately lopsided impression.

Historical writing of a sober cast was losing a good deal of its public everywhere because of the competition between history and many new provinces of scholarship, such as sociology, economics, anthropology, psychology. Increasingly historians became technical specialists; they were researchers rather than writers, experts not artists. They were overwhelmed by the mass of their material, and most of them had neither the courage nor the strength to suggest large perspectives. The myopia of many professional historians gave a big chance to amateurs of talent, and representatives of history as mere belles lettres achieved an exaggerated acclaim.

The latest period of German historiography is notable for a special class of books, written by German victims of Nazi persecution who left their country. Many of these refugees who turned their back on their fatherland for political, religious, or racial reasons had expert knowledge of German affairs. Their reports and interpretations of conditions in their former homeland have come at a time when such information was badly needed and was therefore favourably received as a rule. Yet such men necessarily write under certain liabilities. One of these is a natural and only too well justified feeling of bitterness and resentment, which might, and in some instances did, impede an objective view. Another liability arose from the refugee authors' need to adapt their presentation to the existing level of information on their particular subject within the English-speaking countries, although as relative newcomers they could not themselves appraise this standard confidently. Certain sources of error and misunderstanding thus came into being at times. But on the whole the liabilities were definitely compensated. First, their life in exile secured to many of these refugee authors, who were usually men of already mature years and much experience, the tragic advantage of a large personal fate, the long view. They were forced to re-examine and re-evaluate all their intellectual possessions. Distance and the challenge of a new world made them look at old problems from a fresh perspective and deepened their insight. Many of them acquired considerable command of the English language; some even started writing in the new idiom with success; they were at least able to oversee and control translations of their writing. The result was a literature of a type actually unprecedented. Numerous books were published by authors of merit, full of first-hand information, that were far more understandable to the English-speaking world than anything that had been presented to it by earlier phases of German historiography. Such books certainly have a greater usefulness than some rather theoretical works of earlier days that were written by Germans for an exclusively German audience and were often poorly translated if translated at all.

Two factors have called the authority of German refugee writers into question. The first is general in character and is probably inevitable: the widespread suspicion of anyone who, because of his personal experiences, may have an ax to grind. The second factor has to do with professional standards. National Socialism and the second World War have made historical problems very pressing; therefore certain refugee writers who were not trained historians and had neither the time nor the opportunity to fill their lack by systematic studies started discussing German history, often in a stimulating way, but sometimes without sound results. In a time when the writing of history is undergoing a transformation and incidentally a profound disintegration, a little indulgence for the gifted amateur may be in order; each such book, at any rate, must be judged on its merits.

A. BOOKS PUBLISHED BEFORE THE TREATY OF VERSAILLES

Sybel, Heinrich von: The Founding of the German Empire by William I. Seven volumes, Crowell, 1890–8.

*Janssen, Johannes: A History of the German People at the Close of the Middle Ages. Sixteen volumes, K. Paul, Trench, Trübner, 1896–1903.

Bismarck, Prince Otto: Reflections and Reminiscences. Harper, 1899.

Poschinger, Margarete von: The Life of Emperor Frederick III. Macmillan, 1901.

Hohenlohe-Schillingsfürst, Prince Chlodwig: Memoirs. Macmillan, 1906.

Ringhoffer, Karl: The Bernstorff Papers—The Life of Count Albrecht von Bernstorff. Longmans, Green, 1908.

Bebel, August: My Life. University of Chicago Press, 1912.

Treitschke, Heinrich von: A History of Germany in the Nineteenth Century. Six volumes, McBride, 1915–7.

Radziwill, Princess Catherine: Germany under Three Emperors. Funk & Wagnalls, 1917.

B. BOOKS PUBLISHED BEFORE HITLER'S RISE TO POWER (1933)

Tirpitz, Alfred von: Memoirs. Dodd, Mead, 1919.

Ludendorff, Erich: Ludendorff's Own Story. Harper, 1919.

Bethmann Hollweg, Theobald von: Reflections on the World War. Harper, 1919.

Bernstorff, Count Johann-Heinrich: My Three Years in America. Scribner, 1920.

*Waldersee, Count Alfred: Memoirs. Hutchinson, 1924.

Hammann, Otto: The World Policy of Germany. Alfred A. Knopf, 1927.

Brandenburg, Erich: From Bismarck to the World War. Oxford University Press, 1927.

Oncken, Hermann: Napoleon III and the Rhine. Alfred A. Knopf, 1928.

Prince Max of Baden: Memoirs. Two volumes, Scribner, 1928.

Ponsonby, Frederick, editor: Letters of Victoria, Consort of Emperor Frederick III. Macmillan, 1928.

Wiegler, Paul: William I. Houghton Mifflin, 1929.

Hoffmann, Max: War Diaries and Other Papers. International Publishers, 1929.

Scheidemann, Philip: The Making of New Germany—Memoirs. Two volumes, Appleton, 1929.

Haller, Johannes: The Epochs of German History. Harcourt, Brace, 1930.

*Bülow, Prince Bernhard: Letters. Hutchinson, 1930.

Bülow, Prince Bernhard: Memoirs. Four volumes, Little, Brown, 1931–2.

Olden, Rudolf: Stresemann. Dutton, 1930.

Kessler, Count Harry: Walter Rathenau. Harcourt, Brace, 1930.

*Germany—An Outline of Her Political, Economic, Social, and Cultural Life. Wirtschaftspolitische Gesellschaft, Berlin, 1930.

*Kantorowicz, Ernst: Frederick the Second, 1194–1250. Constable, 1931.

Diesel, Eugen: Germany and the Germans. Macmillan, 1931.

Rosenberg, Arthur: The Birth of the German Republic. Oxford University Press, 1931.

Schultze-Pfaelzer, Gerhard: Hindenburg. Putman, 1931.

*Haller, Johannes: France and Germany—The History of One Thousand Years. Constable, 1932.

Kraus, Herbert: The Crisis of German Democracy. Princeton University Press, 1933.

Nowak, Karl Friedrich: Germany's Road to Ruin. Bobbs Merrill, 1932.

C. BOOKS PUBLISHED DURING THE NATIONAL SOCIALIST PERIOD

Friedjung, Heinrich: The Struggle for Supremacy in Germany, 1859–66. Macmillan, 1935.

Stresemann, Gustav: Diaries, Letters and Papers. Three volumes, Macmillan, 1935–40.

Heiden, Konrad: A History of National Socialism. Alfred A. Knopf, 1935.

Olden, Rudolf: Hitler. Covici-Friede, 1936.

*Seger, Gerhard: A Nation Terrorized. Reilly & Lee, 1935.

*Wolff, Theodor: Through Two Decades. Heinemann, 1936.

*Rosenberg, Arthur: A History of the German Republic. Methuen, 1936.

Brook, Werner Frederick: A Social and Economic History of Germany, 1888–1938. Oxford University Press, 1938.

Grzesinski, A. C.: Inside Germany. Dutton, 1939.

*Behrend, Hans: The Real Rulers of Germany. Lawrence & Wishart, 1939.

*Stutterheim, Kurt von: The Two Germanys. Sidgwick & Jackson, 1939.

*Brandi, Karl: Emperor Charles V. Cape, 1939.

*Valentin, Veit: 1848, Chapters of German History. Allen & Unwin, 1940.

Stolper, Gustav: German Economy, 1870–1940. Reynal & Hitchcock, 1940.

*Borkenau, Franz: The Totalitarian Enemy. Faber & Faber, 1940.

Foerster, Friedrich Wilhelm: Europe and the German Question. Sheed & Ward, 1940.

Rauschning, Hermann: The Revolution of Nihilism. Alliance Book Corporation, 1939.

Rauschning, Hermann: The Voice of Destruction. Putnam, 1940.

Loewenstein, Karl: Hitler's Germany. Macmillan, 1940.

Ludwig, Emil: The Germans — The Double History of a Nation. Little, Brown, 1941.

Koeves, Tibor: Satan in Top Hat — The Biography of Franz von Papen. Alliance Book Corporation, 1941.

*Stern-Rubarth, Edgar: A Short History of the Germans. Duckworth, 1941.

Fraenkel, Ernst: The Dual State. Oxford University Press, 1941.

Fromm, Bella: Blood and Banquets. Harper, 1942.

Fried, H. E.: The Guilt of the German Army. Macmillan, 1942.

Stolper, Gustav: This Age of Fable. Reynal & Hitchcock, 1942.

Heiden, Konrad: Der Fuehrer. Houghton Mifflin, 1943.

*Merker, Paul: Whither Germany? Workers Library Publishers, 1943.

*Schuetz, Wolfgang W.: German Home Front. Gollancz, 1943.

Strasser, Otto: Flight from Terror. McBride, 1943.

Riess, Curt: The Self-Betrayed — The Doom of the German Generals. Putnam, 1943.

Schwarz, Paul: This Man Ribbentrop. Messner, 1943.

*Rehfisch, Hans, editor, for The Club 1943: In Tyrannos — A Symposium. Drummond, 1944.

Brecht, Arnold: Prelude to Silence — The End of the German Republic. Oxford University Press, 1944.

Neumann, Franz: Behemoth — The Struggle and Practice of National Socialism, 1933–44. Second edition with new appendix, Oxford University Press, 1944.

*Rosinski, Herbert: The German Army. New edition, The Infantry Journal, Washington, 1944.

Brecht, Arnold: Federalism and Regionalism in Germany. Oxford University Press, 1945.

Steinberg, Siegfried H.: A Short History of Germany. Macmillan, 1945.

*Spiecker, Karl: Germany from Defeat to Defeat. Macdonald, 1945.

Koch-Weser, Erich: Hitler and Beyond—A German Testament. Alfred A. Knopf, 1945.

Loewenstein, Prince Hubertus: The Germans in History. Columbia University Press, 1945.

Ebenstein, William: The German Record. A Political Portrait. Farrar and Rinehart, 1945.

II. BOOKS BY AMERICAN AND BRITISH AUTHORS

As a result of the Napoleonic wars, when British and German forces joined hands at Waterloo, English historians approached everything German with sympathy for a long while; Americans followed them. History writing in the English-speaking countries was largely influenced by the impressive German school of Leopold von Ranke; certain British scholars indeed were accused of relying too heavily on German methods, while others certainly knew how to combine a great tradition of political insight and skillful presentation, inherited from the English eighteenth century, with German thoroughness of research into sources.

Exponents of a historical point of view that was widely adhered to in the English-speaking countries before the war of 1914–8 showed an increasingly critical attitude toward Germany. Modern German imperialism was analyzed, its origins discussed. Some few studies of Bismarck appeared that were remarkable contributions to learning, although, curiously enough, no biography of Bismarck written in English is comparable to the classic works on Pitt and Gladstone that were produced by German scholars. More radical revision of the conception of modern German history that had become conventional in the English-speaking countries was imposed by Germany's defeat in the first World War, the subsequent revolution, the Weimar episode, Hitlerism, and the outbreak of another World War; strong antipathy and distrust were expressed, and Germanophobia took the place of Germanophilia. It would be an oversimplification, however, to call the older school simply pro-German and the newer anti-German. The two schools of thought coexisted for a long while and showed mutual respect by a sort of gentleman's agreement.

Politically all British historians were inspired by suspicion. Could not, would not, a great Continental power some day unite the Continent against Britain, as France and then Germany had tried to do and as Russia also might? It is common knowledge that different shades of opinion prevailed from time to time in the British Foreign Office and were inclined to support now Germany, now France, now Austria, Italy, or one of the minor Slav states, or now again Russia; in much the same fashion British historians who studied the various countries of Europe betrayed a bias for or against them.

Emotional leanings of this sort remained foreign to American historians at least till into the first World War. It would be interesting to analyze the influence of the German-American element on historical evaluations of Germany that were made in the United States, though this influence was certainly far less than Germany herself had hoped. So far as the spirit of '48 remained alive among German-Americans, it worked against the imperialism of William II rather than for it; even toward the Weimar Republic sympathy took the form of sentimental instead of active patronage; and Hitlerism was hailed only by a German-American minority more noisy than numerous. The German element in the United States exerted no more considerable influence on American historiography than on American foreign policy. Among the scholars in the United States who have made conspicuous contributions to knowledge of Germany and the Germans the number who are of German descent is astonishingly small.

A younger generation of American students of diplomatic history produced a series of critical books that won the sincere admiration of many unbiased German scholars. The most popular question about central Europe in the nineteenth century was the fate of the Duchies of Schleswig and Holstein; the best book that has been written about it so far is the work of an American. The rivalry of Germany and Austria was for many decades a paramount problem; here again an American provided a new interpretation, well documented and fresh in outlook. Still another American scholar advanced decisive evidence against the Prussian legend of the origin of the Franco-German War of 1870–1. The causes of the first World War of 1914–8 provoked voluminous discussion in many countries; what American scholars did in this field is perhaps the most valuable work of all.

Both in Great Britain and in the United States the latest period of German history has called forth a flood of books, and once more historians have had to enlarge and amend their earlier interpretations. The custom of publishing secret government documents in great masses without adequate comment, a trend that was inaugurated in Germany, imposed on historians everywhere a new and marked responsibility as opinion-makers; the writing of diplomatic history took a great spurt, and new specialized studies of Anglo-German and American-German relations appeared.

Current history has always beglamoured many writers who are not professional historians. Journalists lately have seized on particularly rich openings and are putting together a collective picture of the times that will in the long run prove valuable to the professional historian who finds out how to handle it. In a revolutionary and destructive period, when methods of administration are in a state of flux in many countries, even documents lose much of their evidential value, which was once thought unassailable; the real fullness of life was never wholly cabined and confined by historical documents, today less than ever. Films, newspapers, radio broadcasts, tapped wires, all the befogged coming and going of agents and informers amid clouds of risk, tension, and surprise, exert an amazing, though often a hardly ponderable influence on the men and ideas of the day. Anyone who has stood for even a short time within the lines where current historical events take shape knows this all too well. The historian today is under an obligation to every responsible non-professional observer who, through personal experience, can help chart directions in the flood of events.

The present list does not take in books of comment that bear a primary character of propaganda, textbooks, or the welter of periodical literature. It makes no claim to comprehensiveness, but simply reflects personal acquaintance with and to some extent preferences among the more or less standard material that exists in English.

A. ELDER SCHOOL

Headlam, James W.: Bismarck and the Foundation of the German Empire. Putnam, 1899.

*Atkinson, Christopher Thomas: A History of Germany, 1715–1815. Methuen, 1908.

Schevill, Ferdinand: The Making of Modern Germany. McClurg, 1916.

Veblen, Thorstein: Imperial Germany. Macmillan, 1917.

Robertson, Charles Grant: Bismarck. Holt, 1918.

Clapham, J. H.: The Economic Development of France and Germany, 1815–1914. Macmillan, 1921.

Ford, Guy Stanton: Stein and the Era of Reform in Prussia. Princeton University Press, 1922.

Smith, Munroe: Bismarck and German Unity. Columbia University Press, 1923.

Gooch, George P.: Germany. Scribner's, 1925.

Gazley, John G.: American Opinion of German Unification, 1848–71. Columbia University Press, 1926.

*Dawson, W. H.: A History of Germany. Benn, 1928.

Villard, Oswald Garrison: The German Phoenix. Smith & Haas, 1935.

Bruford, Walter H.: Germany in the Eighteenth Century—The Social Background of the Literary Revival. Macmillan, 1935.

*Butler, E. M.: The Tyranny of Greece over Germany. Cambridge University Press, 1935.

B. YOUNGER SCHOOL

Schmitt, Bernadotte: England and Germany, 1740–1914. Princeton University Press, 1916.

*Garfield, Wadsworth: German Disarmament. American Library in Paris, 1926.

Allen, Henry T.: The Rhineland Occupation. Bobbs Merrill, 1927.

Danton, George Henry: Germany Ten Years After. Houghton Mifflin, 1928.

Luehr, Elmer: The New German Republic. Minton Balch, 1929.

Fay, Sidney B.: The Origins of the World War. Macmillan, 1930.

Schmitt, Bernadotte: The Coming of the War. Scribner's, 1930.

Shuster, George: The Germans. Dial Press, 1931.

Lutz, Ralph H.: The Fall of the German Empire. Two volumes, Stanford University Press, 1932.

Steefel, Lawrence D.: The Schleswig-Holstein Question. Harvard University Press, 1932.

Cecil, Algernon: Metternich. Macmillan, 1933.

*Carr, Edward H.: Karl Marx. Dent, 1934.

Clark, Chester W.: Franz Joseph and Bismarck. Harvard University Press, 1934.

Langer, William L.: The Diplomacy of Imperialism, 1890–1902. Alfred A. Knopf, 1935.

Wheeler-Bennett, J. W.: The Wooden Titan—Hindenburg. Morrow, 1936.

Brady, R. A.: The Spirit and Structure of German Fascism. Viking Press, 1937.

*Bithell, Jethro: Germany. Methuen, 1937.

Wedgwood, C. V.: The Thirty Years' War. Yale University Press, 1938.

Watson, Francis: Wallenstein—Soldier under Saturn. Appleton-Century, 1938.

Schuman, Frederick L.: The Nazi Dictatorship. Alfred A. Knopf, 1939.

Sonntag, Raymond J.: Germany and England, 1848–94. Appleton-Century, 1939.

Mowrer, E. A.: Germany Puts the Clock Back. Morrow, 1939.

Shotwell, James T.: What Germany Forgot. Macmillan, 1940.

Miller, Douglas: You Can't Do Business with Hitler. Little, Brown, 1941.

Kneller, G. F.: The Educational Philosophy of National Socialism. Yale University Press, 1941.

Dodd, William E., Jr., and Martha Dodd, editors: Ambassador Dodd's Diary, 1933–38. Harcourt, Brace, 1941.

Hearnshaw, F. J. C.: Germany the Aggressor. Dutton, 1941.

Dewey, John: German Philosophy and Politics. Putnam, 1942.

Butler, Rohan d'Otier: The Roots of National Socialism. Dutton, 1942.

Bischoff, Ralph Frederick: Nazi Conquest through German Culture. Harvard University Press, 1942.

Lochner, Louis: What about Germany? Dodd, Mead, 1942.

*Lorimer, Emily: What the German Needs. Allen & Unwin, 1942.

Jansen, Jon B.: The Silent War—The Underground Movement in Germany. Lippincott, 1943.

Rudin, Harry R.: Armistice 1918. Yale University Press, 1944.

*Taylor, A. J. P.: The Course of German History. Hamilton, 1945.

Fraser, Lindley M.: Germany between the Two Wars. Oxford University Press, 1945.

*Gooch, G. P., and others: The German Mind and Outlook. Chapman & Hall, 1945.

INDEX

INDEX

A NOTE ON THE TYPE
IN WHICH THIS BOOK IS SET

This book was set on the Linotype in Granjon, a type named in compliment to Robert Granjon, but neither a copy of a classic face nor an entirely original creation. George W. Jones based his designs upon the type used by Claude Garamond (1510–61) in his beautiful French books, and Granjon more closely resembles Garamond's own type than do any of the various modern types that bear his name.

Robert Granjon began his career as type-cutter in 1523. The boldest and most original designer of his time, he was one of the first to practise the trade of type-founder apart from that of printer. Between 1557 and 1562 Granjon printed about twenty books in types designed by himself, following, after the fashion of the day, the cursive handwriting of the time. These types, usually known as "caractères de civilité," he himself called "lettres françaises," as especially appropriate to his own country.

This book was composed, printed, and bound by the Kingsport Press, Kingsport, Tennessee. The typographic scheme, the binding design, and the jacket are by EDWARD FISCHER.